the **UNAUTHORIZED GUIDE** to

Windows® 98
Second Edition

Paul McFedries

201 West 103rd Street, Indianapolis, Indiana 46290

The Unauthorized Guide to Windows® 98 Second Edition

Copyright © 1999 by Que Corporation

International Standard Book Number: 0-7897-1912-6

Library of Congress Catalog Card Number: 98-87807

Printed in the United States of America

First Printing: August 1999

01   00   4   3   2

Trademarks

Warning and Disclaimer

Development Editor
Sandy Doell

Managing Editor
Thomas F. Hayes

Project Editor
Lori A. Lyons

Copy Editors
Victoria Elzey
Julie McNamee

Indexer
Tina Trettin

Proofreader
Tricia Sterling

Technical Editor
Kyle Bryant

Interior Designer
Gary Adair

Cover Designer
Karen Ruggles

Copy Writer
Eric Borgert

Layout Technician
Steve Geiselman

Introduction

I Windows 98: Beyond the Basics

1 Beyond the Hype: A Critical Look at What's New in Windows 98

2 Ten Things You Should Know About the Windows 98 Setup

3 Understanding and Controlling the Windows 98 Startup

4 An Insider's Guide to Three Crucial Configuration Tools

5 Getting the Most Out of Your Applications

6 Expert Windows Explorer Techniques

II Advanced Windows 98 Customizing

7 Getting to Know the Control Panel

8 An In-Depth Look at Web Integration and the Active Desktop

9 Customizing the Windows 98 Interface

III Secrets of the Windows 98 File System

10 Powerful Techniques for File Types

11 Taking Advantage of Shortcuts

IV Windows 98 Performance Tuning and Troubleshooting

12 Maximizing Your System's Memory

13 Optimizing Your Hard Disk

14 Making the Move to FAT32

15 Crucial System Maintenance Skills

16 Preparing for Trouble

V Inside Windows 98 Communications and Internet Features

17 Getting the Most Out of Your Modem

18 Getting on the Internet

19 Expert Internet Explorer Techniques

20 Communicating Efficiently and Effectively with Outlook Express

21 Implementing Windows 98's Internet Security Features

VI High-Powered Hardware Techniques

22 Taking the Mystery Out of Hardware

23 Setting Up and Customizing Input Devices

24 Maximizing Multimedia Hardware

25 The Ins and Outs of Windows 98's Notebook Features

VII Windows 98 Networking Skills

26 Understanding Networking

27 Setting Up Your Own Local Area Network

28 A Complete Tour of the Network Neighborhood

29 Connecting Remotely with Dial-Up Networking

VIII Appendixes

A A Glossary of Windows Terms

B Online Resources for Windows 98

C Windows 98 Keyboard Shortcuts

Index

Contents

The Structure of the Book 2

Special Features 5

I Windows 98: Beyond the Basics   7

1 Beyond the Hype: A Critical Look at What's New in Windows 98   9

Web Integration and the Active
  Desktop 10

New Internet Features..........................12

The Windows 98 System Tools...............16

New Hardware Support.........................22

Other New Features..............................26

What's New in Windows 98
  Second Edition 29

What's New Since Windows 3.*x*.............33

Essential Information.........................37

2 Ten Things You Should Know About the Windows 98 Setup   39

Going Beyond the Minimum
  Windows 98 Hardware Requirements.40

Upgrading from DOS or an Existing
  Version of Windows 42

*Upgrading from DOS or
  Windows 3.0....................................42*

Upgrading from Windows 3.1x 44

Upgrading from Windows 95..............45

Dual-Booting Windows 98 with
Another Operating System....................45

Partitioning for Dual-Booting..............46

FAT32 Dual-Boot Considerations 46

*Installing Windows 3.1x After
  Windows 98....................................47*

*Dual-Booting Windows 98 and
  Windows NT...................................49*

Other Dual-Boot Options 51

Performing a Clean Installation..............52

Preparing Your System.........................55
A Preparation Checklist....................55
Better Backup Ideas.........................57

Running the Windows 98 Setup.............58
Using Setup's Switches.....................59
Creating Automated Setup Scripts.....60
Launching Setup...............................62

Adding and Removing
Windows 98 Components 66

Extracting a File from the
Windows 98 Setup Files 67

Customizing Setup Settings in
the Registry.....................................68
Editing Your Username and
Company Name 68
Specifying a New Setup
Source Path 69

Uninstalling Windows 98 69
Running the Uninstall Feature...........71
Uninstalling Windows 98 by Hand......72
Essential Information.........................73

3 Understanding and Controlling the
Windows 98 Startup   75

How the Startup Process Works............76

Notes About `Config.sys` and
`Autoexec.bat` 79

Working with the Windows 98
Startup Menu..................................82

`Win.com` Switches for Startup
Troubleshooting...............................85

Controlling Startup Using the
System Configuration Utility 86

Controlling Startup Using `Msdos.sys`.......91

How the Shutdown Process Works.........97

Creating Custom Startup and
Shutdown Screens...........................98
Essential Information........................100

4 An Insider's Guide to Three Crucial
Configuration Tools   103

An Insider's Guide to the Registry 104
Why Is the Registry So Important?..104
Keeping the Registry Safe 105

Launching the Registry Editor..........110
How the Registry Is Structured 112
Working with Registry Keys
and Settings 113

An Insider's Guide to System Policies ..119
Installing the System Policy Editor...120
Working with a Local Registry 120

An Insider's Guide to Tweak UI 122
Installing Tweak UI..........................122
Running Tweak UI 122
Tweak UI's Boot Options 123
Essential Information......................125

**5 Getting the Most Out of Your
Applications   127**

Installing Applications Safely 127
An Installation Safety Checklist.......128
Installing the Application.................130

Applications and the Registry 131

Launching Applications.......................134

Launching Applications Automatically
at Startup.....................................136
Using the StartUp Folder.................137
Using the Registry 137
Using Win.ini.................................138

Switching Between Running
Applications 139

Special Considerations for DOS
Programs 139
Using MS-DOS Mode 141
Creating Custom Startup
Configurations...........................143
Disabling DOS 145

Uninstalling Applications 146
Using Add/Remove Programs to
Uninstall 32-Bit Applications........146
Uninstalling 16-Bit Applications
by Hand 148
Uninstalling DOS Applications
by Hand 151
Essential Information......................151

6 Expert Windows Explorer Techniques   153

Quick Fixes for Making Windows
Explorer More Usable 153
Displaying the Status Bar................154
Turning on File Extensions...............154
Displaying Hidden Files...................154

Basic File and Folder Chores:
The Techniques Used by the Pros 155
Selecting Files and Folders.............155
Making Sense of Windows 98's
Rules for Moving and Copying......157
Expert Drag-and-Drop Techniques.....159
Taking Advantage of the Send
To Command 160
Creating New Folders and Files........161
Renaming Files and Folders 162
The Recycle Bin: Deleting and
Recovering Files and Folders 162
File Maintenance Using the Open
and Save As Dialog Boxes...........167

Powerful Search Techniques for
Finding Files....................................168

Working with Floppy Disks.................171
Formatting a Floppy Disk.................171
Copying a Floppy Disk 173

Customizing Windows Explorer 174
Changing the View 175
Activating Thumbnails 175
Sorting Files and Folders.................176
Exploring the View Options.............177
Using Windows Explorer's
Command Line Options................179
Essential Information........................180

II **Advanced Windows 98
Customizing   181**

7 **Getting to Know the Control Panel   183**

What Is the Control Panel?.................184

Opening the Control Panel Folder.........184

A Review of the Control Panel Icons 185

Controlling the Control Panel...............188
Understanding Control Panel Files ...188
Hiding and Displaying Control
Panel Icons 190
Control Panel and the Registry........193

Easier Access to the Control Panel......195
Alternative Methods for Opening
Control Panel Icons.....................195
Putting the Control Panel on
the Taskbar..............................196
Putting the Control Panel on
the Start Menu 196
Essential Information........................198

**8 An In-Depth Look at Web Integration
and the Active Desktop   199**

How Does Web Integration Change
Windows 98? 200

Toggling Web Integration On and Off....203

Setting Web Integration Options 205

Viewing Folders As Web Pages 206
Activating the Web View 206
*Creating a Custom Web View
Background...............................207*
*Understanding Web View
Templates 209*
*Under the Hood: The Structure of
a Web View Template 211*
*Inserting Links to Local, Intranet,
and Internet Resources 217*
*Disabling the Annoying "Show Files"
Link 219*

Working with the Active Desktop.........220
*Turning the Active Desktop
On and Off 222*
Working with Desktop Items............222
*Turning the Active Desktop Into
a Web Page 224*
Essential Information........................225

**9 Customizing the Windows 98
Interface   227**

Changing an Icon 227

More Than Just Wallpaper: Customizing
the Desktop 229
*A Quick Look at Windows 98's
Display Settings 229*
Modifying the Desktop Items...........232
*Saving Desktop Settings When
Exiting Windows 98.....................235*
Setting Up Custom Shell Folders......235
*Customizing Windows 98's
System Icons 236*

Renovating the Start Menu 237
*Adding and Removing Start
Menu Shortcuts 238*
*Removing Built-In Start Menu
Items..241*
*Putting System Folders on the Start
Menu...242*
*Creating Accelerator Keys for Start
Menu Shortcuts 243*

Redoing the Taskbar.............................244
  Setting Taskbar Properties *244*
  Moving and Sizing the Taskbar.........*245*
  Customizing the Quick Launch
    Toolbar...............................*245*
  Displaying Other Taskbar Toolbars....*246*

Activating User Profiles.......................247
  Setting Up User Profiles *247*
  Understanding How Windows 98
    Works with User Profiles *250*
  Essential Information......................*251*

III Secrets of the Windows 98
   File System   253

10 Powerful Techniques for File Types   255

Understanding File Types......................256
  File Types and File Extensions.........*256*
  File Types and the Registry *258*
  A Front-End for
  HKEY_CLASSES_ROOT *259*

Opening a Document with an
  Unassociated Application 260

Working with Existing File Types 261
  Editing a File Type............................*261*
  Working with File Type Actions........*263*

Creating a New File Type......................265
  Using Open With to Create a
    Basic File Type.............................*265*
  Using the File Types Tab to Create
    a More Advanced File Type..........*266*

Associating Two or More Extensions
  with a Single Application 267

Customizing the New Menu 268

Figuring Out Browser File Types:
  Internet Explorer Versus Netscape ...270
  Essential Information........................*271*

11 Taking Advantage of Shortcuts   273

Understanding Shortcuts 273
  Windows Shortcut Files....................*274*
  DOS Shortcut Files (PIFs)...............*275*

Creating a Shortcut.............................275

Modifying Shortcut Properties.............276
  Customizing a Windows Shortcut.....*276*
  Customizing a PIF Shortcut *278*

Finding a Moved or Renamed Target 279

Using the Link Check Wizard to Deal
    with Dead Links 280

Some Unauthorized Shortcut Tricks 281
    Viewing Shortcut Extensions *281*
    Disabling the Shortcut to *Text* *282*
    Customizing the Shortcut
        Icon Arrow *282*

Getting the Most Out of Shortcuts.......283
    Essential Information........................*285*

IV Windows 98 Performance
       Tuning and Troubleshooting   287

12 Maximizing Your System's Memory   289

Memory: The Lifeblood of Your
    Computer.......................................290
    The Address Space..........................*290*
    Types of Memory.............................*291*

Determining How Much Memory
    Is Installed....................................292

Restricting Memory Usage 293

How Much Memory Is Enough?............294

Managing the Windows 98 Swap File...296

Tracking and Optimizing System
    Resources.....................................298
    Using the Resource Meter to
        Track System Resources *299*
    Some Ways to Save System
        Resources...................................*301*

More Memory Management
    Techniques.....................................302

Maximizing Memory for DOS Programs 303
    DOS Memory Concepts *303*
    Setting DOS Memory Properties
        for Individual Applications............*304*
    Maximizing Conventional Memory....*306*
    Essential Information........................*310*

13 Optimizing Your Hard Disk   311

Examining Hard Disk Properties 312

Using Disk Cleanup to Remove
    Unnecessary Files 313

Detecting and Repairing Hard Disk
    Errors with ScanDisk.......................316

Optimizing Disk Access Times with Disk
    Defragmenter 320
    Running Disk Defragmenter *320*
    Understanding the Intel
        Application Launch Accelerator....322
Using WinAlign to Speed Up
    Program Launching..........................324
Compressing Files with DriveSpace......325
    Using DriveSpace to
        Compress Files............................*326*
    Using DriveSpace to Compress
        Free Space..................................*328*
    Essential Information......................*329*

14 Making the Move to FAT32   331

Understanding the FAT 331
    The FAT and Cluster Size *333*
    Calculating Cluster Slack *333*
What is FAT32?....................................337
How Much Disk Space Will You Save? .339
Converting a Partition to FAT32 340
    Using FDISK....................................*340*
    Using Drive Converter *341*
    Essential Information......................*342*

15 Crucial System Maintenance Skills   345

Getting the Big Picture: Windows 98
    Information Utilities.........................345
    The System Information Utility.........*346*
    The File Information Utility *348*
    Finding the Version Number
        of a File *350*
Protecting System Files......................350
    Running System File Checker *351*
    Using Version Conflict Manager
        to Deal with Conflicting System
        Files..*355*
Controlling Viruses with Plus! 98's
    McAfee VirusScan 357
    Running VirusScan *359*
    Understanding VShield.....................*360*
    Other Ways to Protect Yourself
        from Viruses................................*361*
    Essential Information......................*362*

16 Preparing for Trouble   365

Putting Together an Emergency
Boot Disk.................................365
*Creating a Windows 98
Startup Disk 366*
Creating a FAT32 Startup Disk........368
Test Driving the Startup Disk..........368

Backing Up Your Files.........................372
Setting Up a Backup Job 374
Notes Towards Easier Backup Jobs..376
Restoring a Backup Job....................377

Using System Recovery to Recover
from a Crash 379

Gathering Troubleshooting Information.383
Essential Information......................384

**V Inside Windows 98
Communications and
Internet Features   385**

17 Getting the Most Out of Your Modem   387

Understanding Modem
Communications............................388

Installing a Modem............................392
*Running the Add New
Modem Wizard 393*
Running Modem Diagnostics............395
Running AT Commands....................396
*Does Your Phone Line Support
56Kbps Transmissions? 398*
Your Modem and the Registry..........398

Setting the Modem's Properties 399
Setting the General Properties 400
Setting the Connection Properties...400
Setting Dialing Properties...............405
Essential Information......................408

18 Getting on the Internet   411

How to Get On the Internet
Using a Phone Line..........................412
*Information You Need Before
Getting Started...........................412*
*Using the Internet Connection
Wizard 414*

*The Internet Connection Wizard
    in Windows 98 Second Edition*.....*416*
Using Dial-Up Networking *417*
*Setting a Few More Connection
    Properties*....................................*419*
*Connection Settings in Windows
    98 Second Edition* *421*
Making the Connection *423*
*Creating Scripts to Automate
    Dial-Ups* *425*
Disconnecting from Your ISP...........*429*

How to Get on the Internet Using a
Local Area Network.........................429
*Information You Need Before
    Getting Started* *429*
*Installing and Configuring the
    TCP/IP Protocol*...........................*430*

Some Internet Utilities You
Should Know 432
Essential Information.......................*433*

19 Expert Internet Explorer Techniques   435

Basic Browsing Techniques 436
*Understanding Web Page
    Addresses* *436*
Opening and Browsing Pages...........*437*
Searching for Sites...........................*438*
Customizing the Links Bar *441*

Address Bar Tricks 442

Using the Favorites Folder to
Save Sites.......................................445
Opening Favorite Sites....................*445*
*Sharing Favorites and Netscape
    Bookmarks*....................................*446*
Maintaining Favorites *447*

Dealing with Subscriptions 448
*Setting Up a Subscription in
    Internet Explorer 4* *449*
*Viewing Pages Offline with
    Internet Explorer 5* *452*

Controlling the Cache...........................454

Internet Explorer's Advanced Options ..455
Essential Information.......................*463*

**20 Communicating Efficiently and
Effectively with Outlook Express   465**

A Quick Look at Some Outlook
  Express Email Basics 466
  Setting Up Mail Accounts................*468*
  Sending a Message *470*
  Retrieving Messages *473*
  Reading a Message *473*
  *Dealing with a Message After
    You've Read It*.............................*474*

Working with Outlook Express Folders .475

Filtering Incoming Messages 476

Finding a Message 480

Finding a Person 482

Customizing Outlook Express..............483
  *Reorganizing the Message List
    Columns*.......................................*483*
  *Rearranging the Layout of the
    Outlook Express Window* *485*
  Essential Information.......................*486*

**21 Implementing Windows 98's
Internet Security Features   489**

Some Thoughts on Email Virus
  Hoaxes 490

Windows 98 Security Updates 491

Internet Security and the TCP/IP
  Protocol 494

Internet Explorer's Security Features ...495
  *Working with Internet Explorer's
    Security Zones* *495*
  More Security Settings....................*502*

Using a Digital ID for Secure Email 503
  *Setting Up an Email Account with
    a Digital ID*.................................*505*
  *Obtaining Another Person's
    Public Key*....................................*506*
  Sending a Secure Message..............*507*
  Receiving a Secure Message...........*508*
  Essential Information.......................*509*

VI High-Powered Hardware Techniques **511**

22 Taking the Mystery Out of Hardware 513

Crucial Hardware Concepts 514
IRQ Lines, I/O Ports, and Other Device Settings.............................514
Understanding Device Drivers 518
How to Make Plug and Play Work (Most of the Time) 520

Installing Device Drivers 521
Using Automatic Hardware Detection......................................522
Installing a Driver by Hand..............524
Working with the Signature Verification Tool...........................525
Using Automatic Skip Driver Agent to Bypass Troublesome Drivers 527

Getting Device Information 528

Dealing with Device Manager 529
Viewing Devices by Resource 531
Working with Device Properties.......532
Essential Information.......................533

23 Setting Up and Customizing Input Devices 535

Working with Your Mouse 535
Customizing the Mouse 536
Working with the IntelliPoint Settings......................................540
Setting the Tweak UI Mouse Properties...................................544

Working with Your Keyboard 546
Customizing the Keyboard 546
Typing Extended Characters 548
Using Keyboard Languages...............551

Calibrating a Game Controller..............553
Essential Information.......................554

24 Maximizing Multimedia Hardware 555

Installing and Configuring a Graphics Adapter..............................555
Changing the Adapter Driver...........557
Configuring the Color Depth and Resolution 558

Working with Windows 98's Monitor
Features 562
Changing the Monitor Type..............*563*
Using Your Monitor's Power
Management Features.................*564*
Setting Up Multiple Monitors...........*564*

Working with Scanners and Digital
Cameras 567
Installing a Scanner........................*567*
Capturing Images *568*

Wiring Windows for Sound 569
Assigning Sounds to Windows 98
Events *569*
Recording a WAV File *572*
Editing a WAV File...........................*573*
Essential Information.......................*574*

25 The Ins and Outs of Windows 98's
Notebook Features   575

Power Management for Notebook
Users 576
Putting the System into
Standby Mode *577*
Setting Up a Power Scheme *577*
Monitoring the Battery *579*

Hot Docking and Hardware Profiles......580

Windows 98's PC Card Support 582

Transferring Files Between Computers
Using Direct Cable Connection 583

Using a Briefcase to Synchronize
File Sharing....................................587

Notes About Infrared Ports 589
Essential Information.......................*592*

VII Windows 98 Networking Skills   593

26 Understanding Networking   595

Network Types: Client/Server Versus
Peer-to-Peer 596

Network Hardware: NICs, Cables,
and More 597
The Connection Point: The Network
Interface Card..............................*597*
The Connection: The Network
Cable *598*

Other Network Hardware 601

Network Topology: Star Versus Bus 603

Network Protocols: NetBEUI, IPX/SPX,
    and TCP/IP 604
    Essential Information 605

**27 Setting Up Your Own Local Area
    Network   607**

Some Preparatory Chores 607

An Eight-Step Guide to Setting Up a
    Network Client 609
    Step 1: Installing a NIC Driver 610
    *Step 2: Installing a Network
        Client Driver* 611
    *Step 3: Installing Network
        Protocols* 611
    *Step 4: Installing Network
        Services* 612
    *Step 5: Setting Up File and Print
        Sharing* 612
    Step 6: Identifying the Computer 613
    Step 7: Specifying Access Control ...614
    *Step 8: Specifying the Network
        Logon* 615
    Finishing Up 616

Creating a Microsoft Mail Postoffice
    for Network Email 616
    Installing the Postoffice 617
    Creating the Postoffice 617
    Creating User Mailboxes 618
    *Installing Microsoft Mail in
        Windows Messaging* 619
    Setting Microsoft Mail Options 621

Sharing a Dial-Up Connection
    Between Network Clients 624
    *Using Internet Connection Sharing
        in Windows 98 Second Edition* 624
    *Other Ways to Share an Internet
        Connection* 627
    Essential Information 628

**28 A Complete Tour of the Network
    Neighborhood   629**

Accessing the Network 629
    Logging On to the Network 629
    *How to Access the Network
        Neighborhood* 632

Understanding the Universal
    Naming Convention *634*
Sharing Your Resources on the
    Network 635
    Working with Share-Level Access *635*
    Working with User-Level Access *637*
Mapping a Shared Resource As a
    Local Disk Drive 639
    Mapping a Resource *640*
    Disconnecting a Mapped Resource ..*641*
Printing Over the Network 641
Customizing the Network
    Neighborhood 642
Some Remote Administration Options ..646
    Administering a Remote Registry *647*
    Other Remote Administration
        Options *647*
    Essential Information *648*

29 Connecting Remotely with Dial-Up
    Networking   **651**
    Configuring the Dial-Up Adapter 651
    Creating and Configuring a
        Network Connection 652
    Connecting to Your Network 654
    Configuring Dial-Up Networking 655
    Setting Up Windows 98 As a
        Dial-Up Server 656
        Setting Up the Dial-Up Server *656*
        Monitoring the Connected User *658*
    Using Microsoft Mail Remotely 659
        Creating a New Remote Mail
            Profile *659*
        Configuring Microsoft Mail for
            Remote Sessions *659*
        Running a Remote
            Microsoft Mail Session *661*
        Essential Information *663*

VIII Appendixes   **665**

    A A Glossary of Windows Terms   **667**

    B Online Resources for Windows 98   **689**
        The World Wide Web 689
        Microsoft Sites *690*

Non-Microsoft Sites *691*

Usenet Newsgroups *694*

C Windows 98 Keyboard Shortcuts   699

Windows 98 Startup Keys *699*

Interface Keys *700*

Application Keys *701*

Dialog Box Keys *702*

Drag-and-Drop Keys *703*

Windows Explorer Keys *703*

Internet Explorer Keys *704*

Doskey Keys *705*

Windows Logo (⊞) Keys *706*

Index   709

Paul McFedries Paul is a computer consultant, programmer, and freelance writer. He is the author of more than two dozen computer books that have sold nearly two million copies worldwide. His titles include the Sams Publishing books *Paul McFedries' Windows 98 Unleashed*, *VBA for Office 2000 Unleashed*, and *Paul McFedries' Microsoft Office 97 Unleashed*, as well as the Que books *The Complete Idiot's Guide to Windows 98* and *The Complete Idiot's Guide to More Windows 98*. You can contact Paul at:

Email: `paul@mcfedries.com`

WWW: `http://www.mcfedries.com/`

About the Author

Dedication

To my friends and family (for being friendly and familiar), and, of course, to Karen.

Acknowledgments

I write computer books for a living, and I always tell people that I think of my job as spending a half hour figuring out how to do something in five minutes, and then giving the reader that five-minute method. I hope, then, that this book makes at least a small part of your life easier and less stressful.

To make my own life easier and less stressful, I need only turn to the dedicated and hard-working folks in the Macmillan Computer Publishing editorial department. These professionals absolutely amaze me with their knowledge, experience, and sheer competence. All I have to worry about is writing the best book that I can, knowing that the Macmillan editors are backing me up by dotting my i's and crossing my t's. Dozens of bright-eyed and energetic folks had a hand in making this book, but there are a few who I worked with directly, so I'd like to single them out for special thanks. They include Associate Publisher Greg Wiegand, Executive Editor Jeff Koch, Acquisitions Editor Jane Brownlow, Development Editor Sandy Doell, Project Editor Lori Lyons, Copy Editor Victoria Elzey, Proofreader Tricia Sterling, and Technical Editor Kyle Bryant. A hearty thanks to all of you for another fantastic job.

Tell Us What You Think!

As the reader of this book, *you* are our most important critic and commentator. We value your opinion and want to know what we're doing right, what we could do better, what areas you'd like to see us publish in, and any other words of wisdom you're willing to pass our way.

As Associate Publisher for Que, I welcome your comments. You can fax, email, or write me directly to let me know what you did or didn't like about this book—as well as what we can do to make our books stronger.

Please note that I cannot help you with technical problems related to the topic of this book, and that due to the high volume of mail I receive, I might not be able to reply to every message.

When you write, please be sure to include this book's title and author as well as your name and phone or fax number. I will carefully review your comments and share them with the author and editors who worked on the book.

Fax: 317.581.4666

Email: consumer@mcp.com

Mail: Greg Wiegand
           Que
           201 West 103rd Street
           Indianapolis, IN 46290 USA

B y definition, what people *create* using a computer is a unique expression of who they are. Whether it's a memo, a letter, a financial model, a presentation, an email message, or a Web page, the fruit of a person's labors is something that only *they* could have produced.

On the other hand, *how* a person uses their computer—or, more to the point, how a person uses Windows—probably isn't unique at all. Most users follow the same Start menu paths to launch programs, use the standard techniques in programs like Windows Explorer and Outlook Express, and perform customizations that don't go much beyond changing the wallpaper. That's because most users find it easier to simply toe the Microsoft party line and follow the techniques outlined in the "Getting Started" booklet and the Help system. To be sure, this is a reasonable approach for novice users who are intimidated by Windows and so prefer to tread carefully to avoid upsetting any digital apple carts.

However, what about those users who qualify as "post-novice"? By that, I mean any person who either knows the basics of Windows 98 or who has some computing experience and is smart enough to figure things out without having their hands held. For those users, doing things the "authorized" way is slower, less efficient, and less powerful because Windows 98 was designed from the ground up so as not to confuse novice users (or, I guess, not to confuse them more than necessary). The result is default settings that restrict your flexibility, interminable wizards that turn two-step tasks into twelve-step sagas, and the hiding of powerful and useful programs behind layers of menus and dialog boxes. To get the most out of Windows 98, the post-novice user needs an "unauthorized" approach that goes where the "Getting Started" booklet and the Help system fear to tread.

Welcome, therefore, to *The Unauthorized Guide to Windows 98*. In this book, I thumb my nose at the standard-issue techniques sanctioned by Microsoft and parroted in other Windows 98 books. Instead, I offer shortcuts for boosting your productivity, customizations for making Windows 98 work the way you do, workarounds for known Windows 98 problems, and warnings for avoiding Windows 98 pitfalls. Along the way, you'll learn about all kinds of insider details, undocumented features, powerful tools, and background facts that help put everything into perspective.

So, is this merely a collection of tips, tricks, and traps? Not at all. This is a *guide* to Windows 98. That means I teach you *how* to use Windows 98, from setup to startup, from performing system maintenance to maintaining system performance, from getting on the Internet to getting on your network. I also cover most of the features new to Windows 98, including Web integration, FAT32, Internet Explorer 4.0, Outlook Express, and much more. As a bonus, I also provide you with coverage of the new and notable features that come with Windows 98 Second Edition.

The Structure of the Book

The Unauthorized Guide to Windows 98 is structured as a work of reference. This means that you can dive into most chapters to learn just the facts or techniques you need now without having to worry that you missed some crucial information in an earlier chapter. The exception to this is Chapter 4, "An Insider's Guide to Three Crucial Configuration Tools." That chapter discusses the Windows 98 Registry, the System Policy Editor, and the Tweak UI customization accessory, and I use all three tools throughout the rest of the book.

Part I: Windows 98: Beyond the Basics

The book begins with a half dozen chapters that discuss some Windows 98 basics with a beyond-the-basics approach. You get a critical look at the new Windows 98 features, a host of Windows 98 Setup tips and techniques, and an inside look at the Windows 98 startup process. I also discuss the Registry, System Policy Editor, and Tweak UI, installing and uninstalling applications, running Windows and DOS programs, and using Windows Explorer for file and disk chores.

Part II: Advanced Windows 98 Customizing

The three chapters in Part II offer loads of customization techniques that go beyond the standard wallpaper-and-color tweaks. You get an in-depth look at the Control Panel, behind-the-scenes coverage of Web integration and the Active Desktop, and powerful methods for customizing the desktop, Start menu, and taskbar.

Part III: Secrets of the Windows 98 File System

This short section contains just two chapters, but it's jam-packed with practical and powerful tips and techniques. Chapter 10, "Powerful Techniques for File Types," discusses file types and file extensions and shows you how to modify existing file types, create new file types, customize Windows 98's New menu, and more. Chapter 11, "Taking Advantage of Shortcuts," teaches you about shortcuts and shortcut files, shows you how to modify shortcut properties, and provides a number of techniques for working with and customizing shortcuts.

Part IV: Windows 98 Performance Tuning and Troubleshooting

Windows 98 is bursting at the seams with powerful system tools, most of which are hidden in the most obscure places. The chapters in Part IV show you where to find these tools and show you how to make best use of them. You'll learn powerful techniques for optimizing memory, revving up your hard disk, taking advantage of FAT32, protecting system files, controlling viruses, creating an emergency boot disk, backing up your files, and recovering easily from a system crash.

Part V: Inside Windows 98 Communications and Internet Features

The five chapters in Part V show you how to get wired with Windows 98. I begin by showing you how to install and configure your modem. From there, you learn how to get on the Internet and how to get the most out of Internet Explorer (for the World Wide Web) and Outlook Express, (for email). I close with a look at some important Internet security considerations.

Part VI: High-Powered Hardware Techniques

Part VI covers Windows 98's extensive hardware features. You start by learning some crucial hardware concepts, including device drivers, device settings—such as interrupt request lines and I/O ports—and Plug and Play. With that background, you then learn about installing device drivers, using Device Manager, creating hardware profiles, setting up input devices, and configuring graphics adapters, monitors, and other multimedia hardware. This section closes with a look at some notebook features, including power management, docking stations, Direct Cable Connection file transfers, infrared ports, and more.

Part VII: Windows 98 Networking Skills

The last four chapters of the book cover Windows 98 networking. You learn network fundamentals such as the difference between peer-to-peer and client/server, networking hardware, and networking architecture. I then show you how to set up a local area network, how to work with and share network resources, and how to connect to a network remotely using Dial-Up Networking.

Part VIII: Appendixes

The book finishes with a few appendixes. You get a glossary of Windows 98 terms, a selection of World Wide Web and Usenet resources for Windows 98, and a complete list of Windows 98 keyboard shortcuts.

Special Features

This book offers the following six special sidebars in the margins that were devised to help you get things done quickly, efficiently, and smartly:

1. "Shortcut"—Tips and shortcuts that save you time.

2. "Watch Out"—Cautions that warn you about potential pitfalls and problems.

3. "Remember"—Valuable information that you'll want to store away for future use.

4. "Inside Scoop"—Insider's facts or anecdotes.

5. "Undocumented"—Important tidbits and techniques that you won't find in the standard documentation.

6. "Quote"—Statements from real people that are intended to be prescriptive and valuable to you.

   We also recognize your need to have quick information at your fingertips and have thus provided the following comprehensive sections at the back of the book:

1. A Glossary of Windows Terms—Definitions of Windows 98 terminology and jargon.

2. Online Resources for Windows 98—An extensive list of Web sites and newsgroups that offer information related to Windows 98.

3. Windows 98 Keyboard Shortcuts—A complete rundown of all the Windows 98 shortcut keys and key combinations.

Windows 98: Beyond the Basics

PART I

GET THE SCOOP ON...
Web integration and Active Desktop features ▪
Windows 98's Internet tools ▪ The new hardware sup-
port, customization features, multimedia programs,
and more ▪ Learning what's new in Windows 98
Second Edition ▪ Moving to Windows 98 from DOS or
Windows 3.*x*

Beyond the Hype: A Critical Look at What's New in Windows 98

WHEN WINDOWS 98 SHIPPED in June of 1998, the technology pundits quickly split into three camps: applause, apathy, and apoplexy. Those in the applause camp bent over backward to extol the virtues of the new operating system, and claimed Windows 98 would solve the world's problems if everyone just gave it a chance. The apathetic ones took Microsoft's relatively low-key marketing campaign and Windows 98's superficially unchanged interface to mean that this was a ho-hum upgrade that was nothing more than "Windows 95 plus 3." The apoplectic ones heard about the 3,000 Windows 95 bugs that were repaired in Windows 98 and railed against the "Microsoft monopoly" and its outright greed in charging money for a mere "bug fix."

The pundits, as usual, are all wrong because it just isn't possible to generalize the overall merits or shortcomings of Windows 98. In the same way that, in art, beauty is in the eye of the beholder, in operating systems, value is in the needs of the user. We all bring a unique set of requirements to an operating system, and the value we receive from that OS depends on how well it meets those needs.

"
It's true that
Windows 98 is
really just a bug-
fixed, tuned-up,
optimized and
enhanced ver-
sion of Windows
95. But that's
exactly why you
should buy it!
—Mike Elgan,
Windows
Magazine
"

My goal in this chapter is to go beyond the hype—both pro and con—surrounding Windows 98. You won't find any useless generalizations or rehashes of Microsoft marketing materials. Instead, I offer a critical look at what's new and noteworthy in Windows 98, so you can decide for yourself. If you've already made the move to Windows 98, this chapter acts as an overview of the general Windows 98 landscape, which should serve you well throughout the rest of this book.

Web Integration and the Active Desktop

Web integration is probably the single most talked about new feature in Windows 98. The basic idea is that, when Web integration is activated, the Windows 98 interface incorporates certain Web browser features and functionality. The goal is to blur the difference between browsing a remote Web page and browsing your local icons and folders. Unfortunately, Microsoft has only partially met this goal. Some Web integration features are next to useless, while some of the most useful features are undocumented. Chapter 8, "An In-Depth Look at Web Integration and the Active Desktop," provides you with the details. In the meantime, this section reviews the basic features.

Single-click to launch icons and programs. When Web integration is turned on, you no longer have to double-click icons and files to open them. Instead, a single-click does the job, the same way you single-click a link in a Web page.

- **Beyond the hype:** After you get used to it, the single-click metaphor is at least an improvement on Windows 95: It's more consistent, it's faster, and it saves some wear-and-tear on your clicking finger. On the other hand, the fact that Web integration is turned off by default tells you that even Microsoft isn't too sure about all this. The main reason, I think, is that some single-click versus double-click confusion remains. For example, even with Web integration activated, users still have to double-click many system tray icons to open them; similarly, to launch a file displayed in the Open dialog box, you have to double-click the filename.

"Hover" to select icons and files. *Hovering* means that you place the mouse pointer over an icon or filename. After a slight delay, Windows 98 then selects the icon or file. You use Ctrl+hover to select multiple files, and Shift+hover to select multiple contiguous files.

Watch Out!
Web integration's single-click launching can also be dangerous. It's almost inevitable that you end up clicking a filename in the hopes of merely selecting the file, but the file then launches. If that file does something drastic—say, if it's a registration (.reg) file that updates the Windows 98 Registry— the results can be calamitous, indeed.

- **Beyond the hype:** Unlike single-click launching, the "hover-to-select" feature does not enhance productivity thanks to the slightly-too-long delay that occurs while Windows 98 gets around to selecting the "hovered" object. Also, if you decide to use arrow keys to select objects, instead, Windows 98 annoyingly continues to select some other object if the mouse pointer happens to be hovering over it.

Navigate folders like Web pages. Folder windows and Windows Explorer come with Back and Forward buttons that work exactly the same as the Back and Forward buttons in a Web browser. That is, they enable you to leap sequentially through the various folders you've viewed.

- **Beyond the hype:** This feature is marginally useful in folder windows that display the contents of one folder at a time. However, most users don't "surf" folders. Instead, they tend to open the folder they need, work with it, and then close down the window. Similarly, this feature isn't all that useful in Windows Explorer thanks to its All Folders list.

Display folder contents as a Web page. The folders in Windows 98 come with a "Web view" that displays the folder contents as though they were inside a Web page (see Figure 1.1). With this feature, you can customize the window background and see previews of certain documents (particularly graphics and HTML files).

- **Beyond the hype:** As on a Web page, folder backgrounds just tend to make the text difficult to read. Also, the design of the Web view is poor as it wastes quite a bit of space. On the plus side, the previews can be quite handy, and the Web view templates are readily customizable to get the look you want.

Figure 1.1
Web view displays folders as Web pages.

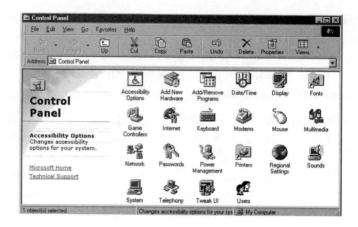

Undocumented
Microsoft's documentation doesn't mention this anywhere, but it's possible to use the Web view to set up links to frequently used folders, drives, and network resources. To my mind, this is by far the most useful thing you can do with the folder Web view. In Chapter 8, see "Inserting Links to Local, Intranet, and Internet Resources," p. 217.

The Active Desktop. Instead of the static desktop of Windows 95, Windows 98's desktop can be customized with dynamic content. This *Active Desktop* can hold objects such as Java applets and ActiveX controls, or it can be transformed into a Web page. The Active Desktop also supports push media—remote content that is sent directly to the desktop.

- **Beyond the hype:** The desktop isn't a great place for active content since it's usually buried under one or more windows. This feature is really only useful for people with a large monitor, a video card able to run at high resolution, or a second monitor/video card combination (more on this later). Even then, the Active Desktop tends to usurp an unseemly amount of Windows 98's resources, so a fast computer with lots of memory is also required.

New Internet Features

Microsoft only jumped on the Internet bandwagon after Windows 95 shipped, so the latter had only a limited number of Internet tools. That's not the case with Windows 98, however, because it comes with a much larger collection of Internet-related programs and features. Although some of these programs are less than impressive, many of them are excellent products that by themselves justify the cost of the Windows 98 upgrade. Here's a review:

Internet Explorer 4.   This version of Internet Explorer boasts a large number of improvements over version 3. These include support for Dynamic HTML, revamped Search and History features, enhanced security, an improved user interface, and a host of customization options. There's also a new feature called *subscriptions*, which enables Internet Explorer to check for changed Web pages, and then notify you of (or even download) the changed content. For insight on these and other Internet Explorer features, see Chapter 19, "Expert Internet Explorer Techniques."

- **Beyond the hype:** Internet Explorer still isn't perfect. For example, it's still too hard to work with your Favorites list, and the status bar's brain dead design often means that crucial information gets truncated. However, Internet Explorer's speed and excellent standards compliance make this a "best-of-breed" browser.

The Internet Connection Wizard.   This wizard takes you step-by-step through the process of setting up a connection for a new or existing Internet account (see Figure 1.2). This can be a complex process, so the wizard's various dialog boxes reduce that complexity by breaking everything down into a simple question-and-answer format.

- **Beyond the hype:** This wizard certainly helps inexperienced users who would otherwise have no way of knowing the appropriate sequence required to set up an Internet account. However, the process is still not idiot-proof because users often have to deal with Internet arcana such as IP addresses and DNS server names. The wizard also makes a few dumb or just plain wrong choices along the way, so more experienced users are usually better off setting up their connections by hand (see Chapter 18, "Getting on the Internet").

Remember
Less than a year after Windows 98 hit the shelves, Microsoft released version 5 of Internet Explorer, which is also part of Windows 98 Second Edition (discussed later in this chapter). So, if you've purchased a new computer recently, it likely comes with Internet Explorer 5.0.

Remember
Although Internet Explorer is built into Windows 98, you can still use another browser such as Netscape Navigator. Setting this up is a bit tricky, however. I show you how it's done in Chapter 10, "Powerful Techniques for File Types." See the "Figuring Out Browser File Types: Internet Explorer Versus Netscape" section, p. 270.

Figure 1.2
The Internet
Connection
Wizard offers
step-by-step
Internet setups.

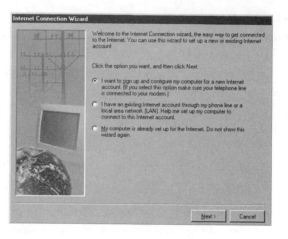

See Also...
"How to Get On
the Internet Using
a Phone Line,"
p. 412

Upgrade Windows 98 online with Windows Update.   During Windows 95's lifetime, Microsoft put out a service pack, several service releases, and a number of other updates. That was the good news. The bad news was how hard it was to get those updates. Windows 98 is destined to become even more of a moving target, so Microsoft created the Windows Update Web site to make it easier to keep up with the latest upgrades. This site examines your system and then lets you know what's new that you can download and install.

- **Beyond the hype:** Windows Update is a welcome tool for staying on top of the inevitable (and sure to be numerous) Windows 98 upgrades. It's convenient having all the new updates listed in a single location, and the downloading and installation of these updates requires only a minimum of user intervention. Unfortunately, the Windows Update download doesn't leave a permanent file on your hard disk, so if you reinstall Windows 98 or want to apply the update to another computer, you have to start from scratch. Also, it remains to be seen if the Windows Update list becomes unwieldy after a large number of upgrades have been released.

Build, publish, and serve Web pages.   Windows 98 ships with three programs for would-be Webmasters: FrontPage Express is a WYSIWYG (what you see is what you get) HTML editor you use to build Web pages; the Web Publishing Wizard takes you step-by-step through the process of getting HTML files, graphics, and other Web site components from your hard disk to your Web directory; and Personal Web Server enables you to turn your Windows 98 machine into a Web server, accessible either via the Internet or an intranet.

- **Beyond the hype:** None of these tools is particularly impressive. FrontPage Express, for example, doesn't support many common features (such as frames) and it has the annoying tendency to add many proprietary tags to a page. Personal Web Server supports only a limited number of connections and doesn't have an FTP service. However, these programs are more than adequate if your Web page publishing needs are simple. And you can't beat the price, especially considering that the total cost of equivalent third-party programs would likely be in the hundreds of dollars.

Work with email and newsgroups using Outlook Express. The Internet email service in Windows 95's Windows Messaging (a.k.a., Microsoft Exchange) was a token gesture, at best. With email far and away the most popular online activity, Windows 98 sensibly ships with an email client designed for the Internet: Outlook Express. You can also use this program to work with Usenet newsgroups. I cover the Outlook Express email features in Chapter 20, "Communicating Efficiently and Effectively with Outlook Express."

- **Beyond the hype:** As an Internet client, Outlook Express is a vast improvement over Windows Messaging thanks to its support for multiple accounts, signatures, HTML messages, Usenet newsgroups, and offline reading and composing. In fact, if it weren't for a few annoying quirks (such as having HTML as the default sending format), Outlook Express would have my vote as the Net's best all-around email client.

Collaborate remotely using NetMeeting. At its simplest, this product enables two users with computers equipped with

Remember
Windows
Messaging and
its sister product
Microsoft Fax are
gone from the
main Windows 98
installation, but
they're not forgotten. You can
install them from
the Windows 98
CD by looking in
the `\tools\`
`oldwin95\`
`message\us` folder.
Run `wms.exe` to
install Windows
Messaging, and
then run
`awfax.exe` to
install Microsoft
Fax.

sound cards and microphones to have voice conversations over the Internet or an intranet. (Users lacking the appropriate sound equipment can still "chat" using text messages.) NetMeeting also supports videoconferencing, file exchanges, and program sharing.

- **Beyond the hype:** The accessories that come with Windows tend to be low-end programs (such as Paint), or dumbed-down versions of existing applications (such as WordPad). Occasionally, however, a truly impressive product makes it into the Windows package. NetMeeting is one of those products. This is an outstanding remote collaboration tool that does just about everything you'd want it to, and throws in a few surprises, to boot. However, for anything other than simple voice or chat conversations, NetMeeting requires a significant amount of bandwidth and so, for now, is best utilized over a local area network.

Dial-Up Networking improvements.   Most people use Dial-Up Networking to connect to the Internet, and Windows 98 offers a few enhancements. For example, you can tell Dial-Up Networking to connect without prompting you for a username and password. Windows 98's Dial-Up Networking also supports dial-up scripts and the ability to set up your computer as a dial-up server. Windows 98 also offers Multilink Bandwidth Aggregation, which enables you to combine bandwidth from multiple phone lines. See Chapter 29, "Connecting Remotely with Dial-Up Networking."

- **Beyond the hype:** Most of these enhancements were available in the Microsoft Plus! add-on for Windows 95. These are all very useful features that deserve to be in the operating system.

The Windows 98 System Tools

In most respects, I have no trouble avoiding becoming a "cheerleader" for Windows 98. However, I do tend to reserve a "rah, rah" or two for Windows 98's fine collection of system tools. No third-party utility or utility suite comes close to the breadth and depth of what the Windows 98 system tools can do (at least not yet). Of course, a cynic would reply that only an operating system that has fundamental problems would require such a large collection of tools. That's true to a certain extent, but it's also true that many of these tools aren't mere troubleshooters. They also serve to enhance performance and ease system maintenance.

Windows 98 boasts over two dozen system utilities. Here's my take on the noteworthy tools that are new or improved.

FAT32 and Drive Converter.   FAT32 is a new file system that Windows 98 supports for storing files on disk. It offers a number of benefits, but the biggest are the ability to work with partitions larger than 2GB, and more efficient file storage (Microsoft claims FAT32 is 28 percent more efficient than FAT16, on average). Windows 98 also ships with Drive Converter, a utility that converts a FAT16 drive to FAT32 without trashing your data. I discuss FAT32 in Chapter 14, "Making the Move to FAT32."

- **Beyond the hype:** In my own testing, I've found that FAT32 is around 35–40 percent more efficient than FAT16, so for once Microsoft is under-hyping something. You have to be careful, however. Once you convert a partition to FAT32, you can't convert it back to FAT16, you can no longer uninstall Windows 98, and you can't compress the partition using DriveSpace.

Registry Checker.   This utility checks the Windows 98 Registry for damage and wasted space, and can repair and compress the Registry files automatically. It also makes backup copies of the Registry each time you launch Windows 98.

- **Beyond the hype:** As you'll see throughout this book (particularly in Chapter 4, "An Insider's Guide to Three Crucial Configuration Tools") the Registry is Windows 98's most vital component. So the Registry Checker is a welcome addition to Windows 98's preventative maintenance arsenal.

Inside Scoop
There are, however, third-party utilities that can convert a FAT32 partition back to FAT16. The best of these tools is PartitionMagic, by PowerQuest Corp (http://www.powerquest.com/).

See Also...
"An Insider's Guide to the Registry,"
p. 104

System File Checker. This program (see Figure 1.3) examines the Windows 98 system files and lets you know if any of these files have been deleted, replaced, or corrupted. The program can then restore the file. System File Checker can also extract a file from one of the Windows 98 installation files. See Chapter 15, "Crucial System Maintenance Skills."

See Also...
"Running System
File Checker,"
p. 351

- **Beyond the hype:** Damaged, missing, or overwritten system files are the chief causes of instability and General Protection Faults in Windows. So the System File Checker's ability to repair these errors should mean a more reliable setup over the long term. This program's ability to extract files from the Windows 98 source files is also a welcome and useful feature. On the downside, however, note that System File Checker does not check for changed and deleted files by default, which is just plain dumb.

Figure 1.3
System File
Checker keeps an
eye on your precious system
files.

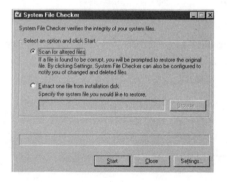

See Also...
"Backing Up Your
Files," p. 372

Backup. The Windows 98 version of the Microsoft Backup program is much improved over its Windows 95 predecessor. For novices, the program includes wizards for backing up and restoring data. It also supports a much larger range of backup devices, has more backup and restore options, and can also back up the Registry files. I cover Backup in Chapter 16, "Preparing for Trouble."

- **Beyond the hype:** Although the Windows 98 Backup is an improvement, this is still not a great backup program. In particular, Backup's inability to schedule unattended backups is a crucial flaw.

System Recovery.   This utility enables you to restore your system from a complete backup should you experience a hard disk crash or other calamity. Given a new or formatted hard disk, System Recovery restores your system to its pre-crash state automatically. I discuss this utility in Chapter 16.

See Also...
"Using System Recovery to Recover from a Crash," p. 379

- **Beyond the hype:** The ability to completely recover your system in the event of a major crash is useful, to say the least, and System Recovery works beautifully. However, it's important to understand that you won't get any use out of this utility if you don't prepare for a possible crash. Moreover, as documented, System Recovery is too rigid to be generally useful. Chapter 16 shows you not only how best to prepare for using System Recovery, but it also provides undocumented methods for making the program more flexible.

Disk Cleanup.   As a matter of course, hard disks accumulate unneeded and temporary files that take up large amounts of disk space. The Disk Cleanup utility (see Figure 1.4) can identify many of these files—as well as files downloaded from the Internet and those in the Recycle Bin—and offer to delete them for you. See Chapter 13, "Optimizing Your Hard Disk."

See Also...
"Using Disk Cleanup to Remove Unnecessary Files," p. 313

- **Beyond the hype:** This feature represents a good first step towards keeping a hard disk free of clutter. However, there are a number of other candidates for deletion that should have been included: zero-byte files, empty folders, and backup files (these files commonly use the bak or old extensions).

Remember
Microsoft Plus! 98 is a collection of extra programs designed for Windows 98. It includes an enhanced version of Disk Cleanup that can delete a far wider range of files.

System Configuration.   This program aids startup troubleshooting by providing an interface for choosing various startup options and for enabling and disabling startup features. For more startup information, see Chapter 3, "Understanding and Controlling the Windows 98 Startup."

Figure 1.4
Use Disk Cleanup
to remove
unneeded files
from your system.

See Also...
"Controlling
Startup Using the
System
Configuration
Utility," p. 86

See Also...
"Optimizing Disk
Access Times
with Disk
Defragmenter,"
p. 320
"Using WinAlign
to Speed Up
Program
Launching,"
p. 324

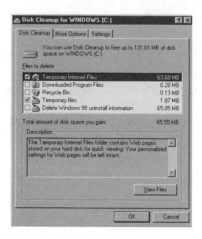

- **Beyond the hype:** In Windows 95, startup troubleshooting was a hit-and-miss experience that required quite a bit of legwork to track down the culprit. System Configuration saves a lot of time by making it easy to try different startup configurations. On the downside, System Configuration's nice interface is wasted if you can't start Windows 98.

Application Launch Accelerator and WinAlign. These two utilities are designed to make your applications launch faster. Application Launch Accelerator works in conjunction with Disk Defragmenter to position frequently used program files for the quickest hard disk access. WinAlign restructures program files so that they can be launched directly from the hard disk cache. The inner workings of these utilities are covered in Chapter 13.

- **Beyond the hype:** Windows 98 has minor performance improvements throughout, but application launching is a source of major improvement. These two technologies significantly improve application launch times. However, Application Launch Accelerator also slows down Disk Defragmenter considerably, and WinAlign is only useful under certain conditions (which is discussed in Chapter 13).

System Information utility. Windows 98 stores a ton of information about your system's hardware and software. Some of that data is viewable via the Registry Editor, and some of it can be reviewed in the Device Manager. However, the place to go for just about any system data is the System Information utility. Note, too, that this utility is also a useful launching pad for tools such as the Registry Checker and the System File Checker (see Chapter 15).

See Also...
"The System Information Utility," p. 346

- **Beyond the hype:** Most of the information in this utility is highly technical, and so it's really designed for tech support engineers. That's not a bad thing, because any extra bit of data you can supply an engineer can only help them to find a solution.

Task Scheduler and the Maintenance Wizard.   These tools enable you to schedule maintenance tasks at regular intervals. The Task Scheduler (really the Scheduled Tasks folder) can run any program at a preset schedule, and the Maintenance Wizard (see Figure 1.5) acts as a front-end for the Task Scheduler.

- **Beyond the hype:** Task Scheduler is a flexible program that's ideal for running maintenance programs such as ScanDisk and Disk Defragmenter regularly (which is the key to proper system maintenance). The Maintenance Wizard is more suited to inexperienced users, but it's also useful as a starting point for quickly scheduling a few tasks that you can later tweak by hand in the Scheduled Tasks folder.

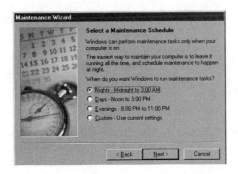

Figure 1.5
Use the Maintenance Wizard to quickly schedule routine Windows 98 maintenance.

New Hardware Support

One of the things an operating system must do well is support a wide range of hardware devices and standards. So one of Windows 98's primary "reasons for being" is to offer the world an operating system that's conversant with the latest gadgets. Much of this support only proves important in the future as devices based on standards such as the Universal Serial Bus, FireWire, and DVD become more common. In that regard, Windows 98 appears to be reasonably "future proof," at least in the medium term. Here's my take on some of the more important hardware innovations in Windows 98.

See Also...
"Setting Up Multiple Monitors,"
p. 564

Multiple monitors. With this feature, if you add a second video card/monitor combination to your PC, Windows 98 expands the desktop across both monitors. You can drag windows from one monitor to the other, display the taskbar on either monitor, and even set up separate display settings for each monitor. Windows 98 supports up to nine video card/monitor combinations. I explain how to set up multiple monitors in Chapter 24, "Maximizing Multimedia Hardware."

"
Multimonitor support is my favorite Win 98 feature.
—Jim Seymour,
PC Magazine
"

- **Beyond the hype:** I've been using two monitors for months and can't imagine going back to a single monitor setup. It is just wildly convenient to have my email client or a window containing research materials on one monitor and my word processor on another. The drawback here is an obvious one: the cost of an extra video card and monitor. Also, only certain PCI and AGP (see below) video cards are supported.

Accelerated Graphics Port (AGP). AGP is a new video bus that offers up to four times the performance of PCI video cards. By bypassing the PCI bus and a few other tricks, AGP cards render graphics—particularly 3D images—faster and with greater detail.

- **Beyond the hype:** AGP seems to be the video card of choice on new Pentium II systems, so it's good to have support for this standard built into the operating system.

Enhanced display settings. Windows 98 offers a number of video adapter enhancements, including the ability to change the color resolution without having to restart your computer, and the ability to set video card refresh rates.

- **Beyond the hype:** These enhancements are the kinds of things you don't have to worry about very often, but when you do need them, you're very glad they're around.

Pentium MMX. Windows 98 offers support for third-party applications that utilize Intel's Multimedia Extensions (MMX) for the Pentium processor.

- **Beyond the hype:** MMX support isn't all that important in mainstream business applications, so this one isn't a big deal unless you plan on running MMX-based games.

Universal Serial Bus (USB). This bus enables users to daisy chain up to 127 devices to a single port and "hot swap" those devices (that is, add and remove devices without turning off the computer). USB also supplies power to devices that need it and offers 12Mbps throughput. Windows 98 has built-in support for USB controllers and USB devices such as keyboards, mice, scanners, speakers, and printers. Your PC must have one or more USB ports to take advantage of this feature.

- **Beyond the hype:** This support actually began in a service release of Windows 95, so technically this isn't a new feature. Still, only a limited number of USB devices were available when Windows 98 shipped. Given the fact that a two-port USB configuration is becoming standard on most new PCs, and the fact that there are now millions of Windows 98 users out there, USB peripherals are being released at an increasing rate. It's pretty clear that USB will be the optimal I/O standard in years to come, so it's great to have native operating system support for it.

IEEE 1394. This competitor to USB offers similar benefits to users: up to 63 devices connected to a single port, hot swapping, and so on. Where IEEE 1394 (also known as "FireWire" or simply "1394") shines is throughout: from 100Mbps to

400Mbps. Windows 98 supports the IEEE 1394 bus and it comes with drivers for 1394 controllers from Adaptec, Intel, and others.

- **Beyond the hype:** Again, IEEE 1394 is a standard whose time has not yet come, at least at the consumer level. Its fast throughput makes it a natural in digital video applications, including videoconferencing. This means that IEEE 1394 and NetMeeting's videoconferencing features are a natural fit (and work beautifully together, in my experience).

DVD-ROM. DVD (which stands for Digital Versatile Disc or possibly Digital Video Disc, depending on who you talk to) is a new optical storage medium. DVD-Video discs are designed for movies and other entertainment, while DVD-ROM discs are a storage medium, not unlike CD-ROM. DVD-ROM discs can hold up to 4.7GB of data, compared with just 650MB for CD-ROM. Windows 98 features an updated CD-ROM device driver that supports DVD-ROM drives. It also supports a new DVD file system called the Universal Disk Filesystem, or UDF.

- **Beyond the hype:** DVD support is not yet a big deal since DVD-Video has failed to capture the public's imagination, and few applications use DVD-ROM discs as a distribution medium. The consensus seems to be that computer-based DVD will not explode until DVD-RAM (with its ability to write data to a DVD disc) appears. The first DVD-RAM drives began shipping in the fall of 1998.

See Also...
"IRQ Lines, I/O Ports, and Other Device Settings," p. 514

IRQ steering. This feature enables Windows 98 to maintain "holders" for some Interrupt Request lines (IRQs), and to assign those holders dynamically as devices need them. I explain IRQs and IRQ steering in Chapter 22, "Taking the Mystery Out of Hardware."

- **Beyond the hype:** This is one of the most underrated of Windows 98's features. On systems that support it, IRQ steering means never again having to worry about conflicting IRQs or not being able to install another device due to a lack of available IRQs. An emphatic thumbs-up for this one.

Scanners and digital cameras.   No longer seen only in high-end graphics shops, image scanners and digital cameras are now popular consumer devices. Windows 98 supports these still-image capture devices and offers the Imaging for Windows applet for importing images from a scanner or camera and for manipulating those images once they're on the hard disk (see Chapter 24).

See Also...
"Working with Scanners and Digital Cameras," p. 567

- **Beyond the hype:** Windows 98 doesn't bring all that much to the table here since it requires existing TWAIN support for scanners and ships with only a limited number of drivers for digital cameras. Imaging for Windows contains a few interesting annotation features, but is otherwise unremarkable.

Power management.   Windows 98 implements Advanced Power Management (APM) 1.2, which includes features such as hard drive spin down, modem wake-on-ring, and support for multiple notebook batteries. Windows 98 offers a Power Management icon in Control Panel for easy power management customization. Windows 98 also implements Advanced Configuration and Power Interface (ACPI) 1.0, which brings power management to the operating system level (where it used to reside at the BIOS level). Power management is mostly of use to notebook users, so I discuss it in Chapter 25, "The Ins and Outs of Windows 98's Notebook Features."

See Also...
"Power Management for Notebook Users," p. 576

- **Beyond the hype:** APM and ACPI are laudable attempts at providing modern power management techniques for PCs. In practice, however, these standards are implemented poorly. For example, Windows 98's default time-outs for turning off the monitor and hard drive are absurdly low on desktop systems. Also, the system standby is often the cause of system lockups and other undesirable behavior. If you want to use these features, you need to change the default settings and exercise some caution until you see how your system reacts.

"

Windows 98: n.
32 bit exten-
sions and a
graphical shell
for a 16 bit
patch to an 8 bit
operating sys-
tem originally
coded for a 4 bit
microprocessor,
written by a 2
bit company,
that can't stand
1 bit of competi-
tion.
—From the
Internet

"

Other New Features

This section closes our look at what's brand new in Windows 98 by running through a mixed bag of features that represent "the best of the rest."

A streamlined Setup program.   The Windows 98 Setup offers a number of improvements over its Windows 95 predecessor. The biggest improvement occurs during a Windows 95 upgrade. Setup can read the existing Registry settings, so it doesn't need to prompt you for very much information. Also, the hardware detection phase (which is skipped on a Windows 95 upgrade) is put off until after Setup has installed most of the Windows 98 files and rebooted the machine.

- **Beyond the hype:** If you're upgrading from Windows 95, Setup is extremely easy and, in my experience, generally runs without mishap. Leaving the hardware detection phase until after the first reboot is an excellent idea since it gives Setup a chance to detect Plug and Play devices first, and it ensures that installation is mostly complete before the often problematic hardware detection occurs. Note, however, that the easiest Setup route can often lead to problems down the road. For more about this, see Chapter 2, "Ten Things You Should Know About the Windows 98 Setup."

The My Documents folder.   Setup creates a folder named My Documents, which you can use to store the documents that you create. Setup also creates a shortcut to this folder on the Windows 98 desktop.

- **Beyond the hype:** Using a folder as a storage area for all your documents has been a central part of good file management techniques for a number of years. It makes it easier to find documents and it makes it easier to back them up. It's nice to see the operating system recognize this. Note, however, that you need to add a number of subfolders within My Documents in order to better organize your files.

Windows Address Book.   Windows 98 has an address book application you can use to store contact data. This Windows Address Book is also used by Outlook Express and Internet Explorer, and it has tie-ins with NetMeeting.

- **Beyond the hype:** The idea of a global address book is a good one since it means you can keep all your contact information in one spot. Unfortunately, not all applications know about the Windows Address Book, so it's not quite global. However, the Windows Address Book does have an import feature, so you should be able to consolidate most of your addresses under one roof.

Accessibility options.   Windows 98 has a new Accessibility Wizard (see Figure 1.6) that makes it easier to customize the interface to suit those with special hearing, vision, or mobility needs. Also new is the Microsoft Magnifier, which enables you to magnify portions of the screen.

- **Beyond the hype:** Windows has always been ahead of the curve when it comes to implementing accessibility features. The large range of accessibility options in Windows 98 proves Microsoft's commitment to making PCs accessible to everyone.

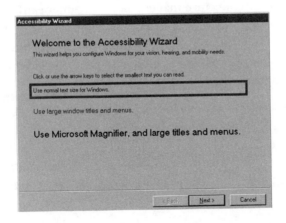

Figure 1.6
The Accessibility Wizard leads you step-by-step through the process of setting up Windows 98's accessibility options.

Start menu customizing.   You can now perform much of your Start menu maintenance and customization by working directly with (that is, by right-clicking) Start menu items.

- **Beyond the hype:** Customizing the Start menu is a great way to boost productivity, and it must be the most common customization task. Therefore, giving users the ability to customize Start menu items directly is a welcome enhancement. I just wish they were a bit smarter about it. For example, you can't rename Start menu items directly, which is frustrating.

Support for the wheel mouse.   Some modern mice (including Microsoft's Intellimouse) have an extra wheel "button" in the middle. Windows 98 now supports this wheel, which means that you can use it to scroll up and down in most Windows 98 windows.

See Also...
"Customizing the
Mouse," p. 536

- **Beyond the hype:** It's good that Windows 98 supports wheel scrolling, particularly in Internet Explorer since Web surfing is often a click-and-scroll business. Unfortunately, older applications don't support wheel scrolling, which leads to an interface inconsistency that can throw you for a loop. Note, however, that there is a way around this, and I tell you about it in Chapter 23, "Setting Up and Customizing Input Devices."

WebTV for Windows.   Windows 98 implements a new Broadcast Architecture that enables a TV tuner card-equipped computer to receive and display TV signals. The WebTV for Windows application can download program listings and offers a Program Guide that enables you to select the station you want to view.

- **Beyond the hype:** This technology is really in its infancy and is not implemented well in Windows 98. The hardware support is meager (only ATI All-In-Wonder TV tuner cards are supported), program listing downloads are often problematic, and WebTV for Windows is flaky, at best. This is a "wait for version 3" technology.

NetShow and streaming content.   Windows 98 comes with the NetShow player, which can run multimedia content (video or audio) streamed over the Internet or an intranet.

- **Beyond the hype:** Streaming media is a real leap forward because you no longer have to wait for an entire file to download. Instead, NetShow processes the content "on-the-fly," so the video or audio plays almost immediately. The downside is that the quality isn't great on slower connections. Note, too, that NetShow has been replaced by the new Media Player, which is available from the Windows Update Web site.

Windows Scripting Host.   This program enables users to create scripts—in either VBScript or JavaScript—that program many aspects of Windows 98, including the Registry, network resources, and shortcuts. And with the Windows Scripting Host's support for ActiveX Scripting, you can program objects from other applications.

- **Beyond the hype:** This is one of those "it's about time" features. There have been third-party utilities that implement Windows "batch" programming for years, but this support really needs to be built into the operating system. The Windows Scripting Host is quite powerful, although it has no editing environment or debugger, so it's not easy to use.

What's New in Windows 98 Second Edition

As I mentioned earlier, Microsoft hasn't been shy about adding new upgrades and fixes to the Windows Update Web site. In fact, Windows Update had so many new components that Microsoft decided to package them together into a new version of the operating system called Windows 98 Second Edition. This is available as an OEM release (meaning that most new computers will ship with Second Edition as the OS), a full retail version, and a retail upgrade. Besides the inevitable bug fixes and security patches, here's a summary of what else is in Windows 98 Second Edition.

Internet Explorer 5.   This new version of Windows 98's default browser is crammed with improvements, including the following: an improved Search feature; easier access to previously typed URLs; importing and exporting of Favorites and Netscape bookmarks; the ability to save Web form data and have it entered automatically the next time you use the form; a Radio toolbar enabling you to listen to a radio station while surfing; and a What's Related feature showing sites related to the current one. Microsoft also claims that Internet Explorer 5 loads pages up to 50 percent faster than Internet Explorer 4. See Chapter 19 to learn more about the new features in version 5.

- **Beyond the hype:** Internet Explorer 5 is a great browser, but it doesn't offer any spectacular improvements over version 4. Most of the new features are usability enhancements so, overall, the browsing experience feels smoother and more efficient. My own load testing didn't show a consistent 50 percent speed boost, but Internet Explorer 5 is definitely faster. (I've found that the actual boost varies widely from site to site.) Finally, the ability to have form data entered automatically is nice, but you wouldn't want to use it when accessing your online bank account!

Outlook Express 5.   This update includes many new features: improved message filtering, easier access to contacts, an improved Find feature, the ability to set up "identities" so that multiple users can share Outlook Express without exposing their messages, and many more customization options.

- **Beyond the hype:** Windows 98's original version of Outlook Express was an excellent email client, and the improvements in version 5 make it even better. I still don't like HTML as the default sending format, but I fear I'm swimming against the tide on this one.

Internet Connection Sharing.   This feature enables a single Net-connected machine to share that connection with other machines on the network.

- **Beyond the hype:** The ability to share an Internet connection among multiple machines on a network has long been a problem for small networks. Previously, you either had to use a dedicated router, or you had to go to third-party software such as WinGate. Internet Connection Sharing is easy to set up (a wizard takes you through), and maintenance is minimal (particularly if you use DHCP to translate IP addresses automatically). Overall, this is a welcome addition to Windows 98's networking arsenal.

Windows Media Player. This program replaces the ActiveMovie control as Windows 98's jack-of-all-media-trades. It's easier to use than ActiveMovie and has support for a large number of media file types, including many audio formats, MIDI, MPEG, MP3, AVI, QuickTime, ASF, and ASX.

- **Beyond the hype:** ActiveMovie not only had a misleading name, but its implementation as an ActiveX control rather than a full-blown application was strange. Media Player is a big improvement with a much nicer interface. The main drawback of Media Player is that it doesn't support RealAudio or RealVideo streaming media.

Renaming Start menu shortcuts. Previously, I mentioned that one of Windows 98's little frustrations was its lack of a Rename command on the context menu for Start menu shortcuts. That oversight has been fixed in Windows 98 Second Edition.

- **Beyond the hype:** It's about time!

Dial-Up Networking 1.3. This iteration of Dial-Up Networking offers extra security features, including the ability to specify that 128-bit encryption is required over a connection, and a new MSCHAP secure mode for virtual private networking (VPN) connections.

- **Beyond the hype:** No one can complain when extra security is offered, so these innovations are welcomed. Now if Microsoft would just fix all those other security holes still waiting to be discovered in Internet Explorer, we could all sleep better at night.

Support for the euro symbol. The default Windows 98 fonts now support the symbol for the new euro currency: €.

■ **Beyond the hype:** With the euro an integral part of the international financial community as of January 1, 1999, many people will appreciate the ability to easily add this symbol to their documents.

Wake-On-LAN. This feature enables a network node to go into suspend mode to save energy, but then to be "wakened" if it detects another machine attempting to access it via the network.

■ **Beyond the hype:** With power management becoming common on not only notebooks, but also desktop systems, making sure suspended machines are still available for network access is crucial. Note, however, that hardware support is limited only to network cards that support the NDIS Power Management Object Identifier. Suspend mode technologies have never really worked consistently well in Windows, so only time and testing will tell if Wake-On-LAN can be used reliably in the field.

WebTV for Windows update. This update supports the BrookTree chipset used by some TV tuner cards, offers improved parental controls, and enables you to launch WebTV tuned to a specific channel.

■ **Beyond the hype:** WebTV with this update is definitely a better product, but most of my earlier reservations still stand. This is "version 1.1" and I'm still waiting for "version 3."

Device Bay support. *Device Bay* is hardware specification developed by Microsoft, Intel, and Compaq. The goal is to enable users to add and upgrade peripherals simply by inserting them into a slot. You don't have to open the case or worry about connecting power or interface cables.

■ **Beyond the hype:** Although no products were shipping as this book went to press, Device Bay looks like a great idea on paper (see http://www.devicebay.org/). The vast majority of users are understandably squeamish about opening their computers, so installing items such as DVD drives and hard drives is beyond most people. To be able to install these and many other devices simply by plugging them into an external bay is a great innovation. And, it goes without saying, having support for this initiative at the operating system level is a no-brainer.

What's New Since Windows 3.*x*

If you bypassed the Windows 95 hoopla and are making the move to Windows 98 from DOS or Windows 3.*x*, you find quite a bit different in both the look and operation of Windows. To help you make the transition, this section runs through a few of the more important changes.

The desktop.   When you start Windows 98, the first thing that should strike you is that Program Manager is gone. Instead, you see a large green area with a few icons on it. That green area is the Windows 98 *desktop*, and it's where you'll do all your Windows work.

- **Beyond the hype:** The desktop is a versatile area in that it's capable of holding all kinds of objects, including program icons, *shortcuts* that point to files (see the next item), and even Web page objects if you turn on the Active Desktop feature. Unfortunately, the desktop tends to get hidden under multiple windows (or even just a single maximized window), so in many cases its usefulness is limited.

Shortcuts.   A shortcut is a tiny file that serves only to point to something else. In the simplest sense, a shortcut that points to an application is more or less identical to a Program Manager icon. In both cases, double-clicking the shortcut or icon launches the application. However, Windows 98 shortcuts are more versatile since they can also point to documents, folders, disk drives, network resources, printers, Web sites, and more. See Chapter 11, "Taking Advantage of Shortcuts."

- **Beyond the hype:** Shortcuts are everywhere in Windows 98, and they really do spare you a lot of the drudgery of having to track down files and other resources. However, shortcuts are only as useful as they are convenient. So it's

66

Microsoft estimates there are 40 million Win3.*x* users out there.
—Amy Helen Johnson, Windows Magazine

99

Inside Scoop
Program Manager is still part of the Windows 98 package. To use it, select Start, Run, type progman in the Run dialog box, and then click OK.

Remember
Windows 98 rarely uses the term *directory*. Instead, these disk storage locations are now usually called *folders*.

See Also...
"Redoing the
Taskbar,"
p. 244

not enough to just create shortcuts, but you also have to give some thought to where you put them. For example, most people put all their shortcuts on the desktop, which isn't convenient if the desktop is hidden behind a bunch of windows. Chapter 9, "Customizing the Windows 98 Interface," offers quite a few techniques for taking control of your shortcuts.

See Also...
"Renovating the
Start Menu,"
p. 237

The Start menu. With Program Manager out of the way, how do you launch programs? That's the job of the Start menu, which you display by clicking the Start button in the lower-left corner of the screen. The menu that appears contains several icons, some of which display submenus, which are the Windows 98 equivalent of program groups (see Figure 1.7).

■ **Beyond the hype:** The Start menu is a more sensible arrangement than Windows 3.*x*'s program groups. However, to get to some Windows 98 features, you have to slog through two or three subfolders. To get the most out of the Start menu, you have to customize it so that the items you use most often are only a click or two away (see Chapter 9).

Figure 1.7
Click the Start button to display the Start menu. From here you can access program files, favorites folders, and other accessories without using the program manager.

The taskbar. This is the gray strip that runs along the bottom of the window. Its job is to display an icon for each running program. You can then switch between programs by clicking these taskbar icons. The Windows 98 taskbar also enables you to create "toolbars" to hold shortcuts.

- **Beyond the hype:** The taskbar icons are very handy because they enable you to tell which applications are currently running with a quick glance. The task-switching abilities of the taskbar are less useful because most people prefer the old Alt+Tab method.

Long filenames.   Windows 98 supports filenames that go well beyond the restrictions of DOS filenames. Primary names can be longer than eight characters and extensions can be longer than three characters. Filenames can include spaces and the following characters:

~ ` ! @ # $ % ^ & ( ) _ – + = [ ] ; ' , .

- **Beyond the hype:** Long filenames are a welcome relief from the onerous "8.3" restrictions enforced by DOS. The tendency for new users is to take full advantage of this feature and create extremely long filenames. However, more seasoned users know that extremely long names are difficult to work with, not only at the DOS prompt, but also in Windows Explorer and the Open and Save As dialog boxes. Two- or three-word filenames are ideal. Note, too, that only applications designed for Windows 9x and Windows NT can understand long filenames. Older applications can still work with these files, but they see only a truncated version of the name. For example, My Web Page.html would be seen as MYWEBP~1.HTM.

Shortcut menus.   These are menus that appear when you right-click an object (such as the desktop, the taskbar, or an icon). They're also known as *context menus* because the menu commands you see depend on which object you right-clicked. For example, if you right-click the desktop, you see some commands for arranging the icons, creating a new icon, and so on. On the other hand, if you right-click an icon, you see commands for opening the icon, renaming it, deleting it, and so on.

- **Beyond the hype:** I use shortcut menus constantly because, as their name implies, they are almost always faster than the equivalent pull-down menu commands. The only trick

Undocumented
So just how long can Windows 98 filenames get? Microsoft claims the limit is 255 characters, but that's not quite right. The actual rule is that the file's full pathname—the drive, folder, and filename—can't exceed 253 characters.

Remember
Here's the general rule that Windows 98 uses for creating an 8.3 filename out of a long filename. For the primary name, remove all the spaces and other illegal characters, take the first six remaining characters, and append "~1". For the extension, take just the first three characters. Note that if this would result in two files having the same 8.3 name, then Windows 98 uses "~2" instead of "~1" in the primary name.

is knowing when to use a shortcut menu, because the commands you see are only a subset of the complete list of commands that are available for a given object.

Property sheets.   Most Windows 98 objects (files, folders, drives, icons, and so on) have a set of *properties* that determine how the object looks and operates. A *property sheet* is a special dialog box that contains controls for all of the object's properties. In most cases, you display the property sheet for an object either by highlighting the object and selecting File, Properties, or by right-clicking the object and then clicking Properties in the shortcut menu. Figure 1.8 shows the desktop's property sheet.

- **Beyond the hype:** Property sheets are invaluable because they gather all of an object's alterable characteristics into a single location for easy customization. Unfortunately, Windows 98 often tries to cram too much into a single property sheet, which can be confusing.

Figure 1.8
Here is the property sheet for the desktop.

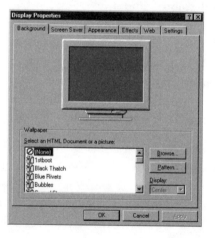

To complete your look at what's new in Windows 98 for DOS and Windows 3.*x* users, Table 1.1 presents a few DOS and Windows tasks and shows you their Windows 98 equivalents.

TABLE 1.1: THE WINDOWS 98 EQUIVALENTS FOR SOME DOS AND WINDOWS 3.x TASKS

Task	DOS/Windows 3.x	Windows 98 Equivalent
Launch a program	Program Manager	Start menu
Switch programs	Alt+Tab	Taskbar or Alt+Tab
Word processing	Write	WordPad
Create pictures	Paintbrush	Paint
Work with files	File Manager	Windows Explorer
Find files	File, Search (File Manager)	Start, Find, Files, or Folders
Undelete a file	UNDELETE (DOS)	Recycle Bin
Repair a disk	SCANDISK (DOS)	ScanDisk
Defragment files	DEFRAG (DOS)	Disk Defragmenter
Compress files	DRVSPACE (DOS)	DriveSpace
Back up files	BACKUP (DOS)	Backup
Control print jobs	Print Manager	Printers folder
Customize Windows	Control Panel group	Control Panel folder
Use a modem	Terminal	HyperTerminal
Connect computers Connection	INTERLNK (DOS)	Direct Cable
Use accessories	Accessories group	Start, Programs, Accessories
Set the time	Control Panel, Clock	Taskbar clock
Get help	Help menu (Program Manager)	Start, Help
Exit Windows	File, Exit (Program Manager)	Start, Shut Down

Shortcut
To reduce clutter on many property sheets (and other dialog boxes), Windows 98 uses *tabbed dialog boxes*. These dialogs have several tabs—reminiscent of notebook tabs—along the top (refer to Figure 1.8). Clicking a tab presents a different set of controls. To cycle through tabs from the keyboard, press Ctrl+Tab or Ctrl+Shift+Tab.

Essential Information

■ Web integration's single-click launching is convenient, but its no-click selecting feature doesn't work well, and the Active Desktop does more harm than good.

■ Windows 98 Internet features are excellent overall, and they include some "best-of-breed" applications, including Internet Explorer, Outlook Express, and NetMeeting.

■ Windows 98 ships with an impressive collection of tools for system monitoring, maintenance, and repair.

- Windows 98 supports many new hardware devices—such as MMX, AGP, USB, IEEE 1394, DVD, and Zip and Jaz disks—which is good news for newer computers that are more likely to use these technologies.

- Other new and improved features include a streamlined Setup program, easier Start menu customization, more accessibility options, WebTV for Windows, and the Windows Scripting Host.

- For those making the move from DOS or Windows 3.*x*, Windows 98 offers a new desktop metaphor, the taskbar, shortcuts, long filenames, shortcut menus, and property sheets.

GET THE SCOOP ON...
Installing to maximize performance ▪ Dual-booting
with other operating systems ▪ Installing to a clean
system ▪ Creating customized and automated installations ▪ Adding and removing Windows 98 components ▪ Uninstalling Windows 98

Ten Things You Should Know About the Windows 98 Setup

Chapter 2

IN ITS PRESS RELEASES and documentation, Microsoft crows that the Windows 98 Setup is the easiest operating system installation routine yet. However, what they don't say is that installing Windows 98 is easy only under certain conditions, and only if you take a few precautions in advance. What Microsoft also won't tell you is that there is often a trade-off involved in how you set up Windows 98. The easiest setup route (installing over Windows 95) often leads to the most problems later on, while following the hardest route (installing on a clean system) most often leads to relatively problem-free computing.

This chapter discusses these and many other Windows 98 Setup issues. I take you behind the scenes to learn some truly useful setup know-how that helps you prepare for the installation process and will help you get through the installation after you decide to take the plunge. You'll also learn a few setup-related chores, such as adding and removing Windows 98 components and uninstalling Windows 98.

"

The Windows 98 Setup Wizard makes changing operating systems easier than ever.

—From Windows 98's "Getting Started" booklet

"

Going Beyond the Minimum Windows 98 Hardware Requirements

The Windows 95 minimum system requirements elicited quite a few chuckles when they were originally published. Yes, it was theoretically possible to run Windows 95 on a 386DX system equipped with a mere 4MB of RAM, but I doubt that anyone who tried ever got any work done. The minimum requirements for Windows 98 have been bumped up to the next level, but so too have Windows 98's resource requirements. And so, once again, a system that can boast nothing more than the bare-bones hardware recommended by Microsoft will have serious performance problems.

Therefore, you should consider the following list of minimum hardware requirements only the starting point for either upgrading or purchasing a system for Windows 98:

- A 486DX processor running at 66MHz.

- 16MB of RAM.

Remember
If you're upgrading over an existing version of Windows, Setup can backup your existing system files, which can take up as much as 65MB of hard disk space. Also, the disk space requirements will be less if you're installing to a FAT32 partition, which stores files more efficiently (see Chapter 14, "Making the Move to FAT32").

- A hard disk with a partition that has enough free space to hold not only the Windows 98 files, but also the temporary files that are installed by the Setup program. If you're upgrading over Windows 95, you'll need at least 170MB of free space; for a clean install, the minimum is approximately 185MB.

- A VGA video card and monitor.

- A CD-ROM drive if you're installing Windows 98 from the CD-ROM; a 3 1/2-inch floppy drive if you're installing Windows 98 from floppy disks.

Depending on what you're used to, this may seem like a reasonable system. Such a machine would positively scream under Windows 3.x, and it would perform quite well under Windows 95, but it's simply not good enough for serious work in Windows 98. The most underpowered machine that I've used with Windows 98 is a Pentium 120 notebook with 16MB of RAM, and I find it only barely usable.

Here are the real minimum hardware requirements for Windows 98:

- A system with a PCI bus and a Plug and Play-compliant BIOS.

- A Pentium MMX processor running at 200MHz.

- 32MB of RAM.

- A hard disk with a partition that has at least 500MB of free space. This will enable you to load as many of the Windows 98 components as you want, and it gives you enough space for other applications to install their program and support files. It also gives you room to install the inevitable updates and patches that will appear over the course of Windows 98's lifetime.

- A Super VGA video card and monitor capable of displaying at least 256 colors at 1,024×768 resolution.

- A Microsoft-compatible mouse; a keyboard with the Windows logo key (⊞); a sound card and speakers; a modem for online and Internet sessions; and a network adapter for connecting to a network.

Other Windows 98 features require further hardware investments. For example, if you want to take advantage of Windows 98's multiple-monitor support, you'll need a second video card/monitor combination. Similarly, if you want to use Windows 98's new WebTV application, you'll need one of the ATI All-in-Wonder TV tuner cards.

To ensure that your system hardware is fully compatible with Windows 98, check out the Microsoft Windows Hardware Compatibility List:

`http://www.microsoft.com/hwtest/hcl/`

This page enables you to search for specific devices to see if they are compatible with Windows 98, or meet Microsoft logo requirements for the PC 97 or PC 98 hardware specifications. For the latter, see the following Web site:

`http://www.microsoft.com/hwdev/pc98.htm`

Remember
If you're installing Windows 98 Second Edition, the Setup procedure is no different from the one used in the original Windows 98.

Upgrading from DOS or an Existing Version of Windows

If your hardware passes muster, the next decision you have to make is how to install Windows 98. You have three choices:

- Upgrade from DOS or over an existing version of Windows.

- Install to dual-boot with an existing operating system.

- Install to a "clean" hard disk that has no existing operating system.

This section discusses upgrading from DOS or Windows. Later sections discuss dual-boot and clean installations.

Shortcut
If your system is DOS-only, but you do have Windows 3.x or Windows 95 on disk or CD-ROM, you don't have to install the old version of Windows in order to use the Windows 98 upgrade. Instead, the Setup program will prompt you to insert your original disk (or disks) to verify that you have an existing version of Windows.

Upgrading from DOS or Windows 3.0

If your system is running DOS only (or Windows 3.0), you can "upgrade" to Windows 98 under the following conditions:

- You must be running DOS 5.0 or later.

- You must have the "full" version of Windows 98: either the full OEM version from your computer manufacturer or the full retail version (the one that says "for PCs without Windows" on the box). The upgrade version looks for an existing version of Windows, so it won't work on a DOS-only machine.

What happens to your existing DOS files after Windows 98 is installed? The original DOS directory remains in place, but certain commands that could cause problems if run within Windows 98 are renamed with the ex~ extension. (For example, defrag.exe becomes defrag.ex~.) These commands are replaced by batch files (for example, defrag.bat) that tell you to use the Windows 98 equivalent of the program.

See Also...
"Working with the Windows 98 Startup Menu,"
p. 82

Other than that, the old version of DOS is still available, and it's possible to boot that version of DOS at any time. (See Chapter 3, "Understanding and Controlling the Windows 98 Startup," to learn how to boot to your old version of DOS.)

Note, too, that Windows 98 DOS is not quite the same as the old (that is, pre-Windows 95) DOS:

- The DOS commands are now stored in the `C:\Windows\Command` subfolder. (The path of this folder may be different depending on where you installed Windows 98.)

- You can work with long filenames at the DOS prompt.

- You can work with network resources at the DOS prompt.

- You can run Windows applications from the DOS prompt.

- DOS programs have a number of configuration options. For example, you can create custom `Config.sys` and `Autoexec.bat` files, and you can use "MS-DOS mode" for DOS programs that require full access to the computer's resources. (See Chapter 5, "Getting the Most Out of Your Applications.")

- The following commands have been deleted from Windows 98 DOS:

APPEND	MIRROR
ASSIGN	MSAV
BACKUP	MSBACKUP
CHKSTATE	POWER
COMP	PRINT
DOSSHELL	RECOVER
EDLIN	REPLACE
FASTHELP	RESTORE
FASTOPEN	SETVER
GRAFTABL	SHARE
GRAPHICS	SIZER
INTERLNK	SMARTMON
INTERSVR	TREE
JOIN	UNDELETE
LOADFIX	UNFORMAT
MEMCARD	VSAFE
MEMMAKER	

Watch Out!
When working at the DOS prompt, bear in mind that you must enclose long file and path-names in quotation marks, as shown in this example:
del "long

Upgrading from Windows 3.1*x*

If you have Windows 3.1*x*—that is, Windows 3.1 or Windows for Workgroups 3.1 or 3.11—you have to decide whether you want to upgrade over your existing Windows installation, or install Windows 98 into a separate directory so you can dual-boot between the two operating systems. (I discuss dual-booting in detail a bit later in this chapter.) To help you decide, let's examine both scenarios.

See Also...
"Dual-Booting
Windows 98 with
Another
Operating
System," p. 45

Upgrading over Windows 3.1*x* offers the following advantages:

- You save the disk space that was used by Windows 3.1*x* (about 10MB).

- Your existing Program Manager groups and icons are translated into submenus and commands on the Windows 98 Start menu.

- File associations, object linking and embedding information, and other Windows 3.1*x* Registry data are carried over automatically to the Windows 98 Registry.

- Settings in the Windows 3.1*x* initialization files—particularly Win.ini, System.ini, and Protocol.ini—are maintained (some stay within the same initialization files, while others are transferred into the Windows 98 Registry). This means that you keep Windows settings, such as the current screen resolution.

- The above three points also mean that you don't have to re-install your existing applications.

Undocumented
If you decide to dual-boot, you may not have to reinstall all your existing applications. In some cases, you can coax a program to run by appending to your PATH statement the locations of the Windows 3.1*x* directory and its System subdirectory. In Autoexec.bat, find the PATH= line and append the following to the end of the line:
;C:\Windows\;C:\Windows\System.

Here are some points in favor of the dual-boot route:

- If you have a Windows 3.1*x* or DOS program that refuses to run under Windows 98, you can always boot to Windows 3.1*x* in order to run the program.

- You ensure that Windows 98 is unencumbered by existing problems in your Windows 3.1*x* setup, including conflicting DLL files, out-of-date device drivers, and corrupted system files.

- You get to keep some Windows 3.1*x* accessories that were dropped from Windows 98. These include Write (replaced by WordPad), Paintbrush (replaced by Paint), Cardfile, Calendar, and Recorder.

Note, too, that you may also decide to wipe out Windows 3.1*x* and install Windows 98 on a clean hard disk. See "Performing a Clean Installation," later in this chapter for the pros and cons of this approach.

Upgrading from Windows 95

Running Windows 98 Setup as an upgrade to Windows 95 is by far the easiest installation path. That's because Windows 98 Setup processes the existing Windows 95 Registry early in the install procedure. It then uses these existing settings as the basis of Windows 98's configuration. This has two main advantages:

- Installation is more robust because Setup just assumes the Registry's current hardware configuration is accurate, and so it doesn't run any hardware detection.

- Installation takes less time, not only because the lengthy hardware detection phase is skipped, but also because you don't have to respond to as many prompts (very few, in fact).

Note, however, that you don't have a choice about whether you upgrade Windows 95 or dual-boot. Windows 98 can only upgrade an existing Windows 95 installation, and offers no way to dual-boot between the two systems.

Dual-Booting Windows 98 with Another Operating System

Here's a summary of the dual-boot information you've seen so far:

- If you install Windows 98 on a DOS-only system, you'll be able to dual-boot between Windows 98 and your previous version of DOS.

- To dual-boot Windows 98 with Windows 3.1*x*, install Windows 98 into a separate directory.

Inside Scoop
It *is* possible to set up a computer to dual-boot Windows 98 and Windows 95. However, you need a third-party boot manager program, such as System Commander (http://www. v-com.com/) or BOOTMENU (http://www. bootmenu.com/).

- Windows 98 does not provide native support for dual-booting with Windows 95.

The rest of this section runs through a few more dual-boot scenarios.

Partitioning for Dual-Booting

A *partition* is a section of a hard disk, and is usually assigned its own drive letter. For example, the default file system used in DOS, Windows 3.1*x*, and Windows 9*x* supports hard disks up to 2GB in size. If your computer comes with a 4GB hard disk, the manufacturer will have split the disk into two 2GB partitions, which will probably be assigned drive letters C: and D:.

If you're considering a dual-boot configuration with some other PC-compatible operating system—Windows NT, OS/2, or Linux—you must create a separate partition that the other OS can use to store its system files. To adjust hard disk partitions, use the DOS FDISK command.

FAT32 Dual-Boot Considerations

When you learn about FAT32 in Chapter 14, you'll see that its pros—improved performance and more efficient storage—must be balanced with a crucial dual-boot con: other operating systems (including DOS and Windows 3.1*x*) won't recognize a FAT32 partition, and Windows 98 actually turns off its dual-boot capabilities.

Here's a workaround that lets you get most of the benefits of FAT32 while still retaining the ability to dual-boot:

- The *boot partition* is the partition that holds the Windows 98 system files (Io.sys and Msdos.sys), and it's usually drive C:. When re-partitioning your system for dual-booting, create a smallish (say, 100MB) boot partition and leave it as FAT16. This will ensure that Windows 98's dual-boot abilities remain activated.

- Create another partition exclusively for Windows 98. Convert this partition to FAT32. (Note that FAT32 partitions must be 512MB or larger.)

- Set up a partition for your programs and convert it to FAT32. Since the other operating system won't see this

> **66**
> If you convert your hard drive to FAT32 using Drive Converter, you can no longer use dual boot to run earlier versions of Windows (Windows 95 [Version 4.00.950], Windows NT 3.*x*, Windows NT 4.0, and Windows 3.*x*).
> —From the Windows 98 Help system
> **99**

partition, you'll need to reinstall your programs in that OS, but you'd probably have to do that anyway.

- Create a partition for your data files. Since you'll probably want to access these files in the other operating system, leave this partition as FAT16.

- Finally, set up a partition for the other operating system. Leave this a FAT16 for now, and then, if you like, format the partition using the operating system's native file system (such as NTFS for Windows NT).

Installing Windows 3.1*x* After Windows 98

You've seen that dual-booting Windows 98 and Windows 3.1*x* is automatic if you install Windows 98 into a directory other than the one used by Windows 3.1*x*. What happens, however, if your system is currently Windows 98-only and you want to install and dual-boot Windows 3.1*x*? If you just try installing Windows 3.1*x*, you'll end up trashing the Windows 98 system files. This section takes you through an undocumented method for getting around this.

Remember
If you don't see the system files, you need to tell Windows 98 to display hidden files. To do so, select Windows Explorer's View, Folder Options command and then display the View tab. Activate the Show all files option, deactivate the Hide file extensions for known file types check box, and click OK.

The first thing you have to do is to copy the Windows 3.1*x* system files to your bootable partition. These files are named Io.sys, Msdos.sys, and Command.com, which are the same names used by the Windows 98 system files. (Now you see why installing Windows 3.1*x* trashes Windows 98: the latter's system files get overwritten!) Therefore, the copies of these files must use another name. Specifically, they must use the dos extension. Here's the procedure to use:

1. Locate your Windows 3.1*x* system files. You'll find these files either on a bootable disk created using Windows 3.1*x*, or on a DOS setup disk. Insert the disk into drive A:.

2. In Windows Explorer, select drive A: and then highlight Io.sys, Msdos.sys, and Command.com. While you're at it, you should also select Config.sys and Autoexec.bat.

3. Copy these files to an empty folder on your hard disk. (Don't copy them to the root folder, or you may overwrite the Windows 98 system files.)

4. Rename each file using the dos extension. You should end up with Io.dos, Msdos.dos, Command.dos, Config.dos, and Autoexec.dos.

5. Copy these files to the root folder of your bootable partition.

See Also...
"Putting Together an Emergency Boot Disk," p. 365

6. If your system needs real mode device drivers for hardware such as a CD-ROM drive or a SCSI adapter, copy the appropriate driver files to the root folder. I discuss these and other boot disk options in Chapter 16, "Preparing for Trouble."

7. In both Config.dos and Autoexec.dos, add or edit the necessary lines that load and configure the device drivers. In particular, make sure the paths used in these lines point to the root folder.

Shortcut
Files with the dos extension (as well as the sys extension; see step 9) aren't associated with any application. To open these files in Notepad, right-click the file, click Open With, highlight NOTEPAD in the Open With dialog box, and then click OK.

8. In the root folder, right-click Msdos.sys, deactivate the Read-only check box, and then click OK.

9. Open Msdos.sys in Notepad.

10. Beneath the [Options] line, add the line BootMulti=1.

11. Save the file and exit Notepad.

12. Right-click Msdos.sys, activate the Read-only check box, and then click OK.

From here, reboot your computer, hold down Ctrl, and then select Previous version of MS-DOS when the Windows 98 Startup menu appears. (I discuss this menu in detail in Chapter 3.) Here's what happens when you do this:

See Also...
"Working with the Windows 98 Startup Menu," p. 82

- Windows 98 temporarily renames Config.sys to Config.w40, Autoexec.bat to Autoexec.w40, and Command.com to Command.w40.

- It renames Config.dos to Config.sys, Autoexec.dos to Autoexec.bat, and Command.dos to Command.com.

This means that you can safely install Windows 3.1x because it will update and modify the old system files, while ignoring the Windows 98 system files.

Dual-Booting Windows 98 and Windows NT

If you want to dual-boot between Windows 98 and Windows NT, the best approach is to install Windows 98 first and then install Windows NT. NT recognizes that Windows 98 is already installed, and it adds a command for it on the NT OS Loader menu:

```
OS Loader V4.00


Please select the operating system to start:


    Windows NT Workstation Version 4.00
    Windows NT Workstation Version 4.00 (VGA mode)
    Microsoft Windows


Use ↑ and ↓ to move the highlight to your choice.
Press Enter to Choose.
```

Select the operating system you want to work with and then press Enter.

Here are a few points to bear in mind when considering this dual-boot scenario:

Shortcut
When you're ready to install Windows NT, start a DOS session in Windows 98, change to the Windows NT source files folder, and then enter the command winnt /w. You need the /w switch to enable the Windows NT installation program to operate under Windows 98.

- Make sure your hard disk has a FAT16 or FAT32 partition into which you can install Windows 98.

- NT can create FAT16 partitions up to 4GB in size. However, Windows 98's FAT16 doesn't support partitions of this size (the maximum is 2GB), so the Setup program won't work.

- Windows 98 does not recognize NT's native NTFS file system, so you won't be able to access NTFS partitions from within Windows 98. (And, as I mentioned earlier, NT won't be able to read Windows 98's FAT32 partitions. However, it is expected that NT 5 will have the ability to work with FAT32.)

- The DriveSpace compression schemes used by Windows 98 and Windows NT 3.51 are incompatible. Therefore, the two operating systems will not be able to work with each other's compressed files.

■ Any applications already installed within one operating system will likely have to be re-installed within the other. This is particularly true for any application that stores values in the Windows Registry or a Windows 98 initialization file (such as Win.ini).

For the latter, you may be able to get away without having to re-install some applications. Certainly any application that doesn't use the Registry or some other initialization file, and that stores all of its files in its own directory, will likely operate without a problem in both operating systems. However, many programs store DLLs and other support files either in the main Windows folder or in the System subfolder. You may be able to get these programs to work in both operating systems by adjusting the PATH variable. (This variable lists a series of folders into which Windows looks when trying to find executable files.) Here's how you do it (I'm assuming here that NT is installed in C:\Winnt and Windows 98 is installed in D:\Windows):

Watch Out!
If the PATH statement already exists and contains other folder paths, be sure not to remove those paths or some of your programs might not work properly. Just append the NT paths (;C:\WINNT;C:\WINNT\SYSTEM32) onto the end of the existing PATH statement.

■ In Windows 98, open Autoexec.bat and edit the PATH statement as follows:

PATH=D:\WINDOWS;D:\WINDOWS\SYSTEM;C:\WINNT;C:\WINNT\SYSTEM32

■ In NT, launch Control Panel and open the System icon. In the System dialog box that appears, highlight the Path line in the System Environment Variables section. In the Value text box, add the following to the end of the existing value:

;D:\WINDOWS;D:\WINDOWS\SYSTEM

Click Set and then click OK.

What do you do if NT is already installed and you want to install Windows 98? That depends on how you installed NT:

■ If you installed NT along with Windows 3.1x (or DOS), NT's OS Loader menu will have a Windows (or DOS) option. Select that option at startup and then install Windows 98 normally.

- If NT is the only operating system, boot from a floppy disk: use either the Boot Disk that comes with the full retail version of Windows 98, or a bootable disk that has a previous version of DOS. Now run Windows 98 Setup. When you're done, insert your NT boot floppy, restart your computer, and then follow the instructions that appear on the screen. You'll eventually end up at the Welcome to Setup screen, which has a Repair option. Press r to select that option and restore the NT boot sector that was damaged during the Windows 98 Setup.

Other Dual-Boot Options

To close your look at dual-booting, here are a few other scenarios to consider:

Dual-booting with OS/2 Warp.   The best way to do this is to install OS/2 and create a "startable" Boot Manager partition. You'll also need a "bootable" FAT16 partition to use with Windows 98. (If you've already installed OS/2, use the FDISK utility to do this.) Restart your machine using a bootable floppy, and then install Windows 98. Setup will disable Boot Manager in order to be able to restart the system during the installation. Once Windows 98 is installed, use the OS/2 boot disk to restart your system, and then use FDISK to restore the Boot Manager partition.

Dual-booting with Linux.   To set this up, install Windows 98 and then install Linux and the Linux Loader (LILO). The latter can recognize and work with Windows, so at startup LILO offers you a choice of loading Linux or "DOS" (that is, Windows 98).

Triple-booting Windows 3.1x, Windows 98, and Windows NT.   If you want all three Windows flavors on your system, install Windows 3.1x first, then install Windows 98, and finally NT. Be sure to follow the dual-boot suggestions that I outlined previously for each case. When you're done, you'll see the NT OS Loader menu at startup. From there, either run NT or Windows. The latter loads Windows 98, and you can then choose to load Windows 3.1x by using the Windows 98 Startup menu.

Watch Out!
If you install Windows 98 on a Linux system, Setup will overwrite LILO if LILO was installed to the Master Boot Record. In this case, use a bootable Linux floppy to restart and then run the LILOCONFIG utility. If, instead, LILO was installed to the root directory—or superblock—of the Linux partition, Setup deactivates LILO. In this case, use FDISK to reactivate the Linux partition.

Performing a Clean Installation

One of the sad facts of computing life is that system performance and reliability both degrade over time. There are a
number of system maintenance techniques that you can use to
stave off this process, and you'll learn about them in Part 4,
"Windows 98 Performance Tuning and Troubleshooting."
Even if you were diligent about these maintenance chores in
your current Windows 3.1x or Windows 95 Setup, your system
will still be slower and less reliable than it was when it was new.

Why is this? The biggest culprit is the intermingling of
Windows files and application files. Windows and most programs use helper files called *dynamic link libraries*, or *DLLs*, for
short. Rather than put all programming code into a single file,
many functions and subroutines are split off into separate DLL
files, which are only loaded when required by the program.
This saves memory and enables multiple programs to easily
reuse the same code. Many Windows features are also housed
in DLLs, including common interface features such as the
Open and Save As dialog boxes.

Many years ago, Microsoft made the fateful decision to
encourage software developers to store all their program's
DLLs in the \Windows\System subdirectory. Unfortunately, this
has led to a number of problems, all of which contribute to system decay:

- DLLs often change over time as features get added or
  changed. Installation programs are supposed to check
  DLL version numbers and only install their version if it's
  later than an existing version on the system. Many sloppily
  programmed applications don't do this, however.

- Some installation utilities install a program's DLLs in the
  program's home directory. This often meant you ended
  up with two or more copies of the same file scattered
  about your system.

- If a program used a DLL with the same name as another
  program's DLL, that latter file would usually get overwritten.

■ It's difficult to know which DLLs correspond to which programs. Unless a program comes with its own uninstall utility, DLLs tossed into the SYSTEM subdirectory were usually in there for good.

The best (albeit the most radical) solution is to start from scratch: Wipe your hard drive clean and then install Windows 98. This removes the DLL detritus that has accumulated over the years and so ensures that Windows 98 begins without having to drag around any excess DLL baggage. There are other benefits to this approach:

■ If you're currently running Windows 95, you get to start with a fresh Registry. The Registry often gets bloated with many unused settings leftover from deleted or uninstalled programs.

■ You rid your system of stray temporary files that might have accumulated over the years. Many programs—and Windows itself—create temporary files while you work. These files are usually deleted when you finish working with the program, but if your system shuts down unexpectedly (due to, say, a power failure), the files remain to clutter your hard disk.

■ You get rid of old device drivers and replace them with the latest versions that ship with Windows 98. These newer device drivers are often faster and more reliable, plus they may support new Windows 98 features.

■ It gives you a good excuse to adjust your hard disk partitions using FDISK. Since FDISK destroys all data anyway, it doesn't hurt to restructure your hard disk. This gives you a chance to create a partition to hold data files, another for program files, and another for any operating system you want to dual-boot with Windows 98.

■ You ensure that there are no computer viruses lurking anywhere on your hard disk. Although you may not have experienced any virus-like behavior, many viruses are timed to release on a certain date, so it's possible your system is infected and you don't know it.

66

Consultant Michael Green...says that 90 percent of the GPFs [General Protection Faults] he's studied are caused by conflicting versions of DLLs.
—Brian Livingston, **99**World

The downside, of course, is that you must re-install your applications and rebuild your directory structure. However, I believe these negatives are greatly outweighed by the positives listed above.

Here's a general procedure to follow for installing Windows 98 to a clean system:

1. Make backup copies of all your data files.

2. Make backup copies of initialization files and other files used to store program customization options. (If you use Microsoft Word, for example, you should back up NORMAL.DOT and any custom templates you created.)

3. Make backup copies of the archive (for example, .ZIP) files for any programs that you downloaded from the Internet or some other online source.

4. Create a bootable disk. Make sure you include on this disk your system startup files—Config.sys and Autoexec.bat—as well as any real-mode device drivers that are loaded within these files (particularly the drivers for your CD-ROM). You'll also need the DOS files Fdisk.exe and Format.com.

5. Insert the bootable disk in drive A: and restart your computer.

6. When you get to the A:\ prompt, run FDISK to repartition your hard disk. Note that you can skip this step if you don't want to repartition the disk.

7. Format drive C: by entering the command format c:/s/u. (I'm assuming here that drive C: will be your bootable partition.) The /s switch makes drive C: bootable by copying the system files, and the /u switch tells FORMAT not to save unformatted data.

8. If necessary, format your other partitions. Use the syntax format d:/u, where "d" is the drive letter of the partition.

9. Copy Config.sys, Autoexec.bat, and your startup device driver files from the bootable disk to drive C: (or your bootable partition).

Remember
Technically, the only partitions you need to format are your bootable partition and, if different, the partition in which your existing version of Windows is stored. If you already have a separate partition for your data files, don't bother formatting it (or backing up your data files, for that matter).

10. Remove the bootable disk and restart your computer so that it can boot from the hard disk.

11. Run the Windows 98 installation.

Preparing Your System

The Windows 98 "Getting Started" booklet (I refuse to call it a manual) offers a brief "Before You Begin" section that runs through the minimum system requirements for installing Windows 98. After that, the only other suggested step to take to prepare your system for installing Windows 98 is to "Close all programs."

A Preparation Checklist

For an operating system installation, such advice is woefully inadequate. Here's a list of what you should do to prepare your system:

Back up data files.   Make backup copies of all your data files, including any custom templates that you created.

Back up application configuration files.   Many applications store their current configuration in .ini files located either in the Windows directory or the application's home directory. If you're using Windows 95, however, most of this configuration data will be stored in the Registry.

Back up Windows configuration files.   Make backup copies of Config.sys, Autoexec.bat, Win.ini, System.ini, and all your password list (.pwl) files. If you're running Windows 3.1x, back up all the program group (.grp) files in the Windows directory. If you're running Windows 95, restart the computer in MS-DOS mode and make backups of the two Registry files: System.dat and User.dat (these are hidden files in the Windows folder).

Back up Windows Messaging files.   If you're using Windows Messaging (or Microsoft Exchange), back up your personal folders file (usually Exchange.pst) and your personal address book (usually Exchange.pab). You'll find these files either in the Windows Messaging folder or in the Windows folder.

Check your system BIOS. Many system vendors—including Compaq, Dell, Hewlett-Packard, IBM, and Toshiba—have reported that some of their older computers won't upgrade to Windows 98 properly unless the machines receive a BIOS update in advance. Check with your system manufacturer to see if a BIOS update is required for your computer.

Disable the Windows 3.1x permanent swap file. This not only saves some disk space, but it also enables Windows 98 to set up its dynamic swap file. Open Control Panel, launch the 386 Enhanced icon, and then click the Virtual Memory button. If you see Permanent in the Type field, click the Change button. If you'll be installing over Windows 3.1x, select None in the Type list. If, instead, you plan on dual-booting Windows 3.1x and Windows 98, select Temporary.

Clean out the Startup group or folder. Setup can migrate your Startup applications to Windows 98, but it's best to wait until Windows 98 is installed and then test these applications to make sure they work properly. If they do, you can add them to Windows 98's Startup folder.

Do a spring cleaning on your hard disk. To free up disk space and prepare for defragmenting (discussed below), clean up your hard disk. This includes uninstalling applications you no longer use, removing stray files from the Windows TEMP directory (usually C:\Windows\Temp), and deleting the DOS backup directory (usually C:\Old_dos.1), if it exists.

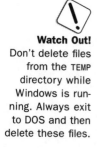

Watch Out!
Don't delete files from the TEMP directory while Windows is running. Always exit to DOS and then delete these files.

Perform a "thorough" ScanDisk check. The thorough check examines the surface of the disk for imperfections. It takes longer, but now is the perfect time to do it.

Run and then disable your antivirus software. If you have antivirus software, use it to check your files and system memory for lurking viruses. Once that's done, disable the software if it's resident in memory. The Windows 98 Setup changes the hard disk's Master Boot Record, which, to an antivirus program, is "virus-like" activity.

Defragment your hard disk.   This ensures that Windows 98 stores its files in a defragmented state, which will improve performance. If you have Windows 3.1x, run the DOS DEFRAG utility; if you have Windows 95, use Disk Defragmenter.

Create a bootable floppy disk.   Just in case the installation procedure fails, you should have a bootable disk at the ready. If you have Windows 95, create a startup disk. If you have Windows 3.1x, insert an expendable disk in drive A:, and then use one of the following methods:

- Run File Manager and select the Disk, Make System Disk command.

- At the DOS prompt, type `format a: /s` and press Enter.

Disable Internet Explorer 4's Web integration.   If you're running Windows 95 with Internet Explorer 4, turn off Web integration. In Windows Explorer, select View, Folder Options and then, in the General tab, activate the Classic style option.

Run a system report.   This will give you a record of your current configuration in case you need to know what device drivers you were using, or some other bit of information useful for troubleshooting. If you have Windows 3.1x, use the Microsoft Diagnostics utility (at the DOS prompt, type `msd` and press Enter). In Windows 95, use Device Manager (right-click My Computer, click Properties, select the Device Manager tab, and then click Print).

Close all running programs.   This ensures that none of these programs can interfere with Windows 98 Setup, and it helps Setup run faster.

Better Backup Ideas

Backing up data files and important configuration files is important, but if something goes awry during Setup, returning to your original configuration will be a time-consuming process. This section looks at some ways to make a completely recoverable backup of your system.

The first thing you need to do is get out of Windows so you avoid backing up the swap file, the existing temporary files, and other flotsam that is specific only to your current Windows session. In other words, you have to do this from DOS. That presents a whole new series of problems, including the speed of the backup and the medium you use to store the backup:

- The simplest solution would be to use the DOS XCOPY command to copy the entire boot partition to another partition on the disk, or to another hard disk altogether. For example, to copy drive C: to drive D:, you'd use the following command:

  ```
  xcopy c:\ d:\ /t /e /h /k
  ```

  This will be quite a slow process, however, and won't have any kind of built-in error checking.

- To increase speed and robustness, you need to turn to third-party programs. One such program is Partition Magic, by PowerQuest (http://www.powerquest.com/). You can use this program to safely make a copy of the boot partition to another hard disk. You can also use Partition Magic to resize the copied partition to remove all unused space, as well as to hide this new partition, which avoids confusion for Setup and disk utilities down the road.

- A third method is to clone the drive and store it either on another disk or on a recordable CD. Here are three programs that can clone a disk drive:

  Drive Image (http://www.powerquest.com/)

  DiskClone (http://www.quarterdeck.com/)

  Norton Ghost (http://www.symantec.com/sabu/ghost/)

Remember
Drive cloning software usually creates a sector-by-sector copy of the disk, which means the clone takes up much less space than the original. This means you can fit a fairly large amount of data onto a recordable CD or small partition.

Running the Windows 98 Setup

At long last, your preparations are complete and you're just about ready to run Setup. This section looks at a couple of ways to run custom installations, and then runs through the actual Setup procedure.

Using Setup's Switches

If you'd like a bit more control over how Setup runs, you can use the various switches that are supported by Setup.exe.

The Setup.exe command uses the following general syntax:

```
setup [batch] switches
```

The optional *batch* portion specifies a Setup script that can automate much of the Setup procedure. I discuss these scripts in the next section. Table 2.1 runs through some of the more useful switches. Bear in mind that these switches are case-sensitive, so enter them exactly as they appear in the table.

TABLE 2.1: SWITCHES YOU CAN USE WITH THE SETUP COMMAND

Switch	What It Does
/?	Displays a description for a few of the switches.
/C	Bypasses loading the SmartDrive disk cache.
/d	Tells Setup not to use your existing copy of Windows (that is, Setup ignores Win.ini, System.ini, and so on).
/id	Bypasses the check for the minimum disk space required to install Windows 98.
/ie	Tells Setup not to prompt you to create a startup disk.
/ih	Runs ScanDisk in the foreground (if you start Setup from within Windows 3.x).
/iL	Loads the Logitech mouse driver rather than the Microsoft mouse driver.
/in	Bypasses the networking portion of Setup.
/iq	Bypasses the check for cross-linked files.
/is	Bypasses the ScanDisk hard disk check.
/it	Bypasses the check for the presence of dirty or deadly terminate-and-stay resident programs.
/iv	Bypasses the "billboards" that tell you about Windows features during the Setup procedure.
/IW	Tells Setup not to display the License Agreement.
/T:dir	Sets dir as the directory in which Setup should store its temporary files. (Note that all the files in this directory are deleted when Setup is finished.)

Shortcut
Use the /id switch if your current Windows directory doesn't have enough space to install Windows 98, but you'll be installing Windows 98 in a different directory that does have enough space.

Creating Automated Setup Scripts

If you install Windows 98 on a clean or DOS-only system, or if you install Windows 98 to a separate directory on a Windows 3.1*x* system, you'll be required to answer quite a few Setup prompts. These include your name and company name, your product ID, the directory to use for installing Windows, the components you want to install, and more. There's a lot to go through, but it's not that much of a burden if you'll only be running Setup once.

However, Setup becomes quite tedious if you have to run it multiple times, either if you're running several installation tests on a single machine, or if you have to install Windows 98 on multiple machines. Rather than trudging through every Setup step each time, you can automate Setup by creating an *installation script.*

An installation script is in an information (.inf) file that contains your answers to Setup's prompts. As you saw in the previous section, you can include the name of an installation script on the Setup command line. When you do this, Setup takes the data it needs from the script and bypasses the prompts. If you set up your script correctly (and make judicious use of Setup's switches), you can run Setup and then never touch your computer again until the installation is complete. Best of all, Windows 98 comes with a utility called Batch 98 that makes it easy to create a script.

Here is the basic procedure for creating and using an installation script:

1. Install Windows 98.

2. Install Batch 98. You'll find it on your Windows 98 CD, in the \tools\reskit\batch folder. Run setup.exe and follow the prompts until the program is installed.

3. Select Start, Programs, Microsoft Batch 98. You'll see the Batch 98 window shown in Figure 2.1.

Undocumented
You need Windows 98 to run Batch 98. However, it is possible to set up a script before you install Windows 98. In the Windows 98 CD, open the \tools\sysrec folder and you'll see a file named msbatch.inf. This is a script used with System Recovery, but feel free to edit it as necessary and use it the first time you install Windows 98.

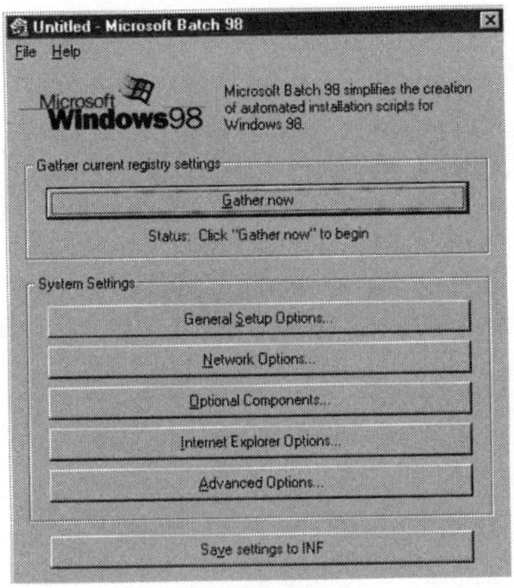

Figure 2.1
Use Batch 98 to create an automated installation script for Windows 98.

4. If you'll be using the script on the same machine, you can write the Setup-related Registry entries to the script by clicking the Gather Now button.

5. To specify other Setup parameters, use the buttons in the System Settings group:

   General Setup Options.   Use this button to enter information such as the Windows 98 product ID, installation directory, user data, desktop icons to be displayed, and time zone. You can also activate or deactivate several Setup prompts.

   Network Options.   Here you can specify various network components to install, including protocols, services, and clients.

   Optional Components.   Click this button to choose the Windows 98 components you want to install.

   Internet Explorer Options.   This module deals with options such as which items appear in the Quick Launch toolbar, whether Web integration is turned on, security settings, and more.

   Advanced Options.   Use this button to specify a Registry file to load, a system policy file, and whether Windows Update is enabled.

6. Click Save settings to INF, select a location and filename in the Save As dialog box, and then click Save.

7. To create another script, select File, New and repeat steps 4–6.

Inside Scoop
The script created with Batch 98 is a text file, so you can edit it using Notepad or WordPad. The entries use the format Name=Value, where Name is the name of the setting and Value is its value. In most of the entries, the value is either a string, the number 0 (the item is deactivated), or the number 1 (the item is activated).

Again, you use the script by specifying its path and filename when running the SETUP command. For example, if you saved the script as msbatch.inf (the default name) to C:\, you'd launch Setup as follows (assuming drive D: contains the Windows 98 CD):

```
d:\setup c:\msbatch.inf
```

Launching Setup

How you get Setup under way depends on how you're installing Windows 98. First, a few notes to bear in mind:

- If you'll be starting Setup from DOS, and if you have the Windows 98 CD, you need to make sure that the appropriate CD-ROM drivers are installed at startup.

- If you don't have CD-ROM drivers, but you do have the full retail version of Windows 98, insert the Boot Disk and then restart your computer. You'll see the following Windows 98 Startup Menu:

```
Microsoft Windows 98 Startup Menu
=====================================

    1. Start Windows 98 Setup from CD-ROM.
    2. Start computer with CD-ROM support.
    3. Start computer without CD-ROM support.
```

Select one of the CD-ROM options.

- If you don't have a CD-ROM drive, you'll need to install Windows 98 via floppy disks. There's a form in the back of the "Getting Started" booklet that you can use to order the appropriate 3 1/2-inch disks.

Here's a summary of the various ways you can launch Setup (I assume in all cases that you have already inserted the Windows 98 CD.):

If you're installing to a clean system. Restart your system with a bootable floppy disk in drive A:. Type `d:\setup` (where *d* is the letter of your CD-ROM drive) and then press Enter.

If you're installing to a system with only DOS or Windows 3.0. Boot to the DOS prompt and then run `d:\setup`.

If you're upgrading over Windows 3.1x. In Program Manager, select File, Run, enter `d:\setup`, and then click OK.

If you're dual-booting with Windows 3.1x. Launch Setup as described in the previous item. When Setup asks you which directory to use for the installation, be sure to enter a directory that's different from the current Windows 3.1*x* directory.

If you're upgrading over Windows 95. When you insert the Windows 98 CD, a dialog box should show up and ask if you want to upgrade to Windows 98, click Yes. If no dialog box appears, select Start, Run, enter `d:\setup`, and click OK.

If you're dual-booting with another operating system. Boot to the DOS prompt, either by using the existing dual-boot capabilities, if they exist, or by restarting with a bootable DOS floppy disk in drive A:. Run the `d:\setup` command.

Here's a behind-the-scenes look at what happens when Setup gets under way:

1. Setup checks your hard disk for errors by running ScanDisk.

2. Setup checks for the existence of antivirus software resident in memory and, if found, asks you to disable the software before continuing.

3. Setup copies its file to a temporary directory named `Wininst0.400` on your hard disk.

Inside Scoop
For a faster installation, run Setup from your hard disk instead of the CD. If you have at least 170MB free on your hard disk (in addition to the space required to install Windows 98), copy the CD's Win98 directory to your hard disk and then install Windows 98 from there. The following DOS command copies the files from drive D: to drive C:. `xcopy d:\ win98 c:\win98\ /s`.

4. During a Windows 95 upgrade, Setup examines the Registry to provide you with an identical Windows 98 configuration.

5. Setup checks your system to make sure it meets the minimum system requirements.

6. Setup checks for and, if necessary, installs both an extended memory manager and a disk drive cache.

7. Setup examines RAM for any terminate-and-stay resident programs and device drivers that are known to cause problems during installation.

8. Setup checks your hard disk for DOS uninstall information, which is typically stored in a directory named Old_dos.1. If found, Setup asks if you want to delete this information.

9. During a Windows 95 upgrade, Setup performs an integrity check on the Registry files.

10. If a problem occurs during the installation, Setup has a Safe Recovery option that appears the next time you run Setup. You are warned that you should use Safe Recovery the next time you reboot. This warning is put in place by adding the following two lines to Autoexec.bat:

```
@if exist C:\WININST0.400\SuWarn.bat call
C:\WININST0.400\SuWarn.bat
@if exist C:\WININST0.400\SuWarn.bat del
C:\WININST0.400\SuWarn.bat
```

11. The Setup wizard is loaded. This wizard takes you step-by-step through the rest of the installation. Note that a Windows 95 upgrade skips most of the following steps.

12. In the "Information Collection" phase of Setup, you're asked to provide data such as the Windows 98 directory, whether you want to save your existing system files, which Windows 98 components you want to install (see Figure 2.2), your name and company name, and your network options.

Shortcut
Although it takes a bit longer, selecting the Custom option gives you complete control over which components are installed. This saves you time down the road because you're less likely to have to add or remove components once the installation is complete.

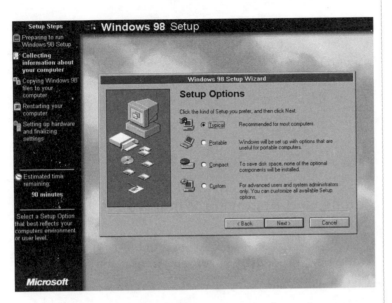

Figure 2.2
During installation, the Setup wizard asks you to select the components you want to install.

13. Setup asks if you want to create a startup disk. This is a bootable floppy disk that contains CD-ROM support and a number of troubleshooting utilities. (If you elect not to create the disk now, you can always create one later. See Chapter 16 for details.)

See Also...
"Putting Together an Emergency Boot Disk," p. 365

14. Setup begins copying the Windows 98 files to your hard disk. If you booted from a floppy, this is a good time to remove it.

15. When the file copying is complete, Setup reboots your computer.

16. Setup detects the Plug and Play hardware on your computer. The appropriate device drivers are installed.

17. If you're not upgrading from Windows 95, Setup begins its "hardware detection" phase to look for legacy devices. Your computer may be rebooted when this phase is complete.

18. Setup asks you to provide your time zone.

19. Setup prompts you to log on to Windows 98 and your network (if applicable).

Remember
The hardware detection phase can take quite a while. If the progress meter stops moving for more than a few minutes, shut off your machine. Wait for a few seconds to give all devices time to completely shut down, and then restart your computer.

See Also...
"Using WinAlign
to Speed Up
Program
Launching,"
p. 324

20. Setup runs through a number of chores to set up items such as the Control Panel, Start menu, and Registry. Setup also runs the WinAlign utility to improve the startup performance of some applications. (This is the "Tune Up Application Start" item on Setup's checklist; see Chapter 13 for more on WinAlign.)

21. When Setup is done, the Welcome to Windows 98 dialog box appears.

Adding and Removing Windows 98 Components

Once Windows 98 is installed, you don't have to rerun Setup to add new components or to remove installed components. You can do it right from within Windows 98:

1. Select Start, Settings, Control Panel to open the Control Panel window.

2. Launch the Add/Remove Programs icon. Windows 98 displays the Add/Remove Programs Properties dialog box.

3. Select the Windows Setup tab. Windows 98 takes a few seconds to figure out which components are installed, and then displays a list similar to the one shown in Figure 2.3.

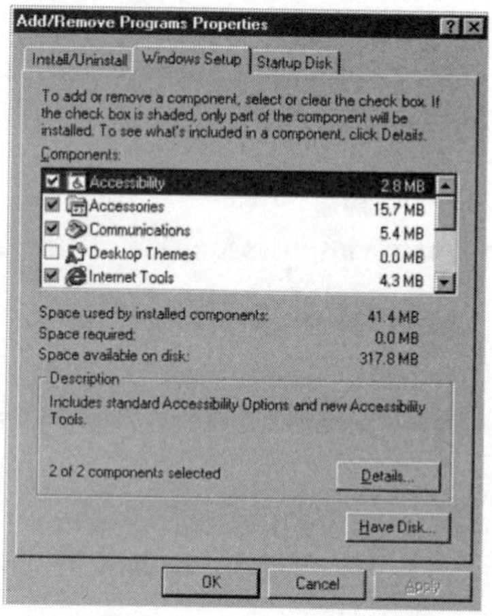

Figure 2.3
Use the Windows
Setup tab to see
which compo-
nents are
installed, and to
add and remove
components.

4. Find the component you want to work with. Here's how to interpret the check boxes:

- An activated check box with a white background means the component is fully installed.

- An activated check box with a gray background means the component is partially installed. To see the various pieces associated with the component, click the Details button.

- A deactivated check box means the component is not installed.

5. To add a component, activate its check box; to remove a component, deactivate its check box. Repeat as necessary.

6. Click OK.

7. If Setup asks you to insert the Windows 98 CD, insert the disc and follow the prompts.

Extracting a File from the Windows 98 Setup Files

One common Windows 98 troubleshooting technique is to extract a single file from the Windows 98 CD and store it on your hard disk. You most often use this technique when you need to replace an existing file that has become corrupted or has been deleted. Unfortunately, you can't simply copy the file from the disc, because most of the files are stored in special compressed archive files called *cabinets* (they use the cab extension). Here's how to extract a file from a cabinet:

1. Insert the Windows 98 CD and use Windows Explorer to open the Win98 folder.

2. Double-click the cabinet file to open it. The folder window that appears shows a list of the files contained in the cabinet.

3. Highlight the file and then select the File, Extract command. (You can also right-click the file and then click Extract.)

4. In the Browse for Folder dialog box that appears, select a folder for the extracted file, and then click OK.

Undocumented
To find out which cabinet contains the file you want, run a search. With the CD's Win98 folder highlighted, run Windows Explorer's Tools, Find, Files or Folders command. Type *.cab in the Named text box, type the name of the file you want to extract in the Containing text box, and then click Find Now.

Note, too, that Windows 98's System File Checker utility offers an easier way to extract files from a cabinet (see Chapter 15, "Crucial System Maintenance Skills").

Customizing Setup Settings in the Registry

In Chapter 4, "An Insider's Guide to Three Crucial Configuration Tools," you'll learn about the Windows 98 Registry, which will play a big part throughout the rest of this book. To give you a taste of what you can do with the Registry, this section shows you how to use it to change a couple of Setup settings. (Since editing the Registry is not a task to be taken lightly, I suggest you read the Registry material in Chapter 4 before running through the techniques in this section.)

Editing Your Username and Company Name

As I mentioned earlier, one of the chores Setup asks you to perform is to enter a username and company name. This data is stored in the Registry, and it's used in a variety of circumstances:

See Also...
"Running System File Checker," p. 351

See Also...
"An Insider's Guide to the Registry," p. 104

- Many 32-bit applications (including Microsoft Office) gather these values from the Registry and use them as the default settings during installation.

- When you open Control Panel's System icon (or right-click My Computer and then click Properties), these values are displayed in the General tab of the System Properties dialog box.

- When you select the Help, About command in most applications, these values are displayed in the About dialog box.

If you'd like to change these values, open the Registry Editor (select Start, Run, type regedit, and click OK) and find the following key:

```
HKEY_LOCAL_MACHINE\Software\Microsoft\Windows\CurrentVersion
```

Here you'll find two settings that hold your registered names:

RegisteredOwner: This is your registered username.

RegisteredOrganization: This is your registered company name.

To change a setting, double-click the setting name, edit the string in the text box that appears, and then click OK.

Specifying a New Setup Source Path

When you add new Windows 98 components or change device drivers, Windows 98 will usually prompt you to insert your Windows 98 CD so that the required files can be installed. If you have two CD-ROM drives, you must insert the Windows 98 disc in the *same* drive that you used to run Setup. That's because Setup recorded the location of the Windows 98 source files (that is, the *d*:\Win98 folder, where *d* is your CD-ROM drive letter) in the Registry, and it expects that location to remain the same.

What if that location changes, however? This could happen in a number of ways:

- If you re-partition your hard disk, add a second hard disk, or add a new removable drive or CD-ROM drive, your drive letters may change. For example, your CD-ROM drive may move from drive D: to drive E:.

- If you copy the Win98 folder from the CD to your hard disk.

- If you originally used floppy disks to run Setup, but you now have the Windows 98 CD-ROM.

To tell Windows 98 the new path to the source files, first use the Registry Editor to find the following key:

HKEY_LOCAL_MACHINE\Software\Microsoft\Windows\Current
Version\Setup

This key contains a setting named SourcePath. Double-click this setting and then change the value to the new path (for example, c:\win98).

Uninstalling Windows 98

I haven't seen any statistics on the percentage of users who stick with Windows 98 after installing it, but my guess is that it's quite high. However, Windows 98 isn't for everyone. Whether it's the

Undocumented
Copying your source files to your hard disk is an excellent idea, and not only because your hard disk is much faster than your CD-ROM drive. It also means that once you adjust the source path as described here, you'll never be prompted to insert your Windows 98 CD since the source files are always available.

"
Bill: "And the
electrical out-
lets? The holes
are round, not
rectangular.
How do I fix
that?"
Contractor:
"Just uninstall
and reinstall the
electrical sys-
tem."
—From "Bill
Gates Buys a
House"

integration of Internet Explorer, an old and treasured program that no longer runs, poor performance, or a multitude
of General Protection Faults caused by installing over a previous version of Windows, you might decide your life would be
better without Windows 98.

Fortunately, Windows 98 does come with an uninstall feature that usually works quite well at expunging the Windows 98
from your machine and restoring the previous operating system. However, you can only use this feature under the following conditions:

- You upgraded over Windows 3.1x or Windows 95.

- You saved the system files of your existing version of Windows
  during Setup, and you haven't deleted those files.

- You haven't compressed your hard disk.

- You haven't changed your hard disk partitions. (This
  means you haven't used Partition Magic or some other
  non-data-destroying partitioning utility to create or
  remove partitions, and that you haven't converted the
  drive to FAT32.)

See Also...
"Controlling
Viruses with Plus!
98's MacAfee
VirusScan,"
p. 357

- Your hard disk isn't infected with a boot sector virus.
  (You'll need to run an antivirus program to check this; see
  Chapter 15.)

How can Windows 98 uninstall itself? The secret lies within
a few files stored in the root folder of your bootable partition.
Here's a summary:

> **Setuplog.txt**: This text file is the log of the entire Setup
> procedure. It contains, among many other things, a set-
> ting that records the location of the Winundo.dat and
> Winundo.ini files (described below).

> **Suhdlog.dat**: This file contains a copy of the master boot
> record and partition boot records as they were configured
> when you installed Windows 98. This is why you can't
> uninstall Windows 98 if your partition configuration has
> changed. Windows 98 would restore this old partition
> information, and you'd almost certainly lose data.

`Winundo.dat`: This file contains a compressed backup of the system files from your old version of Windows.

`Winundo.ini`: This file is an inventory of the files that were backed up into the `Winundo.dat` file. It also contains a list of the new Windows 98 files that Setup installed.

The Uninstall feature also copies the saved system files (`Io.dos`, `Msdos.dos`, `Command.dos`, `Config.dos`, and `Autoexec.dos`) to their original names (`Io.sys`, `Msdos.sys`, `Command.com`, `Config.sys`, and `Autoexec.bat`).

Running the Uninstall Feature

Here are the steps to follow to uninstall Windows 98:

1. Select Start, Settings, Control Panel to open Control Panel, and then launch the Add/Remove Programs icon.

2. In the Install/Uninstall tab, highlight Uninstall Windows 98.

3. Click the Add/Remove button. A dialog box asks if you're sure you want to uninstall Windows 98.

4. Click Yes. Windows 98 displays another dialog box to tell you that Uninstall is about to check for disk errors and remove all the long filename information created by Windows 98.

5. Click Yes. Uninstall runs ScanDisk to check your hard disk for problems. When ScanDisk is done, another dialog box appears to tell you that Uninstall is ready to do its thing.

6. Click Yes. Uninstall shuts down your computer, removes the Windows 98 files, and restores your previous configuration (this process takes several minutes).

7. When Uninstall is finished, remove any floppy disks you might have in your computer and then press Enter to restart your machine and load your previous operating system.

If you want to
uninstall Windows
98 because you
can't get it to
load, you won't be
able to use the
Control Panel
technique.
Instead, boot to
DOS and then run
the command
C:\Windows\
Command\
Uninstall
(assuming that
you installed
Windows 98 in
the C:\Windows

Uninstalling Windows 98 by Hand

There are two situations in which you won't be able to run the Windows 98 uninstall feature:

- If you deleted the uninstall data for the previous version of Windows.

- If you set up Windows 98 to dual-boot with Windows 3.1x.

In either case, it takes quite a bit more work to uninstall Windows 98. Note that you must have a bootable disk that boots your system to the previous version of Windows or DOS, and that this disk must have the Sys.com utility on it.

1. If you're uninstalling to Windows 3.1x, load the file Scandisk.ini into Notepad (select Start, Run, type scan-disk.ini and click OK). In the [ENVIRONMENT] section, change the value of the following two settings to On (save the file when you're done):

   LabelCheck: When On, ScanDisk checks the disk volume labels for invalid characters.

   SpaceCheck: When On, ScanDisk checks for invalid spaces in filenames.

2. Insert a bootable disk in drive A: and restart your computer.

3. At the A:\ prompt, type c: and press Enter to move to drive C:.

4. You're going to need three files: Deltree.exe, Scandisk.exe, and Scandisk.ini, all of which are in the \Windows\Command subdirectory. You'll be deleting this subdirectory, so you have to use the following commands to copy these files to the root:

   ```
   copy c:\windows\command\deltree.exe
   copy c:\windows\command\scandisk.*
   ```

5. If you're uninstalling to Windows 3.1x, type scandisk d: (where d is the letter of the drive where Windows is installed) and press Enter. ScanDisk will remove all volume labels and filenames that Windows 3.1x will consider invalid. Run separate ScanDisk commands for each drive.

6. Run the following `Deltree` commands to delete all the Windows 98 files on your system:

```
deltree /y windows
deltree /y recycled
deltree /y winboot.*
deltree /y io.sys
deltree /y msdos.sys
deltree /y commmand.com
deltree /y config.sys
deltree /y autoexec.bat
deltree /y detlog.txt
deltree /y netlog.txt
deltree /y setuplog.txt
deltree /y suhdlog.dat
deltree /y system.1st
deltree /y d??space.bin
```

7. The following commands rename `Config.dos` to `Config.sys` and `Autoexec.dos` to `Autoexec.bat`:

```
ren config.dos config.sys
ren autoexec.dos autoexec.bat
```

8. Type `a:\sys c:` to transfer the system files for the previous DOS version and overwrite the Windows 98 master boot record.

9. Remove the bootable disk and restart your computer. You should now boot to your previous version operating system.

Essential Information

- To get the most out of Windows 98, go beyond the minimum system requirements and load your machine with a PCI bus, a Plug and Play BIOS, at least 32MB of RAM, a fast Pentium processor, a large hard disk, and a Super VGA card and monitor.

- For maximum reliability, install Windows 98 on a clean system.

- Don't jump blindly into the Windows 98 installation. Run through the checklist provided in this chapter to make sure your system is ready to accept Windows 98.

- Take advantage of Setup's switches to customize your Windows 98 installation.

- If you'll be installing Windows 98 multiple times or on multiple computers, use Batch 98 to create automated Setup scripts.

- Remember that you won't be able to uninstall Windows 98 if you compressed your hard disk or changed your hard disk's partition information.

GET THE SCOOP ON...
The intricacies of the startup process ▪ Whether you
need Config.sys and Autoexec.bat ▪ Techniques for
runningcustom startups ▪ The importance of exiting
Windows 98 properly ▪ Customizing the startup logo
and shutdown display messages

Understanding and Controlling the Windows 98 Startup

O THER THAN A BRIEF SECTION covering the logon procedure, the Windows 98 "Getting Started" booklet is
mute on the subject of the Windows 98 startup.
At first glance, this may seem reasonable. After all, isn't the
startup an uneventful procedure that's nothing more than an
excuse to go grab another cup of coffee? Yes, it is—most
of the time. However, what do you do if one day Windows just
refuses to run? What if an error occurs during startup? What
if you need to do some work at the DOS prompt before
Windows loads? What if you want to boot
to your previous version of Windows or DOS?

To handle all of these non-standard startups, you have to
understand how the startup procedure works, and you have to
know how to wield the various startup tools that Windows 98
offers. This chapter will help you do just that by giving you an
inside look at the Windows 98 startup.

Remember
Here are two terms you should know: real mode and protected mode. *Real mode* is a single-tasking mode that can address only 1MB of memory and that gives applications direct access to system hardware. *Protected mode* is a multitasking mode that can address memory beyond 1MB (virtual memory) and takes advantage of the microprocessor's built-in protection features that enable multiple programs to safely share the same system resources.

How the Startup Process Works

Troubleshooting startup problems, and figuring out which of the many Windows 98 startup options and tools you need, requires an understanding of the entire boot process. In the steps that follow, I ignore most of the hundreds of internal tasks that occur during a typical boot, and instead concentrate solely on those steps that relate to startup troubleshooting and customization:

1. During a *cold boot* (turning the power on or pressing the restart button), the microprocessor locates and runs the ROM BIOS code. On a system with a Plug and Play BIOS, the code enumerates and initializes all Plug and Play devices on the system.

2. The ROM BIOS code then runs the Power-On Self Test (POST), which tests the system memory and initializes various devices (such as the keyboard and disk drives).

3. During the POST, you have the opportunity to change your computer's startup options (these are known variously as the BIOS settings or the CMOS settings). You should see a message on the screen that tells you how to get to these options (pressing Delete is common, as is pressing Esc or Ctrl+Esc).

4. If the POST completes successfully, the computer beeps the speaker once.

5. The ROM BIOS code checks for a disk in drive A: and, if it finds one, checks to see if the disk is bootable. If so, the system boots to the A:\ prompt. If there is no disk in drive A:, the code finds the hard disk's bootable partition and boots the system from there.

6. Windows 98 takes over at this point and processes the system file Io.sys, which is basically just DOS. This is known as the *real mode* portion of the startup sequence.

See Also...
"Hot Docking and Hardware Profiles," p. 580

7. Io.sys processes the settings in the Msdos.sys system file. (See "Controlling Startup Using Msdos.sys," later in this chapter.)

8. If your system has multiple hardware profiles defined (see Chapter 25, "The Ins and Outs of Windows 98's Notebook Features"), Io.sys attempts to detect which hardware profile should be loaded. If it can't tell, you see a menu of hardware profiles so that you can choose which profile to load.

9. The Windows 98 startup logo is displayed.

10. If your system has a Config.sys startup file, Io.sys reads the file and processes its statements (which are usually real mode device drivers).

11. Io.sys loads the following programs, drivers, and DOS environment settings:

    DBLSPACE.BIN or **DRVSPACE.BIN:** The real mode driver for disk compression.

    HIMEM.SYS: The real mode memory manager that enables access to the high memory area.

    DOS=HIGH: This statement loads DOS into the high memory area.

    IFSHLP.SYS: The Installable File System Helper, which ensures that real mode file system calls go through the protected mode file system.

    SETVER.EXE: This program is used when an older application requires that a particular version of DOS be present. If a program requires DOS 6, for example, SETVER intercepts the DOS version number request and tells the program that the current version is 6.

    FILES=60: Sets the number of *file handles* that can be used by DOS programs. Some programs (particularly DOS database programs) require a larger FILES setting. In this case, you add your own FILES=100 (or whatever) line to Config.sys.

    BUFFERS=30: Sets the number of file buffers that can be used during file I/O calls by DOS programs. To specify a larger value, add a BUFFERS line to Config.sys.

Remember

Step 5 shows you why a bootable disk enables you to regain control of your computer even if your hard disk isn't working. By always checking drive A: first, the BIOS code can bypass the hard disk at startup. Most computers have BIOS settings that enable you to change this startup behavior (for example, you can have the BIOS code boot from drive B: or check the hard drive first).

Watch Out!
Placing a FILES line in Config.sys overrides the FILES setting from Io.sys. This also applies to the BUFFERS, STACKS, and FCBS settings. If you add any of these lines to Config.sys, make sure you never use a value lower than the default value used in Io.sys.

Inside Scoop
Step 15 provides a handy troubleshooting technique. If you discover that one of the VxDs in VMM32 isn't loading properly, extract the appropriate VxD file from your Windows 98 CD-ROM and then put the file in the Windows\System\ Vmm32 folder. Windows 98 will then bypass the VxD in Vmm32.vxd and load it from the Vmm32 folder, instead.

See Also...
"An Insider's Guide to the Registry," p. 104

STACKS=9,256: Sets the number of stack frames and the size of each frame. To specify a larger value, add a STACKS line to Config.sys.

FCBS=4: Sets the maximum number of file control blocks that can be open at once. To specify a larger value, add your own FCBS line to Config.sys.

LASTDRIVE=Z: Sets the last drive letter that can be assigned to a disk drive or mapped network resource.

SHELL=Command.com /P: Sets the name of the command-line interpreter.

12. If your system has an Autoexec.bat startup file, Io.sys reads the file and processes its statements.

13. Io.sys runs Win.com.

14. Win.com runs the Virtual Memory Manager (Vmm32.vxd) to handle the real mode loading of virtual device drivers, or *VxDs*. These are the *static* VxDs that Windows 98 needs immediately (as opposed to *dynamic* VxDs that only load when they're required), and they're all contained within the Vmm32.vxd file.

15. VMM32 checks the Windows\System\Vmm32 folder to see if it contains any of the VxDs that are normally found within the Vmm32.vxd file. If it does, the VxDs are loaded from that folder instead of Vmm32.vxd.

16. Vmm32 queries the Windows 98 Registry for the list of static VxDs to load (these are Registry entries that have a StaticVxD setting). This list can be found in the following Registry key (see Chapter 4, "An Insider's Guide to Three Crucial Configuration Tools"):

```
HKEY_LOCAL_MACHINE\System\CurrentControlSet\Services\
VxD
```

17. VMM32 checks the System.ini file for other VxDs listed under the [386 Enh] section.

18. VMM32 switches the processor into protected mode.

19. VMM32 begins loading the protected mode Vxds for system devices and other hardware. Also, Plug and Play device drivers are loaded and the resources used by Plug and Play devices are allocated. If VMM32 detects any new or changed devices, you may be asked to insert your Windows 98 CD-ROM.

20. The three main components of the Windows 98 system are loaded:

    Kernel: The Kernel (`Kernel32.dll` and `Krnl386.exe`) is the heart of Windows 98. Its duties include loading applications, allocating virtual memory, scheduling and running program threads, and handling file input and output.

    GDI: The Graphical Device Interface (`Gdi.exe` and `Gdi32.exe`) manages Windows 98's graphical user interface.

    User: The User component (`User.exe` and `User32.exe`) manages input from the user (keystrokes, mouse clicks, joystick movements, and so on), and output to the user (sending data to an open window, playing sounds in response to events, and so on).

See Also...
"Launching
Applications
Automatically at
Startup," p. 136

21. The values in the `Win.ini` initialization file are processed.

22. The Windows 98 shell is loaded.

23. Windows and network logon dialog boxes are displayed.

24. Shortcuts for programs, documents, and other files are processed from the Startup folder. Also, the Registry's various "Run" keys are processed. See Chapter 5, "Getting the Most Out of Your Applications."

Notes About `Config.sys` **and** `Autoexec.bat`

As you saw in the previous section, `Config.sys` and `Autoexec.bat` are startup files processed during the real mode phase of the Windows 98 boot sequence. These files are holdovers from the pre-Windows 95 days when applications (and DOS) used `Config.sys` and `Autoexec.bat` to load device drivers, set environ-

Shortcut
To prevent the
shortcuts in the
Startup folder
from loading, hold
down the Shift key
while Windows 98
starts.

ment variables, and run programs at startup. Now, however, Io.sys handles most of the Config.sys initialization chores, and Windows 98 has VxDs to manage most devices.

Therefore, chances are good that you can get rid of these two startup files and improve performance in two ways:

- You reduce startup time since Io.sys no longer has to process Config.sys and Autoexec.bat.

- You improve device performance by using a protected mode driver instead of a real mode driver. There are three reasons for this: 1) 16-bit real mode drivers are generally slower than the equivalent 32-bit protected mode driver; 2) Real mode drivers must reside either in conventional memory (the first 640KB) or the Upper Memory Area (the area between 640KB and 1MB), thus reducing the amount of memory below 1MB that's available for DOS programs; and 3) Windows 98 runs in protected mode, so it must perform a time-consuming "context switch" in order to use a real mode driver.

This doesn't mean that you should rush out and delete Config.sys and Autoexec.bat. There may be drivers or settings loading within either file that your system needs. Here's how to find out:

- Rename Config.sys and Autoexec.bat (to, say, Config.98 and Autoexec.98) and then restart your computer. If everything seems to work, then you don't need these files. (I suggest living with this new setup for a week or two, just to be sure.)

- If your system doesn't run properly without these files, restore the names and then try "commenting out" one line at a time. To comment out a line, add REM and a space to the beginning of the line. After editing a line, restart your computer and see if it works properly. When startup fails, you'll know that the previous line you commented out is one that your system requires. Remove the REM from that line.

There are also two `Autoexec.bat` items you should watch out for:

PATH statement: The PATH statement lists a series of directory paths, separated by semicolons. If you ask Windows to launch an executable file (that is, a file with the `.exe`, `.com`, or `.bat` extension), it looks in the current directory. If it doesn't find the file there, it looks in each of the directories specified in the PATH. Some programs add their home directory to the PATH. These programs may not function properly if you delete `Autoexec.bat` or comment out the PATH line because, in both cases, Windows just uses its default PATH:

```
C:\Windows;C:\Windows\System
```

SET statements: These statements set the value of a DOS environment variable. Some programs and devices use these variables as a quick-and-dirty way of storing information. (For example, the Sound Blaster sound card uses a variable named BLASTER to store data about the sound card's current configuration.) Again, your programs might not work if `Autoexec.bat` is missing or if one or more SET statements have been commented out.

Remember
The default PATH will be different if you installed Windows 98 in a folder other than `C:\Windows`.

If a PATH or SET statement is all that's keeping your system from being `Autoexec.bat`-free, there is a workaround—it's called WINSET, and you can find it on your Windows 98 CD in the following folder:

```
\tools\reskit\scrpting
```

The idea is that you can run WINSET to set the PATH or to assign a value to an environment variable. To use it, copy the file `Winset.exe` to the `Windows` folder. Here's the syntax for this program:

```
WINSET variable=string
```

variable	This is the name of the environment variable.
string	This is the value that you want to assign to the variable.

See Also...
"Using the
Startup Folder,"
p. 137

For example, suppose your `Autoexec.bat` file contains the following lines:

```
PATH=C:\Windows;C:\Windows\COMMAND;C:\VISIO
SET DIRCMD=/OGN /P
SET BLASTER=A220 I5 D1 H5 P330 T6
```

To accomplish the same thing with WINSET, you'd enter the following commands:

```
WINSET PATH=C:\Windows;C:\Windows\COMMAND;C:\VISIO
WINSET DIRCMD=/OGN /P
WINSET BLASTER=A220 I5 D1 H5 P330 T6
```

Shortcut
To avoid leaving the DOS session window onscreen when the batch file finishes, open the Startup folder, right-click the batch file shortcut and then click Properties. In the dialog box that appears, select the Program tab, and then activate the Close on Exit check box.

The best way to do this is to use Notepad to create a new text file, enter these lines, and then save the file with the .bat extension (for example, `Set.bat`). Then create a shortcut for this batch file in your Windows 98 Startup folder (see Chapter 5).

Working with the Windows 98 Startup Menu

Unlike Windows 3.*x*, Windows 98 launches automatically at startup. What do you do if you need to prevent Windows 98 from loading, either because you're having trouble getting Windows 98 to run or because you want to boot to the DOS prompt? For these situations, you can invoke the Windows 98 Startup menu, which offers various startup options.

To get to the Startup menu, restart your computer and hold down the Ctrl key during the POST. Once the POST is complete, the Startup menu appears:

```
Microsoft Windows 98 Startup Menu
=======================================
```

Watch Out!
Holding down Ctrl may interfere with some POST chores, such as setting up the keyboard or initializing a SCSI controller. If this happens, just release Ctrl until the POST resumes, and then hold it down again.

```
1. Normal
2. Logged (\BOOTLOG.TXT)
3. Safe mode
4. Step-by-step confirmation
5. Command prompt only
6. Safe mode command prompt only
7. Previous version of MS-DOS
```

To select an item, type its number and then press Enter.

Not surprisingly, the Normal option starts Windows 98 in the usual way. The rest of this section discusses each of the other Startup menu items.

Logged (\BOOTLOG.TXT): This options starts Windows 98 normally, but records each step of the boot procedure to a text file named Bootlog.txt, which is stored in your system's root folder. You use this option when Windows 98 won't start and you want to see where in the boot process the failure occurs. Here's the general procedure for using this option:

1. Restart your computer and then run the Logged (\BOOTLOG.TXT) option.

2. When Windows 98 fails to load, restart your computer.

3. Display the Startup menu once again, but this time select the Command Prompt Only option.

4. At the DOS prompt, type edit bootlog.txt and press Enter to open Bootlog.txt in the MS-DOS Editor.

5. Search for a line that contains LoadFailed:

```
[000DE95B] Loading Vxd = CONFIGMG
[000DE95B] LoadFailed = CONFIGMG
```

6. Reinstall the offending driver or file:

- If the line shows only a filename without an extension or path (for example, CONFIGMG), it's a VxD that's loading from within Vmm32.vxd. In this case, extract the VxD file (see Chapter 2, "Ten Things You Should Know About the Windows 98 Setup") and copy it to the C:\Windows\System\Vmm32 folder.

- If the line shows a filename with an extension but no folder (for example, JAVASUP.VXD), it's a VxD that's loading from the C:\Windows\System folder. Extract the file from the Windows 98 source files (or wherever) and then replace the existing file in the C:\Windows\System\ folder.

- If the line shows a full path (folder plus filename), reinstall the file to that folder.

Safe mode: This command launches a bare-bones version of Windows 98. This means that Config.sys and Autoexec.bat are skipped, the Registry isn't processed, only necessary device dri-

See Also...
"Extracting a File from the Windows 98 Setup Files," p. 67

Undocumented
Not all LoadFailed lines indicate a problem. In some cases, a driver may fail to load simply because the necessary hardware doesn't exist on your system. For example, the driver VPOWERD will fail to load if your system doesn't support Advanced Power Management. False LoadFailed lines may appear with the following drivers: DSOUND, EBIOS, NDIS2SUP, VPOWERD, VSERVER, and VSHARE.

vers are loaded (such as those for the keyboard and mouse), and the display is set to a 16-color, 640×480 resolution using the Standard VGA display driver. This minimal configuration should enable you to load Windows 98 successfully. From there, you can (hopefully) troubleshoot the problem.

Step-by-step confirmation: This command tells Windows 98 to ask you for confirmation before performing a startup task:

```
Load DoubleSpace driver [Enter=Y,Esc=N]?
```

Pressing Enter or Y loads the driver or runs the command. To bypass the task, press Esc or N. This is one of the best methods for isolating a problem. As you step through the tasks, press Enter or Y to load each one. Keep an eye on the screen to see if any error messages show up. If you see such a message, or if your system hangs, then you've found the culprit:

- If it's a Config.sys and Autoexec.bat command, comment out the line that loads the command.

- If it's a Windows device driver, replace the driver (as described earlier).

Command prompt only: This command processes Config.sys and Autoexec.bat and then drops you off at the DOS prompt. (No virtual device drivers are loaded and the Windows 98 GUI is not displayed.) This is useful for running DOS programs such as the MS-DOS Editor (Edit.com) or a command-line utility (such as Scandisk.exe). You also use this command when you want to start Windows 98 using command-line switches, as described in the next section.

When your work at the DOS prompt is complete, you can start Windows 98 by typing win and pressing Enter.

Safe mode command prompt only: This command is the same as Command prompt only, except that Config.sys and Autoexec.bat are not processed. Use this command when you suspect a line in Config.sys and Autoexec.bat is causing a startup problem.

Previous version of MS-DOS: You'll only see this command if you set up Windows 98 to dual-boot with DOS or Windows 3.1x. As I mentioned in Chapter 2, the Windows 98 Setup pro-

Shortcut
You can bypass the Startup menu and select Safe Mode automatically by pressing F5 as soon as you hear the beep that signals the end of the POST.

Shortcut
The shortcut key for the Step-by-step confirmation command is Shift+F8. Remember to press this key combination as soon as your hear the beep that announces the end of the POST.

gram renames your existing startup files—Io.sys, Msdos.sys, Command.com, Config.sys, and Autoexec.bat—with the .dos extension (Io.dos, and so on). Running the Previous version of MS-DOS command causes the following to happen:

- The Windows 98 system files are renamed as follows: Io.sys to Jo.sys, Msdos.sys to Msdos.w40, Command.com to Command.w40, Config.sys to Config.w40, and Autoexec.bat to Autoexec.w40.

- The system files from your previous operating system are renamed as follows: Io.dos to Io.sys, Msdos.dos to Msdos.sys, Command.dos to Command.com, Config.dos to Config.sys, and Autoexec.dos to Autoexec.bat.

With the old system files now restored, the boot continues and your previous operating system loads.

Win.com **Switches for Startup Troubleshooting**

I mentioned earlier that you can boot to DOS using the Startup menu's Command prompt only item, and then load the Windows 98 GUI by typing win and pressing Enter. When you start Windows 98 this way, you're actually running Win.com by hand.

For troubleshooting purposes, you can modify Win.com by using various switches that control how Windows 98 loads. Here's the syntax:

```
WIN [/B] [/D:[F] [M] [S] [V] [X]] [/W] [/WX]
```

/B	This switch does the same thing as selecting the Logged (\BOOTLOG.TXT) command in the Windows 98 Startup menu. That is, it logs the startup procedure to a file named Bootlog.txt in the root folder.
/D:F	This switch disables all 32-bit protected mode disk drivers. Instead, Windows 98 uses only real mode drivers. Try this if your computer is having trouble reading from or writing to the hard disk.

See Also...
"Using MS-DOS
Mode," p. 141

/D:M	This switch starts Windows 98 in Safe mode, so it's the same thing as selecting the Windows 98 Startup menu's Safe mode command.
/D:S	This switch forces Windows 98 not to use the ROM address space between F000:0000 and 1MB for a break point. Use this switch if Windows 98 hangs during startup.
/D:V	This switch tells Windows 98 not to handle interrupt requests from the hard disk controller, and not to bypass the ROM code that processes these requests. Use this switch if Windows 98 has trouble reading from or writing to the hard disk.
/D:X	This switch tells Windows 98 not to scan the Upper Memory Area for unused upper memory blocks. Use this switch if Windows 98 hangs during startup or if you have video problems.
/W	This switch is used when exiting MS-DOS mode. It renames Config.wos to Config.sys and Autoexec.wos to Autoexec.bat, and then prompts you to press any key to start Windows 98. See Chapter 5 to learn more about this switch and MS-DOS mode.
/WX	This switch is also used when exiting MS-DOS mode. This switch works like /W, except that it restarts Windows 98 automatically.

Controlling Startup Using the System Configuration Utility

If Windows 98 won't start, troubleshooting the problem usually involves trying various Startup menu commands and experimenting with different step-by-step sequences. It's almost always a time-consuming and tedious business.

However, what if Windows 98 will start, but you encounter problems along the way? Or what if you want to try a few different startup configurations to see if you can eliminate items in Config.sys and Autoexec.bat or improve Windows 98's overall performance? For these scenarios, don't bother trying out different startup configurations by hand. Instead, take advantage of Windows 98's new System Configuration Utility, which gives you a graphical front-end that gives you precise control over how Windows 98 starts.

To launch the System Configuration Utility, you have two choices:

- Select Start, Programs, Accessories, System Tools, System Information. When the System Information window appears, select Tools, System Configuration Utility.

- Select Start, Run, type msconfig, and click OK.

Either way, the System Configuration Utility window appears, as shown in Figure 3.1.

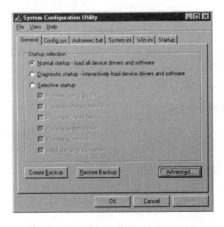

Figure 3.1
Use the System Configuration Utility to select different startup configurations.

Before making any changes, you might want to click the Create Backup button to create backup copies of your configuration files. Config.sys and Autoexec.bat are backed up to Config.pss and Autoexec.pss in the root folder, and System.ini and Win.ini are backed up to System.pss and Win.pss in the Windows folder. To restore these backups later on, click the Restore Backup button.

The General tab has three startup options:

Normal startup: This option loads Windows 98 normally.

Diagnostic startup: This option is equivalent to selecting Step-by-step Confirmation in the Windows 98 Startup menu.

Selective startup: When you activate this option, the check boxes below become available. You use these check boxes to select which portions of the startup should be processed: Config.sys, Autoexec.bat, Winstart.bat, System.ini, Win.ini, and the items in the Startup folder.

Clicking the Advanced button displays the Advanced Troubleshooting Settings dialog box, shown in Figure 3.2. Here's a summary of the settings in this dialog box:

Disable System ROM breakpoint: When you activate this check box, Windows 98 won't use the ROM address space between F000:0000 and 1MB for a system break point. This is equivalent to starting Windows 98 with the command win.com /D:S.

Disable Virtual HD IRQ: When you activate this check box, you're telling Windows 98 not to use its virtual handler for interrupt requests from the hard disk controller. Instead, these requests will be handled by the ROM code that processes controller interrupts. This is equivalent to starting Windows 98 with the command win.com /D:V.

EMM Exclude A000-FFFF: When activated, this check box tells Windows 98 not to look for unused memory blocks in the Upper Memory Area (that is, the addresses from A000 to FFFF). This is equivalent to starting Windows 98 with the command win.com /D:X.

Force Compatibility mode disk access: When you activate this check box, Windows 98 uses only real mode drivers for disk access. When a disk drive uses real mode drivers, it is said to be in *compatibility mode.* This is equivalent to starting Windows 98 with the command win.com /D:F.

VGA 640×480×16: Activate this check box to load Windows 98 using the Standard VGA display driver, which uses 640×480 resolution and only 16 colors.

Use SCSI Double-buffering: Activate this check box if you have a SCSI hard disk and you're experiencing disk access problems. Activating this check box adds the line DoubleBuffer=1 to your Msdos.sys file (explained in the next section). This check box will be grayed out if the line DoubleBuffer=1 already exists in Msdos.sys.

Enable Startup menu: If you activate this check box, the Windows 98 Startup menu appears automatically when you boot. You don't have to hold down Ctrl during the POST.

Disable Scandisk after bad shutdown: If you shut off or reboot your computer without exiting Windows 98, ScanDisk is run automatically during Startup to check for disk errors. If you find yourself constantly rebooting after Windows 98 hangs during startup, these ScanDisk checks can waste time. In this case, activate this check box and then run ScanDisk later once the problem is solved.

Limit memory to _x_ MB: Use this check box to restrict memory usage on your machine to the first _x_ megabytes. For example, some Intel processors suffer performance problems when more than 64MB is installed.

Disable fast shutdown: Windows 98 uses a "fast shutdown" procedure that doesn't unload device drivers, among other things. If you experience shutdown problems, activate this check box.

Disable UDF file system: Activating this check box tells Windows 98 not to use the Universal Disk Format file system for removable media, including DVD discs. You may need to activate this check box if you have a DVD player that doesn't support UDF.

Enable Pentium F0 (Lock CmpXchg) workaround: Pentium and Pentium MMX processors have a bug that causes the system to hang if it encounters a specific illegal instruction sequence. Although this sequence should never

Inside Scoop
If video problems prevent you from using the System Configuration Utility, you can still configure Windows 98 to use the Standard VGA driver by editing System.ini. Boot to the DOS prompt and enter the command edit C:\ windows\system. ini to load System.ini into the MS-DOS Editor. Find the display.drv line and change it to display.drv=vga. drv.

Inside Scoop
The design of Intel's TX chipset allows only a maximum of 64MB to be cached. Therefore, anything loaded above 64MB must be accessed from main memory instead of the faster cache. Windows loads its files from the top of memory on down, so its services are not cached, and therefore overall performance suffers.

occur in practice, you can try activating this check box if your system is hanging. This enables a Windows 98 workaround that prevents the system from locking up.

Figure 3.2
Click the
Advanced button
to display these
advanced startup
settings.

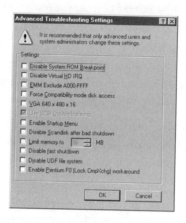

The next four tabs—Config.sys, Autoexec.bat, System.ini, and Win.ini—contain check boxes for the various settings that appear within these files. For example, Figure 3.3 shows some check boxes from a typical Config.sys file. Here's how to work with these settings:

■ Deactivating a check box is equivalent to adding "REM" to the beginning of the line to comment out the settings.

See Also...
"Launching
Applications
Automatically at
Startup," p. 136

■ Use the Move Up and Move Down buttons to change the order of the settings.

■ Click New to add a new setting to the file.

■ To change a setting, highlight it and click Edit.

The final tab—Startup—enables you to work with programs and services that run automatically at startup. These are the items found in your Startup folder, as well as any item found in the following Registry keys (see Chapter 5):

HKEY_LOCAL_MACHINE\Software\Microsoft\Windows\Current Version\Run

HKEY_LOCAL_MACHINE\Software\Microsoft\Windows\Current Version\RunServices

Figure 3.3
The System
Configuration
Utility enables you
to toggle individual
startup settings
on and off, such
as those shown
here for Config.sys.

To prevent an item from loading at startup, disable its check box. If you disable a Startup folder item, Windows 98 creates a new folder named Disabled Startup Items (see Start, Programs, Disabled Startup Items) and moves the disabled item into this folder.

Controlling Startup Using Msdos.sys

Msdos.sys is a special system file that controls various aspects of the Windows 98 startup. For example, you can use Msdos.sys to tell Windows 98 to always display the Startup menu, to adjust the length of time Windows 98 waits before selecting the default Startup menu command, or to disable the Windows 98 startup logo.

Msdos.sys contains some powerful options, so to prevent novice users from accidentally editing or deleting this file, Windows 98 sets the file's read-only, hidden, and system attributes. So the first thing you must do is make sure that Windows 98 is displaying hidden files:

1. Run Windows Explorer and select the View, Folder Options command to display the Options dialog box.

2. Select the View tab.

3. Activate the Show All Files option button.

4. While you're here, you should also deactivate the Hide File Extensions for Known File Types check box.

5. Click OK.

Undocumented
It's possible that you may disable a Startup folder item and then have it reappear later on (if you reinstall an application, for example). In this case, you won't be able to disable the item again because Windows 98 won't let you disable an item if it already exists in the Disabled Startup Items folder. To work around this, delete the item from the Disabled Startup Items folder.

To set up Msdos.sys for editing, you have to perform the following tasks:

1. In the root folder, right-click Msdos.sys and then click Properties. The file's property sheet appears.

2. Deactivate the Read-only check box and click OK.

3. Right-click Msdos.sys once again, but this time click Open With in the shortcut menu.

4. In the Open With dialog box, highlight NOTEPAD (or some other text editor), make sure the Always Use This Program to Open This Type of File check box is deactivated, and then click OK.

5. Edit the file, save your changes, and then exit the text editor.

Watch Out!
To ensure that Msdos.sys isn't accidentally deleted or modified, reinstate the read-only attribute. Right-click Msdos.sys, click Properties, activate the Read-only check box in the dialog box that appears, and then click OK.

That's an awful lot of work to go through just to make some quick edits to Msdos.sys. To avoid this drudgery, create a batch file that performs all of these steps automatically:

1. Right-click the desktop, and then click New, Text Document.

2. Type Edit Msdos.sys.bat and press Enter. (When Windows 98 asks if you're sure you want to change the extension, click Yes.)

3. Right-click the new file and then click Edit.

4. In Notepad, enter the following lines:

```
@ECHO OFF
ATTRIB -R -H -S C:\Msdos.sys
START /W NOTEPAD C:\Msdos.sys
ATTRIB +R +H +S C:\Msdos.sys
```

5. Save the file and exit Notepad.

Figure 3.4 shows a typical Msdos.sys file opened in Notepad.

Msdos.sys contains three sections:

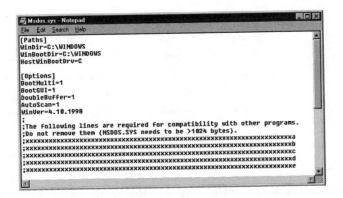

Figure 3.4
Notepad showing a
typical `Msdos.sys`
file.

- The [Paths] section contains settings that specify the main Windows 98 folder (WinDir), the Windows 98 boot folder (WinBootDir), and the letter of the drive from which Windows 98 boots (HostWinBootDrv). You shouldn't change any of these settings.

- The [Options] section contains settings that determine various Windows 98 startup options. I discuss the available settings below.

- The lines that consist mostly of the letter x are there to ensure compatibility with older programs. For example, some older virus checkers expect Msdos.sys to be larger than 1,024 bytes. (Msdos.sys used to be a DOS system file.) All those extra lines are there to make sure that the Msdos.sys file size is at least 1,024 bytes.

The real meat of Msdos.sys is the [Options] section, which accepts various settings for customizing the Windows 98 startup. The default Msdos.sys may contain only four or five settings (depending on your system), but there are many more you can use:

AutoScan: Controls whether Windows 98 runs ScanDisk after an improper shutdown. There are three values you can use:

AutoScan=0—Windows 98 does not run ScanDisk after a bad shutdown.

`AutoScan=1` (the default)—Windows 98 displays a message that your system was shut down improperly and then prompts you to run ScanDisk. Pressing any key starts the ScanDisk check. (Note that on some systems Windows 98 will start ScanDisk automatically without prompting you.)

`AutoScan=2`—Windows 98 runs ScanDisk automatically after a bad shutdown.

BootGUI: Controls whether the Windows 98 graphical user interface (GUI) is loaded at startup:

`BootGUI=0`—`Io.sys` does not load the Windows 98 GUI. This is equivalent to choosing the Command Prompt Only option in the Windows 98 Startup menu.

`BootGUI=1` (the default)—`Io.sys` loads the Windows 98 GUI.

BootKeys: Controls whether the Windows 98 Startup menu's shortcut keys are enabled:

`BootKeys=0`—The shortcut keys are disabled.

`BootKeys=1` (the default)—The shortcut keys are enabled.

BootMenu: Controls whether the Windows 98 Startup menu appears automatically:

`BootMenu=0` (the default)—You must hold down Ctrl during the POST to display the Startup menu.

`BootMenu=1`—The Startup menu appears automatically.

BootMenuDefault: Specifies the Startup menu command that is highlighted automatically when the menu is first displayed. Set this value equal to the number of the menu command, where 1 is the `Normal` command, 2 is the `Logged` (`\BOOTLOG.TXT`) command, and so on.

Remember
You must press a Startup menu shortcut key immediately after you hear the beep that signals the end of the POST. Windows 95 supported an extra `Msdos.sys` option called `BootDelay` that enabled you to specify the number of seconds Windows would wait for a key-press. This option is not supported in Windows 98.

BootMenuDelay: Specifies the length, in seconds, of the countdown that appears when you display the Startup menu. The default value is 30.

BootMulti: Controls whether Windows 98 can dual-boot with your previous version of DOS:

> BootMulti=0—Dual-booting is disabled. The Previous version of MS-DOS command does not appear on the Startup menu.

> BootMulti=1—Dual-booting is enabled. The Previous version of MS-DOS command appears on the Startup menu.

BootSafe: Controls whether Windows 98 boots in Safe mode automatically:

> BootSafe=0 (the default)—You can only start Windows 98 in Safe mode by selecting one of the Safe mode options from the Startup menu.

> BootSafe=1—Windows 98 starts in Safe mode automatically.

BootWarn: Controls whether Windows 98 starts in Safe mode automatically if it encountered problems on the previous boot:

> BootWarn=0—Windows 98 loads normally, even if the previous boot failed.

> BootWarn=1 (the default)—If Io.sys detects that the most recent boot failed, it displays the Startup menu, sets the Safe mode option as the default, and displays a warning message.

BootWin: Controls whether your system boots to Windows 98 or your previous version of DOS:

> BootWin=0—Your previous version of DOS loads at startup. This is equivalent to selecting the Previous Version of MS-DOS option on the Startup menu.

> BootWin=1 (the default)—Windows 98 loads at startup.

DoubleBuffer: Controls whether double-buffering is loaded at startup for memory caching on some hard disk controllers (particularly SCSI controllers):

> DoubleBuffer=0—Double-buffering is not loaded.

> DoubleBuffer=1 (the default)—Double-buffering is loaded only for controllers that need it.

> DoubleBuffer=2—Double-buffering is loaded.

DBLSpace: Controls whether Dblspace.bin (the DOS 6.x disk compression driver) is loaded automatically:

> DBLSpace=0—Dblspace.bin isn't loaded.

> DBLSpace=1 (the default)—Dblspace.bin is loaded automatically.

DRVSpace: Controls whether Drvspace.bin (the Windows 98 disk compression driver) is loaded automatically:

> DRVSpace=0—Drvspace.bin isn't loaded.

> DRVSpace=1 (the default)—Drvspace.bin is loaded automatically.

LoadTop: Controls whether Io.sys loads Command.com and Drvspace.bin into the Upper Memory Area (UMA):

> LoadTop=0—Command.com and Drvspace.bin are not loaded into the UMA, and are loaded into conventional memory, instead. Use this setting if you suspect another program is loading into the UMA and possibly conflicting with either Command.com or Drvspace.bin.

> LoadTop=1 (the default)—Command.com and Drvspace.bin are loaded into the UMA, which increases the amount of free conventional memory.

Inside Scoop
Windows 98 often sets DoubleBuffer=1 on SCSI controllers unnecessarily. If you have a newer controller, try using DoubleBuffer=0 and see if your system starts normally. Disabling double-buffering will reduce your start time slightly and free up a small amount of conventional memory.

Logo: Controls whether the Windows 98 logo is displayed at startup:

> `Logo=0`—The logo isn't displayed. Use this setting if you have a video card that can't handle the graphics mode switch that is required to display the logo.

> `Logo=1` (the default)—The logo is displayed.

How the Shutdown Process Works

Shutting down Windows 98 isn't difficult, but there are a few issues to consider, which is what you'll do in this section.

First off, you should know that Windows 98 has a new *fast shutdown* feature that shuts down your system quite a bit faster than Windows 95. This feature basically just bypasses the unloading of device drivers and other device shutdown chores. The upshot is that your system should shut down in just a few seconds, instead of the 10 or 15 seconds that was typical of Windows 95.

Certainly the most important aspect of shutdown to bear in mind is that you should always exit Windows before you shut off your computer. There are a number of reasons why you need to do this:

- Windows 98 doesn't record some Registry settings until the shutdown process is under way. You'll lose these unsaved settings if you turn off your machine before exiting Windows 98.

- Windows 98 waits for idle processor time before committing some changed data to disk (this is called *write-behind caching*). If you shut down your machine before exiting Windows 98, you'll lose this changed data.

- When you exit Windows 98, it checks to see if any network users are connected to any of the resources you share with the network. If you turn off your machine without exiting Windows 98, network users could get cut off in the middle of a file transfer or print operation.

Shortcut
You can also bypass the Windows 98 logo at startup by pressing Esc once the logo appears.

66
Don't turn off your computer until you see a message telling you that shutdown is complete. If you turn off your computer without shutting it down correctly, you risk losing information.
—From the "Getting Started" booklet
99

Here's the proper Windows 98 shutdown procedure:

1. Close all your applications and save all your work.

2. Select the Start, Shut Down command. Windows 98 displays the Shut Down Windows dialog box shown in Figure 3.5.

Figure 3.5
Selecting the Shut Down command displays this dialog box.

Inside Scoop
For a faster restart, select the Restart option, hold down Shift, and then click OK. Leave the Shift key held down until you see the message Windows is now restarting. This method bypasses the POST and other cold reboot startup chores.

3. Select the shut-down command you want to use:

   Stand by: Places your computer in standby mode, which powers down the monitor and hard disk. This option is only available if your system has support for Advanced Power Management.

   Shut down: Prepares your computer to be turned off. You first see a bitmap with the message Windows is shutting down. A few seconds later, another bitmap appears, this time with the message It's now safe to turn off your computer. Note that some newer Advanced Power Management computers will turn themselves off automatically at this point.

   Restart: Exits Windows 98 and then cold boots the computer to restart it.

   Restart in MS-DOS mode: Exits Windows 98, restarts your computer in MS-DOS mode, and then drops you off at the DOS prompt. I explain MS-DOS mode in Chapter 5.

4. Click OK. Windows 98 runs the selected shutdown option.

Creating Custom Startup and Shutdown Screens

See Also...
"Using MS-DOS Mode," p. 141

When you start Windows 98, a startup logo is displayed to give you something nicer to look at than the boot text displayed during the POST or the processing of Config.sys and Autoexec.bat. You also saw in the previous section that Windows 98 displays two bitmaps during the shutdown process. Interestingly, Windows 98 is happy to display custom bitmaps in place of any of these three images. Here's how:

- To replace the startup bitmap, create a new image or edit an existing image and then save it as Logo.sys in your system's root folder.

- The Windows is shutting down bitmap is a file named Logow.sys in the Windows folder. You can either modify this file, or else replace it with a new or modified image that you save as Logow.sys in the Windows folder.

- The It's now safe to turn off your computer bitmap is a file named Logos.sys in the Windows folder. You can either modify this file, or else replace it with a new or modified image that you save as Logos.sys in the Windows folder.

Note that, in all cases, the file you create or modify must have a width of 320 pixels and a height of 400 pixels.

Here are the steps to follow to replace a logo screen with a new file:

1. To ensure that the existing file doesn't get overwritten, rename it (with, say, the .old extension).

2. Select Start, Programs, Accessories, Paint to launch the Paint program.

3. Select Image, Attributes to display the Attributes dialog box. (You can also press Ctrl+E.)

4. Type 320 in the Width text box, type 400 in the Height text box, and then click OK.

5. Use Paint's tools and colors to construct your image.

6. Select File, Save (or press Ctrl+S) to save the image into the same folder and with the same name as the logo file you want to replace.

> 66
> It has come to our attention that a few copies of the 'Alabama' edition of Windows 98 may have accidentally been shipped outside Alabama. If you have one of the 'Alabama' editions, you may need some help understanding the commands. The Alabama edition may be recognized by looking at the opening screen. It reads WINDERS 98 with a background picture of General Lee superimposed on a Confederate flag.
> —From the rnet

Here are the steps to follow to convert an existing image:

1. To ensure that the existing file doesn't get overwritten, rename it (with, say, the .old extension).

2. Select Start, Programs, Accessories, Paint to launch the Paint program.

3. Select File, Open (or press Ctrl+O) to display the Open dialog box, highlight the file you want to work with, and then click Open.

4. Select Image, Attributes (or press Ctrl+E) to display the Attributes dialog box, note the current values in the Width and Height text boxes, and then click OK.

5. To adjust the width of the image to 320 pixels, select Image, Stretch/Skew (or press Ctrl+W), enter an appropriate percentage in the Stretch group's Horizontal text box, and then click OK.

6. To adjust the height of the image to 400 pixels, select Image, Stretch/Skew (or press Ctrl+W), enter an appropriate percentage in the Stretch group's Vertical text box, and then click OK.

7. Select Image, Attributes (or press Ctrl+E) to confirm that the image's width is 320 pixels and its height is 400 pixels. If you're just a few pixels off, type 320 in the Width text box, type 400 in the Height text box, and then click OK.

8. Use Paint's tools and colors to modify your image, if necessary.

9. Select File, Save (or press Ctrl+S) to save the image into the same folder and with the same name as the logo file you want to replace.

Shortcut

You may decide to start with one of the existing logo screens and modify it. Since these screens use .sys extensions (or .old if you renamed them), they won't appear in the Open dialog box. To work around this, select All Files in the Files of Type dropdown list. Make sure, as well, to use the File, Save As command to save the modified file under a new name.

Essential Information

■ Windows 98 doesn't require Config.sys and Autoexec.bat, so you may be able to improve performance by removing these files, or else by commenting out lines within these files.

- Hold down Ctrl during the Power-On Self Test to invoke the Windows 98 Startup menu, from which you can select various startup options, such as loading Windows 98 in safe mode.

- Windows 98's new System Configuration Utility gives you an easy-to-use graphical front-end for many of Windows 98's startup options.

- `Msdos.sys` is a hidden, read-only text file that supports a large number of options for controlling the Windows 98 startup.

- Before turning off your computer, always select Start, Shut Down to exit Windows 98 properly and ensure that you don't lose data.

- You can customize the startup and shutdown bitmaps by using Paint to create or modify 320×400-pixel images and saving them as `C:\Logo.sys` (for the startup bitmap), `C:\Windows\Logow.sys` (the `Windows is shutting down` bitmap), or `C:\Windows\Logos.sys` (the `It's now safe to turn off your computer` bitmap).

GET THE SCOOP ON...
The importance of the Registry ▪ Techniques backing-
up and keeping the Registry error-free ▪
Understanding the overall structure of the Registry ▪
The Registry Editor ▪ Using the System Policy Editor
that controls a wide range of Windows 98 behavior ▪
Installing and using Tweak UI

An Insider's Guide to Three Crucial Configuration Tools

Chapter 4

M Y GOAL IN THIS BOOK is to help you get the most out of Windows 98, and my premise is that this goal can't be met by "toeing the line" and doing only what the manual or Help system tells you. Rather, I believe you can only reach this goal by taking various "unauthorized" routes that go beyond Windows orthodoxy.

This chapter is a perfect example. The three tools that I'll discuss—the Registry, system policies, and Tweak UI—aren't difficult to use, but they put an amazing amount of power and flexibility into your hands. I discuss them in this early chapter because you'll be using these important tools throughout the rest of the book. However, you can scour the Windows 98 manual and Help system all day long and you'll find only a few scant references to the Registry, and nothing at all on system policies or Tweak UI. To be sure, Microsoft is just being cautious since these *are* powerful tools, and the average user can wreak all kinds of havoc if these features are used incorrectly. However, your purchase of this book is proof that you are not an "average user" so, by following the instructions in this chapter, I'm sure you'll have no trouble at all using these tools.

An Insider's Guide to the Registry

Let's begin with the Registry, which most experts agree is the most important feature on the Windows landscape. In the next few sections, you'll learn why the Registry is so important, how to keep the Registry safe from harm, how the Registry is structured, and how to work with Registry settings. I'll be referring to the Registry constantly in the chapters to come, so your mastery of this material will go a long way to helping you get your money's worth not only out of this book, but also out of Windows itself.

Why Is the Registry So Important?

One of the main reasons that a computer is a more useful tool than, say, a washing machine, is that computers can "remember" things. Files that you create or install are remembered simply by virtue of being stored on your hard disk. But computers are also very good at remembering settings and configurations. If you customize an application's toolbar, for example, chances are the application will remember your customization and display it the next time you use the program. Windows has always done a lot of this. Things like the settings you entered during Setup, the color of the desktop, and the arrangement of the icons are all saved for later use.

In the pre-Windows 95 world, any settings that Windows wanted to remember were stored in simple text files. At first, just Config.sys and Autoexec.bat were used. Subsequent versions of Windows turned to initialization files such as Win.ini and System.ini to hold an ever-growing list of configuration data.

The problem with this design was that these text files were too easily modified or even deleted. Also, the sheer number of .INI files that came to be used made it difficult to find the setting you wanted to work with.

So one of the many innovations born with Windows 95 was the concept of a central storage area to hold all (or almost all) Windows configuration data. This database is called the Registry, and it contains a lot of data:

- Information about all the hardware installed on your computer.

- The resources used by those devices.

- A list of the device drivers that get loaded at startup.

- Settings used internally by Windows 98.

- File type data that associates a particular type of file with a specific application.

- Object linking and embedding data.

- Wallpaper, color schemes, and other interface customization settings.

- Other customization settings for things like the Start menu and the taskbar.

- Settings for accessories such as Windows Explorer and Internet Explorer.

- Internet and network connections and passwords.

- Settings and customization options for many applications.

That may seem like a long list, but it's only a tiny fraction of what's contained within the Registry's walls. The sheer wealth of data stored in one place makes the Registry convenient, but it also makes it very precious. If your Registry went missing somehow, or if it got corrupted, Windows 98 simply would not work.

Keeping the Registry Safe

Now that you see why the Registry is an important piece of business, let's take a moment to run through a few protective measures. The techniques in this section should ensure that Windows 98 never goes down for the count because of a Registry problem.

Copying the Registry Database Files

The first thing you need to understand is that the Registry consists of two files: User.dat and System.dat:

Remember
The Registry may have taken over as Windows' "memory," but that doesn't mean that .INI files have no place in Windows 98. Many older applications still expect to store and retrieve settings from .INI files such as Win.ini, so Windows 98 still ships with many of its old .INI files to ensure compatibility with these legacy programs.

- User.dat is a hidden, read-only system file in the Windows folder. Its job is to store user-specific data, including your Windows 98 customizations, your program configurations, and so on.

- System.dat is also a hidden, read-only system file that resides in the Windows folder. It stores system-specific data, such as your machine's hardware configuration, settings used internally by Windows 98, and settings required by some 32-bit applications.

So one of the simplest ways to keep the Registry safe is to make copies of User.dat and System.dat. Bear in mind, however, that these files are quite large. In particular, System.dat will be between 1.5 and 2MB to start with, and can easily grow to be 4 or 5MB in size. (User.dat begins around 150KB and can grow to several times that size.) This means you can't back up these files to a floppy disk. Instead, you'll have to copy these files to another hard disk, a network folder, or a removable disk such as a Zip or Jaz disk.

See Also...
"Backing Up Your
Files," p. 372

Backing Up the Registry

The Backup program that came with Windows 95 left a lot to be desired. One of its strangest quirks was that it wouldn't allow you to include the Registry files as part of a backup job! The only way to include these files in a backup was to use the default "Full System Backup" set, which was inconvenient, to say the least.

Happily, this absurd behavior didn't make it into the Windows 98 version of Backup, a much-improved product on all counts. I'll be discussing the Backup utility in detail in Chapter 16, "Preparing for Trouble." For now, here are the steps to follow to include the Registry files in a backup job:

1. Select Start, Programs, Accessories, System Tools, Backup.

2. If the Microsoft Backup dialog box appears, click Close.

3. Click Options to display the Backup Job Options dialog box.

4. Select the Advanced tab, as shown in Figure 4.1.

Figure 4.1
Windows 98's Backup program is only too happy to include the Registry files as part of a backup job.

5. Activate the Back Up Windows Registry check box.

6. Click OK.

Inside Scoop
Microsoft Backup will not back up the Registry if you don't also include in the backup job either the Windows folder or at least one file from your computer's boot partition (usually drive C:).

Using the Registry Checker

The only protection Windows 95 offered for the Registry was to make backup copies of the Registry files each time you shut down or restarted your system. Windows 98 beefs up Registry protection considerably thanks to its new Registry Checker utility, which does three things:

- It makes daily backup copies (up to five in all) of the Registry files.

- It checks for corrupted Registry data and tries to fix any problems it finds. If it can't fix the problem, it restores the previous day's backup.

- It checks for unused data blocks. If enough empty blocks are found (more than 500KB), the Registry is optimized to remove the unused space.

Windows 98 itself uses Registry Checker. For example, during a Windows 95 upgrade, Setup runs Registry Checker to ensure that the Windows 95 Registry is working properly. Also, Windows 98 runs Registry Checker each time you start your computer. In this case, Registry Checker makes copies of the Registry files (Win.ini and System.ini are also included for good measure) and combines everything into a .cab file. This file is then stored in the Windows\Sysbckup folder. Registry Checker stores up to five backups, and they usually take the filenames rb000.cab to rb004.cab.

When Registry Checker runs at startup, it will automatically restore the previous day's backup if it detects a problem with the Registry. However, you can also restore the previous day's backup by hand by booting to DOS and running the following command at the DOS prompt:

SCANREG /RESTORE

Registry Checker loads and then displays a list of the available backups and the dates on which they were created. Select the .cab file you want to use and then click Restore.

If you're in Windows 98, you can restore any previous backup, and any individual file within that backup, by following these steps:

1. Use Windows Explorer to open the Windows\Sysbckup folder.

2. Find the rb00x.cab file you want to work with (select View, Details to use Explorer's Details view to see the file dates).

3. Open the file. Windows 98 displays the contents of the .cab file in a folder window.

4. Highlight the file or files you want to restore and then select File, Extract. The Browse for Folder dialog box appears.

5. Highlight the Windows folder and then click OK.

Registry Checker actually comes in two versions:

■ Scanreg.exe is the real mode version, which is suitable for use at the DOS prompt. This file is located in the Windows\Command folder.

■ Scanregw.exe is the protected mode version, which you can use while within Windows. This file is located in the Windows folder.

Remember
A .cab file is a cabinet archive file that stores multiple files in a compressed format.

Shortcut
You should include Scanreg.exe in your Windows 98 emergency boot disk. (In Chapter 16, see "Putting Together an Emergency Boot Disk," p. 365.) This will enable you to run scanreg /restore just in case a Registry problem prevents you from starting Windows 98.

Here's the syntax used by these files:

```
SCANREG [/BACKUP] [/RESTORE] [/FIX] [/COMMENT="text"]
SCANREGW [/BACKUP] [/AUTORUN] [/FIX] [/COMMENT="text"]
```

/BACKUP	Backs up the system files, even if they have already been backed up today.
/RESTORE	Displays a list of backups so you can select the one you want to restore.
/AUTORUN	Runs Registry Checker without prompting. If you don't include this switch and today's backup has already been created, Registry Checker asks if you want to back up the files again.
/FIX	Repairs and optimizes the Registry if no backup copy is available.
/COMMENT="text"	Adds the string specified by text to the .cab file.

Registry Checker maintains a small list of settings that control how the program runs. As you can imagine, it would make no sense to store these settings within the Registry itself. Instead, the settings can be found in the file Scanreg.ini in the Windows folder.

Select Start, Run, type scanreg.ini, and then click OK to open this file in Notepad. When you do, you'll see four settings:

Backup: When this value is set to 1, Registry Checker backs up the configuration files. If you set this value to 0, Registry Checker doesn't perform the backup.

Optimize: When this value is set to 1, Registry Checker looks for blank space within the Registry files and then removes that space to optimize the file. (The optimization only occurs when there is more than 500KB of unused space.) If you set this value to 0, Registry Checker doesn't perform the optimization.

MaxBackupCopies: This setting specifies the maximum number of backups that Registry Checker can store in Sysbckup. The default value is 5. If you're thinking about

Inside Scoop
The bigger the Registry, the more conventional memory Registry Checker requires. You may need to optimize conventional memory to get Registry Checker to run. Also, Registry Checker requires extended memory, so most of its functions won't run if you boot using the Safe Mode Command Prompt Only option. The only function that does work without extended memory is the /RESTORE switch.

increasing this value, remember that each .cab backup file consumes from 500KB to over 1MB, depending on the size of the original files.

BackupDirectory: When this setting is blank, Registry Checker uses the Windows\Sysbckup folder to store the .cab backup files. If you'd prefer to use another location (say, on a separate hard disk or on a removable disk), enter the full path you want to use.

Scanreg.ini also lets you specify one or more other files to include in the backup. You do this by adding one or more lines with the following syntax:

```
Files=[dir code,]file1,file2,file3
```

Here, dir code is a two-digit code that represents a prede-fined path, as described in Table 4.1.

TABLE 4.1: DIRECTORY CODES FOR USE IN SCANREG.INI

Code	What It Represents
10	The main Windows 98 folder (usually C:\Windows)
11	The System subfolder (usually C:\Windows\System)
30	Your system's boot folder (usually C:\)
31	Your system's boot host folder (usually C:\)

Otherwise, you just enter the full path and filename of the file or files you want to include in the backup. Here are some examples:

```
Files=10,control.ini,paul.pwl
Files=11,desktop.ini,folder.htt
Files=30,autoexec.bat,config.sys
Files=c:\msoffice\normal.dot
```

Launching the Registry Editor

System.dat and User.dat are binary files, so you can't edit them directly. Instead, you use a program called the Registry Editor, which enables you to view, edit, add, and delete any Registry set-ting. It also has a search feature to help you find settings, and an export feature that enables you to save settings to a text file.

There are two methods you can use to launch Registry Editor:

- Select Start, Run to display the Run dialog box, type `regedit`, and then click OK.

- In Windows Explorer, open the `Windows` folder and then launch the file `Regedit.exe`.

Figure 4.2 shows the Registry Editor window. Here are some notes about this window:

- The left side of the window—which I'll call the *Keys pane*—contains a hierarchical list of the Registry's *keys*. I'll explain which keys in the next section.

- To see more keys, either click the plus sign (+) beside a key, or else highlight a key and then press plus (+) on your keyboard's numeric keypad.

- To hide exposed keys, either click the minus sign (-) beside a key, or else highlight a key and then press minus (-) on your keyboard's numeric keypad.

- The Registry has many levels of keys. To keep straight where you are in the hierarchy, watch the status bar, which always shows the full path of the currently highlighted key.

- The right side of the window—which I'll call the *Settings pane*—displays the settings found within the currently highlighted key.

- The Settings pane is divided into two columns. The Name column shows the name of each setting, and the Data column shows the value associated with each setting.

- Registry settings come in three types: string values, binary values (a series of hexadecimal numbers), and DWORD (double word) values (a 32-bit hexadecimal value arranged as eight digits).

Remember
You can adjust the size of the panes by using your mouse to drag the vertical split bar that separates the two panes. Alternatively, select View, Split, use the left and right arrow keys to move the split bar, and then press Enter.

Figure 4.2
Use the Registry
Editor to work
with Registry set-
tings.

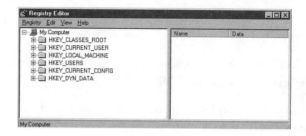

How the Registry Is Structured

When you first open the Registry Editor, you see My Computer at
the top, followed by six keys. These are known as the Registry's
root keys. Here's a summary of what kind of data is stored within
each root key:

See Also...
"Activating User
Profiles," p. 247

HKEY_CLASSES_ROOT: This key is mostly concerned with file
types: which file extensions are associated with which
applications. For example, it's thanks to this key that
Windows 98 knows that a file with a .txt extension
should be opened using the Notepad Text Editor. This
key also contains data related to object linking and
embedding. Note, too, that this key is exactly the same as
the following key:

HKEY_LOCAL_MACHINE\Software\Classes

HKEY_CURRENT_USER: This key contains a number of user-
specific settings, such as the current wallpaper and color
scheme. (This is, in other words, the data from User.dat.)
If you set up Windows 98 with multiple user profiles (see
Chapter 9, "Customizing the Windows 98 Interface"), this
key contains the settings for whichever user is currently
logged on.

HKEY_LOCAL_MACHINE: This key (which is basically
System.dat) contains a large number of settings related to
your hardware and software. In particular, the bulk of the
settings used by Windows 98 can be found here:

HKEY_LOCAL_MACHINE\Software\Microsoft\Windows\Current
Version

HKEY_USERS: If you haven't set up Windows 98 for user profiles, this key contains the same data as HKEY_CURRENT_USER. Otherwise, this key contains three subkeys: .DEFAULT (which contains default settings for users logging in for the first time), Software (which can be ignored), and a key for the current user (which is the same as HKEY_CURRENT_USER).

HKEY_CURRENT_CONFIG: This key contains settings related to the current hardware profile.

HKEY_DYN_DATA: Changes to System.dat and User.dat are written to disk periodically. For fast access, however, some data needs to remain in memory. This data is stored in the HKEY_DYN_DATA key.

Working with Registry Keys and Settings

Now let's examine the Registry Editor techniques that you'll need throughout the rest of this book. In particular, you need to know how to find data, edit settings, rename, create, and delete keys and settings, and how to import and export Registry data. The next few sections provide the specifics.

Finding a Key, Setting, or Value

The Registry contains hundred of keys and thousands of values, so it helps to know how to search for the item you want to work with. To run a search, follow these steps:

1. Select a starting point for the search. For example, if you know the item you want is in the HKEY_LOCAL_MACHINE root key, highlight HKEY_LOCAL_MACHINE in the Keys pane. If you're not sure, highlight My Computer at the top of the Keys pane.

2. Select Edit, Find, or press Ctrl+F, to display the Find dialog box, shown in Figure 4.3.

3. Use the Find What box to enter the text you want to locate.

4. Use the check boxes in the Look At group to specify what parts of the Registry you want to search.

Figure 4.3
Use the Find dialog box to search for strings within the Registry.

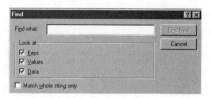

Shortcut
After you close the Find dialog box, you can resume your search without having to display the dialog box all over again. To do so, select Edit, Find Next, or press F3.

5. Find usually tries to match your string with any part of a key or setting. If you prefer to find the exact string you entered, activate the Match Whole String Only check box.

6. Click Find Next until you find the string you want (or until the entire Registry has been checked).

Changing the Value of a String Setting

Most of the Registry settings that you'll work with will be strings. To edit a string setting, follow these steps:

1. Find the string setting you want to work with and then click it to highlight it.

2. Select Edit, Modify. The Edit String dialog box appears, as shown in Figure 4.4.

Figure 4.4
You use the Edit String dialog box to modify a string setting.

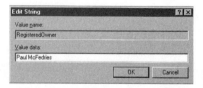

3. Use the Value Data text box to edit the string.

4. Click OK.

Changing the Value of a Binary Setting

Working with binary settings is slightly different than working with strings. Here are the steps to follow:

Shortcut
You can also open a setting for editing by double-clicking it, or by right-clicking it and then clicking Modify in the shortcut menu.

1. Find the binary setting you want to work with and then click it to highlight it.

2. Select Edit, Modify. The Edit Binary Value dialog box appears, as shown in Figure 4.5.

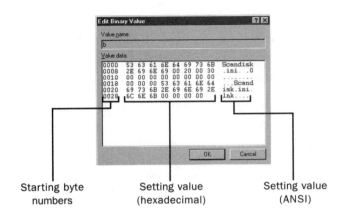

Starting byte numbers

Setting value (hexadecimal)

Setting value (ANSI)

Figure 4.5
You use the Edit Binary Value dialog box to modify a binary setting.

3. Use the Value Data text box to edit the value. You use the text box's three columns:

- The left column contains the starting byte numbers. You can't edit these values.

- The middle column contains the value of the setting expressed as hexadecimal numbers. This value is displayed in rows consisting of eight two-digit hexadecimal numbers, where each two-digit number represents one byte. You can edit these values.

- The right column contains the value of the setting expressed as ANSI characters. That is, each character is the ANSI equivalent of the corresponding hexadecimal byte value in the middle column. You can edit these values.

4. Click OK.

Renaming a Key or Setting

You won't often need to rename existing keys or settings. Just in case, though, here are the steps to follow:

1. Find the key or setting you want to work with and then click it to highlight it.

2. Select Edit, Rename, or press F2.

3. Edit the name and then press Enter.

Creating a New Key or Setting

Many Registry-based customizations don't involve editing an existing setting or key. Instead, you have to create a new setting or key. Here's how you do it:

1. Highlight the key in which you want to create the new sub-key or setting.

2. Select Edit, New.

3. In the cascade menu, select one of the following: Key, String Value, Binary Value, or DWORD Value.

4. Type a name for the new key or setting.

5. Press Enter.

Deleting a Key or Setting

Here are the steps to follow to delete a key or setting:

1. Highlight the key or setting that you want to delete.

2. Select Edit, Delete, or press Delete. The Registry Editor asks if you're sure.

3. Click Yes.

Exporting a Key to a Registration (.reg) File

Earlier I showed you a number of methods for backing up the Registry. Another approach is to back up only part of the Registry. For example, if you're about to make changes within the HKEY_CURRENT_USER key, you could back up just that key.

The way you do this is to export the key to a registration file, which is a text file that uses the .reg extension. Here's how it works:

1. Highlight the key you want to export.

2. Select Registry, Export Registry File to display the Export Registry File dialog box shown in Figure 4.6.

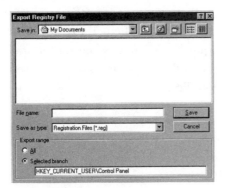

Figure 4.6
Use this dialog box to export a key to a registration file.

3. Select a location for the file.

4. Use the File Name text box to enter a name for the file (without the extension).

5. If you only want to export the currently highlighted key, make sure the Selected Branch option is activated. If you'd prefer to export the entire Registry, activate the All option.

6. Click Save.

If you want to make changes to the registration file, highlight the file in Windows Explorer and then select File, Edit. Windows 98 will open the file in Notepad (unless the file is too large, in which case Windows 98 offers to use WordPad, instead).

Importing a Registration (.reg) File

If you need to restore the key that you backed up to a registration file, follow these steps:

1. Select Registry, Import Registry File to display the Import Registry File dialog box.

2. Find and highlight the file you want to import.

3. Click Open.

Inside Scoop
If you need to make global changes to the Registry, export the entire Registry and then load the resulting registration file into WordPad or some other word processor or text editor. Use the application's Replace feature (carefully!) to make changes throughout the file. You can then import the changed file back into the Registry (as described in the next section).

Note, too, that you can create registration files from scratch and then import them into the Registry. This is a handy technique if you have some customizations that you want to apply to multiple systems. Here's the general structure of a registration file:

Shortcut
You can also import a registration file without opening the Registry Editor. To do so, highlight the file using Windows Explorer and then select the File, Merge command (you can also double-click the file).

```
REGEDIT4


[KEY_PATH]
"StringSetting"="String value"
"BinarySetting"=hex:xx,yy,,zz
"DWORDSetting"=dword:nnnnnnnn
etc.
```

Here's what the various placeholders mean:

KEY_PATH	The full path of the Registry key that will hold the settings you're adding.
StringSetting	The name of a string setting. Notice the name is surrounded by quotation marks.
String value	The value of the string setting, surrounded by quotation marks.
BinarySetting	The name of a binary setting. Again, the name is surrounded by quotation marks.
hex:xx,yy,zz	The binary value of the setting. Separate each two-digit hexadecimal number with a comma.
DWORDSetting	The name of a DWORD setting, surrounded by quotation marks.
dword:nnnnnnnn	The eight-digit DWORD value of the setting.

You can add as many keys and as many settings as you like. Here's an example:

```
REGEDIT4


[HKEY_LOCAL_MACHINE\Software\Microsoft\Windows\Current
Version]
"RegisteredOwner"="Paul McFedries"
"Install Type"=hex:03,00
```

```
[HKEY_CURRENT_USER\Software\Microsoft\Windows\Current
Version\Policies\WinOldApp]
"NoRealMode"=dword:00000001
```

An Insider's Guide to System Policies

Another measure of the importance of the Registry is the number of front-ends that Windows 98 offers for working with Registry settings:

The Registry Editor: As you've seen, the Registry Editor gives you a hierarchical menu of all the keys and settings available with the Registry.

System Configuration Utility: As you saw in Chapter 3, this utility controls a number of startup options, several of which are Registry-related.

Device Manager: This tool provides a summary of many of the hardware-related Registry items. See Chapter 22, "Taking the Mystery Out of Hardware."

System Information Utility: This program offers a more complete picture of the hardware and software items in the Registry. See Chapter 15, "Crucial System Maintenance Skills."

System Policy Editor: This feature gives you access to a number of *system policies*, which are customization options set by adding or modifying Registry values.

Tweak UI: This utility offers a long list of interface customization options, many of which control Registry settings.

This section discusses system policies and the System Policy Editor. I'll discuss Tweak UI later in this chapter.

To reiterate, system policies are settings that control how Windows 98 works. You can use them to customize the Windows 98 interface, specify your own folders for things like the Start menu, the desktop, and the Startup group, restrict access to certain areas, and much more.

System policies are mostly used by system administrators who want to make sure that novice users don't have access to

See Also...
"Dealing with Device Manager," p. 529

See Also...
"The System Information Utility," p. 346

"
Using System Policy Editor (Poledit.exe) incorrectly can cause serious problems that may require you to reinstall Windows. Microsoft cannot guarantee that problems resulting from the incorrect use of System Policy Editor can be solved. Use System Policy Editor at your own risk.
—From the Microsoft Knowledge Base
"

dangerous tools (such as the Registry Editor), or who want to ensure a consistent computing experience across multiple machines. However, system policies are also useful on stand-alone machines, as you'll see throughout this book.

Installing the System Policy Editor

To work with system policies, you use the System Policy Editor. Here's how to install this tool:

1. Insert your Windows 98 disc into the CD-ROM drive.

2. Select Start, Settings, Control Panel and, in the Control Panel window, launch the Add/Remove Programs icon.

3. Display the Windows Setup tab. Windows 98 takes a few moments to collect data on the installed components.

4. Click Have Disk. The Install From Disk dialog box appears.

5. Type the following path into the Copy Manufacturer's Files From text box, where *d* is the letter of your CD-ROM drive (you can also use the Browse button to select this path):

   `d:\tools\reskit\netadmin\poledit\`

6. Click OK. The Have Disk dialog box appears.

7. Activate the System Policy Editor check box.

8. Click Install. Windows 98 installs the System Policy Editor.

9. Click OK.

With the System Policy Editor installed, you can run it by selecting Start, Programs, Accessories, System Tools, System Policy Editor.

Working with a Local Registry

As I've said, the System Policy Editor acts as a front-end for various Registry settings. So the first step in working with the System Policy Editor is to open this front-end, which you do by selecting the File, Open Registry command. This adds two icons to the System Policy Editor, as shown in Figure 4.7:

Local Computer: This icon contains system policies that correspond to some of the settings in the Registry's HKEY_LOCAL_MACHINE key.

Local User: This icon contains system policies that correspond to some of the settings in the Registry's HKEY_CURRENT_USER key.

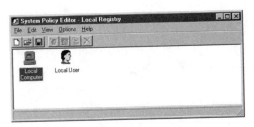

Figure 4.7
The Local Computer and Local User icons appear when you open the Registry.

To work with individual system policies, double-click either Local Computer or Local User. The dialog box that appears contains a hierarchical menu of policy categories. In Figure 4.8, for example, I opened the Local Computer icon, then opened Windows 98 System, Network Paths.

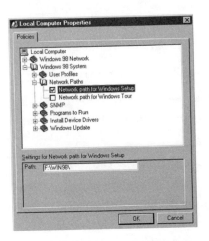

Figure 4.8
The System Policy Editor's icons offer a hierarchical list of policies.

As you can see, each policy has a check box that toggles the policy on and off. In many cases, activating the policy's check box also activates a text box or some other control, which appears in the Settings area in the bottom half of the dialog box. For example, the Network path for Windows Setup policy

See Also...
"Specifying a New Setup Source Path," p. 69

Inside Scoop
If you think you'll be reinstalling Windows 98 down the road, or if you'd like to apply a set of policies to another computer, create a policy (.pol) file. Select File, New Policy, set up your policies, and then select File, Save and save the settings as Config.pol. To use this policy file, open Local Computer and select Windows 98 Network, Update, Remote Update. Select Manual as the Update Mode and use the Path For Manual Update text box to enter the name and location of Config.pol.

has a Path text box in the Settings area. In this case, you would use this text box to specify the location of the Windows 98 source files. Recall from Chapter 2, "Ten Things You Should Know About the Windows 98 Setup," that this corresponds to the SourcePath setting in the following Registry key:

HKEY_LOCAL_MACHINE\Software\Microsoft\Windows\Current
Version\Setup

An Insider's Guide to Tweak UI

The third tool I'll discuss in this chapter is Tweak UI, which acts as a front-end for a large number of user interface customization options. Most of these options are controls for adding and working with Registry settings. As with the Registry Editor and the System Policy Editor, I'll be using various Tweak UI settings throughout the rest of this book.

Installing Tweak UI

Tweak UI isn't part of the main Windows 98 package, but it is on the Windows 98 CD. Here are the steps to follow to install Tweak UI:

1. Insert the Windows 98 CD-ROM.

2. Select Start, Programs, Windows Explorer.

3. Display the CD's \tools\reskit\powertoy folder.

4. Right-click tweakui.inf and then click Install in the shortcut menu. Once the installation is complete, a Help window appears.

5. Press Alt+F4 or click the Close button.

Running Tweak UI

To launch Tweak UI, select Start, Settings, Control Panel and then open the Tweak UI icon. You'll see the window shown in Figure 4.9. Some notes about this window:

- The tabs across the top take you to different categories of options.

■ Tweak UI displays only six tabs at first, but there are actually 13 tabs in all. To scroll through the tabs, either click the left and right arrows to the right of the tabs, or press Ctrl+Tab and Ctrl+Shift+Tab.

■ Many of the tabs have a Restore Factory Settings button. Click this button to reset a tab's settings to their Windows 98 defaults.

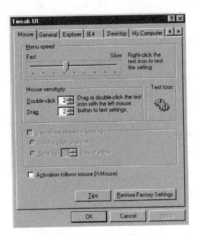

Figure 4.9
Tweak UI offers a simple interface for customizing a wealth of Windows 98 options.

Tweak UI's Boot Options

To give you an example of how much easier it is to use Tweak UI rather than the default Windows 98 tools, let's run through an example. In Chapter 3, "Understanding and Controlling the Windows 98 Startup," I showed you how to modify your system's startup by editing Msdos.sys. Recall that this wasn't a particularly convenient exercise since you had to remove the read-only attribute before you could edit Msdos.sys.

Fortunately, Tweak UI offers an attractive interface for the most useful of the Msdos.sys settings. You'll find them on the Boot tab, as shown in Figure 4.10. Here's a rundown of the various controls:

> **Function keys available:** When this check box is activated, the Windows 98 Startup menu's shortcut keys are enabled. This is the same as setting BootKeys=1 in Msdos.sys.

> 66
> Great care has been taken to ensure that Tweak UI operates as it should. But please keep in mind, this tool is not a part of Windows and is not supported by Microsoft. For this reason, Microsoft Technical Support is unable to answer questions about TweakUI.
> —From the POWERTOY folder's README.TXT file
> 99

See Also...
"Controlling Startup Using Msdos.sys," p. 91

Inside Scoop
For some unfath-
omable reason,
Microsoft removed
Tweak UI from the
Windows 98
Second Edition
disc. Grrrr.
Although
Microsoft doesn't
recommend it, you
can get the
Windows 95 ver-
sion of TweakUI
by downloading
the Power Toys
Set from here:
http://www.
winmag.com/win98/
software.htm.

Start GUI automatically: When this check box is activated, the Windows 98 GUI is loaded at startup. This is
equivalent to adding `BootGUI=1` to `Msdos.sys`.

Display splash screen while booting: When this check box
is activated, the Windows 98 startup logo appears during
the boot. This is the same as setting `Logo=1` in `Msdos.sys`.

Allow F4 to boot previous operating system: When this
check box is activated, Windows 98 can dual-boot with
your previous operating system. This is equivalent to setting `BootMulti=1` in `Msdos.sys`.

Autorun Scandisk: Use this drop-down list to decide when
and how ScanDisk runs after an improper shutdown.
`Never` is the same as `AutoScan=0` in `Msdos.sys`; After prompting is the same as `AutoScan=1`; Without prompting is the
same as `AutoScan=2`.

Always show boot menu: Activate this check box to force
the display of the Windows 98 Startup menu during each
boot. This is the equivalent of adding `BootMenu=1` to
`Msdos.sys`.

Continue booting after *x* seconds: Use this spinner to set
the length, in seconds, of the countdown that appears
when you display the Startup menu. This is the same as
setting `BootMenuDelay=x` in `Msdos.sys`.

Figure 4.10
Use the controls
in the Boot tab to
set some useful
startup options.

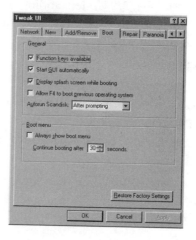

Essential Information

- The Registry is a central storage area for thousands of settings related to your hardware and software.

- Since the Registry is so crucial, always make a backup copy before making major changes.

- The Registry Editor (`Regedit.exe`) offers a hierarchical view of the Registry's keys and settings. You can use the Registry Editor to change values, add new keys and settings, delete keys and settings, and more.

- System policies are settings that control various aspects of Windows 98. Each policy corresponds to a Registry setting, and the System Policy Editor provides a convenient front-end for working with these settings.

- Tweak UI is another Registry front-end that provides an easier method for setting up user interface customizations.

GET THE SCOOP ON...
Installing applications safely ▪ Understanding Registry
changes upon new installations ▪ Launching programs
at system startup ▪ Switching between running programs ▪ Using MS-DOS mode and custom `Config.sys`
and `Autoexec.bat` files to run DOS applications ▪
Uninstalling 32-bit, 16-bit, and DOS applications

Getting the Most Out of Your Applications

I T'S A RARE (AND NO DOUBT UNPRODUCTIVE) user who does
nothing but run Windows on her computer. After all, once
Windows starts, it doesn't do much of anything. No, to get
full value for your computing dollar, you have to run an application or two. As an operating system, it's Windows' job to help
make it easier for you to run your programs. Whether it's loading them into memory, managing their resources, or printing
their documents, Windows has plenty to do behind the scenes.
Windows 98 also comes with a few tools and techniques that
you can use to make your applications run faster and more reliably. In this chapter, I'll show you how to install applications
safely, how to launch applications, how to switch between running programs, and how to uninstall applications you no
longer need.

Installing Applications Safely

Outside of hardware woes and user errors (see the Quote side-
bar), most computer problems are caused by improperly
installing a program or installing a program that doesn't mesh
correctly with your system. It could be that the installation
makes unfortunate changes to your configuration files, or that

the program replaces a crucial system file with an older version, or that the program just wasn't meant to operate on a machine with your configuration.

An Installation Safety Checklist

Whatever the reason, you can minimize these kinds of problems by following a few precautions before installing a new software package. Here's a checklist:

- **Have a bootable disk ready:** If a program installation creates a big enough mess, you may not be able to restart your computer. In that case, you'll be glad you have a bootable floppy disk that will give you control of your machine once again. See Chapter 16, "Preparing for Trouble."

- **Examine** readme.txt **Text Files:** Most programmers hate to write, so if your application comes with a readme.txt file or some other "read me first" material, chances are it contains important information. For example, this kind of documentation often tells you what you need to do to prepare for the installation, what the program will alter on your system, program changes that went into effect after the manual was produced, and so on.

- **Back up your data files:** If the program is an upgrade, make backup copies of all your data files. Many upgrades include new file formats for documents created with the program. These upgrades are usually upward compatible (the upgrade can read documents that use an older file format), but rarely downward compatible (previous versions of the software can't work with the new file format). Having backup copies of files in the old format will ensure you can still use your documents in the event that you uninstall the program.

- **Back up your configuration files:** Installation programs can cause all kinds of trouble by making imprudent changes to your system's configuration files. Therefore, always back up the Registry, Config.sys, Autoexec.bat, Win.ini, and System.ini.

❝
PEBCAK: Tech support shorthand for Problem Exists Between Chair And Keyboard.
—Julie Danis, The Chicago Tribune
❞

See Also...
"Putting Together an Emergency Boot Disk," p. 365

- **Check downloaded programs for viruses:** If the program you're about to install was downloaded from the Internet or an online service, use a virus checker to examine the setup file for viruses.

- **Always run "custom" installations:** Most install programs offer you both a "typical" installation and a "custom" installation. The typical option installs the program with just the default options and very little interaction. The custom option usually enables you to control many aspects of the installation, including where the files are stored, which program options are installed, whether configuration files are updated automatically, and so on. The custom route is more work, but it's always better to have the extra control.

Shortcut
The easiest way to do back up all your configuration files is to use Windows 98's Registry Checker. I showed you how to use this utility in Chapter 4's "Using the Registry Checker" section, p. 107.

Another safe setup technique I recommend is to compare the contents of some folders before and after the installation. Windows programs like to add all kinds of files to the Windows and Windows\System folders. To troubleshoot problems, it helps to know which files were installed.

To figure this out, write directory listings for both folders to text files. The following two DOS statements use the DIR command to produce alphabetical listings of the Windows and Windows\System folders and redirect (using the > operator) these listings to text files:

```
dir c:\windows /a-d /on > c:\windir.txt
dir c:\windows\system /a-d /on > c:\sysdir.txt
```

Once the installation is complete, run the following commands to save the new listings to a second set of text files:

```
dir c:\windows /ad /on > c:\windir2.txt
dir c:\windows\system /ad /on > c:\sysdir2.txt
```

The resulting text files will be quite long, so comparing the before and after listings will be time consuming. To make this chore easier, use the DOS FC (File Compare) command. Here's the simplified syntax to use with text files:

```
FC /L filename1 filename2
```

/L	Compares files as ASCII text.
filename1	The first file you want to compare.
filename2	The second file you want to compare.

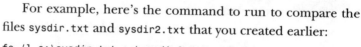

Remember
The FC command can also compare binary files, display line numbers, perform case-insensitive comparisons, and much more. For the full syntax, enter the command fc /? at the DOS prompt.

Inside Scoop
The FC command is useful for more than just directory listings. You can also use it to compare your configuration files—particularly Config.sys, Autoexec.bat, Win.ini, and System.ini—before and after an installation. You could also export Registry keys before and after and then use FC to compare the resulting registration (.reg) files.

For example, here's the command to run to compare the files sysdir.txt and sysdir2.txt that you created earlier:

```
fc /l c:\sysdir.txt c:\sysdir2.txt > fc.txt
```

This statement redirects the FC command's output to a file named fc.txt. Here's an example of the kind of data you'll see in this file:

```
Comparing files sysdir.txt and sysdir2.txt
****** sysdir.txt
WINSPOOL DRV           23,040  05-11-98  8:01p WINSPOOL.DRV
WINTRUST DLL            9,943  05-11-98  8:01p WINTRUST.DLL
****** sysdir2.txt
WINSPOOL DRV           23,040  05-11-98  8:01p WINSPOOL.DRV
WINTOP   VXD           14,102  06-22-96  5:04a WINTOP.VXD
WINTRUST DLL            9,943  05-11-98  8:01p WINTRUST.DLL
******
```

In this case, you can see that a file named WINTOP.VXD has been added between WINSPOOL.DRV and WINTRUST.DLL.

Installing the Application

After you've run through this checklist, you're ready to install the program. Here's a summary of the various methods you can use to install a program in Windows 98:

Add/Remove Programs wizard: This wizard is the standard Windows 98 method for installing all types of applications. To use this wizard, select Start, Settings, Control Panel and then open the Add/Remove Programs icon. In the Add/Remove Programs Properties dialog box, display the Install/Uninstall tab and then click Install. The wizard's dialog boxes will lead you through finding the installation program and launching it. The wizard departs at this point and you follow the installation program's instructions.

AutoPlay install: If the program comes on a CD that supports AutoPlay, it's likely that the installation program will launch automatically once you insert the disc into the CD-ROM drive. To prevent the install program from launching automatically, hold down the Shift key while you insert the disc.

Run `setup.exe`: For most applications, the installation program is named `setup.exe` (sometimes its `install.exe`). Use Windows Explorer to find the install program and then double-click it. Alternatively, select Start, Run, enter the path to the `setup.exe` file (such as `a:\setup`), and click OK.

Install from an `.inf` **file:** Some applications (such as the Tweak UI utility discussed in Chapter 4) install via an information (`.inf`) file. To install these programs, select the Windows Setup tab in the Add/Remove Programs Properties dialog box, and then click Have Disk. In the Install from Disk dialog box, enter the path of the folder containing the .inf file and click OK. You should now see a Have Disk dialog box with a list of components to install. Activate the check boxes for the components you need, and then click Install.

See Also...
"An Insider's Guide to Tweak UI,"
p. 122

Install in MS-DOS mode: Some DOS programs will not install properly unless Windows 98 is running in MS-DOS mode (discussed later in this chapter). In this case, select Start, Shut Down, activate the Restart in MS-DOS Mode option, and then click OK.

Applications and the Registry

I mentioned in Chapter 4, "An Insider's Guide to Three Crucial Configuration Tools," that the Registry is perhaps Windows 98's most important component because it stores thousands of settings that Windows needs. The Registry is important for your applications, as well, because most Windows applications (particularly those designed for Windows 95 or Windows 98) use the Registry to store configuration data and other settings.

Shortcut
An easier way to install from an .inf file is to right-click the file and then click Install in the shortcut menu that appears.

When you install an application, it typically makes a half dozen different Registry modifications:

- Program settings

- User settings

- File types

- Application-specific paths

- Shared DLLs

- Uninstall settings

Program settings: These are settings related to the application as a whole: where it was installed, the serial number, and so on. The program settings are placed in a new subkey of HKEY_LOCAL_MACHINE\Software:

HKEY_LOCAL_MACHINE\Software\Company\Product\Version

Here, Company is the name of the program vendor, Product is the name of the software, and Version is the version number of the program. Here's an example:

HKEY_LOCAL_MACHINE\Software\Netscape\Netscape Navigator\4.01

User settings: These are user-specific settings such as the user's name, preferences and options the user has selected, and so on. The user settings are stored in a subkey of HKEY_CURRENT_USER\Software:

HKEY_CURRENT_USER\Software\Company\Product

File types: This refers to the file extensions used by the program's documents. These extensions are associated with the program's executable file so that double-clicking a document loads the program and displays the document. The extensions and file types are stored as subkeys within HKEY_CLASSES_ROOT. (See Chapter 10, "Powerful Techniques for File Types," for details.)

Remember
A file's *primary name* is the part of the filename to the left of the period (.). For example, the primary name of the file Excel.exe is excel.

If the application comes with OLE support, it will have a unique *class ID*, which will be stored as a subkey within HKEY_CLASSES_ROOT\CLSID.

Application-specific paths: The DOS PATH statement is a list of directories that DOS looks in to try and find an executable (.exe, .com, or .bat) file. Windows 98 uses a variation on this theme called *application-specific paths*. The idea is that if you enter only the primary name of a program's executable file in the Run dialog box (select Start, Run), Windows 98 will find and run the program. For example, WordPad's executable file is Wordpad.exe, so you enter just wordpad in the Run dialog box and WordPad will open.

These application-specific paths are set up in the following key:

HKEY_LOCAL_MACHINE\Software\Microsoft\Windows\Current
Version\AppPaths

Each application that supports this feature adds a subkey that uses the name of the application's executable file (for example, Wordpad.exe). Within that subkey, the value of the Default setting is the full pathname (drive, folder, and file-name) of the executable file. Note, too, that many applications also create a Path setting that specifies a default folder for the application.

Shared DLLs: It's quite common for multiple applications to share a common DLL (dynamic link library) file. Windows 98 uses settings in the following key to keep track of how many applications are sharing a particular DLL:

HKEY_LOCAL_MACHINE\Software\Microsoft\Windows\Current
Version\SharedDLLs

As you can see in Figure 5.1, the name of each setting is the full pathname of a DLL, and the value is the number of applications that share the file.

Undocumented
It's possible to set up your own application-specific paths. Just add a new subkey to the AppPaths key, and name it whatever word you want to use to launch your application, followed by .exe. In this new subkey, open the Default setting and enter the full pathname of the executable file that runs the application.

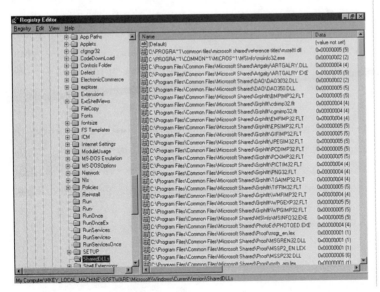

Figure 5.1
The SharedDLLs key keeps a running total of the number of applications that share a particular DLL file.

During the installation of most 32-bit applications, the setup program checks to see if any DLLs that it requires are already on the system. If so, it finds the appropriate settings within the SharedDLLs key and increases their values by 1.

Uninstall settings: Most 32-bit applications also use the Registry to hold data related to uninstalling the application. To store this data, the setup program creates a subkey for the application within the following key:

```
HKEY_LOCAL_MACHINE\Software\Microsoft\Windows\Current
Version\Uninstall
```

Launching Applications

Although you'd never know it from the "Getting Started" booklet, Windows 98 rarely gives you just one way to do anything. In fact, most operations have two or three routes you can take. This isn't just mere overkill on Windows' part because one procedure is usually better than another under a given set of circumstances. For example, a keyboard technique (such as pressing a shortcut key) might be preferred over a mouse technique (such as right-clicking an object) if your fingers are already poised over the keyboard.

Launching applications is a classic example of a destination that has many roads leading to it. That makes sense since not only is launching applications one of the primary jobs of an operating system, but we also have to deal with many different types of applications. Here's a summary of the various Windows methods available for launching applications (I discuss some ways to launch programs automatically in the next section):

Use the Start menu: Click the Start button, open menus until you see the item you want, and then click the item.

Double-click the executable file: Use Windows Explorer to find the application's executable file, and then double-click that file.

"Most of the programs installed on your computer are available from one convenient location—the Programs section of the Start menu.
—From the "Getting Started" booklet"

Double-click a shortcut: If a shortcut points to a program's executable file, double-clicking the shortcut will launch the program.

Double-click a document: If you can use the application to create documents (these include word processing files, spreadsheets, graphics, and so on), double-clicking one of those documents should launch the program and load the document automatically.

Use the Run dialog box: Select Start, Run to display the Run dialog box shown in Figure 5.2. Use the Open text box to specify the application (click OK when you're done):

■ If the application resides within the `Windows` or `Windows\Command` folder, if it's in your DOS PATH statement, or if it has an application-specific path in the Registry, just type the primary name of the executable file.

■ For all other applications, enter the full pathname (drive, folder, and filename) for the executable file.

■ If you're not sure about the application's executable file, click Browse and then use the Browse dialog box to track down the file you need.

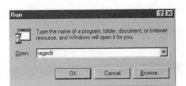

Use the Quick Launch toolbar: Windows 98's new Quick Launch toolbar (to the right of the Start button) offers one-click access for launching programs. I'll show you how to add your own programs to this toolbar in Chapter 9, "Customizing the Windows 98 Interface."

Use the Task Scheduler: The Task Scheduler can run programs automatically at a given date and time, or on a regular schedule. See Chapter 15, "Crucial System Maintenance Skills."

Remember
If Web integration is activated, you only have to single-click the executable file.

Shortcut
If you have a keyboard with the Windows logo key (⊞), press ⊞ +R to open the Run dialog box.

Figure 5.2
Use the Run dialog box to launch a program's executable file.

See Also...
"Customizing the Quick Launch Toolbar," p. 245

Watch Out!
To avoid errors
when working at
the DOS prompt,
either use a file's
8.3 filename, or
else surround the
long filename with
quotation marks.

See Also...
"Controlling
Startup Using
Msdos.sys," p. 91

Inside Scoop
It's possible to set
up your machine
to only run certain
programs. In the
System Policy
Editor, open the
Registry and then
open Local User,
Windows 98
System,
Restrictions.
Activate the Only
Run Allowed
Windows
Applications box
and then click
Show to display
the Show Contents
dialog box. Click
Add, enter the
name of the pro-
gram's executable
file, and click OK.

Enter the executable path at the DOS prompt: At the
DOS prompt, enter the full pathname of the executable
file. Note that you need only use the file's primary name
if the application resides within the current folder, the
Windows folder, or Windows\Command folder, or if it's in your
DOS PATH statement.

Use the Start command at the DOS prompt: To launch
Windows applications from the DOS prompt, use the
Start command:

START [/M] [/MAX] [/R] [/W] *program*

/M   Starts the application minimized.

/MAX   Starts the application maximized.

/R   Starts the application restored (neither min-
            imized nor maximized); this is the default.

/W   Waits for the application to finish before
            you're returned to the DOS prompt. This is
            useful in batch files when you need an oper-
            ation to complete before continuing with the
            rest of the batch file. For an example, see
            Chapter 3, "Understanding and Controlling
            the Windows 98 Startup."

program   The full pathname of the program's exe-
            cutable filename. If the application resides
            within the current folder, the Windows folder,
            or Windows\Command folder, if it's in your DOS
            PATH statement, or if it has an application-
            specific path in the Registry, use the file's pri-
            mary name only.

Launching Applications Automatically at Startup

Besides all those methods for launching applications by hand,
Windows 98 also offers several techniques for launching applications automatically at startup. The next few sections discuss
three methods: the StartUp folder, the Registry, and Win.ini.

Using the StartUp **Folder**

The idea behind the StartUp folder is that any program or document (or more likely, a shortcut to a program or document) within this folder is launched automatically each time Windows 98 starts. (If you've used Windows 3.*x*, you'll recognize the StartUp folder as being the Windows 98 equivalent of the old StartUp group in Program Manager.)

To add a shortcut to the StartUp folder, follow these steps:

1. In Windows Explorer's All Folders list, display the following folder (see Figure 5.3):

   `Windows\Start Menu\Programs\StartUp`

Shortcut
If you can no longer see the StartUp folder, drag the file to the top of the All Folders list (to scroll the list down) or to the bottom of the list (to scroll up).

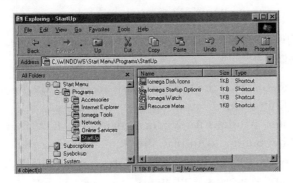

Figure 5.3
To launch applications automatically at startup, create shortcuts in the StartUp folder.

2. Locate the executable file or document you want to launch.

3. Right-drag the file (that is, hold down the right mouse button and drag the file) and drop it on the StartUp folder.

4. In the shortcut menu that appears, click Create Shortcut(s) Here.

Using the Registry

If you have quite a few items in your StartUp folder, you may find yourself often holding down Shift at startup to get Windows 98 up and running quicker. What do you do, however, if you have one or two items that you *always* need to be launched at startup? In this case, bypassing the StartUp folder is a hassle because it means you have to launch these items by hand. (One way to do this is to select Start, Programs, StartUp and then select the item you want to launch.)

Remember
You can avoid loading the StartUp folder items by holding down the Shift key while Windows 98 starts.

An easier way is to remove those important items from the StartUp folder and put them into the Registry's Run key. Items in this key are also run automatically at startup, but they aren't bypassed when you hold down the Shift key.

Follow these steps:

1. In the Registry Editor, open the following key:

   HKEY_LOCAL_MACHINE\Software\Microsoft\Windows\Current Version\Run

2. Select Edit, New, String Value.

3. Type a name for the new setting and press Enter. It doesn't matter what name you use, but something descriptive (such as the name of the program) is best.

4. Open this new setting and enter the full pathname of the executable file.

Note, too, that the Run key is also accessible via the System Policy Editor. Once you've opened your Registry, select Local Computer, Windows 98 System, Programs to Run, Run. Click the Show button to display the Show Contents dialog box, which offers a list of the programs. You can use this dialog box to add and remove startup items.

Using Win.ini

The third and final method for launching applications automatically at startup involves the Win.ini file. If you open this file (which you can do by selecting Start, Run, typing win.ini, and clicking OK), you'll see a line that begins run= near the top of the file. Use this line to add the full pathname of the executable file you want to launch. To include multiple entries, separate each path with a semi-colon (;).

Note, however, that this method is obsolete as most applications use either the StartUp folder or the Registry's Run key. However, it's good to know about the run= line in Win.ini just in case you're trying to track down a program that starts automatically on your system.

Switching Between Running Applications

Windows is superior to DOS in countless ways, but perhaps its single most useful superiority is its ability to *multitask*—to run multiple programs at the same time. I'm sure the vast majority of Windows users typically have two or three programs running all the time. (Having said that, I think it's also true that very few Windows users regularly run more than four or five applications at a time. Windows 98's unfortunate resource limitations (discussed in Chapter 12) guarantee that you can't run a large number of applications at once for very long.)

Of course, multitasking is only useful as long as you can switch easily and quickly from one program to another. Windows 98 offers no less than four ways to do this:

- If you can see part of the window you want, use your mouse to click inside that window.

- Click the application's taskbar button.

- Hold down Alt and tap the Tab key. Windows 98 displays a box showing an icon for each running program. With each tap of the Tab key, Windows 98 highlights the next icon in the list. When the icon that represents the program you want is highlighted, release Alt.

- Hold down Alt and tap the Esc key. This is the same as Alt+Tab, except in this case Windows 98 cycles through the running applications by displaying each application's window. When you see the window you want, release Alt.

Special Considerations for DOS Programs

Windows 98 works best with programs designed to run under Windows 95 or Windows 98. However, there are still lots of old DOS programs (particularly games) kicking around, so it pays to know a few tricks for getting these old programs to work well within Windows 98. The next few sections will take you through a few of these tricks.

Before moving on, however, it's important that you take a quick look under the DOS hood and understand exactly what

Watch Out!
Generally speaking, the more applications you launch at startup, the longer Windows 98 will take to load. Also, all running programs use up memory and resources. Therefore, make sure that every program you load automatically at startup is one you'll use right away and often. Otherwise, you're better off launching the application when you need it.

See Also...
"Tracking and Optimizing System Resources," p. 298

Windows 98 does when you start any DOS session. The Windows 98 component that handles this is called the Virtual Machine Manager (VMM). Its job is to create a "virtual machine" for DOS to run in.

The first thing the VMM does is set aside 1MB of virtual memory for the exclusive use of the DOS session. Even though this is virtual memory (that is, memory that resides past the 1MB mark), the DOS session will think that it's working with the first 1MB on the system (640KB of conventional memory and 384KB of upper memory).

The second thing the VMM does is put together a full DOS environment for the session. This DOS environment is based on the following:

- The default settings in Io.sys.

- Any Config.sys entries that duplicate (and hence take precedence over) items in Io.sys.

- Any other lines you have in your Config.sys and Autoexec.bat files.

In other words, the VMM sets things up so that you have the virtual equivalent of a DOS-only machine that was booted with the following Config.sys and Autoexec.bat files:

Config.sys:

```
DEVICE=C:\Windows\HIMEM.SYS
DEVICE=C:\Windows\IFSHLP.SYS
DEVICE=C:\Windows\SETVER.EXE
DOS=HIGH
FILES=30
BUFFERS=30
STACKS=9,256
FCBS=4
LASTRIVE=Z
```

Autoexec.bat:

```
PROMPT=$P$G
PATH=C:\Windows;C:\Windows\COMMAND
SET TMP=C:\Windows\TEMP
```

```
SET TEMP=C:\Windows\TEMP
SET COMSPEC=C:\Windows\Command.com
SET windir=C:\Windows
SET winbootdir=C:\Windows
```

Using MS-DOS Mode

One of the most common complaints about DOS programs is that they often will simply refuse to run within a Windows 98 DOS session. The usual culprit here is that the DOS program expects to have full control over all the computer's resources: hardware, memory, ports, you name it. To get around this, Windows 98 will try to fool the DOS program into thinking it has full control over the computer. This works fine with most DOS applications, but there are always a few for which this just isn't good enough.

For these stubborn DOS apps, Windows 98 offers *MS-DOS mode*, where Windows 98 takes a back seat and hands over the controls of the computer to the DOS program. In MS-DOS mode, you're really running just a pure DOS machine. You can't multitask, long filename support is gone, no protected mode drivers are used, and so on.

Windows 98 will often recognize if a particular program requires MS-DOS mode, and it will adjust accordingly. However, you can also set things up to run a program in MS-DOS mode on your own. You have two choices:

- Select Start, Shut Down, activate the Restart in MS-DOS mode option, and click OK. Once you get to the DOS prompt, start your program.

- Configure the DOS program to start in MS-DOS mode automatically.

Here are the steps to follow to configure a program to start in MS-DOS mode:

1. Right-click the program's executable file and then click Properties.

2. In the property sheet that appears, select the Program tab.

Remember
Actually, the MS-DOS mode session isn't quite pure. A small 4KB stub from Windows 98 remains in memory (to keep an eye on things, I suppose).

3. Click the Advanced button. Windows 98 displays the Advanced Program Settings dialog box.

4. Activate the MS-DOS mode check box, as shown in Figure 5.4.

Figure 5.4
Activate the MS-DOS mode check box to start a program in MS-DOS mode.

5. To have Windows 98 display a warning before it switches to MS-DOS mode to run the program, leave the Warn Before Entering MS-DOS Mode check box activated.

6. Select one of the following options:

   Use current MS-DOS configuration: If you select this option, Windows 98 boots to MS-DOS mode using the settings from the default virtual DOS machine.

   Specify a new MS-DOS configuration: If you select this option, Windows 98 enables you to create a new virtual DOS machine configuration and will then boot to MS-DOS mode using this new machine. See "Creating Custom Startup Configurations," later in this chapter.

7. Click OK to return to the property sheet.

8. If you want to reboot back to Windows 98 automatically when you shut down the program, make sure the Close on Exit check box is activated.

9. Click OK.

When you run the program, Windows 98 closes all running applications, unloads its protected mode device drivers, shuts down, and then reboots into a real-mode DOS machine.

Creating Custom Startup Configurations

The default DOS virtual machine is probably fine for most DOS applications running in MS-DOS mode. However, if you have some applications that require special settings, Windows 98 enables you to specify custom Config.sys and Autoexec.bat files. Here are the steps to follow:

1. Follow steps 1–3 from the previous section to display the Advanced Program Settings dialog box.

2. Select the Specify a New MS-DOS Configuration option. As you can see in Figure 5.5, two text boxes become available:

   Config.sys for MS-DOS mode: This text box displays the default commands used in the custom Config.sys file.

   Autoexec.bat for MS-DOS mode: This text box displays the default commands used in the custom Autoexec.bat file.

3. Click Configuration. Windows 98 displays the Select MS-DOS Configuration Options dialog box, shown in Figure 5.6. These are items you can include in your custom startup files.

Inside Scoop
One other chore that Windows 98 performs while switching to MS-DOS mode is to run the Dosstart.bat batch file, if it exists. If Windows 98 Setup commented out any lines from your original Autoexec.bat file, those lines are added to Dosstart.bat (which resides in the Windows folder). Feel free to add your own commands and settings to this file.

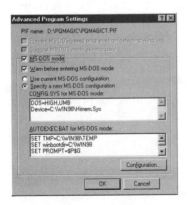

Figure 5.5
Activate Specify a New MS-DOS Configuration to create custom Config.sys and Autoexec.bat files.

4. Activate the check boxes beside the items you want, and then click OK. The items that appear in this dialog box depend on how your system is configured. However, you should see at least the following:

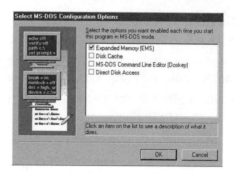

Expanded Memory (EMS): This is EMM386.EXE, the DOS memory manager that provides access to upper memory blocks (UMBs) and extended or expanded memory.

Disk Cache: This is SMARTDrive, the real-mode disk cache. Although not all DOS programs can take advantage of a disk cache, those that do will see a major performance improvement.

MS-DOS Command Line Editor (Doskey): This is Doskey.com, the DOS command-line editor that enables you to edit commands, recall commands, and more. It's excellent if you'll be working at the DOS prompt.

Direct Disk Access: This is the Lock command. It enables DOS applications to work with disk data structures directly.

5. Modify the custom Config.sys and Autoexec.bat files as necessary.

6. Click OK to return to the property sheet.

7. Click OK.

When you run the program now, Windows 98 goes through a few extra chores. In particular, it renames Config.sys to Config.wos and Autoexec.bat to Autoexec.wos. It then creates the custom Config.sys and Autoexec.bat files for the MS-DOS mode session. Note, however, that the files created by Windows 98 aren't quite the same as the ones you specified earlier.

Config.sys is the same as you specified, except that it includes the following line at the beginning:

```
DOS=SINGLE
```

This just tells the computer to boot using MS-DOS mode (SINGLE means single-tasking).

Autoexec.bat is the same as you specified, except that it includes the following lines at the end:

```
REM
REM The following lines have been created by Windows. Do
not modify them.
REM
drive:
CD \folder
CALL program
C:\Windows\WIN.COM [/W, /WX]
```

Here, *drive*, *folder*, and *program* are the drive letter, folder name, and filename, respectively, of the DOS program's executable file, which is launched using the CALL command.

When you exit the program, the last Autoexec.bat line is executed. As you can see, this line runs Win.com to start Windows 98, but Win.com is modified by one of the following switches:

/W   This switch is used if you deactivated the Close on Exit check box. In this case, Windows 98 prompts you to press a key to continue loading Windows 98.

/WX   This switch is used if you activated the Close on Exit check box. In this case, Windows 98 restarts automatically.

Disabling DOS

When I was running Windows 95, I had a machine that simply would not run DOS. Every time I tried to start a DOS session or run a DOS application, the machine would lock up completely and not even Ctrl+Alt+Delete would work. All my troubleshooting was in vain, so my solution was to completely disable DOS on that system.

Remember
Ctrl+Alt+Delete
(variously known
as the "three-
fingered salute" or
the "Vulcan nerve
pinch") displays
the Close Program
dialog box. Press
these keys if you
have a stuck pro-
gram, and the
Close Program dia-
log box will display
(not responding)
beside the pro-
gram name.
Highlight the pro-
gram and then
click End Task to
shut down the
offending program.

If you're having trouble with DOS, or if you don't want other people who use your computer to run DOS programs for some reason, you can disable both access to the DOS prompt and the ability to run programs in MS-DOS mode.

The easiest way to do this is to set some system policies. In the System Policy Editor, open the Registry and then open Local User, Windows 98 System, Restrictions. Activate Disable MS-DOS Prompt and Disable Single-Mode MS-DOS Applications.

To do this via the Registry, head for the following key:

```
HKEY_CURRENT_USER\Software\Microsoft\Windows\CurrentVer
sion\Policies
```

If necessary, add a new subkey named WinOldApp. Now add two DWORD values to this subkey:

Disabled: Set this value to 1 to disable the DOS prompt.

NoRealMode: Set this value to 1 to disable MS-DOS mode.

Uninstalling Applications

There's no law that says humans and software have to get along. You might end up with a program that doesn't do what you want, is too buggy or slow, or takes up too much hard disk real estate. In that case, the best approach is to uninstall the program and get on with your life.

Using Add/Remove Programs to Uninstall 32-Bit Applications

I mentioned earlier that most 32-bit programs add uninstall data to the Registry in the following key:

```
HKEY_LOCAL_MACHINE\Software\Microsoft\Windows\CurrentVersion
\Uninstall
```

Each application adds its own subkey that includes two settings: DisplayName—the name of the application—and UninstallString—the command that Windows 98 must run in order to start the uninstall process.

All of this means that you can remove these programs from your system by following this simple procedure:

1. Select Start, Settings, Control Panel to open the Control Panel folder.

2. Launch the Add/Remove Programs icon. As you can see in Figure 5.7, the bottom part of the Install/Uninstall tab lists the programs and features that can be uninstalled (note that your system will almost certainly display a different list of programs than the one shown in Figure 5.7):

   Delete Windows 98 uninstall information: This item refers to the system files that you saved from your previous version of Windows or DOS. If you remove this item, you won't be able to run Windows 98's automatic uninstall feature.

   Uninstall Windows 98: This item runs the Windows 98 uninstall feature.

   All others: Everything else in the list is a program or component that can be uninstalled automatically.

3. Highlight the item you want to uninstall, and then click Add/Remove. Windows 98 launches the uninstall program.

Undocumented
When you attempt to uninstall an application, you may receive an error message that tells you the `Uninstallation has been cancelled`. This likely means that the program has already been uninstalled manually. Head for the `Uninstall` key in the Registry and then delete the subkey for the application. This will remove the application from the uninstall list in Add/Remove Programs.

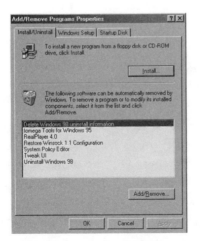

Figure 5.7
The Install/ Uninstall tab lists the programs that you can uninstall automatically.

4. Some applications (such as Microsoft Office) may ask that you insert their source CD at this point. Follow the instructions onscreen.

5. If the uninstall program asks if you're sure you want to remove the program, click Yes.

6. The uninstall program decrements the appropriate setting in the Registry's SharedDLLs key for each DLL used by the application. If the usage counter for a DLL is now 0, you'll see a dialog box asking if you want to remove the DLL file, as shown in Figure 5.8. If you're certain that the DLL was used only by the application you're removing, click Yes. If you're not sure, click No.

Figure 5.8
You'll see this dialog box if a DLL's usage is down to 0 in the SharedDLLs Registry key.

Watch Out!
It's possible that a DLL with a usage counter of 0 could still be used by another program, particularly a 16-bit program that doesn't know about the SharedDLLs Registry key. A better approach would be to make a note of the DLL's filename, click No, and then move the DLL to another folder. If none of your programs misses the file after a while, it's safe to delete it.

7. When the uninstall is complete, restart your computer. (This is not strictly necessary in most cases, but it's a good idea, particularly if device drivers and other system files were involved in the uninstall.)

Uninstalling 16-Bit Applications by Hand

16-bit Windows programs don't know about the Uninstall Registry key, so they can't be removed using Add/Remove programs. If the program doesn't come with its own uninstall tool, you have to remove the program from your system by hand.

The first step is to figure out which files to delete. If the program installed all of its files into its own folder, then you need look no further. On the other hand, many 16-bit Windows programs add a number of support files to the Windows folder and the Windows\System folder.

Earlier I mentioned that you should save DIR command listings before and after installing an application. If you did that, then you know which files the program installed. Otherwise, you have to do some detective work.

One of the best ways to determine which files a program uses is the Quick View utility. This program is normally used to examine what's inside a document without having to open (or even install) the original application. However, it also works for executable files:

1. In Windows Explorer, find the program's executable file.

2. Highlight the executable file and select File, Quick View. (You can also right-click the file and click Quick View in the shortcut menu.)

3. Scroll down until you find a section called either Imported-Name Table or Import Table. This section provides a list of the DLLs that the program uses, as shown in Figure 5.9. (Note that, in some cases, just the file primary names are shown.)

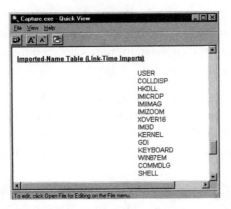

Figure 5.9
Use Quick View to see a list of the DLLs that a program uses.

4. Make a note of the DLL filenames.

5. Only some of these DLLs will be specific to the program. Others will be common DLLs used by other applications. Here are three ways to tell the difference:

   • Check the Registry SharedDLLs key to see if any of the listed DLLs are being used by other applications.

   • The files for most applications have a common date and time stamp. See if the listed DLLs use the same date and time stamp.

- The DLLs for some applications often have file-names that begin with the same two or three letters. For example, WordPerfect uses a number of DLLs that begin with the letters WP.

Again, if you're not certain whether you can safely delete a DLL, just move it to another folder for now.

Here are the steps to follow to delete a 16-bit Windows application by hand:

1. Just in case you decide to reinstall the application down the road, make backup copies of any data files you created using the program.

2. In Windows Explorer, highlight the application's folder in the All Folders list and select File, Delete. Click Yes when Windows Explorer asks you to confirm the deletion.

3. If the application added any submenus or shortcuts to the Start menu, open the Start menu and, for each item added by the application, right-click and then click Delete in the shortcut menu.

4. Select Start, Run, type sysedit, and then click OK. This opens the System Configuration Editor, which offers the following files for editing: Autoexec.bat, Config.sys, Win.ini, System.ini, and Protocol.ini (see Figure 5.10).

Undocumented
One way to check if other programs use a particular DLL is to run a search for files that reference the DLL. Select Start, Find, Files or Folders to display the Find window. In the Containing text box, type the primary name of the DLL. In the Look In box, type c:\windows. Click Find Now to run the search.

Figure 5.10
The System Configuration Editor gives you easy editing access to five configuration files.

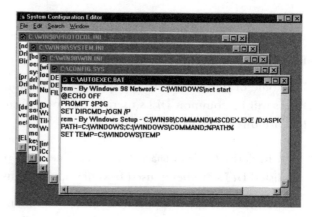

5. Check each file and remove any traces of the application. When you're done, save your changes and select File, Exit.

6. The one part of the Registry that 16-bit Windows applications do use is HKEY_CLASSES_ROOT. In the Registry Editor, delete any keys and settings related to the program (file extension keys, file type keys, CLSID keys, and so on).

7. Restart your computer.

Uninstalling DOS Applications by Hand

DOS programs almost always store all their files in their home directory, which makes it much easier to uninstall these programs:

1. Just in case you decide to reinstall the application down the road, make backup copies of any data files you created using the program.

2. In Windows Explorer, highlight the application's folder in the All Folders list and select File, Delete. Click Yes when Windows Explorer asks you to confirm the deletion.

3. Open the System Configuration Editor, as described in the previous section. Delete any references to the program from Config.sys and Autoexec.bat.

Essential Information

- To ensure a safe installation, back up configuration files, read readme.txt files, and perform other preparatory chores before launching an application's setup program.

- Windows 98 offers quite a number of methods for launching programs, including the Start menu, the Run dialog box, double-clicking the executable file or a document, the Task Scheduler, and more.

- You have three methods for launching applications automatically at startup: the StartUp folder, the Registry's Run key, and the run= line in Win.ini.

- To switch to another running application, click the window, click the taskbar button, press Alt+Tab, or press Alt+Esc.

- If you run DOS applications, they may not start unless you set them up to use MS-DOS mode.

- Use Control Panel's Add/Remove Programs icon to uninstall 32-bit applications automatically.

GET THE SCOOP ON...
Techniques for routine file maintenance ▪ Recovering
deleted files ▪ Searching for files ▪ Formatting and
copying floppy disks ▪ Customizing the Windows
Explorer environment

Expert Windows Explorer Techniques

W HETHER YOU'RE LOOKING TO MASTER Windows 98 or just get your work done quickly and efficiently, a thorough knowledge of the techniques available for working with files, folders, and floppy disks is essential. Or perhaps I should say that a thorough knowledge of certain techniques is essential. That's because, like the rest of Windows 98, Windows Explorer (the file management accessory) offers a handful of methods for accomplishing most tasks. Not all of these techniques are particularly efficient, however. Therefore, my goal in this chapter is to not only tell you how to do file management chores, but also to tell you the best ways to do those chores.

Quick Fixes for Making Windows Explorer More Usable

Before we get to the specifics, there are a few Windows Explorer tweaks you should perform in advance. These tweaks will slightly modify the default Windows Explorer setup to make it less oriented towards novice users.

For starters, get Windows Explorer onscreen by selecting Start, Programs, Windows Explorer. Now you'll do three things:

- Display the status bar.

- Turn on file extensions.

- Display hidden files.

Shortcut
If you have a keyboard with the Windows logo key (⊞), you can start Windows Explorer by pressing ⊞+E.

Displaying the Status Bar

Windows Explorer doesn't display its status bar by default, presumably to avoid confusing beginning users. However, the status bar displays all kinds of useful data: the number of files or folders currently selected, the total number of kilobytes or megabytes selected, the amount of free space on the current drive, and more. To turn on this much-needed feature, activate the View, Status Bar command.

Turning on File Extensions

When you read Chapter 10, "Powerful Techniques for File Types," you'll see that file extensions are one of the most crucial Windows 98 concepts. That's because file extensions define the file type and automatically associate files with certain applications. Microsoft figures that, crucial or not, the file extension concept is just too hard for new users to grasp. Therefore, right out of the box, Windows Explorer doesn't display file extensions. To overcome this limitation, follow these steps:

Shortcut
You can display the Folder Options dialog box even when Windows Explorer isn't running. To do so, select the Start, Settings, Folder Options command.

1. Select View, Folder Options to display the Folder Options dialog box.

2. Select the View Tab.

3. Deactivate the Hide File Extensions for Known File Types check box, as shown in Figure 6.1. (Note that the View tab has a slightly different layout in Windows 98 Second Edition.)

4. Click OK.

You'll need this dialog box again in the next section, so you may as well leave it onscreen for now.

Displaying Hidden Files

Windows 98 also insists upon hiding system files. This makes sense for novice users since they could accidentally delete or rename an important file. However, it's a pain for more advanced users who require access to certain system files—such as Config.sys and Msdos.sys. Here's how to force Windows 98 to display system files:

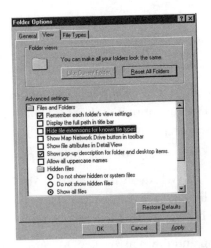

Figure 6.1
For easier file and
folder mainte-
nance, tell
Windows Explorer
to display file
extensions.

1. Select View, Folder Options to display the Folder Options dialog box.

2. Select the View Tab.

3. Activate the Show All Files option, as shown previously in Figure 6.1.

4. Click OK.

Basic File and Folder Chores: The Techniques Used by the Pros

With Windows Explorer in fighting trim, it's time to put it through a workout. I'll begin in this section with a few basic file and folder chores: selecting, moving and copying, and renaming.

Selecting Files and Folders

Before you can do anything in Windows Explorer—whether it's copying a file, renaming a folder, or deleting a shortcut—you have to *select*—or *highlight*—the object or objects you want to work with. (For simplicity's sake, I'll use the generic term *object* to refer to any file or folder.)

Selecting a Single Object

Selecting a single object with the mouse is straightforward, but the technique you use depends on whether Web integration is

Watch Out!
If you elect not to display file exten-sions, note that you won't be able to edit the exten-sion when you rename a file. For example, suppose you have a text file named Index.txt, which will be dis-played only as Index with file extensions hidden. If you edit the file-name to Index.htm, Windows 98 actually renames the file to Index.htm.txt! To rename exten-sions, you must display them.

Remember
The Windows Explorer screen is divided into two main areas. On the left side, the All Folders list shows the contents of your computer: the disk drives, the folders within those drives, and a few other special folders. On the right side, the Contents list displays the files and other objects that reside in the currently selected folder.

See Also...
"Toggling Web Integration On and Off," p. 203

Watch Out!
If you're using the keyboard selection techniques while Web integration is turned on, first move the mouse away from any objects. Otherwise, if the mouse pointer is hovering over an object, Windows Explorer may keep trying to select that object, which will undermine your keyboard efforts.

turned on (see Chapter 8, "An In-Depth Look at Web Integration and the Active Desktop"):

- If Web integration is off, click the object's name.

- If Web integration is on, position the mouse pointer over the object's name until it's selected. (This is known as *hovering* the mouse pointer over the object.)

From the keyboard, follow this two-step procedure:

1. Pressing Tab cycles you through the All Folders list, the Contents list, and the Address bar. Therefore, press Tab to move the highlight into the area you want.

2. Use the up and down arrow keys to move the highlight to the object you want to select.

Here are some notes to keep in mind when using the keyboard to select an object:

- If the Contents list shows objects displayed in two or more columns, use the left and right arrow keys to move between columns.

- If the current folder contains a large number of items, use the Page Up and Page Down keys to jump through the list quickly.

- Press Home to select the first object in the list; press End to select the last object in the list.

- If you press a letter, Windows Explorer will jump down to the first object that has a name that begins with that letter. Press that letter again to move to the next object that begins with the letter.

Selecting Multiple Objects

Here are the mouse techniques for selecting two or more objects:

- If Web integration is off, click the first object, then hold down Ctrl and click the rest of the objects. If the objects are contiguous, click the first object, then hold down Shift and click the last object.

- If Web integration is on, hover over the first object, then hold down Ctrl and hover over each of the rest of the objects. If the objects are contiguous, hover over the first object, then hold down Shift and hover over the last object.

From the keyboard, use the following techniques:

- To select objects individually, use the navigation keys (the arrow keys, Page Up and Page Down, and so on) to select the first object. Now hold down the Ctrl key. For each of the other objects you want to select, use the navigation keys to move the selector to the object, and then press the Spacebar.

- To select multiple contiguous objects, use the navigation keys to select the first object, hold down Shift, and then use the navigation keys to select the last object.

- To select every object in the current folder, run the Edit, Select All command, or press Ctrl+A.

- To reverse the current selection—that is, to deselect everything that's currently highlighted and to select everything that's currently unhighlighted—run the Edit, Invert Selection command.

Making Sense of Windows 98's Rules for Moving and Copying

If you've used Windows before, you know that you can move text from one part of a document to another by cutting it and then pasting it in the new location. One of Windows 95's innovations was to bring this "cut-and-paste" metaphor to file and folder copying and moving:

- If you want to copy an object, select it and then run the Edit, Copy command, or press Ctrl+C. If you want to move an object instead, select it and then run Edit, Cut, or press Ctrl+X.

- To perform the move or copy, go to the destination folder and then select Edit, Paste, or press Ctrl+V.

An alternative—and often faster—method for moving and copying objects is to "drag-and-drop" them. In Windows, to

Inside Scoop
If you need more room for your selecting, you can place Windows Explorer in full-screen mode by holding down Ctrl and clicking the Maximize button. This mode takes over the entire screen, shrinks the toolbar buttons, and removes the title bar, menu bar, status bar, and Address bar. To restore the window, press Alt+Spacebar and then select the Restore command.

drag-and-drop an object means to use the following generic technique:

1. Move the mouse pointer over the object, and then press and hold down the left mouse button.

2. Move the mouse to the destination. As you move the mouse, the object follows the pointer (the effect is as though you are using the mouse to *drag* the object along with the pointer).

3. Release the mouse button (that is, you *drop* the object on the destination).

You can use this drag-and-drop technique to move or copy files. Unfortunately, Windows 98 uses a fairly arcane set of rules for how this works:

- If you drag an object to a destination on the *same* drive, Windows 98 will move the object.

- If you drag an object to a destination on a different drive, Windows 98 will copy the object. While you're dragging, the mouse pointer sprouts a small plus sign (+) as a visual indicator that you're copying the object.

- If you drag an executable file, Windows 98 will create a shortcut for the object. While you're dragging, the mouse pointer displays a small arrow to indicate that you're cre-ating a shortcut for the object.

To work around the last rule, and to avoid trying to remember the first two rules, use the following techniques:

Move an object: Hold down the Shift key while you drag-and-drop.

Copy an object: Hold down the Ctrl key while you drag-and-drop.

Right-drag an object: Right-drag means that you drag the object while holding down the *right* mouse button. In this case, when you drop the object, Windows 98 displays a shortcut menu similar to the one shown in Figure 6.2. Click the command you want to run.

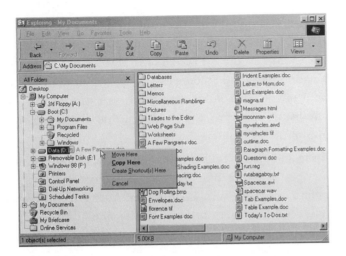

Figure 6.2
When you right-drag
an object and then
drop it, Windows
98 displays this
shortcut menu.

Inside Scoop
If your mouse is
missing a right but-
ton, you can simu-
late a right-drag by
holding down both
Ctrl and Shift while
you drag-and-drop
using the left
mouse button.

Expert Drag-and-Drop Techniques

You'll use drag-and-drop throughout your Windows career. To
make drag-and-drop even easier and more powerful, here are
a few pointers to bear in mind:

> **"Lassoing" multiple files:** If the objects you want to select
> are displayed in a block within the Contents list, you can
> select them by dragging a box around the objects, as
> shown in Figure 6.3. This is known as lassoing the objects.

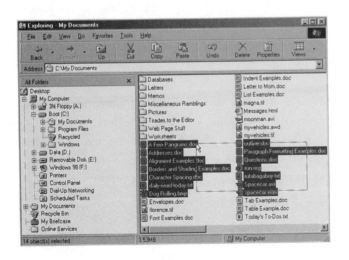

Figure 6.3
To select multiple
objects, drag a box
around the objects
to "lasso" them.

Inside Scoop
You can't drop an object on a running program's taskbar icon, but you can get the next best thing. Drag the mouse over the appropriate taskbar button and wait a second or two. Windows will then bring that application's window to the foreground, and you can then drop the object within the window.

Drag-and-scroll: Most drag-and-drop operations involve dragging an object from the Contents list and dropping it on a folder in the All Folders list. If you can't see the destination in the All Folders list, drag the pointer to the bottom of the All Folders list. Windows Explorer will scroll the list up. To scroll the list down, drag the object to the top of the All Folders list.

Drag-and-open: If the destination is a subfolder within an unopened folder branch, drag the object and hover the pointer over the unopened folder. After a second or two, Windows Explorer opens the folder branch.

Inter-window dragging: You can drag an object outside of the window and then drop it on a different location, such as the desktop.

Drag between Explorers: Windows 98 lets you open two or more copies of Windows Explorer. If you have to use several drag-and-drops to get some objects to a particular destination, open a second copy of Windows Explorer and display the destination in this new window. You can then drag from the first window and drop into the second window.

Canceling drag-and-drop: To cancel a drag-and-drop operation, either press Esc or click the right mouse button. (If you're right-dragging, click the left mouse button to cancel.)

Taking Advantage of the Send To Command

For certain destinations, Windows 98 offers an easier method for copying or moving files or folders: the Send To command. To use this command, select the objects you want to work with and then run one of the following techniques:

- Select File, Send To.

- Right-click the selection and then click Send To in the shortcut menu.

Either way, you see a submenu of potential destinations, as shown in Figure 6.4. Note that this menu is completely customizable, so you can add and delete destinations. These destinations are just shortcuts, so I'll explain how it's done in Chapter 11, "Taking Advantage of Shortcuts."

See Also...
"Creating a Shortcut," p. 275

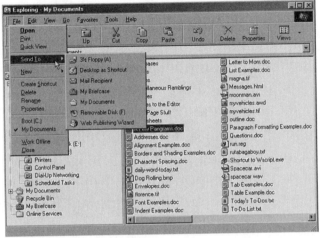

Figure 6.4
The Send To command offers a menu of possible destinations.

Click the destination you want and Windows 98 will send the object there. What do I mean by "send"? I suppose "drop" would be a better word because the Send To command acts like the drop part of drag-and-drop. Therefore, Send To follows the same rules as drag-and-drop:

- If the Send To destination is on a different disk drive, the object is copied.

- If the Send To destination is on the same disk drive, the object is moved.

- If the object is an executable file, Windows 98 asks if you want to create a shortcut. Click Yes if you do.

Inside Scoop
As with drag-and-drop, you can force the Send To command to copy or move an object. To force a move, hold down Shift when you select the Send To command. To force a copy, hold down Ctrl when you select the Send To command.

Creating New Folders and Files

You'll find yourself requiring a new folder quite often. For example, one of Windows 98's new features is the My Documents folder, which you use to store the documents that you create. This is a good start, but it makes no sense to stuff all your documents into a single folder. Instead, you'll want to create a number of subfolders to store different types of documents (memos, worksheets, presentations, and so on).

See Also...
"Customizing the
New Menu,"
p. 268

Here are the steps to follow to create a new folder:

1. Open the folder in which you want to create the new folder. For example, if you want to create a subfolder within My Documents, open the My Documents folder.

2. Select File, New, Folder. (You can also right-click an empty part of the Contents list and then click New, Folder.) Windows 98 creates a new folder and surrounds its name with a text box.

3. Edit the text box with the name of your folder, and then press Enter.

When you select the New command, notice that the submenu that appears contains not only the Folder command, but a number of other commands: Shortcut, Text Document, Bitmap Image, and so on. Selecting any of these commands creates a new file of the selected type. This new file is empty, of course, so you need to open it to add your content.

I'll show you how to customize the New menu in Chapter 10.

Renaming Files and Folders

Renaming files and folders is very easy in Windows 98:

Shortcut
There are three other methods you can use to get the text box around an object's name: Press F2; right-click the object and then click Rename; click the object's name, wait a second or two, and then click the object's name again.

1. Select the file or folder you want to rename. (You can only work with one object at a time.)

2. Select File, Rename. Windows 98 places a text box around the name.

3. Edit the name and then press Enter.

Bear in mind that you should only rename objects that you've created yourself. Renaming objects used by Windows or any of your applications can cause all kinds of problems.

The Recycle Bin: Deleting and Recovering Files and Folders

In my conversations with Windows users, I've noticed an interesting trend that has become more prominent in recent years: People don't delete files as often as they used to. I'm sure the reason for this is the absolutely huge hard disks that are offered these days. Even entry-level systems come equipped with multi-gigabyte disks, and double-digit gigabyte capacities (10GB and up) are no longer a big deal. So unless someone's working with digital video files, even a power user isn't going to put a dent in these massive disks any time soon. So why bother deleting anything?

While it's always a good idea to remove files and folders you don't need (it makes your system easier to navigate, it speeds up defragmenting, and so on), avoiding deletions does have one advantage: you can never delete something important by accident.

Just in case you do, however, Windows 98's Recycle Bin can bail you out. The Recycle Bin icon on the Windows 98 desktop is actually a front-end for a collection of folders named `Recycled` that exist on each hard disk partition. The idea is that when you delete a file or folder, Windows 98 doesn't actually remove the object from your system. Instead, the object is just moved to the `Recycled` folder on the same drive. If you delete an object by accident, you can go to the Recycle Bin and return the object to its original spot. Note, however, that the Recycle Bin can hold only so much data. When it gets full, it permanently deletes its oldest objects to make room for newer ones.

Deleting a File or Folder

To delete a file or folder, use either of the following methods:

- Highlight the object (or objects) and then select File, Delete. Pressing the Delete key, right-clicking the selection and clicking Delete, and clicking the Delete toolbar button will also work.

- Drag the object and drop it either on the desktop's Recycle Bin icon, or on the `Recycled` folder in the same drive.

Whichever method you use, Windows 98 displays a dialog box asking if you're sure you want to send the object to the Recycle Bin. Click Yes to continue with the deletion, or click No to cancel it.

Inside Scoop
If you're absolutely
sure you don't
need an object,
you can perma-
nently delete it
from your system
(that is, bypass
the Recycle Bin) by
highlighting it and
pressing
Shift+Delete.

Please note that Windows 98 bypasses the Recycle Bin and permanently deletes an object under the following circumstances:

- You delete the object from a floppy disk or any removable drive.

- You delete the object from the DOS prompt.

- You delete the object from a network drive.

However, there *is* a method you can use to recover these supposedly permanent deletions, and I'll show you that method a bit later.

Setting Some Recycle Bin Options

The Recycle Bin has a few properties you can set to control how it works. To view these properties, right-click the desktop's Recycle Bin icon and then click Properties. Windows 98 displays the property sheet shown in Figure 6.5.

Figure 6.5
Use this property
sheet to configure
the Recycle Bin to
your liking.

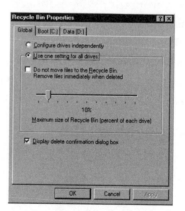

Here's a rundown of the various controls:

Configure drives independently: By default, the Recycle Bin uses the same settings on all your drives. To set up separate configurations for each drive, activate this option and then click the other tabs to configure the drives.

Use one setting for all drives: This is the default setting for the Recycle Bin. It means that, for the next two controls, the configuration that you select is used for all your drives.

Do not move files to the Recycle Bin. Remove files immediately when deleted: If you activate this option, all deletions are permanent.

Maximum size of Recycle Bin (percent of each drive): Use this slider to set the maximum size of the Recycle Bin as a percentage of the total capacity of the drive. The higher the percentage, the more deleted files the Recycle Bin can hold, but the less disk space you have available. (Unless you work with very large files, a maximum size of 3–5 percent is more than adequate.)

Display delete confirmation dialog check box: If you don't want Windows 98 to ask for confirmation when you delete an object, deactivate this option.

Click OK to put the new settings into effect.

Recovering a File or Folder

If you accidentally delete the wrong file or folder, you can return it to its rightful place by using the following method:

1. Open the desktop's Recycle Bin icon, or open any `Recycled` folder in Windows Explorer.

2. Highlight the object.

3. Select File, Restore. (You can also right-click the file and then click Restore.)

Recovering a "Permanently" Deleted File or Folder

According to the official Microsoft party line, an object is permanently deleted from your system under the following circumstances:

■ You deleted the object from a floppy disk, removable disk, or the DOS prompt.

■ You bypassed the Recycle Bin with Shift+Delete.

■ You deleted the object from the Recycle Bin, or you emptied the Recycle Bin.

Remember
You can clean out your Recycle Bin at any time by right-clicking the desktop's Recycle Bin icon and then clicking Empty Recycle Bin. The Recycle Bin contents can also be purged using Windows 98's Disk Cleanup utility.

Inside Scoop
If deleting the file or folder was the last action you performed in Windows Explorer, you can recover the object by selecting the Edit, Undo Delete command. Note, however, that Windows 98 Second Edition lets you undo the 10 most recent actions.

Microsoft may call these deletions "permanent," but they're not totally unrecoverable. The reason is that under all of the circumstances mentioned above, Windows 98 doesn't delete the file's contents. Instead, it changes the first letter of the file's name to the Greek lowercase sigma, and it alerts the file system that the file's clusters are free to be used by another file. Therefore, as long as you act before the file's clusters are overwritten, the file can indeed be recovered.

How? By using the DOS 6 UNDELETE command, which you can run from your original DOS disks. Failing that, you can obtain a copy from Microsoft:

```
http://support.microsoft.com/download/support/mslfiles/
PD0646.EXE
```

Here are the steps to follow:

1. Select Start, Shut Down, activate the Restart in MS-DOS Mode option, and click OK.

2. You must give the UNDELETE command direct access to the disk. Therefore, when you get to the DOS prompt, type `lock` and press Enter.

3. When you're asked to confirm, press y and Enter.

4. Change to the folder from which you deleted the file.

5. Type `undelete filename`, where `filename` is the 8.3 name of the file you want to recover. UNDELETE displays a message similar to this:

```
UNDELETE - A delete protection facility
Copyright (C) 1987-1993 Central Point Software, Inc.
All rights reserved.

Directory C:\
File Specification: SAVEME.TXT

    Delete Sentry control file not found.

    Deletion-tracking file not found.
```

```
MS-DOS directory contains    1 deleted files.
Of those,    1 files may be recovered.
```

```
Using the MS-DOS directory method.
```

```
    ?AVEME   TXT    41894   2-28-99  5:47p  ...A
Undelete (Y/N)?
```

Watch Out!
If the file you recover had a long filename, this name will be lost and the recovered file will use only its 8.3 filename.

6. Press y. UNDELETE displays the following prompt:

   ```
   Please type the first character for ?AVEME   .TXT:
   ```

7. Press the appropriate character. UNDELETE recovers the file.

8. Type unlock and press Enter to disable direct disk access.

9. Restart Windows 98.

File Maintenance Using the Open and Save As Dialog Boxes

One of the best-kept secrets of Windows 98 is the fact that you can perform many of these file maintenance operations within two of Windows 98's standard dialog boxes:

Open: In most applications, you display this dialog box by selecting the File, Open command.

Save As: You usually display this dialog box by selecting File, Save As, or, if you're working with a new, unsaved file, by selecting File, Save.

There are three techniques you can use within these dialog boxes:

- To perform maintenance on a particular file or folder, right-click the object to display a shortcut menu like the one shown in Figure 6.6.

- To create a new object, right-click an empty section of the file list, and then click New to get the New menu.

- To create a new folder within the current folder, click the Create New Folder button.

Figure 6.6
You can perform
most basic file
and folder mainte-
nance right from
the Open and
Save As dialog
boxes.

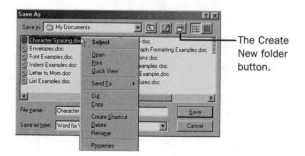

The Create
New folder
button.

> **66**
> Data expands to
> fill the space
> available for
> storage.
> —Parkinson's
> Law of Data
> **99**

Shortcut
If you have a key-
board with the
Windows logo key
(⊞), you can
start Find by press-
ing ⊞ + F. Also, if
you're in Windows
Explorer or if you
click the desktop,
you can start Find
by pressing F3.

Powerful Search Techniques for Finding Files

I mentioned earlier that hard disks are getting huge, so people
don't delete as much as they used to. Another consequence of
these large disk capacities is that users don't move files to
archival storage as much as they used to. Why bother when a
multi-gigabyte drive can store tens of thousands of files?
Keeping the file on disk is much more convenient, but *only* if
you can find the file you want, and there's the rub.

Fortunately, Windows 98 comes with a decent Find utility
that offers some reasonably powerful search options for tracking down files.

Here's how to get started:

- To search within a specific folder, highlight the folder in
  Windows Explorer, and then select Tools, Find, Files or
  Folders, or press F3.

- Select Start, Find, Files or Folders.

  Figure 6.7 shows the Find window that appears.

Figure 6.7
The Find window
will help you
search for files on
your system.

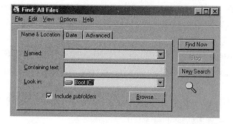

Here are the steps to follow to run a search:

1. Use the Named text box to enter the name of the file you want to locate (this is optional). If you're not sure of the exact name, you can enter a *file specification*, which uses a partial name or a wildcard character or two. Here are some pointers for using the Named text box:

    - Find doesn't differentiate between uppercase and lowercase letters.

    - If the filename contains one or more spaces, surround the name with quotation marks.

    - Find always looks for filenames that *contain* the text you enter. Therefore, if you're not sure about a file-name, just enter part of the name.

    - Another way to broaden your search is to use wildcard characters. Use the question mark (?) to substitute for a single character (for example, memo5?.txt); use an asterisk (*) to substitute for a group of characters (for example, *.doc).

    - To search for multiple file specifications, separate each one with a space, comma, or semicolon.

    - The Named control doubles as a drop-down list box, so you can repeat a search later on by selecting the file specification from the list.

2. Use the Containing text box to enter a word or phrase con-tained within the file (this is optional). Note that if you enter multiple words, Find will only match documents that contain the exact phrase you enter.

3. Use the Look In combo box to either type the drive or folder you want to check or select one of the predefined locations. To specify multiple locations, separate each path with a semicolon.

4. If you want Find to search all the folders contained within the Look in location, leave the Include Subfolders check box activated.

Remember
If you'd rather run a case-sensitive search, activate the Options, Case Sensitive com-mand.

5. The controls on the Date tab (see Figure 6.8) enable you to narrow the search using the file date and time stamps. To use this feature, activate the Find All Files option, and then use the list to select Modified, Created, or Last Accessed.

Figure 6.8
Use the Date tab to enter date criteria for your search.

6. Now choose the date range:

   between: If you activate this option, use the two calendar controls to select the first and last dates between which you want to find the file.

   during the previous x month(s): If you activate this option, use the spinner to select how many months back you want to search.

   during the previous x day(s): If you activate this option, use the spinner to select how many days back you want to search.

7. The controls in the Advanced tab (see Figure 6.9) enable you to narrow your search even further:

   Of type: Use this drop-down box to choose the type of file you want to find.

   Size is: Use the first list to select either At Least or At Most. Then use the spinner to enter a size in kilobytes.

8. Click the Find Now button to begin the search. If Find locates any matching files, they appear in a list at the bottom of the Find window.

Figure 6.9
Use the Advanced
tab to narrow your
search by file type
or file size.

Remember
If you entered a
complex set of cri-
teria that you
think you might
use again, you can
save your search
by selecting File,
Save Search. Find
gathers the search
criteria and saves
them to a file on
your desktop.
Open this file to
run the search
again.

Working with Floppy Disks

You've concentrated so far in this chapter on files and folders,
so let's talk about disks for a while. Windows 98 ships with a
large collection of disk utilities. Most of these tools deal with
disk maintenance and repair, so I'll hold off on them until I discuss performance tuning and troubleshooting. (In particular,
see Chapter 13, "Optimizing Your Hard Disk.") In this section,
I'll discuss two floppy disk techniques: formatting and copying.

Formatting a Floppy Disk

Floppy disks are a magnetic storage medium. When you place
a file on a floppy disk, the file is divided up and placed in magnetic storage areas called *sectors*, which are arranged in *tracks*.
These sectors and tracks are not present in a new floppy disk
so, before you can store any files, you must *format* the disk to
create the magnetic sector/track pattern. (Nowadays, however,
many new floppy disks come pre-formatted.)

Formatting is also important for older disks:

- You can run a "quick" format, which is an easy way to completely erase a floppy disk.

- A format can "freshen" a disk's sectors and tracks, thus
  making the disk more reliable.

- Formatting can identify corrupted areas of the disk and
  mark them so they aren't used in the future.

- Many computer viruses are transported via floppy disk, so
  a format ensures that no viruses are hiding within the disk.

Undocumented
You may find that
Windows 98 con-
stantly accesses
your floppy drive
whenever you per-
form any type of
file activity (such
as opening or sav-
ing). This is
caused by having
a recently used
floppy disk file on
your Documents
menu (select
Start, Documents).
To fix this, open
the Documents
menu, right-click
the floppy disk file,
and then click
Delete.

Here are the steps to plow through to format a floppy disk:

1. Insert the floppy disk you want to work with.

2. In Windows Explorer, right-click the floppy disk drive and then click Format. Windows 98 displays the Format dialog box, shown in Figure 6.10.

Figure 6.10
Use the Format dialog box to launch your floppy disk format.

Watch Out!
For a used disk, formatting completely erases whatever is currently on the disk. Therefore, check the disk's contents before formatting it to ensure you aren't wiping out anything important.

3. The proper disk capacity and size should be selected in the Capacity drop-down list. If not, use this list to select the capacity of your disk.

4. Select one of the three formatting options in the Format Type group:

   Quick (erase): Select this option if you only need to erase the files on an already-formatted disk. Format skips the bad-sector check, so this option takes only a few seconds.

   Full: Select this option to run a complete format that erases the disk files and checks the disk for bad sectors. This option is a must for new, unformatted disks. It's also useful for very old disks that are more likely to have bad sectors.

   Copy system files only: Select this option to make the disk bootable by copying the Windows 98 system files. Four files are copied in all: Io.sys, Drvspace.bin, Msdos.sys, and Command.com. Note that this isn't technically a format since existing files on the disk aren't erased.

5. Make your choices from the Other Options group:

   Label: Use this text box to enter a label that will be written to the disk during the format (you'll be able to see this label by displaying the disk's property sheet). You can enter up to 11 characters.

   No label: Activate this check box to remove the label from the disk and disable the Label text box. (This is the same as leaving the Label text box blank.)

   Display summary when finished: When this check box is activated, Windows 98 displays the Format Results dialog box, which offers a few disk statistics, including the total disk space, the total bytes used by system files and bad sectors, and the size of each cluster ("allocation unit").

   Copy system files: Activate this check box if you want to format the disk *and* make the disk bootable by copying the Windows 98 system files to the disk.

6. Click Start to launch the format. The Windows 98 Format tool is a 32-bit, multitasking program. Therefore, unlike previous versions of Windows, Windows 98 enables you to carry on with your work while the format proceeds.

7. When the formatting is complete, Windows 98 displays the Format Results dialog box. (Assuming, of course, that you activated the Display Summary When Finished check box.) Click OK.

8. Click Close.

Copying a Floppy Disk

If a floppy disk contains just a few files, you can copy those files to another floppy by selecting them, copying them, inserting the second disk, and then pasting the files. However, if you need an exact copy of the disk—including the disk label and serial number—you need to run a sector-by-sector copy using the Copy Disk command:

1. Insert the source disk (that is, the disk that you want to copy).

Inside Scoop
You can use the Format command to format a hard disk partition, although Windows 98 won't let you format the partition containing the Windows 98 files. Once you format a hard drive, it will no longer be set up for long filenames. You have to either restart your computer or else highlight the drive in Windows Explorer and select View, Refresh (or press F5).

Watch Out!
Windows 98 will
only copy a floppy
disk to another
disk of the same
size and capacity.

Figure 6.11
You make an exact
copy of a floppy
disk by using the
Copy Disk dialog
box.

Remember
The "Removable
disk" shown in
Figure 6.11, is in
this case, a
100MB Zip disk.
Windows 98 can
work with many
removalbe disk
media, including
the popular Zip
and Jazz formats.
You use these
disks more or less
like any other
disk. About the
only difference is
that if you right-
click the disk, in
most cases
Windows 98 offers
an Eject command
that will eject the
disk form its drive.

2. If your computer has a second floppy disk drive of the *same* type, insert the destination disk (that is, the disk you want to use for the copy) in the second drive.

3. Right-click the source disk drive and then click Copy Disk. The Copy Disk dialog box appears, as shown in Figure 6.11.

4. In the Copy From list, highlight the drive that contains the source disk.

5. In the Copy To list, highlight the drive you want to use for the destination disk. If your system has only one floppy drive (or only one drive that has the capacity of the source and destination disks), highlight the same drive in both lists.

6. Click the Start button. Windows 98 reads the data from the source disk. When that's done, you're prompted to insert the destination disk (assuming you're using the same drive for the copy).

7. Insert the destination disk into the drive and then click OK. Windows 98 copies the source disk data to the destination disk.

8. Click Close when the copy operation is done.

Customizing Windows Explorer

I'll close this chapter by examining various ways to customize the Windows Explorer interface. You'll likely be spending a lot of time with Windows Explorer over the years, so customizing it to your liking will make you more productive.

Changing the View

The icons in Windows Explorer's Contents list can be viewed in five different ways. To see a list of these views, either pull down the View menu or pull down the Views button in the toolbar. Here are your choices:

as Web Page: Displays the Contents list within a Web page structure. See Chapter 8.

Large Icons: Increases the size of the Contents list icons and displays those icons in rows across the List pane.

Small Icons: Decreases the size of the icons and displays them in columns that you must scroll vertically.

List: Icons are the same size as in the Small Icons view, but the icons are arranged in columns that you must scroll horizontally.

Details: Displays a vertical list of icons, where each icon has four columns: Name, Size, Type, and Modified.

Here are some techniques to remember when working with the Details view:

- You can change the order of the columns by dragging the column headings to the left or right.

- You can adjust the width of a column by pointing the mouse at the right edge of the column's heading (the pointer changes to a two-headed arrow) and dragging the pointer left or right.

Activating Thumbnails

Windows 98 also supports a sixth view: thumbnails. The idea is that in Thumbnails view, you see the contents of the file instead of just its name. This works for many graphics formats—including BMP, GIF, JPG, and TIF—as well as for Web pages (HTML files).

Here's how to use this view:

1. Open the folder you want to work with.

2. Right-click an empty section of the Contents list, and then click Properties.

See Also...
"Viewing Folders As Web Pages," p. 206

Undocumented
To adjust all the columns so that they're exactly as wide as their widest data, press Ctrl+plus sign (+), where the plus sign is the one on your keyboard's numeric keypad.

3. In the folder's property sheet, activate the Enable Thumbnail View check box (see Figure 6.12), and then click OK.

4. Select View, Thumbnails or drop-down the Views toolbar button and click Thumbnails. (If you don't see this command, move to a different folder and then move back to the original folder.)

Figure 6.12
Activate the
Enable Thumbnail
View check box.

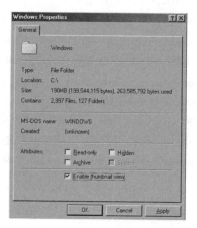

Sorting Files and Folders

The icons in the Contents list are sorted alphabetically by name, with folders displayed before files. You can change this sort order by selecting View, Arrange Icons (or right-clicking the Contents list and clicking Arrange Icons), and then selecting one of the following commands:

by Name: Select this command to sort the folder alphabetically by name (this is the default).

by Type: Select this command to sort the folder alphabetically according to file type.

by Size: Select this command to sort the folder numerically according to file size, with the smallest sizes at the top.

by Date: Select this command to sort the folder by date, with the most recent dates at the top.

Auto Arrange: Activate this command to have Windows Explorer sort the folder automatically whenever you move icons or change the size of the window. Note that this command only works with the Large Icons and Small Icons views.

Exploring the View Options

The Windows 98 version of Windows Explorer boasts a large number of customization options that you need to be familiar with. To see these options, you have two choices:

- In Windows Explorer, select the View, Folder Options command.

- Select Start, Settings, Folder Options.

Either way, the view options can be found, appropriately enough, on the View tab, as shown in Figure 6.13.

Shortcut
An easier way to sort a folder is to click the column headers in Details view. For example, click the Size column to sort the folder by file size. Clicking the same column header toggles the sort order between ascending and descending.

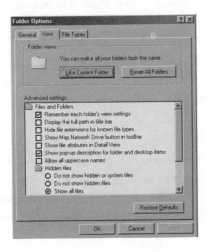

Figure 6.13
The View tab has quite a few options for customizing Windows Explorer.

The Folder views group contains two command buttons that you use to define a common view for all your folders:

Like Current Folder: Use Windows Explorer's View menu to customize a folder the way you want. Then display the Folder Options dialog box and click Like Current Folder. This tells Windows Explorer to display every folder using the same view options as the current folder.

Reset All Folders: If you prefer to set up a unique view for each folder, click Reset All Folders to revert everything back to the default Windows 98 view.

Here's a complete look at the various options in the `Files` and `Folders` branch:

Remember each folder's view settings: Activate this check box to have Windows Explorer keep track of the view options you set for each folder. The next time you display a folder, Windows Explorer will "remember" the view options and use them to display the folder.

See Also...
"Mapping a Shared Resource As a Local Disk Drive," p. 639

Display the full path in title bar: Activate this check box to place the full pathname of the current folder in the Windows Explorer title bar. The full pathname includes the drive, the names of the parent folders, and the name of the current folder.

Hide file extensions for known file types: As you saw earlier in this chapter, you deactivate this check box to force Windows Explorer to display file extensions.

Show Map Network Drive button in toolbar: Activate this check box to add the Map Network Drive and Disconnect Network Drive buttons to the Windows Explorer toolbar. See Chapter 28, "A Complete Tour of the Network Neighborhood."

Remember
To adjust the attributes of a file or folder, right-click the object and then click Properties. The property sheet that appears contains check boxes for the attributes (see Figure 6.12, earlier in this chapter).

Show file attributes in Detail View: Activate this check box to bolster the Details view with an extra Attributes column, which shows the current attributes of each object: `A` for archive, `H` for hidden, `R` for read-only, and `S` for system.

Show pop-up description for folder and desktop items: Some icons display a pop-up banner when you point the mouse at them. For example, WordPad documents display `Author: Name` (where `Name` is the name of the document author), and the default desktop icons display an InfoTip that describes each icon. Use this check box to turn these pop-ups on and off.

Allow all uppercase names: If you rename a file or folder with all uppercase letters, Windows 98 will usually adjust the name so that only the first letter is capitalized. To preserve your all uppercase names, activate this check box.

Hidden files: You use these options to tell Windows Explorer which files to display:

- **Do not show hidden or system files:** Activate this option to avoid displaying objects that have the hidden or system attribute set.

- **Do not show hidden files:** Activate this option to avoid displaying objects that have the hidden attribute set.

- **Show all files:** Activate this option to display every file.

Using Windows Explorer's Command Line Options

The Windows Explorer executable file is `Explorer.exe`, and it resides in the `Windows` folder. `Explorer.exe` supports various command line parameters, which you can take advantage of to control how Windows Explorer starts. Here's the syntax for `Explorer.exe`:

`explorer [/n]¦[/e][,/root,folder][,subfolder]`

/n	Start Windows Explorer using the My Computer view (just the Contents list).
/e	Starts Windows Explorer using the Explorer view (both the All Folders list and the Contents list).
/root,*folder*	Tells Windows Explorer to display *folder* at the top of the All Folders list. You can only view *folder* and all of its subfolders.
subfolder	Specifies a subfolder of *folder* that will be highlighted in the All Folders list.

The following command opens Windows Explorer with
`C:\Windows` as the root and `C:\Windows\System` highlighted:

```
explorer /e,/root,c:\windows,c:\windows\system
```

Essential Information

- To make Windows Explorer more usable, display the status
  bar, turn on file extensions, and display hidden and system
  files.

- To select multiple objects with your mouse, hold down Ctrl
  and click each object. For contiguous objects, click the
  first object, hold down Shift, and click the last object. (If
  Web integration is on, replace "click" with "hover over.")

- Windows 98 copies objects dragged to a different drive,
  and moves objects dragged to the same drive. To force a
  move, hold down Shift; to force a copy, hold down Ctrl.

- Select the File, Send To command to send objects to a
  floppy drive, removable drive, or another predetermined
  destination.

- To rename an object, highlight it and either select File,
  Rename or press F2.

- Deleted items are sent to the Recycle Bin, which represents the Recycled folders on your hard disks. To restore an
  accidentally deleted file, highlight it in the Recycle Bin
  and select File, Restore.

- Select View, Folder Options to customize Windows
  Explorer view options.

Advanced Windows 98 Customizing

PART II

GET THE SCOOP ON...
Understanding the Control Panel ▪ Each Control Panel
icon ▪ Working with individual Control Panel files ▪
Displaying and hiding Control Panel icons and tabs ▪
Easier methods of accessing the Control Panel icons

Getting to Know the Control Panel

Chapter 7

A N EASY WAY TO DISTINGUISH a novice user from an experienced user is that the former rarely customizes her system. Most new users are wary of doing the wrong thing, so they leave the interface as they found it. Moreover, it's been my experience that new users don't even consider the possibility of customization, and are surprised to learn that it can be done. Microsoft encourages this passive attitude by providing only perfunctory customizing instructions in the Windows 98 documentation.

On the other hand, experienced users customize their systems to the hilt. They know that strategic customizing is the royal road not only to improved productivity, but also to a more interesting and enjoyable computing experience.

In the broadest sense, "customizing" means changing a system's default settings. So you could say that this book is entirely about customizing Windows 98 since its goal is to eschew the Windows 98 defaults and examine the "unauthorized" side of things. On a narrower level, however, customizing involves adapting the user interface to suit your personal taste and working style. To that end, this chapter is the first in a three-chapter series that examines the wide range of cus-

"
customize, *verb*,
transitive: To
make or alter to
individual or per-
sonal specifica-
tions.
—Webster's
College
Dictionary
"

"
Control Panel
A group of tools
you use to
change hardware
and software
settings.
—From the
"Getting Started"
booklet
"

See Also...
"Adding and
Removing
Windows 98
Components,"
p. 66

tomization options available for transforming the Windows 98 interface. You begin here with a look at "Customization Central"—the Control Panel.

What Is the Control Panel?

The Control Panel is a folder that contains a large number of icons—there are a couple of dozen in the default Windows 98 Setup, but depending on your system configuration, there could be 30 or more icons available. Each of these icons deals with a specific area of the Windows 98 configuration: hardware, applications, fonts, printers, multimedia, and much more.

Opening an icon displays a dialog box containing various properties related to that area of Windows. For example, you saw back in Chapter 2, "Ten Things You Should Know About the Windows 98 Setup," that you can use the Add/Remove Programs icon to add and remove Windows 98 components.

The Control Panel is a folder. However, unlike the Windows 3.*x* Control Panel, which was a mere program group like any other, the Windows 98 Control Panel is a special Windows 98 system folder. (It's actually an ActiveX component.) This gives you much more flexibility when working with the Control Panel:

- The Control Panel folder can appear within Windows Explorer and My Computer.

- You can hide Control Panel icons.

- Other applications can easily add new icons to the Control Panel.

- You can display the Control Panel just about anywhere you like, including the Start menu and taskbar.

I'll discuss these and other Control Panel techniques throughout the rest of this chapter.

Opening the Control Panel Folder

To display the Control Panel folder, use any of the following techniques:

- Select Start, Settings, Control Panel.

- In Windows Explorer's All Folders list, select the Control Panel folder.

- Open the desktop's My Computer icon and then open Control Panel.

Figure 7.1 shows a typical Control Panel window. Again, the icons you see in your Control Panel vary depending on your system configuration, what applications you have installed, and so on.

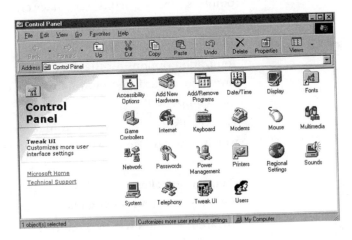

Figure 7.1
The Windows 98 Control Panel.

A Review of the Control Panel Icons

To help you familiarize yourself with what's available in the Control Panel, this section offers summary descriptions of 28 Control Panel icons.

Shortcut
The Control Panel folder shown in Figure 7.1 is displayed in Web view, which gives you a brief description of any selected icon. To display the Control_Panel folder in Web view, activate the View, as Web Page command.

 Accessibility Options: Enables you to customize input—the keyboard and mouse—and output—sound and display—for users with special mobility, hearing, or vision requirements.

 Add New Hardware: Launches the Add New Hardware Wizard, which searches for new Plug-and-Play devices on your system, and can run a more in-depth hardware detection to look for non-Plug-and-Play devices.

Add/Remove Programs: Enables you to install and uninstall applications, add and remove Windows 98 components, and create a startup disk.

Date/Time: Use this icon to set the current date and time and to select your time zone.

Desktop Themes: Enables you to customize the Windows 98 interface with a theme that affects the wallpaper, mouse pointers, desktop icons, screen saver, and so on.

Display: Offers a large number of customization options for the desktop, screen saver, video card, monitor, and other display components.

Remember
The Infrared icon only appears if Windows 98 detects an infrared device on your system.

Fonts: Displays the Fonts folder, from which you can view, install, and remove fonts.

Game Controllers: Enables you to calibrate joysticks and other game devices.

Infrared: Enables you to monitor infrared connections and specify options for infrared devices.

Internet: Displays a large collection of settings for modifying Internet properties (how you connect, the Internet Explorer interface, and so on).

Keyboard: Enables you to customize your keyboard, work with keyboard languages, and change the keyboard driver.

Mail: Used for configuring Windows Messaging settings. (Note that on some systems this icon is named Mail and Fax.)

Microsoft Mail Postoffice: Runs the Workgroup Postoffice Administration program, which enables you to set up and maintain a Microsoft Mail Postoffice.

 Modems: Used for installing and configuring a modem.

 Mouse: Displays the Mouse Properties dialog box, which enables you to set various mouse options and to install a different mouse device driver.

 Multimedia: Enables you to specify settings for audio, video, MIDI, CD music, and multimedia devices.

 Network: Used for setting up a Windows 98 network client, including installing client software and network protocols, identifying your computer, and setting various networking options.

 Passwords: Enables you to change your Windows and networking passwords, enable remote administration of your computer, and turn on user profiles.

 PC Card (PCMCIA): Used for setting PC Card options and enabling PC Card sockets.

 Power Management: Enables you to configure Advanced Power Management properties for powering down system components (such as the monitor and hard drive) and for defining low-power alarms for notebook batteries.

 Printers: Displays the Printers folder, from which you can install, configure, and remove printers.

Inside Scoop
The Mail icon only appears if you had Windows Messaging installed when you upgraded over Windows 95. Similarly, the Microsoft Mail Postoffice icon only appears if Microsoft Mail was installed in Windows 95. You can also get both icons by installing Windows Messaging from the Windows 98 CD. In the folder \tools\oldwin95\ message\us, run the file named wms.exe.

Remember
The PC Card (PCMCIA) icon only appears if Windows 98 detects a PC Card controller on your system.

Regional Settings: Enables you to configure international settings for country-dependent items such as numbers, currencies, times, and dates.

Scanners and Cameras: Enables you to install and configure scanners and digital cameras.

Sounds: You use this icon to map sounds to specific Windows 98 events, such as closing a program and minimizing a window.

System: Displays the System Properties dialog box, which gives you access to the Device Manager, hardware profiles, and various performance settings.

Telephony: Used for configuring modem-dialing locations and for configuring telephony drivers.

TweakUI: Provides an extensive collection of user interface customization options. As discussed in Chapter 4, you must install TweakUI from the Windows 98 CD.

See Also...
"An Insider's Guide
to Tweak UI,"
p. 122

Users: Enables you to configure user profiles.

Controlling the Control Panel

To help you get the most out of the Control Panel, this section runs through a few techniques for controlling how this folder operates. You'll learn about the files that are at the heart of the Control Panel, how to hide and display Control Panel icons, how to customize Control Panel dialog boxes, and more.

Understanding Control Panel Files

Each Control Panel icon is represented by a *Control Panel extension* file, which uses the .cpl extension. All of these files reside in the Windows\System folder. When you open the Control Panel, Windows 98 scans the System folder looking for these .cpl files, and then displays an icon for each one. (Windows 98 also checks `Control.ini` to see if any icons are not supposed to be displayed. More on this later in this chapter; see "Hiding and Displaying Control Panel Icons.")

These `.cpl` files offer an alternative method for launching individual Control Panel dialog boxes. The idea is that you run `Control.exe` and specify the name of a `.cpl` file as a parameter. This bypasses the `Control Panel` folder and opens the icon directly. Here's the syntax:

```
C:\Windows\Control.exe Cplfile.cpl [module]
```

`Cplfile.cpl`	The name of the `.cpl` file.
`module`	An optional module name for `Main.cpl`, which contains several Control Panel modules.

Table 7.1 lists the various Control Panel icons and the appropriate command line to use.

Remember
Not all the Control Panel icons appear in Table 7.1, because a few—particularly Add New Hardware, PCMCIA (PC Card), and Sounds—can't be accessed by running `Control.exe`.

TABLE 7.1: COMMAND LINES FOR LAUNCHING INDIVIDUAL CONTROL PANEL ICONS

Control Panel Icon	Command Line
Accessibility Options	`C:\Windows\Control.exe Access.cpl`
Add/Remove Programs	`C:\Windows\Control.exe Appwiz.cpl`
Date/Time	`C:\Windows\Control.exe Timedate.cpl`
Desktop Themes	`C:\Windows\Control.exe Themes.cpl`
Display	`C:\Windows\Control.exe Desk.cpl`
Fonts	`C:\Windows\Control.exe Main.cpl Fonts`
Game Controllers	`C:\Windows\Control.exe Joy.cpl`
Infrared	`C:\Windows\Control.exe Infrared.cpl`
Internet	`C:\Windows\Control.exe Inetcpl.cpl`
Keyboard	`C:\Windows\Control.exe Main.cpl Keyboard`
Mail	`C:\Windows\Control.exe Mlcfg32.cpl`
Microsoft Mail Postoffice	`C:\Windows\Control.exe Wgpocpl.cpl`
Modems	`C:\Windows\Control.exe Modem.cpl`
Mouse	`C:\Windows\Control.exe Main.cpl Mouse`
Multimedia	`C:\Windows\Control.exe Mmsys.cpl`
Network	`C:\Windows\Control.exe Netcpl.cpl`
Passwords	`C:\Windows\Control.exe Password.cpl`

continues

TABLE 7.1: CONTINUED

Control Panel Icon	Command Line
Power Management	`C:\Windows\Control.exe Powercfg.cpl`
Printers	`C:\Windows\Control.exe Main.cpl Printers`
Regional Settings	`C:\Windows\Control.exe Intl.cpl`
Scanners and Cameras	`C:\Windows\Control.exe Sticpl.cpl`
System	`C:\Windows\Control.exe Sysdm.cpl`
Telephony	`C:\Windows\Control.exe Telephon.cpl`
TweakUI	`C:\Windows\Control.exe Tweakui.cpl`

Hiding and Displaying Control Panel Icons

If you find your `Control Panel` folder is bursting at the seams, you can trim it down to size by removing those icons you never use. Windows 98 offers three methods for doing this:

- Move Control Panel files

- Customize `Control.ini`

- Use TweakUI

- Use the System Policy Editor

The next four sections discuss each of these techniques.

Moving Control Panel Files

Watch Out!
Don't try to move a .cpl file while the Control Panel is open. If you do, Windows 98 may display an error message telling you the file is in use.

To remove a Control Panel icon, the most obvious point of attack is simply to take the appropriate .cpl file out of the `Windows\System` folder. That way, when Windows 98 scours the `System` folder for .cpl files, it won't find the moved file and it won't display the icon. Since you never know when you might need the icon again in the future, don't delete the .cpl file. Instead, I recommend creating a subfolder within the `System` folder (named, say, `CplBackup`) and moving the unwanted .cpl files into that subfolder.

Customizing with `Control.ini`

Rather than messing with the .cpl files directly, you can prevent an icon from appearing in the `Control Panel` folder by modifying the file `Control.ini`. Here's how it's done:

1. Select Start, Run, type `control.ini` in the Run dialog box, and then click OK. This opens the file in Notepad.

2. Scroll down until you come to the section named `[don't load]`.

3. Directly under that section name, type the name of the `.cpl` file for the icon you want to hide, followed by `=no`. For example, to hide the Telephony icon, you'd add the following line:

   `telephon.cpl=no`

4. Save the file and exit Notepad.

5. If the Control Panel is already open, switch to it and press F5 to update the icons. (Note that you may need to press F5 twice to refresh the icons completely.)

You might think that changing a `[don't load]` value in `Control.ini` from `no` to `yes` would display the icon once again. Unfortunately, that's not the case. Instead, you either have to delete the line completely, or else "comment out" the line by adding a semicolon (;) at the beginning.

For example, Windows 98 does not automatically detect non-Plug-and-Play scanners or digital cameras, and it doesn't display the Scanners and Cameras Control Panel icon by default. However, you can use this icon to run the Scanner and Camera Installation Wizard and tell Windows 98 about your scanner or camera. How do you get around this "buried shovel" situation? By forcing Windows 98 to display the Scanners and Cameras icon. To do this, comment out the `sticpl.cpl` line in `Control.ini`, like so:

`;sticpl.cpl=no`

Customizing Control Panel with TweakUI

Perhaps the easiest way to hide and display Control Panel icons is to use TweakUI. As you can see in Figure 7.2, TweakUI's Control Panel tab offers check boxes for each `.cpl` file. Activate a check box to display the icon; deactivate a check box to hide the icon.

> 66
> **Buried shovel,**
> *noun*: A tool that is required to perform a certain task, but that is only available after you perform that task.
> —The Word Spy
> (http://www.mcfedries.com/WordSpy/)
> 99

Figure 7.2
Use TweakUI's
Control Panel tab
to toggle Control
Panel icons on
and off.

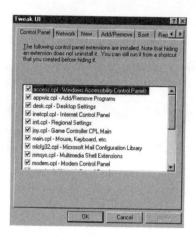

Customizing Control Panel with the System Policy Editor

The System Policy Editor enables you not only to hide and display Control Panel icons, but also to customize the dialog boxes that are displayed by several of the icons. Specifically, you can hide one or more dialog box tabs.

To see how this works, follow these steps:

1. Select Start, Programs, Accessories, System Tools, System Policy Editor.

2. Run the File, Open Registry command to load the Registry.

3. Open the Local User icon and select Windows 98 System, Control Panel. This branch contains five sub-branches that correspond to five Control Panel icons: Display, Network, Passwords, Printers, and System.

4. Open the sub-branch you want to work with, and then activate the check box. For example, if you want to work with the Display icon, open the Display branch and activate the Restrict Display Control Panel check box, as shown in Figure 7.3.

5. To hide the icon in Control Panel, activate the Disable icon Control Panel check box, where icon is the name of the icon (for example, Disable Display Control Panel).

Figure 7.3
The Control Panel branch enables you to set up restrictions for several Control Panel icons.

6. To hide a tab within the icon's dialog box, activate the appropriate Hide *tab* page check box, where *tab* is the name of the dialog box tab (for example, Hide Background page).

7. When you're done, click OK.

8. Select File, Save to put the settings into effect.

If you elected to hide certain dialog box tabs, the settings for this are stored in the following Registry key:

```
HKEY_CURRENT_USER\Software\Microsoft\Windows\Current
Version\Policies\System
```

Each hidden tab is represented by a setting that has a DWORD value of 1. For example, if you hide the Background tab in the Display Properties dialog box, a setting named NoDispBackgroundPage is added to this key. You can reinstate the tab by setting this value to 0 (or, of course, by using the System Policy Editor).

Control Panel and the Registry

You saw in the previous section that the Registry plays a hand in hiding individual tabs from the Control Panel icon dialog boxes. The Registry and the Control Panel have other ties, as well, and I'll tell you about them in this section.

Windows 98 settings that can be modified via the Control Panel are scattered throughout the Registry. However, one location in particular stores almost all of the interface customizations you'll be working with in the next couple of chapters. That location is the following Registry key:

`HKEY_CURRENT_USER\Control Panel\`

This key can contain up to eight subkeys (the exact number you see depends on your system configuration):

Accessibility: This subkey stores the settings from Control Panel's Accessibility icon.

Appearance: This subkey stores the settings from Control Panel's Display icon. In particular, it deals with the various interface appearance schemes that you can work with in the Appearance tab of the Display Properties dialog box.

Colors: This subkey stores the settings from Control Panel's Display icon. It tracks the colors you can apply to various Windows 98 interface components in the Appearance tab of the Display Properties dialog box. (This subkey only appears if you've made changes to the colors.)

Cursors: This subkey stores the settings from Control Panel's Mouse icon. It tracks and lists the mouse pointer scheme, as specified in the Pointers tab of the Mouse Properties dialog box.

Desktop: This subkey stores the settings from Control Panel's Display icon. It deals with the desktop-related settings from the Background and Effects tabs of the Display Properties dialog box.

Infrared: This subkey stores the settings from Control Panel's Infrared icon.

International: This subkey stores the settings from Control Panel's Regional Settings icon.

PowerCfg: This subkey stores the settings from Control Panel's Power Management icon.

Besides the storage of settings, the Registry also contains data about the Control Panel ActiveX control itself. Here's the key to look for:

```
HKEY_CLASSES_ROOT\CLSID\{21EC2020-3AEA-1069-A2DD-
08002B30309D}
```

Easier Access to the Control Panel

The Control Panel is certainly a useful and important piece of the Windows 98 package. It's even more useful if you can get to it easily. I'll close this chapter by looking at a few methods for gaining quick access to individual icons and the entire folder.

Alternative Methods for Opening Control Panel Icons

Access to many Control Panel icons is scattered throughout the Windows 98 interface, meaning that there's more than one way to skin a Control Panel cat. Many of these methods are faster and more direct than using the Control Panel folder. Here's a summary:

Inside Scoop
The CLSID key contains a long list of subkeys that are all 16-byte (32-digit hexadecimal) values. These are the *class IDs* for all the registered ActiveX objects, and they're unique (hence they're also known as Globally Unique Identifiers, or GUIDs).

 Date/Time: Double-click the clock in the taskbar's system tray.

 Display: Right-click the desktop and then click Properties.

 Fonts: In Windows Explorer, select the Windows\Fonts folder.

 Infrared: Double-click the Infrared icon in the taskbar's system tray.

 Internet: In Internet Explorer, select View, Internet Options.

 Modems: Available through various Windows 98 components, including Dial-Up Networking, HyperTerminal, and Device Manager.

 Network: Right-click the desktop's Network Neighborhood icon and then click Properties.

 PC Card (PCMCIA): Double-click the PC Card icon in the taskbar's system tray.

 Power Management: Right-click the Power Meter icon in the taskbar's system tray.

Printers: Select Start, Settings, Printers. Alternatively, in Windows Explorer, select the Printers folder.

 System: Right-click the desktop's My Computer icon and then click Properties.

Putting the Control Panel on the Taskbar

For one-click access to the icons, create a new Control Panel taskbar toolbar by following these steps:

Shortcut
With the icon titles turned off, you may forget what a particular icon represents. To find out, move your mouse pointer over the icon. After a second or two, the icon title appears inside a banner (see Figure 7.4).

1. Right-click an empty section of the taskbar and then click Toolbars, New Toolbar. The New Toolbar dialog box appears.

2. Select Control Panel and then click OK.

3. To fit all the Control Panel icons on your screen, turn off the icon titles by right-clicking the left end of the Control Panel taskbar (where the Control Panel title appears) and then clicking Show Text to deactivate it.

4. Drag the top of the toolbar up one notch to double the size of the taskbar. Your taskbar should now look something like the one shown in Figure 7.4.

Figure 7.4
The Windows 98 taskbar with a new toolbar of Control Panel icons.

Putting the Control Panel on the Start Menu

You can add individual Control Panel icons to the Start menu by following these steps:

1. Open the Control Panel folder.

2. Drag the icon you want and hover it over the Start button. After a second or two, the Start menu appears.

3. Drag the icon into the Start menu and drop it where you want the icon to appear.

4. When Windows 98 asks if you want to create a shortcut, click Yes.

Rather than putting individual icons on the Start menu, you might prefer to add the entire Control Panel. Unfortunately, dragging the `Control Panel` folder onto the Start menu will only create a shortcut to the folder. What you really want is to be able to open a submenu that contains all the Control Panel icons. To create this submenu, follow these steps:

1. In Windows Explorer, open the `Windows\Start Menu` folder.

2. Select File, New, Folder.

3. Give the new folder the following name:

   `Control Panel.{21EC2020-3AEA-1069-A2DD-08002B30309D}`

   `{21EC2020-3AEA-1069-A2DD-08002B30309D}` is the class ID for Control Panel, as defined in the Registry. By specifying this value as part of the folder name (the text before the period can be whatever you want), you're telling Windows 98 that you want to use the Control Panel ActiveX component. As you can see in Figure 7.5, this procedure produces a true submenu that displays each Control Panel icon.

Remember
You don't have to put your shortcut icons on the Start menu. You can drag-and-drop Control Panel icons to other areas of Windows 98, including the desktop.

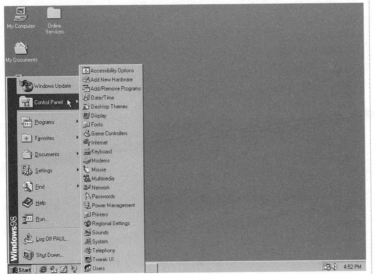

Figure 7.5
The Start menu with a submenu of Control Panel icons.

Essential Information

- The Control Panel is a special Windows 98 system folder that stores numerous icons for customizing and tweaking hardware, software, the Windows 98 interface, and more.

- Select Start, Settings, Control Panel to open the Control Panel folder. You can also view this folder from within Windows Explorer.

- Each Control Panel icon is generated by a .cpl file in the Windows\System folder.

- You can hide Control Panel icons by moving the .cpl files, editing Control.ini, or by using either TweakUI or the System Policy Editor.

- You can display the Control Panel icons on the taskbar. To get a cascade menu of Control Panel icons on the Start menu, create a new folder that uses Control Panel's class ID.

GET THE SCOOP ON...
Web integration and the Windows 98 interface ▪
Specifying custom Web integration settings ▪
Displaying folders as Web pages ▪ The Active Desktop

An In-Depth Look at Web Integration and the Active Desktop

Chapter 8

ONE OF WINDOWS 98's most talked about (and most controversial) innovations is the integration of Internet technologies within the operating system. In particular, Windows 98 incorporates many of the technologies and techniques used on the World Wide Web. Hence the name *Web integration* for these innovations.

Web integration isn't the sea change that many pundits (and Microsoft marketers) make it out to be. Overall, it represents a relatively minor update to the existing user interface. That's not to say that Web integration should be ignored, far from it. This may be a minor interface course correction, but the new direction is a definite improvement over the tired desktop metaphor that has dominated the Windows interface ever since version 3.0.

To get excited about Web integration, and to truly appreciate this new direction, you have to go "under the hood" and take an in-depth look at how Web integration works. Once you understand the inner workings of this technology, you'll be able to use it in powerful new ways that go well beyond the "authorized" uses prescribed by Microsoft. This chapter shows you everything you need to know.

How Does Web Integration Change Windows 98?

Before diving in, let's run through a short glossary of terms that you'll need to know when working with Web integration:

Background image: In a Web page, an image that is tiled to cover the entire window and serves as a background for the page text and graphics.

HTML (HyperText Markup Language): The collection of codes that's used to structure and format a Web page. HTML consists of a series of *tags* that define links, page formatting, graphics, and more.

Hypertext: Text that's defined as a *link*.

Java: A programming language designed to create small programs called "applets" that run inside a Web page.

JavaScript: A scaled-down version of Java that's used to create "scripts" that are embedded within a Web page. These scripts add limited programming constructs to the page.

Link: A word or phrase that, when clicked, sends the user to a different Web page or to a different location on the same Web page.

Tag: An element of HTML that defines a specific Web page object or format. Each tag is surrounded by angle brackets (< and >). For example, the tag for bolding is <B>. Most tags have a corresponding end tag that closes the tag. For example, the end tag for <B> is </B>. Here's an example:p

```
<B>This text appears in bold.</B>
```

URL (Uniform Resource Locator): An address that specifies the location of a resource on the Internet. Most URLs use the following general format:

```
protocol://host.domain/directory/file.name
```

protocol   The TCP/IP protocol to use for retrieving the resource. Web pages use http.

Remember
You need to be familiar with HTML in order to get the most out of Web integration. If you're looking for an HTML tutorial, may I humbly suggest my book *The Complete Idiot's Guide to Creating an HTML 4 Web Page*. You can find out more about the book from my Web site (http://www.mcfe dries.com/).

host.domain	The domain name of the host computer that stores the resource.
directory	The host computer directory that contains the resource.
file.name	The filename of the resource.
Web browser:	A program designed to display and navigate pages on the World Wide Web.
Web page:	A World Wide Web document, constructed using *HTML tags*.
Web server:	A server program that processes Web page requests from a Web browser. Also, the computer that runs the Web server program.
Web site:	A collection of related *Web pages*.

With these concepts in mind, let's examine the specific ways that Web integration alters the lay of the Windows land.

"Clickable" Windows objects look like Web page links: In most Web pages, links have the following characteristics:

- The link text appears underlined.

- When you position the mouse over a link, the mouse pointer changes to a small hand with a pointing finger.

Figure 8.1 shows a simple Web page with a link and the changed mouse pointer.

You get the same effect with Web integration: icon titles and filenames are underlined, and the mouse pointer changes to a hand when positioned over an icon or filename.

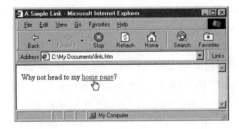

Figure 8.1
In a Web page, links are underlined and the mouse pointer for a link is a hand with a pointing finger.

Watch Out!
Until you get used to the new single-click metaphor (which doesn't take long), you'll occasionally lapse into the old ways and try to select an object by clicking it. This, of course, launches the object, which can have disastrous consequences. For example, if you accidentally launch a registration (.reg) file, it will update the Windows 98 Registry, which could lead to problems.

You now single-click to launch icons and programs: Web page links require just a single-click to activate them, and Web integration brings the same idea to Windows 98. That is, you can launch icons and files by single-clicking them instead of the usual double-clicking required in the classic Windows interface.

You now select objects by hovering the mouse over them: As you saw in Chapter 6, "Expert Windows Explorer Techniques," you normally select an object by clicking it. With Web integration turned on, you select an object by positioning the mouse pointer over the object for a second or two (this is called *hovering* over the object). See Chapter 6 for the details on selecting multiple files with this new technique.

You can navigate folders as you do Web pages: A Web browser keeps a list of the pages you've visited and enables you to retrace your steps by offering Back and Forward buttons. Windows 98's folder windows also have Back and Forward buttons that operate the same way. As you can see in Figure 8.2, you can drop down the buttons to jump quickly to any folder you've visited.

Figure 8.2
Drop down the Back and Forward buttons to navigate to a folder you've visited in the current Windows Explorer session.

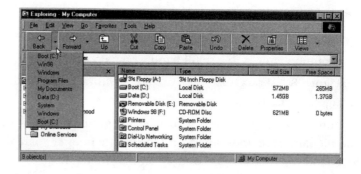

See Also...
"Selecting Files and Folders," p. 155

You can display folder contents within a local Web page: Windows 98's folders have a new *Web view* that displays the folder contents within a Web page structure. The Web view creates a new margin to the left of the contents and, when you select an object, this margin displays some information about the object. As you can see in Figure 8.3, this *information panel* also displays a thumbnail image for certain files, particularly graphics, HTML documents, and some Microsoft Office documents. (Figure 8.3 also points out a few other features of the information panel that you'll be dealing with later in this chapter.)

Folder icon   Folder name   Horizontal line

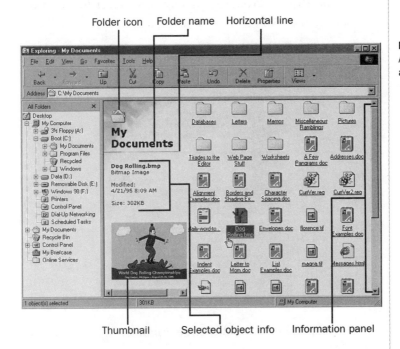

Figure 8.3
A folder viewed as a Web page.

Thumbnail   Selected object info   Information panel

You can activate the Active Desktop: The new Active Desktop enables you to display "wallpaper" that's really a Web page, and to place Web page objects (such as Java applets) on the desktop.

Toggling Web Integration On and Off

Some Web integration features are available full-time in Windows 98. These include using the Back and Forward buttons to navigate folders and the ability to display a folder as a Web page. The rest of the Web integration features—objects that appear as links, single-click launching, and no-click selecting—have to be activated.

To turn Web integration on, display the Folder Options dialog box by using any of the following techniques:

Remember
To open the Display Properties dialog box, either launch the Control Panel's Display icon, or right-click the desktop and then click Properties.

- Select Start, Settings, Folder Options.

- In any folder window (such as Windows Explorer or Control Panel), select View, Folder Options.

- In the Display Properties dialog box, select the Web tab and then click Folder Options.

Figure 8.4 shows the dialog box that appears.

Figure 8.4
Use the Folder Options dialog box to turn on Web integration and set some Web integration options.

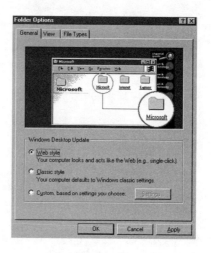

See Also...
"Turning the Active Desktop Into a Web Page," p. 224

The General tab provides three options:

Web style: Select this option to activate all the Web integration features. It also turns on the Active Desktop and, in some cases, displays the default Windows 98 Web page wallpaper. More on this later in this chapter.

Classic style: Select this option to use the old Windows 95 interface.

Custom, based on the settings you choose: Select this option to turn specific Web integration features on and off and to customize those features (see the next section).

If you activate Web style and click OK, Windows 98 displays the Single-click dialog box asking if you want to use the single-click technique. Select Yes or No, and then click OK.

Setting Web Integration Options

To gain some measure of control over the Web integration features, activate the Custom, based on the settings you choose option in the Folder Options dialog box. This enables the Settings button, and clicking this button displays the Custom Settings dialog box. This section presents a survey of the settings in this dialog box.

The options in the Active Desktop group toggle the Active Desktop on and off. I'll discuss these options later in this chapter.

See Also...
"Working with the Active Desktop,"
p. 220

When you click a link in a Web page, the new page usually opens in the same browser window. The two options in the Browse folders as follows group determine whether a new window appears when you navigate folders in Windows 98:

Open each folder in the same window: If you activate this option, each time you click a folder the new folder opens in the same window.

Open each folder in its own window: If you activate this option, each time you click a folder the new folder appears in a separate window.

The options in the View Web content in folders group determine when Windows 98 displays a folder in Web view:

See Also...
"Activating the Web View," p. 206

For all folders with HTML content: If you activate this option, Windows 98 uses the Web view automatically for every folder.

Only for folders where I select "as Web Page" (View menu): If you activate this option, you have to turn on the Web view by hand, as explained later in this chapter.

The options in the Click items as follows group determine how you launch and select icons and files:

Single-click to open an item (point to select): If you activate this option, Windows 98 accepts single-clicks to launch objects, and hovering to select objects. You also get two ways to determine how Windows 98 underlines objects:

See Also...
"Internet Explorer's
Advanced
Options," p. 455

Underline icon titles consistent with my browser settings: If you activate this option, Windows 98 underlines icon and file links the same way that Internet Explorer is set up to underline Web page links. I tell you how to control Internet Explorer underlining in Chapter 19, "Expert Internet Explorer Techniques."

Underline icon titles only when I point at them: If you activate this option, Windows 98 only underlines an object when you point at it.

Double-click to open an item (single-click to select): If you activate this option, Windows 98 accepts double-clicks to launch objects, and single-clicks to select objects.

Inside Scoop
I suggest that you select the Underline icon titles consistent with my browser settings option. This will give you a strong visual clue that single-clicking is activated, so you'll be less likely to launch icons and files accidentally.

Viewing Folders As Web Pages

The most customizable—and therefore the most powerful—aspect of Web integration is the Web view for folders. The following sections run through some Web view basics, and then take you beyond the basics by looking at the technology that makes Web view work.

Activating the Web View

If you're running Windows 98 using the "classic" style, or if you activated the `Only for folders where I select "as Web Page"` (`View menu`) option in the Custom Settings dialog box, you have to turn on the Web view by hand. Windows 98 gives you a couple of ways to do this:

- Select the View, as Web Page command.

- Drop down the Views toolbar button and then click as Web Page.

Shortcut
You can also activate the Web view by right-clicking an empty section of the folder and then selecting View, as Web page.

The Web view will typically look something like the folder shown earlier in Figure 8.3. However, if the window is too small (less than 400 pixels wide), Windows 98 will display a Web view variation that shows only the folder title at the top, as shown in

Figure 8.5. (This is called the *mini banner* view.) To get the standard (and more useful) Web view, widen the window until the mini banner disappears.

Mini banner

Figure 8.5
Windows 98 displays this version of the Web view when the window is too small.

Creating a Custom Web View Background

Windows 98 only gives you a single "authorized" method for customizing the Web view: specifying a background image. Here are some things to keep in mind:

- When you set a background for a folder's Web view, all the icons and filenames are displayed on this background.

- The background affects only the Contents list. It doesn't change the background of the information panel that runs down the left side of the Web view.

- If your image is smaller than the Contents list, Windows 98 tiles the image so that it covers the entire list.

- Using the default Windows 98 method, you can only specify a background for one folder at a time.

  Here's how it works:

1. Open the folder you want to work with.

2. Select View, Customize this Folder. The Customize this Folder Wizard appears.

3. Activate the Choose a background picture option, and then click Next.

Shortcut
You can also launch the Customize this Folder Wizard by right-clicking an empty section of the folder and then clicking Customize this Folder.

Watch Out!
Make sure the image you select doesn't hamper the readability of the folder text. For example, a dark image may make it impossible to read black filenames or icon titles. Note, however, that you can also change the color of the text (see step 5).

4. In the dialog box that appears, select the image you want to use as the background by using either of the following methods:

   • Highlight an item in the Background picture for this folder list (see Figure 8.6).

   • Click Browse and use the Open dialog box to choose the image file you want to use. Note that you can select an image file on a network folder.

5. To change the color of the folder text, click the Text button, choose a color in the Color dialog box, and click OK.

6. To change the color of the text background, activate the Background check box and click the button beside it. Select a color in the Color dialog box and then click OK.

Figure 8.6
Select the image you want to use as the folder background.

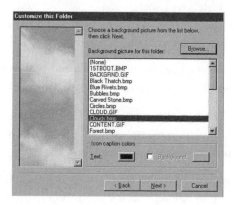

Undocumented
To create a solid-color background, use Paint to create a small image consisting only of the background color you want. Save this image into the Windows directory, and it will appear in the list of backgrounds displayed by the Customize this Folder Wizard.

7. Click Next. Windows 98 displays a summary of the choices you made.

8. Click Finish. Windows 98 applies the background and colors to the folder.

Windows 98 keeps track of the background image and text colors by means of a hidden file named Desktop.ini, which is stored within the folder.

The background is specified by an IconArea_Image line, as in this example:

```
IconArea_Image=C:\WINDOWS\Clouds.bmp
```

The text foreground and background colors are specified by the `IconArea_Text` and `IconArea_TextBackground` lines:

```
IconArea_Text=0x00rrggbb
IconArea_TextBackground=0x00rrggbb
```

For each value, *rrggbb* is an RGB color code where *rr* (the red component), *gg* (the green component), and *bb* (the blue component) are two-digit hexadecimal values between 00 and FF.

To remove the formatting from a folder, you have two choices:

- Select View, Customize this Folder, activate the `Remove customization` option, click Next, click Next again, and then click Finish.

- Delete the `Desktop.ini` file.

Understanding Web View Templates

Customizing the background and text within a folder is a step up from what you could do in Windows 95, but it's not particularly exciting or useful. The real meat of the Web view matter comes when you work with the underlying structure of the Web view. This structure comes in the form of *hypertext template* files, which use the `.htt` extension. This is a text file that contains references to special ActiveX controls for displaying folder-specific items such as the contents, the folder icon, and data about the highlighted object. The rest of the file is pure HTML and JavaScript, just like you'd see in a Web page. The beauty of this is that you can easily modify the template with your own tags and text to create a customized Web view.

There are three ways to go about this:

- Modify the `Windows\Web\Folder.htt` file. This is the default template that Windows 98 uses to display the Web view in most folders. If you modify this file, you customize the Web view for all of those folders at once.

- Select View, Customize this Folder, activate the `Create or edit an HTML document` option, and then click Next until `Folder.htt` is opened in Notepad. Bear in mind that this is

Inside Scoop
You might think that you can customize the background of another folder just by giving it a copy of the `Desktop.ini` file. That would be handy, but it doesn't work. Windows 98 won't apply the customization until you run the Customize this Folder Wizard. In any case, a better way to customize multiple folders is to use Web view templates, as discussed in the next few sections.

a copy of `Windows\Web\Folder.htt`. This copy will be saved in the folder and will override the default template to create a custom Web view for the folder.

- Modify one of the folder-specific templates that come with Windows 98:

  `Program Files\folder.htt`: The Web view template for the Program Files folder.

  `Windows\folder.htt`: The Web view template for the Windows folder.

  `Windows\System\folder.htt`: The Web view template for the Windows\System folder.

  `Windows\System32\folder.htt`: The Web view template for the Windows\System32 folder.

  `Windows\Web\Controlp.htt`: The Web view template for the Control Panel folder.

  `Windows\Web\Dialup.htt`: The Web view template for the Dial-Up Networking folder.

  `Windows\Web\Mycomp.htt`: The Web view template for the My Computer folder.

  `Windows\Web\Nethood.htt`: The Web view template for the Network Neighborhood folder.

  `Windows\Web\Printers.htt`: The Web view template for the Printers folder.

  `Windows\Web\Recycle.htt`: The Web view template for the Recycle Bin folder.

  `Windows\Web\Safemode.htt`: The Web view template displayed by the Active Desktop if an error occurs.

  `Windows\Web\Schedule.htt`: The Web view template for the Scheduled Tasks folder.

The Registry keeps track of the name of the folder where the default Web view is stored. Rather than modifying `Folder.htt`, you could create your own custom template file and then modify the Registry to point to your file.

Shortcut
It's best to work with the hypertext templates within Notepad. (You may be tempted to work with FrontPage Express, but it doesn't understand all of the elements in the templates.) To set up Notepad as the default application for .htt files, right-click any .htt file and then click Open With. In the Open With dialog box, use the list box to highlight NOTEPAD, activate the Always use this program to open this type of file check box, and then click OK.

The path and filename for the default folder template is stored in the `PersistMoniker` setting in the following Registry key, as shown in Figure 8.7:

```
HKEY_CLASSES_ROOT\Directory\shellex\ExtShellFolderView\
[ic:ccc]{5984FFE0-28D4-11CF-AE66-08002B2E1262}
```

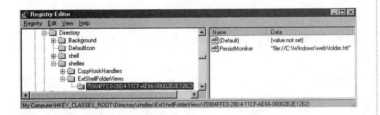

Figure 8.7
The Registry tracks the location and name of the default folder template.

Under the Hood: The Structure of a Web View Template

Before you can create your own custom Web view, you have to understand the structure of the hypertext templates. These files appear quite complex at first blush, but by breaking them down into their component parts, you'll see that understanding how they work isn't that difficult.

I'll use the default folder template—`Windows\Web\folder.htt`—as an example in this section. So that you can recover gracefully should something untoward happen to this file while you are editing it, I suggest making a copy of the file in another folder and then working on this copy until you're comfortable with the structure of the file.

The Web view templates, like all Web pages, are divided into two main areas:

Undocumented
The names and locations of the templates used with the Control Panel, the `Printers` folder, and the other folders listed earlier are also stored in the Registry. Run a search on the appropriate template name to find these settings.

The header: The first part of the template contains support data for displaying the Web view. This support data includes various "styles" that determine how the folder appears, and various JavaScript functions that are executed under different circumstances.

The body: The rest of the template contains the text, ActiveX control references, and HTML tags that govern what you see when the folder is in Web view.

The following two sections offer detailed discussions of each part of the template.

Understanding the Template Body

I'll begin with the body section since it's easier to understand and it's where you'll perform most of your customizing. To get to the body, scroll down until you see the following line:

```
<body scroll=no onload="Init()">
```

Figure 8.8 shows the first part of the body and points out a few interesting landmarks. Note that these correspond to the Web view features that I pointed out earlier in Figures 8.3 and 8.5.

Mini banner

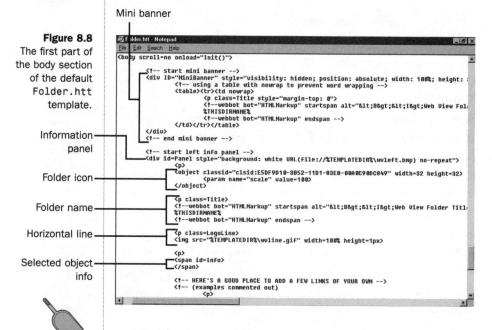

Figure 8.8
The first part of the body section of the default Folder.htt template.

Information panel

Folder icon

Folder name

Horizontal line

Selected object info

Here's a brief explanation of each part:

Mini banner: This is a banner that displays the name of the folder at the top of the Contents list if the window is less than 400 pixels wide (see Figure 8.5). The folder name is given by the %THISDIRNAME% environment variable. The banner is encompassed by a set of <div> and </div> tags named MiniBanner (ID="MiniBanner"). The <div> tag is used to divide a Web page into sections. As you'll see later, it's possible to hide entire sections.

Inside Scoop
In the <body> tag, the onload="Init()" part means that Windows 98 runs a JavaScript function named Init() whenever you open a folder. I'll talk about this and other JavaScript functions when I discuss the header section a bit later.

Information panel: This is the information panel that appears in the left margin if the window is at least 400 pixels wide. It's encompassed by a second set of `<div>` and `</div>` tags named `Panel` (ID=Panel).

Folder icon: This `<object>` tag is used to display the folder icon. You can eke out a bit more room in the information panel by either deleting the entire `<object></object>` construct, or preferably, by commenting it out.

Folder name: This section uses the `%THISDIRNAME%` environment variable to display the folder name. (You can ignore all the "webbot" tags that are scattered throughout the file. These are used for compatibility with the FrontPage and FrontPage Express HTML editors.)

Horizontal line: This `<img>` tag defines the horizontal line that appears below the folder name.

Selected object into: This `<span>` and `</span>` set marks the spot where the data on the currently selected object appears. For later use, note the name of this span is `Info` (id=Info).

Figure 8.9 shows the rest of the template body.

Once again, let's run through the particulars:

Insert links: You can insert links to local and remote resources here. See "Inserting Links to Local, Intranet, and Internet Resources," later in this chapter.

Thumbnail: This `<object>` tag (id=Thumbnail) represents the Thumbnail Viewer ActiveX control that displays thumbnails for images, Web pages, and other documents.

Status message: This `<div>` tag (id=Status) displays a status message while Windows 98 is generating the thumbnail.

ActiveMovie control: This `<div>` tag (id=Media) displays the ActiveMovie control, which can be used to play movies, sound files, and other media supported by ActiveMovie. Note that this feature is turned off by default.

Undocumented
You can use the `<div ID=Panel...>` tag to set up a custom background for the information panel. To do so, replace `%TEMPLATEDIR%\wvl eft.bmp` with the full path to the image you want to use. If you want the image to be tiled to cover the entire panel, delete the `no-repeat` attribute.

Remember
To comment out a section of HTML code, place `<!—` at the beginning and `—>` at the end.

Figure 8.9
The rest of the
body section of
the default
`Folder.htt` tem-
plate.

Status message　Thumbnail　Insert links

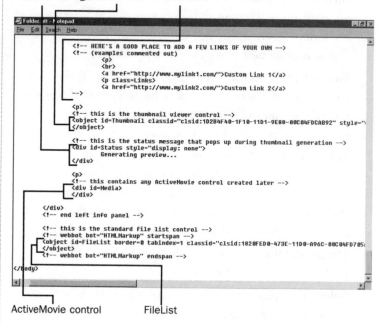

ActiveMovie control　　　　　FileList

Inside Scoop
To turn on the
ActiveMovie con-
trol feature, scroll
up near the top of
the file and
look for
the line `var`
`wantMedia`. Change
the value of this
variable from
`false` to `true`.

FileList: This `<object>` tag (id=FileList) displays the FileList ActiveX control, which displays the contents of the folder.

Understanding the Template Header

Now that you know the structure of the template body, you'll be able to understand what happens within the header. Most of the header consists of various JavaScript functions, so I won't go into as much detail.

Undocumented
Some templates
don't put the style
sheet inside the
`.htt` file. Instead,
they link to
an external style
sheet named
`webview.css`.
You find this text
file in the
`Windows\Web`
folder.

For starters, Figure 8.10 shows the top part of the header, and points out two main features:

Style sheet: The lines between the `<style>` and `</style>` tags define the styles used within the information panel. For example, the `body` line defines the default font as 8- or 10-point Verdana. You could customize this line to set a larger font size or a different typeface.

Variable declarations: These `var` lines declare and initial-ize a large number of variables used by the JavaScript functions.

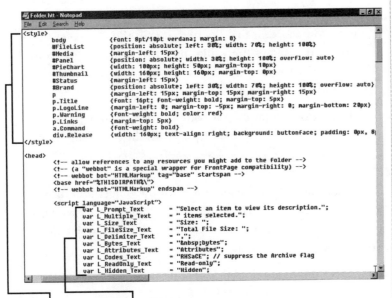

```
Folder.htt - Notepad                                                    _ B X
File  Edit  Search  Help
<style>
        body            {font: 8pt/10pt verdana; margin: 0}
        #FileList       {position: absolute; left: 30%; width: 70%; height: 100%}
        #Media          {margin-left: 15px}
        #Panel          {position: absolute; width: 30%; height: 100%; overflow: auto}
        #PieChart       {width: 100px; height: 50px; margin-top: 10px}
        #Thumbnail      {width: 160px; height: 160px; margin-top: 0px}
        #Status         {margin-left: 15px}
        #Brand          {position: absolute; left: 30%; width: 70%; height: 100%; overflow: auto}
        p               {margin-left: 15px; margin-top: 15px; margin-right: 15px}
        p.Title         {font: 16pt; font-weight: bold; margin-top: 5px}
        p.LogoLine      {margin-left: 0; margin-top: -5px; margin-right: 0; margin-bottom: 20px}
        p.Warning       {font-weight: bold; color: red}
        p.Links         {margin-top: 5px}
        a.Command       {font-weight: bold}
        div.Release     {width: 160px; text-align: right; background: buttonface; padding: 0px, 8
</style>

<head>
        <!-- allow references to any resources you might add to the Folder -->
        <!-- (a "webbot" is a special wrapper for FrontPage compatibility) -->
        <!-- webbot bot="HTMLMarkup" tag="base" startspan -->
        <base href="%THISDIRPATH%\">
        <!-- webbot bot="HTMLMarkup" endspan -->

        <script language="JavaScript">
                var L_Prompt_Text       = "Select an item to view its description.";
                var L_Multiple_Text     = " items selected.";
                var L_Size_Text         = "Size: ";
                var L_FileSize_Text     = "Total File Size: ";
                var L_Delimiter_Text    = " ,";
                var L_Bytes_Text        = " bytes";
                var L_Attributes_Text   = "Attributes";
                var L_Codes_Text        = "RHSaCE"; // suppress the Archive flag
                var L_ReadOnly_Text     = "Read-only";
                var L_Hidden_Text       = "Hidden";
```

└─ Style sheet   └─ Variable declarations

Figure 8.10
The top part of
the header section
of the default
Folder.htt
template.

The rest of the header is a series of JavaScript functions. Here's a summary of what each function does:

FixSize(): This function adjusts the size of the information panel each time the window is resized. In particular, it checks the width of the window and, if it's less than 400 pixels, the mini banner is displayed instead of the information panel. This is accomplished by setting the MiniBanner object's style.visibility property to visible, and by setting the Panel object's style.visibility property to hidden.

FormatNumber(): This function formats large numbers by inserting commas for the thousands separators. For example, this function formats 1000 as 1,000.

Properties(): This function displays an object's property sheet when you click the Attributes link in the information panel. (In other words, this is equivalent to right-clicking the object and then clicking Properties.) Note that the Attributes link only appears if the Show file attributes in Detail View check box is activated. (To see this check box, select View, Folder Options and then select the View tab.)

Undocumented
The width at which the mini banner is displayed is set by the threshold variable that's declared within the FixSize() function. This variable is initialized to 400. To force Windows 98 never to display the mini banner, change the value of the threshold variable to 0.

Inside Scoop
The `innerHTML` property represents all the text and HTML tags within an object. Therefore, in the `Init()` function, `Info.innerHTML` represents the text and tags within the `Info` object, which is the information panel.

`Init():` This function initializes the folder and is run when the folder is first opened. It calls the `FixSize()` function and displays the initial message in the information panel. For the latter, the `Info.innerHTML` property is set to the variable `L_Prompt_Text`.

The rest of the JavaScript code specifies handlers for various events. The first of these begins with the following line:

```
<script language="JavaScript" for="FileList"
event="SelectionChanged">
```

Recall that `FileList` is the name of the object that displays the folder's contents. Here, the event is `SelectionChanged`, so this routine runs every time you select a different object. Here are the basics of what happens:

1. To represent the folder, the code assigns the variable `fldr` to the `Folder` property of `FileList`.

2. The information panel is cleared: pending status messages are cancelled, thumbnails are hidden, and media players are removed.

3. The code assigns the variable `data` to the number of items selected.

4. What happens next depends on how many items are selected:

   • If nothing is selected, the information panel displays just the prompt text, and the code ends.

   • If multiple items are selected, the total size of the objects is calculated, the names of the objects are placed into the `text` string, and then all of this is displayed in the information panel. The code then stops.

   • If only one item is selected, the rest of the code executes.

5. The code assigns the variable `items` to the `SelectedItems().Item(0)` property of `FileList`. This represents the selected object.

6. The code uses different calls to the `GetDetailsOf` function to grab the object's name, file type, last modified date, file size, file attributes (if activated), and any extra data associated with the object. Each of these is appended to the `text` variable.

7. The line `innerHTML = text` displays the object's data in the information panel.

8. The ActiveMovie control is displayed if the selected object is a media file (and the `wantMedia` variable is set to `true`, as described earlier).

9. If necessary, a thumbnail for the file is generated.

The header closes with another event handler:

```
<script language="JavaScript" for="Thumbnail"
event="OnThumbnailReady">
```

This code displays the thumbnail after it has been generated.

Inserting Links to Local, Intranet, and Internet Resources

One of the most useful ways to customize a Web view template is to add links that appear within the information panel. You can enter links to other folders (local), network resources (intranet), or even the Internet.

Here's the general syntax for a link:

```
<A HREF="address">Link text</A>
```

Here, *address* is the local, network, or Internet address of the resource, and *Link text* is the text that you click.

Here are three examples that demonstrate links for local, intranet, and Internet resources:

```
<A HREF="C:\Windows\">A local link</A>
<A HREF="\\SERVER\Data\">An intranet link</A>
<A HREF="http://www.mcfedries.com/">An Internet link</A>
```

You can place these links anywhere within the body. The template suggests just below the `Info` object (see Figure 8.9), which is as good a place as any.

Note, too, that you can format all your links by adjusting the `p.Links` class in the header's style sheet. In my own template, I create some vertical room between each link by setting the `margin-top` style to 5 pixels, and I indent the links from the left by setting the `margin-left` style to 25 pixels:

```
p.Links   {margin-top: 5px; margin-left: 25px}
```

Here is the code I use for my links:

```
<P>
<B>Local Links:</B>
<P class=Links>
<A HREF="C:\Windows\">C:\Windows</A>
<P class=Links>
<A HREF="D:\Books\">D:\Books</A>
<P class=Links>
<A HREF="D:\Databases\">D:\Downloads</A>
<P>
<B>Network Links:</B>
<P class=Links>
<A HREF="\\ZEUS\htdocs\">HTDOCS on ZEUS</A>
<P class=Links>
<A HREF="\\ZEUS\D\Website\logs\">LOGS on ZEUS</A>
<P class=Links>
<A HREF="\\HERMES\figures\">FIGURES on HERMES</A>
<P>
<B>Internet Links:</B>
<P class=Links>
<A HREF="http://www.mcfedries.com/">Home</A>
<P class=Links>
<A HREF="http://www.mcfedries.com/WordSpy/">Word Spy</A>
<P class=Links>
<A HREF="http://www.mcp.com">Macmillan Computer
Publishing</A>
```

Figure 8.11 shows how they look in Web view.

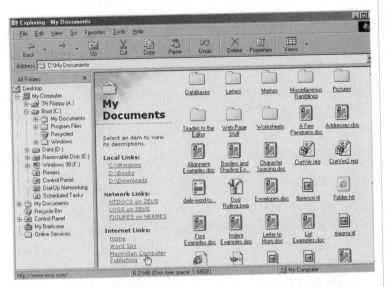

Figure 8.11
A customized Web view showing links to local, network, and Internet resources.

Disabling the Annoying "Show Files" Link

As you can see in Figure 8.12, when you open the Windows folder, Windows 98 doesn't display the contents. Instead, it displays a warning message about the possible negative consequences of modifying anything in this folder. It then presents a Show Files link that you must click in order to see the folder's contents. Note that the same thing occurs when you open the Windows\System folder.

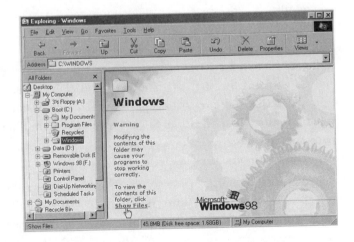

Figure 8.12
Windows 98 doesn't show the contents of the Windows folder automatically.

To get around this annoying extra step, follow this procedure:

1. Click Show Files to display the folder's contents.

2. Find the file Folder.htt and open it in Notepad. (Recall that both the Windows folder and the Windows\System folder have their own Folder.htt template.)

3. Scroll down to the Init() function.

4. Create a new line at the end of this function (that is, after the Info.innerHTML) line.

5. You now want to tell Windows 98 to run the ShowFiles() function. This is a special function that's called when you click the Show Files link. On the new line you created, add the following statement:

   ShowFiles();

6. Save the file and exit Notepad.

Working with the Active Desktop

Some wag once defined confidence as "being wrong at the top of your voice." If that's true, then Wired Magazine is confident, indeed. Their March, 1997 issue displayed "PUSH!" in Second Coming type on the front cover, and told readers to "Kiss your browser goodbye." Why? Because push technology—data sent to your desktop rather than you going out to the Internet to "pull" it in—was going to be the Next Big Thing. However, people just didn't buy into the hype. The content was never that good, the technology couldn't do what its champions had claimed, and most people despised the very concept of pushed data because it just felt too much like television. So, as I write this more than two years later, push is effectively dead, its bandwagon just about out of gas and with only a few diehards on board.

One of those diehards is Microsoft, as evidenced by the push technology they built into Windows 98's new Active Desktop. The technology is a series of *channels* that display pushed content from the likes of Disney, MSNBC, and PointCast. However, I think it's safe to say that these channels are easily the most ignored of the new Windows 98 features thanks to their lame content, confusing implementation, and unappealing push model.

So what about the rest of the Active Desktop? Well, again, Microsoft just didn't think things through. The idea behind the non-push part of the Active Desktop is to get away from the static, do-nothing desktop of Windows 95. In its place, the Active Desktop offers a three-tiered replacement:

- The top level contains the regular desktop icons, such as My Computer and the Recycle Bin.

- The middle level is the *desktop items layer*. You use this layer to display dynamic content on the desktop. Possible items include Web pages, images, Java applets, ActiveX controls, and more.

- The bottom level is the *HTML desktop background layer*. This level replaces the wallpaper with an HTML document that can display anything that would normally be available in a Web page.

This all sounds interesting, but it requires that your desktop be visible. However, most users—power users in particular—cover their desktop either with multiple open windows or with maximized windows. (In its defense, Microsoft did give users an easy route to the desktop by including a new Show Desktop icon in the Quick Launch toolbar.) Not only that, but the Active Desktop tends to eat a lot of system resources, and, at least in my experience, isn't particularly robust. (Hence, as mentioned earlier, the need for the "safe mode" folder template—Safemode.htt—that displays if the Active Desktop crashes.)

That's not to say that the Active Desktop should be written off completely. It does have a few interesting technical aspects, it runs well on systems with lots of memory (at least 64MB), and keeping an eye on the desktop might not be a problem for users who are running multiple monitors or who have a large monitor running at high resolution. If you fall into any of these categories, the rest of this chapter shows you how to get the most out of the Active Desktop.

> **“**
> Active Desktop was supposed to be one of the coolest and widely used new features of Internet Explorer 4.0 and Windows 98. But today, almost nobody uses it.
> —Mike Elgan, Windows Magazine
> **”**

Turning the Active Desktop On and Off

The Active Desktop is on by default after you install Windows 98. Here are the techniques to use to toggle the Active Desktop on and off:

- Right-click the desktop, and then click Active Desktop, View As Web Page.

- Select Start, Settings, Active Desktop, View As Web Page.

- Open Control Panel's Display icon, select the Web tab, and then toggle the View my Active Desktop as a web page check box.

Shortcut
You can jump directly to the Web tab by selecting Start, Settings, Active Desktop, Customize my Desktop. You can also right-click the desktop, and then click Active Desktop, Customize my Desktop.

Working with Desktop Items

The desktop items layer is actually a stripped-down Web browser. (Technically, it's an ActiveX control called *WebBrowser.*) This means that you can set up the desktop items layer with all types of Web page content. Here's how to get started:

1. Select Start, Settings, Active Desktop, Customize my Desktop. The Display Properties dialog box appears with the Web tab displayed.

2. Click New. Windows 98 asks if you want to connect to the Active Desktop Gallery Web site.

3. You now have two choices.

    - If you want to connect to the Gallery, click Yes. In this case, Windows 98 starts Internet Explorer and displays the Web site. Once you've found an item you want, click the Add to Active Desktop button. In the dialog box that appears, click OK.

    - If you'd prefer to specify your own content, click No. In this case, Windows 98 displays the New Active Desktop Item dialog box. Enter the address of the HTML document that contains the resource you want to add, and then click OK.

The items you add are displayed in the Web tab of the Display Properties dialog box, as shown in Figure 8.13. Use the following techniques to work with these items:

- To remove an item from the Active Desktop, deactivate its check box.

- To delete an item, highlight it and click Delete.

- If an item has properties, you can view them by highlighting the item and clicking Properties.

- To return the Active Desktop to its default state, click Reset All and then click Yes when Windows 98 asks if you're sure.

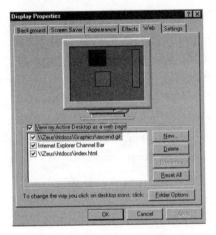

Figure 8.13
The Web tab keeps tracks of your desktop items.

Undocumented
If you want to add a Java applet to the Active Desktop, place the appropriate <APPLET> tag inside an HTML document (you don't need anything else inside this file). Then use the New Active Desktop Item dialog box to choose that document.

You can also work with the desktop items directly. When you position the mouse pointer over a desktop item, a border appears around the item. When you move the mouse pointer to the top of the item, a larger bar appears on top of the item. Given this, you can use these techniques to work with the item:

- To resize the item, drag its border.

- To move the item, drag the top bar.

- To display the item's Control menu, click the arrow that appears on the left side of the top bar.

- To remove the item from the desktop, click the Close button that appears on the right side of the top bar.

Turning the Active Desktop Into a Web Page

As I mentioned earlier, the HTML desktop background layer enables you to convert the desktop into a Web page. Here's how it's done:

1. Right-click the desktop and then click Properties to get the Display Properties dialog box onscreen.

2. Make sure the Background tab is selected.

3. In the Wallpaper list, select Windows98.

4. Click OK. If the Active Desktop is not currently activated, Windows 98 asks if you want to enable it.

5. Click Yes.

The "wallpaper" you selected is actually an HTML document named Windows98.htm, which you'll find in the Windows\Web\Wallpaper folder. Feel free to edit the document to customize the default Active Desktop wallpaper.

Alternatively, you may prefer to create your own HTML document and use it as your Active Desktop wallpaper. Here are a few things to keep in mind when designing your wallpaper:

Shortcut
Rather than working around the regular desktop icons, you may prefer to turn them off while the desktop is displayed as a Web page. To do this, select Start, Settings, Folder Options, display the View tab, and then activate the Hide icons when desktop is viewed as Web page check box.

- Make sure any elements in your HTML document won't be hidden behind the regular desktop icons.

- You can't scroll the wallpaper, so make sure the layout of the HTML document fits inside your desktop.

- Your HTML document must reside either on your hard disk or on a network drive. You can't use Internet pages.

- When specifying images and other elements, use items either on your hard disk or on your network. Again, Internet-based items are not allowed.

Once your page is ready, follow these steps to set it as your Active Desktop wallpaper:

1. Right-click the desktop and then click Properties to get the Display Properties dialog box onscreen.

2. Make sure the Background tab is selected.

3. Click Browse to display the Browse dialog box.

4. Select your HTML document and then click Open.

5. Click OK. If the Active Desktop is not currently activated, Windows 98 asks if you want to enable it.

6. Click Yes.

Shortcut
You'll be able to select your HTML document directly from the Wallpaper list if you place the file in the Windows\ Web\Wallpaper folder.

Essential Information

- Web integration displays objects as links, and it enables you to launch objects by single-clicking, and select objects by hovering.

- To turn on Web integration, select Start, Settings, Folder Options and activate the Web style option.

- Select View, as Web Page to display a folder in Web view.

- Customize the .htt folder template files to set up Web view to your liking.

- Right-click the desktop and then select Active Desktop, View As Web Page to turn on the Active Desktop.

GET THE SCOOP ON...
Advanced desktop customizing ▪ Saving your desktop
settings ▪ Methods for reconstructing the Start menu ▪
Moving, sizing, and customizing the taskbar ▪ Working
with user profiles

Customizing the Windows 98 Interface

MICROSOFT READILY ADMITS to a sense of "ownership" when it comes to the look and feel of the Windows 98 interface, which explains why they refuse to let computer manufacturers implement custom desktops on the machines they sell. This sense of ownership probably also explains why Microsoft doesn't supply users with all that much information about customizing.

What's weird about this is that Microsoft loaded Windows 98 with a large number of customization features. Whether you want to customize the desktop, the Start menu, the taskbar, or the look of everything from window menu bars to icon title text, Windows 98 has what you need to get the job done. And if you dig a little deeper, tools such as the Registry, the System Policy Editor, and Tweak UI enable you to customize system icons and other "built-in" components. This chapter introduces you to Windows 98's basic customizing features, and then pulls out the heavy artillery for some truly "unauthorized" customizing.

Changing an Icon

In several places in this chapter, and in other places throughout this book, you'll customize an object by changing its icon. So I'll begin this chapter by showing you the generic steps for selecting a different icon.

227

How you get started will depend on the object you're working with. However, in all cases you'll eventually end up at the Change Icon dialog box shown in Figure 9.1. Here are some notes about working with this dialog box:

- In Windows 98, icons are usually stored within executable files, particularly .exe and .dll files. Files with the .ico extension are pure icon files.

- If the icon you want isn't displayed in the Change Icon dialog box, use the File Name text box to enter the name of an icon file and then press Tab. Here are a few suggestions:

  C:\Windows\System\Shell32.dll

  C:\Windows\System\Pifmgr.dll

  C:\Windows\System\User.exe

  C:\Windows\Explorer.exe

  C:\Windows\Moricons.dll

  C:\Windows\Progman.exe

- If you're not sure about which file to try, click the Browse button and choose a file in the dialog box that appears.

Click the icon you want to use and then click OK.

Undocumented
To use a bitmap image (.bmp) file as an icon, change the file's extension to .ico. (You might want to make a copy of the .bmp file first.) Windows automatically resizes the image to the appropriate size for an icon and reformats the image to 16 colors.

Figure 9.1
The Change Icon dialog box lists the icons that are available in an executable or icon file.

In some cases, especially when you're working within the Registry, you'll need to know the *icon number* that an icon uses within an executable or icon file. To figure this out, use the

Change Icon dialog box to open the executable or icon file. Now count the icons, as follows:

- The first icon (the one in the upper-left corner) is 0.

- If the file contains more than four icons, they'll be displayed in columns. Be sure to count down each column and work your way across the columns. For example, the first icon in the second column will be icon 4.

Shortcut
An often faster method for getting to the Display Properties dialog box is to right-click an empty section of the desktop and then click Properties.

More Than Just Wallpaper: Customizing the Desktop

Let's now examine a few methods for customizing the desktop. Most of the standard Windows 98 methods for touching up the desktop are very straightforward, so I'll only include brief descriptions of them so that I can concentrate on more powerful methods.

A Quick Look at Windows 98's Display Settings

Most of Windows 98's basic desktop customizing happens within the Display Properties dialog box, shown in Figure 9.2. To get this dialog box onscreen, open the Control Panel and then launch the Display icon.

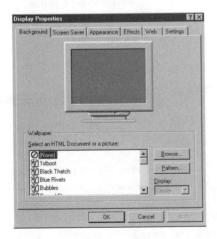

Figure 9.2
Use the various tabs in the Display Properties dialog box to customize the desktop and a few other Windows 98 interface features.

Here's a brief summary of the kinds of customizations you can perform with each tab:

Background: Use the Wallpaper list to select a wallpaper pattern to sit on the desktop. Note that most wallpaper files are only small squares, so you need to select Tile in the Display list in order to cover the entire desktop. For a larger image that doesn't quite fit the desktop, try selecting Stretch in the Display list.

As an alternative to wallpaper, click Pattern to cover the desktop with a pattern.

Screen Saver: Use the Screen Saver list to select an animated screen saver pattern that will appear after your system has been idle for a specified amount of time. After you've chosen a screen saver, the following controls become active:

Settings: Click this button to customize the screen saver.

Preview: Click this button to get a full-screen preview of the screen saver.

Password protected: If you activate this check box, the screen saver won't exit to the desktop unless you enter the correct password. Click Change to set the password.

Wait: Use this spin box to set the number of minutes your computer must be idle (no keyboard or mouse input) before the screen saver kicks in.

Your Screen Saver tab may also have a group named Energy saving features of monitor. I'll discuss power management for monitors in Chapter 24, "Maximizing Multimedia Hardware."

Appearance: Use this tab to customize the colors and fonts that Windows 98 uses. You have two ways to proceed:

- To use one of Windows 98's predefined color schemes, select an item from the Scheme list.

- To create your own scheme, select objects from the Item list and use the rest of the controls to set the size, color, and font of the object.

Watch Out!
Almost every video-related problem I've had with every version of Windows I've ever worked with has been screen saver-related. There is just something about the mode switch required to activate the screen saver that causes a machine to lock up. Therefore, I always recommend that users not activate any screen saver.

Effects: Use the Desktop icons group to pick out a new icon for several desktop stalwarts, including My Computer, My Documents, Network Neighborhood, and Recycle Bin in its full and empty states. This tab also offers the following check boxes:

See Also...
"Using Your Monitor's Power Management Features," p. 564

Hide icons when the desktop is viewed as a Web page: As you saw in the previous chapter, when this check box is activated, Windows 98 hides the regular desktop icons when you view the desktop as a Web page.

Use large icons: Activate this check box to increase the size of every icon from 32 pixels per side to 48 pixels per side.

Show icons using all possible colors: When this check box is activated, Windows 98 uses every available color to render the icons, thus giving them extra detail. You should only deactivate this check box if you have a graphics card that doesn't display the icons properly.

Animate windows, menus, and lists: This check box is activated by default, and it tells Windows 98 to use animation when displaying or hiding certain items. Specifically, windows "slide" down to the taskbar when minimized, and menus and lists "scroll" onto the screen when opened. These objects show up marginally faster if you deactivate this feature.

Smooth edges of screen fonts: Activate this option to have Windows 98 smooth the jagged edges that appear when you use a large font. Unless you use a large font regularly, leave this option deactivated for better performance.

Show window contents while dragging: When this check box is deactivated, Windows 98 displays just an outline when you use your mouse to drag a window. If you activate this check box, Windows 98 leaves the window intact while you drag it (this is called *full-window drag*), which usually makes it easier to position windows.

Web: As you saw in the previous chapter, this tab is used to work with the Active Desktop.

Remember
Full-window drag is a useful setting to activate. However, remember that some older video cards may not have enough horsepower to handle this feature. Most newer cards can handle this, as can older cards that have plenty of video memory.

See Also...
"Working with Desktop Items," p. 222

Settings: This tab offers a number of controls for working with your video card and monitor. See Chapter 24 for details.

Modifying the Desktop Items

This section looks at a few methods for customizing the desktop items (by "item," I mean an icon and its text). I'll show you how to select different icons, hide items, and work with specific items such as My Documents and Recycle Bin.

Changing the Desktop Icons

You saw earlier that the Effects tab in the Display Properties dialog box enables you to choose a different icon for some of the desktop items. For the rest, the Registry is required.

All of the desktop items have their own subkey within the following Registry key:

`HKEY_CLASSES_ROOT\CLSID`

The subkeys in this branch are all 32-digit (16-byte) hexadecimal class ID values. Table 9.1 lists the class IDs for most of the desktop icons.

TABLE 9.1: CLASS IDS FOR THE DESKTOP ITEMS

Desktop Item	Class ID
My Computer	{20D04FE0-3AEA-1069-A2D8-08002B30309D}
My Documents	{450D8FBA-AD25-11D0-98A8-0800361B1103}
Network Neighborhood	{208D2C60-3AEA-1069-A2D7-08002B30309D}
Recycle Bin	{645FF040-5081-101B-9F08-00AA002F954E}
Set Up the Microsoft Network	{4B876A40-4EE8-11D1-811E-00C04FB98EEC}
Internet Explorer	{3DC7A020-0ACD-11CF-A9BB-00AA004AE837}
My Briefcase	{85BBD920-42A0-1069-A2E4-08002B30309D}

Watch Out!
To ensure that you can recover your default desktop at any time, export the `HKEY_CLASSES_ROOT \CLSID` key before performing any of the customizations mentioned in the next few sections.

If you examine these branches, you'll see a subkey named `DefaultIcon`. The `Default` setting in this subkey uses the following general format:

`IconFile,IconNumber`

IconFile	This string is the full pathname of the file that contains the icon used by the desktop item.
IconNumber	This number specifies the icon position within IconFile (recall that the first icon is 0).

See Also...
"Configuring the Color Depth and Resolution,"
p. 558, and "Working with Windows 98's Monitor Features,"
p. 562

For example, here's the setting used by the Network Neighborhood item:

`c:\windows\system\shell32.dll,17`

To specify a different icon, you have two choices:

- Change the icon number to another in the same file.

- Specify a different icon file and select a new icon number within that file.

Editing the Desktop Item InfoTips

If you hover your mouse pointer over most desktop items, a banner appears with a brief description of what the item does. This banner is called an InfoTip, and it can be changed by editing the Registry.

To try this, select the class ID of the desktop item you want to work with. Figure 9.3 shows the class ID for the My Computer item. As you can see, the item's class ID key has an InfoTip setting that stores the banner text. Edit this string value to modify the InfoTip text.

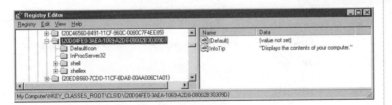

Figure 9.3
Edit the InfoTip setting to create a custom banner for a desktop item.

Hiding Desktop Items

As you saw earlier, you can hide desktop items when you view the Active Desktop as a Web page. Windows 98 also enables you to hide the desktop items even when you're not using the Active Desktop. Here's how:

Inside Scoop
Activating the Hide All Items on Desktop check box not only hides the desktop items, it also disables the desktop. This means you can't right-click the desktop, and you can't display Active Desktop items. Note, however, that the desktop items are still available if you select Desktop at the top of Windows Explorer's All Folders list.

1. Open the System Policy Editor.

2. Select File, Open Registry to load the local Registry.

3. Launch the Local User icon and then select Windows 98 System, Shell, Restrictions.

4. Activate the Hide All Items on Desktop check box.

5. Click OK.

6. Select File, Save to write the change to the Registry.

7. Exit and restart Windows.

Working with the My Documents Icon

One of the easiest ways to make backing up files easier is to store all your documents in one place, such as a folder or hard drive partition. This saves you from the time-consuming chore of having to track down documents that may be scattered throughout the drive. Windows 98 encourages this sensible approach by providing a folder named My Documents, which is located on the same drive that you used to install Windows 98 (the likely path is C:\My Documents).

Windows 98 also creates a handy shortcut to this folder: the My Documents icon on the desktop. This is no ordinary shortcut, however. The My Documents icon is known as a *shell extension shortcut* because it's a shortcut that's also part of the Windows 98 shell. One consequence of this is that it's easy to remove and restore the My Documents icon:

- To remove the icon, right-click it and then click Remove from Desktop. When Windows 98 asks you to confirm, click OK.

- To restore the icon, right-click the desktop and then click New, My Documents Folder on Desktop.

You can also change the target of the My Documents shortcut:

1. Right-click My Documents and then click Properties. The My Documents Properties dialog box appears.

2. Use the Target text box to enter the full path for the folder you want to use (or click Browse to use the Browse for Folder dialog box).

3. Click OK.

Renaming the Recycle Bin

You can rename most of the desktop items by right-clicking them and then clicking Rename in the shortcut menu. This doesn't work for the Recycle Bin, unfortunately. To rename this item, first find its class ID subkey in the Registry:

```
HKEY_CLASSES_ROOT\CLSID\{645FF040-5081-101B-9F08-
00AA002F954E}
```

To rename the item, edit the string in the Default setting. To put the new name into effect, click the desktop and then press F5 to refresh it.

Saving Desktop Settings When Exiting Windows 98

Windows 98 should save the current state of your desktop automatically when you shut down. If it doesn't, the culprit may be a setting in the following Registry key:

```
HKEY_CURRENT_USER\Software\Microsoft\Windows\CurrentVersion\
Policies\Explorer
```

Look for a binary value named NoSaveSettings. If you see it, edit the value to the following:

```
00 00 00 00
```

If you'd prefer that Windows 98 not save your settings, change the NoSaveSettings value to the following:

```
01 00 00 00
```

Setting Up Custom Shell Folders

Windows 98 defines a number of *shell folders*—special folders used by Windows 98 and its applications. These shell folders define what's included on the desktop, the Send To menu, the Fonts folder, and various Start menu folders (including the Start menu itself). You can use the Registry to set up alternative shell folders that contain the icons you want to work with.

Undocumented
You can also tell Windows 98 to save your settings by using the System Policy Editor. Open the Registry, launch the Local User icon, and then select Windows 98 System, Restrictions. Deactivate the Don't Save Settings At Exit check box.

The various shell folders are defined in the following key:

```
\HKEY_CURRENT_USER\Software\Microsoft\Windows\Current
Version\Explorer\Shell Folders
```

Most of the settings in this key are straightforward. For example, the location of the Send To menu's folder is given by the `SendTo` setting. Note, however, that the My Documents shortcut's current target is stored in the Registry as the `Personal` setting.

The `Desktop` setting also requires a bit more explanation. Most of the desktop items are built into the Windows 98 desktop. However, some of the items—including My Briefcase and Online Services—appear on the desktop only by virtue of being located in the `Windows\Desktop` folder (or whatever is specified in the `Desktop` setting in the `Shell Folders` key). Therefore, specifying another folder for the desktop will only replace some of the desktop items.

Customizing Windows 98's System Icons

The *system icons* are the icons Windows 98 uses for file types, folders, drives, Start menu items, and more. Most system icons can be customized with just a simple Registry tweak.

To see how, check out Figure 9.4, which shows the icons contained in `\Windows\System\Shell32.dll`. This file is where most of the Windows 98 system icons are stored. As you can see, the first icon (which is, you'll remember, icon 0) is the system icon for an unregistered file type, the second icon (icon 1) is below it, and it's the system icon for a WordPad document.

Undocumented
Many of these custom shell folders may be more easily defined using the System Policy Editor. To see how, open the Local User icon and then select Windows 98 System, Shell, Custom Folders. This branch contains six check boxes that enable you to specify custom shell folders for the desktop, the Start menu, and more.

Figure 9.4
The `Shell32.dll` file contains most of the Windows 98 system icons.

To specify custom icons, first head for the following Registry key:

```
HKEY_LOCAL_MACHINE\SOFTWARE\Microsoft\Windows\Current
Version\explorer\Shell Icons
```

The idea is that, for each system icon you want to customize, create a new string setting in this key, and give the setting the same name as the position in Shell32.dll of the icon you want to work with. For example, the "unregistered file type" icon is in position 0, so to customize this icon you'd create a new string setting named 0. Similarly, to customize the WordPad icon (icon 1), create a new string setting named 1.

Once you've done that, edit this new setting and give it the following value:

```
shell32.dll,IconNumber
```

     IconNumber   The icon position within Shell32.dll of the icon you want to use.

For example, the following value specifies the "globe" icon (number 13):

```
shell32.dll,13
```

Renovating the Start Menu

Messing around with icons and colors is fine for rugged individualists who enjoy fritterware. If you're more into boosting your productivity, spending a few minutes now to reconstruct your Start menu will pay off handsomely over time. Why? Simply because the default Windows 98 Start menus are a model of poor design. Features that you might use only rarely (such as the MS-DOS Prompt) are relatively handy on the Programs menu, while crucial features (such as Backup and ScanDisk) are buried four menus deep.

The next few sections show you how to customize the Start menu. Using these techniques, you can perform the following Start menu productivity boosts:

- Move important features closer to the beginning of the Start menu hierarchy.

Undocumented
The system icons are stored in a hidden file named ShellIconCache in the Windows folder. To put your new system icons into effect, you have to force Windows 98 to refresh this file. The easiest way to do this is to right-click the desktop, click Properties, and select the Appearance tab. In the Item list, select Icon, modify the Size value, and then click Apply. Return Icon to its original value, and then click OK.

66

fritterware, *noun*: Feature-laden software that seduces people into spending inordinate amounts of time tweaking various options for only marginal gains in productivity.
—The Word Spy (http://www. mcfedries.com/ WordSpy/)

99

- Remove features you don't use.

- Add new commands for features not currently available on the Start menu (such as the Registry Editor).

I'll also show you a few tricks for making it easier to select Start menu commands.

Adding and Removing Start Menu Shortcuts

On the main Start menu (the one that appears when you click the Start button), the commands from Programs on down are built into the Windows 98 system. This means the following:

- Everything else on the Start menu and its submenus is a shortcut that points to a program or document.

- You can't add new shortcuts to the area that contains the built-in commands. You can add shortcuts above Programs, or you can add shortcuts to the Programs menu (or any of its submenus).

- You can't hide the built-in commands directly, although it *is* possible to hide some of these commands indirectly (see "Removing Built-In Start Menu Items," later in this chapter).

Windows 98 offers no less than four methods for adding and removing Start menu shortcuts, and I explain each of them in the next four sections.

Using the Create Shortcut Wizard

The Create Shortcut wizard is available by selecting Start, Settings, Taskbar & Start Menu to display the Taskbar Properties dialog box. Select the Start Menu Programs tab and you'll see three buttons in the Customize Start menu group:

Add: Click this button to launch the Create Shortcut wizard. This is a cumbersome method, and I recommend it only for novices.

Remove: Click this button to display the Remove Shortcuts/Folders dialog box, from which you can delete a Start menu shortcut.

Advanced: Click this button to open Windows Explorer and display the Start Menu folder, which I describe a bit later in this chapter (see the section "Working with the Start Menu Folder").

Dragging-and-Dropping Onto the Start Button

The quickest way to add a shortcut is to drag an executable file from Windows Explorer and then do either of the following:

- Drop it on the Start button. This creates a shortcut on the main Start menu, above the Programs command.

- Hover over the Start button. After a second or two, the main Start menu appears. Now drag the file into the Start menu and drop it where you want the shortcut to appear.

Working with the Start Menu Folder

All the Start menu shortcuts are stored in the Windows\Start Menu folder, as shown in Figure 9.5. As you can see, this folder contains only the Programs menus, its submenus, and any shortcuts displayed above the Programs menu.

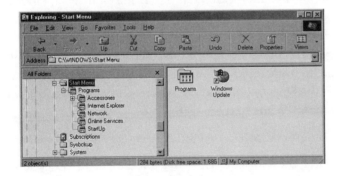

By working with this folder, you get the most control over not only where your Start menu shortcuts appear, but also the names of those shortcuts. Here's a summary of the techniques you can use:

- You can drag existing Start Menu shortcuts from one folder to another.

Watch Out!
Clicking the Advanced button displays Windows Explorer with the Start Menu folder as the root. This means you can't access the other folders and drives on your system, which is inconvenient if you want to add new shortcuts. Only click the Advanced button if you need to rename or delete Start menu short-cuts.

Figure 9.5
The Start menu shortcuts are stored in the Start Menu folder.

Remember
If you drag the file to the Programs command, the Programs sub-menu opens, and you can then con-tinue dragging within that sub-menu. Repeat as necessary.

Shortcut
A quick way to get to the `Start Menu` folder is to right-click the Start button and then click Explore.

Inside Scoop
If you have user profiles enabled on your system, each user will have his own `Start Menu` folder, which will be located at `Windows\Profiles\ User\Start Menu` (where `User` is the person's user-name).

- To create a new shortcut, drag the executable file and drop it inside the folder you want to use. (Remember that if you want to create a shortcut for a document or other non-executable file, right-drag the file and then select Create Shortcut(s) Here when you drop the file.)

- To make a shortcut appear on the main Start menu (above the Programs command), create the shortcut in the `Start Menu` folder.

- You can create your own folders within the `Start Menu` hierarchy and they'll appear as submenus within the Start menu.

- You rename a Start menu shortcut the same way you rename any file.

- You delete a Start menu shortcut the same way you delete any file.

Working with Start Menu Shortcuts Directly

When I'm examining a new version of Windows, I generally ignore the headline-grabbing "big" features. Instead, I look for the small tweaks and features that directly affect efficiency and productivity, because those are the ones that save time in the long run. A perfect example of such a feature is Windows 98's ability to work with Start menu shortcuts directly. That is, you open the Start menu, find the shortcut you want to work with, and then use any of these techniques:

- Drag the shortcut to another section of the Start menu.

- Drag the shortcut to another folder or to the Recycle Bin.

- Right-click the shortcut and then select a command (such as Delete) from the context menu.

Unfortunately, this timesaving new feature is marred by the inexplicable lack of a Rename command on the shortcut's context menu. Since renaming Start menu shortcuts is a common task, it would have been great to be able to do it right from the Start menu. Instead, you have to do it within the `Start Menu` folder.

That's the bad news. The good news is that Microsoft listened to everyone's bellyaching on this and added the Rename command to the context menu in Windows 98 Second Edition. (You also get it if you have Internet Explorer 5.0 installed.)

Removing Built-In Start Menu Items

I mentioned earlier that most of the commands on the main Start menu (those below and including Programs) are part of the operating system, and can't be worked with directly. However, Windows 98 does offer some methods for hiding or customizing most of these commands. Here's a summary:

Programs: To hide this command, use the System Policy Editor to edit the Registry. Open Local User, select Windows 98 System, Custom Folders, then activate the Hide Start Menu subfolders check box.

Favorites: To hide this command, in Tweak UI, select the IE4 tab and deactivate the Show Favorites on Start Menu check box.

Documents: To hide this command, in Tweak UI, select the IE4 tab and deactivate the Show Documents on Start Menu check box. To clear the Documents menu, select Start, Settings, Taskbar & Start Menu, display the Start Menu Programs tab, and then click Clear in the Documents menu group.

Settings: There are two ways to customize this submenu. To begin, use the System Policy Editor to open the Registry, open Local User, and then select Windows 98 System, Shell, Restrictions. To hide the Control Panel and Printers commands, activate the Remove Folders from Settings in the Start Menu check box. To hide the Taskbar & Start Menu command, activate the Remove Taskbar from Settings in the Start Menu check box.

Find: To hide this command, use the System Policy Editor to edit the Registry. Open Local User, select Windows 98 System, Shell, Restrictions, then activate the Remove Find Command check box.

Inside Scoop
You can also clear the Documents menu by deleting all the shortcuts in the Windows\Recent folder.

Help: No customizations are possible with this command.

Run: To hide this command, use the System Policy Editor to edit the Registry. Open Local User, select Windows 98 System, Shell, Restrictions, then activate the Remove Run Command check box.

Log Off: To hide this command, in Tweak UI, select the IE4 tab and deactivate the Allow Logoff check box.

Shut Down: To hide this command, use the System Policy Editor to edit the Registry. Open Local User, select Windows 98 System, Shell, Restrictions, then activate the Disable Shut Down Command check box.

Putting System Folders on the Start Menu

See Also...
"Putting the
Control Panel on
the Start Menu,"
p. 196

In Chapter 7, "Getting to Know the Control Panel," I showed you how to customize the Start menu with a submenu for the Control Panel icons. The secret was to head for the Start Menu folder and create a new folder with the following name:

`Control Panel.{21EC2020-3AEA-1069-A2DD-08002B30309D}`

That long, 32-digit value is the class ID of the Control Panel. Other Windows 98 system folders have a unique class ID, so you can use the same technique to add one or more of those folders to the Start menu. Here's a list of the folders you can work with and the folder names to use:

The Printers folder:

`Printers.{2227A280-3AEA-1069-A2DE-08002B30309D}`

The Recycle Bin:

`Recycle Bin.{645FF040-5081-101B-9F08-00AA002F954E}`

The Scheduled Tasks folder:

`Scheduled Tasks.{D6277990-4C6A-11CF-8D87-00AA0060F5BF}`

The Subscriptions folder:

`Subscriptions.{F5175861-2688-11d0-9C5E-00AA00A45957}`

The URL History folder:

`URL History.{FF393560-C2A7-11CF-BFF4-444553540000}`

Creating Accelerator Keys for Start Menu Shortcuts

When you open the main Start menu, you notice that the built-in commands each have an accelerator key. This means that you can select one of these commands quickly by pressing the letter of its accelerator key. For example, press p to select Programs.

All the other Start menu shortcuts have an implied accelerator key, which is the first character of the shortcut name. If multiple shortcuts share the same first character, pressing the character repeatedly will select each item in turn. In the Accessories menu, for example, press c to select the Communications menu, and press c again to select Calculator.

You can take advantage of this behavior to create custom accelerator keys that are quick to press and are unique. The secret? Rename the shortcuts so that each one begins with a different single-digit number. For example, if you have a shortcut named "Registry Editor," renaming this to "1. Registry Editor" means that you can select this shortcut by pressing 1. Figure 9.6 shows a Start menu that uses this technique.

Remember
For all of these folder names, the string to the left of the period can be whatever you like. Note that this string is what appears on the Start menu.

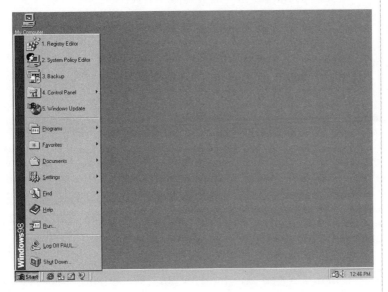

Figure 9.6
Add numbers to the start of shortcut names to create unique accelerator keys.

Redoing the Taskbar

Fixing the Start menu is a great way to streamline your Windows work. Another way to enhance efficiency is to customize the taskbar. Windows 98 gives you quite a few ways to do this, and I'll discuss them all in the next few sections.

Setting Taskbar Properties

Let's begin by looking at a few properties that enable you to customize the look of the taskbar. To see these properties, select Start, Settings, Taskbar & Start Menu. In the Taskbar Properties dialog box that appears, the Taskbar Options tab contains the following check boxes:

Shortcut
A quicker way to get to the Taskbar Properties dialog box is to right-click an empty section of the taskbar and then click Properties in the context menu.

Always on top: If you deactivate this check box, open windows—particularly maximized windows—can cover the taskbar. This is useful when you need some extra screen real estate.

Auto hide: If you activate this check box, Windows 98 shrinks the taskbar down to a thin gray strip at the bottom of the screen. To display the full taskbar, move your mouse to the bottom edge of the screen.

Inside Scoop
If you deactivate Always on Top and then maximize a window, the taskbar disappears. To see it again, press Ctrl+Esc or the Windows logo key (⊞).

Show small icons in Start menu: This option has nothing to do with the taskbar, so I'm not sure why it's here. Anyway, if you activate this check box, Windows 98 uses slightly smaller icons within the Start menu. This enables you to get more shortcuts onto each menu. However, these smaller icons are difficult to see if you're running at a high-video resolution.

Show clock: This check box toggles the system tray's Clock on and off.

The taskbar's context menu also offers a few commands for working with open windows. Right-click an empty part of the taskbar to see the following commands:

Cascade Windows: Select this command to arrange the non-minimized windows in an overlapping, diagonal pattern.

Tile Windows Horizontally: Select this command to arrange the non-minimized windows into horizontal strips that cover the desktop.

Tile Windows Vertically: Select this command to arrange the non-minimized windows into vertical strips that cover the desktop.

Minimize All Windows: Select this command to clear the desktop by minimizing each open window.

Moving and Sizing the Taskbar

Somewhat surprisingly, the position and size of the taskbar are not set in stone. Here are the techniques you can use:

To move the taskbar: You can move the taskbar to any edge of the screen. To try this, position the mouse pointer over an empty section of the taskbar, drag the taskbar to a screen edge, and then drop the taskbar.

To size the taskbar horizontally: The Windows 98 taskbar can be sized horizontally, which is useful if you need more room to display other taskbar toolbars. To size the taskbar, drag the left edge of the taskbar to the left or right.

To size the taskbar vertically: The default taskbar uses a single row to display the icons of your open windows. If you often have half a dozen or more programs running, the taskbar can appear crowded. To remedy this, you can add more rows by dragging the top edge of the taskbar up.

Customizing the Quick Launch Toolbar

Windows 98's taskbar includes a new Quick Launch toolbar on the left. These icons offer one-click access to some Windows 98 features:

Launch Internet Explorer Browser: Runs Internet Explorer.

Launch Outlook Express: Runs Outlook Express.

Show Desktop: Minimizes all open windows.

Launch WebTV for Windows: Runs WebTV (this icon only appears if you have WebTV for Windows installed).

View Channels: Displays the Active Channels page.

Shortcut
If you have the Microsoft Natural Keyboard or its equivalent, you can minimize all windows by pressing + D. Alternatively, click the Show Desktop icon in the Quick Launch toolbar.

Undocumented
The maximum number of taskbar rows depends on the current screen resolution. If you're running at 640×480, the taskbar can have 9 rows. If you're running at 1,280×1,024, you can create up to 20 rows.

These icons are a good start, but that one-click access is too good to leave just to these five features. The good news is that you can populate the Quick Launch toolbar with your own shortcuts, just as you can the Start menu. The secret is that the Quick Launch icons all reside in the following folder:

```
Windows\Application Data\Microsoft\Internet Explorer\Quick Launch
```

Any shortcuts you add to this folder are automatically displayed in the Quick Launch toolbar.

Once you start adding icons to the Quick Launch toolbar, you'll probably run out of room, so you may need to resize the taskbar to compensate. Alternatively, create two taskbar rows and display the Quick Launch toolbar on its own row. If you have a large number of icons, consider dragging the Quick Launch toolbar off the taskbar and positioning it on another edge of the screen.

Shortcut
You can also create Quick Launch shortcuts by dragging an executable file and dropping it inside the Quick Launch toolbar. (For non-executable files, remember to right-drag, drop the file, and then click Create Shortcut(s) Here.) Make sure you drop the file in between one of the existing icons.

Displaying Other Taskbar Toolbars

Windows 98's taskbar is happy to share some screen space with other toolbars. The Quick Launch toolbar, discussed in the previous section, is but one example. To see the others, follow these steps:

1. Right-click the taskbar to display its context menu.

2. Click Toolbars to see a list of the available toolbars:

   Address: This is the same Address bar that appears in Windows Explorer, folder windows, and Internet Explorer. You can use it to enter local addresses (folder paths), network addresses (UNC paths), or Internet addresses (URLs).

   Links: This is the Links bar that appears in Internet Explorer.

   Desktop: This toolbar displays the desktop icons, which is handy if you usually run applications maximized and don't see the desktop.

   New Toolbar: Use this command to display another folder as a toolbar.

3. Click the command you want.

4. If you clicked New Toolbar, the New Toolbar dialog box appears. Use this dialog box to select the folder you want to use, and then click OK.

You can customize a toolbar by right-clicking the left edge of the toolbar to display its context menu. You can then click one of the following commands:

View: Use this command to set the size of the toolbar icons. When you click View, a submenu appears with two options: Large and Small.

Show Text: Click this command to turn the icon titles on and off.

Refresh: Click this command to refresh the toolbar's contents.

Show Title: Click this command to turn the toolbar title on and off. (The title is displayed on the left side of the toolbar.)

Activating User Profiles

If multiple people use your computer, it's best to set up folders for each person to store their own documents and programs. However, what do you do about the individual customizations that each user will inevitably make to the system? After all, one person's attractive wallpaper is another person's hideous eyesore.

To solve these kinds of problems, activate Windows 98's user profiles feature. This feature enables each user to set up his own interface customizations, and it gives each user his own desktop, Start menu, My Documents folder, and more.

Setting Up User Profiles

Getting user profiles established on your computer involves the following tasks:

■ Activate user profiles and set up a default profile for yourself.

■ Set up profiles for the other users.

Inside Scoop
Toolbars can be dragged off the taskbar and dropped on the desktop to get a floating "palette." If you want this palette to always appear on top of your other windows, right-click an empty section of the palette and then click Always on Top.

Setting Up the Default Profile

To activate user profiles and set up your default profile, follow these steps:

1. Open the Control Panel's Users icon. The Enable Multi-user Settings dialog box appears.

2. Click Next. The Add User dialog box appears.

3. Enter your username and then click Next.

4. You now see one of the following dialog boxes:

   Enter New Password: You see this dialog box if Windows 98 doesn't recognize your username. In this case, enter a password for your profile twice and then click Next.

   Enter Password: You see this dialog box if you've logged on to Windows 98 with the username you entered in step 3. In this case, enter your password and click Next. Skip to step 7.

5. If you entered a new username, the Personalized Items Settings dialog box appears, as shown in Figure 9.7. In the Items group, activate the check boxes for those folders that you want included in the profile. Also, use the following option buttons to choose how you want the personalized folders created:

   Create copies of the current items and their content: Select this option to have the existing folder items copied to your profile. This is the option to choose to preserve your existing customizations.

   Create new items to save disk space: Select this option to start out with empty folders in the user profile.

6. Click Next. Windows 98 creates the profile.

7. Click Finish. Windows 98 asks if you want to restart.

8. Click Yes.

Figure 9.7
Use this dialog box
to select the items
that should be
included in the
new user profile.

Setting Up the Profiles for Other Users

When Windows 98 restarts, log in under your username. To create profiles for the other users, follow these steps:

1. Open the Control Panel's Users icon. The User Settings dialog box appears.

2. Click New User. The Add User dialog box appears.

3. Click Next.

4. Follow steps 3–7 from the previous section to create the new user profile.

5. Repeat this procedure for each user.

Remember
The User Settings
dialog box also
enables you to
work with your pro-
files. With a user
highlighted, click
Change Settings
to alter the user's
profile, click Set
Password to
change his pass-
word, and click
Delete to remove
the profile.

Logging On

Each time you start Windows 98, you'll see one of the following dialog boxes:

Enter Password: You see this dialog box if your computer doesn't have a network card (see Figure 9.8). To log on, highlight your username in the Select User Name list, enter your Password, and then click OK.

Welcome to Windows: You see this dialog box if your computer has a network card. Enter your User Name, enter your Password, and click OK.

Figure 9.8
You see this dia-
log box at startup
if your computer
doesn't have a
network card.

Understanding How Windows 98 Works with User Profiles

To complete your look at user profiles, this section gives you a bit of background information on how Windows 98 works with user profiles.

Watch Out!
If you install a
Windows program
after the user pro-
files are in place,
the shortcut for the
program will only
appear on the
Start menu for the
current user.

User Folders

The individual user settings are stored in special folders set up for each user. You'll find these folders within the Windows\Profiles folder. Figure 9.9 shows an example. Here are some points to bear in mind:

- The name of each subfolder is the name of each user.

- Each user has a subfolder for things like the Start menu, My Documents, and Favorites. (The number of subfolders depends on which options you chose in the Personalized Items Settings dialog box.)

- Each user has his own copy of the User.dat Registry file.

Figure 9.9
Each user gets his
own subfolder
within
Windows\Profiles.

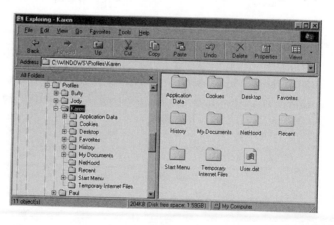

User Profiles and the Registry

I mentioned in the previous section that each user gets his own copy of User.dat. Recall from Chapter 4, "An Insider's Guide to Three Crucial Configuration Tools," that User.dat stores user-specific settings, so it makes sense that each user gets a unique copy of this file.

Recall, too, that these user-specific settings are stored in the HKEY_CURRENT_USER key. When a user logs in, Windows 98 reads his personal User.dat file from his profile folder, and writes this data to the appropriate settings in HKEY_CURRENT_USER. Note, too, that the HKEY_USERS key always has a subkey for the current user. HKEY_CURRENT_USER is an alias for this HKEY_USERS subkey.

Finally, the list of user profiles is stored in the following key:

```
HKEY_LOCAL_MACHINE\Software\Microsoft\Windows\Current
Version\ProfileList
```

Essential Information

- The Registry, the System Policy Editor, and Tweak UI offer some powerful desktop customization methods that go well beyond the standard wallpaper and color customizations.

- Rearranging the shortcuts on your Start menu is an excellent way to improve your day-to-day productivity. In particular, be sure to move commonly used shortcuts closer to the beginning of the Start menu hierarchy.

- For maximum flexibility, work with the Start Menu folder when customizing the Start menu.

- You can access some Start menu operations by right-clicking a shortcut.

- The taskbar can be moved, sized, shrunk to a line, or displayed behind windows.

See Also...
"How the Registry is Structured," p. 112

Remember
To deactivate user profiles, open Control Panel's Passwords icon to display the Passwords Properties dialog box. Select the User Profiles tab and then activate the All users of this computer use the same preferences and desktop settings option.

- The Quick Launch toolbar's one-click icon launching makes it an excellent place to store shortcuts for frequently used programs and documents.

- Use Windows 98's Users Control Panel icon to activate and maintain user profiles on your system.

Secrets of the
Windows 98
File System

PART III

GET THE SCOOP ON...
Understanding file types ▪ Opening documents in
alternate applications ▪ Editing file type actions ▪
Creating new file types ▪ Adding more choices to the
New menu ▪ Web browser file types

Powerful Techniques for File Types

Chapter 10

I AM CONTINUALLY AMAZED by the long list of useful and powerful Windows 98 features that are either ignored or given short shrift in the official Microsoft documentation. Whether it's the Windows 98 startup options, the Registry, or the Web view templates (to name a few that have been discussed so far in this book), Microsoft prefers that curious users figure these things out for themselves. (With, of course, the help of their favorite computer book authors.)

The subject of this chapter is a prime example. The idea of the *file type* can be described, without hyperbole, as the very foundation of the Windows 98 file system. Not only does Microsoft offer scant documentation and tools for working with file types, but they even seem to have gone out of their way to hide the whole file type concept. As usual, the reason is to block out this aspect of Windows 98's innards from the sensitive eyes of the novice user. Ironically, however, this just creates a whole new set of problems for beginners, and more hassles for experienced users.

This chapter brings file types out into the open. I'll explain the concept and then offer a number of powerful techniques for using file types to take charge of the Windows 98 file system.

Understanding File Types

To get the most out of this chapter, you need to understand some background about what a file type is and how Windows 98 determines and works with file types. The next couple of sections tell you everything you need to know to get you through the rest of the chapter.

File Types and File Extensions

One of the fictions that Microsoft has tried to foist on the computer-using public is that we live in a "document-centric" world. That is, that people care only about the documents they create and not about the applications they use to create those documents.

66
The Start button's
Documents menu...helps
users think of their work in terms of documents (a concept known as *document-centricity*), rather than applications.
—From the "Windows 98 Reviewer's
99

This is pure hokum. The reality is that applications are still too difficult to use and the ability to share documents between applications is still too problematic. In other words, we can't create documents unless we learn the ins and outs of an application, and we can't share documents with others unless we use compatible applications.

Unfortunately, we're stuck with Microsoft's worship of the document and all the problems that this worship creates. A good example is the hiding of file extensions. As you learned in Chapter 6, "Expert Windows Explorer Techniques," Windows 98 turns off file extensions by default. Here are just a few of the problems this allegedly document-centric decision creates:

See Also...
"Quick Fixes for
Making Windows
Explorer More
Usable," p. 153

Document confusion: If you have a folder with multiple documents that use the same primary name, it's often difficult to tell which file is which. For example, Figure 10.1 shows a folder with 15 different files named Project. Windows 98 unrealistically expects users to be able to tell files apart just by examining their icons.

The inability to rename extensions: If you have a file named index.txt and you want to rename it to index.html, you can't do it with file extensions turned off. If you try, you'll just end up with a file named index.html.txt.

The inability to save a document under an extension of your choice: Similarly, with file extensions turned off, Windows 98 forces you to save a file using the default extension associated with an application. For example, if you're working in Notepad, every file you save must have a .txt extension.

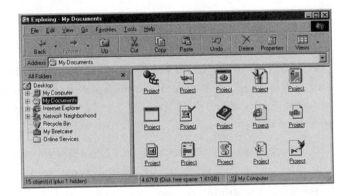

Figure 10.1
With file extensions turned off, it's often difficult to tell one file from another.

You can overcome all of these problems simply by turning on file extensions. Why does the lack of file extensions cause such a fuss? Because they solely and completely determine the file type of a document. In other words, if Windows 98 sees that a file has a .txt extension, then it knows the file uses the Text Document file type. Similarly, a file with the extension .bmp uses the Bitmap Image file type.

The file type, in turn, determines the application that's associated with the extension. If a file has a .txt extension, Windows 98 associates that extension with Notepad, so the file will always open in Notepad. Nothing else inherent in the file determines the file type so, at least from the point of view of the user, the entire Windows 98 file system rests on the shoulders of the humble file extension.

This method of determining file types is, no doubt, a poor design decision. (For example, there is some danger that a novice user could render a file useless by imprudently renaming its extension.) However, it also leads to some powerful methods for manipulating and controlling the Windows 98 file system, as you'll see in this chapter.

Inside Scoop
There are two ways to get around the inability to save a document under an extension of your choice. 1) In the Save As dialog box, surround the filename you want to use with quotation marks. 2) In the Save as type list, select the All Files (*.*) option, if it exists.

Remember
To turn on file extensions, select Start, Settings, Folder Options, display the View tab, and deactivate the Hide file extensions for known file types check box.

File Types and the Registry

As you might expect, everything Windows 98 knows about file types is defined in the Registry. You'll be using the Registry to work with file types throughout this chapter, so let's see how things work. Open the Registry Editor and then examine the HKEY_CLASSES_ROOT key. You'll see that it's divided into two sections:

- The first part of HKEY_CLASSES_ROOT consists of dozens of file extension subkeys (such as .bmp and .txt). There are over 175 such subkeys in a basic Windows 98 installation, and there could be 400 or more on a system with many applications installed. Each of these subkeys represents a file extension that has been *registered* with Windows 98.

- The second part of HKEY_CLASSES_ROOT lists the various file types that are associated with the registered extensions.

To see what this all means, take a look at Figure 10.2. Here, I've highlighted the .txt key, which has txtfile as its Default value.

Figure 10.2
The first part of the HKEY_CLASSES_ROOT key contains sub-keys for all the registered file extensions.

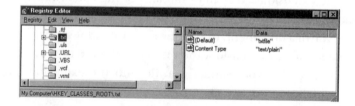

That Default value is a pointer to the extension's associated file type subkey in the second half of HKEY_CLASSES_ROOT. Figure 10.3 shows the txtfile subkey associated with the .txt extension. Here are some notes about this file type subkey:

Inside Scoop
HKEY_CLASSES_ROOT also stores information on ActiveX controls in its CLSID subkey. Many of these controls also have corresponding subkeys in the second half of HKEY_CLASSES_ROOT.

- The Default value is a description of the file type (Text Document, in this case).

- The DefaultIcon subkey defines the icon that's displayed with any file that uses this type.

- The shell subkey determines the *actions* that can be performed with this file type. These actions vary depending on the file type, but open and print are common. The open action determines the application that's associated with the file type. For example, the `open` action for a Text Document file type is the following:

```
C:\WINDOWS\NOTEPAD.EXE %1
```

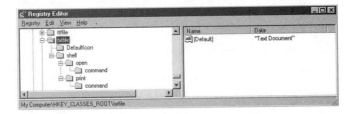

Figure 10.3
The second part of `HKEY_CLASSES_ROOT` contains the file type data associated with each extension.

A Front-End for `HKEY_CLASSES_ROOT`

For much of the work you do in this chapter, you won't have to deal with the Registry's `HKEY_CLASSES_ROOT` key directly. Instead, Windows 98 offers a dialog box tab that acts as a front-end for this key. Follow these steps to display this tab:

1. Select Start, Settings, Folder Options to display the Folder Options dialog box.

2. Select the File Types tab.

Figure 10.4 shows the File Types tab. The Registered File Types list shows all the file types known to Windows 98. When you highlight a file type, the tab shows you the extension associated with the file type, and the primary name of the executable file associated with the file type.

Inside Scoop
The "%1" at the end of the command is a placeholder that refers to the document being opened (if any). If you double-click a file named memo.txt, for example, the %1 placeholder is replaced by memo.txt, which tells Windows to run Notepad and open that file.

Figure 10.4
The File Types tab offers a front-end for working with Windows 98's registered file types.

Shortcut
You can also get to the Folder Options dialog box by selecting View, Folder Options in Windows Explorer or any folder window.

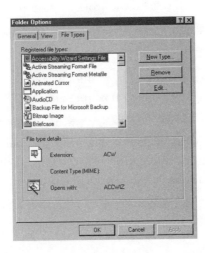

Opening a Document with an Unassociated Application

From the preceding discussion, you can see the process that Windows 98 goes through when you double-click a document:

1. Look up the document's extension in HKEY_CLASSES_ROOT.

2. Examine the Default value to get the name of the file type subkey.

3. Look up the file type subkey in HKEY_CLASSES_ROOT.

4. Get the Default value in the shell\open\command subkey to get the command line for the associated application.

5. Run the application and open the document.

What do you do if you want to bypass this process and have Windows 98 open a document in an unassociated application? (That is, an application other than the one with which the document is associated.) For example, what if you want to open a text file in WordPad?

One possibility would be to launch the unassociated application and open the document from there. To do so, you'd run the File, Open command (or whatever) and, in the Open dialog box, select All Files (*.*) in the Files of type list.

That will work, but it defeats the convenience of being able to launch a file right from Windows Explorer or some other folder window. Here's how to work around this:

1. In Windows Explorer, highlight the document you want to work with.

2. Hold down the Shift key and then select File, Open With. The Open With dialog box appears.

3. In the Choose the Program You Want To Use list, highlight the unassociated application in which you want to open the document (see Figure 10.5). If the application you want to use isn't listed, click Other and then select the executable from the dialog box that appears.

Shortcut
A faster method for displaying the Open With dialog box is to hold down Shift, right-click the document, and then click Open With in the content menu.

Figure 10.5
Use the Open With dialog box to select the unassociated application you want to use to open the document.

4. To prevent Windows 98 from changing the file type to the unassociated application, make sure the Always use this program to open this type of file check box is deactivated.

5. Click OK to open the document in the selected application.

Working with Existing File Types

In this section you'll learn how to work with Windows 98's existing file types. I'll show you how to change the file type description, modify the file type's actions, and more.

Editing a File Type

To make changes to an existing file type, follow these steps:

1. Open the Folder Options dialog box and display the File Types tab, as described earlier.

2. Use the Registered file types list to highlight the file type you want to work with.

3. Click Edit. The Edit File Type dialog box appears. Figure 10.6 shows the Edit File Type dialog box for the Text Document type.

4. Make your changes using the following controls:

   Change Icon: Click this button to display the Change Icon dialog box. Use this dialog box to select a new icon for the file type.

Inside Scoop
Windows 98 determines which applications appear in the Open With dialog box by examining HKEY_CLASSES_ROOT. Specifically, it runs through the file type subkeys and looks for those that have a shell\open\ command subkey. For those that do, the executable file's primary name is extracted and that's what appears in the Open With dialog box.

Figure 10.6
Use the Edit File
Type dialog box to
make changes to
an existing file
type.

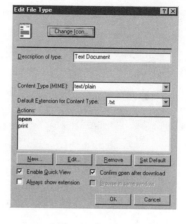

Inside Scoop
The complete
database of MIME
content types is
stored in the
HKEY_CLASSES_ROOT
key. Look in the
MIME\Database\Con
tent Type subkey.

Description of type: This text box describes the file type. This description appears in the Registered file types list and in the New menu (right-click a folder and then click New).

Content Type (MIME): This list contains all the MIME content types supported by Windows 98. A MIME content type is the Internet equivalent of a file type. It tells a Web browser what kind of file it's downloading so the browser knows whether to display the file in the browser or to call a helper application.

Default Extension for Content Type: This list contains one or more extensions associated with the MIME content type. Use this list to set the default extension.

Actions: This list shows the actions defined for the file type. I'll discuss file type actions in more detail in the next section.

Enable Quick View: When this check box is activated, Windows 98 adds a Quick View command to the context menu of any document that uses this file type. Selecting this command displays the Quick View program, which displays the contents of the file. If you activate this check box, Windows 98 adds the file type extension to the HKEY_CLASSES_ROOT\QuickView key.

Always show extension: If you activate this check box, Windows 98 shows this file type's extension even if you hide extensions globally.

Confirm open after download: When this check box is activated, Internet Explorer asks whether you want to save or open a downloaded file. Otherwise, Internet Explorer just opens the file according to the value in the Content Type (MIME) box. Here are two points to bear in mind:

- Despite the name of this check box, Internet Explorer prompts you before you download the file.

- The prompt only appears if you leave the Content Type (MIME) box blank.

Browse in same window: When this check box is activated, the file type opens within Internet Explorer instead of its associated application. This applies only to Microsoft Office file types that are capable of being displayed within Internet Explorer.

5. Click Close to return to the File Types tab. (This button will still be named OK if you didn't make any changes.)

6. Click OK.

Working with File Type Actions

In the Edit File Type dialog box, the Actions list displays the defined actions for the file type. You'll usually see two types of actions:

- An action shown in boldface represents the default action for the file type. This is the action that's performed when you double-click one of these files (or highlight a file and press Enter). This action also appears in bold on the context menu for the file type.

- All other actions are listed on the context menu for the file type.

The buttons below the Actions list enable you to work with the file type's actions:

Undocumented
What if you want Windows 98 to never show a file type's extension, even if extensions are turned on globally? To set this up, find the appropriate file type subkey in HKEY_CLASSES_ROOT, add a new string value named NeverShowExt, and leave its value as the empty string. You may need to restart Windows to put this into effect.

Shortcut
When you want to open a folder window in the two-paned Explorer view, you have to right-click the folder and then click Explore. To make the latter the default action for a folder, edit the Folder file type, highlight Explore in the Actions list, and then click Set Default.

Inside Scoop
You can assign an accelerator key to the action by preceding a letter in the action name with an ampersand (&). For example, if you enter Open in &MS-DOS Editor (see Figure 10.7), the M becomes the accelerator key.

New: Click this button to create a new action for the file type. (I'll describe this process in more detail after this list.)

Edit: Click this button to make changes to the highlighted action.

Remove: Click this button to delete the highlighted action.

Set Default: Click this button to make the highlighted action the default for this file type.

To demonstrate how these actions work, let's run through an example. In this case, I'll create a new action for the Text Document type. Specifically, I'll create an "Open in MS-DOS Editor" action that opens a text file in the MS-DOS Editor (Edit.com):

1. In the Edit File Type dialog box, click New. Windows 98 displays the New Action dialog box.

2. In the Action text box, type in a name for the new action. This name will appear in the file type's content menu.

3. In the Application used to perform action text box, enter the drive, path, and filename of the executable file you want to use. Here are a few notes to keep in mind:

   - If the action will be opening the file, add the %1 placeholder at the end.

   - If you want the action to print the file, add /P at the end.

   - If the path or filename contains spaces, enclose the text within quotation marks.

4. Figure 10.7 shows a completed dialog box. Click OK when you're done. Windows 98 adds your new action to the Actions list.

5. If you want the new action to be the default, highlight it and click Set Default.

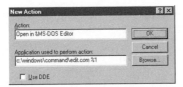

Figure 10.7
Use the New
Action dialog box
to define a new
action for the file
type.

6. Click Close to return to the File Types tab.

7. Click Close.

In Figure 10.8, I right-clicked a text file. Notice how the new action appears in the content menu.

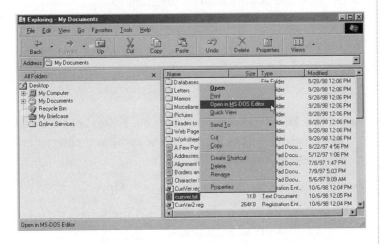

Figure 10.8
The new action
appears in the file
type's content
menu.

Inside Scoop
Text files, in par-
ticular, seem to
come with all
kinds of non-stan-
dard (that is,
unregistered)
extensions. Rather
than constantly
setting up file
types for these
extensions or
using the Open
With dialog box, I
created a shortcut
for Notepad in my
Windows\SendTo
folder. That way, I
can open any text
file by right-click-
ing it and then
selecting Send To,
Notepad.

Creating a New File Type

Windows 98 comes with a long list of registered file types, but it can't account for every extension you'll face in your computing career. For rare extensions, it's best just to use the Open With dialog box. However, if you have an unregistered extension that you encounter frequently, you should register that extension by creating a new file type for it. The next two sections provide a couple of methods for doing this.

Using Open With to Create a Basic File Type

Our old friend the Open With dialog box provides a quick-and-dirty method for creating a simple file type for an unregistered extension:

1. In Windows Explorer, highlight the file you want to work with.

2. Select File, Open With to get the Open With dialog box onscreen.

3. Use the Description of .*EXT* files text box (where .EXT is the extension of the file) to enter a description for the new file type.

4. In the Choose the program you want to use list, highlight the application you want to use to open the file.

5. Activate the Always use this program to open this type of file check box.

6. Click OK.

This method creates a new file type with the following properties:

- In the File Types tab, the new file type appears in the Registered file types list under the name you entered into the Description box.

- The file type has only a single action: Open.

- The icon associated with the file is the same as the one used for WordPad documents.

- In the Registry, the new HKEY_CLASSES_ROOT file type name is *EXT*_auto_file, where EXT is the file's extension.

Undocumented
Why does Windows 98 use the WordPad document icon? Because that's the first icon in Shell32.dll that applies to a registered file type. (Recall that the first icon in Shell32.dll is the one used for an unregistered file. See Chapter 9's "Changing an Icon" section, page 227.)

Using the File Types Tab to Create a More Advanced File Type

If you want more control over your new file type, use the File Types tab instead of the Open With dialog box. This method enables you to select an icon, set up multiple actions, and more. Here are the steps to follow:

1. Open the Folder Options dialog box and display the File Types tab.

2. Click New Type. Windows 98 displays the New File Type dialog box shown in Figure 10.9.

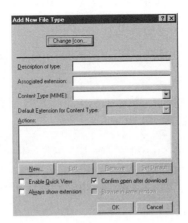

Figure 10.9
Use the Add New
File Type dialog
box to define your
new file type.

3. Click Change Icon to select an icon for the file type.

4. Use the Description of type text box to enter a description of the new file type.

5. Use the Associated extension text box to enter the file type's extension (you don't have to enter the period).

6. Fill in the other options as described earlier in the "Working with Existing File Types" section.

7. Click OK.

Associating Two or More Extensions with a Single Application

The problem with creating a new file type is that you often have to reinvent the wheel. For example, let's say you set up a new file type for the .dos files that store your old system settings (Config.dos, Autoexec.dos, and so on). These are text files, so you probably associated them with Notepad, which meant repeating some or all of the existing Text Document file types. To avoid this, it's possible to tell Windows 98 to associate a second extension with an existing file type. Here's how:

1. Open the Registry Editor and, in HKEY_CLASSES_ROOT, find the extension subkey of the existing file type.

2. Make a note of the Default value, which is, you'll recall, the name of the file type. For example, the file type for text documents is txtfile.

Remember
To confirm that the new extension is now associated with the existing file type, display the File Types tab and highlight the file type. The Extension field should now show both the original extension and the new extension.

See Also...
"Creating New Folders and Files," p. 161

3. Highlight HKEY_CLASSES_ROOT, select Edit, New, Key, and enter the name of the new extension that you want to associate with the file type. (For the .dos file example, enter .dos.)

4. Change the Default value in this new key to the name of the file type from step 2.

If you ever need to remove the new extension's association with the existing file type, find the new extension's subkey in HKEY_CLASSES_ROOT and change the Default setting to the empty string.

Customizing the New Menu

In Chapter 6, "Expert Windows Explorer Techniques," I showed you how to create new documents by using the New menu. That is, you either select File, New or right-click and then click New in the context menu. As you can see in Figure 10.10, the New menu includes a Folder command, and commands for six different file types. (You may see more commands, depending on which applications you have installed.)

Figure 10.10
The New menu enables you to create new documents on-the-fly.

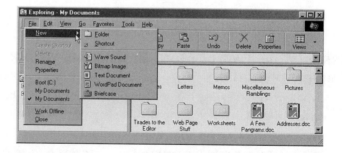

The New menu is a handy tool, but it gets even handier if you customize it by adding your own commands and by removing existing commands that you don't need. This is all possible through the Registry.

To understand how this works, let's see how those New menu commands got there in the first place. In the Registry, open HKEY_CLASSES_ROOT and then open the .bmp subkey. As you can see in Figure 10.11, this subkey includes a ShellNew subkey. The existence of ShellNew tells Windows 98 to include this file type on the New menu.

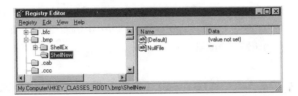

Figure 10.11
If an extension key has a `ShellNew` subkey, Windows 98 includes the file type on the New menu.

How Windows 98 creates the new file is determined by extra settings (other than `Default`) in `ShellNew`. There are four different settings used:

Remember
The `ShellNew` folder contains a dozen (or more) templates, including files named `Excel.xls` and `Lotus.wk4`. The reason these items don't show up on the New menu is that they don't have a corresponding registered file type.

NullFile: When Windows 98 sees this string setting, it creates an empty document of the associated file type. This is the method used by the Bitmap Image (`.bmp`) and Text Document (`.txt`) file types.

FileName: The value of this string setting is always a filename. When Windows 98 sees this setting, it looks in the `Windows\ShellNew` folder for that filename, and then creates the new file by making a copy of the file that's in `ShellNew`. This method is used by the Wave Sound (`.wav`) and WordPad Document (`.doc`) file types. For the latter, the filename (`winword.doc`) is defined in the following key:

`HKEY_CLASSES_ROOT\.doc\Wordpad.Document.1\ShellNew`

Command: The value of this string setting is a command. When Windows 98 sees this setting, it creates the new document by running the command. This is the method used by the Shortcut (`.lnk`) and Briefcase (`.bfc`) file types.

Data: This setting is set to a binary value. When Windows 98 sees this setting, it creates a new document of the associated file type and copies the binary value into the document.

Given all this, it's relatively easy to add file types to and remove file types from the New menu:

To add a file type to the New menu: In `HKEY_CLASSES_ROOT`, find the extension subkey for the file type and add a new subkey named `ShellNew`. Within this new subkey, create a setting using one of the four names discussed above.

To remove a file type from the New menu: In `HKEY_CLASSES_ROOT`, open the extension subkey for the file type and delete the `ShellNew` subkey.

Figuring Out Browser File Types: Internet Explorer Versus Netscape

Watch Out!
If you think you may need to use the file type on the New menu once again down the road, don't delete the `ShellNew` subkey. Instead, just rename it. That way, you can recover it later simply by renaming it back to `ShellNew`.

❝
Competition is supposed to be good for consumers: It keeps prices down and innovation up. But rather than bombarding you with advertisements or promotions, Microsoft and Netscape are using the Windows Registry to win you over.
—David A. Karp, Windows Sources
❞

One of the unfortunate consequences in the ongoing Battle of Browsers is that Internet Explorer and Netscape often use your computer as a battleground. That is, each program wants to be your default browser, and they'll often use unscrupulous means to achieve this end. In this section, I'll show you how to make peace reign on your desktop.

The first thing you should do is make sure the browser you want to use as your default is set up as such. That is, the next time you start the browser, if it asks you if it can be your default browser, click yes to make it so.

Note that the browser's executable is stored in the various URL file types, such as `URL:Hypertext Transfer Protocol` and `URL:File Transfer Protocol`. You'll see a list of about 15 or so of these file types in the File Types tab. In most cases, these file types refer to the protocol prefix used in an Internet address. For example, the `URL:Hypertext Transfer Protocol` is used in Web page addresses that begin with `http`. Note, too, that each of these file types has a corresponding Registry entry at `HKEY_CLASSES_ROOT\`*`protocol`*, where *`protocol`* is the protocol prefix. For example, data on the `URL:Hypertext Transfer Protocol` file type can be found here:

`HKEY_CLASSES_ROOT\http`

Now you need to force both browsers to stop pestering you to make them your default browser.

To do this in Internet Explorer, select View Internet Options to display the Internet Options dialog box. Display the Programs tab and then deactivate the Internet Explorer should check to see whether it is the default browser check box.

To tell Navigator not to check whether it's the default browser, you have two choices:

- If Internet Explorer is currently your default browser, at startup Netscape will ask if you'd like to register Navigator as the default. Make sure you activate the Do not perform this check in the future check box.

- You can also do this via the Registry. Open the Registry Editor and head for the following key:

```
\HKEY_CURRENT_USER\Software\Netscape\Netscape
Navigator\Main
```

Set the Ignore DefCheck value to yes. (Note that you may need to create this string value if it doesn't exist.)

Watch Out!
With Navigator as default, the Start, Windows Update command won't work. Instead, you have to open Internet Explorer and connect by hand by entering the address windowsupdate. microsoft.com.

Essential Information

- The file type of a document is determined solely by its extension.

- Registered file extensions and their associated file types are stored in the Registry in the HKEY_CLASSES_ROOT key.

- To open a document in an unassociated application, hold down Shift and select File, Open With.

- Use the File Types tab (select View, Folder Options) to edit existing file types and create new file types.

- The items in the New menu are determined by the various ShellNew subkeys in the extension keys in HKEY_CLASSES_ROOT.

GET THE SCOOP ON...
Different methods for creating shortcuts •
Customizing shortcut properties • Getting rid of the
Shortcut to
text • Other shortcut tricks

Taking Advantage of Shortcuts

chapter 11

O NE OF THE PROBLEMS with the "authorized" way of doing things in Windows 98 is that it tends to be the long and inefficient way, as well. Whether it's a needlessly tedious wizard, a poorly laid out Start menu structure, or faulty defaults, doing Windows "by the book" is often not the best way to work. Fortunately, as you've seen throughout this book, there are plenty of "unauthorized" detours you can take to route around Windows' inefficiencies.

In this chapter, you'll see one of those rare instances where the authorized Windows way is actually pretty good. As their name implies, *shortcuts*—the topic of this chapter—offer all kinds of opportunities to streamline your work. I'll run through these opportunities, and along the way I'll explain how shortcuts work and offer a few undocumented tricks for getting even more out of this useful feature.

Understanding Shortcuts

You've seen and worked with shortcuts quite often so far in this book:

- Some of the items on the default Windows 98 desktop—such as the Connect to the Internet icon—are shortcuts.

- Other than the built-in items (from Programs on down), everything you see on the Start menu is a shortcut.

273

- The items on the Send To menu are shortcuts stored in the Windows\SendTo folder.

- Some of the items in the Quick Launch toolbar—such as the Launch Internet Explorer icon—are shortcuts.

From all of this, it's not hard to figure out just what a shortcut is: It's a special file that points to another object, such as a program's executable file or a document. From this definition, you may be tempted to conclude that Windows 98 shortcuts are more or less the same as the program items found in Windows 3.*x* program groups. That's not true, however. The crucial difference is that Windows 98 shortcuts are standalone files. By contrast, each Windows 3.*x* program item was merely an element within a program group (.grp) file. Having a shortcut as a separate file offers two main advantages:

- You can create, copy, or move shortcuts within any Windows 98 folder.

- Like all files in Windows 98, shortcuts have properties that you can customize.

The other big advantage enjoyed by Windows 98 shortcuts is flexibility. Whereas Windows 3.*x* program items could point to only application executables and documents, Windows 98 shortcuts can also point to folders, printers, disk drives, and much more.

Windows 98 actually uses two different types of shortcuts: one for Windows objects and another for DOS programs. The next two sections discuss each type.

Windows Shortcut Files

Shortcuts for Windows objects are stored in special files that use the .lnk (short for *link*) extension. If you examine HKEY_CLASSES_ROOT (as described in the previous chapter), you'll see that the .lnk extension is associated with the lnkfile file type:

```
HKEY_CLASSES_ROOT\lnkfile
```

> **shortcut:** An icon that links to a file or folder. When you double-click a shortcut, the original item opens.
> —From the "Getting Started" booklet

> A shortcut doesn't change the location of a file—the shortcut is just a pointer that lets you open the file quickly. If you delete the shortcut, the original file isn't deleted.
> —From the "Getting Started" booklet

As you can see in Figure 11.1, this subkey's Default value is Shortcut, and it also includes three other settings:

EditFlags: When this value is 01 00 00 00, Windows 98 prevents this file type from appearing in the File Types tab of the Folder Options dialog box.

IsShortcut: When this setting is present, Windows 98 overlays a small arrow on the file's icon to indicate that it's a shortcut.

NeverShowExt: When this setting is present, Windows 98 suppresses the file's extension, even if extensions are turned on globally.

See Also...
"File Types and the Registry," p. 258

I'll show you how to customize some of these settings a bit later in this chapter (see "Some Unauthorized Shortcut Tricks").

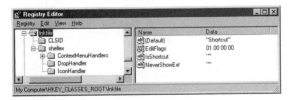

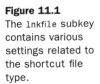

Figure 11.1
The lnkfile subkey contains various settings related to the shortcut file type.

DOS Shortcut Files (PIFs)

The shortcut files that point to DOS programs are a different kettle of fish entirely. They're called *program information files*, or PIFs, for short. These files contain special DOS-related data that governs how the program runs in DOS, what its DOS window looks like, and more. PIFs use the .pif extension, which is associated in the Registry with the piffile file type:

`\HKEY_CLASSES_ROOT\piffile`

This subkey contains the same settings that I described in the previous section for Windows shortcuts.

Creating a Shortcut

Windows 98's genius (if that's the right word) for offering us too many ways to perform a task applies equally well with shortcuts. Below is the long list of methods you can use to cre-

Undocumented
You can use the EditFlags setting to customize other aspects of the File Types dialog box. For example, to disable the Edit button for a file type, set EditFlags to 08 00 00 00. To disable the Remove button for a file type, set EditFlags to 10 00 00 00. To disable both buttons, set EditFlags to 18 00 00 00.

ate a shortcut. I've arranged this list more or less with the easiest methods first:

- Drag an executable (.exe or .com) file and drop it on the
  destination.

- Right-drag any file or folder, drop it on the destination,
  and then click Create Shortcut(s) Here in the context
  menu that appears.

- Drag any file or folder, hold down both Ctrl and Shift, and
  drop it on the destination.

- Copy a file or folder, open the destination, and then select
  Edit, Paste Shortcut.

- In Windows Explorer or a folder window, select File, New,
  Shortcut. (You can also right-click and then click New,
  Shortcut in the context menu.) This launches the Create
  Shortcut wizard, which takes you step-by-step through the
  process of selecting the shortcut's target, name, and icon.

To create a PIF shortcut for a DOS executable file, you have
two choices:

- Use any of the above methods.

- Make changes to the properties for the DOS executable.
  See "Customizing a PIF Shortcut," later in this chapter.

Modifying Shortcut Properties

Shortcuts have a number of properties you can manipulate to
customize them to your liking. The next two sections take you
through the available options for both Windows and PIF shortcuts.

Customizing a Windows Shortcut

To see the property sheet for a shortcut, either highlight the
shortcut and select File, Properties, or right-click the shortcut
and then click Properties in the context menu. Figure 11.2
shows the property sheet's Shortcut tab.

Here's a summary of the available controls:

Target: This text box tells you what the shortcut points to. If the shortcut points to a file, for example, this text box displays the file's full pathname (drive, folder, and filename). You should only need to edit this text box if the target gets moved or renamed.

Start in: If the target is an application or document, this text box displays the folder in which the target resides. This will be the application's default folder (that is, the one that first appears when you display the Open or Save As dialog box).

Shortcut key: When this text box is active and you press a key, Windows 98 inserts a key combination of the form Ctrl+Alt+*character*, where *character* is the letter or number you pressed. You can then press this key combination to launch the shortcut. Here are some notes about this setting:

- Other key combinations are possible by holding down Ctrl+Shift, Alt+Shift, or Ctrl+Alt+Shift.

- The shortcut key only works if the shortcut resides in the Start menu hierarchy or on the desktop.

- For any shortcut, the key combination *will* work while the target application is running. That is, pressing the key combination will switch to the target application.

- Not all programs respond to the shortcut key.

Inside Scoop
Another good reason to edit the Target text is to add parameters or switches that modify how the shortcut starts the target. For example, if the target is Windows Explorer, you could add any of the Explorer.exe command-line switches. (In Chapter 6, see "Using Windows Explorer's Command Line Options," page

Shortcut
To help you remember which key combination applies to which shortcut, include the key combination in the shortcut's name.

See Also...
"Changing an Icon," p. 227

Remember
I offer in-depth coverage of all the PIF property sheet options in my books *Windows 98 Unleashed* and *Paul McFedries' Windows 98 Unleashed Professional*

Figure 11.3
This is the property sheet you see for a DOS program and its PIF shortcut.

Watch Out!
If you plan on making any adjustments to the Target text box, make sure you add quotation marks around any file or folder names that include spaces.

Run: For applications and documents, this list specifies how the application's window appears. You can select Normal window (for the application's default window), Minimized, or Maximized.

Find Target: Click this button to open the folder that contains the target.

Change Icon: Click this button to select a different icon for the shortcut, as explained in Chapter 9, "Customizing the Windows 98 Interface."

Customizing a PIF Shortcut

The properties available for both a DOS program and its PIF shortcut are identical. Therefore, to view the property sheet, highlight either the program's executable file or the PIF, and then select File, Properties. (Remember that if the PIF doesn't exist, Windows 98 creates it automatically after you make changes to the DOS program's properties.) Alternatively, right-click either file and then click Properties in the context menu. Figure 11.3 shows the Program tab of the property sheet that appears.

Use the text box at the top of the Program tab to change the name of the PIF, if necessary. Here's a summary of the rest of the controls in the Program tab:

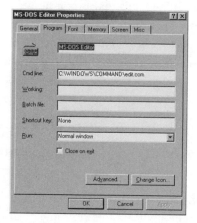

Cmd line: This is the same as the Target text box in a Windows shortcut's property sheet.

Working: This is the same as the Start in text box in a Windows shortcut's property sheet.

Batch file: Use this text box to specify the path and file-name for a batch file or DOS command. Windows 98 will run this batch file or command before it loads the DOS program.

Shortcut key: This is the same as the Shortcut key text box in a Windows shortcut's property sheet.

Run: This is the same as the Run text box in a Windows shortcut's property sheet.

Close on exit: When this check box is activated, Windows 98 shuts down the DOS session when you exit the program. If you deactivate this check box, you'll have to shut down the DOS session manually.

Advanced: This button sets the MS-DOS mode options for the program. See Chapter 5, "Getting the Most Out of Your Applications."

Change Icon: This is the same as the Change Icon button in a Windows shortcut's property sheet.

I discuss the Memory tab in Chapter 12, "Maximizing Your System's Memory."

The rest of the tabs—Font, Screen, and Misc—offer a large number of options for controlling the look of the DOS window, memory settings for the application, and much more. Unfortunately, the proverbial space limitations prevent me from discussing these options.

Finding a Moved or Renamed Target

A shortcut points to an object—the *target*—so what happens if the target gets moved, renamed, or even deleted? When you attempt to launch the shortcut, Windows 98 will be unable to locate the target and it will then initiate a search for the object. While the search is in progress, Windows 98 displays the Missing Shortcut dialog box, shown in Figure 11.4. (This dialog

Undocumented
If you'd like Windows 98 to prompt you for program parameters when you launch the shortcut, add a space and a question mark (?) to the end of the value in the Cmd line text box.

Shortcut
Many people like to run the Doskey command-line editor after they start a DOS session. To ensure that this useful utility is loaded automatically, select Start, Programs, right-click MS-DOS Prompt, and click Properties to get the property sheet onscreen. In the Program tab, type doskey.com in the Batch file text box.

See Also...
"Using MS-DOS Mode," p. 141

See Also...
"Setting DOS Memory Properties for Individual Applications," p. 304

box is misnamed since it's the target that's missing, not the shortcut.) Click Browse to find the target yourself, or click Cancel to abandon the search (for example, if you know the target has been deleted).

Figure 11.4
If Windows 98 can't find the target, it starts looking for it.

If Windows 98 can't find a file with the same name, it looks for a file that has the same size, file type, and date and time stamp. If it finds a matching file, the shortcut is updated and the target loads. If Windows 98 isn't sure, it will display a Problem with Shortcut dialog box similar to the one shown in Figure 11.5. If this is the correct target, click Yes.

Figure 11.5
You see this dialog box if Windows 98 isn't quite sure that it has found the file.

Watch Out!
Windows 98 won't find the file if you moved it off your hard disk (for example, to a removable drive or a network drive). Also, Windows 98's search will be unsuccessful if the letter of the drive where the target is stored changes.

Using the Link Check Wizard to Deal with Dead Links

In Windows parlance, a *dead link* refers to any shortcut that points to a target that no longer exists. There are all kinds of reasons dead links can appear on your system. For example, you could delete the target, or an application's uninstall program might not remove a Start menu or desktop shortcut.

To help you weed out these dead links, the Windows 98 CD offers the Link Check Wizard, which scours your hard disk looking for shortcuts without a target. Here's how it works:

1. Insert the Windows 98 CD and head for the `\tools\reskit\desktop` folder.

2. Launch the file `chklnks.exe`. The Link Check Wizard appears.

3. Click Next. The wizard scans your system and then displays a list of the dead links (if any), as shown in Figure 11.6.

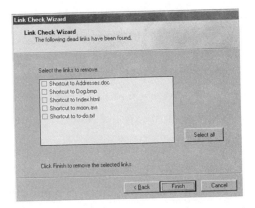

Figure 11.6
The Link Check
Wizard scours your
hard disk for dead
links and then dis-
plays them.

4. To find out more about a shortcut, right-click the dead link. The dialog box that appears tells you the filename, its location, its target, and the reason the link is dead. Click OK when you're done.

5. Activate the check box for each dead link you want to remove. If you want to get rid of all the dead links, click Select all.

6. Click Finish to remove the dead links.

7. When the wizard acknowledges that the operation is complete, click OK.

Some Unauthorized Shortcut Tricks

Shortcuts are relatively straightforward to work with, but there are still a few items in the "Unauthorized Bag of Tricks" that you might consider using. The next three sections show you how to view shortcut file extensions, tell Windows 98 not to include Shortcut to in the shortcut filename, and tell Windows 98 not to use the icon arrow.

Viewing Shortcut Extensions

You saw earlier that the Registry's shortcut file type key— HKEY_CLASSES_ROOT\lnkfile—contains a setting named NeverShowExt. The presence of this setting tells Windows 98 not to display the extension for any Windows shortcut file, even if file extensions are activated globally.

Shortcut
If you think you'll be using the Link Check Wizard regularly (which is a good idea), copy chklnks.exe to your hard disk (the Windows folder is a good spot) so you can run it without inserting the Windows 98 CD. Create a shortcut for this file in the Start menu's System Tools submenu.

If you'd prefer to see the .lnk extension in a shortcut's file-name, change the name of this setting to AlwaysShowExt.

Note, too, that if you want to see the .pif extension for a DOS PIF shortcut, head for HKEY_CLASSES_ROOT\piffile and rename the NeverShowExt setting to AlwaysShowExt.

In both cases, you must exit and restart Windows 98 to put the change into effect.

Disabling the Shortcut to Text

When you create a shortcut, Windows 98 names the shortcut file Shortcut to *object*, where *object* is the name of the target. Many people prefer to delete the extraneous Shortcut to text. Rather than doing this every time, you can save some work by telling Windows 98 not to add the Shortcut to text. You can do this either via the Registry or via Tweak UI.

To do it in the Registry, load the Registry Editor and head for the following key:

```
HKEY_CURRENT_USER\Software\Microsoft\Windows\CurrentVersion
\Explorer
```

Inside Scoop
When you view the link setting originally, it will likely have a value such as 1c 00 00 00. The link setting is a hexadecimal value that tracks the Shortcut to text. When you create a shortcut, this value is incremented by 1; when you delete the Shortcut to text, this value is decremented by 5. When the value reaches 0, Windows 98 will automatically stop adding the

Change the value of the link setting to 00 00 00 00 and then exit and restart Windows 98.

To do the same thing with Tweak UI, follow these steps:

1. Open Tweak UI from the Control Panel.

2. Display the Explorer tab.

3. Deactivate the Prefix "Shortcut to" on the New Shortcuts check box.

4. Click OK. Tweak UI tells you to log off Windows.

5. Exit and restart Windows 98.

Customizing the Shortcut Icon Arrow

Besides adding the Shortcut to text to the filename, Windows 98 also indicates a shortcut by overlaying a small arrow in the lower-left corner of the target's default icon. You can customize this arrow either by choosing a different overlay icon or by telling Windows 98 not to use any overlay.

To specify a different icon, open the Registry Editor and select the following key:

```
HKEY_LOCAL_MACHINE\Software\Microsoft\Windows\Current
Version\explorer\Shell Icons
```

Recall from Chapter 9 that you change a system icon by creating a new setting in this key, and giving the setting the same name as the icon's position within `Shell32.dll`. The default shortcut icon overlay is the 29th icon in `Shell32.dll`, so create a new text value named `29`. Change this setting to the full pathname of the icon file you want to use, followed by the position of the icon within that file. Here's an example:

```
C:\Windows\System\Shell32.dll,30
```

If you'd prefer that Windows 98 not use any overlay, open the Registry's shortcut file type keys — `HKEY_CLASSES_ROOT\lnkfile` for a Windows shortcut, and `HKEY_CLASSES_ROOT\piffile` for a DOS shortcut—and rename the `IsShortcut` setting.

See Also...
"Customizing
Windows 98's
System Icons,"
p. 236

Once again, Tweak UI can help with these customizations:

1. Open Tweak UI from the Control Panel.

2. Display the Explorer tab.

3. In the Shortcut overlay group, select one of the following options:

   Arrow: This is the default shortcut arrow.

   Light arrow: This is an alternative arrow overlay that comes with Tweak UI.

   None: Select this option to get rid of the overlay.

   Custom: Select this option to display the Change Icon dialog box and select the new overlay.

Remember
To put the new overlay icon into effect, you have to refresh the `ShellIconCache` file. See Chapter 9 to learn how to do this.

4. Click OK. The new setting goes into effect immediately.

Getting the Most Out of Shortcuts

So far, I've concentrated mostly on creating shortcuts to files—either application executables or documents. However, Windows 98 supports shortcuts to all kinds of other objects, and you should be familiar with these techniques in order to wring the most out of your shortcuts. Here's a look at the other kinds of objects you can work with:

Document scraps: A *document scrap* is a shortcut to a section of text or to an image. To create the scrap, highlight the data in the source application, drag the data, and then drop it where you want the scrap to appear. (If you can't drop the data, it means that the application doesn't support scraps.) When you double-click the scrap, the source application opens and loads the data. Note that this only works for applications that support object linking and embedding.

Folders: You create shortcuts to folders just as you do any non-executable file. (That is, you must either hold down Ctrl+Shift while you drag the folder, or else right-drag the folder.)

Disk drives: You can create a shortcut for each disk drive on your system. This gives you quick access to the drive you want, and also enables you to perform some disk-related operations right from the shortcut. For example, you can right-click a floppy drive shortcut and then click Format to format the disk that's currently in the drive. Note that the default drag operation for disk drives is to create a shortcut.

Network computers: You can create a shortcut for any computer that appears in the Network Neighborhood. If you connect to your network remotely, launching the shortcut will invoke Dial-Up Networking automatically. The default drag operation for network computers is to create a shortcut.

Printers: If you create a shortcut to a printer, you can drag a document and drop it on the printer shortcut. Windows 98 will then print the document without further prompting. The printer shortcut also gives you quick access to the printer's queue, which means you can easily double-click the shortcut to make changes to pending print jobs. The default drag operation for printers is to create a shortcut.

Dial-Up Networking connections: Creating a shortcut to a Dial-Up Networking connection means you can establish the connection by launching the shortcut, and thus avoid-

Inside Scoop
By default, Windows 98 displays folder shortcuts in the single-paned My Computer view. If you prefer the two-paned Windows Explorer view, open the folder shortcut's property sheet. In the Target text box, add `explorer. exe /e`, before the folder name (for example, `explorer.exe /e, "C:\My`

ing the `Dial-Up Networking` folder. To create these shortcuts, you must either hold down Ctrl+Shift while you drag the connection, or else right-drag the connection.

Control Panel icons: If you have some Control Panel icons you use regularly (such as Tweak UI), create a shortcut on the desktop or Start menu. The default drag operation for Control Panel icons is to create a shortcut. I showed you a few other methods for accessing Control Panel icons back in Chapter 7, "Getting to Know the Control Panel."

Web sites: Shortcuts to Web sites give you quick access to sites you visit often. To create a shortcut for the current page in Internet Explorer, either select File, Send, Shortcut to Desktop, or right-click the page and then click Create Shortcut. (You can also drag the URL icon shown in the Address bar and drop it where you want the shortcut created.) To create a Web site shortcut from a link, drag the link and drop it on the destination.

See Also...
"Easier Access to the Control Panel," p. 195

Essential Information

- A shortcut is a pointer to a program, document, or other target that gets launched automatically when you open the shortcut.

- Windows shortcuts use the `.lnk` extension, while DOS shortcuts are program information files (PIFs) that use the `.pif` extension.

- Dragging and dropping an executable file (`.exe` or `.com` extension) automatically creates a shortcut.

- For non-executable files, either hold down Ctrl+Shift while dragging the file, or else right-drag the file.

- Right-click a shortcut file and then click Properties to customize the shortcut's icon or target, or to set up a shortcut key.

- You can create shortcuts to document scraps, folders, disk drives, network computers, printers, Web sites, and more.

Windows 98 Performance Tuning and Troubleshooting

PART IV

GET THE SCOOP ON...
Understanding conventional memory and virtual
memory ▪ Optimizing your memory configuration ▪
The Windows 98 swap file ▪ Getting the most out of
Windows 98's system resources ▪ Optimizing conven-
tional memory for DOS applications

Maximizing Your System's Memory

Chapter 12

THIS CHAPTER BEGINS A FIVE-PART series on performance tuning and troubleshooting. The series includes chapters on optimizing your hard disk, working with the new FAT32 file system, wielding Windows 98's collection of system tools, and preparing for and recovering from trouble.

To get you started, this chapter covers what is probably the most important performance tuning technique: optimizing your system's *random access memory*, or RAM, for short. There are two main reasons why this topic is so crucial:

- When you open an application or a document, the underlying files are copied from the hard disk to RAM. So, in a sense, everything you do with a computer happens within RAM.

- Small improvements in RAM usage can lead to significant improvements in performance.

According to the authorized Microsoft party line, there isn't much you can do to improve how Windows 98 uses memory. While that's true in many cases, there are a few "unauthorized" techniques that you can use to eke out maximum performance. This chapter gives you both sides of the story.

Memory: The Lifeblood of Your Computer

Why do computers need memory in the first place? Why not simply run programs and data right from the hard disk? The answer is simple: *speed.* A typical hard disk has an access time of approximately 12 milliseconds, while a typical memory chip has an access time of roughly 60 nanoseconds, or about *20,000 times* quicker! This enormous speed difference is the main reason why RAM is such an important performance component.

Before discussing the specifics of Windows 98 memory management, let's run through a few concepts that you'll need to know to get through the rest of the chapter.

Remember
The latest main memory chips boast access times as low as 10 nanoseconds! There are even cache memory chips with access times as low as 2 nanoseconds.

The Address Space

The individual memory locations within a memory chip can hold a single byte of data. These locations are connected to the microprocessor via *address lines,* each of which carries a single bit: either a low current or a high current. This binary state is represented internally using, naturally enough, the binary number system: 0 for the low current state (off) and 1 for the high current state (on).

Therefore, the total number of possible memory locations—the *address space*—is a function of the number of address lines and these two states. In the simplest case, a machine with only one address line could deal with two memory locations: 0 (when the address line has low current) and 1 (when the address line has high current). Similarly, a system with two address lines could deal with four memory locations: 00 (both lines off), 01 (first line off and second line on), 10 (first line on and second line off), and 11 (both lines on). In general, the total amount of addressable memory is 2 to the power of the number of address lines.

The 8088 processor in the original IBM PC came with 20 address lines, meaning it had an address space of 1,048,576 bytes (2 to the power of 20), or 1MB. The 80386, 80486, and Pentium processor all use 32 address lines, which yields an address space of 4,294,967,296 bytes (2 to the power of 32), or 4GB.

Types of Memory

Your computer actually contains a number of different memory subsystems, all of which come into play when discussing memory optimization. Here's a quick summary of the various memory categories available on a typical system:

Main memory: This is RAM that your system uses for running programs and opening documents. On most systems, main memory consists of one or more *memory modules*, which are circuit boards that contain memory chips. These modules are packaged either as Single In-Line Memory Modules (SIMMs) with chips along one side of the circuit board, or as Dual In-Line Memory Modules (DIMMs) with chips along both sides of the circuit board. The boards plug into special slots (*banks*) on your system's motherboard.

Disk cache: In computer parlance, a *cache* is a chunk of RAM that stores frequently used data for later use. The idea is that the cache is faster than the source from which the data normally comes, so keeping at least some data within the cache should improve performance. For example, rather than simply grabbing code and data from the hard disk as it's needed, modern systems make educated guesses about what data might be required in the future. This "popular" data is then stored in a separate section of main memory called the *disk cache*.

Level 1 (L1) cache: As fast as main memory is, it's still slower than the processor. For example, a 60ns access time is equivalent to approximately 16MHz, far slower than the 200MHz to 450MHz processors found on modern systems. To help ease this bottleneck, most modern systems incorporate a RAM cache right into the processor. This Level 1 cache (L1, for short) uses super-fast (and super-expensive) Static RAM (SRAM) memory that runs as fast as the processor. This cache is used to hold processor instructions and data that would otherwise be accessed from main memory.

Remember

If you're looking to buy more main memory for your computer, make sure you buy the right memory modules. Check your system manual to learn the module size you need (30-pin, 72-pin, or 168-pin), the appropriate RAM access time (such as 70ns or 60ns), and whether you need parity or non-parity modules.

Inside Scoop
Windows 98 "only" makes the first 2GB available to 32-bit applications. The address space between 2GB and 3GB is used for the core Windows 98 components (User, GDI, and Kernel), 16-bit applications, and the DLLs and ActiveX objects that are shared by applications. The address space between 3GB and 4GB is set aside exclusively for virtual device drivers and some 32-bit system components.

Level 2 (L2) cache: The L2 cache is a secondary processor cache that sits outside of the processor. Larger than the L1 cache (128KB to 512KB versus 16KB to 32KB), the L2 cache also runs a bit slower, with access times equivalent to the motherboard in which the cache resides (typically 15ns, which is equivalent to about 66MHz). Note, however, that newer L2 caches reside within the processor housing, so these models boast access times as low as 5ns (equivalent to 200MHz).

Virtual memory: If your system has only 16MB or 32MB of main memory, does that mean your computer's ability to address up to 4GB of memory is mostly wasted? Not at all. Your computer can still address memory beyond what is physically installed. This non-physical memory is called *virtual memory,* and it's implemented by using a piece of your hard disk that's set up to emulate physical memory. This hard disk storage is actually a single file called a *swap file* (or sometimes a *paging file*). When physical memory is full, Windows 98 makes room for new data by taking some data that's currently in memory and swapping it out to the hard disk.

Determining How Much Memory Is Installed

If you're not sure how much memory you have in your system, Windows 98 makes it easy to find out:

- Open the Control Panel's System icon (or right-click My Computer and then click Properties). As you can see in Figure 12.1, the System Properties dialog box shows you the number of megabytes of RAM on your system.

- Select Start, Programs, Accessories, System Tools, System Information to open the System Information utility. Make sure System Information is highlighted at the top of the tree. The right pane shows you the number of megabytes on your system.

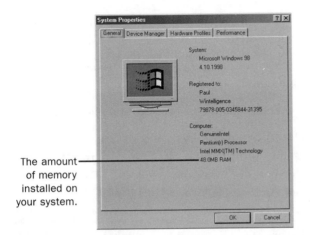

Figure 12.1
The System
Properties dialog
box tells you how
much RAM you
have.

The amount
of memory
installed on
your system.

Restricting Memory Usage

Whatever the amount of RAM you have installed, Windows 98 has a new feature that enables you to restrict how much memory is available to the system. Why would you want to restrict memory usage? Here are three good reasons:

- In the next section, I'll tell you about some tests that I ran to determine whether Windows 98 has a memory "sweet spot," beyond which performance increases only marginally no matter how much memory you have. Systematically restricting memory usage is a better way to test this than adding and removing memory circuit boards.

- A fault in physical memory may be causing Windows 98 to throw fatal exception errors. If you restrict the amount of memory available to Windows 98 and the problem goes away, then you know you have a defective memory chip.

- Many Pentium systems use Intel's 430TX or 430VX chipset. Unfortunately, the L2 cache on these chipsets can only cache data from the first 64MB of main memory. Anything beyond that isn't cached, so installing more than 64MB of main memory in these systems can actually *reduce* performance. In this case, you'd want to restrict memory usage to the first 64MB.

Undocumented
The failure of the TX and VX chipsets to cache memory beyond 64MB is particularly hard on Windows' performance. The reason is that Windows loads its files into the top of memory, so on a system with more than 64MB, the Windows files don't ever hit the L2 cache.

Here are the steps to follow to restrict the amount of memory used on your system:

1. Load the System Configuration Utility using either of the following methods:

   - Select Start, Run, type msconfig, and click OK.

   - Select Start, Programs, Accessories, System Tools, System Information. In the Microsoft System Information window, select Tools System Configuration Utility.

2. In the General tab, click Advanced to display the Advanced Troubleshooting Settings dialog box.

3. Activate the Limit memory to check box, as shown in Figure 12.2.

Figure 12.2
Use this dialog box to restrict the amount of memory that is used on your system.

4. Use the spinner to select the maximum number of megabytes that your system will use.

5. Click OK to return to the System Configuration Utility.

6. Click OK. Windows 98 asks if you want to restart your computer.

7. Click Yes.

Watch Out!
Even though the Limit memory to spinner can go as low as 4MB, Windows 98 requires 16MB to operate. Therefore, never select a value less than 16MB.

How Much Memory Is Enough?

The Windows 98 *Getting Started* booklet laconically states that "More memory improves performance." That seems like an obvious statement, but is it true? That is, if you just keep adding memory, will Windows 98's performance improve accordingly?

To test this hypothesis, I ran a series of application benchmark tests using various memory configurations: 16MB, 24MB, 32MB, 40MB, 48MB, 64MB, and 96MB. Figure 12.3 shows the results.

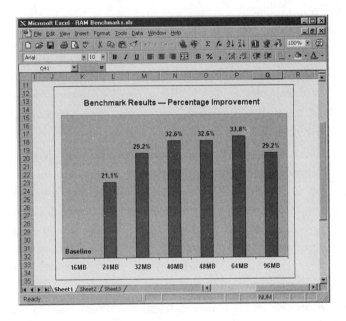

Figure 12.3
Benchmark results for various memory configurations.

As you can see, the answer to the above questions is "Yes, to a point." That is, Windows 98 seems to have a memory "sweet spot" that gives you the biggest bang for your memory dollar. Looking at the chart in Figure 12.3, you can see that Windows 98's performance improved dramatically by increasing memory from 16MB to 24MB and performance improved a smaller amount (although still substantially) by moving to 32MB. Upping the memory to 40MB increased performance by only a few percentage points, and subsequent memory boosts had little or no effect on performance.

Therefore, on my test system, the memory sweet spot seems to be 32MB, and that's probably the case on most systems.

However, the sweet spot will be higher if you deal with massive databases or immense graphics files that benefit from having access to large amounts of main memory.

Managing the Windows 98 Swap File

No matter how much main memory your system boasts, Windows 98 will still create and use a swap file for virtual memory. To maximize swap file performance, you should make sure that Windows 98 is working with the swap file optimally. Here are some techniques that will help you do just that:

Store the swap file on the hard disk that has the fastest access time: You'll see later in this section that you can tell Windows 98 which hard disk to use for the swap file. If you have multiple hard disks, you should store the swap file on the disk that has the fastest access time.

Store the swap file on an uncompressed hard disk: Windows 98 is happy to store the swap file on a compressed hard disk (assuming you're using a protected mode compression driver). However, as with all file operations on a compressed disk, the performance of swap file operations suffers thanks to the compression and decompression required. Therefore, you should store the swap file on an uncompressed disk.

Store the swap file on a defragmented hard disk: Windows 98 can store the swap file in noncontiguous clusters, but the more fragmented the file is, the slower the swap file paging will be. Therefore, always keep the swap file drive defragmented.

Store the swap file on the hard disk that has the most free space: Windows 98 expands and contracts the swap file dynamically depending on the system's needs. To give Windows 98 the most flexibility, make sure the swap file resides on a hard disk that has lots of free space.

Watch the swap file size: Windows 98's System Monitor (Start, Programs, Accessories, System Tools, System Monitor) can track the size of the swap file. Select Edit, Add Item, highlight Memory Manager in the Category

Remember

If you'd like to try your own benchmark testing, Winstone 98 is an excellent tool. It runs a series of tests using mainstream business applications such as Word, Excel, PowerPoint, WordPerfect, and CorelDraw. You can find out more by visiting the Ziff-Davis Benchmark Operation at http://www.zdbop.com.

list, highlight Swapfile Size in the Item list, and then click OK. If you see that this value is approaching the amount of free space left on the disk, you might want to run the Disk Cleanup utility to free up some disk space.

The swap file is named Win386.swp, and it's usually stored in the Windows folder. Here's how to change the hard disk that Windows 98 uses to store the swap file:

1. If necessary, defragment the hard disk that you'll be using for the swap file. See Chapter 13, "Optimizing Your Hard Disk."

2. Open the Control Panel's System icon to display the System Properties dialog box.

3. Select the Performance tab.

4. Click the Virtual Memory button. Windows 98 displays the Virtual Memory dialog box.

5. Activate the Let me specify my own virtual memory settings option, as shown in Figure 12.4.

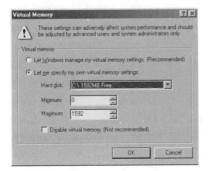

6. Use the Hard disk list to select the hard disk you want to use.

7. Click OK. Windows 98 asks you to confirm the change.

8. Click Yes to return to the System Properties dialog box.

9. Click Close. Windows 98 asks if you want to restart your computer.

10. Click Yes.

Inside Scoop
If you hear your hard disk working even when you're not using your computer, that's usually a sign that Windows 98 is compacting the swap file. It usually leaves that chore until your computer has been idle for a while.

See Also...
"Optimizing Disk Access Times with Disk Defragmenter," p. 320

Figure 12.4
Use the Virtual Memory dialog box to select a different hard disk to store the swap file.

In Figure 12.4, you can see that activating the Let me specify my own virtual memory settings option also activates the Minimum and Maximum spinners. Should you bother with those? Some folks think you should. It has become almost conventional wisdom that you should set these two values to 2.5 times the amount of main memory on your system. (For example, on a 32MB system, set them to 80MB each.) The idea is that by doing this, you're telling Windows 98 to use a fixed-size swap file. Theoretically, this prevents Windows 98 from having to waste time resizing the file.

Practically, however, this just doesn't work. In my benchmark testing I've found that doing this actually *decreases* overall performance, albeit very slightly. I've found about a one-percent performance decrease in a general application benchmark, and about a three-percent decrease in a subsystem benchmark. So this is one of those rare times when the authorized Windows way is also the right way.

Tracking and Optimizing System Resources

One of the ironies of Windows memory management is that, for many computers, certain small pieces of memory are more important than the entire memory system. These small pieces comprise the *system resources*. They're special memory areas called *heaps* that Windows 98 uses to store data structures for things like windows, menus, toolbars, fonts, ports, and more. The irony lies in the frustrating fact that your computer can have megabytes of free memory, but if the system resource heaps reach their limits, your programs may crash and Windows itself may refuse to run.

The good news is that Windows 98's system resource management has been much improved over that of Windows 3.*x*. The latter used four 16-bit heaps that could hold a mere 64KB of data each. By contrast, Windows 98 mostly uses a single 32-bit heap, which is capable of addressing 2GB. (For compatibility reasons, Windows 98 retains one of the old 16-bit heaps.) This enabled the Windows 98 designers to greatly increase the system resource limits. For example, in Windows 3.*x* you could install no more than 250 or 300 fonts, but with Windows 98, that number is closer to 1,000.

Besides increasing the heap size, Windows 98 continues the system resource management improvements that were introduced in Windows 95:

- Windows 98 monitors and, if necessary, cleans up after 32-bit applications. Windows 98 examines the heap after a 32-bit program shuts down and then removes any allocated resources that remain on the heap.

- 16-bit applications often intentionally leave some resources allocated after shutdown so that other processes can use those resources. This is efficient, so Windows 98 waits until all 16-bit applications have been closed before it removes allocated resources from the heap.

Unfortunately, all this good news doesn't mean that you never have to worry about system resources. Windows 98's system resource limits may be larger and better managed, but they are still limits, nonetheless. On my main computer (which has 128MB of RAM), I still need to reboot every three or four days because Windows 98 runs low on system resources.

Using the Resource Meter to Track System Resources

I'll discuss a few ways to keep system resources under control in the next section. For now, let's see how you track the current system resource levels to avoid getting into trouble.

The tool to use is the Resource Meter (`Rsrcmtr.exe`), which you launch by selecting Start, Programs, Accessories, System Tools, Resource Meter. The first time you open the utility, a dialog box warns you that the Resource Meter itself uses up some system resources. To avoid being reminded of that obvious fact each time you use this tool, activate the Don't Display This Message Again check box, and then click OK.

The Resource Meter adds an icon to the taskbar's system tray. This icon offers a graphical view of the current resource level. The more green you see, the more system resources are available. To get an exact measure, use either of the following techniques:

- Position the mouse pointer over the Resource Meter icon. After a second or two, a banner displays the current resource percentages.

- Double-click the Resource Meter icon to display a dialog box that shows the current levels.

Figure 12.5 demonstrates both techniques. In both cases, you see three values:

User: This is the percentage of system resource available in the User heap, which holds the data structures for things like windows and menus.

GDI: This is the percentage of system resource available in the Graphical Device Interface heaps, which hold the data structures for things like fonts, pens, and brushes.

System: This is the lower of the User and GDI values.

Figure 12.5
You get the current values for the system resources either by hovering over the Resource Meter icon, or by double-clicking the icon.

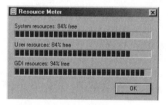

The color of the Resource Meter icon also gives you a clue to the current state of the system resources:

- When the Resource Meter icon is green, you have plenty of system resources available.

- When the Resource Meter icon is yellow, it means that the System value has dropped below about 34 percent. You should now be cautious about opening more applications and windows, and you might consider trying some of the resource-saving techniques that I discuss in the next section.

- When the Resource Meter icon is red, it means that the System value has dropped to 15 percent or less. It's time to quit some applications before the meter drops any further.

- If the System value drops to 10 percent or less, Windows 98 displays the Low Resources dialog box shown in Figure 12.6. (This warning appears even if the Resource Meter isn't running.) Windows is in imminent danger of running out of resources, which means possible application lockups or a system crash. You should immediately save your work and start shutting down applications you don't need.

Figure 12.6
This dialog box appears when system resources drop to 10 percent or less.

Some Ways to Save System Resources

Although there isn't any way to prevent Windows 98 from eventually running out of system resources, there are some things you can do to stave off the inevitable. Here's a rundown of a few methods that will save and recover system resources:

- Shut down any applications you're not using.

- Many programs use up system resources as you work, and the longer the program is open, the more unnecessary resources will be allocated. You can rid the system of these unnecessary resources by exiting and restarting the application.

- Each open document window uses up some resources, so close any documents you don't need.

- Other application features—such as toolbars and status bars—use up resources, so shut down any of these features that you don't use.

- Some applications are huge system resource hogs. Internet Explorer, for example, seems to use an inordinate amount of resources, particularly if it is running for a long time. Keep an eye on your resources as you use your programs to determine which ones seem to use up a large amount of resources. Use those programs as sparingly as possible, and never leave them running for long periods of time.

Watch Out!
When your resources get into the red, Windows 98 never really can recover. That is, although you may be able to get back into the green zone by shutting down your applications, it won't take much to push the resources back down into the yellow or red zones. Therefore, you should exit and restart Windows 98 to get a fresh set of system resources.

- Turn off the Active Desktop.

- Don't use wallpaper, animated cursors, or desktop themes.

- Run your DOS applications full-screen instead of in a window.

More Memory Management Techniques

Finding your memory sweet spot and keeping an eye on system resources are good starting points for proper Windows 98 memory management. Here are a few other techniques to bear in mind:

Shut down unnecessary applications: This is probably the most obvious piece of advice, but it's one that people seem to constantly ignore. For example, many users leave Windows Explorer open all day long even though they may need it only a few times a day. It's much better to restructure the Windows 98 interface—by, say, rearranging the Start menu and taking advantage of the Quick Launch toolbar—so that programs can be launched quickly when you need them.

Don't load unnecessary programs and services at startup: Similarly, don't load up your Startup folder or Run Registry key with applications that run at startup. Use the System Configuration Utility to remove all unnecessary startup items (see Chapter 3, "Understanding and Controlling the Windows 98 Startup").

Keep the Clipboard's contents small: The Clipboard resides in main memory, so anything cut or copied to the Clipboard not only usurps some memory, but it remains in memory until the next time you cut or copy something. If the current Clipboard contains a large image or other object, having it sit there just wastes memory. To clear the Clipboard, either copy a small item (such as a single character), or select Start, Programs, Accessories, System Tools, Clipboard Viewer, and then select Edit, Delete to clear the Clipboard.

Use only minimal network services: If you're running Windows 98 on a network, only use a single network client and use only the network protocols that you need for network access.

See Also...
"Controlling Startup Using the System Configuration Utility," p. 86

Optimize conventional memory for DOS programs: DOS programs run best when they have lots of conventional memory to roam around in. I tell you how to optimize conventional memory in the next section.

Load SmartDrive for MS-DOS mode programs: You'll greatly improve the performance of MS-DOS mode programs by including the SmartDrive disk cache in your MS-DOS mode configuration. See Chapter 5, "Getting the Most Out of Your Applications."

See Also...
"Creating Custom Startup Configurations," p. 143

Maximizing Memory for DOS Programs

Some DOS programs are quite finicky when it comes to memory. That's not surprising since 32-bit Windows programs can address up to 2GB of memory, but DOS programs are often stuck with a mere 640KB. To ensure that your DOS programs load and run optimally, you need to maximize the memory resources available to these programs. This section shows several methods for doing just that.

DOS Memory Concepts

Before getting to the specifics of DOS memory management, here are a few concepts you need to be familiar with:

Conventional memory: This is the first 640KB of main memory. DOS programs must operate within this memory region. Why only 640KB? As I mentioned earlier, the original IBM PC could address up to 1,024KB (1MB). The computer designers decided to reserve 384KB for system use (this is the upper memory area discussed next), which left only 640KB for DOS programs.

> **66**
> 640K ought to be enough for anybody.
> —Bill Gates in 1981
> **99**

Upper memory area (UMA): This is the 384KB area that lies between 640KB and 1MB. In the original IBM PC it was set aside to hold video buffers, ROM BIOS code, and other system data. Not all of the UMA was used, however.

Gaps called *upper memory blocks* (UMBs) are always present, and can be used to store device drivers and terminate-and-stay-resident (TSR) programs that would otherwise reside in conventional memory.

High memory area (HMA): This is the first 64KB segment beyond 1MB. You can use this area to store some DOS code that would otherwise take up room in conventional memory.

Expanded memory: This is a special type of memory that's used to give DOS programs access to memory outside of conventional memory. Expanded memory usually comes on a separate circuit board. To use this memory, an *expanded memory manager* (EMM) sets up a 64KB *page frame* inside the UMA. The EMM then uses this page frame to swap data between the expanded memory board and a DOS program that can work with expanded memory.

Extended memory: This is memory beyond 1MB, and it consists of memory chips plugged into your computer's motherboard. For DOS programs that can work with extended memory, an *extended memory manager* shuffles bits of program code and data between the memory chips and conventional memory.

Setting DOS Memory Properties for Individual Applications

One way to control the memory available to a DOS program is to customize the PIF shortcut for the program's executable file. (See Chapter 11, "Taking Advantage of Shortcuts.") Right-click the PIF shortcut file (or the program's executable, if no PIF has been created), click Properties, and then display the Memory tab, shown in Figure 12.7.

See Also...
"DOS Shortcut
Files (PIFs),"
p. 275

The Conventional memory group offers three controls:

Total: This drop-down list contains various kilobyte values that you use to restrict how much conventional memory Windows 98 supplies to the program. By setting this value to a little more than what the program requires, the program's virtual machine will use less memory overall. If you'd prefer that Windows 98 handle this, leave the value as Auto.

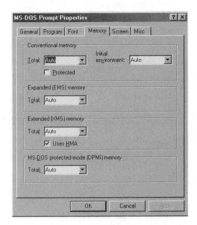

Figure 12.7
The Memory tab offers a number of properties for customizing how a DOS program uses memory.

Initial environment: This drop-down list contains various byte values that you use to set the size of the DOS environment. The latter is a small memory area that stores environment variables such as PATH, PROMPT, and DIRCMD. Some DOS programs also set a few environment variables. If you get an Out of environment space error when you run the program, try increasing the size of the environment.

Shortcut
You can see the current environment variables within a DOS session by typing set and pressing Enter at the DOS prompt.

Protected: Activate this check box to write-protect the system area of conventional memory. While you're in a DOS session, the system area of conventional memory holds a couple of Windows 98 drivers. If Windows 98 crashes when you run the DOS program, it probably means that the system area is getting overwritten by the program. Activating the Protected check box will prevent that from happening.

The rest of the tab determines how Windows 98 supplies various types of memory to the program:

Expanded (EMS) memory: The Total drop-down list contains various kilobyte values that determine how much expanded memory is provided to the DOS program.

Watch Out!
Instead of the
Total list, you may
see a message
stating that The
computer is not
configured for
expanded memory
in MS-DOS ses-
sions. This is
because your
Config.sys file has
the line C:\WIN-
DOWS\EMM386.EXE
NOEMS. The NOEMS
tells Windows 98
not to use
expanded memory.
You must change
the NOEMS parame-
ter to RAM in order
to use expanded
memory.

(This is true even if your system has no expanded memory. Windows 98 will use extended memory to emulate expanded memory.)

Extended (XMS) memory: The Total drop-down list contains various kilobyte values that set the amount of extended memory that's provided to the DOS program. When the Uses HMA check box is activated, Windows 98 gives the program access to the HMA. If you deactivate this check box, Windows 98 uses the HMA for DOS.

MS-DOS protected-mode (DPMI) memory: The Total drop-down list contains various kilobyte values that specify the amount of DOS protected-mode memory that is supplied to the program.

Maximizing Conventional Memory

Most large DOS programs run best when there is as much conventional memory available as possible. Unfortunately, the full 640KB is never available because DOS and Windows take up some space and because there are usually several device drivers and TSRs loaded. However, as you'll see in this section, it's possible to tweak DOS memory settings to maximize the amount of free conventional memory.

To set up a benchmark for measuring your progress, use the DOS MEM program:

```
mem /c /p
```

The /c switch gives you a detailed listing of what's loaded in conventional memory, and the /p switch pauses the output (which will be more than one screenful). The report you get will look something like the following:

```
Modules using memory below 1 MB:
```

Name	Total	Conventional	Upper Memory
MSDOS	17,840 (17K)	17,840 (17K)	0 (0K)
ASPI8DOS	9,680 (9K)	9,680 (9K)	0 (0K)
ASPICD	11,648 (11K)	11,648 (11K)	0 (0K)
HIMEM	1,168 (1K)	1,168 (1K)	0 (0K)

ASPI8HLP	592	(1K)	592	(1K)	0	(0K)
IFSHLP	2,864	(3K)	2,864	(3K)	0	(0K)
SETVER	832	(1K)	832	(1K)	0	(0K)
WIN	3,568	(3K)	3,568	(3K)	0	(0K)
vmm32	1,008	(1K)	1,008	(1K)	0	(0K)
MSCDEX	41,008	(40K)	41,008	(40K)	0	(0K)
COMMAND	7,408	(7K)	7,408	(7K)	0	(0K)
DOSKEY	4,688	(5K)	4,688	(5K)	0	(0K)
Free	552,896	(540K)	2,896	(540K)	0	(0K)

Memory Summary:

Type of Memory	Total	Used	Free
Conventional	655,360	102,464	552,896
Upper	0	0	0
Reserved	393,216	393,216	0
Extended (XMS)	49,283,072	229,376	49,053,696
Total memory	50,331,648	725,056	49,606,592
Total under 1 MB	655,360	102,464	552,896

Total Expanded (EMS)	49,790,976	(47M)
Free Expanded (EMS)	16,777,216	(16M)
Largest executable program size	552,880	(540K)
Largest free upper memory block	0	(0K)

MS-DOS is resident in the high memory area.

Here's a summary of the various sections of this report:

Modules using memory below 1MB: This list shows the programs and device drivers currently loaded in both conventional memory and upper memory. MEM also shows how much memory (in bytes and kilobytes) each module is using. The Free line at the bottom of this section tell you how much conventional memory and upper memory is available. The conventional memory number is the one you want to maximize.

Memory summary: This section shows you the Total, Used, and Free memory (in bytes) for five areas: conventional, upper (upper memory blocks), reserved (the upper memory area), extended, and expanded.

Inside Scoop
Recall that the
NOEMS parameter
tells Windows 98
not to create the
expanded memory
page frame in
upper memory,
which opens up a
64KB upper mem-
ory block. If you
know you have
DOS programs
that require
expanded mem-
ory, change NOEMS
to RAM.

Largest executable program size: This line tells you, in bytes and kilobytes, the size of the largest DOS program you can run in the current configuration.

Largest free upper memory block: This line tells you, in bytes and kilobytes, the largest available UMB.

MS-DOS is resident in the high memory area: This line tells you that Windows 98 has loaded most of DOS (about 60KB) into the HMA.

To optimize conventional memory, you need to get as many device drivers and TSRs as possible out of conventional memory and into upper memory blocks. To do this, you need to add the following lines to your Config.sys file:

```
DEVICE=C:\WINDOWS\EMM386.EXE NOEMS
DOS=HIGH,UMB
```

EMM386 is the Windows 98 device driver that manages the upper memory area. The line DOS=HIGH,UMB does two things:

- The HIGH part tells Windows 98 to load DOS into the high memory area.

- The UMB part tells EMM386 to look for available upper memory blocks and make them available for device drivers and TSRs.

Watch Out!
Since Windows 98
loads DOS into the
HMA by default,
you may be
tempted to insert
only DOS=UMB into
your Config.sys.
Unfortunately, this
won't work
because that line
in Config.sys
supercedes the
DOS=HIGH line in
Io.sys, which
means DOS does
not get loaded
into the HMA.

With upper memory blocks ready for action, you must now tell Windows 98 to load device drivers and TSRs into the high memory area. You do that in Config.sys by changing the word DEVICE to DEVICEHIGH. For example, suppose your Config.sys file contains the following lines:

```
DEVICE=ASPI8DOS.SYS /D /Z
DEVICE=ASPICD.SYS /D:ASPICD0
```

You should edit them as follows:

```
DEVICEHIGH=ASPI2DOS.SYS /D /Z
DEVICEHIGH=ASPICD.SYS /D:ASPICD0
```

You perform a similar task in Autoexec.bat. In this case, you add LOADHIGH (or just LH) to the beginning of each line that launches a TSR:

```
LOADHIGH C:\WINDOWS\COMMAND\DOSKEY.COM
```

```
LOADHIGH C:\WINDOWS\COMMAND\MSCDEX.EXE /D:ASPICD0 /L:H
/M:12 /S
```

When you've completed these steps, reboot your computer
to put the changes into effect and run MEM again. Here's my
new listing:

```
Modules using memory below 1 MB:


Name        Total           Conventional   Upper Memory
_____

SYSTEM      17,872   (17K)    9,984 (10K)     7,888  (8K)
HIMEM        1,168    (1K)    1,168  (1K)         0  (0K)
EMM386       4,320    (4K)    4,320  (4K)         0  (0K)
WIN          3,568    (3K)    3,568  (3K)         0  (0K)
vmm32       80,640   (79K)    1,472  (1K)    79,168 (77K)
COMMAND      7,408    (7K)    7,408  (7K)         0  (0K)
ASPI8DOS     9,680    (9K)        0  (0K)     9,680  (9K)
ASPICD      11,648   (11K)        0  (0K)    11,648 (11K)
ASPI8HLP       592    (1K)        0  (0K)       592  (1K)
IFSHLP       2,864    (3K)        0  (0K)     2,864  (3K)
SETVER         832    (1K)        0  (0K)       832  (1K)
MSCDEX      41,008   (40K)        0  (0K)    41,008 (40K)
DOSKEY       4,688    (5K)        0  (0K)     4,688  (5K)
Free       627,200  (613K)  627,200 (613K)       0  (0K)


Memory Summary:


Type of Memory      Total        Used          Free
_____       _____        ____          ____

Conventional       655,360      28,160       627,200
Upper              158,368     158,368             0
Reserved           393,216     393,216             0
Extended (XMS)   49,283,072     140,640    49,142,432
_____       _____        ____          ____

Total memory     50,490,016     720,384    49,769,632


Total under 1 MB    813,728     186,528       627,200


Largest executable program size        627,184   (612K)
Largest free upper memory block               0    (0K)
MS-DOS is resident in the high memory area.
```

With the device drivers and TSRs now loaded into upper memory blocks, the Free line shows 613KB available in conventional memory, which is enough for even the largest DOS program.

Essential Information

- Windows 98 can address up to 4GB of memory.

- For memory needs beyond what is physically installed, Windows 98 uses virtual memory: a hard disk swap file that emulates physical memory.

- Windows 98 has a memory "sweet spot" that maximizes performance gains. If you add memory beyond that, performance improvements are only marginal.

- For best virtual memory performance, move the swap file to an uncompressed, defragmented drive that has the fastest access time and the most free space.

- To make the most of Windows 98's limited system resources, use the Resource Meter to track the current levels, close applications you don't need, close documents you're not using, turn off toolbars, status bars, wallpaper, and animated cursors, and run DOS programs full-screen.

- To optimize conventional memory for DOS applications, load EMM386 in Config.sys, enable upper memory blocks, and then load device drivers and TSRs into upper memory.

Inside Scoop
Why is there no space left in the upper memory area? Because after all the device drivers and TSRs have been allocated their upper memory blocks, Windows 98's Vmm32 driver grabs the remaining UMA space for its own uses.

GET THE SCOOP ON...
Removing unneeded files ■ Hard disk problems and
repairing them ■ Defragmenting files ■ The new
WinAlign utility ■ Using disk compression ■
Partitioning your hard disk

Optimizing Your Hard Disk

chapter 13

I N THE CHAPTER 12, I showed you that optimizing Windows 98's memory management was crucial because all your work happens within the confines of memory and you need to take full advantage of the approximately 20,000-fold access time difference between memory and the hard disk.

However, that's not to say that you should ignore the hard disk in your quest for maximum performance. Quite the opposite, in fact:

■ All your work may be done in memory, but all that work has to be read from the hard disk at some point, and then written back to the disk when you're done.

■ As explained in the previous chapter, if you run out of physical memory, Windows 98 uses a part of your hard disk as virtual memory.

■ What hard disks lack in speed (at least compared to RAM), they make up for in their ability to act as a permanent storage medium for programs and data.

All of this means that there are no less than four different optimization categories for your hard disk: speed, reliability, storage capacity, and storage efficiency. This chapter takes you through several Windows 98 techniques for improving hard disk performance in all four categories.

Examining Hard Disk Properties

A disk drive is an object in Windows 98, so it comes with various properties you can examine. These include the disk label, the total capacity of the disk, and the free space on the disk. Windows 98 offers several methods for examining these properties:

Remember
If you have the Windows Explorer status bar turned off, you can still see a hard disk's capacity and free space by activating Web View (select View, as Web Page). The information area shows the disk capacity, used space, and free space, along with a pie chart for the latter two values.

- In Windows Explorer, the All Folders list displays the hard disks using their label followed by the drive letter, such as Boot (C:).

- If you highlight a hard disk in the All Folders list, Windows Explorer displays the disk's capacity in the status bar.

- If you select My Computer in the All Folders list and then highlight a hard disk in the Contents list, the status bar displays both the disk's capacity and its free space.

- If you right-click a hard disk and then click Properties, Windows 98 displays the property sheet shown in Figure 13.1. This dialog box shows the disk Label in an editable text box, as well as the disk type, the file system, the used and free space, and the disk capacity. Note, too, that you can click Disk Cleanup to launch the Disk Cleanup utility (see "Using Disk Cleanup to Remove Unnecessary Files," later in this chapter).

Figure 13.1
The property sheet for a hard-disk supplies you with disk data such as the label, capacity, and free space.

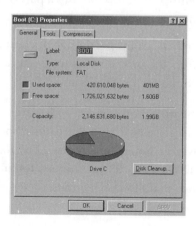

The Tools tab gives you access to three hard-disk utilities in the following groups:

Error-checking status: This group deals with ScanDisk. It tells you when you last ran ScanDisk on the hard disk and offers the Check Now button to launch ScanDisk. See "Detecting and Repairing Hard Disk Errors with ScanDisk," later in this chapter.

Backup status: This group deals with Microsoft Backup. It tells you when you last used this utility to back up files from the hard disk, and offers the Backup Now button to run Microsoft Backup. I discuss this program in Chapter 16, "Preparing for Trouble."

See Also...
"Backing Up
Your Files,"
p. 372

Defragmentation status: This group deals with the Disk Defragmenter utility. It shows you when you last used the program on the hard disk and offers the Defragment Now button to start the program. See "Optimizing Disk Access Times with Disk Defragmenter," later in this chapter.

Using Disk Cleanup to Remove Unnecessary Files

The easiest form of hard-disk maintenance is simply to delete any file and folder detritus that has accumulated over the years. This will free up disk space, make your system easier to navigate, and slightly improve hard-disk performance.

Windows 98 comes with a new Disk Cleanup utility that enables you to remove certain types of files quickly and easily. Before discussing this utility, let's look at a few methods you can use to perform a spring cleaning on your hard disk by hand:

Uninstall programs you don't use: With the Internet and online services only a modem call away, it's easier than ever to download new software for a trial run. Unfortunately, that also means it's easier than ever to have unused programs cluttering your hard disk. Chapter 5, "Getting the Most Out of Your Applications," shows you how to uninstall these and other rejected applications.

See Also...
"Uninstalling
Applications,"
p. 146

Delete downloaded program archives: Speaking of program downloads, your hard disk is also probably littered with ZIP files or other downloaded archives. For those programs you use, you should consider moving the archive files to a removable medium for storage. For programs you don't use, you should delete the archive files.

Remove Windows components that you don't use: If you don't use some Windows 98 components, use the Control Panel's Add/Remove Programs icon to remove those components from your system.

See Also...
"Powerful Search
Techniques for
Finding Files,"
p. 168

Delete application backup files: Applications often create backup copies of existing files and name the backups using either the .bak or .old extension. Use the Find utility to locate these files and delete them (see Chapter 6, "Expert Windows Explorer Techniques").

Delete empty files: Your system will often accumulate empty files that just take up directory entries unnecessarily. Again, you can use Find to locate these files (in the Advanced tab, set the Size Is control to At Most 0KB).

Delete the Windows 98 uninstall data: If you elected to save your system files during the Windows 98 installation, Setup will store those files in a hidden file called Winundo.dat in your hard disk's root folder. This file could be over 65MB, so if you're sure you want to stick with Windows 98, you should delete the uninstall data.

Watch Out!
The Windows 98 uninstall data is actually spread across multiple files. The best way to remove all of this data safely is to run the Control Panel's Add/Remove Program icon and then select the Delete Windows 98 uninstall information item.

In earlier versions of Windows, the preceding techniques were the only methods available for cleaning out a hard disk, short of what third-party programs offered. Windows 98 fixes that by offering the Disk Cleanup utility, which can automatically remove some of the preceding categories, as well as several other types of files. It's not the most powerful tool in the world, but it's not bad. Here's how it works:

1. Select Start, Programs, Accessories, System Tools, Disk Cleanup. The Select Drive dialog box appears.

2. Choose the disk drive you want to work with and then click OK. Disk Cleanup scans the drive to see which files can be deleted, and then displays a window similar to the one shown in Figure 13.2.

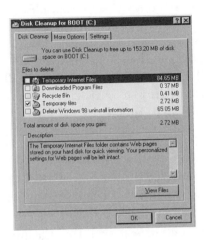

Figure 13.2
Disk Cleanup can automatically and safely remove certain types of files from a disk drive.

3. In the Files to delete list, activate the check box beside each category of file you want to remove (note that for most of these items you can click View Files to see what you'll be deleting):

   Temporary Internet Files: This is a collection of HTML files, images, and other Web page data that Internet Explorer stores just in case you revisit a Web site. These files are from the Windows\Temporary Internet Files folder.

   Downloaded Program Files: This is a collection of Java applets and ActiveX controls that were used by some of the Web sites you've visited. These files are from the Windows\Downloaded Program Files folder.

   Recycle Bin: This is the collection of deleted files in the drive's Recycle Bin.

   Temporary Files: This is the collection of files in Windows 98's Temp folder, which is usually Windows\Temp. Windows 98 and most Windows applications use this folder to store working files that they need temporarily. These files are

Shortcut
Windows 98 offers two methods for bypassing the Select Drive dialog box. One is to click the Disk Cleanup button in a disk drive's property sheet (see Figure 13.1). The other is to select Start, Run, and enter cleanmgr /d*drive*, where *drive* is the letter of the drive you want to work with (for example, cleanmgr /dc).

usually deleted when you either shut down the application or exit Windows. Activating this check box deletes only old temporary files that are not currently being used.

Delete Windows 98 uninstall information: This item represents the Windows 98 uninstall files that I mentioned earlier.

4. The buttons in the More Options tab enable you to remove Windows 98 components, uninstall programs, and convert your drive to FAT32. I'll discuss the latter in Chapter 14, "Making the Move to FAT32."

5. Windows 98 monitors the free space on your hard disks. If the free space gets low, Windows 98 will alert you to the problem and ask if you want to run Disk Cleanup. If you'd prefer that Windows 98 not display this alert, select the Settings tab and deactivate the If this drive runs low on disk space, automatically run Disk Cleanup check box.

6. Click OK. Disk Cleanup asks if you're sure you want to delete the files.

7. Click Yes. Disk Cleanup deletes the selected files.

Remember
The Microsoft Plus! 98 add-on comes with an enhanced version of Disk Cleanup that can delete a large number of "non-critical" files. These include archives, application backup files, empty files and folders, setup files, screen savers, wallpapers, and much more. See the following page on Microsoft's site: http://www. microsoft.com/ windows98/guide/ win98plus/ features/.

Detecting and Repairing Hard Disk Errors with ScanDisk

Hard disk errors and crashes are an unfortunate fact of computing life. Not only can events such as a power surge or an improper shutdown wreak havoc on a hard disk's file system, but most hard disks simply wear out after a few years, the victims of deterioration and the daily grind of constant disk accesses. Here's a rundown of just a few of the maladies that can befall the modern hard disk:

Lost file fragments: The File Allocation Table (FAT, for short; see Chapter 14) tracks which hard-disk clusters belong to which file. If a cluster has a non-zero entry in the FAT, it indicates that the cluster is part of a file. However, if one of those non-zero clusters isn't part of any file's cluster chain, the result is a *lost file fragment* (sometimes called a *lost cluster*).

Cross-linked files: This error occurs when the FAT assigns the same cluster either to two different files or twice to the same file.

Invalid filenames: This error occurs when a filename contains an invalid character.

Invalid dates and times: This error occurs when a file has a date and time stamp that use an illegal date or time (such as 31/31/98).

Duplicate filenames: This rare error occurs when two or more files in the same folder have the same name.

Invalid DOS name length: This error occurs when the full DOS "8.3" path and name for a file exceeds 66 characters. This is never a problem in a Windows DOS session, but it can lead to errors when you switch to MS-DOS mode.

Fortunately, Windows 98's ScanDisk utility can check for and fix all of these errors. It can also examine the surface of the hard disk to make sure there are no flaws—called *bad sectors*—that could render a file unreadable. If ScanDisk does find such a bad sector, it updates the FAT to mark the flaw so that no file uses the sector for storage.

Here are the steps to follow to run ScanDisk:

1. Select Start, Programs, Accessories, System Tools, ScanDisk. Figure 13.3 shows the ScanDisk window that appears.

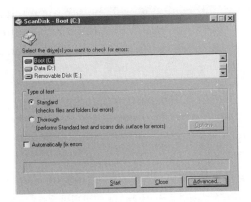

See Also...
"Understanding the FAT," p. 331

Remember
The following characters are illegal in Windows 98's long filenames:
~ ` ! @ # $ % ^ & ( ) _ - + = [ ] ; ' ,

Figure 13.3
Use ScanDisk to check for and repair hard-disk errors.

2. Pick out the drive you want to check by highlighting it in the Select the drive(s) you want to check for errors list. You can select multiple drives, if necessary.

3. Select the Standard option to check just the disk's files and folders. If you'd like ScanDisk to also check the disk surface, activate the Thorough option.

4. If you chose the Thorough scan, the Options button becomes available. Clicking this button displays the Surface Scan Options dialog box with the following settings:

   Areas of the disk to scan: These options tell ScanDisk which part of the disk to scan. The *system area* is the disk location that stores the master boot record and other data structures used by the file system. The *data area* is the disk location that stores the files and folders. I recommend activating the System and data areas option.

   Do not perform write-testing: To ensure data integrity, the surface scan reads whatever data a sector contains and then writes it back to the disk. This is a good idea, but it can slow down the surface scan. For a faster scan, activate this check box. I recommend leaving this check box deactivated.

   Do not repair bad sectors in hidden and system files: If ScanDisk finds a bad sector where a file is stored, it "repairs" the file by moving it to a different location on the disk. This can be a problem for some hidden or system files because applications often expect these files to be in specific disk locations. To avoid these kinds of problems, activate this check box. I recommend leaving this check box deactivated.

5. Click the Advanced button to display the ScanDisk Advanced Options dialog box, which contains the following groups:

   Display summary: Use these options to determine whether ScanDisk displays a summary of disk statistics and problems repaired at the end of the check.

Watch Out!
ScanDisk usually won't be able to fix bad sectors in the system area. However, it's still worthwhile checking this area because errors here are indications that hard-disk failure may be imminent.

Log file: These options determine whether and how ScanDisk creates a log that summarizes the errors found and fixed during the check. (The log file is named Scandisk.log, and it's stored in the drive's root folder.)

Cross-linked files: These options specify what ScanDisk does if it comes across any cross-linked files. Note that Make copies is probably your best option because then at least one of the files involved will probably remain valid.

Lost file fragments: These options specify the action ScanDisk takes when it discovers a lost file fragment. Select Free to allow other files to use the cluster, or select Convert to files to convert the fragments to files.

Check files for: These check boxes control whether ScanDisk performs the indicated checks.

Check host drive first: If you have a compressed drive on your system, errors on this drive are almost always caused by errors on the uncompressed host drive. Leave this check box activated to have ScanDisk check the host drive before checking the compressed drive.

Report MS-DOS mode name length errors: Activate this check box to have ScanDisk look for DOS names that are too long.

6. If you activate the Automatically fix errors check box, ScanDisk repairs any errors it finds by using the options outlined in step 5. This is useful if you'll be running ScanDisk unattended. Otherwise, I recommend leaving this check box deactivated.

7. Click Start to begin the check.

8. If ScanDisk detects a problem, it displays a dialog box to let you know. For example, Figure 13.4 shows the dialog box that appears if ScanDisk finds lost file fragments. Choose the repair option you want and then click OK.

9. When the check is complete, ScanDisk displays a summary. Click OK.

10. Click Close to exit ScanDisk.

Inside Scoop
If you'll be running ScanDisk unattended while checking multiple drives, be sure to select Never in the Display summary group. Otherwise, ScanDisk will display the summary after checking the first drive and won't continue until you dismiss the dialog box.

Inside Scoop
The files created from the lost fragments are root folder files with names like File0000.chk and File0001.chk. The latter are almost always unusable, so freeing up the affected cluster is usually the best approach.

Figure 13.4
ScanDisk displays
a dialog box such
as this when it
comes across an
error.

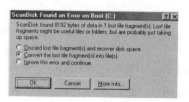

Optimizing Disk Access Times with Disk Defragmenter

Except for very small files, most of the files on your hard disk are stored in multiple clusters (this is called a *cluster chain*), and everything is tracked by the FAT. When you delete a file, the FAT marks that file's clusters as free, and after several deletions, you end up with gaps throughout the FAT. When you save new files (or install a program), the FAT uses these gaps to store the files.

Undocumented
Fragmented files
not only slow disk
access, but they
also make the
disk cache less
effective. The
cache uses a
read-ahead tech-
nology that
assumes the next
cluster in the FAT
is the one most
likely to be
accessed. This is
less likely to be
true when files are
fragmented.

This is an efficient way to work, but it results in *file fragmentation*: files whose clusters are scattered throughout the hard disk. This can drastically reduce disk performance because although it probably takes only about 2 ms to read a 4KB cluster, the seek time to another, noncontiguous cluster could take 10 or 12 ms.

To optimize disk access, you need to *defragment* your hard disk so that all the files reside in contiguous clusters. Windows 98's Disk Defragmenter tool does this by physically rearranging each file's clusters so they're contiguous (and adjusting the FAT accordingly).

Running Disk Defragmenter

Disk Defragmenter can take up to several hours to complete its chores, so you should wait until you won't be using your computer for a while before running the optimization. I usually run it overnight. Here are the steps to follow to use Disk Defragmenter:

1. Select Start, Programs, Accessories, System Tools, Disk Defragmenter. The Select Drive dialog box appears.

2. Choose the drive you want to work with by highlighting it within the Which drive do you want to defragment? list. To defragment all hard disks, select All Hard Drives at the bottom of the list.

3. To set some Disk Defragmenter options, click Settings to display the dialog box shown in Figure 13.5. You have the following options (click OK when you're done):

   Rearrange program files so my programs start faster: When this setting is activated, Disk Defragmenter arranges the clusters of some application startup files so that they are more easily accessed on the disk. See the next section, "Understanding the Intel Application Launch Accelerator," for details.

   Check drive for errors: When this setting is activated, Disk Defragmenter runs ScanDisk behind the scenes before it defragments the disk.

   I want to use these options: Use these settings to tell Disk Defragmenter when you want to use the options you've selected.

Shortcut
One way to avoid the Select Drive dialog box is to display the property sheet for the drive you want to defragment, select the Tools tab, and then click Defragment Now. Another way is to select Start, Run, enter defrag d: (where *d* is the letter of the drive you want to work with), and then click OK.

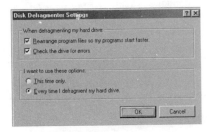

Figure 13.5
Use this dialog box to work with some Disk Defragmenter settings.

4. Click OK. Disk Defragmenter runs ScanDisk (assuming you left the Check drive for errors setting activated) and then starts defragmenting the drive. If you'd like to watch the clusters getting rearranged, click Show Details.

5. When the defragmenting is complete, the program asks if you want to exit. Click Yes to exit, or else click No to optimize another drive.

Undocumented
During the defragmenting, the Disk Defragmenter window displays the percentage of the operation that has been completed. It may appear that the operation is stalled at 10%. However, that's the part where Disk Defragmenter optimizes your program startup files, so it's really not a problem. After that's done, the operation proceeds normally.

Understanding the Intel Application Launch Accelerator

When you launch an application, you're running an executable file—generally an `.exe` or `.com` file. However, most large applications hoist themselves into memory by also calling a number of other support files, mostly `.dll` files. Not only that, but programs typically load part of one file, then call another file, load more of the first file, and so on. For example, Word 97 begins by loading `winword.exe`, which then loads `wwintl32.dll`, then `mso97.dll`, then `mso7enu.dll`, then `Normal.dot`, then more of `mso97.dll`, and so on.

In other words, defragmenting an application's startup files probably won't produce the fastest load times. For optimal startup performance, it would be better to take all of the files that an application uses at startup and then arrange the clusters sequentially—that is, in the order that they load when you start the application.

That's the premise behind the Intel Application Launch Accelerator (IALA) technology included in Windows 98. Each time you start Windows 98, a small (28KB) program called Task Monitor (`Windows\Taskmon.exe`) is loaded into memory automatically via the `TaskMonitor` setting in the following Registry key:

```
HKEY_LOCAL_MACHINE\Software\Microsoft\Windows\Current
Version\Run
```

Task Monitor runs in the background and watches out for application launches. When it detects an application loading, it monitors the progress of the startup at the cluster level. It then writes the entire launch process to a log file in the hidden `Windows\Applog` folder. The bulk of the log is stored in a text file with the `.lgd` extension (for example, `Winword.lgd`), although other files are used as well. Note, too, that Task Monitor also tracks how many times you run each program.

When you run Disk Defragmenter (and assuming you have the `Rearrange program files so my programs start faster` setting activated), the program examines the Task Monitor's log files and then uses IALA to optimally arrange the clusters of the startup files. Also, programs you launch most often are placed closer to the start of the disk for fastest access.

When the optimization is complete, Disk Defragmenter creates a text file named Optlog.txt in the Applog folder. An example of this file is shown in Figure 13.6. This file is divided into five sections:

Program Eligible for Optimization: This section lists all the programs that were optimized. The programs are arranged with the most used at the top, and you get the number of uses, the last time you launched the program, the path of the program's executable file, and more.

Maximum Number of Programs Eligible for Optimization Reached: IALA will only optimize the 50 most-launched programs. All other programs are listed in this section.

Programs Ineligible for Optimization: This section lists the programs that, for one reason or another, could not be optimized. The Flag column displays one or more letter codes that tell you why the program was not optimized.

Control parameters: This section tells you some of the settings that IALA uses:

Use app profile: When this is Yes, IALA uses the Task Monitor log to optimize the program.

Minimum log size: This is the minimum size, in bytes, that a log file must be in order for IALA to optimize the program. The idea here is that a program with a small log file must be loading only a few files at startup, and so wouldn't benefit from optimization. The default value is 1000.

Maximum no use days: This setting is the maximum number of days a program can go unused before it's no longer eligible for optimization. The default value is 90.

Maximum apps: This is the maximum number of applications that IALA will optimize. The default value is 50.

> 66
> The IALA-enabled PC launched all three Microsoft Office applications—Microsoft Word, Microsoft Excel and Microsoft PowerPoint—in approximately 3.2 seconds, compared to 12.3 seconds required to launch the same applications on the PC without IALA technology.
> —Rick Coulson, Intel Platform Architecture Lab
> 99

Flags for Ineligible Programs: This section gives you a key to the letter codes used in the Flags column of the Programs Ineligible for Optimization section.

Figure 13.6
A summary of the optimized programs is written to the Optlog.txt file.

Inside Scoop
The Optlog.txt file isn't read by Disk Defragmenter, so editing the settings in this file won't change how IALA operates.

See Also...
"Types of Memory," p. 291

```
Optlog.txt - Notepad                                                    _|&|x
File  Edit  Search  Help
Program Launch Optimization Log - Created Thu Sep 03 17:31:13 1998

Programs Eligible for Optimization:
Ord Flag ProgName  Uses  LastExecDate  Program Path
1        FINDFAST  3433  1998.09.02    D:\MICROSOFT OFFICE\OFFICE\FINDFAST.EXE
2        C2        362   1998.08.18    C:\PROGRAM FILES\VB\C2.EXE
3        RUNDLL32  355   1998.09.03    C:\WINDOWS\RUNDLL32.EXE
4        EXPLORER  315   1998.09.03    C:\WINDOWS\EXPLORER.EXE
5        NOTEPAD   242   1998.09.02    C:\WINDOWS\NOTEPAD.EXE
6        MSACCESS  155   1998.09.03    D:\MICROSOFT OFFICE\OFFICE\MSACCESS.EXE
7        OUTLOOK   154   1998.09.03    D:\MICROSOFT OFFICE\OFFICE\OUTLOOK.EXE
8        UEDIT32   124   1998.09.03    D:\ULTRAEDIT\UEDIT32.EXE
9        WINHLP32  92    1998.09.03    C:\WINDOWS\WINHLP32.EXE
10       WINWORD   82    1998.08.19    D:\MICROSOFT OFFICE\OFFICE\WINWORD.EXE
11       LINK      77    1998.09.02    C:\PROGRAM FILES\VB\LINK.EXE
12       OSA       77    1998.09.02    D:\MICROSOFT OFFICE\OFFICE\OSA.EXE
13       PSP       58    1998.09.03    D:\PAINT SHOP PRO 5\PSP.EXE
14       REGSUR32  58    1998.09.02    C:\WINDOWS\SYSTEM\REGSUR32.EXE
15       BSHELF98  53    1998.09.03    C:\PROGRAM FILES\MICROSOFT\REFERENCE\BOOKSHELF 98\BSHELF98.
16       REALPLAY  51    1998.08.11    D:\REAL\PLAYPLUS\REALPLAY.EXE
17       WINZIP32  40    1998.08.20    D:\WINZIP\WINZIP32.EXE
18       USCHED    39    1998.09.03    D:\MCAFEE VIRUSSCAN\USCHED.EXE
19       WSCRIPT   36    1998.09.03    C:\WINDOWS\WSCRIPT.EXE
20       SPOOL32   35    1998.09.03    C:\WINDOWS\SYSTEM\SPOOL32.EXE
21       NETSCAPE  34    1998.09.03    D:\NETSCAPE\NAVIGATOR\PROGRAM\NETSCAPE.EXE
22       UB5       34    1998.08.18    C:\PROGRAM FILES\VB\UB5.EXE
23       QBW       31    1998.09.03    D:\QBOOKSW\QBW.EXE
24       USHWIN32  31    1998.09.02    D:\MCAFEE VIRUSSCAN\USHWIN32.EXE
25       VIDSUR    28    1998.09.02    C:\PROGRAM FILES\TV VIEWER\VIDSUR.EXE
26       REGEDIT   26    1998.09.03    C:\WINDOWS\REGEDIT.EXE
27       RUNONCE   23    1998.09.03    C:\WINDOWS\SYSTEM\RUNONCE.EXE
28       EXCEL     22    1998.09.03    D:\MICROSOFT OFFICE\OFFICE\EXCEL.EXE
29       INFOVIEW  21    1998.09.03    D:\TECHNET\INFOVIEW.EXE
30       TWUNK_16  17    1998.07.28    C:\WINDOWS\TWUNK_16.EXE
31       LVIEWPRO  17    1998.07.28    D:\LVIEWPRO\LVIEWPRO.EXE
32       TVX       15    1998.09.02    C:\PROGRAM FILES\TV VIEWER\TVX.EXE
```

Using WinAlign to Speed Up Program Launching

I mentioned in Chapter 12, "Maximizing Your System's Memory," that Windows 98 sets up a disk cache in main memory. The purpose of this cache is to store frequently used bits of program code. This improves performance because it reduces the number of times the system has to read code from the much slower hard disk.

Even though the disk cache gives Windows 98 a big performance boost, there is still some overhead involved:

- The system must copy the required code from the cache to the memory space used by the program.

- You end up with two copies of the code in memory.

You could eliminate both sources of overhead by executing the code right from the disk cache. Unfortunately, that's problematic because memory uses 4KB pages and most programs are divided into 512-byte sections. So, if the system tried to execute a code snippet directly from the cache, it's unlikely (one chance in eight) that the snippet would be an exact multiple of 4KB, so it would fail.

To solve this problem, Microsoft has done four things:

- They have compiled all of the Windows 98 executable files so that they now come aligned on 4KB boundaries.

- They have encouraged developers to align their executables on 4KB boundaries.

- They have included a new tool in Windows 98 called WinAlign that restructures existing executables so that they are aligned on 4KB boundaries.

- They have included a new technology in Windows 98 called MapCache that can run aligned code directly from the disk cache.

If the Windows 98 Setup program locates Microsoft Office 97 executables, it runs WinAlign to optimize these files on 4KB boundaries. Also, WinAlign (`Windows\System\Walign.exe`) is set up to run automatically once a month in the Scheduled Tasks folder. (See the `Tune-up Application Start` item.)

Compressing Files with DriveSpace

The days of having to squeeze every last megabyte out of our hard disks are more or less a thing of the past. Today's modern hard disks are digital behemoths that boast multi-gigabyte capacities, so even power users will be hard-pressed to fill them up. Not only that, but the per-megabyte price of these drives has dropped dramatically over the past couple of years, so even if an upgrade becomes necessary, it will usually be well within the budget of most users.

However, there are still some scenarios where you'll want to get the most out of your hard-disk investment. For example, you may have donated a used machine to the kids, you may have an older notebook machine that can't be upgraded, or you may need to cram a few extra files onto a limited-capacity removable disk, such as a Zip disk or a Jaz disk.

For these situations, Windows 98 offers the DriveSpace disk compression utility. DriveSpace works by compressing files so that they take up much less disk space (for some files, up to 50% less space). You have two ways to proceed:

Compress files: In this scenario, DriveSpace compresses your existing files and, depending on the size of the disk, whatever free space is left on the disk. This gives you the maximum amount of space on the disk.

Compress free space: In this scenario, DriveSpace sets up some or all of the remaining free space on the disk as a separate, compressed drive. This is useful if you have only certain files that you want to compress.

To get started, select Start, Programs, Accessories, System Tools, DriveSpace. Windows 98 displays the DriveSpace 3 window, which includes a list of your system's disk drives.

The next two sections show you how to run the two compression methods mentioned above.

Using DriveSpace to Compress Files

When you compress files and free space, DriveSpace performs the following chores:

1. The drive is hidden and its letter is changed to H (or to the first free drive letter). This new drive letter is known as the *host* for the compressed data.

2. For each file on drive H, DriveSpace compresses the file and appends it to a special file called the *compressed volume file* (CVF) named Drvspace.000.

3. The attributes of the CVF are set to hidden, read-only, and system.

4. The CVF is assigned the drive letter (say, C) of the original disk.

The upshot of all this is that your system looks and acts exactly as it did before compression. (Although there will be a slight performance decrease due to the compression and decompression that Windows 98 must go though to work with each file.)

Here are the steps to follow to compress files:

1. Highlight the drive you want to compress.

2. Select the Drive, Compress command. The Compress a Drive dialog box appears, as shown in Figure 13.7. (If the drive's capacity is less than 1GB, you'll see a slightly different dialog box.)

3. Click Options to display the Compression Options dialog box shown in Figure 13.8. This dialog box offers the following settings (click OK when you're done):

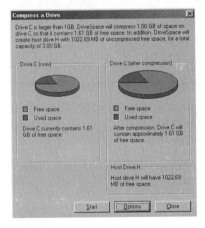

Figure 13.7
This dialog box appears if your drive's capacity is greater than 1GB.

Shortcut
To avoid having to select the drive you want to work with, display the drive's property sheet, select the Compression tab, and then click Compress Drive.

Drive letter of host drive: Use this list to choose the drive letter you prefer for the host drive.

Free space on host drive: Use this text box to adjust the amount of free space on the host.

Hide host drive: If you activate this check box, DriveSpace hides the host drive so that it doesn't appear within Windows Explorer. Don't activate this option if the host drive will have more than the minimum 2MB of free space. This will enable you to still work with the host drive.

Remember
You can't reduce the host's free space to less than 2MB, and you can't increase it to more than about 1GB.

4. Click Start to begin the compression. DriveSpace asks if you want to create or update your startup disk. (The updated disk will contain real-mode compression drivers so that your compressed disk is available when you boot from the floppy.)

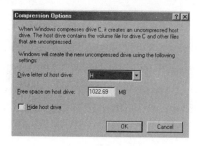

5. If you need to create or update the startup disk, click Yes; otherwise, click No.

6. DriveSpace now gives you an opportunity to back up your files. If you want to take advantage of this, click Back Up Files.

7. To launch the compression, click Compress Now. DriveSpace runs ScanDisk in the background and then starts the compression. (DriveSpace might have to restart Windows 98 if the drive you're compressing contains the Windows 98 system files.)

8. When the compression is complete, click Close.

9. If DriveSpace asks if you want to restart your computer, click Yes.

Using DriveSpace to Compress Free Space

If you decide to compress only the free space on a disk, DriveSpace will use the free space to create a new compressed drive. Here are the steps to follow:

1. In the DriveSpace 3 window, select the Advanced, Create Empty command. DriveSpace displays the Create New Compressed Drive dialog box (see Figure 13.9).

2. Set the following options for your new drive:

   Create a new drive named: Select the drive letter you want to use for the new drive.

   using: Set the number of megabytes of free space that you want to use for the new drive. (The maximum is about 1022MB.)

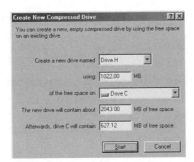

Figure 13.9
This dialog box
appears, then you
create a new com-
pressed drive from
an existing drive's
free space.

of the free space on: Select the drive from which you want to convert the free space.

The new drive will contain about: Instead of adjusting the using text box, you can use this text box to specify how much free space you want on the new drive (up to about 2,043MB).

Afterwards, drive _X_ will contain: Set the number of megabytes of free space you want to preserve on the original drive.

3. Click Start to launch the compression. (You may have to run through some or all of steps 5–9 from the previous section.)

Essential Information

- The property sheet for a disk drive tells you the disk's label, the amount of free and used space, the total capacity of the disk, and it provides shortcuts to Disk Cleanup, ScanDisk, Disk Defragmenter, and more.

- The Disk Cleanup utility offers an easy method for ridding your system of temporary local files, temporary Internet files, downloaded controls and applets, and Recycle Bin files.

- To ensure the good health of your hard disk, run ScanDisk regularly to look for lost file fragments, cross-linked files, bad sectors, and other disk errors.

- Disk Defragmenter improves hard-disk access times by rearranging file clusters so that they're contiguous.

- WinAlign restructures executable files so that their sections reside on 4KB boundaries, which enables MapCache to execute code directly from the disk cache.

- To gain more disk space, use DriveSpace to either compress files or convert free space into a new compressed drive.

Making the Move to FAT32

I N THE PREVIOUS CHAPTER, I discussed DriveSpace and showed you that it can create extra hard disk room by compressing files and free space. On the downside, I mentioned that the cost of DriveSpace is a slight performance hit because of the extra time required to decompress and compress files when reading them to and from memory.

If you want a bit more disk space, but don't want any kind of performance drop-off, Windows 98 offers an alternative to DriveSpace: FAT32. As you'll see in this chapter, FAT32 enables your hard disk to store files more efficiently. This means your existing files take up less room on the disk, thus effectively increasing your disk space. And because the files themselves aren't altered, there's no performance hit. True, FAT32 doesn't net you as much extra disk real estate as DriveSpace, but FAT32 also brings a few other improvements to the file allocation table, including support for very large hard disks. This chapter discusses these advantages, and a few disadvantages, and shows you how to convert a hard disk to FAT32.

Understanding the FAT

You don't need to understand how FAT32 works in order to use it successfully. However, a bit of background on the underlying technology will help you decide whether to convert a disk to FAT32. The next two sections guide you through the inner mysteries of this new Windows 98 file system.

chapter 14

Remember

Clusters (or *file allocation units* as they're often called) aren't the fundamental storage unit on the disk. That honor belongs to the *sectors*, which are 512-byte divisions of the disk's magnetic medium. Because a typical disk has so many sectors (over 2 million per gigabyte), the file system groups them into clusters, which range in size from 2,048 bytes (four sectors) to 32,768 bytes (64 sectors).

When a hard disk is partitioned using the FDISK command, a number of data structures are written to the disk, including the Master Boot Record. When you then format the disk, more data structures are created, including the root directory and the file allocation table (FAT). Besides these *system area* structures, the format also creates a *data area*, which consists of (usually) thousands of *clusters* (the exact number depends on the capacity of the disk).

To keep track of everything on the disk, the file system uses two structures:

- A file directory
- The FAT

A *file directory* is a list of all the files and subfolders within a folder. Each file directory entry is a 32-byte value that tracks the data shown in Table 14.1.

TABLE 14.1: THE DATA TRACKED BY EACH FILE DIRECTORY ENTRY

Data	Size
Primary name	8 bytes
Extension	3 bytes
Attributes (hidden, read-only, and so on)	1 byte
Reserved for future use	6 bytes
Date the file was last modified	2 bytes
Exclusive access handle	2 bytes
Time the file was created	2 bytes
Date the file was created	2 bytes
Starting cluster number in the FAT	2 bytes
File size in bytes	4 bytes

The *FAT* is a database of all the disk's clusters. It contains 16-bit values that track what's in each cluster:

- If the value is 0, it means that no file is using the cluster.
- If the value is non-zero, it means a file is using the cluster. The FAT value is a hexadecimal number that points to the cluster that stores the next part of the file.

- If the value is a special EOF marker, it means the cluster represents the end of a file.

From all of this, you can now deduce how the file system tracks an individual file:

1. The file is located in the file directory.

2. The file's starting cluster number is read from the file directory (refer to Table 14.1).

3. The cluster number is found in the FAT.

4. If the FAT entry points to another cluster number, repeat step 3.

5. Stop when the FAT entry contains the EOF marker.

Inside Scoop
The FAT also uses a special value (FFF7 in hexadecimal) to indicate that a cluster has at least one bad sector. Clusters marked with this value are not used to store data.

The FAT and Cluster Size

The key thing about the FAT is its "16-bitness." 16 bits can be arranged in up to 65,536 ways, which means that no hard disk can have more than 65,536 clusters. How does this jibe with the fact that hard-disk partition capacities range from a few-dozen megabytes to a couple of gigabytes? The relationship is simple: the larger the partition, the larger the cluster size, as shown in Table 14.2.

TABLE 14.2: CLUSTER SIZES FOR VARIOUS PARTITION SIZES

Partition Size	Cluster Size
16–127MB	2,048 bytes
128–255MB	4,096 bytes
256–511MB	8,192 bytes
512–1023MB	16,384 bytes
1024–2047MB	32,768 bytes

Inside Scoop
Floppy disks and other disks with partitions less than 16MB use a 12-bit FAT with 4,096-byte cluster sizes.

Calculating Cluster Slack

Earlier I told you that the FAT maps out a disk at the cluster level, so finer divisions aren't possible. This means that even the smallest file takes up an entire cluster. Similarly, if a file spans multiple clusters, you could have a tiny piece of the file using up a whole cluster. For example, suppose a partition uses 2,048-byte clusters and you have a 2,049-byte file. The fist 2,048 bytes take up one cluster, but that last byte doesn't fit, so it takes up its own cluster. The difference between the size of a cluster and the amount of data stored in the cluster is called the *cluster slack* (or sometimes the *cluster overhang*).

To see cluster slack in action, open a DOS session and run the following command in any folder:

```
dir /a /ogn /v
```

The /a switch displays hidden and system files, the /ogn switch sorts the listing by name with directories first, and the /v switch initiates verbose mode, which tells you, among other things, the number of bytes allocated to each file. Here's a sample listing for a 2GB partition that uses 32,768-bytes clusters:

```
Volume in drive C is BOOT
Volume Serial Number is 101B-18F7
Directory of C:\
File Name          Size        Allocated      Modified
Accessed   Attrib


MYDOCU~1         <DIR>                       09-11-98  6:18p
09-11-98      D       My Documents
PROGRA~1         <DIR>                       09-11-98  5:53p
R    D        Program Files
RECYCLED         <DIR>                       09-21-98  4:24p
09-21-98   HS D       RECYCLED
WINDOWS          <DIR>                       09-11-98  5:42p
R    D       WINDOWS
AUTOEXEC DOS        162       32,768   09-11-98  5:46p
10-15-98       A     AUTOEXEC.DOS
AUTOEXEC BAT        195       32,768   10-14-98 10:47p
10-19-98             AUTOEXEC.BAT
COMMAND  DOS      54,645      65,536   05-31-94  6:22a
10-09-98       A     COMMAND.DOS
COMMAND  COM      93,880      98,304   05-11-98  8:01p
10-09-98       A     COMMAND.COM
CONFIG   DOS        177       32,768   09-11-98  5:46p
10-15-98       A     CONFIG.DOS
CONFIG   SYS        230       32,768   10-14-98  3:52p
10-19-98       A     CONFIG.SYS
IO       DOS      40,774      65,536   05-31-94  6:22a
RHS   A      IO.DOS
IO       SYS     222,390     229,376   05-11-98  8:01p
```

```
09-29-98  RHS        IO.SYS
MSDOS     DOS       38,138        65,536   05-31-94  6:22a
RHS  A       MSDOS.DOS
MSDOS     SYS        1,694        32,768   09-30-98  9:16a
10-19-98  RHS       MSDOS.SYS
SETUPLOG  TXT      121,824       131,072   09-11-98  6:15p
09-11-98    H   A   SETUPLOG.TXT
SUHDLOG   DAT        7,798        32,768   09-11-98  6:03p
09-28-98  RH        SUHDLOG.DAT
SYSTEM    1ST      544,800       557,056   09-11-98  6:03p
09-28-98  RH        SYSTEM.1ST
USBLOG    TXT          120        32,768   10-05-98  8:58a
10-15-98      A     usblog.txt
WINUNDO   DAT    5,407,171     5,439,488   09-11-98  5:53p
09-28-98  RH        WINUNDO.DAT
WINUNDO   INI      298,320       327,680   09-11-98  5:53p
09-28-98  RH        WINUNDO.INI
          16 file(s)       6,832,318 bytes
           4 dir(s)        7,208,960 bytes allocated
                       1,729,495,040 bytes free
                       2,146,631,680 bytes total disk space,
19% in use
```

Note, in particular, the difference between the values in the Size and Allocated columns. For example, the AUTOEXEC.DOS file is a mere 162 bytes, but it takes up an entire 32,768-byte cluster, resulting in cluster slack of 32,606 bytes! This means that about 99.5% of that cluster is wasted. On the other hand, the WINUNDO.DAT file is 5,407,171 bytes and is allocated 5,439,488 bytes (166 clusters). The slack is 32,317 bytes. This is nearly an entire cluster, but that represents a mere 0.6% of the total allocated space.

These two extreme examples demonstrate the reality of file storage on FAT partitions: Very small files waste large amounts of space, wnereas very large files waste only small amounts of space. But what about the overall slack on your disk? Here's how to find out this crucial value:

1. In Windows Explorer's All Folders list, click the drive you want to work with.

2. Either run the Edit, Select All command, or press Ctrl+A. Windows Explorer selects every object in the Contents list.

3. Right-click any selected object, and then click Properties. Windows Explorer takes a few seconds to perform some calculations and then displays both the size of selected files and the number of bytes they use on the disk. In Figure 14.1, for example, you can see the files in this partition constitute 281,444,787 bytes, but the total number of bytes allocated in clusters is 398,852,096.

Figure 14.1
The property sheet for the selected objects shows you the total size of the objects and the number of bytes allocated in clusters.

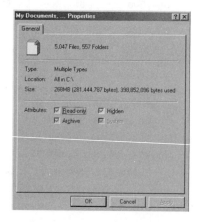

4. Subtract the size from the bytes allocated to get the total cluster slack.

5. Divide the slack by the total bytes allocated to get the percentage of wasted space.

In the example shown in Figure 14.1, the slack is a whopping 117,407,309 bytes, or about 112MB! (To get the number of megabytes, divide the value by 1,048,576). This means that a little more than 29% of the used disk space in this partition is wasted.

In one sense, this is a worst-case scenario because of the 32,768-byte clusters used on this partition. However, the worst case is quickly becoming the most common case because gigabyte-sized partitions (the ones that use 32,768-byte clusters) are becoming the norm. Most multi-gigabyte hard disks arrive now with multiple 1GB–2GB partitions, so cluster slack is automatically a problem for most people.

Watch Out!
To get a true slack value, make sure Windows Explorer is displaying hidden and system files. Select View, Folder Options, display the View tab, and then activate the Show all files option.

What can be done about this waste? Until recently, your only recourse was to use the DOS command FDISK to divide a drive into smaller partitions that use smaller clusters. However, Windows 98 offers a much more attractive alternative: FAT32. The next section shows you how FAT32 can help overcome the problem of cluster slack.

What is FAT32?

Besides wastefully large cluster sizes, the FAT file system has a few other drawbacks:

- The capacity of a FAT partition is limited to 2GB. That limit is derived by multiplying the maximum number of clusters (65,536) by the maximum cluster size (32,768 bytes).

- When you format a disk, the root directory is created in a fixed location. If a bad sector appears within this area, the root directory could be trashed.

- The root directory's fixed location also means the root has a fixed size. For a hard disk, this means the root can't contain more than 512 entries.

To solve all of these problems, Windows 98 has built-in support for a new file system architecture called FAT32. Originally introduced in a limited fashion in Windows 95 OSR2, FAT32 offers the following advantages over FAT16 (as the old file architecture is now called):

Support for partitions larger than 2GB: The "32" in FAT32 tells you that this architecture uses 32-bit values. Six of those bits are reserved for future use, so that leaves 26 bits, or 67,108,864 possible cluster values (2 to the power of 26). Multiplying this by the 32,768-byte cluster limit gives a maximum partition size of 2,199,023,255,552 bytes. This is 2,048GB or 2TB (terabytes).

Dynamic partitioning: Under FAT32, the root folder no longer has a fixed location or a fixed size. This means that it's possible to convert a partition to FAT32 without losing

> **66**
> We've figured out a better way to store data on a hard drive. It's called FAT32 and we've built it into Microsoft Windows 98. So if you put Windows 98 on the computer you're using now, not only will you discover an average of 28% more space on your hard drive, but suddenly YOU'RE A BIG GEEK, using all kinds of fancy-dancy file allocation technology.
> —From a Microsoft ad
> **99**

Undocumented
Although FAT32 partitions can be up to 2TB, the maximum size of the boot partition is only 7.8GB because of BIOS hardware limitations.

data. Theoretically, it also means you can resize a partition on-the-fly, again without losing data. (So far, the latter is only possible by using third-party utilities.)

Better reliability: The fact that the root directory no longer has a fixed location means that it can be moved to avoid bad sectors. Also, FAT32 maintains backup copies of the FAT and a few other data structures.

What about cluster slack? That's probably the biggest advantage of all because FAT32 has dramatically improved storage efficiency, as attested by Table 14.3.

TABLE 14.3: CLUSTER SIZES FOR VARIOUS PARTITION SIZES IN FAT32

Partition Size	Cluster Size
512MB to 8GB	4,096 bytes
8–16GB	8,192 bytes
16–32GB	16,384 bytes
Over 32GB	32,768 bytes

As you can see, partitions up to 8GB now use only 4,096-byte clusters, a vast improvement over the 32,768-bytes clusters that FAT16 uses in gigabyte-sized partitions.

FAT32 sounds like the file system cat's pajamas, but it does have some caveats and disadvantages you should be aware of:

Remember
Windows 2000 has built-in support for FAT32 partitions.

- Other file systems—such as FAT16, NTFS, and HPFS—aren't compatible with FAT32. That is, if you boot to a partition that uses one of these file systems, you won't be able to see any FAT32 partitions on your computer.

- The latter also implies that you can't dual-boot with another operating system if you convert your boot partition to FAT32.

- FAT32 works only on 512MB or larger partitions. (This implies that you can't convert Zip or floppy disks to FAT32.)

- FAT32 works only on uncompressed partitions. If you've compressed a partition using DriveSpace, you won't be able to convert the partition to FAT32.

- After you convert a partition to FAT32, Windows 98 offers no method for converting it back to FAT16.

- FAT32 slightly changes the structure of the file directory entries shown earlier in Table 14.1. Specifically, the size of the "Starting cluster number in the FAT" entry has been increased from 2 bytes (16 bits) to 4 bytes (32 bits) to allow for the new 32-bit cluster numbers. (To compensate, the number of bytes "reserved for future use" has dropped from 6 to 4.) This means that file system utilities that expect to use the old file directory structure will not work under FAT32.

Inside Scoop
Many of these FAT32 problems have been solved by third-party partitioning utilities. The best of these utilities is Partition Magic, by PowerQuest Corporation (http://www.powerquest.com/).

How Much Disk Space Will You Save?

For most people, the main issue when deciding whether to convert a partition to FAT32 is how much disk space they'll save in the process. That's a tricky question because it depends on the composition of your files. If your system has many large files, you'll save less space because large files consist mostly of full clusters. If you have lots of small files, however, you'll save more disk space because small files create all that wasted space inside relatively large clusters.

These distinctions are crucial when deciding whether to convert your partitions to FAT32. To help take some of the guesswork out of this decision, Microsoft has a small (87KB) program called the FAT32 Conversion Information utility that will scan a partition and let you know how much space you'll gain by converting.

Here are the steps to follow to use this program:

1. Insert the Windows 98 CD.

2. In Windows Explorer, open the \tools\reskit\config\ folder.

3. Launch the file named fat32win.exe. The FAT32 Conversion Information window appears.

4. Highlight the drive you want to work with.

Shortcut
If you don't have the Windows 98 CD, you can download the FAT32 Conversion Information utility from the Microsoft Web site at http://www.microsoft.com/windows/downloads/bin/W98FAT32.EXE.

5. Select Scan. The program checks the drive and then reports how much disk space you'll save.

6. Click OK. This returns you to the FAT32 Conversion Information window, which shows various disk statistics, including the amount of additional space you'll get. As you can see in Figure 14.2, my drive would gain an extra 115.49MB in the 397.52MB of used space, or about a 29% increase.

7. If you want to convert the drive to FAT32, click the Convert button to launch Windows 98's Drive Converter utility (discussed in the next section).

Figure 14.2
The FAT32 Conversion Information dialog box tells you how much extra space you get when converting to FAT32.

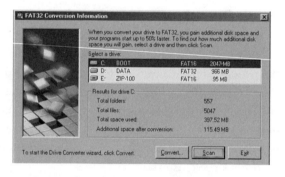

Converting a Partition to FAT32

If you decide to take the FAT32 plunge, Windows 98 offers a couple of different methods for performing the conversion. The next two sections discuss those methods.

Using FDISK

FDISK is the command-line partitioning program that has been around since the earliest days of DOS. It's used to set up primary and extended partitions, specify the boot partition, and to set the size of each partition.

Fortunately, the version of FDISK that comes with Windows 98 has been updated to include FAT32 support. Unfortunately, FDISK is still as destructive as ever. That is, if you use FDISK to repartition your hard disk, you'll lose all the information on the disk. (In fact, each partition will have to be reformatted.)

Shortcut
Before attempting to convert a drive to FAT32, you should check to see if the drive is FAT16. The FAT32 Conversion Information utility tells you what file system a drive uses, as does the drive's property sheet.

Therefore, go the FDISK route only if you plan on wiping out your disk anyway.

Boot to the DOS prompt, and then type `fdisk` and press Enter. When FDISK loads, you'll probably see a long message followed by a prompt:

```
Do you wish to enable large disk support (Y/N)..........?
```

This message and prompt appear only if your hard disk's capacity is 512MB or more. If you press **y** and Enter at this prompt, FDISK will automatically convert all partitions larger than or equal to 512MB to FAT32.

Using Drive Converter

If you'd prefer to keep your data intact during the conversion to FAT32, you need to use the new Drive Converter utility that comes with Windows 98. This utility is easy to use and takes only a few minutes (although the disk defragmentation that runs automatically after the conversion can tack on an hour or two).

To get the Drive Converter utility started, Windows 98 offers the following methods:

- Select Start, Programs, Accessories, System Tools, Drive Converter (FAT32).

- In the Disk Cleanup utility (see Chapter 13, "Optimizing Your Hard Disk"), select the More Options tab and then click Convert.

- In the FAT32 Conversion Information window, click Convert.

With the utility started, follow these steps to run the conversion:

1. Click Next in the initial dialog box. Drive Converter displays a list of drives on your system, as shown in Figure 14.3.

2. Click the drive you want to convert, and then click Next. Drive Converter displays a warning that other operating systems won't be able to access the FAT32 drive.

Watch Out!
Although I have never heard of a user losing data during the conversion to FAT32, you should probably assume the worst. Therefore, you should back up the drive before converting it. Note that Drive Converter gives you a chance to do this before proceeding with the conversion.

See Also...
"Using Disk Cleanup to Remove Unnecessary Files," p. 313

Inside Scoop
You can also run Drive Converter from the MS-DOS mode command line. Use the command `cvt d: /cvt32`, where *d* is the letter of the drive you want to convert.

Figure 14.3
Use this dialog
box to select the
drive you want to
convert to FAT32.

Undocumented
Iomega Jaz drives
come in 1GB and
2GB sizes, so
they're candi-
dates for FAT32.
To run the conver-
sion, however,
you must make
sure that the
drive supports
Interrupt 13 BIOS
calls. In the
Control Panel,
launch the
System icon and
then select the
Device Manager
tab. Open the
Disk drives
branch, highlight
the Jaz drive, and
then click
Properties. In the
Settings tab,
make sure the Int
13 unit check box
is activated.

3. Click OK. Drive Converter scours your system for antivirus checkers and disk utilities that aren't FAT32-compatible.

4. Drive Converter displays a list of the incompatible programs (if any), and offers a Details button to get more information about each one. Note that you may need to disable these utilities, reboot, and then start Drive Converter again.

5. When you're ready to proceed, click Next. Drive Converter now gives you a chance to back up the drive. If you want to back up the drive, click Create Backup to launch Microsoft Backup.

6. When you get back to Drive Converter, click Next. Drive Converter lets you know that it has to restart your computer in MS-DOS mode.

7. Click Next. Drive Converter boots into MS-DOS mode, runs the conversion, and then reboots back into Windows 98.

8. When Drive Converter reappears, click Next >.

9. Click Finish. Drive Converter launches Disk Defragmenter.

Essential Information

- The file allocation table (FAT) is a database of all the clusters on a disk.

- From the FAT's perspective, a cluster is the smallest unit of storage on the disk, so files that don't fill in an entire cluster create wasted space called cluster slack.

- The larger the partition, the larger the cluster size, and the greater the amount of cluster slack.

- FAT32 reduces cluster slack by using 4,096-byte clusters on partitions up to 8GB.

- FAT32 also supports partitions up to 2TB and improves the reliability and flexibility of the root directory.

- Use the FAT32 Conversion Information utility to determine in advance how much disk space you'll save when you convert a partition to FAT32.

- If you're partitioning a disk, the Windows 98 version of FDISK can automatically convert all partitions greater than or equal to 512MB to FAT32.

- To save your data during the conversion, use the Drive Converter utility.

GET THE SCOOP ON...
Information about hardware and software ▪ Checking
for corrupted, changed, or deleted system files ▪
Making your system more robust by resolving system
file conflicts ▪ Protecting your computer from viruses

Crucial System Maintenance Skills

Chapter 15

WHEN YOU ATTEND Microsoft-related conferences and trade shows, the authorized Windows worldview is a pleasant one where systems are up "24/7" and bad things never happen. However, this "don't worry, be happy" attitude is belied by the fact that Windows 98 ships with over two dozen maintenance, information, and troubleshooting tools, and that's not counting the Resource Kit Sampler utilities found on the CD.

It's a good thing Windows 98 has all those tools, too, because here in the real world, bad things can and do happen. Luckily, a few of those Windows 98 system tools enable you to perform important maintenance tasks that can at least help you stave off trouble. This chapter discusses the System Information and File Information utilities, System File Checker, and Version Conflict Manager. I also discuss McAfee VirusScan, an antivirus program that ships on the Microsoft Plus! 98 CD.

Getting the Big Picture: Windows 98 Information Utilities

Let's begin by looking at a couple of programs—System Information and File Information—that aren't maintenance tools, as such. Instead, they're information tools that provide you with data that's useful for troubleshooting problems or understanding the information provided by other programs.

The System Information Utility

See Also...
"An Insider's
Guide to the
Registry,"
p. 104

Troubleshooting problems is often a matter of having a good supply of information about your system's hardware and software components. To its credit, Windows 98 is willing to provide power users with a generous supply of system data. The biggest repository of system info is the Registry, which, as you learned in Chapter 4, "An Insider's Guide to Three Crucial Configuration Tools," is Windows 98's central storehouse for hardware and software settings.

See Also...
"Dealing with
Device Manager,"
p. 529

Another good source of hardware data is Device Manager. As you'll see in Chapter 22, "Taking the Mystery Out of Hardware," Device Manager presents a list of the hardware on your system, as well as the drivers, settings, and resources used by each device.

But probably the most comprehensive source of system data is the new System Information utility. There are two methods you can use to load this program:

- Select Start, Programs, Accessories, System Tools, System Information.

- Select Start, Run, type `msinfo32.exe`, and click OK.

Figure 15.1 shows the window that appears.

Figure 15.1
The System Information program gives you a comprehensive picture of what's on your system.

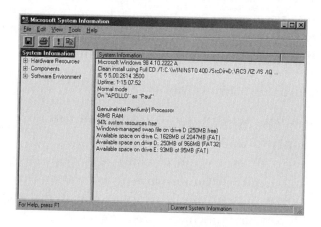

The tree on the left contains various information categories, while the pane on the right displays data for the currently selected category. In the opening view, the left pane shows four main categories:

System Information: This top-level category displays general information about your system, including the Windows 98 version number, the Internet Explorer version number, the uptime (the total time since you last rebooted), the amount of RAM installed, the current system resource level, and basic hard-disk data.

Hardware Resources: This section contains six categories that show you the resources used by the devices on your system. Of particular note is the Conflicts/Sharing category, which will tell you if any devices on your system use conflicting resources. (If your system supports IRQ steering, this category shows you the resources that are shared between devices.)

Remember
The component categories also show color-coded messages if any hardware problems are detected. For example, if the device isn't working properly, you'll see This Device Has a Problem in red type, followed by a description of the problem. Similarly, if a device driver isn't installed, the message Driver Not Installed appears in blue type. See also the Problem Devices category.

Components: This section contains a long list of categories that represent the various hardware components on your system. For each category, you get three viewing options:

- **Basic Information:** Select this option to see the resources allocated to the device and the drivers used by the device.

- **Advanced Information:** Select this option to see the basic information as well as the device's Registry key, all of its possible resource configurations, and the drivers used by the device.

- **History:** Select this option to view a chronological account of the updates made to a device (such as installing a new driver). If you're suddenly having problems with a device, check its history to see what changes were made. (Note, too, that the Components section has a History category that provides a full history of device changes.)

Software Environment: This section contains various categories that tell you about the software running on your system, including the device drivers loaded, the 16-bit and 32-bit executables loaded, the background tasks that are currently running, the programs that run at startup (and where they run from), and much more.

The File Information Utility

When maintaining or troubleshooting Windows, you'll often find yourself dealing with arcane Windows 98 system files of every persuasion from DLLs to VXDs. If you find yourself scratching your head about what a particular file does, you can get at least a bit more information about the file by using the File Information utility that comes on the Windows 98 CD's Resource Kit Sampler.

You can't run this program from the Windows 98 CD. To get it on your hard disk, you have two choices:

- Explore the CD and open the `tools\reskit\diagnose` folder. Copy the files `fileinfo.exe` and `win98.mfi` to your hard disk. When that's done, right-click `win98.mfi` and then click Properties. In the property sheet, deactivate the Read-only check box and then click OK. In this case, you run the program by launching the `fileinfo.exe` file.

- Install the Resource Kit Sampler by launching `setup.exe` from the CD's `tools\reskit` folder. After that's done, you launch the program by first selecting Start, Programs, Windows 98 Resource Kit, Tools Management Console. Now double-click `Tools A to Z`, highlight `D to O`, then double-click `Microsoft File Information`.

Here are the steps to follow when using this program to get information about a Windows 98 file:

1. Select the File Information tab, shown in Figure 15.2.

2. Choose the file you want to work with by using one of the following tabs:

Select By Filename: Use the `First Letter` column to select the first letter of the filename, and then use the `Select File Name` column to highlight the file.

Select By File Extension: Use the `File Extension` column to select the extension used by the file, and then use the `Select File Name` column to highlight the file.

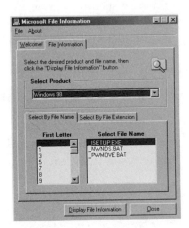

Figure 15.2
Use the File Information tab to pick out the file you want to work with.

3. Click the Display File Information button. The File Information dialog box appears. Figure 15.3 shows the dialog box for `Kernel32.dll`. Notice how you get the file size, its installed location, its location on the Windows 98 CD and floppy disks, the date stamp, and a description of the file. (Not all files will display a description.)

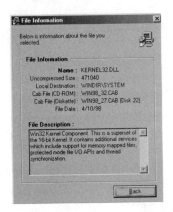

Figure 15.3
The File Information dialog box displays all kinds of useful data about Windows 98's files.

4. Click Back to close the dialog box.

Finding the Version Number of a File

System files and support files are always stamped with a version number to differentiate the various incarnations that the files have gone through. In general, the higher the version number, the newer the file (although, unfortunately, this isn't universally true).

As you'll see in the next section, the version number is crucial when deciding between multiple instances of a system file. Here's one way to determine the version number of a file:

1. In Windows Explorer, highlight the file you want to check.

2. Select File, Properties to display the property sheet for the file.

3. Display the Version tab. As you can see in Figure 15.4, the File version line tells you the version number.

4. Click OK.

Figure 15.4
In a file's property sheet, the Version tab tells you the file's version number.

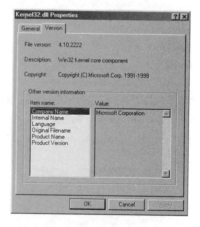

Protecting System Files

Like most programs, Windows 98 comes with support files that provide various services. There are .dll files (dynamic link libraries), .ocx files (ActiveX controls), .vxd and .drv files (device drivers), and of course lots of .exe files (applications). Together, these constitute the Windows 98 system files, and there are well over 1,000 of them located in the Windows and Windows\System folders.

It is by no means a stretch to say that the health of Windows 98 as a whole is dependent on the health of these system files. If one of these files becomes corrupted, gets deleted, or gets overwritten by an older version, you could experience program crashes, at best, or system lockups, at worst.

Windows 98 offers several tools for keeping these system files from harm:

- The standard file installation functions compare existing files with those that a setup program is trying to install and automatically ensure that only more recent files are installed.

- The hidden Windows\Sysbckup folder contains a few dozen system files that are commonly overwritten by older installation programs. If Windows 98 detects that one of these files has been replaced, it automatically restores the file from Sysbckup.

- Windows 98 also keeps a list of system files that are less commonly overwritten by setup programs. If an install application tries to replace one of these files, a dialog box shows up to warn you and ask if you want to keep the newer file.

- The System File Checker can look for system files that have been corrupted, changed, or deleted, and can restore a file from the Windows 98 source disc. See the next section, "Running System File Checker."

- The Version Conflict Manager can restore versions of system files that were replaced during the Windows 98 installation. See "Using Version Conflict Manager to Deal with Conflicting System Files," later in this chapter.

Running System File Checker

When you install Windows 98, one of the chores that Setup performs is to create a baseline *verification data file*. This file specifies all the Windows 98 files that were installed, where they were installed, the date and time stamps of the files, their

Undocumented
Why does Windows 98 allow installation programs to overwrite crucial system files in the first place? It all began back when Windows 3.1 was released. It included handy features such as common dialog boxes that could be used by all applications, and these features were implemented as new or updated .dll files. To ensure that applications taking advantage of these features would run under Windows 3.0, Microsoft allowed developers to install the appropriate .dll files.

sizes and version numbers, and a cyclical redundancy check (CRC) value. All of this data is stored in a file named `Default.sfc`, which is then stored in the `Windows` folder.

The `sfc` extension stands for System File Checker, which is a new Windows 98 utility that uses the data in the verification data file to see if any of the system files have been corrupted, changed, or deleted. System File Checker can then restore system files from the Windows 98 source disc.

To start System File Checker, use either of the following methods:

- Run the System Information utility, as described earlier, and then select Tools, System File Checker.

- Select Start, Run, type `sfc.exe`, and click OK.

Figure 15.5 shows the System File Checker window that appears.

Figure 15.5
Use System File
Checker to scan
for corrupted,
changed, or
deleted system
files.

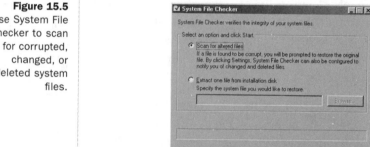

Changing System File Checker Settings

Before getting to the actual check, let's examine the various settings you can use to customize how System File Checker goes about its business. To see these settings, click the Settings button to display the dialog box shown in Figure 15.6.

Let's start with the options in the Settings tab:

Back up file before restoring: You use these options to specify what System File Checker does with an existing file before it restores a file from the source disc. Restoring a file from the Windows 98 source disc could break some updated components. Therefore, backups, whether prompted or automatic, are always a good idea.

Default backup location: If you choose to back up existing files, this line tells you where to find them.

Log file: Use these options to determine how (or if) System File Checker maintains a log. The log is a text file named Sfclog.txt (it's in the Windows folder), and it tracks the changes made to the verification data file (Default.sfc).

Check for changed files: Activate this check box to have System File Checker look for changed system files. Although this option is deactivated by default, I recommend that you activate it.

Check for deleted files: Activate this check box to have System File Checker look for deleted system files. Again, this option is deactivated by default, but I recommend that you activate it.

The System File Checker Settings dialog box also includes two other tabs that you probably won't need to use that often:

Search Criteria: This tab specifies which folders System File Checker looks in, and which file extensions it checks.

Inside Scoop
A cyclical redundancy check is a checksum value that can be used to determine whether a file has changed. The idea is that you add up all the binary 1s and 0s in a file to get a sum. If you run a CRC on the file later and the checksum is different, it means that the file either has changed (if other values such as the date and time stamp are different, as well) or has become corrupted (if everything else in the verification data file is unchanged).

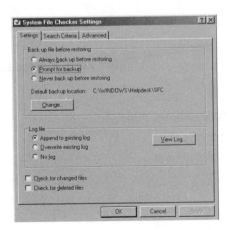

Figure 15.6
Use the System File Checker Settings dialog box to customize System File Checker.

Watch Out!
Strangely, System
File Checker's
default backup
location doesn't
exist! (There is no
Windows\Helpdesk
folder.) To use a
different folder,
click Change.

Advanced: You use this tab to create your own verification data file. Also, if you have already run System File Checker and it has updated Default.sfc, you can click Restore Defaults to use the original verification data file created by Windows 98 Setup.

Starting the Check

To launch the check, make sure the Scan for altered files option is activated, and then click the Start button. System File Checker then busies itself examining the system files. If it comes across a file that doesn't jibe with the verification data file, it displays a dialog box to let you know. The options in the dialog box depend on whether System File Checker thinks the file is corrupted, changed, or deleted. For example, Figure 15.7 shows the dialog box that appears for a corrupted file. You have the following choices:

Shortcut
If you asked
System File
Checker to look
for changed files,
the File Changed
dialog box that
appears will have
an extra option
named Update
verification
information for
all changed files.
If you know you
have quite a few
changed files (if
you've installed a
Windows update,
for example), acti-
vate this option to
avoid getting
prompted for
every file.

> **Update verification information:** If you activate this option, System File Checker will update Default.sfc with the new information about the file. Select this option only if you're sure the current file is legitimate.
>
> **Restore file:** If you activate this option, System File Checker will prompt you to replace the existing file with the original file from the Windows 98 source disc. (A Restore File dialog box is displayed to let you pick the source and destination locations. This dialog box is identical to the Extract File dialog box shown later in Figure 15.8.)
>
> **Ignore:** If you activate this option, System File Checker will skip this file.

Extracting Windows 98 Files

Back in Chapter 2, "Ten Things You Should Know About the Windows 98 Setup," I showed you a method for extracting a file from the Windows 98 source disc. Happily, System File Checker offers an even easier route, as shown in the following steps:

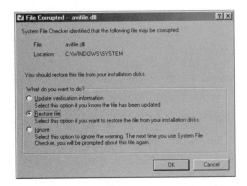

Figure 15.7
System File
Checker displays
this dialog box for
a corrupted file.

1. Make sure the Extract one file from installation disk option is activated.

2. In the Select the system file you would like to restore text box, type the name of the system file you want to extract. (Alternatively, click Browse and then use the Select File to Extract dialog box to pick the file.)

3. Click Start. The Extract File dialog box appears, as shown in Figure 15.8.

See Also...
"Extracting a File
from the Windows
98 Setup Files,"
p. 67

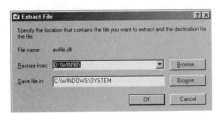

Figure 15.8
Use this dialog
box to set the
source and desti-
nation locations
for the extracted
file.

4. Edit the Restore from and Save file in text boxes, if necessary.

5. Click OK. System File Checker extracts the file and then lets you know the operation was successful.

6. Click OK.

Using Version Conflict Manager to Deal with Conflicting System Files

When you install a Windows 98 upgrade, Setup checks the system files to look for existing files that are the same as the ones being installed. If it finds such a file, it compares the version numbers of the existing file and the Windows 98 file to see which one is newer:

- If the existing file is older than the Windows 98 file being installed, Setup replaces the existing file.

- If the existing file is newer than the Windows 98 file being installed, Setup still replaces the existing file, but it makes a backup copy of the file in the Windows\VCM folder.

The "VCM" part of this folder name stands for Version Conflict Manager, a new Windows 98 tool for managing these kinds of system file conflicts.

If you find that one of your applications crashes, displays error messages, or exhibits other aberrant post-Windows 98 installation behavior, the cause could be a replaced system file. Windows 98's replacement of an older file shouldn't do any damage, but its replacement of a newer file can be problematic:

- The newer file may have contained functionality required by the application.

- The application may expect the system file to have a version number greater than or equal to a particular value. Because the Windows 98 file has a lower version number, the application may decide not to operate with the older file.

If this happens, you can use Version Conflict Manager to restore the newer system file that was backed up by Setup to the VCM folder. To start Version Conflict Manager, use either of the following methods:

- Run the System Information utility, as described earlier, and then select Tools, Version Conflict Manager.

- Select Start, Run, type vcmui.exe, and click OK.

Either way, you see the Version Conflict Manager window shown in Figure 15.9. As you can see, the version numbers in the Current Version column are lower than those in the Backed Up Version column.

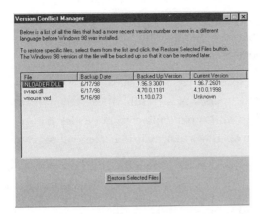

Figure 15.9
Use Version
Conflict Manager
to restore newer
system files
backed up by
Windows 98
Setup.

To restore a file, highlight it and then click Restore Selected Files. Version Conflict Manager does two things:

1. It moves the older Windows 98 system file into the VCM folder and renames it with the 000 extension.

2. It moves the newer system file from the VCM folder to the appropriate folder (such as Windows\System).

Note that this procedure is reversible. That is, if you want to restore the older Windows 98 version of the system file, run Version Conflict Manager again, select the file, and then click Restore Selected Files.

Controlling Viruses with Plus! 98's McAfee VirusScan

Computer viruses are small programs that attach themselves to a host system without authorization. The goal of these programs is either disruption (such as disabling application functionality or distorting the screen) or destruction (such as trashing data or preventing the computer from booting). Either way, they are nasty nuisances that every computer user hopes to avoid.

Unfortunately, avoiding them is becoming increasingly difficult:

- Virus crackers are creating hundreds of new virus programs each month, and would-be crackers are finding it increasingly easy to obtain copies of new and existing viruses.

> ❝
> John Gray, Microsoft's group manager for Windows 98...freely admits that version conflicts are a problem and says Microsoft is actively looking for ways to make it less of one in the future. For example, the company may limit the number of Windows system files that third parties (for example, other software vendors) may redistribute with their apps.
> —Fred Langa, Windows Magazine
> ❞

Watch Out!
Microsoft reports that on some systems, a bug in Version Conflict Manager prevents the program from backing up the older Windows 98 versions of system files to the VCM folder. This occurs when you select multiple files to restore. Microsoft recommends that you restore only one file at a time.

Remember
A *cracker* is an expert user who creates programs or breaks into systems for malicious purposes. The cracker is the evil twin of the more benevolent *hacker*, who simply enjoys programming and other high-level computer pursuits for their own mer-

- With tens of millions of people now online, file downloads have become the predominant mechanism for transmitting viruses.

- Online security has become exceedingly complex over the past few years. As a result, most email programs, Web browsers, and other online technologies have design flaws, bugs, or openings that malicious users can take advantage of.

- *Macro viruses* reside in macros attached to documents created in Word, Excel, and other productivity software. These files are routinely traded via floppy disks, network connections, or e-mail messages, and so are easily propagated.

Besides the relatively new macro viruses just mentioned, viruses also come in three other strains:

Boot sector virus: This type of virus replaces the hard disk's master boot record (or a floppy disk's boot sector), which enables the virus to load itself into memory at startup.

File infector: This type of virus latches on to an application's executable file and runs when you launch the application.

Trojan horse: This type of virus masquerades as a legitimate program, but its true intentions become clear when you run the program.

The bad news is that Microsoft—probably out of fear of antitrust violations—has chosen not to include antivirus software in Windows 98. The good news is that there are many such programs on the market, and most of them are reasonably priced. In this section, I'll discuss one antivirus program in particular: the version of McAfee VirusScan that comes on the Microsoft Plus! 98 add-on.

McAfee VirusScan has two components:

VirusScan: This component scans your system's memory and files to look for virus infections.

VShield: This is a memory-resident component that monitors your system for virus-like activity.

The next two sections discuss these components.

Running VirusScan

The VirusScan program checks your system's memory, your hard disk's master boot record, and all your executable files for virus code. If VirusScan finds a viral intruder, it can disinfect the system. Here's how it works (I'm assuming here that the VirusScan portion of Plus! 98 is installed):

1. Select Start, Programs, Microsoft Plus! 98, McAfee VirusScan, VirusScan. The program loads and scans your system's memory for lurking viruses.

2. If this is the first time you've run the program, you may be prompted to perform an online update of VirusScan. This is always a good idea, so you should go ahead and run the Update. I'll assume, however, that you just clicked OK to continue. In this case, you see the McAfee VirusScan window shown in Figure 15.10.

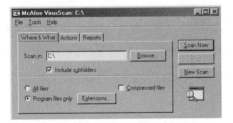

3. Use the Scan in text box to select the folder you want to scan. (If you want the scan to include subfolders, leave Include subfolders checked.)

4. By default, VirusScan checks Program files only. You can customize this by clicking Extensions to add or remove the file extensions to include in the check. (For example, you could add the doc and dot extensions to check for macro viruses in Microsoft Word documents and templates.) Alternatively, select All files to check everything.

5. In the Actions tab, use the When virus is found list to select what VirusScan does when it finds a virus.

Remember
VirusScan has an Advanced view that gives you even more scanning options. To see this view, select the View, Advanced command.

Shortcut
To scan only a specific folder for viruses, use Windows Explorer to right-click the folder icon, and then click Scan for Viruses in the context menu. This is a useful technique if you have a separate folder that you use to hold the files extracted from a downloaded archive. Each time you download an archive and extract its files, scan the folder for viruses *before* you install the program. Later, I'll show you how to scan .zip file archives.

6. In the Reports tab, use the controls to determine how VirusScan alerts you to a potential virus and how it logs its activity.

7. When you're ready to proceed, click Scan Now to begin the check. (This can take quite a while, depending on how many files VirusScan has to check.)

Understanding VShield

Scanning files is only half the antivirus battle because a virus program could infect your system between scans. To protect against these sudden outbreaks, VirusScan's VShield component stays memory-resident to watch for virus activity. After you install Plus! 98 and restart your computer, you see a new VShield icon in the taskbar's system tray. This icon tells you that VShield is resident and on the job.

VShield comes with a few detection options that are worth looking at. To see these options, use either of the following techniques:

- Right-click the VShield icon and then click Properties.

- Select Start, Programs, Microsoft Plus! 98, McAfee VirusScan, VShield Configuration.

Figure 15.11 shows the Detection tab in the VShield Configuration dialog box that appears.

Here's a quick rundown of the controls on this tab:

Scan files on: These check boxes determine when VShield scans a file. Because file infectors and Trojan horses operate when you run a file, you should at least keep the Run check box activated.

Scan floppies on: These options determine when VShield scans floppy disks. Boot sector viruses like to infect floppy disk boot sectors, so you should leave these check boxes activated.

What to scan: As with VirusScan, these options determine which files VShield scans.

General: These check boxes determine whether VShield loads at startup, whether it can be disabled (by right-clicking the VShield icon and then clicking Disable), and whether the icon appears in the system tray.

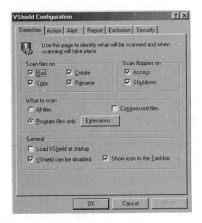

Figure 15.11
Use the Detection tab to determine how VShield monitors your system for viruses.

Other Ways to Protect Yourself from Viruses

Besides running ScanDisk regularly and having VShield monitor your system, there are other things you can do to keep your system virus-free. Here are a few tips and techniques to consider:

Always scan downloaded files: Many downloads come in the form of .exe files that contain self-extracting archives. VirusScan can scan individual .exe files, so you should always check these files before running them. To scan a file, right-click it and then click Scan for Viruses in the context menu.

Install Plus! 98's compressed folder support: Another handy tool in Plus! 98 is support for *compressed folders*. This means that Windows 98 can view and create .zip compressed archive files. It also gives VirusScan the ability to scan individual .zip files, which is a common download file type.

Write-protect boot floppies: If a virus does manage to trash your system, your only recourse will be to boot to a floppy disk. To ensure that the virus doesn't infect your

Watch Out!
If your system doesn't have much memory, VShield's constant behind-the-scenes activity can adversely affect performance. In this case, I recommend deactivating the Load VShield at startup check box and leaving the other General options activated. That way, you can start VShield only when you need it (such as when you want to install a program). To launch VShield by hand, select Start, Programs, Microsoft Plus! 98, McAfee VirusScan, VShield.

boot floppy, write-protect the disk. To do this on a 3 1/2-inch disk, turn the disk over and slide the small, plastic, movable tab to the edge of the disk.

Disable boot-sector writes: Some computers have a BIOS setting that prevents any application from writing to the boot sector. Activating this setting will thwart boot sector viruses.

Format used floppy disks: If you plan on using an older floppy disk, particularly one that you received from someone else, be sure to run a full format on the disk to eradicate any viruses that it may contain.

Visit the Windows Update Web site regularly: In the first few months after Windows 98 shipped, a number of security flaws were found in Outlook Express and Internet Explorer. Microsoft put together patches to fix these problems, and then posted the patches on the Windows Update site (http://windowsupdate.microsoft.com/). Keep an eye on this site to look for other security patches, and be sure to install these fixes as soon as possible.

Remember
Your bootable floppy won't be of much use if it doesn't have antivirus software on it. Unfortunately, the VirusScan files are too large to fit on your Windows 98 startup disk, so you'll need to set up a separate disk. The easiest way to create such a disk is to select Start, Programs, Microsoft Plus! 98, McAfee VirusScan, Create VirusScan Emergency Disk.

Update your virus library regularly: To ensure the utmost protection, always keep VirusScan's list of viruses up-to-date. You can update the program at any time by launching VirusScan and selecting the File, Update VirusScan command. Note, too, that you can see the complete list of viruses by selecting Tools, Virus List.

Essential Information

■ The System Information utility provides an extensive look at the hardware and software resources on your system, while the File Information utility offers useful details on Windows 98 system files.

■ To get the version number of a file, right-click the file, click Properties, and then select the Version tab.

■ System File Checker examines the Windows 98 system files to see if any have been corrupted, changed, or deleted.

■ You can also use System File Checker as an easy method for extracting a file from the Windows 98 source files.

■ Use Version Conflict Manager to restore system files backed up by the Windows 98 Setup program.

■ Run Plus! 98's VirusScan program regularly to check for viruses on your system.

■ Make regular visits to the Windows Update Web site (`http://windowsupdate.microsoft.com/`) to look for security patches, bug fixes, enhanced programs, and more.

Remember
System mainte-
nance is only
effective when it
is regular, so you
should run all of
Windows 98's sys-
tem maintenance
tools as often as
is practical.
Windows 98 helps
in this by offering
the Scheduled
Tasks folder for
setting up tasks
to run at regular
intervals. This
folder is accessi-
ble either within
Windows Explorer
or by selecting
Start, Programs,
Accessories,
System Tools,
Scheduled Tasks.
Note, too, that the
Maintenance
Wizard is a quick
way to set up
tasks for
ScanDisk, Disk
Defragmenter, and
other system
tools. See Start,
Programs,
Accessories,
System Tools,
Maintenance
Wizard.

GET THE SCOOP ON...
Creating and using an emergency boot disk ▪
Backing up your files ▪ Backing up and restoring your
system after a system crash ▪ Gathering troubleshooting data to recover from and solve problems

Preparing for Trouble

Chapter 16

THE PAST FEW CHAPTERS HAVE RUN through many of Windows 98's system tools and other features that are designed to keep your computer running smoothly. Regular application of those tools and techniques should keep Windows 98 humming along quite nicely. However, despite your best maintenance efforts, your system may give up the ghost thanks to a hardware failure, virus, power surge, rogue application, or incorrect Windows configuration.

Anyone who has used a computer for more than a couple of years will tell you that it's not a matter of *if* these kinds of problems will occur, but *when.* In fact, the savviest of users assume their systems are going to fail and take steps to ensure they're prepared when the fateful day arrives. To help you pre-pare for the inevitable, this chapter runs through a few tech-niques that will not only get you ready for a crash, but will help you recover gracefully when (not if) it happens.

Putting Together an Emergency Boot Disk

If you do nothing else to prepare your system for trouble, at the very least you should create a bootable floppy disk. That way, if your hard disk goes down for the count, you can boot to drive A and thus regain some control over your recalcitrant machine.

Inside Scoop
The bootable disk
works because
once the POST is
complete, the
BIOS code checks
for a floppy disk in
drive A. If no disk
is present, the
BIOS boots from
the hard disk's
active partition.
However, if drive A
does contain a
bootable disk, the
BIOS ignores the
hard disk and
loads the operat-
ing system (DOS)
from the floppy.
You should check
your computer's
BIOS settings to
make sure that
it's set up to
check drive A
before the hard
disk.

See Also...
"Formatting a
Floppy Disk,"
p. 171

66
Startup disks
created with
previous ver-
sions of
Windows aren't
compatible with
Windows 98.
—From the
"Getting
Started" booklet
99

Of course, regaining control is one thing, but actually doing something useful after you have control is another. Therefore, the ideal boot disk will contain an extensive collection of utilities and programs for troubleshooting and repairing problems. Such a disk then becomes a full-fledged *emergency boot disk.*

Creating a Windows 98 Startup Disk

One way to create an emergency boot disk would be to first format a floppy disk with the Windows 98 system files, as described in Chapter 6, "Expert Windows Explorer Techniques." You would then copy the necessary DOS utilities to the disk.

That works, but an easier method is to have Windows 98 create a *startup disk* and then customize the result to get an emergency boot disk that suits your needs. Here's how to create the startup disk:

1. In the Control Panel, open the Add/Remove Programs icon to display the Add/Remove Programs Properties dialog box.

2. Display the Startup Disk tab.

3. Click Create Disk. Windows 98 prompts you to insert your source disc, and then gathers the files it needs. When it's done, it prompts you to insert a disk in drive A.

4. Insert the disk. (Make sure this disk doesn't contain valuable data. Windows 98 formats the disk, so all the existing data is lost.)

5. Click OK. Windows 98 formats the disk and copies a number of files.

6. When the disk is done, click OK to close the Add/Remove Programs Properties dialog box.

7. Write-protect the disk.

Table 16.1 shows you the names and descriptions of the two dozen files that are copied to the startup disk.

TABLE 16.1: THE FILES THAT ARE COPIED TO THE WINDOWS 98 STARTUP DISK

Filename	Description
Aspi2dos.sys	Device driver for Adaptec SCSI adapter models AIC-6260/6360/6370
Aspi4dos.sys	Device driver for Adaptec SCSI adapter models AHA-154X/1640
Aspi8dos.sys	Device driver for Adaptec SCSI adapter models AIC-75XX/78XX
Aspi8u2.sys	Device driver for Adaptec SCSI adapter models AIC-789X
Aspicd.sys	Device driver for an Adaptec SCSI CD-ROM drive
Autoexec.bat	Startup batch file
Btcdrom.sys	Device driver for a Mylex/BusLogic SCSI CD-ROM drive
Btdosm.sys	Device driver for a Mylex/BusLogic SCSI adapter
Command.com	DOS command interpreter
Config.sys	Startup configuration file
Drvspace.bin	Real-mode disk compression driver
Ebd.cab	Cabinet archive file containing several DOS utilities
Ebd.sys	Startup disk system file
Extract.exe	Extracts files from a .cab file
Fdisk.exe	Partitions the hard disk
Findramd.exe	Finds a RAM drive
Flashpt.sys	Device driver for a BusLogic FlashPoint SCSI adapter
Himem.sys	Extended memory manager
Io.sys	Windows 98 startup system file
Msdos.sys	Windows 98 startup system file
Oakcdrom.sys	Device driver for an IDE CD-ROM drive
Ramdrive.sys	Creates a temporary disk drive in RAM
Readme.txt	Text file containing information about the startup disk
Setramd.bat	Sets the letter used by the RAM drive

Undocumented
The startup disk has approximately 240KB of free space, so you can include other files on it. To create a startup disk and have Windows 98 automatically include other files, first copy those files to the Windows\Command\Ebd folder. Then switch to the Windows\Command folder and run the command boot-disk a:. Unlike the Add/Remove Programs method (which gathers the startup disk files from the Windows 98 CD), this method gathers the files from the Ebd folder.

Watch Out!
The startup disk doesn't include Uninstal.exe, the program that uninstalls Windows 98. I suggest you copy this file from the Windows\Command folder to the startup disk, just in case you need it.

Creating a FAT32 Startup Disk

If you've converted a hard disk partition to FAT32 (as described in Chapter 14, "Making the Move to FAT32"), you won't see this partition when you boot from the Windows 98 startup disk. If you need support for FAT32 from a bootable floppy, the Windows 98 CD has a tool that will do the job. Follow these steps:

1. Insert the Windows 98 CD.

2. In Windows Explorer, open the CD's `tools\mtsutil\fat32ebd` folder.

3. Launch `fat32ebd.exe`. A DOS session opens and you're prompted to insert a floppy disk in drive A.

4. Insert the floppy, press y, and then press Enter. The program formats the disk and extracts the utilities.

5. When the process is complete, close the DOS session.

The FAT32 emergency boot disk doesn't have the same structure as the regular Windows 98 startup disk. In particular, no RAM drive is created and there is no `Ebd.cab` file (see the following section for details). Instead, the DOS utilities are placed on the disk as individual files.

Test Driving the Startup Disk

After your startup disk is created, you should test it out right away to make sure it works properly. Insert the disk in drive A (if it's not in there already), select Start, Shut Down, activate the Restart option, and then click OK.

When your computer reboots, the version of `Io.sys` on the floppy disk takes over the boot process after the POST is complete. The following menu appears:

```
Microsoft Windows 98 Startup Menu
==================================


    1. Start computer with CD-ROM support.
    2. Start computer without CD-ROM support.
    3. View the Help file.
Enter a choice:
```

Remember
If you've installed the McAfee VirusScan antivirus utility from the Microsoft Plus! 98 package, creating an antivirus startup disk is a must. In Chapter 15, "Crucial System Maintenance Skills," see "Controlling Viruses with Plus! 98's McAfee VirusScan," page 357.

The startup disk's Config.sys file—shown in Figure 16.1—is configured to display this menu and process your selection.

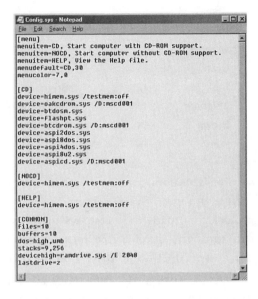

Figure 16.1
The startup disk's
Config.sys file.

Config.sys is divided into five sections:

The [menu] section: This section sets up the menu that you see onscreen. Each menu command is created by a menuitem line:

menuitem=block, [text]

In each line, block is the name of another configuration block (such as [cd]) within Config.sys, and text is the command that you see when the menu is displayed (such as Start computer with CD-ROM support). The [menu] block also contains two other features:

- The menudefault line specifies the command that will be selected automatically and the number of seconds after which that command will be selected.

- The menucolor line sets the menu's foreground (the first value) and background (the second value) colors, as given by the values in Table 16.2.

TABLE 16.2: COLOR VALUES TO USE WITH THE MENUCOLOR STATEMENT

Value	Color	Value	Color
0	Black	8	Gray
1	Blue	9	Bright blue
2	Green	10	Bright green
3	Cyan	11	Bright cyan
4	Red	12	Bright red
5	Magenta	13	Bright magenta
6	Brown	14	Yellow
7	White	15	Bright white

The [CD] **section:** This configuration block is processed if you select the first menu item (Start computer with CD-ROM support). The block first loads the himem.sys memory manager, and then runs through a list of device lines that try all the IDE, SCSI adapter, and SCSI CD-ROM drivers on the disk.

All those device lines in the [CD] block are unnecessary and serve only to slow down the floppy boot sequence. There are two ways you can customize this section:

Undocumented
If you have both an IDE and a SCSI CD-ROM drive, the default startup configuration will set up only one of the drives because all the CD-ROM driver device lines use the same ID—mscd001. To enable support for both drives, change one of the driver IDs to mscd002. In Autoexec.bat, add /D:mscd002 to the line that loads Mscdex.exe.

- Comment out each device line that's not required by your system. You comment out a line by placing REM and a space at the beginning of the line. This tells DOS not to process the line. Remember that SCSI CD-ROMs need both the SCSI adapter driver and the SCSI CD-ROM driver. If you're not sure, do a step-by-step boot (by pressing Shift+F8) to see which lines load successfully.

- If none of these lines is appropriate for your system, comment out all of them and add the appropriate device statement (or statements) for your CD-ROM drive.

The [NOCD] **section:** This block is processed if you select the second menu command (Start computer without CD-ROM support). It loads only himem.sys.

The [HELP] **section:** This block is processed if you select the third menu command (View the Help file). Again, it loads only himem.sys. (The Help file itself gets loaded when Autoexec.bat gets processed, as described below.)

The [COMMON] **section:** This block is processed no matter what menu command you select. Most of these statements set up the DOS environment. Of particular interest, however, is the following statement:

```
devicehigh=ramdrive.sys /E 2048
```

This statement carves out a 2,048KB piece of RAM to use as a disk drive. (The /E switch creates the drive in extended memory.) I'll explain why this RAM disk is needed a bit later.

After you select a menu command (by pressing the command's number and then pressing Enter), Io.sys processes Config.sys and then runs the Autoexec.bat batch file. Figure 16.2 shows most of this file. The numbers on the figure correspond to the numbered steps that follow.

```
Autoexec.bat - Notepad                                    _ □ ×
File  Edit  Search  Help
@ECHO OFF
set EXPAND=YES
SET DIRCMD=/O:N
set LglDrv=27 * 26 Z 25 Y 24 X 23 W 22 V 21 U 20 T 19 S 18 R 17 Q 16 P 15
set LglDrv=%LglDrv% O 14 N 13 M 12 L 11 K 10 J 9 I 8 H 7 G 6 F 5 E 4 D 3 C
cls
call setramd.bat %LglDrv%
set temp=c:\
set tmp=c:\
path=%RAMD%:\;a:\;%CDROM%:\
copy command.com %RAMD%:\ > NUL
set comspec=%RAMD%:\command.com
copy extract.exe %RAMD%:\ > NUL
copy readme.txt %RAMD%:\ > NUL

:ERROR
IF EXIST ebd.cab GOTO EXT
echo Please insert Windows 98 Startup Disk 2
echo.
pause
GOTO ERROR

:EXT
%RAMD%:\extract /y /e /l %RAMD%: ebd.cab > NUL
echo The diagnostic tools were successfully loaded to drive %RAMD%.
echo.

IF "%config%"=="NOCD" GOTO QUIT
IF "%config%"=="HELP" GOTO HELP
LH %ramd%:\MSCDEX.EXE /D:mscd001 /L:%CDROM%
echo.
GOTO QUIT

:HELP
cls
```

1.
2.
3.
4.
5.
6.
7.
8.

Figure 16.2
The startup disk's Autoexec.bat file.

Remember
The ramdrive.sys command uses the first available drive letter for the RAM drive. However, the letter for your CD-ROM drive isn't set until Autoexec.bat is executed. Therefore, your CD-ROM drive letter will be one letter higher than what you would normally use. For example, if your CD-ROM is normally drive D, it will be drive E when you boot with the startup disk.

Here's what happens:

1. Several environment variables are set.

2. The setramd.bat batch file is run. This batch file calls the Findramd.exe program to determine the drive letter being used by the RAM drive. The batch file then sets the RAMD environment variable to that letter.

3. The `path` is set up to include the RAM drive, and then `Command.com` is set up to run from the RAM drive.

4. `Extract.exe` and `Readme.txt` are copied to the RAM drive.

5. If the file `ebd.cab` exists, skip to the `EXT` label.

6. Extract all the files from `ebd.cab` and store them on the RAM drive.

7. If one of the non-CD menu options was selected, skip to the appropriate label. Otherwise, run `Mscdex.exe` to initialize the CD-ROM drive and set its drive letter.

8. Process the rest of the file (not shown in Figure 16.2).

After `Autoexec.bat` is processed, you're dropped off at the `A:\` prompt. Table 16.3 lists the files in `Ebd.cab` that get copied to the RAM drive.

TABLE 16.3: FILES STORED IN EBD.CAB

Filename	Description
Attrib.exe	Sets and removes file attributes
Chkdsk.exe	Checks a disk for errors; can repair some errors
Debug.exe	Tests, edits, and debugs binary files
Edit.com	Text editor that's useful for editing configuration files
Ext.exe	Extracts files from a .cab archive
Format.com	Formats a disk
Help.bat	Displays the Readme.txt file
Mscdex.exe	Initializes the CD-ROM drive
Restart.com	Reboots the computer
Scandisk.exe	Scans and repairs a disk
Scandisk.ini	Contains configuration options for ScanDisk
Sys.com	Transfers Windows 98 system files to a disk

Shortcut
You can view the syntax for many of the RAM drive programs by typing the name of the program, followed by /? (for example, `attrib /?`) and then Enter.

Backing Up Your Files

I'd like to have a megabyte of memory for every computer book and computer magazine article that has regaled the reader with stories of hard-disk crashes, office fires, and stolen computers as a way to underline the importance of backups. (I've been the author of quite a few of those finger-waggings, myself.)

You'll be happy to know that you'll be getting no such lectures from me this time. As a savvy Windows 98 user, you know the importance of backups and you don't need me or anyone else nagging you about it. What you probably need are a few techniques for making backups less of a chore. After all, the more inconvenient it is to back up, the less likely you are to do it regularly. This section shows you how to take control of the backup process and how to streamline it to make it as painless as possible.

The first thing you should know is that the Backup utility in Windows 98 is a big improvement over its Windows 95 predecessor. It has wizards for common tasks, a wider variety of options—including the welcome ability to include the Registry in any backup job—and it supports a much wider range of backup hardware, including SCSI, IDE/ATAPI, parallel port units, and the following media:

- 8-millimeter tapes

- DAT (DDS1 and DDS2) tapes

- DC 6000 tapes

- Digital line tapes (DLTs)

- QIC-80, 80 Wide, 3010, 3010 Wide, 3020, and 3020 Wide tapes

- Travan TR1, TR2, TR3, TR4 tapes

- Removable media such as floppy disks, Zip disks, Jaz disks, and SyQuest cartridges

Of course, you can also use a second hard disk or a shared network folder as the backup destination.

To launch Microsoft Backup, select Start, Programs, Accessories, System Tools, Backup. The first time you launch Backup, it checks to see if you have a backup tape device

66

You should perform a full backup of your system regularly to have a current backup of your entire system available to restore in case of hard disk failures.
—Windows 98 Resource Kit

99

Remember
The Windows 98 version of Microsoft Backup does not support QIC-40 tapes.

Shortcut
If you'd prefer
that Backup not
show this initial
dialog box at
startup, select
Tools,
Preferences,
deactivate the
Show startup
dialog when
Microsoft Backup
is started check

attached to your machine. If you don't, a dialog box asks if you want to run the Add New Hardware Wizard to look for the device. If you do have a backup device that Windows 98 hasn't yet recognized, click Yes. Otherwise, click No to continue.

You'll now see a dialog box that welcomes you to Microsoft Backup. This dialog box appears each time you start Backup, and it offers the following options:

Create a new backup job: This option runs the Backup Wizard, which leads you through the steps required to create a backup job.

Open an existing backup job: This option displays a dialog box from which you can open an existing backup job.

Restore backed up files: This option runs the Restore Wizard, which takes you step by step through the process of restoring files from a backup.

It's my goal in this section to show you the nuts and bolts of Backup, so I won't discuss these options, which are in any case aimed at beginning users. Click Close to remove the dialog box and get to the Microsoft Backup window, shown in Figure 16.3.

Figure 16.3
You'll use the
Microsoft Backup
window to define
and work with
your backup jobs.

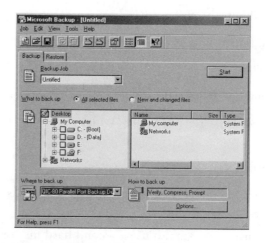

Setting Up a Backup Job

A *backup job* consists of the files you want backed up, the options you want to use for the backup, and the destination for the backup file. Here are the steps to follow to create a backup job:

1. Select the drives, folders, and files you want to include in the backup. The two panes in the middle of the Microsoft Backup window work much like the All Folders pane and the Contents pane in Windows Explorer. In this case, each drive, folder, and file has a check box beside it. To include an object in the backup job, activate its check box.

2. Use the Where To Back Up list to select a backup device or file. If you select the latter, a text box appears so you can enter the path and filename for the backup.

3. Click Options to display the Backup Job Options dialog box shown in Figure 16.4. Here's a summary of the tabs in this dialog box:

   General: The Compare Original And Backup Files... check box toggles backup verification on and off (although it's slower, it's best to leave this on). You can also set the compression used and what Backup does if the media already contains a backup.

   Password: Use this tab to protect the backup file with a password.

   Type: This tab determines how Backup treats the selected files. If you activate All Selected Files, every file is included in the backup job. Otherwise, activate New And Changed Files Only and then select either Differential Backup Type or Incremental Backup Type.

   Exclude: Use this tab to exclude certain file types from the backup job.

   Report: After the backup is complete, Microsoft Backup displays a report that summarizes the backup operation. Use the check boxes in this tab to customize the contents of that report.

   Advanced: Activate the Back Up Windows Registry check box to include the Registry files in the backup job (highly recommended).

Inside Scoop
If you're using tape, you might need to make some media adjustments before beginning. The Tools, Media command displays a submenu of tape commands, including Initialize (erase the media), Format (set up the tape to hold files), and Retension (perform a fast forward and rewind to eliminate slack and even out the tape tension).

Remember
A *differential backup* is one that includes just the files that have changed since the last full backup. An *incremental backup* is one that includes just the files that have changed since the last full or differential backup.

Figure 16.4
Use this dialog
box to set options
for your backup
job.

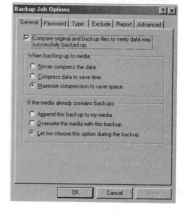
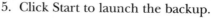

Figure 16.4
Use this dialog
box to set options
for your backup
job.

Shortcut
If you want to
know the size of
the backup job,
run the View,
Selection
Information com-
mand.

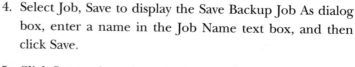

Remember
One thing that
would make your
backup life easier
would be the abil-
ity to schedule
unattended
backups.
Unfortunately,
Microsoft Backup
offers no such
feature, an inex-
plicable oversight
that has left many
a Windows 98
user scratching
his head and say-
ing "Gee, I
thought those
folks at Microsoft
were supposed to
be smart."

4. Select Job, Save to display the Save Backup Job As dialog box, enter a name in the Job Name text box, and then click Save.

5. Click Start to launch the backup.

Notes Towards Easier Backup Jobs

I think the main reason most people don't back up is that it's often a difficult or inconvenient process. However, there are a few things you can do to make backing up easier. Here are some notes:

Forget floppies, if possible: Backing up to floppy disks ranks just above "root canal" on the Top Ten Most Unpleasant Chores list. The reason, of course, is that a standard 3 1/2-inch floppy disk holds a mere 1.39MB (not 1.44MB) of data. If your hard disk contains hundreds of megabytes, you'll have to back up to hundreds of floppy disks, which hurts just to think about it.

Try a tape drive: Tape drives are the *de facto* backup standard, and come in many different capacities. You can back up several hundred megabytes at an extremely low cost.

Other backup media: The big downfall for tape drives is their relatively slow access times. Fortunately, there are much faster media available. These include floppy-compatible drives such as the SuperDisk (120MB) and the HiFD (200MB); removable media such as Iomega's Zip (100MB) and Jaz (1GB and 2GB) drives and SyQuests's EZFlyer (230MB) and SparQ (1GB) drives; a second hard disk (not a second partition on the same hard disk!); a network folder.

Consider online backups: Some companies offer remote backups over the Internet where you pay for a certain amount of storage space. Some of the companies that offer this service are @Backup (`http://www.atbackup.com/`), Atrieva (`http://www.atrieva.com/`), and Connected (`http://www.connected.com/`).

Back up data, not programs: Although you'll see in the next section that a full system backup can come in handy, it isn't always necessary. The only irreplaceable files on your system are those you created yourself, so they're the ones you should spend the most time protecting.

Keep data together: You'll save an immense amount of backup time if you store all your data files in one place. It could be the `My Documents` folder, a separate partition, or a separate hard disk. In each case, you can select all the data files for backup simply by activating a single folder or drive check box.

Back up downloaded archives: If space is at a premium, you can leave program files out of your backup job because they can always be reinstalled from their source disks. The exceptions to this are downloaded programs. To avoid having to find and download these files again, make backup copies of the archives.

Don't always run the full backup: You can speed up your backup times by running differential and incremental backups. You might consider running an incremental backup each day, a differential backup each week, and a full backup each month.

Watch Out!
Make sure you close all programs before launching a backup. Some programs lock files while they're open, so Backup won't be able to use those files.

Restoring a Backup Job

Backup's Restore component is one of those features that you hope is just a waste of disk space that you'll never have to use.

If disaster does strike, however, Restore will be a most welcome tool. If you like the step-by-step approach, you can run the Restore Wizard by selecting the Tools, Restore Wizard command. Alternatively, you can run the restore manually by following these steps:

1. In the Microsoft Backup window, select the Restore tab.

2. If Backup asks if you want to refresh the current view, click Yes and then skip to step 6.

3. In the Restore From list, select the backup source you want to work with.

4. Click Refresh. Backup asks if you want to refresh the current view.

5. Click Yes. Backup accesses the media and displays a list of backup jobs.

6. Select a backup job and then click OK. The backup job's drives, folders, and files appear in the What To Restore panes.

7. Use the check boxes to select the drives, folders, and files you want to restore.

8. In the Where To Restore list, select a destination for the restored files—either Original Location or Alternate Location. If you select the latter, a text box appears below the Where To Restore list. Use this text box to set the new destination for the restored files.

9. Click Options to display the Restore Options dialog box shown in Figure 16.5. Here's a summary of the tabs in this dialog box:

   General: These options determine what Backup does if a file that it's trying to restore already exists in the destination folder. You can leave the existing file, replace the existing file if it's older, or replace the existing file no matter what.

   Report: When the restore operation is done, Backup displays a report. Use the check boxes in this tab to customize the contents of that report.

Figure 16.5
Use this dialog box
to set options for
restoring the
backup job.

Advanced: Activate the Restore Windows Registry check box to include the Registry files in the restore.

10. Click Start to launch the restoration.

11. If Backup displays the Media Required dialog box, insert the backup media containing the backup job, and then click OK.

12. If your backup job included the Registry, Backup will ask if you want to replace the existing Registry. Click Yes to replace it, or click No to leave the existing Registry files.

13. If your backup job included the Registry, Backup will ask if you want to restore the Registry's hardware and software settings. Again, click Yes or No, as appropriate.

Using System Recovery to Recover from a Crash

The worst-case scenario for PC problems is a system crash that renders your hard disk or system files unusable. Your only recourse here is to start from scratch either with a reformatted hard disk or a new hard disk. This usually means that you have to reinstall Windows 98 and then reinstall and reconfigure all your applications. In other words, you're looking at the better part of a day or, more likely, a few days, to recover your system.

However, Windows 98 comes with a new utility called System Recovery that, with a little advance planning on your part, can help you recover from a crash in just a few steps. What kind of advance planning is required? Just two things:

- You must create a Windows 98 bootable disk, as described earlier in this chapter.

- You must run a full backup (including the Registry) of the your system.

I'll run through the specific steps required to use System Recovery a bit later. For now, let's see how it works.

Shortcut
If you're not
replacing your
hard disk and if
you have your
data files on a
separate parti-
tion, you don't
have to back
up that
partition because
you won't be
formatting it.

See Also...
"Using Setup's
Switches," p. 59

See Also...
"Creating
Automated Setup
Scripts," p. 60

The starting point is a batch file called `pcrestor.bat`. You run this batch file after you've formatted (or replaced) your hard disk. The chief function of this batch file is to run the following command:

```
setup.exe c:\restore\msbatch.inf /is /id /iq /im /ie /IW
```

Here, `setup.exe` is the Windows 98 Setup program. Recall from Chapter 2, "Ten Things You Should Know About the Windows 98 Setup," that all those switches modify how Setup performs the installation. See that chapter for details.

The other interesting detail in this command is the use of an installation script named `msbatch.inf`. In Chapter 2, I showed you how an installation script can be used to supply Setup with default values for things like the Windows 98 folder, networking information, and much more. That's exactly what `msbatch.inf` does here. However, it also contains some settings that are crucial for System Recovery:

```
[Install]
AddReg=RegistrySettings
DelReg=DelRegistrySettings

[RegistrySettings]
HKLM,%KEY_RUN%,BatchReg1,,"%11%\srw.exe"

[DelRegistrySettings]
HKLM,%KEY_RUN%,Welcome

[Strings]
KEY_RUN="SOFTWARE\Microsoft\Windows\CurrentVersion\Run"
```

Among other things, these lines tell Setup to modify the following key in the Registry:

```
HKEY_LOCAL_MACHINE\Software\Microsoft\Windows\Current
Version\Run
```

This key lists programs that run automatically at startup. In this case, the script inserts a setting that runs `srw.exe`. This is the System Recovery Wizard, which takes you through the process of recovering your backed up system data after Windows 98 is reinstalled.

Before proceeding, there are two aspects of System Recovery's default configuration that you should customize. These are the installation source folder and the Windows 98 destination folder.

System Recovery assumes the installation source directory is `C:\win98`. If you look at `pcrestor.bat`, you see the following lines just before `setup.exe` is launched:

```
cd\
cd\
cd\
cd win98
```

These (comically inefficient) lines switch to the `win98` directory on whatever drive you're using to run `pcrestor.bat`. To use the Windows 98 CD, you must have the batch file switch to the CD-ROM drive and then select the `win98` directory. For example, if your CD-ROM uses drive D, replace the above lines with the following:

```
d:
cd\win98
```

The Windows 98 destination folder is hardwired into System Recovery's `msbatch.inf` file:

```
InstallDir="C:\Windows"
```

To install Windows 98 on a different drive or in a different folder, edit this line accordingly.

After you've customized System Recovery to suit your needs, copy the new `pcrestor.bat` and `msbatch.inf` files to your Windows 98 startup disk.

Should you ever need to recover from a crash, here are the steps to use System Recovery:

Inside Scoop
Another aspect of `msbatch.inf` you should customize is your Windows 98 product ID. In the [Setup] section, add the line `ProductKey="ID"`, where `ID` is your 25-digit product ID.

Undocumented
To make System Recovery more compatible with your current configuration, create your own version of `msbatch.inf` using Batch 98 (again, as explained in Chapter 2). Just be sure to add the lines that modify the Registry (as shown earlier) from the System Recovery version of `msbatch.inf`. If you see similar lines in your version of `msbatch.inf`, it's okay to delete them because you'll be restoring the Registry later on.

1. Insert your Windows 98 startup disk and then reboot with CD-ROM support.

2. Insert the Windows 98 CD.

3. Format your Windows 98 partition, if necessary.

4. If you customized `pcrestor.bat` and `msbatch.inf` as described above, skip to step 5. Otherwise, you must perform two chores:

    • Create a folder named `win98` on drive C and then copy all the files from the CD's `win98` folder into `C:\win98`.

    • From the `tools\sysrec` folder on the your Windows 98 CD-ROM, copy the files `pcrestor.bat` and `msbatch.inf` to the root folder of drive C.

5. Run `pcrestor.bat`. A welcome message appears.

6. Press any key to launch the Windows 98 Setup.

7. When Setup is done, the System Recovery wizard appears. Figure 16.6 shows the initial dialog box.

Figure 16.6
The System Recovery wizard takes you through the process of restoring your system to its pre-crash state.

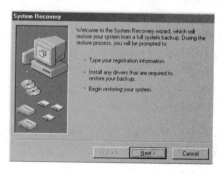

8. Click Next. System Recovery asks for your name and your company name.

9. Type in your name and your company name (the latter is optional), and then click Next.

10. Insert the backup media that you used for the full system backup.

11. Click Finish. System Recovery starts Microsoft Backup.

12. Use Backup's Restore feature to restore the files from your full system backup. Here are some things to note:

    - In Backup's Restore tab, click Options and then, in the General tab, activate the Always Replace the File on My Computer option.

    - When Backup asks whether you want to restore the Registry, click Yes.

    - When Backup asks if you want to restore the Registry's hardware and software settings, click Yes.

13. When Backup is finished and asks if you want to restart your computer, click Yes.

Gathering Troubleshooting Information

One of the keys to recovering gracefully from a problem is having information about the state of your system at the time the problem occurred, as well as data about the problem itself. Luckily, Windows 98 has many tools for gathering this type of data. Here are the most useful ones:

Print out system information: The System Information utility (see Chapter 15) contains an exhaustive inventory of the current hardware and software configuration. Printing out this data will provide you with detailed configuration information, and should be useful for a tech-support engineer. Note, however, that this printout will be at least 75 pages.

Run Dr. Watson: If you have programs that are causing general protection faults, exception errors, or other problems, try loading the Dr. Watson utility into memory. Dr. Watson monitors the system and traps application errors. It then takes a snapshot of the system, records data about the application and the error, and writes everything to a log file in the Windows\Drwatson folder. This data will be useful for a tech-support engineer to diagnose your system. To run Dr. Watson, use either of the following techniques:

See Also...
"The System Information Utility," p. 346

Inside Scoop
Rather than printing out the System Information data, print it to a .prn file and then save that file to a floppy. You can then print out the data when and if you need it. (To print a .prn file, type filename.prn > lpt1, where filename.prn is the name of the file.) To print to a file, add a new printer and, when prompted for the port, select FILE.

- Select Start, Run, type `drwatson.exe`, and click OK.

- Select Start, Programs, Accessories, System Tools, System Information, and then run the Tools, Dr. Watson command.

  Use the Windows Report Tool: You use this tool to describe a problem you're having with your computer. It combines this description with the data found in the System Information utility, compresses everything into a `.cab` file, and then uploads the data to a Microsoft support technician. You should then receive a response via email. (Note, however, that in practice this response can take quite a while.) To run this tool, use either of the following techniques:

- Select Start, Run, type `winrep.exe`, and click OK.

- Select Start, Programs, Accessories, System Tools, System Information, and then run the Tools, Windows Report Tool command.

Essential Information

- A Windows 98 startup disk is an essential component of any troubleshooting and recovery toolkit.

- You should customize the startup disk to suit your SCSI and CD-ROM setup (if necessary) and to add other troubleshooting tools.

- Use `fat32ebd.exe` from the Windows 98 CD to create a boot disk that can work with FAT32 partitions.

- To make backing up easier, bypass floppy disks in favor of tape, higher-capacity removable media, or another hard disk, and put most of your energy into protecting your data files.

- To easily recover your system in the event of a crash, create a startup disk, run a full system backup, and then modify the System Recovery files—`pcrestore.bat` and `msbatch.inf`—to suit your needs.

- Use the System Information utility, Dr. Watson, and the Windows Report Tool to gather information that's useful for troubleshooting problems.

Inside Windows 98
Communications
and Internet Features

PART V

GET THE SCOOP ON...

Understanding modems ▪ Configuring serial ports ▪
Installing, configuring, and testing modems ▪
Tweaking modem settings for fastest performance ▪
Setting up your modem for long distance calls, call-
ing cards, and other dialing properties

Getting the Most Out of Your Modem

chapter 17

NOT SO LONG AGO, THE MODEM was a humble and obscure piece of equipment used only by hobbyists, hackers, and other members of a small coterie of online aficionados. The rest of the computing world either ignored the modem or scratched their heads over its strange jargon and even stranger noises.

Nowadays, however, it's rare to see a new PC ship without a modem. People are even giving modems as Christmas presents and birthday gifts, which surely qualifies as a "sign of the times." The reason for the modem's newfound cachet is, of course, the rapidly escalating popularity of online services, remote computing, and the Internet. And although there are many ways to connect to remote computers, using a modem to do so is far and away the most common method.

But although modems may be more ubiquitous, that does-n't make them any less mysterious. This chapter attempts to lift some of that mystery by first explaining how modems work, and then helping you use that knowledge to configure your modem for optimum performance.

Understanding Modem Communications

Telephones and telephone lines are analog transmission devices. When you speak into a telephone handset, your voice sound wave causes a diaphragm to vibrate, which sets up an electromagnetic wave. This wave traverses the phone line to the remote end, where it's picked up by the receiving handset. This causes another diaphragm in the receiver to vibrate, which reproduces the original voice sound wave.

Computers store data by using tiny electronic devices called *gates*, which are either open (electricity flows through) or closed (no electricity flows through). These two states are represented using the binary number system, where 1 means open and 0 means closed. These *bits*—a blend of *binary* and *digits*—are discrete units, which give computers their digital character.

How, then, can a digital computer interact with an analog telephone line? The answer is that it's possible to convert the computer's bits into tones that are compatible with the telephone system, and can thus be sent along a telephone line. This conversion process is known as *modulation*. For the computer attached to the receiving end, it's possible to convert the incoming tones back into bits. This is called *demodulation*.

This entire process—from modulating the bits into tones, to sending the tones along the telephone lines, to receiving the tones on the far end, to demodulating the tones back into bits—is handled by a piece of equipment called a *modulator/demodulator*, or *modem*, for short. To understand how a modem accomplishes this task quickly, efficiently, and reliably, you have to understand a few concepts:

bits per second (bps): This is the rate at which the modem sends data along the phone line. Various *modulation standards* specify how a modem performs the modulation so that the receiving modem can successfully demodulate incoming signals. Part of each modulation standard is a transmission speed specification. The most common stan-

66

analog,
adjective:
Pertaining to or being a device or signal having the property of continuously varying in strength or quantity, such as voltage or audio.
—Microsoft Bookshelf 98

99

66

modem Hardware that transmits data from one computer to another, often across phone lines.
—From the "Getting Started" booklet

99

dards in use today are V.32bis (14,400bps), V.32fast or V.FC (28,800bps), V.34 (33,600bps), and V.90 (56,000bps).

baud rate: The number of signal changes (which might be variations in voltage or frequency, depending on the modulation standard being used) per second that can be exchanged between two modems. Although many people use baud rate and bps interchangeably, they are rarely the same thing. That's because, for the vast majority of modems, each signal change incorporates multiple bits. For example, a 2,400-baud modem might incorporate 6 bits within each signal change, which results in a transmission speed of 14,400bps.

data bits: This is the number of bits used to represent a single character of information. PCs use 8 bits (1 byte) to represent a character, but many mainframes use only 7 bits. Therefore, the modem must tell the receiving system the number of data bits it will use for the transmission.

parity: This is an extra bit of data used as a very basic form of error-checking. For receiving systems that use 7 data bits, the sending system modifies the eighth bit according to the type of parity used. The most common is *even parity*, which means the sum of the 1s used when transmitting a single character must add up to an even number. For example, if the character is 0001011, the sum of the 1s is 3. Therefore, the eighth bit is set to 1 to get an even number: 10001011. If the receiving system gets a character that has an odd number of 1s, then it knows an error occurred (that is, a bit changed value), so the character must be sent again. Systems that use 8-bit characters have no extra bit, so parity isn't used.

stop bits: This is extra data used to help frame a transmitted character. Line noise and other disturbances can add extraneous "data" to the incoming signal. To make sure the receiving modem knows exactly where a character begins

Remember
Most modern modems don't rely solely on the parity bit to detect errors. Instead, modems typically support some type of *error correction standard*, which uses sophisticated protocols to ensure that data arrives intact. The current error correction standard is

and ends, the transmitting modem frames each character with a start bit and one or more stop bits. The start bit is always the same, but receiving systems vary in the number of stop bits required: 1, 1.5, or 2.

For a successful modem connection, these parameters must match on both the sending system and the remote system. The last three—data bits, parity, and stop bits—have two combinations that are used with the vast majority of connections:

- 7 data bits, even parity, 1 stop bit. Usually abbreviated as 7-E-1, this combination is most often used when connecting to mainframes.

- 8 data bits, no parity, 1 stop bit. This is usually shortened to 8-N-1 and is most often used when connecting to a bulletin board system (BBS) or another PC.

Besides these settings, there are two other parameters that need to be considered when trying to get your computer and a remote machine to exchange data:

Terminal emulation: When you dial in to a remote computer, your machine essentially acts like a *terminal* that's attached to the remote system. The problem, however, is that the keystroke codes sent out by your computer may not make any sense to the remote machine (particularly if it's a mainframe or minicomputer). To overcome this, you use *terminal emulation* to translate your computer's keystrokes into codes that the remote system understands. To do this successfully, you need to know what type of terminal emulation the remote computer expects.

File transfer protocol: To coordinate the transfer of files, communications programs use a *file transfer protocol*, which defines various aspects of the exchange (starting and stopping, error handling, and so on). For this to work, both systems must use the same protocol.

The next aspect of modem communications that you need to understand is the *serial port* (which also goes by the names *COM port* and *RS-232 port*). External modems plug into a 9-pin

Remember
The HyperTerminal program that comes with Windows 98 supports a number of file transfer protocols, including Xmodem, 1K Xmodem, Kermit, Ymodem, and Zmodem. The latter is the most commonly used protocol.

or 25-pin female port in the back of the computer, whereas internal modems use a built-in serial port. In all cases, data transfers between the computer and the modem are handled by sending bits back and forth through each pin. Table 17.1 shows the pin configuration for a 9-pin serial port.

TABLE 17.1: PIN DESCRIPTIONS FOR A 9-PIN SERIAL PORT

Pin	Name	Direction	Used by...
1	Carrier Detect (CD)	Input	The modem to indicate whether it has received a valid data signal from a remote system
2	Receive Data (RD)	Input	The modem to send data to the computer
3	Transmit Data (TD)	Output	The computer to send data to the modem
4	Data Terminal Ready (DTR)	Output	The computer to indicate whether it's ready to communicate with the modem
5	Signal Ground	N/A	The other communications lines as a reference voltage
6	Data Set Ready (DSR)	Input	The modem to indicate whether it's ready to communicate with the computer
7	Request To Send (RTS)	Output	The computer to signal whether it's ready to receive data
8	Clear To Send (CTS)	Input	The modem to signal whether it's ready to send data
9	Ring Indicator	Input	The modem to indicate whether a ringing signal has been received from a remote system

Inside Scoop
If you have an external modem, it probably has several LED indicators, some of which correspond to the serial port pins. For example, the CD light corresponds to the Carrier Detect pin; CS corresponds to Clear To Send; RD corresponds to Receive Data; RS corresponds to Request To Send; SD corresponds to Transmit Data; and TR corresponds to Data Terminal Ready.

As you can see from Table 17.1, data flows from the computer to the modem via the TD pin, whereas data flows from the modem to the computer via the RD pin. In both cases, the data flows one bit at a time. However, the computer likes to deal with data at the byte level, which is to say 8 bits at a time. How do the computer and modem manage to translate bytes into bits, and vice versa?

The secret is a chip called the *Universal Asynchronous Receiver/Transmitter* (*UART*) that's part of the serial port. The UART spends most of its time breaking down outgoing bytes into bits for the modem's consumption, and assembling incoming bits into bytes for the computer. The UART uses up to 16 transmit and receive buffers for storing outgoing and incoming bytes until the CPU can process them.

The final piece of the modem communications puzzle is *flow control*. This determines how the computer and the modem communicate with each other to coordinate the flow of data between them. There are two types:

XON/XOFF flow control: Also known as *software flow control*, the computer and the modem send ASCII characters to each other to indicate whether they're ready to send or receive data. XON (ASCII 17) means "go ahead" and XOFF (ASCII 19) means "hold on." This form of flow control is rarely used today.

RTS/CTS flow control: Also known as *hardware flow control*, this method uses the serial port's RTS and CTS pins (refer to Table 17.1). This is by far the most common type of flow control.

Installing a Modem

If Windows 98 didn't detect your modem during Setup, or if you have a new modem, you need to install your modem before you can use it with any communications software. This section shows you how to install and test a modem in Windows 98.

Many newer modems support Plug and Play, so it's possible that Windows 98 may recognize your modem after you install it and restart your computer. In this case, Windows 98 will offer to search for the best driver for the modem. When choosing search locations, be sure to include the location of your Windows 98 source files. If you also have the manufacturer's drivers, specify their location as well. See Chapter 22, "Taking the Mystery Out of Hardware," to learn more about installing device drivers.

Undocumented
XON/XOFF flow control normally operates behind the scenes. However, you can usually stop and start data transfers manually by pressing Ctrl+S for XOFF or Ctrl+Q for XON. Note, too, that you can often resume a stuck data transfer by pressing Ctrl+Q.

If Windows 98 didn't recognize your modem at startup, you can install it by using the Add New Modem wizard. Before doing so, run through the following modem installation checklist:

See Also...
"Installing
Device Drivers,"
p. 521

- Many modems offer different configurations for things like the IRQ line. Internal modems use jumper switches, whereas external modems use DIP switches. See your modem's documentation to check whether the default configuration will conflict with an existing device on your system.

- Windows 98 will send signals to the serial port in an attempt to communicate with the modem. Therefore, make sure your external modem is turned on and connected to the serial port.

- Make sure you don't have any communications software running.

- If you have a device driver from the manufacturer, insert the disk in the appropriate drive so that it's ready for use.

Running the Add New Modem Wizard

The Add New Modem wizard takes you step by step through the installation process. How you launch this wizard depends on whether you're setting up your first modem:

If you're setting up your first modem: In this case, open the Control Panel's Modems icon and the Install New Modem wizard will appear automatically.

If you're setting up another modem: In this case, opening the Control Panel's Modems icon displays the Modems Properties dialog box. To launch the Add New Modem wizard, click the Add button.

With the wizard up and running, follow these steps to install your modem:

1. In the initial wizard dialog box, click Next. The wizard interrogates your system's serial ports to look for an attached modem, and then displays a dialog box showing the name of the modem.

2. Click Next. The wizard installs your modem.

3. Depending on how Windows 98 was set up on your computer, you may now see the Location Information dialog box. You use this dialog box to specify some settings that control how Windows 98 dials the modem. Fill in your country's code, area code, the number you dial for an outside line (if any), and whether your phone system uses tone or pulse dialing. Click Next.

4. Click Finish. The wizard opens the Modems Properties dialog box with your modem displayed, as shown in Figure 17.1.

Figure 17.1
The Modems Properties dialog box lists your installed modems.

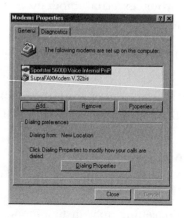

If the wizard failed in its quest to find your modem, or if you prefer to install the manufacturer's drivers, you can install the modem by hand. There are three ways to get started:

- Launch the Add New Modem wizard and in the initial dialog box activate the Don't detect my modem; I will select it from a list check box and then click Next.

- If the wizard found the wrong modem, click the Change button in the dialog box that shows the name of the modem.

- If the wizard didn't find any modem, it will display a dialog box to let you know. Click Next.

You'll now see the Install New Modem dialog box shown in Figure 17.2.

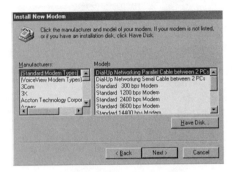

Figure 17.2
Use this dialog box to select your modem manufacturer and model.

Here are the steps to follow:

1. Use the Manufacturers list to highlight the modem maker, use the Models list to highlight your modem, and then click Next. If you want to install the manufacturer's drivers, click Have Disk and follow the instructions that appear.

2. The next dialog box asks you to select the port to which the modem is attached. Click the port and then click Next to install the modem.

3. Fill in the Location Information dialog box, if it appears, and click Next.

4. Click Finish to return to the Modems Properties dialog box.

Shortcut
If you're not sure what type of modem you have, select (Standard Modem Types) in the Manufacturers list, and then use the Models list to select one of the standard types.

Running Modem Diagnostics

With your modem installed, you should run a test to make sure Windows 98 can communicate with the modem. Here are the steps to follow:

1. In the Modems Properties dialog box, display the Diagnostics tab, shown in Figure 17.3.

Figure 17.3
Use the
Diagnostics tab
to test your
modem.

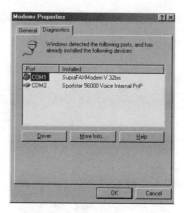

2. If you have multiple modems, click the port that corresponds to the modem you want to test.

3. Click More Info.

4. If Windows 98 can communicate with your modem, it displays the More Info dialog box with data such as the port, IRQ, I/O address, UART type, highest speed, and a list of AT commands. Otherwise, you get an Error dialog box that tells you the modem failed to respond. Click OK in either case.

Watch Out!
Outside the obvious reasons
(modem not turned on, not connected, and so on), one common reason that a modem may fail to respond is an IRQ conflict with the serial port. COM1 and COM3 both use IRQ 4, and COM2 and COM4 both use IRQ 3. If you have, say, a mouse on COM1 and an internal modem on COM3, the resulting conflict will cause problems. Either adjust the modem's jumpers to use another IRQ, or else use Device Manager to change a port's IRQ.

Running AT Commands

Another way to test your modem is to send it *AT* (short for "Attention") commands. For example, most modems will go "off hook" and sound the dial tone if you enter the ATDT (ATtention Dial Tone) command. Similarly, you hang up the modem by entering the ATH (ATtention Hang up) command. See your modem manual for the complete list of AT commands supported by the modem.

The following method should work for most modems:

1. Select Start, Programs, Accessories, Communications, HyperTerminal to display the HyperTerminal folder.

2. Launch the Hypertrm.exe icon. The Connection Description dialog box appears.

3. Click Cancel to get to the HyperTerminal window.

4. If you have multiple modems, select File, Properties to display the New Connection Properties dialog box, make sure the modem you want to test is selected in the Connect Using list, and click OK.

5. Use the HyperTerminal window to type an AT command and press Enter. If you receive OK or some data in response to the command, then HyperTerminal can communicate with your modem. If there's a problem, you'll see ERROR or some other problem indicator.

The above method doesn't work on some internal modems. To work around this, try these steps:

1. Use HyperTerminal to create a new connection (such as the connection for the US Robotics BBS created in the next section).

2. Select File, Properties to display the New Connection Properties dialog box.

3. Click Configure to open the property sheet for the modem, and then display the Options tab.

4. Activate the Bring up terminal window before dialing check box, and then click OK.

5. Click OK to return to HyperTerminal.

6. Select Call, Call to display the Connect dialog box, and then click Dial. HyperTerminal displays the Pre-Dial Terminal Screen.

7. Enter your AT commands. Figure 17.4 shows an example.

8. When you're done, click Cancel (or press F3) to cancel the connection.

Shortcut
You may also want to use AT commands to set up the modem before using it. Rather than entering the commands by hand, Windows 98 enables you to specify the commands as a property of the modem. This means the commands get executed automatically whenever you use the modem. See "Working with Advanced Connection Settings," later in this chapter.

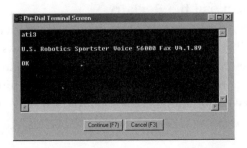

Figure 17.4
Use the Pre-Dial Terminal Screen to send AT commands to the modem.

Undocumented
A third method
for running AT
commands is to
"echo" them to
the serial port
from the DOS
prompt. The
general format is
ECHO ATx > COMn,
where *x* is the rest
of the AT com-
mand and *n* is the
number of the
COM port. For
example, entering
ECHO ATDT > COM1
gets you a dial
tone from the
modem attached
to COM1.

Does Your Phone Line Support 56Kbps Transmissions?

After your modem is tested and working, you may also want to know whether you'll be able to take full advantage of your 56Kbps modem. To do this, you need to find out if your phone system is 56Kbps-capable (some phone lines can't handle such traffic). Here are the steps to follow:

1. Select Start, Programs, Accessories, Communications, HyperTerminal. The HyperTerminal folder appears.

2. Launch the Hypertrm.exe icon. The Connection Description dialog box appears.

3. Type US Robotics BBS in the Name text box, select an Icon, and click OK. HyperTerminal displays the Connect To dialog box.

4. Type 847 in the Area Code text box, type 262-6000 in the Phone Number text box, make sure your modem is displayed in the Connect Using list, and then click OK. HyperTerminal displays the Connect dialog box.

5. Click OK. HyperTerminal dials the modem and then connects you with the US Robotics BBS.

6. The system first asks if you want to display graphics. Press Enter for yes, or press N and Enter for no.

7. When the system asks you for your first name, type line test and press Enter. The system then checks your phone line and displays the results.

8. The system also disconnects the call, so you can now exit HyperTerminal.

Your Modem and the Registry

Windows 98 stores lots of data about your modem in the Registry. Most of this data was supplied to Windows 98 when the Add New Modem wizard interrogated your modem during the installation. To see your modem's Registry settings, open the Registry Editor and find the following key:

```
HKEY_LOCAL_MACHINE\System\CurrentControlSet\Services\Class\
Modem
```

Here you'll find keys for each installed modem: 0000, 0001, and so on. These keys contain general settings such as the manufacturer and model. There are also many subkeys related to specific modem features and commands. Two are particularly interesting:

Init: The values in this subkey are the initialization strings sent to the modem each time you make a connection.

Settings: The values in this subkey are all the AT commands supported by the modem. Note that the commands are shown without the "AT" part (that's specified in the Prefix setting). For example, on most internal modems, you can set the speaker volume to high by entering the command ATL3. So, in this subkey, you'll probably see a setting named SpeakerVolume_High; its value will be L3.

Setting the Modem's Properties

With your modem installed and working, you can now turn to customizing the modem to suit your needs and to troubleshoot problems. The next few sections take you through the various controls in the modem's property sheet. To get the property sheet onscreen, highlight the modem in the Modems Properties dialog box, and then click Properties. Figure 17.5 shows the dialog box that appears.

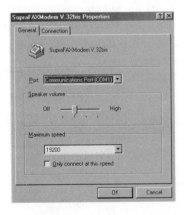

Figure 17.5
Use the modem's property sheet to customize various connection settings.

Setting the General Properties

The General tab displays the name of the modem and also offers the following controls:

Port: This list displays the port to which the modem is attached. If you have multiple serial ports, you can use this list to select a different port. Internal modems have built-in serial ports that can't be changed. Therefore, the Port list is disabled for these modems.

Speaker volume: Use this slider to set the volume level for your modem. This is particularly useful for internal modems (most external modems have a volume knob you can operate).

Maximum speed: This list sets the *data terminal equipment* (*DTE*) transmission speed, which is the speed at which data is transmitted between the CPU and the modem. You can usually get away with bumping this value up to a higher speed if you have a fast computer (at least a Pentium). If the computer and the modem can't connect at the selected speed, Windows 98 will try slower values. To prevent it from doing this, activate the Only connect at this speed check box. Note that not all modems support this feature.

Inside Scoop
If setting the Speaker Volume slider to Off doesn't completely mute your modem, the command ATM0 might do it. See "Working with Advanced Connection Settings," later in this chapter.

Setting the Connection Properties

Figure 17.6 shows the Connection tab, which enables you to set parameters such as the data bits and stop bits, how the modem makes calls, and much more.

Figure 17.6
Use the Connection tab to customize how the modem connects to remote systems.

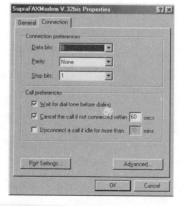

Here's a summary of the options in this dialog box:

Connection preferences: Use these lists to set the connection parameters you want to use for Data bits, Parity, and Stop bits.

Wait for dial tone before dialing: When activated, this option tells the modem to wait until it has detected a dial tone before it begins dialing. There are three circumstances in which you might want to deactivate this option:

- Your phone system gives you an immediate dial tone. In this case, deactivating this check box may slightly decrease the connection time because the modem no longer waits for the dial tone.

- The modem can't recognize the dial tone (this often happens in foreign countries).

- You have to dial manually or with the assistance of an operator.

Cancel the call if not connected within *x* secs: When this check box is activated, Windows 98 gives the modem the specified number of seconds to connect to the remote system. If the connection doesn't happen within that time, Windows 98 cancels the call. If you're connecting to a system that takes a long time to connect (such as an international call), adjust the number of seconds accordingly (you can enter any integer value between 1 and 254).

Disconnect a call if idle for more than *x* mins: If you activate this check box, Windows 98 monitors the connection for activity. If there is no activity within the specified number of minutes, Windows 98 disconnects the call.

The Connection tab also has two command buttons named Port Settings and Advanced buttons. I explain these buttons in detail in the next two sections.

Working with Port Settings

Figure 17.7 shows the Advanced Port Settings dialog box that appears when you click the Port Settings button. You use this dialog box to control the first-in, first-out (FIFO) buffers used

Watch Out!
Forgetting that your modem is connected to a remote system is easy to do. If you pay money for your connection time—either a per-minute connect fee or a long distance charge—be sure to activate the Disconnect a call if idle for more than x mins check box. For the idle time, enter a value between 1 and 42 minutes.

by the serial port's UART chip. (This applies only to serial ports that have a 16550-compatible UART. The type of UART you have is one of the things displayed in the modem diagnostics test I told you about earlier.)

Figure 17.7
Use the controls in this dialog box to adjust how the UART generates interrupts from the FIFO buffers.

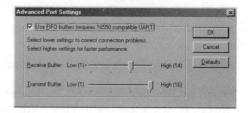

Recall from our earlier discussion that the purpose of the UART is to convert the CPU's outgoing bytes into bits for modem transmission, as well as to convert the modem's incoming bits into bytes for the CPU. The FIFO buffers are storage areas that the UART uses to hold incoming (the *receive buffers*) and outgoing (the *transmit buffers*) bytes. When a certain number of these buffers are full, the UART generates an interrupt to let the CPU know what's going on.

The two sliders determine when these interrupts are sent:

- Moving the sliders to the right means that more buffers must be full before an interrupt is sent. This means that fewer interrupts are generated, so performance increases.

- Moving the sliders to the left means that fewer buffers must be full before an interrupt is sent. This gives the CPU more opportunity to deal with the buffers, so you're less likely to have transmission problems.

Working with Advanced Connection Settings
Figure 17.8 shows the Advanced Connection Settings dialog box that appears when you click the Advanced button in the Connection tab. You use this dialog box to customize error control, flow control, specify extra AT commands, and more.

Figure 17.8
Use this dialog box to set a few advanced connection-related options.

Here's a rundown of the controls in this dialog box:

Use error control: Most modern modems support some sort of error-checking protocol (such as V.42). This check box toggles the modem's built-in error-checking on and off.

Required to connect: When this check box is activated, the modem will connect to a remote modem only if the latter supports error-checking. Although you should leave this option deactivated to support a wider variety of remote modems, you may have no choice but to activate it if your phone system uses lines that are particularly noisy (and, hence, error-prone).

Compress data: Most modern modems support some sort of data compression protocol. For example, the V.42bis standard enables data compression of up to 4:1. This check box toggles the modem's built-in compression on and off.

Use cellular protocol: Some PC Card modems support error-correction protocols designed for cellular connections. This check box (which is available only for modems that support these cellular protocols) toggles the protocols on and off.

Use flow control: Use this check box to toggle flow control on and off. When this check box is activated, you can set the flow control to either Hardware (RTS/CTS) (recommended) or Software (XON/OFF).

Watch Out!
If you have trouble establishing a connection to the remote modem, activating Use error control may be the culprit. This also applies to the other check boxes in this group. Try deactivating these check boxes one at a time to see if that improves your connections.

Undocumented
You can get most modems to dial faster by changing the value of the S11 register, which sets the number of millisec-onds between numbers dialed. The default on most modems is about 70, so try lowering this num-ber gradually until the dialing no longer works. On my modem, I use ATS11=40 in the Extra Settings text box.

Modulation type: This list determines whether the modem uses its default modulation protocol (the Standard option) or some other proprietary protocol.

Extra settings: Any text you enter into this box is used by Windows 98 to initialize the modem. Use this text box to add AT commands or other initialization settings, as described in your modem manual. Note that these com-mands are sent to the modem *after* Windows 98 has sent the modem's default initialization string (see Figure 17.9).

Append to log: Activating this check box tells Windows 98 to log the progress of the connection to a text file. This file is named *Modem.log*—where *Modem* is the name of the modem—and it's stored in the Windows folder. You can open the log in Notepad by clicking the View Log button. As you can see in Figure 17.9, the log shows the various commands sent to the modem, the modem's responses, and other useful troubleshooting data.

Figure 17.9
The modem's log file tracks the progress of the connection.

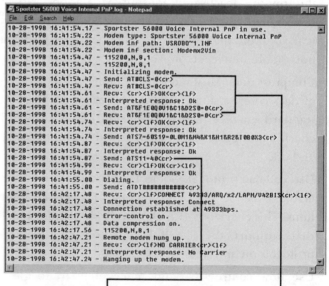

Custom initialization string entered into the "Extra settings" text box   Default initialization strings

Setting Dialing Properties

When you set up your modem, Windows 98 probably asked you for information about your location, such as your country code, your area code, whether you use tone or pulse dialing, and so on. For most users, that information stays constant over time. However, a growing number of users take notebook computers on the road with them (or just back and forth between home and the office). For these users, their location data often changes, so how they dial the phone changes, as well. For example, dialing a number in the 317 area code from your home may be a long distance call, but it will be a local call when you're in the 317 area. Similarly, travelers often need to use a calling card or a long distance service, which usually requires entering ID numbers, passwords, and other extra digits.

All of this affects how your modem dials, as well. To help you manage this, Windows 98 enables you to set up different *dialing locations* that specify an area code, numbers to dial to get an outside line, calling card numbers, and much more.

To set up and modify dialing locations, open the Control Panel's Modems icon. When the Modems Properties dialog box appears, click the Dialing Properties button to get the Dialing Properties dialog box onscreen, as shown in Figure 17.10.

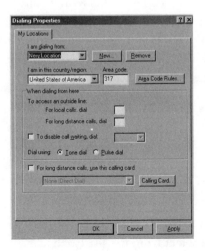

Figure 17.10
Use this property sheet to set up and customize dialing locations.

Let's look at the options in this dialog box:

I am dialing from: This is the list of defined dialing locations. A new location is started for you automatically. Feel free to edit the New Location name. To create another new location, click New, click OK when Windows 98 tells you the new location was created, and then edit the new location name.

I am in this country/region: This is the location's country code.

Area code: This is the location's area code.

Area Code Rules: Click this button to display the Area Code Rules dialog box. You'll see two groups:

> **When calling within my area code:** If your phone company requires that you use 10-digit dialing (area code plus phone number) when making calls to your own area code, activate the Always dial the area code (10-digit dialing) check box. If some calls to your own area code are long distance calls, click New to specify the phone number prefixes that Windows 98 must dial as long distance.

> **When calling to other area codes:** If your phone company has split off part of your area code into a separate area code, it's likely that calls between the two codes aren't treated as long distance. To tell Windows 98 not to dial calls to the other area code as long distance, click New and specify the other area code.

To access an outside line: If you're dialing through a PBX system at an office or hotel, you'll usually have to dial a number to get an outside line. Use these text boxes to enter the appropriate numbers to get an outside line for local calls (such as 9) and long distance calls (such as 8).

To disable call waiting, dial: Activating this check box tells Windows 98 to disable call waiting by sending whatever code you select from the list (such as *70) or entering by hand.

Dial using: Select the type of dialing used by the phone system: Tone dial or Pulse dial.

For long distance calls, use this calling card: If you want to use a calling card or a long distance carrier, activate this check box and then select the card or carrier you want to use from the list.

Calling card: Click this button to customize an existing calling card or carrier or to define a new calling card or carrier. I explain how this works below.

If you plan on using a calling card, you'll need to modify the card setup to add your PIN number. And if Windows 98 doesn't come with a predefined calling card or long distance carrier that you use, you must define a new one. Here are the steps to follow:

1. In the Dialing Properties dialog box, click the Calling Card button. Windows 98 displays the Calling Card dialog box, shown in Figure 17.11.

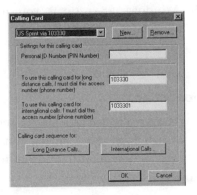

2. You have two ways to proceed:

   - If you want to work with an existing item, use the list box at the top of the dialog box to select the calling card or long distance carrier.

   - If you want to create a new item, click New, enter a name for the new item, and then click OK. When Windows 98 tells you that you must enter dialing rules, click OK.

Watch Out!
Call waiting signals an incoming call by sending extra tones. Unfortunately, those tones can throw the modem for a loop and disrupt communications. Therefore, you should always disable call waiting.

Figure 17.11
Use this dialog box to modify or create a calling card or long distance carrier.

3. If you're working with a calling card, enter your PIN number in the Personal ID Number (PIN Number) text box.

4. Use the To Use This Calling Card for Long Distance calls... text box to enter the access number that must be dialed to initiate a long distance call.

5. Use the To Use This Calling Card for International Calls... text box to enter the access number that must be dialed to initiate an international call.

6. Calling card and long distance calls must follow a sequence. For example, you dial the number, wait for a tone, enter your PIN, and so on. To adjust the sequences used for calls, click the Long Distance Calls and International Calls buttons. In each case, the dialog box that appears has various steps that you fill in. You enter what should be dialed and what the system should wait for before moving on to the next step in the sequence. Click OK when you're done.

7. Click OK. Windows 98 returns you to the Dialing Properties dialog box.

8. Click OK.

Essential Information

- *Modem* is short for *modulator/demodulator*, and its purpose is to modulate digital bits into analog tones, send those tones over a phone line, and then demodulate the tones back into bits on the receiving end.

- Modem transmission speeds are measured in *bits per second* (bps), with common speeds being 14,400bps (V.32bis), 28,800bps (V.32fast), 33,600bps (V.34), and 56,000bps (V.90).

- Common communications parameters are *data bits* (the number of bits in a character), *parity* (how error-checking is performed), and *stop bits* (the bits that signal the end of a character).

- To install a modem and work with modem properties, open the Control Panel's Modems icon.

- In the Modems Properties dialog box, click Properties to work with settings such as the speaker volume, connection parameters, error control, flow control, and extra initialization strings.

- To specify dialing location settings such as the country code, area code, calling card data, and how to disable call waiting, click Dialing Properties in the Modems Properties dialog box.

GET THE SCOOP ON...
Running through a checklist of information required
to set up an Internet connection ■ Creating a dial-up
Internet connection ■ Automating dial-up connections
using scripts ■ Using TCP/IP to create an Internet
connection through your local area network ■ Working
with Windows 98's Internet utilities such as PING
and TRACERT

Getting on the Internet

Chapter 18

THE INTERNET HAS BEEN a big deal for four or five years now. In that time, thousands of books, stories, and articles have been published in an effort to explain what the Internet is, to outline what users can do with it, and to come to grips with this phenomenon's good, bad, and ugly sides. In other words, the Internet needs no introduction.

So, you'll no doubt be happy to hear that you won't be getting any kind of "Internet 101" from me. This chapter assumes you've had it up to here with the "it all began with the Department of Defense" histories, "network of networks" definitions, and gee-whiz descriptions of how great the Web and email are. You already know the what and why, and now all you need is the how. This chapter provides you with plenty of that. I'll tell you the information you need to get started, and then put that data to good use in setting up a dial-up Internet connection. If you're on a local area network that has an Internet gateway, I'll show you how to get your machine to access that connection. You'll also learn about some of Windows 98's Internet utilities, connection tricks, and much more.

How to Get On the Internet Using a Phone Line

Most home users access the Internet by using a dial-up connection over a phone line. These accounts typically offer a certain number of hours of connection time for a monthly fee, with extra time being billed hourly. Connecting these accounts is usually straightforward, and some Internet service providers (ISPs) make it very easy:

- Online services such as America Online offer Internet gateways as part of their regular service. In these cases, getting on the Internet is a simple matter of installing the service's software. If this is the route you want to take, click the Online Services icon on the desktop and then click the icon for the service you want to install.

- Some ISPs offer installation programs that create the appropriate connection for you automatically (as well as install some Internet software).

All other connections require some sort of setup within Windows 98. This section shows you how to get your connection established.

Information You Need Before Getting Started

The Internet is all about information, so it's appropriate (or ironic, depending on how you look at it) that the key to getting connected to the Internet is having adequate information. Fortunately, most ISPs are pretty good at supplying you with the information you need. The following list runs through all the data that you *might* need to get your connection going (note, however, that many setups require only some of these items):

- The phone number you must dial to connect to the ISP.

- The username and password for your ISP account.

- Whether logging in to the ISP requires any special instructions.

- Whether you need to enable or disable certain modem features—such as error control and data compression—in order to connect to the ISP successfully.

- The type of flow control used by the ISP's modems.

- Whether the ISP assigns you an *IP (Internet Protocol) address* automatically when you log in. If not, you need to know your permanent IP address and the *subnet mask* that goes along with it. (Your IP address identifies your computer when you're on the Internet. That is, when you request data, it's sent to your IP address. Each IP address uses *dotted-decimal notation*, which takes the form *aaa.bbb.ccc.ddd*, where *aaa* and so on are numbers between 1 and 255.)

- Whether the ISP assigns the IP address of its *DNS (Domain Name System) server* automatically when you log in. If not, you need to know the address of the DNS server. Most ISPs give you addresses for both a primary DNS server and a secondary DNS server. (A *domain name* is an English language equivalent to an IP address. For example, the IP address of my Web server is 209.146.148.66, but its domain name is `www.mcfedries.com`. The DNS is a technology that handles the translation of IP addresses to domain names, and vice versa.)

Remember
IP is the fundamental protocol of the Internet. It defines the structure of all the data that's sent over the Internet, as well as the addresses of all the Internet's resources.

- The type of connection. Most ISPs use PPP (Point-to-Point Protocol) connections, although some still use SLIP (Serial Line Interface Protocol) connections.

If you plan on using Internet email, you'll need to gather the following:

- Your email account username and password, if they're different from your login username and password.

- The type of email account (POP3 or IMAP).

- The domain name of the ISP's incoming (POP3 or IMAP) email server and its outgoing (SMTP) email server. Note that most ISPs use the same server for both incoming and outgoing mail.

If you plan on working with Usenet newsgroups, you need the following data:

- The domain name of the ISP's *news server* (which is sometimes called an *NNTP server* or a *news host*).

- Whether you need to log in to the news server.

- Your login name and password, if you do have to log in to the news server.

If your ISP supports an *Internet directory service* (often called an *LDAP—Lightweight Direct Access Protocol—service*) for finding people on the Internet, you need the following data:

- The domain name of the ISP's *directory server*

- Whether you need to log in to the directory server

- Your login name and password, if you do have to log in to the directory server

With this information at the ready, Windows 98 offers two ways to create the connection:

- Use the Internet Connection Wizard.

- Create a Dial-Up Networking connection by hand.

The next three sections explore both routes. The first two sections examine the Internet Connection Wizard: The first section discusses the wizard as it appears in the original version of Windows 98, and the second section discusses the Windows 98 Second Edition version of the wizard (see "The Internet Connection Wizard in Windows 98 Second Edition" later in this chapter).

Using the Internet Connection Wizard

The Internet Connection Wizard takes you through the process of setting up an Internet connection in the usual wizardly, step-by-step fashion. You get things started either by launching the desktop's Connect to the Internet icon, or by selecting Start, Programs, Internet Explorer, Connection Wizard. Either way, the Internet Connection Wizard appears, as shown in Figure 18.1.

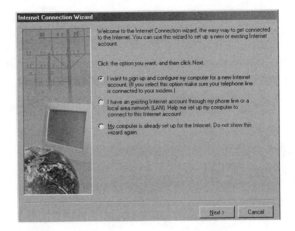

Figure 18.1
The Internet
Connection Wizard
takes you through
the process of set-
ting up a connec-
tion.

The initial dialog box offers three choices:

■ **I Want to Sign Up and Configure My Computer for a New Internet Account:** If you choose this option, the wizard dials your modem and connects to the Microsoft Referral Service to download a list of ISPs in your area. Each of these ISPs will configure your Internet connection automatically.

■ **I Have an Existing Internet Account Through My Phone Line or a Local Area Network (LAN):** Select this option to configure your dial-up account.

■ **My computer Is Already Set Up for the Internet:** Choose this option if you already have an Internet connection set up. This replaces the Connect to the Internet icon on the desktop with icons for Internet Explorer and Outlook Express.

After you activate the I Have an Existing Internet Account Through My Phone Line or a Local Area Network (LAN) option and click Next, you then follow these steps:

1. The next wizard dialog box asks how you'll be accessing the Internet. Activate the Select This Option If You Are Accessing the Internet Using an Internet Service Provider or a Local Area Network (LAN) button, and then click Next.

66

Using the Internet
Connection wizard,
you can quickly
set up an Internet
account and con-
nection. After you
set up a connec-
tion, you can also
use the wizard to
set up email,
newsgroups, and
directory services.
—From the
"Getting Started"
booklet

99

Inside Scoop

One of the wizard's dialog boxes is titled Logon Procedure. If you activate the I Need to Log On Manually option, the wizard doesn't set things up properly. To fix this, open the Dial-Up Networking folder, open the property sheet for the connection, click Configure, and then display the Options tab. Deactivate the Bring Up Terminal Window Before Dialing option, and activate the Bring Up Terminal Window After Dialing option.

2. In the next wizard dialog box, activate the Connect Using My Phone Line option, and then click Next.

3. The wizard checks your system and may perform one or more of the following tasks:

   - It may install Dial-Up Networking. If so, you should restart your computer and run through this procedure again.

   - It may launch the Install New Modem Wizard if you haven't yet installed a modem.

   - If you have multiple modems installed, it asks which modem you want to use for the connection.

4. From here, you run through a long series of dialog boxes in which you fill in some or all of the information listed in the previous section.

The Internet Connection Wizard in Windows 98 Second Edition

Windows 98 Second Edition offers a different version of the Internet Connection Wizard. Although the new wizard boasts some extra features, overall it's a more streamlined process (mostly because it eliminates the procedures for setting up a news account and an LDAP account).

The first change is that although the Connect to the Internet icon remains on the desktop, the Start menu path to the wizard has changed: Start, Programs, Accessories, Internet Tools, Connection Wizard. The new wizard also uses a different startup dialog box, as shown in Figure 18.2. You now have the following three choices:

- **I Want to Sign Up for a New Account:** Choose this option to open an account via one of Windows 98's preselected ISPs.

- **I Want to Transfer My Existing Internet Account to This Computer:** If you already have an account, the wizard may be able to download its settings automatically by choosing this option. Note, however, that only certain ISPs support this feature (the wizard supplies you with a list of those ISPs).

■ **I Want to Set Up My Internet Connection Manually...:** This is the option to choose if you'll be specifying the account details by hand. Again, you follow the various wizard dialog boxes and plug in the values I listed earlier. If your account requires entering IP addresses, specifying PPP or SLIP, or specifying a manual logon, click the Advanced button in the step 1 of 3 dialog box.

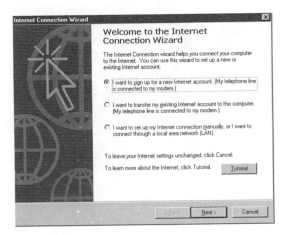

Figure 18.2
The Internet Connection Wizard dialog box used by Windows 98 Second Edition.

Using Dial-Up Networking

Using the Internet Connection Wizard is a good way to make sure you don't miss anything when setting up your Internet connection. However, it's not the quickest or the most efficient way to go about things. This is particularly true when you realize that all the wizard is really doing is gathering data to create a Dial-Up Networking connection. If you already have Dial-Up Networking installed, and you've already told Windows 98 about your modem, it's often easier to set up your connection directly from the Dial-Up Networking folder:

1. Select Start, Programs, Accessories, Communications, Dial-Up Networking.

2. The next step depends on how Dial-Up Networking started:

- If this is the first time you've launched Dial-Up Networking, the Welcome to Dial-Up Networking dialog box appears. In this case, click Next.

- Each subsequent time you launch Dial-Up Networking, the Dial-Up Networking folder appears. In this case, click the Make New Connection icon.

3. In the initial dialog box, enter a name for your connection and, if you have multiple modems, choose the modem you want from the Select a Device list (see Figure 18.3).

Figure 18.3
Enter a name for your connection and select a modem.

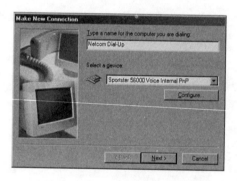

4. If your ISP requires you to log in, click Configure to display the modem's property sheet, select the Options tab, activate the Bring Up Terminal Window After Dialing check box, and click OK.

5. Click Next.

6. In the next dialog box, enter the ISP's Area Code, Telephone Number, and Country Code, and then click Next.

7. Click Finish. An icon for your new connection appears in the Dial-Up Networking folder.

8. Highlight the connection and then select File, Properties to display the connection's property sheet.

9. Display the Server Types tab.

10. If your ISP uses a PPP server, make sure you select the PPP option in the Type of Dial-Up Server list. If your provider uses SLIP, choose the SLIP option, instead.

11. Deactivate the Log On to Network check box.

12. Activate or deactivate the other check boxes in the Advanced Options group, as necessary. (For most connections, you can use the default selections.)

13. In the Allowed Network Protocols Group, deactivate the NetBEUI and IPX/SPX check boxes.

14. Make sure the TCP/IP check box is activated and click the TCP/IP Settings button to display the TCP/IP Settings dialog box.

15. Choose one of the following options:

    Server Assigned IP Address: Select this option if your ISP assigns you an IP address each time you log in.

    Specify an IP Address: Select this option if your ISP has assigned you a permanent IP address. Use the IP address boxes to enter your address.

16. Choose one of the following options:

    Server Assigned Name Server Address: Select this option if your ISP assigns a DNS server IP address each time you log in.

    Specify Name Server Addresses: Select this option if your ISP has given you IP addresses for its DNS server. Use the Primary DNS and Secondary DNS boxes to enter the addresses (see Figure 18.4).

17. Click OK to return to the connection's property sheet.

18. Click OK to return to the Dial-Up Networking folder.

Setting a Few More Connection Properties

Your Internet connection is now ready to go. Before connecting, however, there are a few other settings that you might want to work with. To see these settings, click the Internet icon on the Control Panel to display the Internet Properties dialog

Shortcut
You can also get to the connection's property sheet by highlighting the icon and then clicking the Properties button in the toolbar, or by right-clicking the icon and then clicking Properties.

Inside Scoop
Windows 98 makes it easy to share Dial-Up Networking connections with other Windows 98 machines or users. Open the Dial-Up Networking folder and copy the connection you want to work with to a floppy disk, removable disk, or network drive. On the other machine, open the Dial-Up Networking folder and then copy the connection into that folder. Adjust the properties of the copied connection to select a different modem, if necessary.

box, select the Connection tab, and then click the Settings button. Figure 18.5 shows the Dial-Up Settings dialog box that appears. (The Windows 98 Second Edition version of this dialog box has a different layout, which I'll discuss in the next section.)

Figure 18.4
Use this dialog box to fill in your IP address and your ISP's DNS server addresses, if necessary.

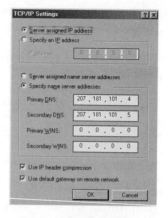

Figure 18.5
Use this dialog box to adjust some settings related to your Internet connection.

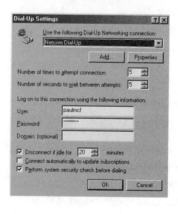

Let's run through the available options in this dialog box:

Shortcut
Right-click the Internet Explorer icon on the desktop and then click Properties to get the Internet Properties dialog box onscreen quickly.

- **Use the Following Dial-Up Networking Connection:** If you have multiple connections, use this list to select the one you want to use. (Note, too, that you can click Add to create a new connection and you can click Properties to make changes to the selected connection.)

- **Number of Times to Attempt Connection:** Use this spinner to set the maximum number of dial-up attempts Windows 98 performs if it can't connect with the ISP.

- **Number of Seconds to Wait Between Attempts:** Use this spinner to set the amount of time Windows 98 waits before attempting another connection.

- **Log On to This Connection Using the Following Information:** Use these text boxes to adjust your User Name and your Password. (You probably don't need to enter a Domain.)

- **Disconnect If Idle for *x* Minutes:** Leave this option activated to have Windows 98 automatically disconnect from your ISP if the connection is idle for the number of minutes selected in the spinner.

- **Connect Automatically to Update Subscriptions:** Activate this check box to enable Windows 98 to connect to your ISP automatically to update Internet Explorer's subscriptions (explained in the next chapter).

- **Perform System Security Check Before Dialing:** Leave this check box activated to have Windows 98 perform a security check with each dial-up. This security check examines your system to see if the TCP/IP protocol is bound to the File and Print Sharing service. See Chapter 21, "Internet Security Features for the Sophisticated Surfer."

Watch Out!
The automatic connection feature works only if you don't log in to your ISP. If you do have to log in, you can still use this feature if you create a script to automate the login. See "Creating Scripts to Automate Dial-Ups," later in this chapter.

See Also...
"Internet Security and the TCP/IP Protocol," p. 494

Connection Settings in Windows 98 Second Edition

To adjust the settings for your dial-up connection in Windows 98 Second Edition, you again open the Internet Properties dialog box and display the Connection tab. From here, use the Dial-Up Settings list to highlight the connection you want to work with, and then click Settings. Figure 18.6 shows the dialog box that appears.

This dialog box offers a set of options substantially different from those in the original version, so let's take a closer look:

Automatically Detect Settings: This check box toggles whether the connection will use a network server to automatically configure Internet and Internet Explorer settings. If the server supports this feature and uses DNS and

Dynamic Host Control Protocol (DHCP), activate this check box. This means that your settings will be configured automatically when you start your browser.

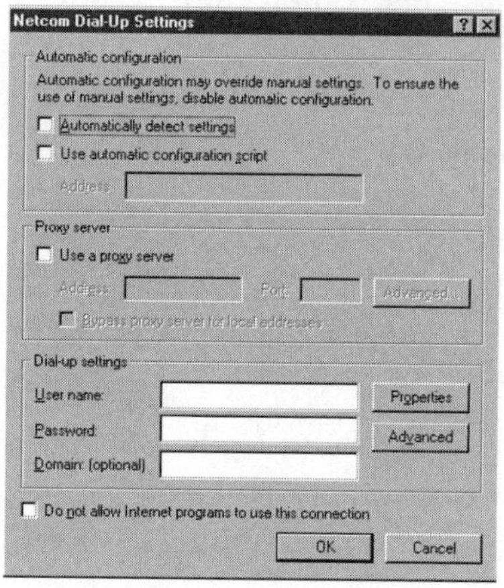

Figure 18.6
Use the Netcom
Dial-Up Settings
dialog box to
adjust your dial-up
connection.

Use Automatic Configuration Script: If your network administrator has created a configuration script (an .ins file), activate this check box and enter the path to the script in the Address text box.

Use a Proxy Server: Activate this check box if you want your connection to go through a proxy server. (A proxy server is used as a security barrier between your local network and the Internet.) You must also specify the Address and Port used by the proxy server. If you need to set up specific addresses and ports for different protocols (HTTP, FTP, and so on), click Advanced. Finally, if you want to use the proxy server for intranet addresses, activate the Bypass Proxy Server for Local Addresses check box.

Dial-Up Settings: Use this group to enter your dial-up User Name and Password. In the unlikely event that your ISP specified a domain for you, enter it in the Domain text box. Click Properties to get to the connection's property sheet, and click Advanced to specify the values for dial attempts and disconnect times.

Do Not Allow Internet Programs to Use this Connection:
This check box may be ignored because we're dealing
with Internet connections here.

Making the Connection

No matter what method you use to create a dial-up connection, you'll end up with an icon for the connection in the Dial-
Up Networking folder. So, one way to get on the Internet is to
launch that connection by following these steps:

1. Select Start, Programs, Accessories, Communications,
   Dial-Up Networking.

2. Use any of the following methods to launch the icon:

   • Double-click the icon.

   • Highlight the icon and then either select
     Connections, Connect, or click the toolbar's Dial
     button.

   • Right-click the icon and then click Connect.

3. The Connect To dialog box that appears (see Figure 18.7)
   has fields for your User Name and Password. Make sure
   these are filled in correctly. You can save yourself a bit of
   work in the future if you activate the Save Password check
   box. This tells Windows 98 to enter your password automatically.

Remember
If you choose to
have Windows 98
enter your pass-
word automati-
cally, there's a
good chance
you'll eventually
forget the pass-
word through dis-
use. You should
write down your
password and
store it in a safe
place just in case
Windows 98 ever
"forgets" the
password (believe
me, it happens).

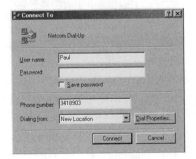

Figure 18.7
When you initiate
a Dial-Up
Networking con-
nection, the
Connect To dialog
box appears.

Shortcut
If you don't do anything in the Connect To dialog box other than click Connect, you can streamline the connection by telling Windows 98 not to display this dialog box. In the Dial-Up Networking folder, select Connections, Settings, deactivate the Prompt for Information Before Dialing check box, and click OK.

4. Adjust the Phone Number field, if necessary.

5. If you have multiple dialing locations defined, select the location you want to use from the Dialing From list. You can also click Dial Properties to adjust the selected dialing location.

6. Click Connect. Dial-Up Networking dials your modem to connect to the ISP. If you have to log in (and if you activated the Bring Up Terminal Window After Dialing option, as described earlier), you'll see the Post-Dial Terminal Screen, shown in Figure 18.8.

7. Fill in the prompts to log in, and then either click Continue or press F7. Dial-Up Networking displays the Connection Established dialog box.

8. This dialog box doesn't give you much useful data, so you can avoid having it displayed in subsequent dial-ups by activating the Do Not Show This Dialog Box in the Future check box.

9. Click Close.

Figure 18.8
Use the Post-Dial Terminal Screen to log in to your ISP.

Remember
When you complete the login, you may see a stream of garbage characters appear in the Post-Dial Terminal Screen. This is normal and it goes away after you click Continue.

Another way to connect with your ISP is to launch an Internet program or resource. For example, click the Launch Internet Explorer icon in the Quick Launch toolbar. In this case, you see the Dial-up Connection dialog box shown in Figure 18.9. (The version of this dialog box that comes with Windows 98 Second Edition uses a slightly different layout.) The default Dial-Up Networking connection is the one you selected earlier in the Dial-up Settings dialog box. Click Connect to dial up your ISP.

Figure 18.9
This dialog box appears when you attempt to run an Internet program or connect to an Internet resource.

Creating Scripts to Automate Dial-Ups

Connecting to the Internet can become a chore if you find yourself dialing up your ISP several times a day and you have to enter login data each time. To streamline the login, Windows 98 supports *scripts* that look for prompts (such as Login:) and then send the appropriate responses (such as your username) automatically.

A script is a text file that uses the .scp extension and contains simple programming commands and functions. Let's begin by examining the four most commonly used scripting commands: delay, halt, waitfor, and transmit.

The delay command tells Dial-Up Networking to wait for a specified number of seconds before moving on to the next command in the script:

delay *seconds*

> *seconds*   This is the number of seconds Dial-Up Networking must wait.

The halt command tells Dial-Up Networking to stop processing the script. This is useful if a problem occurs and you need to abandon the login.

The waitfor command tells Dial-Up Networking to check the incoming characters from the ISP and look for a specific string:

```
waitfor "string" [, matchcase] [then label] [until seconds]
```

string	This is the remote text Dial-Up Networking should watch for.
matchcase	This optional parameter tells Dial-Up Networking to look for text that exactly matches the uppercase and lowercase letters used in string.
then label	This optional parameter tells Dial-Up Networking to jump to the script line that begins with label when it receives the string prompt.
until seconds	This optional parameter sets the number of seconds that Dial-Up Networking waits for the string prompt.

Consider the following example:

```
waitfor "User Name:" then Continue until 30
halt
Continue:
waitfor "Password:"
...
```

This partial script uses waitfor to look for the User Name: prompt. If it arrives within 30 seconds, the script jumps down to the Continue: label. Otherwise, the script just runs the halt command to stop the script.

The transmit command tells Dial-Up Networking to send text to the ISP's computer:

```
transmit "string" [,raw]
```

string	This is the text you want to send.
raw	This optional parameter tells Dial-Up Networking to treat the string as is and not interpret it as a string literal. For example, "^M" is a string literal that represents a carriage return. If you include raw, the string is sent just as a caret and the letter M.

Table 18.1 lists the string literals supported by the transmit command.

TABLE 18.1: STRING LITERALS YOU CAN USE WITH THE TRANSMIT **COMMAND**

String Literal	Sends
^char	A control character. For example, "^M" sends Ctrl+M, which is the control character for a carriage return.
<cr>	Carriage return
<lf>	Line feed
\"	Quotation mark
\^	Caret
\<	Less-than sign
\\	Backslash

Scripts also recognize several system variables. These are outlined in Table 18.2.

TABLE 18.2: SYSTEM VARIABLES SUPPORTED BY DIAL-UP NETWORKING SCRIPTS

Variable	What It Represents
$USERID	The contents of the User Name field in the Connect To dialog box
$PASSWORD	The contents of the Password field in the Connect To dialog box
$SUCCESS	True or false. Commands such as waitfor set the value of this variable. For example, if waitfor doesn't find the prompt it's looking for, it sets $success to false.

Place all your script commands within the following structure:

```
proc main
    Type your commands in here.
endproc
```

Here's a sample script that automates a simple login that requests a username and password:

```
proc main
    ; Delay for 3 seconds to allow the remote system
    ; enough time to send the initial characters.
    delay 3
    ; Now wait for the remote system to prompt for
    ; the user name. When it does, send the $USERID
    ; followed by a carriage return.
```

Inside Scoop

To use the $USERID and $PASSWORD variables, you must enter your correct username and password in the Connect To dialog box. If you activate the Save Password check box, Dial-Up Networking will remember your username and password and enter them automatically the next time you connect. You can then opt not to display the Connect To dialog box, as outlined earlier.

Remember

Dial-up scripting supports a few more commands, as well as programming constructs such as if…endif and while…endwhile. To learn about these other features, see the file Script.doc in the Windows folder.

```
    waitfor "user name:"
    transmit $USERID
    transmit "<cr>"
    ; Now wait for the remote system to prompt for
    ; the password. When it does, send the $PASSWORD
    ; followed by a carriage return.
    waitfor "Password:"
    transmit $PASSWORD
    transmit "<cr>"
endproc
```

After your script is ready, follow these steps to assign it to a Dial-Up Networking connection:

1. In the Dial-Up Networking folder, display the property sheet for the connection you want to work with.

2. Select the Scripting tab.

3. Use the File Name text box to enter the path and filename for your script (see Figure 18.10). Alternatively, click Browse to select the script file using the Open dialog box.

Figure 18.10
Use the Scripting tab to assign a script to a Dial-Up Networking connection.

4. To test your script, activate the Step Through Script check box. With this option turned on, Dial-Up Networking steps through the script one line at a time. This enables you to watch the progress of the login to ensure that everything works properly. After you're sure your script is working, deactivate this check box.

5. To follow the prompts from the ISP, leave the Start Terminal Screen Minimized check box deactivated. After your script is working, you can activate this check box to avoid displaying the terminal screen.

6. Click OK to return to the Dial-Up Networking folder.

Disconnecting from Your ISP

When you've completed your Internet labors, you disconnect from your ISP by using any of the following techniques:

- Double-click the Dial-Up Networking icon in the system tray, and then click Disconnect.

- Right-click the Dial-Up Networking icon in the system tray, and then click Disconnect.

- In the Dial-Up Networking folder, right-click the connection's icon and then click Disconnect.

- If you connected by running an Internet application, close the application. When Windows 98 asks if you want to disconnect, click Yes.

How to Get on the Internet Using a Local Area Network

If your computer is part of a local area network (LAN) that has an Internet gateway, connecting to the Internet requires a different configuration. Specifically, you have to set up the TCP/IP networking protocol to use your network's gateway as your connection to the Internet. This section shows you how it's done.

Information You Need Before Getting Started

Before starting, you need to gather information from your network administrator. Here's a checklist that tells you the information you need to set up the connection:

- Whether your network assigns you an IP address automatically. If not, you need your permanent IP address as well as the subnet mask that goes along with your address.

Shortcut
Windows 98 ships with some sample scripts for automating CompuServe dial-ups, logins that require selecting menu choices, and more. You'll find them in the `C:\Program Files\Accessories` folder. If you create your own script, save it in this folder for easier access later on.

Watch Out!
Because you no longer have to enter login data by hand, make sure you tell Dial-Up Networking not to display the Post-Dial Terminal Screen. In other words, display the connection's property sheet, click Configure, select the Options tab, and then deactivate the Bring Up Terminal Window After Dialing check box.

- Whether your network uses the Windows Internet Name System (WINS) or the Dynamic Host Configuration Protocol (DHCP) to resolve computer network names and IP addresses. If your LAN uses WINS, you'll need the IP address of one or more WINS servers.

- The IP address of your network's Internet gateway.

- Your computer's host name and your network's domain name.

- The IP address of one or more DNS servers used by your network.

- Whether your network uses a proxy server and, if so, the name of the proxy server.

Installing and Configuring the TCP/IP Protocol

With all your data in hand, follow these steps to set up TCP/IP for the Internet connection:

Shortcut
A quick way to get to the Network dialog box is to right-click the desktop's Network Neighborhood icon and then click Properties.

1. Click the Network icon on the Control Panel to display the Network dialog box. In the Configuration tab, check the list of installed components to see if the TCP/IP protocol is bound to your network adapter. This appears as TCP/IP -> *Adapter*, where *Adapter* is the name of your adapter (see Figure 18.11). If you see this, skip to step 4.

2. Click Add, highlight Protocol, and click Add again. The Select Network Protocol dialog box appears.

3. Highlight Microsoft in the Manufacturers list, highlight TCP/IP in the Network Protocols list, and then click OK.

4. In the list of components, highlight the item that represents TCP/IP bound to your network adapter, and then click Properties.

5. In the IP Address tab, select one of the following options:

   Obtain an IP Address Automatically: Select this option if your network assigns you an IP address automatically.

   Specify an IP Address: Select this option if you have a permanent network IP address. In this case, fill in the IP Address and Subnet Mask boxes.

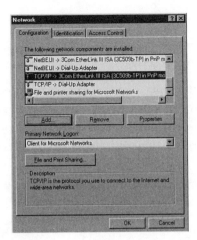

Figure 18.11
Find the compo-
nent that repre-
sents TCP/
IP bound to the
network adapter.

6. In the WINS Configuration tab, activate the Enable WINS Resolution option if your network uses WINS. Use the WINS Server Search Order box to add the IP address for one or more WINS servers. If your LAN uses DHCP, activate the Use DHCP for WINS Resolution option, instead.

7. In the Gateway tab, enter the IP address of one or more Internet gateways used by your LAN.

8. In the DNS Configuration tab, enter your computer's Host name and your network's Domain name. Use the DNS Server Search Order box to enter the IP address of one or more DNS servers used by your LAN.

9. In the Bindings tab, deactivate the File and Print Sharing for Microsoft Networks check box.

10. Click OK to return to the Network dialog box.

11. Click OK.

12. When Windows 98 asks if you want to restart your computer, click Yes.

If your Internet access is filtered through a proxy server, you need to configure the proxy server by following these extra steps:

1. Click the Internet icon on the Control Panel and, in the Internet Properties dialog box that appears, select the Connection tab.

Watch Out!
Disabling the File and Print Sharing for Microsoft Networks check box in the Bindings tab tells Windows 98 not to bind file and print sharing to TCP/IP. In other words, you're preventing your shared resources from being share with entire Internet! For details on this, see Chapter 21's "Internet Security and the TCP/IP Protocol" section, page 494.

See Also...
"Internet Security and the TCP/IP Protocol" p. 494

Remember
In Windows 98
Second Edition,
click the LAN
Settings button to
display the Local
Area Network
(LAN) Settings
dialog box. This
dialog box con-
tains the same
automatic config-
uration and proxy
server options
that I discussed
earlier in this
chapter (see
"Connection
Settings in
Windows 98
Second Edition").

Inside Scoop
Use System
Monitor to keep
an eye on your
Internet connec-
tion's perfor-
mance. In the
System Monitor
window, choose
Edit, Add Item,
highlight the
Dial-Up Adapter
category, high-
light the Bytes
Received/Second
item, and click
OK.

2. Activate the Access the Internet Using a Proxy Server check box.

3. Enter the proxy server's Address and Port.

4. If you want to specify proxy servers for specific protocols, click Advanced and use the Proxy Settings dialog box to enter addresses and ports for the various protocols. Note, too, that you can also use the Exceptions group to enter IP addresses (such as 123.231.*.*) or domain names (such as *.mcfedries.com) for sites that shouldn't go through the proxy server. Click OK.

5. If you don't want to use the proxy server for intranet addresses, activate the Bypass Proxy Server for Local (Intranet) Addresses check box.

6. Click OK.

Some Internet Utilities You Should Know

Now that you can actually get on the Internet, the next three chapters will focus on various Internet applications and tools. Before that, let's take a quick look at some useful TCP/IP utilities:

PING: You use the PING utility to see if you can access a remote system. The idea is that PING sends out special IP *echo packets* that ask the remote server to send back a response. If the response is received, then you know the remote computer is accessible. At the DOS prompt, type **ping *host***, where ***host*** is the IP address or domain name of the remote host you want to use. This syntax sends out four packets. If you would prefer to have PING send out packets indefinitely, use the syntax **ping** -t *host*. (You can interrupt the pinging by pressing Ctrl+C.)

TRACERT: This utility also sends out echo packets, but it traces the route that the packets take. If PING can't reach a remote host, it could be because the echo packets are getting stuck at some intermediate host. TRACERT (trace route) can tell you if this is the case. At the DOS prompt, enter **tracert** *host*, where *host* is the IP address or domain name of the remote host.

WINIPCFG: This utility can tell you your current IP address, which is often useful if your ISP or network assigns IP addresses dynamically. To launch this utility, select Start, Run, type **winipcfg.exe**, and then click OK. In the IP Configuration dialog box that appears, click More Info to get the expanded version of the dialog box shown in Figure 18.12.

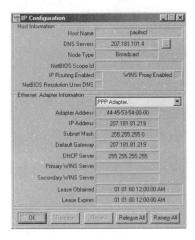

Figure 18.12
The IP Configuration dialog box shows you your current IP address.

Inside Scoop
To use PING to test your Internet connection, first try pinging the loopback address: 127.0.0.1. If that doesn't work, uninstall and then reinstall TCP/IP. Next try your IP address. If that ping doesn't work, check your IP address and the subnet mask for errors. Next try your LAN's Internet gateway. If that doesn't work, make sure TCP/IP is bound to your network adapter.

Essential Information

■ Before creating your Internet connection, gather the information you need, such as the dial-up number, your username and password, your IP address, the IP addresses of your ISP's DNS servers, and so on.

■ To run the Internet Connection Wizard, click the Connect to the Internet icon on the desktop.

■ To create a connection by hand, select Start, Programs, Accessories, Communications, Dial-Up Networking and then click the Make New Connection icon.

■ Click the Internet icon on the Control Panel and select the Connection tab to adjust some connection settings.

■ To connect to your ISP, either launch the icon from the Dial-Up Networking folder, or open an Internet application or resource.

■ Connecting to the Internet via a LAN gateway requires installing and configuring the TCP/IP protocol.

GET THE SCOOP ON...
Using Internet Explorer's browsing tools ▪ Getting the
most out of the Address bar ▪ Using subscriptions to
keep abreast of Web site changes and to view pages
offline ▪ How and where Internet Explorer stores its
temporary files ▪ What's new in Internet Explorer 5,
the browser that ships with Windows 98 Second
Edition ▪ The extensive list of advanced options for
customizing Internet Explorer

Expert Internet Explorer Techniques

Chapter 19

W HEN YOU COMPLETE THE Internet Connection Wizard, it replaces the desktop's Connect to the Internet icon with two icons: Internet Explorer and Outlook Express. (If you elected to bypass the wizard and set up your Internet connection by hand, you can still get these icons on the desktop. Run the wizard, select My Computer Is Already Set Up for the Internet, and click Next.) That these icons get privileged positions on the Windows 98 desktop isn't surprising because Web surfing and email represent the two most popular online activities. This chapter shows you how to use Internet Explorer to browse sites on the World Wide Web. (Outlook Express is covered in the next chapter.)

We will pass quickly over the basics of Web browsing and concentrate more on Internet Explorer's powerful features, including the Search bar, the Address bar, the Favorites folder, subscriptions, the cache, and Internet Explorer's advanced options. See also Chapter 21, "Internet Security Features for the Sophisticated Surfer," to learn about implementing security in Internet Explorer.

Basic Browsing Techniques

The Windows 98 "Getting Started" booklet contains almost no information on the basic techniques for browsing Web sites, yet it devotes a little less than six pages to two next-to-useless topics: the Active Desktop and channels. I'll try to fix that skewed perspective by offering a quick synopsis of all the ways you can use Internet Explorer to browse the Web.

See Also...
"Internet
Explorer's
Security
Features," p. 495

Understanding Web Page Addresses

Let's begin by examining that strange creature, the World Wide Web address. Officially known as a *Uniform Resource Locator* (URL), a Web page's address usually takes the following form:

http://*host.domain*/*directory*/*file.name*

> *host.domain:* The domain name of the host computer where the page resides.
>
> *directory:* The host computer directory that contains the page.
>
> *file.name:* The page's filename. Note that most Web pages use the extensions .html and .htm.

Consider these notes about URLs:

- The http part of the URL signifies that the TCP/IP protocol to be used to communicate with the server is HTTP (Hypertext Transfer Protocol), which is used for standard Web pages. Other common protocols are https (Secure Hypertext Transfer Protocol: secure Web pages) and ftp (File Transfer Protocol: file downloads).

- Most Web domains use the www prefix and the com suffix (for example, www.mcfedries.com). Other popular suffixes are edu (educational sites), gov (government sites), and org (non-profit sites).

- Directory names and filenames are case sensitive on most Web hosts (those that run UNIX servers, anyway).

Opening and Browsing Pages

Using Internet Explorer to open and "surf" Web pages is straightforward and easy (which is one reason Microsoft decided to adapt the browsing metaphor to folders, disk drives, and other local resources). The following is a review of the techniques you can use to open a page:

Inside Scoop
Most Web sites use one or more default filenames, the most common of which are index.html and index.htm. If you omit the filename from the URL, the Web server will display the default page.

- **Type a URL in the Run dialog box:** Select Start, Run, type the URL you want in the Run dialog box, and click OK.

- **Type a URL in any Address bar:** Internet Explorer and all folder windows have an Address bar. To open a page, type the URL in the Address bar and press Enter.

- **Select a URL from the Address bar:** Internet Explorer's Address bar doubles as a drop-down list that holds the last 25 addresses you entered.

- **Use the Open dialog box for remote pages:** Choose File, Open (or press Ctrl+O) to display the Open dialog box, type the URL, and click OK.

- **Use the Open dialog box for local pages:** If you want to view a Web page that's on your computer, display the Open dialog box, click Browse, find the page, click Open, and then click OK.

- **Click a Links bar button:** The Links bar contains seven buttons that take you to predefined Web pages. For example, the Microsoft button takes you to the Microsoft home page. (You can add buttons to the Link bar, remove existing buttons, and more. See "Customizing the Links Bar," later in this chapter.)

After you've opened a page, there are more techniques you can use to navigate to other pages:

Click a link: Most Web pages contain several *hypertext links*: text that, when clicked, loads another page into the browser. Links usually appear underlined and in a different color than the rest of the text. To see the URL of a linked page before you go there, hover the mouse pointer over the link and the URL will appear in the status bar.

Click an imagemap: Some Web page graphics are *imagemaps* where different sections of the image are linked to different Web pages.

Open a link in another window: If you don't want to leave the current page, you can force a link to open in another Internet Explorer window by right-clicking the link and then clicking Open in New Window. (You can open a new window for the current page by choosing File, New, Window, or by pressing Ctrl+N.)

Retrace the pages you've visited: Click Internet Explorer's Back button to return to a page you visited previously in this session. (Alternatively, choose Go, Back or press Alt+Left arrow.) After you've gone back to a page, click the Forward button to move ahead through the visited pages. (You can also choose Go, Forward or press Alt+Right arrow.) Note, too, that the Back and Forward buttons also serve as drop-down lists. Click the downward-pointing arrow to the right of each button to see the list.

Return to the start page: When you launch Internet Explorer without specifying a URL, you end up at MSN, the default start page (`http://home.microsoft.com/`; in Internet Explorer 5, the start page address is `http://www.msn.com/`). You can return to this page at any time by choosing Go, Home Page, or by clicking the Home button on the toolbar.

Use the History bar: If you click the toolbar's History button or choose View, Explorer Bar, History, Internet Explorer adds a History bar to the left side of the window. This bar lists the sites you've visited over the past 20 days. Just click a URL to go to a site. Note that the items you see in the History bar are based on the contents of the `Windows\History` folder.

Undocumented
Hold down Shift and click a link to open that link in a new browser window.

Searching for Sites

Although most new Web users prefer just to surf around and see what serendipity brings, most veteran users prefer a more targeted approach that enables them to find information and do research. The bad news is that the Web is home to hundreds of millions of pages, so finding what you want is no easy task. The good news is that there's no shortage of indexes and search engines that can at least narrow things down a bit. To help you get started, Internet Explorer offers some default searching options.

For quick searches, use the Search bar:

- Click the Search toolbar button.

- Choose View, Explorer Bar, Search.

Internet Explorer adds a Search bar to the left side of the window, as shown in Figure 19.1. (At this point, you may see a Security Warning asking if you want to install an update to the Search bar. This update gives you access to more search engines and more customization options, so it's a good idea to install it.) The Search bar offers a scaled-down version of a Web search engine, such as the Lycos engine shown in Figure 19.1. The layout of the Search bar depends on the engine (and on which version of Internet Explorer you're using; Figure 19.1 shows the one that comes with version 5), but in all cases you get a text box into which you enter your search terms. You then click Search (or Seek or Find or whatever) and the bar is updated with the results. You then click a resulting match to display the page in the main part of the Internet Explorer window.

If you prefer to use another search engine, the Search bar is easily customizable. However, the steps you take to do this vary depending on which version of Internet Explorer you're running.

Customizing the Search Bar in Internet Explorer 4

In the Internet Explorer 4 Search bar, click Choose a Search Engine and then click the engine you want to use. If you installed the Search bar update, follow these steps to set up a permanent engine for the Search bar:

Remember
You can change the default start page and customize some History bar options by choosing View, Internet Options and displaying the General tab. Use the Home Page group to specify a new URL for the start page. Use the History group to specify the number of days of history you want to keep. You can also click Clear History to start afresh.

Figure 19.1
Use the Search
bar to enter quick
searches.

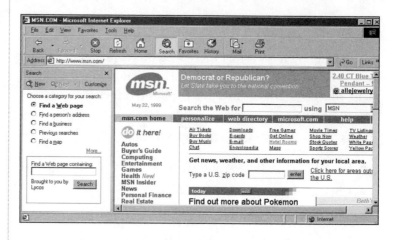

Inside Scoop
Most good search
engines offer
Boolean searches.
This means you
separate search
terms with partic-
ular keywords. For
example, separat-
ing two terms
with AND means
you want to
match sites that
contain both
terms. Similarly,
OR means you
want to match
only sites that
match at least
one of the terms.
You can also use
NOT to exclude
sites that contain
a particular term.

1. Click Choose a Search Engine.

2. Click List of All Search Engines. The main part of the Internet Explorer window displays the Pick a Search Engine page.

3. Click the search engine you want to use.

A more extensive search feature is available by using either of the following techniques:

- In Internet Explorer, choose Go, Search the Web.

- Select Start, Find, On the Internet.

Either way, you get the Search the Web page, which offers access to a large number of general and specialty search engines.

It's possible to customize the page that appears when you choose Go, Search the Web or Start, Find, On the Internet. Open the Registry Editor and head for the following key:

```
\HKEY_CURRENT_USER\Software\Microsoft\Internet
Explorer\Main
```

Change the Search Page setting to the URL of the search engine you prefer to use.

Customizing the Search Bar in Internet Explorer 5

The Search bar that comes with Internet Explorer 5 offers a greater range of customization options. Here's a review:

- **Repeating the same search on a different search engine:** After you've run a search, the Search bar's Next button becomes enabled. Click this button to repeat the search using the next search engine in the list. Alternatively, select the search engine you want to use from the Next drop-down list.

- **Customizing the list of search engines:** You can customize the Next list by clicking the Customize button on the Search bar. Internet Explorer displays the Customize Search Settings window, shown in Figure 19.2. In the Find a Web Page section, use the check boxes to add or remove search engines from the Next list.

- **Reordering the search engines:** The order in which the search engines appear in the Next list is determined by the order they appear in the Find a Web Page list. You can change this order by highlighting an engine and then clicking the up and down arrows below the list.

Customizing the Links Bar

I like the *idea* of the Links bar: one-click access to Web sites. However, I don't really like the *execution* of the Links bar because I use only a couple of the predefined Web sites. That's not a problem, however, because the Links bar is easily customized:

Shortcut
Internet Explorer 5 supports searches from the Address bar. When you enter a word or phrase, the Address bar list drops down and you see `Search for "text,"` where `text` is the word or phrase you typed. Press Enter to run a search on the text. To specify the search engine used for this type of search, display the Customize Search Settings window, click Autosearch settings, and then use the dialog box that appears to choose the search engine.

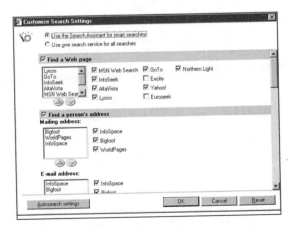

Figure 19.2
Use this window to customize the Search bar.

- **Removing a button:** To delete a button from the Links bar, right-click it and then click Delete.

- **Changing a button's URL:** Right-click a button and then click Properties to display the button's property sheet. Use the Target URL text box to change the URL, and then click OK.

- **Renaming a button:** To do this you have to access the Windows\Favorites\Links folder. Once there, you'll see that a URL shortcut file represents each button. Use the usual file renaming techniques.

- **Adding a button for the current page:** Drag the icon in the Address bar and drop it inside the Links bar.

- **Adding a button for a link:** Drag the link and drop it inside the Links bar. If you've already saved the page as a Favorite, choose the Favorites menu, drag the icon from the menu and drop it inside the Links bar.

- **Moving a button:** Drag the button left or right within the Links bar.

Watch Out!
Don't add subfold-
ers to the Links
folder. Some
users report prob-
lems using the
Links bar after
adding subfolders.

Address Bar Tricks

One of Windows 98's new features is the expansion of the Address bar's territory from Internet Explorer to all folder windows (as well as to Windows Explorer). When you enter a URL into the Address bar of a folder window, the window morphs into Internet Explorer, complete with the appropriate toolbars and menus. You can even place a version of the Address bar on the taskbar. Right-click an empty section of the toolbar, and then choose Toolbars, Address. Entering a URL into this Address bar loads Internet Explorer to display the page.

Shortcut
After you have
your Links bar
customized to suit
your style, you
can make it even
more convenient
by displaying it as
part of the
taskbar. To do
this, right-click an
empty section of
the taskbar, and
then choose
Toolbars, Links.

However, the Address bar is more than a mere click-and-type mechanism. It's useful for many things, and comes with its own bag of tricks for making it even easier to use. Here's a rundown:

- Press F4 to select the Address bar text and drop its list down. Use the Up and Down Arrow keys to select an item from the list. To work with only the text box, press Esc to close the list.

- You can create a shortcut for whatever object is displayed in the Address bar by dragging the object's icon (it's on the left side of the text box) and dropping it on the desktop or some other location.

- The Address bar's AutoComplete feature monitors the address as you type. If a previously entered address matches your typing, the rest of that address is displayed automatically. You can press Enter to select that address, press Delete to remove the rest of the address, or just keep typing.

- You can also use AutoComplete to view a list of associated URLs. To try this, type a URL in the Address bar until the AutoComplete portion appears. Then hold down the Ctrl key and click the drop-down arrow in the toolbar. You'll see a complete set of related URLs.

- Internet Explorer assumes any address you enter is for a Web site. Therefore, you don't need to type the `http://` prefix because Internet Explorer will add it for you automatically.

- If you're not sure which domain suffix a site uses, just type the domain and press Enter. For example, the World Wide Web Consortium is known as the W3C, so you could find it by typing just **w3c** and pressing Enter. Internet Explorer then invokes its Autoscan feature and tries various prefixes and suffixes to see if it can find the site. Autoscan uses this order:

w3c

www.w3c.com

www.w3c.edu

www.w3c.org

w3c.com

w3c.edu

w3c.org

> 66
> By default, the Address Bar shows your current location, whether it's a folder or a Web page. You can browse to another location by typing an address—a URL, a path, or even a program name.
> —From the "Getting Started" booklet
> 99

Notice that Autoscan doesn't check the gov or net suffixes, nor does it check any country domains, such as ca (Canada) or uk (United Kingdom). You can tell Autoscan to check these and other suffixes by adding values to the following Registry key:

```
\HKEY_LOCAL_MACHINE\Software\Microsoft\Internet
Explorer\Main\UrlTemplate
```

For example, to have Internet Explorer check for gov addresses, add a new string value, name it **7**, and then change its value to **www.%s.gov**.

Undocumented
The numbers used with each value represent the order that Autoscan uses to check the various domain combinations. You can change this order by renumbering the values in the UrlTemplate key.

- Internet Explorer also assumes that most Web addresses are of the form www.something.com. Therefore, if you simply type the "something" part and press Ctrl+Enter, Internet Explorer automatically adds the www prefix and the com suffix. For example, you can get to my home page (www.mcfedries.com) by typing **mcfedries** and pressing Ctrl+Enter.

- You can run Web searches from the Address bar. Just type a question mark (or the words **Go** or **Find**), a space, and then one or more search terms. (This process is slightly different with Internet Explorer 5. See "Customizing the Search Bar in Internet Explorer 5," earlier in this chapter.) When you press Enter, Internet Explorer connects to a search engine and then asks it to run a search using your terms. To control which search engine is used, launch Tweak UI, select the General tab, and then select an item from the Search Engine list. (If you select the Custom item, a dialog box asks you for the URL and search syntax to use.) The result is stored in the Default setting in the following Registry key:

```
HKEY_CURRENT_USER\Software\Microsoft\Internet
Explorer\SearchUrl
```

- Some Web sites use *frames* to divide a Web page into multiple sections. Some of these sites offer links to other Web sites but, annoyingly, those pages appear within the first site's frame structure. To break out of frames, drag a link into the Address bar.

Using the Favorites **Folder to Save Sites**

If you come across a Web page that you want to read later or that you think you'll be visiting regularly, you can use the Windows\Favorites folder to store a shortcut that points to the page's URL. Follow these steps to do so:

1. Open the Web page you want to save. (If you want to set up a link as a favorite, right-click the link, click Add to Favorites, and then skip to step 3.)

2. Choose Favorites, Add to Favorites to get the Add Favorite dialog box onscreen.

3. I'll discuss subscriptions in the next section, so for now make sure the No, Just Add the Page to My Favorites option is selected. (In Internet Explorer 5, make sure the Make Available Offline check box is deactivated.)

4. If you want to place the page into a subfolder, click the Create In button to expand the dialog box as shown in Figure 19.3. (The Internet Explorer 5 version of this dialog box has a different layout.) From here, click either the folder you want to use, or New Folder to add a folder to the Favorites hierarchy.

5. Click OK.

Opening Favorite Sites

To browse to a favorite site, use any of the following techniques:

■ In Internet Explorer, Windows Explorer, or any folder window, choose the Favorites menu and then select the favorite.

Shortcut
If you enter multiple words separated by spaces, Internet Explorer assumes you're running a search, so you don't need the leading question mark.

Shortcut
Internet Explorer offers two methods for quickly adding a site to the Favorites folder. If the current page has a link to the site you want to save, drag the link to the Favorites menu. If you want to save the current page, instead, drag the icon from the Address bar to the Favorites menu. When the menu pulls down, drag the item to the position you want (you can even hover over submenus to open them) and then drop the item.

Figure 19.3
The expanded ver-
sion of the Add
Favorite dialog
box.

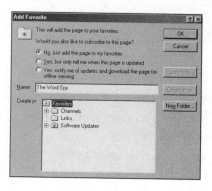

- In Internet Explorer, Windows Explorer, or any folder window, either click the Favorites button in the toolbar, or
  choose View, Explorer Bar, Favorites. This adds a Favorites
  bar to the left side of the window. From there, click the
  favorite you want to open.

- Select Start, Favorites and then click the favorite.

- In Windows Explorer, open the Windows\Favorites folder
  and then double-click the icon for the favorite.

Sharing Favorites and Netscape Bookmarks

Many users like to run both Internet Explorer and Netscape
Navigator on their machines. Unfortunately, the two browsers
store saved sites differently: Internet Explorer uses favorites
whereas Navigator uses bookmarks. However, Internet
Explorer 5 has a new feature that enables you to either export
favorites to a bookmark file, or import bookmarks as favorites
as described in the following steps:

1. In Internet Explorer 5, choose File, Import and Export.
   The Import/Export Wizard appears.

2. Click Next.

3. Highlight one of the following:

   Import Favorites: Select this option to import Navigator
   bookmarks as favorites. When you click Next, the wizard
   asks you for the path to the bookmark.htm file. Click Next
   when you're done.

Export Favorites: Select this option to export your favorites as Navigator bookmarks. When you click Next, the wizard first asks you which Favorites folder you want to export. Click Next again and the wizard prompts you to enter the path to the `bookmark.htm` file. Click Next after you've done that.

4. The wizard performs the requested operation and then displays a dialog box to let you know when it's complete. Click Finish.

Maintaining Favorites

When you have a large number of favorites, you'll need to do some regular maintenance to keep things organized. This involves creating new subfolders, moving favorites between folders, changing URLs, deleting unused favorites, and more. Here's a summary of a few maintenance techniques you'll use most often:

- To change the URL of a favorite, choose the Favorites menu, find the item you want to work with, and right-click it. In the shortcut menu, click Properties and then use the property sheet to adjust the URL.

- To move a favorite, choose the Favorites menu, find the item you want to work with, and then drag the item to another spot on the menu (or into a submenu).

- To delete a favorite, choose the Favorites menu, find the item you want to work with, right-click it, and then click Delete.

- To work with the `Favorites` folder, choose Favorites, Organize Favorites to display the dialog box shown in Figure 19.4. (The Organize Favorites dialog box that ships with Internet Explorer 5 has a different layout than the one you see in Figure 19.4.) From here, you can use the standard file maintenance techniques to move, copy, rename, and delete the shortcut files.

- You can also work with the `Favorites` folder directly by launching Windows Explorer and selecting the `Windows\Favorites` folder.

Inside Scoop
If you also run Netscape Navigator and Internet Explorer 4, there isn't any way to use a common list of favorites (or *bookmarks*). One partial solution is to set up the list of Navigator bookmarks as a favorite. This list is stored in an HTML file called `bookmark.htm`, which can usually be found in the `Netscape\Users\user\` folder (where *user* is your Netscape username). Note, too, that Microsoft has a Bookmark Converter utility available at `ftp://ftp.microsoft.com/mslfiles/winbm2fv`.

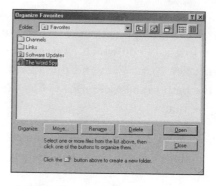

Undocumented
You can also open
the Organize
Favorites dialog
box by pressing
Ctrl+B. Note, too,
that this dialog
box is sizable.
Use your mouse
to drag any edge
to get the size
you want.

Dealing with Subscriptions

The Favorites folder is a useful place to save important or interesting sites for future reference. The Favorites folder is particularly handy for two categories of sites:

- **Sites that remain relatively constant over time:** These are sites that contain good information for research or fun features for entertainment. These sites are usually accessed only as needed.

- **Sites that change frequently:** These are sites that have constantly updated information, such as news or "something-of-the-day" features. (For an example of the latter, see my Word Spy site: http://www.logophilia.com/WordSpy.) I store these types of sites in a Favorites subfolder named Daily Links and I browse each favorite daily to look for new content.

However, the majority of sites fall into a third category: sites that change content only occasionally. If you like such a site enough to store it as a favorite, how do you know when the site's content has changed? You could just run through your favorites once a week or once a month, but you might miss some changes. Besides, this becomes impractical when your list of favorites grows to a few dozen sites or more.

The solution is to use the new *subscription* technology that comes with Windows 98 and Internet Explorer 4. (If you're running Internet Explorer 5, you use a slightly different process. See "Viewing Pages Offline with Internet Explorer 5," later in this chapter.) A subscription to a page tells Internet Explorer to check that page at regular intervals. If the page has changed content, Internet Explorer offers a variety of methods for letting you know (including downloading the page for offline viewing).

Setting Up a Subscription in Internet Explorer 4

To get started, you have two choices:

> **For a page that's already set up as a favorite:** In this case, choose the Favorites menu, right-click the favorite, and then click Subscribe. Figure 19.5 shows the Subscribe Favorite dialog box that appears.

> **For all other pages:** In this case, open the page in Internet Explorer and then choose Favorites, Add to Favorites. The Add Favorite dialog box appears, as shown earlier in Figure 19.3.

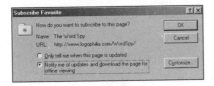

Figure 19.5
This dialog box appears when you subscribe to a favorite.

Although the wording is slightly different, the Only Tell Me When This Page Is Updated option and the Notify Me of Updates and Download the Page for Offline Viewing options offer the same subscription features as the two choices we just looked at.

If you choose the Only Tell Me When This Page Is Updated option, Internet Explorer indicates that a site has changed by adding a red asterisk to the left of the site's name in the Favorites menu. You can customize this option as follows:

1. Click Customize. The Subscription Wizard appears and asks if you also want to receive an email message notifying you that the site has changed content.

2. Choose No to bypass the notification, or Yes to accept the notification. For the latter, if you have multiple email

addresses, click the Change Address button to specify a different address.

3. Click Next. The wizard asks if the site requires a password.

4. Choose No if it doesn't, or Yes if it does. For the latter, use the User Name and Password text boxes to enter the site's login data.

5. Click Finish.

Remember

Unfortunately, you can't set up a custom schedule when you cus- tomize this option. To change the schedule, you have to adjust the properties of the subscription, as explained later in this section.

If you choose the Notify Me of Updates and Download the Page for Offline Viewing option, you can ask Internet Explorer to send you an email message letting you know the site has changed content. You can also elect to have the page downloaded so that you can read it offline later on, and you can specify an update schedule. Here are the steps to follow to customize this option:

1. Click Customize. The Subscription Wizard asks how you want to download the page for offline viewing.

2. Choose Download the Page to download only the sub- scribed page. Alternatively, choose Download This Page and Pages Linked to It to download the page and its linked pages.

3. Click Next. If you chose the Download This Page and Pages Linked to It option, the wizard asks how many levels of linked pages you want to download.

4. Use the spinner to select the number of levels, and then click Next. The wizard asks if you want to receive an email message notifying you that the site has changed content.

5. Choose No to bypass the notification, or Yes to accept the notification. As before, you can specify a different address.

6. Click Next. The wizard displays a dialog box for setting up the subscription schedule.

7. To have Internet Explorer check the site automatically, choose the Scheduled option and then choose a prede- fined schedule from the list. (You can also click Edit or

New to change the predefined schedule or create a new one.) If you prefer to update the subscriptions yourself, choose Manually.

8. Click Next. The wizard asks if the site requires a password.

9. Choose No if it doesn't, or Yes if it does. For the latter, use the User Name and Password text boxes to enter the site's login data.

10. Click Finish.

If you need to adjust a subscription, you have to open its property sheet. To do this, first choose Favorites, Manage Subscriptions to open the Subscriptions folder. (You can also display the Windows\Subscriptions folder in Windows Explorer.) Now highlight the subscription and choose File, Properties.

If you're using a scheduled update and you connect to the Internet using a modem, follow these pointers to make sure everything works properly:

Watch Out!
If you use a dial-up connection, make sure you select the Dial As Needed If Connected Through a Modem option.

- Make sure you leave your computer and modem turned on.

- If you must log in to your ISP, you'll need to set up a script that automates the login. See Chapter 18, "Getting on the Internet."

- When setting up the subscription schedule, activate the Dial As Needed If Connected Through a Modem option. If you didn't do this, you can still activate the option by opening the subscription's property sheet. You'll find the option in the Schedule tab.

- Make sure Internet Explorer is set up to AutoDial. To do this, in Internet Explorer choose View, Internet Options. In the Internet Options dialog box, display the Connection tab, click Settings, and then activate the Connect Automatically to Update Subscriptions check box.

See Also...
"Creating Scripts to Automate Dial-Ups," p. 425

Watch Out!
If you scheduled a subscription to update during the day and it doesn't seem to be working, open the subscription's property sheet. In the Schedule tab, deactivate the Don't Update This Subscription When I'm Using My Computer option.

You can run the following updating techniques by hand:

Updating all subscriptions: Choose Favorites, Update All Subscriptions. Alternatively, open the Subscriptions folder and then click Update All.

Updating a single subscription: Choose the Favorites menu, right-click the favorite, and then click Update Now. Another approach is to open the Subscriptions folder, highlight the subscription, and then click Update.

Skipping an update: If you're present while the update is running, you'll see the Downloading Subscriptions dialog box. To skip the update of any site, click Details to expand the dialog box, highlight the subscription, and then click Skip.

Viewing Pages Offline with Internet Explorer 5

Internet Explorer 5 does away with the subscription model. In its place, you have a "synchronization" model, which enables you to set up favorite sites for offline viewing. The idea is that Internet Explorer 5 maintains a version of the page on your computer. You then synchronize your local version with the online version to ensure you have the latest data. As with subscriptions, you can also set up a schedule for the synchronization process.

Again, you have two ways to get started:

- **For a page that's already set up as a favorite:** Choose the Favorites menu, right-click the favorite, and then click Make Available Offline.

- **For all other pages:** Open the page in Internet Explorer 5 and then choose Favorites, Add to Favorites. In the Add Favorite dialog box, select the Make Available Offline check box and then click Customize.

Either way, the Offline Favorite Wizard appears. Follow these steps to wield this wizard:

1. The first dialog box just offers an introduction, so click Next. (You might want to activate the In the Future, Do Not Show This Introduction Screen check box to avoid this useless dialog box down the road.)

2. As shown in Figure 19.6, the next wizard dialog box wonders if you also want to view pages that are linked to the favorite page:

   No: Tells Internet Explorer 5 not to bother downloading linked pages.

   Yes: Tells Internet Explorer 5 to download linked pages. Use the Download Pages *X* Links Deep from This Page spin box to specify how many levels of links you want downloaded.

3. Click Next. The wizard now asks how you want the page synchronized:

   Only When I Choose Synchronize from the Tools Menu: Choose this option to perform the synchronization by hand. Click Next and skip to step 5.

   I Would Like to Create a New Schedule: Choose this option to set up a schedule for automatic synchronizations. Click Next and proceed to step 4.

4. If you elected to set up a schedule, the wizard displays a dialog box with the following controls (click Next when you're done):

   Every *x* Days: Set the interval, in days, that Internet Explorer 5 uses to run the synchronization.

   at: Set the time at which Internet Explorer 5 runs the synchronization.

Undocumented
Subscriptions are also useful for reading Web sites offline. Browse the main page of the site, and then set up a subscription to the page. Make sure you choose to download the page and its linked pages, and make sure you select the Manually option for updating. After the subscription is set up, update it manually and Internet Explorer will download the page and its linked pages. After that's done, you can read all the pages while offline.

Figure 19.6
Use the Offline Favorite Wizard to set up a page for offline viewing.

Name: Make up a name for this new synchronization schedule.

If My Computer Is Not Connected...: Tells Internet Explorer 5 to connect to the Internet automatically to perform the synchronization.

5. The wizard now asks if the page requires a password. If not, choose No; if so, choose Yes and then enter your User Name and Password (twice).

6. Click Finish.

With all that done, you can synchronize your offline content at any time by choosing Tools, Synchronize. In the Items to Synchronize dialog box, leave the check boxes activated for the pages you want to download, and then click Synchronize.

Controlling the Cache

In the same way that a disk cache stores frequently used data for faster performance, Internet Explorer also keeps a cache of files from Web pages you've visited recently. This cache is the Windows\Temporary Internet Files folder, and Internet Explorer uses these saved files to display Web pages quickly the next time you ask to see them.

To control the cache, choose View, Internet Options (in Internet Explorer 5, choose Tools, Internet Options) and make sure the General tab is displayed. The Temporary Internet Files group has two buttons:

- **Delete Files:** Clicking this button cleans out the Temporary Internet Files folder.

- **Settings:** Clicking this button displays the Settings dialog box (see Figure 19.7).

You have the following options:

Check for newer versions of stored pages: Choose an option to determine when Internet Explorer checks for updated versions of cache files. Choosing Every Visit to the Page always ensures that you see the most current data, but it can delay the loading of a page. Choosing Every Time You Start Internet Explorer causes the cache to be updated only at startup. If you don't want the cache checked at all, choose Never.

Amount of Disk Space to Use: Use this slider to set the size of the cache as a percentage of the hard disk's capacity. A larger cache speeds up Web site browsing.

Move Folder: Clicking this button enables you to change the folder used for the cache. Note that you'll lose all your subscriptions if you move the cache folder.

View Files: Clicking this button displays the Temporary Internet Files folder.

View Objects: Clicking this button displays the Downloaded Program Files folder, which holds the Java applets and ActiveX controls that have been downloaded and installed on your system.

Remember
No matter which cache update option you choose, you can view the most up-to-date version of a page at any time by choosing View, Refresh. (You can also press F5.)

Internet Explorer's Advanced Options

To complete our look at Internet Explorer, this section examines the huge list of customization features found in the Advanced tab of the Internet Explorer property sheet. To begin, use any of the following techniques to get the Internet Explorer Properties dialog box onscreen:

- In Internet Explorer 4, choose View, Internet Options. In Internet Explorer 5, choose Tools, Internet Options.

- Click the Internet icon on the Control Panel.

- Right-click the desktop's Internet Explorer icon and then click Properties.

Whichever method you choose, select the Advanced tab, as shown in Figure 19.8 (this is the Internet Explorer 5 version of this tab).

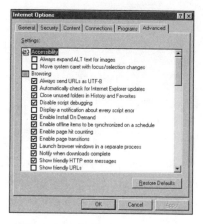

The Accessibility group has two options:

- **Always Expand ALT Text for Images:** Most Webmasters define a text description for each image they include on a page. If you tell Internet Explorer not to show images (see the discussion of the Show Pictures check box in the Multimedia branch list of options), all you see are boxes where the images should be, and each box contains the text description (which is known as *alt text*, where alt is short for alternate). Activating this check box tells Internet Explorer to expand the image box horizontally so that the alt text appears on a single line.

- **Move System Caret with Focus/Selection Changes:** Activating this check box tells Internet Explorer to move the system caret whenever you change the focus. This is useful if you have a screen reader or screen magnifier that uses the position of the system caret to determine what part of the screen should be read or magnified.

The Browsing branch boasts quite a few options:

- **Always send URLs As UTF-8:** Tells Internet Explorer to send Web page addresses using the UTF-8 standard, which is readable in any language. If you're having trouble accessing a page that uses non-English characters in the URL, the server may not be able to handle UTF-8, so deactivate this check box.

- **Automatically Check for Internet Explorer Updates:** Tells Internet Explorer to check (approximately every 30 days) to see whether a newer version of the program is available.

- **Close Unused Folders in History and Favorites:** Internet Explorer 5 keeps unused folders closed when you display the History bar and the Favorites bar.

- **Disable Script Debugging:** Toggles the script debugger (if one is installed) on and off.

- **Display a Notification About Every Script Error:** Internet Explorer 5 displays a dialog box to alert you to JavaScript or VBScript errors on a page. If you leave this option deactivated, Internet Explorer 5 displays an error message in the status bar. To see the full error message, double-click the status bar message.

- **Enable Install On Demand:** Internet Explorer 5 examines each Web page for elements that require a specific browser feature. If that feature isn't installed, the program asks if you want to install it.

- **Enable Offline Items to Be Synchronized on a Schedule:** (in Internet Explorer 4, this option is named Enable Scheduled Subscription Updates) Toggles the synchronization (or subscription) updates on and off. Deactivating this check box is a good idea if you're going out of town for a few days and don't want offline pages updated while you're away.

- **Enable Page Hit Counting:** Sites—such as those defined in the Channel bar—that use the Channel Definition Format (CDF) can request logs of user activity within a channel. These are anonymous logs that just tell which pages were visited. If you don't want to supply the site with such logs, deactivate this check box.

Remember
The system caret is a visual indication of what part of the screen currently has the focus. If a text box has the focus, the system caret is a blinking, vertical bar; if a check box or option button has the focus, the system caret is a dotted outline of the control name.

- **Enable Page Transitions:** Toggles Internet Explorer's support for page transitions on and off. Web sites that use a server that supports FrontPage extensions can define various page transitions (such as wipes and fades). However, these transitions often slow down your browsing, so turning them off is recommended.

- **Launch Browser Windows in a Separate Process:** (in Internet Explorer 4, this option is named Browse in a New Process) Tells Windows 98 to create a new thread for each open Internet Explorer window. This is useful if you find that Internet Explorer crashes are also causing Windows Explorer crashes (the two applications share the same thread).

- **Notify When Downloads Complete:** Toggles the Download Complete dialog box message that Internet Explorer displays when a file download is finished. If you often run unattended downloads, leave this check box activated so you know that a file was received properly.

- **Show Friendly HTTP Error Messages:** Internet Explorer 5 intercepts the error messages generated by Web servers and replaces them with its own messages that offer more information as well as possible solutions to the problems.

Watch Out!
Selecting the Launching Browser Windows in a New Process check box means that Internet Explorer and Windows Explorer require far greater amounts of system resources and memory. Activate this option only if your system has plenty of resources and memory.

- **Show Friendly URLs:** Determines how URLs appear in the status bar when you hover the mouse over a link or imagemap. Activate this check box to see only the filename of the linked page; deactivate this check box to see the full URL of the linked page. (Note, however, that thanks to the poor design of the Internet Explorer status bar, lengthy URLs are often cut off on the right.)

- **Show Go button in Address Bar:** Internet Explorer 5 adds a Go button to the right of the Address bar. You click this button to open whatever URL is shown in the Address bar. The usefulness of this button is dubious, but it doesn't hurt anything.

- **Show Internet Explorer on the Desktop:** Toggles the desktop's Internet Explorer icon on and off.

- **Underline Links:** Specifies when Internet Explorer should format Web page links with an underline. The Hover option means that the underline appears only when you position the mouse pointer over the link.

- **Use Inline AutoComplete for Web Addresses:** (in Internet Explorer 4, this option is named Use AutoComplete) Toggles the Address bar's AutoComplete feature on and off.

- **Use Inline AutoComplete for Windows Explorer:** Enables you to use the AutoComplete feature while working with folders in Windows Explorer's Address bar.

- **Use Smooth Scrolling:** Toggles a feature called *smooth scrolling* on and off. When you activate this check box to enable smooth scrolling, pressing Page Down or Page Up causes the page to scroll down or up at a preset speed. If you deactivate this check box, pressing Page Down or Page Up causes the page to instantly jump down or up.

- **Use Web Based FTP:** Allows you to view only FTP directories and download files. When this check box is turned off, Internet Explorer 5 gives you an interface with full access to FTP features, including file uploading, downloading, renaming, and deleting, as well as the ability to work with FTP directories.

- **Show Channel Bar at Startup (If Active Desktop Is Off):** (available only in Internet Explorer 4) Toggles the Channel bar on and off at startup. Note, however, that this option has no effect if you have the Active Desktop turned on (in that case, the Channel bar always appears at startup).

- **Launch Channels in Full Screen Window:** (available only in Internet Explorer 4) Toggles the full-screen mode on and off for active channel Web pages.

- **Launch Browser in Full Screen Window:** (available only in Internet Explorer 4) Toggles the full-screen mode on and off at startup for Internet Explorer.

Undocumented
With Internet Explorer 4, the Show Internet Explorer on the Desktop option also says (requires restart). You can ignore this, however. To put this option into effect, click OK or Apply, click the desktop, and then press F5 to refresh it.

- **Show Welcome Message Each Time I Log On:** (available only in Internet Explorer 4) Toggles the Welcome to Windows 98 startup message on and off. (You can view the Welcome to Windows 98 screen at any time by selecting Start, Run, typing **welcome**, and clicking OK.)

The check boxes in the HTTP 1.1 settings branch determine whether Internet Explorer uses the HTTP 1.1 protocol:

- **Use HTTP 1.1:** Toggles Internet Explorer's use of HTTP 1.1 to communicate with Web servers. (HTTP 1.1 is the standard protocol used on the Web today.) You should deactivate this check box only if you're having trouble connecting to a Web site. This tells Internet Explorer to uses HTTP 1.0, which may solve the problem.

- **Use HTTP 1.1 Through Proxy Connections:** Toggles on and off the use of HTTP 1.1 only when connecting through a proxy server.

Shortcut
You can toggle the Internet Explorer window (and, indeed, any folder window) between regular and full-screen mode by pressing F11.

The check boxes in the Java VM branch are related to Internet Explorer's Java Virtual Machine:

- **Java Console Enabled (Requires Restart):** Toggles the Java console on and off. The Java console is a separate window in which the output and error messages from a Java applet are displayed. If you activate this option (which requires that you restart Internet Explorer), you can view the Java console by choosing View, Java Console command.

- **Java Logging Enabled:** Toggles Internet Explorer's Java logging on and off. When it's on, Internet Explorer logs Java applet error messages to a file named Javalog.txt in the Windows\Java folder. This is useful for troubleshooting Java problems.

- **JIT Compiler for Virtual Machine Enabled:** (in Internet Explorer 4, this option is named Java JIT Compiler Enabled) Toggles Internet Explorer's internal "just-in-time" Java compiler on and off. This compiler is used to compile and run Java applets using native Windows code.

In many cases, this causes the Java applet to run much faster than the regularly compiled code. However, it may break some applets, or cause them to run slower than normal.

The options in the Multimedia branch toggle various multimedia effects on and off:

- **Always Show Internet Explorer Radio Bar:** Internet Explorer 5 adds a new Radio toolbar. You can use this toolbar to listen to a radio station using streaming audio. However, this feature is useful only if you have a fast connection.

- **Play Animations:** Toggles animated GIF images on and off. Again, if you want to view an animation, right-click the box and then click Show Picture.

- **Play Sounds:** Toggles Web page sound effects on and off. Because the vast majority of Web page sounds are extremely bad MIDI renditions of popular tunes, turning off sounds will save your ears.

- **Play videos:** Toggles Internet Explorer's support for inline AVI files on and off. If you turn this setting off, the only way to view a video is to turn the option back on and then refresh the page.

- **Show Image Download Placeholders:** Internet Explorer 5 displays a box that is the same size and shape as the image it is downloading.

- **Show Pictures:** Toggles Web page images on and off. If you're using a slow connection, turn off this option and Internet Explorer will show only a box where the image would normally appear. (If the designer has included alt text, that text will appear inside the box.) If you want to view a picture, right-click the box and then click Show Picture.

- **Smart Image Dithering:** Toggles image dithering on and off. Dithering is a technique that slightly alters an image to make jagged edges appear smooth.

The Printing branch has an option that affects how you print Web pages:

- **Print Background Colors and Images:** Determines whether Internet Explorer includes the page's background when you print the page. Many Web pages use solid colors or fancy images as backgrounds, so you'll print these pages faster if you deactivate this setting.

The options in the Search from the Address Bar branch control Internet Explorer 5's Address bar searching:

- **Display Results and Go to the Most Likely Site:** Displays the search engine's results in the Search bar and displays the best match in the main browser window.

- **Do Not Search from the Address Bar:** Disables Address bar searching.

- **Just Display the Results in the Main Window:** Displays a list of the sites that the search engine found in the main browser window.

- **Just Go to the Most Likely Site:** Displays the search engine's best match in the main browser window.

The options in the Searching branch (Internet Explorer 4 only) determine how Internet Explorer reacts if you enter an incorrect URL:

- **Autoscan Common Root Domains:** Toggles the Address bar's Autoscan feature on and off.

- **Search When URL Fails:** Controls another feature that allegedly kicks in when Internet Explorer can't find a URL.

The Security branch has many options related to Internet Explorer security. I'll hold off discussing these until I discuss security in Chapter 21.

Use the options in the Toolbar branch (Internet Explorer 4 only) to customize the Standard Buttons toolbar:

- **Show Font Button:** Toggles the toolbar's Fonts button on and off. When you click this button, Internet Explorer displays a menu of font sizes and language choices.

- **Small Icons:** Toggles the toolbar buttons between the regular icons and smaller versions of the icons. This is supposed to give you more room for content, but the size difference between the two types of icons is negligible.

Essential Information

- Web page addresses are called Uniform Resource Locators (URLs) and take the form `http://host.domain/ directory/file.name`, where `file.name` is the name of the page, `directory` is the name of the directory that contains the page, and `host.domain` is the domain name of the Web site.

See Also...
"Internet Explorer's Security Features," p. 495

- You enter URLs using the Address bar, the Open dialog box (choose File, Open), or the Run dialog box (select Start, Run).

- Internet Explorer offers a number of Explorer bars (choose View, Explorer Bar), including History (displays the pages you've visited over the past 20 days), Search (displays a search engine), and Favorites (displays the contents of the `Favorites` folder).

Inside Scoop
If you have a mouse with a wheel button, hold down Ctrl while pressing and turning the wheel. This changes the onscreen font size on-the-fly.

- Use the `Windows\Favorites` folder to store sites you want to visit again later on.

- To maintain your favorites, either choose Favorites, Organize Favorites (or press Ctrl+B) or else work with the `Favorites` folder directly.

- For sites that have content that changes irregularly, set up a subscription by choosing Favorites, Add to Favorites and then selecting one of the two subscription options.

GET THE SCOOP ON...
Setting up your email account ▪ Outlook Express basic
functions ▪ Adding, moving, and deleting message
folders ▪ Using message filters ▪ Updated coverage of
Outlook Express 5 ▪ Customizing message columns
and window layout

Communicating Efficiently and Effectively with Outlook Express

Chapter 20

T HE WORLD WIDE WEB IS POPULAR because it offers lots of eye candy and, once in a while, some useful information. But study after study has shown that the main reason people get connected to the Internet is to send email messages. Whether it's client contact, communicating with peers, or keeping in touch with friends and family, folks from the four corners of the world are busy sending out over 150 million email messages each day.

The huge popularity of Internet email was not lost on the designers of Windows 98. They realized that Windows 95's email client, Windows Messaging (née Microsoft Exchange), was woefully inadequate for the rigors of Internet email. So they dropped Windows Messaging and replaced it with a new client called Outlook Express that was built from the ground up to handle only Internet email. Outlook Express uses Internet standards such as SMTP, POP3, IMAP, and LDAP, can handle multiple email accounts, and supports goodies such as automatic signatures, HTML messages, and digital ID security.

Remember
Windows
Messaging may be
gone, but it's not
completely forgot-
ten. It's still avail-
able, tucked away
in an obscure nook
in the Windows 98
CD. Look in the
`tools\oldwin95\`
`message\us` folder.
Run `wms.exe` to
install Windows
Messaging, and
run `awfax.exe` to
install Microsoft
Fax. If you want to
use only Microsoft
Fax, you still need
to install Windows
Messaging,
although it works
with Microsoft
Outlook (not
Outlook Express),
as well.

See Also...
"Using a Digital
ID for Secure
Email,"
p. 503

"
Windows 98
gives you more
than a great Web
browser. Its
e-mail program
Outlook Express
ranks among the
best mail pro-
grams in exis-
tence and is built
into the operating
system.
—Edward
Mendelson, PC
Magazine
"

This chapter takes you through most of these features. (Although see Chapter 21, "Implementing Windows 98's Internet Security Features," to learn about the Outlook Express security features.) My emphasis is on those tools and techniques that help you get the most out of Outlook Express and help you communicate efficiently. I'll also show you some of what's new in Outlook Express 5, which ships with Windows 98 Second Edition and Internet Explorer 5. If you're new to Internet email, you might want to take a look at the email primer that I have on my Web site:

`http://www.mcfedries.com/Ramblings/email-primer.html`

A Quick Look at Some Outlook Express Email Basics

Let's begin by running through some of the day-to-day chores that you'll perform most often with Outlook Express, including setting up accounts, sending messages, retrieving and reading messages, and sending out replies and forwards.

To get started, use any of the following techniques to launch Outlook Express:

- Select Start, Programs, Internet Explorer, Outlook Express. (If you're running Windows 98 Second Edition, select Start, Programs, Outlook Express.)

- Click the Launch Outlook Express icon in the Quick Launch toolbar.

- Double-click the desktop's Outlook Express icon.

- If you have Internet Explorer 4 open, select the Go, Mail command. (This assumes that you have Outlook Express set up as your default mail client. To check, select View, Internet Options, display the Programs tab, and then select Outlook Express in the Mail list.)

- If you have Internet Explorer 5 open, select Tools, Mail and News, Read Mail. (To check whether Outlook Express is your default mail client, select Tools, Internet Options, display the Programs tab, and then select Outlook Express in the E-mail list.)

The first time you launch the program, you see the Browse for Folder dialog box. (This doesn't happen in Outlook Express 5.) You use this dialog box to choose the folder in which Outlook Express stores your messages. The default folder is Windows\Application Data\Microsoft\Outlook Express. Select a different folder, if necessary, and click OK. Figure 20.1 shows the Outlook Express window that appears.

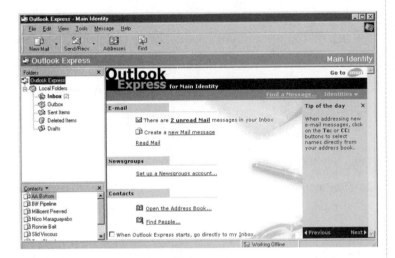

Figure 20.1
This is the Outlook Express window you see when you first start the program.

Inside Scoop
Because you'll probably want to include your Outlook Express messages when you back up your data, consider storing the messages in the same drive or folder that you use to store all your data (such as a subfolder within the My Documents folder).

The left side of the window contains a hierarchical list of the Outlook Express folders, which are used to store messages. There are five default folders:

Inbox: Messages that you've received

Outbox: Messages waiting to be sent

Sent Items: Messages that have been sent

Deleted Items: Messages that you've deleted

Drafts: Messages that you're currently working on (that is, they've been saved but not sent)

Outlook Express opens with the top-level Outlook Express folder selected. When this folder is selected, the right side of the window displays various icons for common tasks.

In Outlook Express 5, the left side of the window also includes a new Contacts list, which displays the names of the people in your Address Book.

Setting Up Mail Accounts

If you didn't define your Internet email account when you set up your Internet connection, or if you have multiple accounts and need to set up others, this section shows you how to do it within Outlook Express.

Shortcut

It's more efficient to start with the Inbox folder selected, so activate the When Outlook Express starts, then go directly to my Inbox check box.

You have two choices for getting started:

- Click the Inbox folder. The first time you do this, the Internet Connection Wizard launches automatically.

- Select Tools, Accounts to display the Internet Accounts dialog box. Click Add and then click Mail.

The wizard will ask you to enter the following data:

- A display name. This is the name that will appear in the "From" field when you send a message.

- The email address for the account.

- The type of email server (POP3 or IMAP) and the server domain names for incoming and outgoing mail.

- The account user name and password.

- A "friendly name" for the account. This is the name that appears in the list of accounts. (Note that this step is skipped in the Windows 98 Second Edition version of the wizard.)

- How you connect to the Internet. (Again, this step is skipped in the Windows 98 Second Edition version of the wizard.) If you use a dial-up connection, you have two choices:

  Connect using my phone line: If you go this route, you'll be asked to select a modem and a Dial-Up Networking connection. Each time you start Outlook Express, it will offer to connect to the Internet for you.

  I will establish my Internet connection manually: If you select this option, you won't have to enter any other data, and Outlook Express won't prompt you to connect to the Internet at startup.

When the wizard completes its labors, your new account appears in the Mail tab of the Internet Accounts dialog box, as shown in Figure 20.2. While you're in this dialog box, this is as good a time as any to check out some account properties.

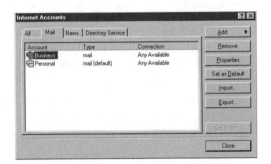

Figure 20.2
Your Internet email accounts are listed in the Mail tab.

The first property to work with is the default account. If you have multiple accounts, the default account is the one Outlook Express uses automatically when you send a message. To set the default account, highlight it in the Mail tab and then click Set as Default.

To work with the other properties, highlight an account and then click Properties. The property sheet that appears contains five tabs:

Remember
It is possible to send a message using any of your accounts. However, sending a message using anything other than the default account requires an extra step. See "Sending a Message," later in this chapter.

General: Use this tab to set the name of the account, as well as your display name, organization name, and email address. By default, replies to your messages are sent to your email address. If you'd prefer to have replies sent somewhere else, use the Reply address field to enter the other address. There's also a check box named Include this account when receiving mail or synchronizing. (In Outlook Express 4, this check box is named Include this account when doing a full Send and Receive. As you'll see later, Outlook Express has a Send and Receive command that normally works with all accounts. If you'd prefer to exclude this account from the Send and Receive operation, deactivate this check box.

Servers: Use this tab to set the mail server domain names, and the account user name and password.

Connection: Use this tab to set the type of Internet connection you use and, for dial-ups, the Dial-Up Networking connection to use.

Security: Use this tab to specify a digital ID for secure messages. Again, I discuss email security in Chapter 21.

Advanced: This tab contains a large number of relatively obscure options. However, there are useful settings in the Delivery and Sending groups. In the Delivery group, activate the Leave a copy of messages on server check box to download only a copy of each incoming message while leaving the original messages intact on the server. This is useful if you need to download the messages using another email program or another computer. The two other check boxes in this group determine when Outlook Express deletes the messages from the server. In the Sending group, activate the Break apart messages larger than x KB check box if you'll be sending messages to older servers that can't handle large messages.

Sending a Message

With your email account (or accounts) set up, it's time to try things out. Here are the steps to follow to compose and send a message:

1. Use any of the following techniques to get started:

    - Select Message, New Message (in Outlook Express 4, select Compose, New Message), or press Ctrl+N.

    - Click the New Mail (in Outlook Express 4, Compose Message) toolbar button.

    - If you're using Internet Explorer 5, select Tools, Mail and News, New Message (in Internet Explorer 4, select File, New Message).

    - If you want to use one of Outlook Express' predefined stationery patterns as a background, select Message, New Message Using (in Outlook Express 4, select Compose, New Message using) and then select

Shortcut
If you've been using another email client, you can make your life easier by importing the client's address book, message, and accounts into Outlook Express. Select File, Import and then select one of the following commands: Address Book, Messages, or Mail Account Settings.

a stationery from the submenu that appears. Alternatively, drop down the New Mail (in Outlook Express 4, Compose Message) toolbar button and click the stationery you want to use.

2. Figure 20.3 shows the New Message window that appears. Use the To, Cc (carbon copy), and Bcc (blind carbon copy) text boxes to enter the addresses of the recipients. In each text box, you can enter multiple addresses by separating each one with a semi-colon (;). If you're running Outlook Express 5 and you have multiple accounts defined, use the From list to select the account from which you want to send the message.)

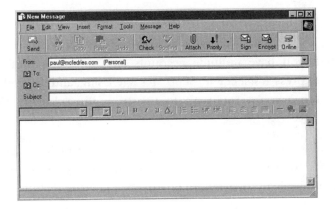

Figure 20.3
Use this window to compose your message.

Remember
Click the icons beside the To, Cc, and Bcc fields to open the Windows Address Book. From there you, can define commonly used recipients and then insert them into the To, Cc, and Bcc fields. Note, too, that the Address Book is also available within Outlook Express by selecting Tools, Address Book, pressing Ctrl+Shift+B, or by clicking the Address Book toolbar button.

3. Enter a brief description for the email in the Subject text box.

4. Pull down the Format menu and select the message style: Rich Text (HTML) or Plain Text. Note that if you select the Rich Text (HTML) command, your recipient must have an email client (such as Outlook Express, Outlook 98 or later, and Netscape Mail) that can handle HTML formatting.

5. Use the large text box below the Subject line to compose the message body. If you selected the Rich Text (HTML) style, use the Formatting toolbar and the commands on the Format menu to format the message.

Inside Scoop
To create a signature, switch to the Outlook Express window and select Tools, Options, display the Signature tab, and click New. (in Outlook Express 4, select Tools, Stationery and click the Signature button.)Enter the signature in the Text box. (Alternatively, select File and specify a text file with the signature text.) If you want Outlook Express to add the signature automatically, activate the Add Signatures To All Outgoing Messages check box.

Watch Out!
After Outlook Express connects to the server and sends the messages, it does not hang up the connection. If you'd prefer that Outlook Express hang up after it's finished, select Tools, Options, select the Dial-Up tab, and activate the Hang up when finished check box.

6. To attach a file to the message, select Insert, File Attachment, find the file in the Insert Attachment dialog box, and then click Attach.

7. To set the message priority, select Message, Set Priority (in Outlook Express 4, select Tools, Set Priority) and then select High, Normal, or Low in the submenu that appears.

8. If you've defined a signature, you can add it to the message by selecting Insert, Signature.

When the message is ready to ship, how you send it depends on whether you have multiple accounts and on whether you want to send the message now or later. If you want to send the message now, use either of the following techniques:

- If you have only a single account, select File, Send Message.

- If you have multiple accounts and are using Outlook Express 4, select File, Send Message Using, and then select the account you want to use from the submenu that appears.

If you prefer to send the message later (which is a good idea if you're using a dial-up connection and you're composing multiple messages), use one of the following techniques:

- If you have only a single account, select File, Send Later.

- If you have multiple accounts and are using Outlook Express 4, click the Send button (or press Alt+S) to send the message from your default account.

- If you have multiple accounts and are using Outlook Express 4, select File, Send Later Using, and then select the account you want to use from the submenu that appears.

With each of the above techniques, Outlook Express displays a dialog box letting you know that the message will be stored in the Outbox folder. When you're ready to send the

Outbox messages, return to Outlook Express and select the Tools, Send and Receive, Send All command (in Outlook Express 4, select Tools, Send). If Outlook Express asks whether you want to go online, click Yes.

Retrieving Messages

To receive the messages that have been sent to your account, Outlook Express offers a number of options:

- If you have a single email account, select Tools, Send and Receive, or click the Send/Recv (in Outlook Express 4, Send and Receive) toolbar button. (You can also press Ctrl+M or F5.) Note that this method not only receives the incoming messages, but it also sends any messages waiting in the Outbox folder.

- If you have multiple email accounts, click the Send/Recv (in Outlook Express 4, Send and Receive) toolbar button (or press Ctrl+M or F5) to send and receive messages from the default account.

- If you have multiple email accounts, select Tools, Send and Receive and then select the account you want to work with.

- In Outlook Express 4, the Tools, Download All command (Ctrl+Shift+M is the shortcut key) is supposed to only receive messages for all your accounts. However, a bug in Outlook Express 4 causes this command to also send any waiting messages. To avoid sending messages, you must first move any waiting messages out of the Outbox folder.

Reading a Message

The messages you receive are stored in the Inbox folder, which has five columns:

Exclamation mark: Indicates the priority of the message: A red exclamation mark means high priority, a blue, downward-pointing arrow means low priority.

Paper clip: A paper clip icon in this column indicates that the message has an attached file.

Shortcut
Outlook Express can check for new messages automatically. Select Tools, Options and, in the General tab of the Options dialog box, activate the Check for new messages every *x* minutes check box. Use the spinner to set the frequency of the checks (between 1 and 480 minutes). For this to work with a dial-up connection, make sure Outlook Express isn't working offline (deactivate the File, Work Offline command.) Also, in Outlook Express 4, activate the Automatically dial when checking for new messages check box in the Dial Up tab.

Flag: You can put a flag icon in this column to remind yourself to take some kind of action on the message.

From: The name (or sometimes just the email address) of the person who sent the message.

Subject: The Subject line of the message.

Received: The date and time the message was received from the server.

Messages that you haven't read yet are displayed in bold. To read a message, you have two choices:

- Highlight the message to view it in the preview page.

- To open the message in its own window, double-click it. Alternatively, highlight the message and press either Enter or Ctrl+O, or select File, Open.

Dealing with a Message After You've Read It

Here's a list of actions you can take after you've read a message:

Reply to the author of the message: Select Message, Reply to Sender (in Outlook Express 4, select Compose, Reply to Author), or press Ctrl+R. Outlook Express appends Re: to the Subject line and the existing message text is included in the reply.

Reply to all the message recipients: Select Message, Reply to All (in Outlook Express 4, select Compose, Reply to All), or press Ctrl+Shift+R.

Forward the message: Select Message, Forward (in Outlook Express 4, select Compose, Forward), or press Ctrl+F. Outlook Express appends Fw: to the Subject line and the existing message text is included in the forward.

Forward the message as an attachment: Select Message, Forward As Attachment (in Outlook Express 4, select Compose, Forward as Attachment). Outlook Express appends Fw: to the Subject line and the existing message is attached. Use this option if you want the recipient to see the message exactly as you received it.

Shortcut
If you'd like to add a sender to your address book, open the message and then select Tools, Add To Address Book, Sender. Alternatively, right-click the sender and then click Add To Address Book.

Watch Out!
When you reply to a message, Outlook Express 5 has an annoying habit of adding the author of the original message to your Address Book. To turn off this dumb behavior, select Tools, Options, display the Send tab, and deactivate the Automatically put people I reply to in my Address Book check box.

Save an attachment: In the preview pane, click the paper clip icon in the upper-right corner, and then click the filename. In the Open Attachment Warning dialog box, select either Open It or Save It To Disk. If the message is open, select File, Save Attachments, and then click the file. You can also drag the file's icon from the message.

Move the message to another folder: Drag the message header from the Inbox folder and drop it on the destination folder. If the message is open, select File, Move To Folder.

Copy the message to another folder: Hold down Ctrl and drag the message header from the Inbox folder and drop it on the destination folder. If the message is open, select File, Copy To Folder.

Print the message: Select File, Print, or press Ctrl+P.

Flag the message: Select Message, Flag Message. This adds a flag icon beside the message to the Flag column. This is useful if you want to remind yourself to take some kind of action on the message.

Delete the message: In the Inbox folder, select Edit, Delete, or press Delete. If the message is open, select File, Delete, or press Ctrl+D). You can also drag the message header to the Deleted Items folder.

Working with Outlook Express Folders

No savvy user would ever consider organizing her hard disk so that all her data files were stored in a single folder. But that, essentially, is the way Outlook Express is organized by default. The messages that you don't delete remain in the Inbox folder. That's not a big deal at first, but it gets messy after you have a few dozen messages stored. To reduce the clutter and help you find messages, you should create new folders and subfolders to store related messages. Here's how it's done:

1. Select File, Folder, New (in Outlook Express 4, select File, Folder, New Folder). Outlook Express displays the Create Folder dialog box.

Watch Out!
Outlook Express 4 has a bug that can cause a malicious user to execute code on your computer if an attachment has an extremely long filename. (The code can run even if you don't open the attachment.) To find out more, see Chapter 21's "Windows 98 Security Updates" section, page 491.

Watch Out!
If you delete a message by accident, open the Deleted Items folder and move the message to another folder. If you'd like Outlook Express to clean out the Deleted Items folder each time you exit the program, select Tools, Options and, in the Maintenance tag (in Outlook Express 4, use the General tab), activate the Empty messages from the 'Deleted Items' folder on exit check box.

2. Enter the name of the new folder in the Folder name text box.

3. Use the list to highlight the folder in which you want to create the new folder.

4. Click OK. Outlook Express creates the folder.

The File, Folder submenu contains a number of other commands. Here's what they do:

Move: Moves the highlighted folder to another location.

Rename: Renames the highlighted folder. (You can also highlight the folder and press F2.)

Delete: Deletes the highlighted folder. This is a permanent action, so Outlook Express warns you that it can't be undone. To give yourself the flexibility of undoing the deletion later on, try moving the folder to the Deleted Items folder, instead. (Watch out, however, if you've set up Outlook Express to empty this folder when exiting.)

Compact: Reduces the size of the files that store the highlighted folder's contents.

Compact All Folders: Reduces the size of the folder files for all the existing folders.

Undocumented
The contents of each folder are stored on the hard disk using an .mbx file for the messages and an .idx file as an index to the messages. Deleting messages causes gaps to appear in these files. Compacting the folder removes these gaps and reduces the size of the files.

Filtering Incoming Messages

Just a couple of years ago, my email chores took up only a few minutes of each workday. Now it takes me two or three hours to get through the hundreds of messages I receive every day. What's interesting about this is that it's by no means unusual. Most people find that after they really get into Internet email, the messages really start to pile up quickly.

To help ease the crunch, Outlook Express offers *mail rules* (this feature was called the Inbox Assistant in Outlook Express 4). You can set up these rules to handle incoming messages for you automatically. Of course, these rules are limited in what they can do, but what they *can* do isn't bad:

■ If you'll be out of the office for a few days, or if you go on vacation, you can create a rule to mail out an automatic reply that lets the sender know you received their message but won't be able to deal with it for a while.

- If you have multiple email accounts, you can set up a rule to redirect incoming messages into separate folders for each account.

- You can create a rule to redirect incoming messages into separate folders for specific people, projects, or mailing lists.

- If you receive unwanted messages from a particular source (such as a spammer), you can set up a rule to automatically delete those messages.

For the latter, note that Outlook Express 5 also comes with a Blocked Senders list. If you put an address on this list, Outlook Express 5 watches for messages from that address and deletes them automatically. To use this feature, follow these steps:

1. Highlight a message that comes from the address you want to block.

2. Select Message, Block Sender. Outlook Express 5 adds the address to the Blocked Senders list and asks if you want to delete all messages from that address.

3. Click Yes to delete the messages, or click No to leave them be.

To view the Blocked Senders list, select Tools, Message Rules, Blocked Senders List. Outlook Express 5 opens the Message Rules dialog box and displays the Blocked Senders tab.

For more general situations, you need to set up mail rules. How you do this depends on which version of Outlook Express you're using. Let's start with the Outlook Express 5 route:

1. Select the Tools, Message Rules, Mail command. Outlook Express 5 displays the New Mail Rule dialog box.

2. In the Select the Conditions for your rule list, activate the check box beside the criterion you want to use to pick out a message from the herd. Outlook Express 5 adds the con-

Inside Scoop
One of the problems with redirecting messages to other folders is that it's less convenient to read those messages. Outlook Express helps by bolding the name of any folder that contains unread messages. (It also tells you how many unread messages are in each folder.) Outlook Express also opens the folder tree to reveal any folders that have unread messages. (To make sure this option is turned on, select Tools, Options and, in the General tab, check that the Automatically display folders with unread messages setting is activated.)

dition to the Rule Description text box, as shown in Figure 20.4. Note that you're free to select multiple conditions.

Figure 20.4
Use this dialog
box to set up a
mail rule in
Outlook Express
5.

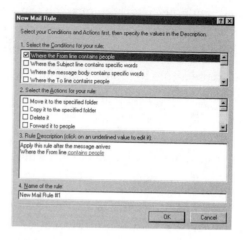

3. The condition will probably have some underlined text. You need to replace that underlined text with the specific criteria you want to use (such as a word or an address). To do that, click the underlined text, enter the criteria in the dialog box that appears, and click OK.

4. In the Select the Actions for your rule list, activate the check box beside the action you want Outlook Express 5 to take with messages that meet your criteria. Again, you may have to click underlined text to complete the action. Also, you can select multiple actions.

5. Use the Name of the rule text box to enter a descriptive name for the rule.

6. Click OK. Outlook Express 5 drops you off at the Mail Rules tab of the Message Rules dialog box.

To give Outlook Express 4's Inbox Assistant a whirl, select the Tools, Inbox Assistant command). In the dialog box that appears, click Add to display the Properties dialog box shown in Figure 20.5. The purpose of this dialog box is to create a *rule* that tells the Inbox Assistant when and how to deal with incoming messages.

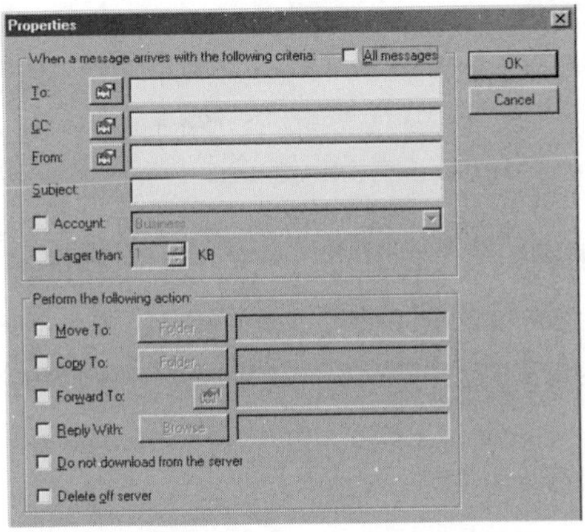

Figure 20.5
Use this dialog
box to define the
Inbox Assistant
rules for filtering
messages.

You start by defining the conditions under which the rule
will be invoked. That is, to which incoming messages will the
rule be applied. That's the job of the options in the When a
message arrives with the following criteria group. You have two
ways to proceed:

- If you want the rule to apply to every message that arrives,
  activate the All messages check box. You would do this if,
  for example, you were going out of town and wanted to
  send out an automatic reply for each incoming message.

- If you want the rule to apply only to certain messages, use
  the other controls in the group to specify the criteria. For
  example, if you want to use the rule on messages received
  from a particular email address, enter that address in the
  From text box.

With the criteria set, you must now tell the Inbox Assistant
what to do with any message that meets the criteria. The
Perform the following action group offers six choices:

Move To: Inbox Assistant moves the message to the specified folder. For example, to delete the message, move it
to the Deleted Items folder.

Copy To: Inbox Assistant copies the message to the
specified folder.

Forward To: Inbox Assistant forwards the message to the
specified address.

Undocumented
To create a file in the Mail format, compose a message that contains the text you want to use in the reply, and then send the message to yourself. After you receive the message, open it, select File, Save As, make sure Mail(*.eml) is selected in the Save As Type list, and then click Save.

Reply With: Inbox Assistant sends a reply using the specified file. Four file formats are supported: News (.nws), Mail (.eml), HTML (.htm), or Text(.txt).

Do not download from server: Inbox Assistant doesn't download the message, but it leaves the message intact on the server.

Delete off server: Inbox Assistant doesn't download the message, and it deletes the message from the server.

After your rule is defined, click OK to add it to the list in the Inbox Assistant dialog box.

Whichever method you used, here are a few notes to bear in mind when working with the list of rules:

Toggling rules on and off: Use the check box beside each rule to turn the rule on and off.

Setting rule order: Some rules should be processed before others. For example, if you have a rule that deletes spam, you want Inbox Assistant to process that rule before sending out a vacation reply. To adjust the order of a rule, highlight it and then click either Move Up or Move Down.

Applying the rules to another folder (Outlook Express 4 only): By default, the rules apply to the Inbox folder. To apply the rules to another folder, click Apply To.

Modifying a rule: To edit a rule, highlight it and click Modify (in Outlook Express 4, click Properties).

Deleting a rule: Highlight the rule and click Remove.

Finding a Message

Although you'll delete many of the messages that come your way, it's unlikely that you'll delete all of them. So, over time, you'll probably end up with hundreds, or more likely thousands, of messages stored throughout various folders. What happens if you want to find a particular message? Even if you curmudgeonly delete everything that comes your way, your Sent Items folder will still eventually contain copies of the hundreds or thousands of missives you've shipped out. What if you want to find one of those messages?

For both incoming and outgoing messages, Outlook Express offers a decent Find Message feature that can look for messages based on addresses, subject lines, body text, dates, and more.

To try it out, select the Edit, Find, Message command (in Outlook Express 4, select Edit, Find Message), or press Ctrl+Shift+F. Outlook Express displays the Find Message dialog box. (Figure 20.6 shows the Outlook Express 5 version of this dialog box.) Use the following controls to set the search criteria:

Browse (**Look in** in Outlook Express 4): Select the folder to search. If you want the search to include the subfolders of the selected folder, activate the Include subfolders check box.

From: Enter one or more words that specify the email address or display name of the sender you want to find.

To (**Sent to** in Outlook Express 4): Enter one or more words that specify the email address or display name of the recipient you want to find.

Subject: Enter one or more words that specify the Subject line you want to find.

Message (**Message body** in Outlook Express 4): Enter one or more words that specify the message body you want to find.

Received after (**After** in Outlook Express 4): Select the earliest received date for the message you want to find.

Received before (**Before** in Outlook Express 4): Select the latest received date for the message you want to find.

Message has attachment(s): Activate this check box to find only messages that have attached files.

Message is flagged (Outlook Express 5 only): Activate this check box to find only messages that have been flagged.

After your search criteria are defined, click Find Now. If Outlook Express finds any matches, it displays them in a message list at the bottom of the dialog box. From here, you can

Remember
The Find Messages feature performs Boolean "AND" searches. That is, if you enter multiple words, Outlook Express matches only those messages that contain all the words.

open a message or use any of the commands in the menus to work with the messages (reply, forward, move to another folder, delete, and so on).

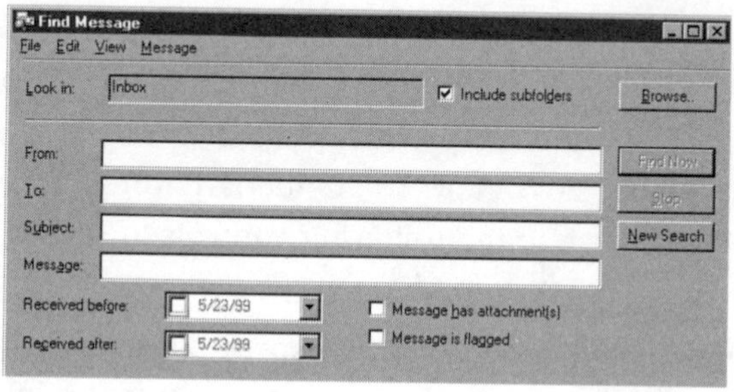

Figure 20.6
Use the Find
Message dialog
box to look for
specific messages
in a folder.

Finding a Person

In an effort to create a kind of White Pages for the Internet, a number of companies have set up *directory servers* that contain databases of names and email addresses. Using a standard Internet protocol called the Lightweight Directory Access Protocol (LDAP), email clients and other programs can use these directory servers to perform simple searches for names and addresses.

Outlook Express supports LDAP and is set up to provide ready access to several of the most popular directory servers. To see the complete list, select Tools, Accounts and then display the Directory Service tab. If your company runs its own directory server, you can add it to this list by clicking Add, Directory Service and following the Internet Connection Wizard's dialog boxes.

To perform a search on a directory server, or to search the Windows Address Book, follow these steps:

1. Select the Edit, Find, People command (in Outlook Express 4, select Edit, Find People). Outlook Express displays the Find People dialog box.

2. Use the Look in list to select either Address Book (to search the Windows Address Book) or a directory service.

3. You have two searching options:

- If you know the name of a person and want to find out his email address, use the Name text box to enter the person's name. (You can enter the exact name or a partial name.)

- If you know the email address of a person and want to find out her name, use the E-mail text box to enter the person's exact email address.

4. Click Find Now. Outlook Express accesses the directory server and runs the query. If the server reports any matches, they're displayed at the bottom of the dialog box.

Remember
To get more information about the selected directory service, click the Web Site button to open the service's home page in Internet Explorer. Note, too, that in most cases you can use the Web site to add your own name and address to the service.

Customizing Outlook Express

I'll close this look at Outlook Express with a few pointers for customizing the program. I'll discuss sorting messages, customizing the message columns, changing the Outlook Express layout, creating a custom toolbar, and much more.

Reorganizing the Message List Columns

As you've seen, the columns in the message list display the basic header data associated with each message. You can also use these columns to sort the messages, change the order of the header data, and even display other header fields. Here's a summary:

Sorting the messages: Click a column heading to sort the messages on the values in that column. Clicking the heading repeatedly toggles between a descending sort and an ascending sort. (You can also right-click the column heading and then click either Sort Ascending or Sort Descending.) Alternatively, select the View, Sort By command, and then select a column from the submenu that appears.

Displaying only unread messages: Select the View, Current View, Hide Read Messages command (in Outlook Express 4, select View, Current View, Unread Messages). To display all the messages again, select View, Current View, Show All Messages (in Outlook Express 4, select View, Current View, All Messages).

Changing the column width: Move your mouse to the right edge of the heading of the column you want to adjust. Then drag the mouse left (to create a narrower column) or right (to create a wider column).

Moving a column: Drag the column heading left or right.

Changing the size of the message list: To change the width of the message list, drag the vertical split bar that separates the folder list from the message list and the preview pane. To change the height of the message list, drag the horizontal split bar that separates the message list pane from the preview pane.

Shortcut
To adjust the width of a column so that it's as wide as its widest entry, position the mouse over the right edge of the column heading and then double-click.

Adding and removing columns in Outlook Express 4: Select View, Columns to display the Columns dialog box. To add a column, highlight it in the Available columns list and then click Add. To remove a column, highlight it in the Displayed columns list, and then click Remove. Note, too, that you can reposition a column by highlighting it and clicking the Move Up and Move Down buttons.

Adding and removing columns in Outlook Express 5: Select View, Columns to display the Columns dialog box, shown in Figure 20.7. To add a column, activate its check box in the list. To remove a column, deactivate its check box. Note, too, that you can reposition a column by highlighting it and clicking the Move Up and Move Down buttons.

Figure 20.7
Use this dialog box to add and remove columns, and to change the column order.

Rearranging the Layout of the Outlook Express Window

One of the nice features of Outlook Express is that its window layout is quite flexible and customizable. To see how, select the View, Layout command to display the Window Layout Properties dialog box, shown in Figure 20.8. (This is the Outlook Express 5 version of this dialog box.)

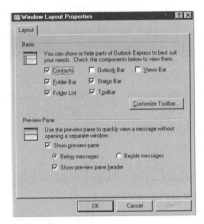

Figure 20.8
Use this dialog box to rearrange the Outlook Express window to your liking.

Inside Scoop
If you decide to hide the folder list, Outlook Express offers a number of folder navigation techniques you can use. For starters, select Go, Inbox (Outlook Express 4 only) or press Ctrl+Shift+I to select the Inbox folder. If you're in a subfolder, you can move up the parent folder by selecting Go, Up One Level (Outlook Express 4 only). Finally, you can move to any folder by selecting View, Go to Folder (select Go, Go To Folder in Outlook Express 4) or by pressing Ctrl+Y.

The Basic group enables you to toggle certain window features on and off by using the following four check boxes:

Contacts: This is Outlook Express 5's new Contacts list that's displayed under the Folder list.

Folder Bar: This is displayed above the message list. It shows the name of the currently selected folder.

Folder List: This is the folder list.

Outlook Bar: This is displayed as a strip down the left side of the Outlook Express window. It contains icons for the Outlook Express folders.

Status Bar: This is the status bar that runs across the bottom of the window.

Toolbar: This is the toolbar that runs across the window below the menu bar.

Views Bar: This is a drop-down list that is displayed below the toolbar. You can use this list as a quick way to change the view.

Tip of the Day (Outlook Express 4 only): This is a short tip that appears in the Outlook Express folder.

The Toolbar group (Outlook Express 4 only) enables you to control the position and look of the Outlook Express toolbar:

Top, Left, Bottom, Right: These options specify the toolbar's position within the Outlook Express window.

Show text on toolbar buttons: If you deactivate this check box, Outlook Express displays only the toolbar icons without their titles. This gives you some extra vertical room in the Outlook Express window.

Customize Toolbar: Click this button to display the Customize Toolbar dialog box, which you can use to add and remove toolbar buttons, as well as to change the order of the buttons.

The Preview Pane group enables you to customize several aspects of the preview pane:

Shortcut
You can access all of these toolbar customization features by right-clicking the toolbar and then selecting a command in the shortcut menu that appears.

Show preview pane: Toggles the preview pane on and off

Below Messages: Positions the preview pane below the message list (this is the default position)

Beside Messages: Positions the preview pane between the folder list and the message list

Show preview pane header: Toggles the header that appears at the top of the preview pane on and off

Essential Information

- Select Tools, Accounts to define new email accounts and to adjust the properties of existing accounts.

- To send a message, select Compose, New Message, enter the recipient addresses, the Subject line, and the message text, and then click Send.

- To retrieve a message, select Tools, Send and Receive and, if you have multiple accounts, select the account you want to use.

- Organize your incoming messages by creating folders to store related messages, such as those from specific people, projects, or mailing lists.

- Select the Tools, Inbox Assistant command to set up rules to filter incoming messages based on the recipient, Subject line, account, and more.

- To customize Outlook Express, select View, Columns to add and remove columns, and select View, Layout to rearrange the Outlook Express window.

GET THE SCOOP ON...
Avoiding email virus hoaxes and chain mail scams ▪
The latest Windows 98 security patches ▪ Avoiding
security holes created by the TCP/IP protocol ▪
Internet Explorer security options ▪ Digital IDs for
secure email in Outlook Express

Implementing Windows 98's Internet Security Features

Chapter 21

A S MORE PEOPLE, BUSINESSES, and organizations establish a presence online, the world becomes an increasingly connected place. And the more connected the world becomes, the more opportunities there are for communicating with others, doing research, sharing information, and collaborating on projects. The flip side to this new connectedness is the increased risk of connecting with a remote user whose intentions are less than honorable. It could be a "packet sniffer" who steals your password or credit card number, a cracker who breaks into your Internet account, a virus programmer who sends a Trojan horse virus attached to an email, or a Web site operator who uses Web browser security holes to run malicious code on your machine.

Admittedly, online security threats are relatively rare and are no reason to swear off the online world. However, these threats *do* exist and people fall victim to them every day. Luckily, protecting yourself from these and other e-menaces doesn't take much effort or time, as you'll see in this chapter. I'll discuss a number of security issues, and I'll show you how to work with the Internet security tools built into Windows 98.

❝

packet sniffer,
noun: Software
that monitors
network traffic
to steal pass-
words, credit
card numbers,
and other sensi-
tive data. Also,
the person who
uses such soft-
ware.
—The Word Spy
(http://www.
logophilia.com/
WordSpy)
❞

Some Thoughts on Email Virus Hoaxes

Once you're online, it probably won't be long until you receive an email message along the following lines:

> There is a computer virus that is being sent across the Internet. If you receive an email message with the subject line "Good Times," DO NOT read the message, DELETE it immediately. Some miscreant is sending email and files under the title "Good Times." If you receive this file, do not download it. It has a virus that rewrites your hard drive, obliterating anything on it. Please be careful and forward this mail to anyone you care about.

Heeding the last sentence, the sender will most likely have forwarded this warning to a few dozen friends, relatives, and colleagues. That's awfully thoughtful of him, but there's only one problem: This message is a hoax! There is no such virus, and even if it existed, it couldn't possibly do what the message suggests. That is, it's impossible to execute code on your system simply by reading an email message. (However it is possible to unleash a virus by opening a file attached to an email message. Also, see the Outlook Express "File Attachment" Security Update, discussed in the next section.)

"Good Times" is the oldest (it's been around since 1994) and most famous of the email virus hoaxes. It is not, unfortunately, the only one. While writing this book, I received many "warnings" forwarded by concerned readers about an alleged email virus called "Win a Holiday." Other hoaxes include the "Penpal Greetings" virus, the "Deeyenda" virus, and the "Irina" virus. All of these are variations on the "Good Times" theme.

❝

Ironically, well-
meaning com-
puter users
often include the
phrase "Good
Times" (or one
of the other evil
phrases) in the
subject line of
their message
when alerting
others!
—Computer
Virus Myths

❞

Other email hoax annoyances take the form of chain letters. Some of these messages claim to be from malicious hackers who will do something nasty to your computer if you don't forward the message to ten of your friends. One of my favorites is the "Bill Gates $1,000" hoax, where a message allegedly from Bill Gates tells you to forward the message to everyone you know and, when 1,000 people have received it, you'll win $1,000.

The ironic thing about all this is that these messages end up as a kind of virus themselves. With thousands of people naively forwarding tens of thousands of copies of the message all over the Internet, they end up wasting bandwidth and wasting the time of those people who must refute their claims.

The Internet offers many sources of information on these virus hoaxes. One of the best is the Computer Virus Myths Web site:

```
http://kumite.com/myths/
```

Windows 98 Security Updates

Windows 98 has millions of lines of code, and it must work with thousands of legacy software and hardware products, as well as the latest and greatest goodies such as USB and FireWire. This staggering complexity has one inevitable downside: *bugs*. Lots and lots of bugs. (A computer academic has proved that it's impossible for a sufficiently complex software program to be bug-free.) Most of these bugs are either benign or obscure. However, for those Windows 98 components that are related to the Internet, these bugs more often than not create some gaping security loophole.

Even years after Windows 98 hit the market, there have been a large number of security issues of varying severity discovered in either Outlook Express or Internet Explorer. It's likely that more will have been found by the time you read this.

The good news is that Microsoft quickly released patches for all of these issues and made them available on the Windows Update Web site. These patches are listed in the Critical Updates section, as shown in Figure 21.1. (Note, too, that all the patches are incorporated into Windows 98 Second Edition.)

Let's examine six of the updates so you can get an idea of the types of security problems that can arise:

Untrusted Scripted Paste Issue: This patch fixes an Internet Explorer bug that could enable a Web site operator to download a file (such as your Windows 98 password file) from your computer. If the user knows the exact path of a file (not a stretch for common Windows files), he could use a script to paste the path and filename into Internet Explorer's built-in upload control. The

Figure 21.1
Patches for secu-
rity vulnerabilities
are listed in the
Critical Updates
section of the
Windows Update
Web site.

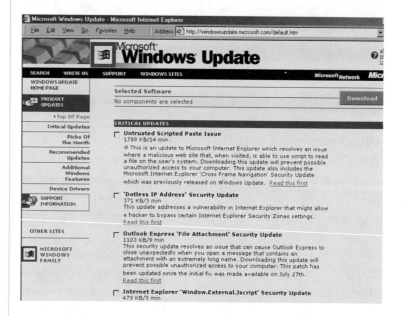

remote script could then submit a form behind the scenes, and the file would be included in the submission.

"Cross Frame Navigation" Security Update: This is an Internet Explorer bug that enables a malicious Web site operator to use JavaScript to open a text or HTML file from your computer (he would need to know the exact path and name of the file) and then send that file to an arbitrary host. The fix for this bug is part of the Untrusted Scripted Paste Issue update.

"Frame Spoof" Fix: This bug enables malicious Web site operators to create a Web page frame that encapsulates the page of a legitimate site. If the user attempts to send data to the legitimate site, it would be sent instead to the malicious user.

"Dotless IP Address" Security Update: This patch fixes an

Internet Explorer bug that occurs when the program comes across a "dotless" IP address. A dotted IP address—such as 123.45.67.89—can be represented as a single number—such as 2066563929. However, while a URL such as http://123.45.67.89 may refer to a site in the Internet security zone, Internet Explorer interprets the dotless version—http://2066563929—as the name of a computer on an intranet, and therefore places the site in the Local Intranet zone. (I'll discuss these security zones later; see "Internet Explorer's Security Features.") Because the user may have set up less stringent security settings in the Local Intranet zone, a malicious Web site could run ActiveX controls or Java applets without the user knowing.

Inside Scoop
To get the dotless IP address, you multiply the first number in the IP address by 16,777,216 (256 cubed), the second number by 65,536 (256 squared), and the third number by 256. You then add these three products to the fourth number.

Outlook Express "File Attachment" Security Update: This is a bug in Outlook Express that can cause problems if a message arrives with an extremely long—200 characters or more—filename. The long filename causes an internal buffer overrun. The result is that portions of the message header actually end up in the memory space reserved for executable code! This means a malicious sender could make Outlook Express run arbitrary commands at the user's privilege level, including sending messages, running a Trojan horse virus, or formatting the user's hard drive. Because these commands are embedded in the message header, which is processed when the message is read, the evil code can execute when the message is read, and not just when the file attachment is opened.

The potential impact of this vulnerability could be very high. Everyone who uses the affected E-Mail/ News readers needs to patch their systems as soon as possible.
—The Computer Incident Advisory

99

Internet Explorer "Windows.External.Jscript" Security Update: This patch fixes an Internet Explorer bug that could cause a malicious Web site operator to run arbitrary code on your computer. If the remote Web site runs the JavaScript Window.External function with a carefully crafted, very long string argument, Internet Explorer may run code embedded in the string.

As I write this, there are no known instances of users being adversely affected by any of these vulnerabilities. However, the publicity generated by these bugs, and the relative ease with which some of them can be exploited, mean that you should install all the patches as soon as possible.

Note, too, that the Windows Update site also contains a Windows Critical Update Notification patch. Installing this patch adds a Windows Critical Update Notification item to the `Scheduled Tasks` folder. When you're connected to the Internet, this item checks with Windows Update to see if there are any critical updates available to install.

Internet Security and the TCP/IP Protocol

When you launch your Internet connection, you may see the System Security Check dialog box shown in Figure 21.2. This warning appears if your system has the TCP/IP protocol bound to the file and printer sharing service. TCP/IP is used for connecting to the Internet, and file and printer sharing is used to enable network users to see and work with shared files and printers on your computer. (It's also used with the Direct Cable Connection feature.) If the two are bound together,

Figure 21.2
This dialog box appears if your Internet connection isn't secure.

then it could mean that someone on the Internet would be able to work directly with the files on your computer!

Note, however, that this scenario applies only to the version of TCP/IP that's bound to whatever mechanism you use to connect to the Internet:

- If you use a dial-up connection, it applies only to the TCP/IP protocol bound to the Dial-Up Adapter.

- If you use a local area network connection, it applies only to the TCP/IP protocol bound to your network adapter.

The easiest way to fix this problem is to click Yes in the System Security Check dialog box. Alternatively, open the Control Panel's Network icon, highlight the appropriate TCP/IP component, as described above, and click Properties. Display the Bindings tab and deactivate the check box beside File and printer sharing for Microsoft Networks.

Internet Explorer's Security Features

Internet Explorer implements security along two different lines:

Outgoing security: This involves data that you send, which could be a credit card number, data in a form, or a username and password.

Incoming security: This involves data sent to your computer, which could be a Java applet or ActiveX control embedded inside a page, a script, or a file download.

For outgoing security, Internet Explorer offers the following features:

- A warning dialog box is displayed when you enter or leave a secure site. (A secure site is one that uses encryption and other features to ensure that the data you send can't be read by a third party.)

- A lock icon appears in the status bar (see Figure 21.3).

- If the site uses Netscape's Secure Sockets Layer (which implements RSA encryption, among other things), the URL protocol is displayed as https—Secure Hypertext Transport Protocol (again, see Figure 21.3).

The next two sections discuss the long list of Internet Explorer features that deal with incoming security.

Working with Internet Explorer's Security Zones

When implementing security for Internet Explorer 4, Microsoft realized that different sites have different security needs. For example, it makes sense to have fairly stringent secu-

Remember
If you don't see this dialog box when you connect, make sure that Windows 98 is set up to perform the security check. Open the Control Panel's Internet icon and display the Connection tab. If you're running Internet Explorer 4, you also need to click Settings. Check to see if the Perform system security check before dialing option is activated.

rity for Internet sites, but you can probably scale the security back a bit when browsing pages on your corporate intranet.

To handle these different types of sites, Internet Explorer 4 defines various *security zones*, and you can customize the secu-

Figure 21.3
When you access a secure page, Internet Explorer displays a lock icon in the status bar and changes the protocol to *https*.

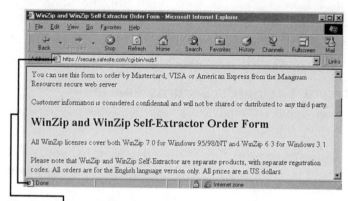

Shortcut
Another way to get to the Security tab is to double-click the security zone shown in the Internet Explorer status bar.

The protocol and the lock icon indicate a secure site.

rity requirements for each zone. The current zone is displayed in the status bar (refer to Figure 21.3).

To work with these zones, either select View, Internet Options in Internet Explorer, or open the Control Panel's Internet icon. In the Internet Properties dialog box that

Figure 21.4
Use the Security tab to set up security zones and customize the security options for each zone.

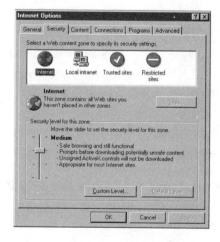

appears, select the Security tab, shown in Figure 21.4. (Note that this is the version of this tab that comes with Internet Explorer 5.)

The following list contains the four types of zones available:

Internet: Web sites that aren't in any of the other three zones. The default secuasdfkrity level is Medium.

Local intranet: Web pages on your computer and your network (intranet). The default security level is Medium-low (it's just Medium in Internet Explorer 4).

Trusted sites: Web sites that implement secure pages and that you're sure have safe content. The default security level is Low.

Restricted sites: Web sites that don't implement secure pages or that you don't trust, for whatever reason. The default security level is High.

Adding and Removing Zone Sites

Three of these zones—Local intranet, Trusted sites, and Restricted sites—enable you to add sites. To do this, select the zone you want to work with and then click Add Sites.

If you selected the Local intranet zone, you'll see a dialog box with three check boxes:

Include all local (intranet) sites not listed in other zones: When activated, this option includes all intranet sites in the zone. If you add specific intranet sites to other zones, those sites aren't included in this zone.

Include all sites that bypass the proxy server: When this check box is activated, sites that you've set up to bypass your proxy server are included in this zone.

Include all network paths (UNCs): When this check box is activated, all network paths that use the Universal Naming Convention are included in this zone.

If you want to add sites, click Advanced. This displays a dialog box like the one shown in Figure 21.5 that appears for the Trusted sites zone.

Remember
Some sites—particularly online banks—allow you to access their secure pages only if you have a browser that implements 128-bit encryption. This is approximately 300 trillion trillion times more secure than the 40-bit encryption that comes with Windows 98's version of Internet Explorer. To upgrade, head to http://www.microsoft.com/windows/ie/download/128bit.htm on Microsoft's site. Note, however, that's it's illegal to export 128-bit encryption outside the U.S. and

Figure 21.5
Use this dialog
box to add sites
to a zone.

Remember
The Universal
Naming
Convention is a
standard format
used with network
addresses. They
usually take
the form
\\server\resource,
where *server* is
the name of the
network server
and *resource* is
the name of a
shared network
resource.

Two of these dialog boxes (Local intranet zone and Trusted sites zone) have a `Require server verification (https:) for all sites in this zone` check box. If you activate this option, then each site address you enter must begin with the `https` protocol.

To add a site, enter the address in the `Add this Web site to the zone` text box, and then click Add. Note, too, that you can include an asterisk as a wildcard character, as shown in Figure 21.5. For example, the address `http://*.microsoft.com` adds every `microsoft.com` domain, including `www.microsoft.com`, `support.microsoft.com`, `windowsupdate.microsoft.com`, and so on.

To remove a site, highlight it and then click Remove.

Changing a Zone's Security Level

To change the security level for a zone, select it in the list and then use the slider to set the level. (With Internet Explorer 4, select one of the following options: High, Medium, Low, or

Figure 21.6
Use this dialog
box to set up cus-
tomized security
levels for the
selected zone.

Custom.) To set up your own security settings, click Custom Level. (With Internet Explorer 4, activate the Custom option, and then click the Settings button that becomes available.) This displays the Security Settings dialog box shown in Figure 21.6.

The dialog box provides you with a long list of possible security issues, and your job is to specify how you want Internet Explorer to handle each one. You usually have three choices:

Enable: Security is turned off. For example, if the issue is whether to run an ActiveX control, the control is run automatically.

Prompt: You're asked how you want to handle the issue. For example, whether you want to accept or reject an ActiveX control.

Disable: Security is turned on. For example, if the issue is whether to run an ActiveX control, the control is not run.

Let's take a quick look at the various security issues covered in this dialog box. I'll begin with the options in the ActiveX controls and plugins branch:

Download signed ActiveX controls: Determines whether ActiveX controls that have a valid security signature can be downloaded.

Download unsigned ActiveX controls: Determines whether ActiveX controls that don't have a valid security signature can be downloaded.

Initialize and script ActiveX controls not marked as safe: Determines whether Web page scripts can interact with ActiveX controls that don't have a digital signature that marks them as safe for scripting.

Run ActiveX controls and plugins: Determines whether ActiveX controls embedded in a Web page and browser plug-in modules required by Web page objects can be run.

Script ActiveX controls marked safe for scripting: Determines whether Web page scripts can interact with ActiveX controls that have a security certificate that marks

Remember
A *security certifi-cate* is a digital guarantee that a control comes from a trustwor-thy publisher.

them as safe for scripting.

The options in the Cookies branch determine whether Internet Explorer 5 accepts cookies. A cookie is a small text file that a remote site stores on your computer in the Windows\Cookies folder. Cookies are normally used to *preserve state*—that is, to remember selections you've made so that they can be referred to in other pages you visit. There are two settings:

Watch Out!
Some sites require cookies and won't work properly if you disable them. On the other hand, some sites use cookies only to track your movements within their site. In subsequent visits, the sites may use this data to display targeted advertising. Most reputable sites will warn you when cookies are required.

Allow cookies that are stored on your computer: Determines whether Internet Explorer 5 accepts stored cookies.

Allow per-session cookies (not stored): Determines whether Internet Explorer 5 accepts cookies that are only valid for the current browser session.

The Downloads branch has two settings:

File download: Determines whether file downloads are enabled.

Font download: Determines whether font downloads are enabled.

The Java permissions branch controls the permissions assigned to Java applets run within the zone. Java applets are executed on your computer, so they can potentially work with your local files and network resources, run programs, display dialog boxes (including the Open dialog box), access system information, print documents, and create temporary files. Select one of the following: Low safety, Medium safety, High safety, or Disable Java. Alternatively, you can define your own permissions by selecting Custom and then clicking the Java Custom Settings button that appears.

The Miscellaneous branch contains a grab bag of security settings:

Access data sources across domains: This is the fix for the "Cross-Frame Navigation" vulnerability I described earlier. Leave this option disabled to ensure that this problem never affects you.

Drag and drop or copy and paste files: Determines whether Web page files (such as graphics) can be dragged or copied from the Web page and then dropped or pasted locally.

Installation of desktop items: Determines whether Active Desktop items can be installed.

Launching applications and files in an IFRAME: Determines whether programs can be run and files can be downloaded from a floating frame window (defined by the <IFRAME> tag in HTML).

Navigate sub-frames across different domains: This is the fix for the "Frame Spoof" vulnerability I described earlier. To ensure that you don't fall victim to this spoof, disable this option.

Software channel permissions: Determines whether an Active Channel can download and install software. Choose one of Low safety (the software is downloaded and installed automatically), Medium safety (the software is downloaded automatically and then you're prompted to launch the installation), and High safety (you're prompted to launch the download and the installation).

Submit nonencrypted form data: Determines whether forms can be submitted from sites that don't use SSL (that is, that don't encrypt the form data).

Userdata persistence: Determines whether Internet Explorer 5 allows persisted userData structures in a Web page. The userData structure enables a Web developer to maintain (persist) data about users across sessions (similar to what a cookie does).

The Scripting branch contains three options:

Active scripting: Determines whether Web page scripts are allowed to run.

Allow paste operations via script: Determines whether Internet Explorer 5 allows Web page scripts to paste data

Inside Scoop
Setting the Submit non-encrypted form data option to Prompt (this is the default for Medium security) will thwart the Untrusted Scripted Paste Issue, discussed earlier. If you're prompted about submitted unencrypted data, but there's no form in sight, then you know a malicious site is trying to submit data secretly.

into Explorer controls.

Scripting of Java applets: Determines whether Web page scripts can interact with Java applets.

The User Authentication branch determines how HTTP authentication is implemented for sites that require a username and password:

Automatic logon only in Intranet zone: On your intranet only, uses Windows NT Challenge/Response to supply the server with your current username and password.

Anonymous logon: You're logged in as a Guest on the server.

Prompt for user name and password: Displays a dialog box asking you for your username and password.

Automatic logon with current username and password: Uses Windows NT Challenge/Response to supply the server with your current username and password.

More Security Settings

While you have the Internet Properties dialog box onscreen, display the Advanced tab and scroll down to the Security branch. You'll find the following settings:

Check for publisher's certificate revocation (in Internet Explorer 4, this option is named Check for certificate revocation): If you enable this option, Internet Explorer examines a site's digital security certificates to see if they have been revoked.

Check for server certificate revocation (requires restart): When activated, this option also checks the security certificate for the Web page's server.

Do not save encrypted pages to disk: If you enable this option, Internet Explorer will not store encrypted files in the Temporary Internet Files folder.

Empty Temporary Internet Files folder when browser is closed (in Internet Explorer 4, this option is named Delete saved pages when browser closed): If you enable

Watch Out!
Most large sites use some form of JavaScript on their pages. Therefore, for the best surfing experience, don't disable the Active scripting option.

this option, Internet Explorer will remove all files from the `Temporary Internet Files` folder when you exit the program.

Enable Profile Assistant: Toggles the Profile Assistant on and off. Your *profile* is just an extra entry in the Windows Address Book that stores your personal information (name, address, and so on). The Profile Assistant can work with some Web sites to share this data, which prevents you from having to enter this data by hand. To edit your profile, see the options in the Content tab's Personal information group.

Use Fortezza: When this option is activated, Internet Explorer 5 can set up a secure connection to any Fortezza-Web site. (Fortezza is the U.S. Department of Defense cryptographic security standard.)

Use PCT 1.0: Toggles support for Microsoft's Private Communications Technology security protocol on and off. PCT is an upgrade to SSL.

Use SSL 2.0: Toggles support for the Secure Sockets Layer Level 2 security protocol on and off. This version of SSL is currently the Web's standard security protocol.

Use SSL 3.0: Toggles support for SSL Level 3 on and off. SSL 3.0 is more secure than SSL 2.0 (it can authenticate both the client and the server), but isn't currently as popular as SSL 2.0.

Use TLS 1.0: Toggles support for Transport Layer Security on and off. This is a relatively new protocol, so few Web sites implement it.

Warn about invalid site certificates: When activated, this option tells Internet Explorer to display a warning dialog box if a site is using an invalid digital security certificate.

Warn if changing between secure and not secure mode: When activated, this option tells Internet Explorer to display a warning dialog box whenever you enter and leave a secure site.

Warn if submitted form is being redirected: When activated, this option tells Internet Explorer to display a warning dialog box if a form submission is going to be sent to a site other than the one hosting the form.

Using a Digital ID for Secure Email

When you connect to a Web site, your browser sets up a direct connection—called a *channel*—between your machine and the Web server. Because the channel is a direct link, it's relatively easy to implement security because all you have to do is secure the channel, which is what PCT and SSL do.

However, email security is entirely different and much more difficult to set up. The problem is that email messages don't have a direct link to an SMTP email server. Instead, they must usually "hop" from server to server until the final destination is reached. Combine this with the open and well-documented email standards used on the Internet, and you end up with three email security issues:

The privacy issue: Because messages often pass through other systems and can even end up on a remote system's hard disk, it isn't that hard for someone with the requisite know-how and access to the remote system to read a message.

The tampering issue: Because a user can read a message passing through a remote server, it will come as no surprise that he can also change the message text.

The authenticity issue: With the Internet email standards an open book, it isn't difficult for a savvy user to forge or *spoof* an email address.

To solve these issues, the Internet's gurus came up with the idea of *encryption*. When you encrypt a message, a complex mathematical formula scrambles the message content to make it unreadable. In particular, a *key value* is incorporated into the encryption formula. To unscramble the message, the recipient feeds the key into the decryption formula.

This *single-key encryption* works, but its major drawback is that the sender and the recipient must both have the same key. *Public-key encryption* overcomes that limitation by using two related keys: a *public key* and a *private key*. The public key is available to everyone, either by sending it to them directly or through an online key database. The private key is secret and is stored on the user's computer.

Here's how public-key cryptography resolves the issues discussed earlier:

Resolving the privacy issue: When you send a message, you obtain the recipient's public key and use it to encrypt the message. The encrypted message can now be decrypted only by using the recipient's private key, thus assuring privacy.

Resolving the tampering issue: An encrypted message can still be tampered with, but only randomly because the content of the message can't be seen. This thwarts the most important skill used by tamperers: making the tampered message look legitimate.

Resolving the authenticity issue: When you send a message, you use your private key to digitally sign the message. The recipient can then use your public key to examine the digital signature to ensure the message came from you.

If there's a problem with public-key encryption, it is that the recipient of a message must obtain the sender's public key from an online database. (The sender can't just send the public key because the recipient would have no way to prove that the key came from the sender.) Therefore, to make all of this more convenient, a *digital ID* is used. This is a digital certificate that states the sender's public key has been authenticated by trusted certifying authority. The sender can then include her public key in her outgoing messages.

Setting Up an Email Account with a Digital ID

To send secure messages using Outlook Express, you first have to obtain a digital ID. Here are the steps to follow:

1. In Outlook Express, select Tools, Options to display the

Inside Scoop
As a further anti-tampering measure, the secure email system—it's called S/MIME or Secure Multipurpose Internet Mail Extension—uses an algorithm that creates a unique digest of the message. If the digest created by the recipient's mail client doesn't match the original digest, then the message has been tampered with.

Options dialog box.

2. Display the Security tab.

3. Click Get Digital ID. Internet Explorer loads and takes you to the Outlook Express digital ID page on the Web.

4. Click a link to the certifying authority (such as VeriSign) you want to use.

5. Follow the authority's instructions for obtaining a digital ID.

With your digital ID installed, the next step is to assign it to an email account:

1. In Outlook Express, select Tools, Accounts to get the Internet Accounts dialog box onscreen.

2. Use the Mail tab to highlight the account you want to work with and then click Properties. The account's property sheet appears.

3. Display the Security tab.

4. Activate the Use a digital ID when sending secure messages from check box, which also enables the Digital ID button.

5. Click the Digital ID button to display the Select Default Account Digital ID dialog box.

6. Use the Issuer: Subject list to click your digital ID, and then click OK. Your name appears in the Security tab.

7. Click OK.

Obtaining Another Person's Public Key

Before you can send an encrypted message to another person, you must obtain his or her public key. How you do this depends on whether you have a digitally signed message from that person.

If you do have a digitally signed message, follow these steps:

1. Open the message, as described later in this chapter in the "Receiving a Secure Message" section.

Inside Scoop
To make a backup copy of your digital ID, open Internet Explorer and select View, Internet Options. Display the Content tab and click Personal to see a list of your installed certificates. Click your digital ID and then click Export.

2. Select File, Properties. Outlook Express opens the property sheet for the message.

3. Display the Security tab.

4. Click the Add Digital ID to Address Book button. Outlook Express opens the property sheet for the new contact. The sender's digital ID appears in the Digital IDs tab.

5. If necessary, use the property sheet to enter other information about the sender.

6. Click OK to get back to the message property sheet.

7. Click OK.

Watch Out!
Outlook Express will often fail to enter the digital ID correctly if the sender is already set up as a contact in the Address Book. For best results, delete the existing contact and then add the digital ID.

If you don't have a digitally signed message for the person you want to work with, you have to visit a certifying authority's Web site and find the person's digital ID. For example, you can go to the VeriSign site (`http://www.verisign.com/`) to search for a digital ID and then download it to your computer. After that's done, follow these steps:

1. Open the Windows Address Book.

2. Open the person's contact info, or create a new contact.

3. Enter one or more email addresses, and fill in the other data as necessary.

4. Display the Digital IDs tab.

5. In the Select an e-mail address list, select the address that corresponds with the digital ID you downloaded.

6. Click the Import button to display the Select digital ID file to import dialog box.

7. Find and highlight the downloaded digital ID file, and then click Open.

8. Click OK.

Sending a Secure Message

After your digital ID is installed, you can start sending out secure email messages. You have two options:

- Digitally sign a message to prove that you're the sender. With the New Message window open, either activate the Tools, Digitally Sign command, or press the Digitally Sign Message toolbar button. A small, red "seal" icon appears to the right of the Subject field. When you send the message, Outlook Express displays a dialog box letting you know the message was signed using your private key.

- Encrypt a message to avoid snooping and tampering. In the New Message window, either activate the Tools, Encrypt command, or press the Encrypt Message toolbar button. A blue lock icon appears to the right of the Subject field.

Receiving a Secure Message

The technology and mathematics underlying the digital ID are complex, but there's nothing complex about handling incoming secure messages. Outlook Express handles everything behind the scenes, including the authentication of the sender (if the message was digitally signed) and the decryption of the message (if the message was encrypted). For the latter, a dialog box tells you that your private key has been used to decrypt the message.

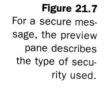

Figure 21.7
For a secure message, the preview pane describes the type of security used.

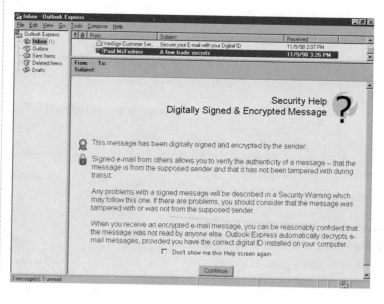

As you can see in Figure 21.7, the preview pane gives you a few visual indications that you're dealing with a secure message:

- The message text doesn't appear in the preview pane.

- The preview pane title is Security Help and the subtitle tells you the type of security used: Digitally Signed or Encrypted.

- The preview pane text describes the security used in the message.

To read the message, click the Continue button at the bottom. (If you'd rather not see this security preview in the future, activate the Don't show me this Help screen again check box.)

Essential Information

- If you receive an email message that either warns you of a message that can run a virus or asks you to forward the message to a number of recipients, delete the message for it is worthless spam.

- Microsoft has posted a number of security patches for both Internet Explorer and Outlook Express, all of which can be downloaded and installed from the Windows Update

Undocumented
If you change your mind and decide you prefer to see the preview screen, you have to edit the Registry. Open the Registry Editor and head for the key named HKEY_CURRENT_ USER\Software\ Microsoft\ Outlook Express\ Dont Show Dialogs. Open the Digital Signature Help setting and change its value to 0.

High-Powered
Hardware Techniques

PART VI

GET THE SCOOP ON...
Understanding device drivers, IRQ lines, I/O ports,
DMA channels, and other hardware settings ▪ Making
Plug and Play work properly ▪ Installing device drivers
▪ Using the Signature Verification Tool ▪ Using Device
Manager

Taking the Mystery Out of Hardware

Chapter 22

LTHOUGH I'VE BEEN A PROGRAMMER for nearly 25 years (ouch!), I've always enjoyed working with hardware. When writing a book such as this, for example, I relish the idea of prying open the cases of my test computers to see how Windows 98 reacts to different configurations: internal modems, SCSI controllers, network interface cards, graphics adapters, memory chips, and so on. Until recently, however, the part I truly disliked about these "machine-ations" was the endless tweaking and configuring required to get the devices to cooperate with each other. Now, thanks to Plug and Play and other automatic hardware configuration technologies, all that fiddling is a thing of the past for me.

In this chapter, my goal isn't so much to get you to "relish" the idea of working with hardware. (That would be asking a lot, I know.) Instead, I aim only to remove some of the mystery surrounding hardware, and to help you configure your own system. If you have an older machine or if you have legacy devices, you'll learn how to avoid the conflicts that can cause hardware to fail. If you have a newer system and Plug and Play devices, you'll see how easy Windows 98 makes it to create a problem-free setup.

Crucial Hardware Concepts

That hardware seems a mysterious and arcane subject is probably due to the fact that the underlying concepts are, at first blush, confusing and obscure. However, the good news is that these concepts are not unexplainable. The next few sections take you through some hardware basics that will serve you well not only through the rest of this chapter, but also in the next three chapters where I discuss specific devices.

IRQ Lines, I/O Ports, and Other Device Settings

One of Windows 98's core responsibilities is to coordinate the interaction of hardware and software. In general, that means sending signals from software to hardware (such as printing instructions) and relaying signals from hardware to software (such as displaying characters in response to keystrokes). All these signals going back and forth need some sort of communications channels, and most devices use one or more of the following: interrupt request lines, input/output ports, Direct Memory Access channels, and memory addresses.

"
Windows 98 has added support for a wide range of new devices. In fact, it is likely that more effort was devoted to increased hardware support than to any other area in Windows 98.
—Keith Pleas, PC Magazine
"

Interrupt Request Lines

An *interrupt request line* (IRQ) is a wire built into the computer's motherboard or a device slot. It's used by the processor and a device to send signals to each other. In other words, the device uses the wire to send a "request" to the processor to "interrupt" whatever the latter is doing (and vice versa).

For example, recall from Chapter 17, "Getting the Most Out of Your Modem," that most serial ports incorporate a special chip called a UART. Its job is to convert bits coming in from the modem into bytes that can be processed by the computer. (The UART also converts the computer's outgoing bytes into serial bits for transmission via the modem across the phone line.) Most UARTs use special buffers to hold these incoming bytes. When a specified number of those buffers is full, the UART uses an IRQ line to send a signal to the processor that there are bytes to take care of. The processor then goes through the following (greatly simplified) steps:

See Also...
"Understanding Modem Communications," p. 388

1. The processor saves its current state in a special memory area called a *stack.*

2. The processor accesses the *interrupt vector table,* which contains a list of memory locations that correspond to each IRQ line. In particular, the processor uses the table to determine the memory location of the device driver that works with whatever device initiated the interrupt request.

3. The processor gets the device driver to handle the interrupt request.

4. The original contents of the processor are restored off the stack and the processor continues what it was doing prior to the interrupt.

The crucial step here is when the processor uses the interrupt vector table to look up the required device driver. This works because, in a typical system, a single IRQ line is assigned to each device that requires one. Table 22.1 lists the IRQ line assignments in a typical PC.

TABLE 22.1: IRQ LINE ASSIGNMENTS IN A TYPICAL PC

IRQ Line	Device
0	System timer
1	Keyboard
2	Programmable interrupt controller
3	Serial port 2 (COM2)
4	Serial port 1 (COM1)
5	Available, sound card, or parallel port 2 (LPT2)
6	Floppy disk controller
7	Parallel port 1 (LPT1)
8	Real-time clock
9	Available
10	Available
11	Available
12	Available or motherboard mouse port
13	Math coprocessor
14	Primary IDE controller
15	Available or secondary IDE controller

Inside Scoop
A stack is a memory location that stores data in a last-in, first-out (LIFO) format. The STACKS parameter in CONFIG.SYS determines the size of the stack used by the processor. (Note, however, that Windows 98 manages this value automatically in IO.SYS and therefore it need not be adjusted manually.)

Inside Scoop
The *programmable interrupt controller* on IRQ 2 is a second IRQ controller chip. The main IRQ controller chip takes care of IRQ lines 0 through 7, which were all that were available in the original IBM PC. For the IBM AT, a second IRQ controller chip was added to bring the total number of IRQ lines to 16 (8 through 15). The main chip has IRQ 2 available, so that line is used to coordinate the two chips.

As you can see, as many as six and as few as three IRQ lines are available, depending on your system configuration. Therein lies the rub because so many other devices require IRQ lines: graphics adapters, network interface cards, SCSI controllers, PC cards, infrared ports, and more. The IRQ line number used by a device is configured usually either by adjusting a jumper or DIP switch, or by running a setup program. (This assumes the device is not Plug and Play-compatible.)

All of this leads to three possible IRQ problems:

- Two devices configured to use the same IRQ line

- An interrupt vector table that doesn't correctly match an IRQ line with the IRQ line used by a device

- No available IRQ lines for a new device

These are among the most common PC hardware headaches and are the source of many system lock-ups and bizarre device behavior. As you'll see in many places throughout the rest of this chapter, Windows 98 not only gives you tools to properly configure IRQs, but it also supports a number of new technologies that aim to eliminate IRQ conflicts. Perhaps the most important of these is *IRQ steering*. This technology enables Windows 98 to manage some of the available IRQ lines to enable multiple devices to share a single IRQ line. This lets you install more devices than you have IRQ lines.

Input/Output Ports

An *Input/Output port* (or I/O port) is a small block of memory (typically 8 bytes, 16 bytes, or 32 bytes) that acts as a communications channel between a device and the processor or a device driver. Each I/O port address is expressed as a range of hexadecimal numbers. For example, the first I/O port on most systems is used by the Direct Memory Access controller, and its address is the 16-byte range 0000–000F.

Most devices "listen in on" (or *poll*) their I/O port looking for new data, and then process that data when it's found. The processor, too, will poll the used I/O ports looking for incoming data from a device. For a high-speed device such as a SCSI controller, IRQ lines and I/O ports are used together to avoid the inherent inefficiency of polling. Let's see how things work if the processor needs some data from a SCSI hard disk:

1. The processor places the initial location of the data into the SCSI controller's I/O port.

2. The processor sends an interrupt request to the SCSI controller to let it know that data is waiting for it in the I/O port.

3. The SCSI controller accesses the I/O port and gets the location.

4. The SCSI controller finds the required data and then places it inside the I/O port.

5. The SCSI controller sends an interrupt request to the processor.

6. The processor retrieves the data from the I/O port.

7. Steps 1–6 are repeated as necessary to get all the required data.

Almost all devices use an I/O port, but there are 65,536 bytes of memory available for these ports, so there is no danger of ever running out of ports. As with IRQ lines, however, an I/O port conflict where two devices are configured to use the same I/O port can lead to problems.

Direct Memory Access Channels

In the preceding section, you saw how the processor and a device pass data back and forth by using an I/O port. However, if there is a large amount of data to exchange, the relatively tiny size of the I/O port forces the processor and the device to interact frequently, thus slowing system performance. Some devices overcome this by using a *Direct Memory Access channel* (DMA channel). This is a connection maintained by a DMA controller chip that enables a device to transfer data directly to and from memory. The processor tells the DMA controller chip what device to work with and what data is needed. The DMA controller chip then uses the channel to perform the complete data transfer without involving the processor.

Like IRQ lines, modern computers come with only a limited number of DMA channels, as outlined in Table 22.2.

TABLE 22.2: DMA CHANNEL ASSIGNMENTS IN A TYPICAL PC

DMA Channel	Device
0	Available
1	Available
2	Floppy disk controller
3	Available
4	DMA controller chip
5	Available
6	Available
7	Available

Some of the available channels are usually taken up by devices such as a sound card, an ISA SCSI controller, or an ECP printer port. DMA channel conflicts can cause problems, but it's a rare machine that uses up all eight available channels.

Remember
PCI systems also implement a technique that's similar to DMA: *bus mastering*. In this case, the processor delegates I/O control over the PCI bus to the PCI controller. (That is, the PCI controller becomes the "master" of the bus.) This enables the PCI controller to work directly with I/O devices (such as a PCI SCSI controller).

Memory Addresses

The final medium for device communication is *system memory*, including the 384KB of upper memory that resides between conventional memory (up to 640KB) and extended memory (1MB and beyond). This memory is used by a variety of devices for a variety of uses:

- Graphics adapter video RAM—the pixel values that appear on your monitor

- Graphics adapter BIOS code

- BIOS code for other adapters (such as a PCI SCSI adapter)

- Motherboard BIOS code

Again, no two devices can use the same memory block.

Understanding Device Drivers

A *device driver* is a small software program that acts as a kind of digital equivalent to the proverbial one-trick pony: all it does is act as a go-between for a device and other programs (including Windows). The device driver is intimately "familiar" with the instructions and code required to make a device perform a specific task. When a program needs the device to perform that task, it simply tells the device driver what needs to be done and the driver handles everything from there.

Other than obtaining and installing the correct driver for a device (see "Installing Device Drivers," later in this chapter), the most important concept to bear in mind is the difference between real mode device drivers and virtual device drivers:

- Real-mode drivers are 16-bit, so they're generally slower than the 32-bit virtual device drivers.

- Real-mode drivers are loaded via either Config.sys or Autoexec.bat, so they slow down system startup. Virtual device drivers are loaded via the Virtual Memory Manager.

- Real-mode drivers are loaded into either conventional memory or upper memory blocks, which reduces available memory for DOS programs. Virtual device drivers are loaded in extended memory.

- To use a real-mode driver, Windows 98 has to switch from its native protected mode to real mode, which slows performance. Virtual device drivers run in protected mode, so no context switch is required.

- The processor offers no built-in protection for real-mode operations, so a crashed real-mode driver can lock up the system. Virtual device drivers can take advantage of the processor's protected-mode security and so are inherently more robust.

Therefore, you should try wherever possible to rid your system of real-mode drivers. Windows 98 has virtual drivers for most, if not all, the components that formerly required real-mode drivers, including SCSI controllers, CD-ROM drivers, network devices, MSCDEX.EXE, SHARE.EXE, SmartDrive, and DriveSpace.

> 66
> Windows 98 includes hundreds of new printer, modem, and other hardware drivers, making hardware installation and setup more efficient than ever.
> —*From the* "Getting Started"
> 99

Shortcut
The easiest way to avoid loading real-mode device drivers at startup is to rename your Config.sys and Autoexec.bat files (to, say, Config.old and Autoexec.old). Alternatively, open these files in a text editor and comment out the device driver lines by adding REM and a space to the beginning of each line.

One of the innovations introduced in Windows 95 was the *universal driver/mini-driver architecture* for device drivers. (This idea actually began with the printer support Windows 3.*x*, but it was extended to all device classes in Windows 95). There are two components:

Universal driver: This is a driver that contains all the code needed for any device in a particular class of devices to work with the appropriate subsystem of the operating system. For example, the universal printer driver enables any printer to interact with the Windows 98 printing subsystem.

Mini-driver: This is a smaller driver that contains the code required to implement the specific functionality of a particular device.

How to Make Plug and Play Work (Most of the Time)

As you could tell even from my simplified explanations of IRQ lines, I/O ports, DMA channels, and memory addresses given earlier, configuring a device to avoid conflicts is a tricky operation. This untenable situation existed for many years until three companies—Compaq, Intel, and Phoenix Technologies—decided to do something about it. The result was an industry standard called *Plug and Play* with a simple, yet very tantalizing, purpose: to define a system in which *all* device configuration occurred automatically and without any user intervention.

Plug and Play was introduced in 1995, and, despite all the promise (and all the hype), it immediately flopped. Why? Well, it wasn't because it was an imperfect standard, to be sure. No, Plug and Play got off to a bad start simply because it was just ahead of the technology curve and, therefore, ahead of its time. You see, for Plug and Play to work, it requires hardware and software (an operating system) that meet certain rigid restrictions. Back in 1995, the operating system existed (Windows 95), but the requisite hardware didn't exist in the mainstream. Most users had only *legacy devices* (as non-Plug-and-Play hardware is now called), so the full Plug-and-Play equation wasn't satisfied.

So just what *is* required for Plug and Play to work? Three things:

A Plug-and-Play BIOS: This BIOS adds a few extra steps to the Power-On Self Test code that runs at system startup. Specifically, the code enumerates all the Plug-and-Play-compliant devices installed on the system and interrogates each device to determine its resource requirements. The code then checks for and resolves conflicts automatically.

Windows 98 (or some other Plug-and-Play-compatible operating system): Windows 98's Configuration Manager component gathers all the data on the system's Plug and Play devices and stores everything in the Registry. (Configuration Manager either uses the data gleaned by the Plug and Play BIOS or, if no such BIOS is present, enumerates and configures the Plug and Play devices directly.) It also monitors the system to watch for *hot swapping*—Plug and Play devices added and removed while the system is running. In this case, Windows 98 will automatically reconfigure the system, reallocate resources, and alert running applications of the hardware change.

Plug-and-Play devices: These are the key to the entire Plug and Play exercise. If you don't use Plug-and-Play devices, neither a Plug and Play BIOS nor Windows 98 will be able to do much in the way of automatic configuration. When purchasing a device, always check to see if it's Plug-and-Play-compatible.

Installing Device Drivers

As I mentioned earlier, whatever device you install on your system, you must also install a device driver so that Windows 98 can work with the device. This isn't something you have to worry about if the device is Plug-and-Play-compatible. In this case, Windows 98 reacts in one of the following ways:

Remember
If you purchased your computer within the last couple of years, it will almost certainly have a Plug and Play BIOS. If you're not sure, check with your manufacturer. If you don't have the correct BIOS, your manufacturer should be able to supply you with either a new BIOS chip or a program that will upgrade the BIOS code.

Shortcut
The following devices are automatically Plug and Play-compatible: PCI devices, USB devices, and IEEE 1394 (FireWire) devices.

- If you *hot-swapped* a device such as a PC Card or a printer, Windows 98 will recognize the device immediately and install the driver for it. (You'll likely need to insert your Windows 98 CD at this point.)

- If you turned your computer off to install the device, Windows 98 will recognize it the next time you start the machine, and Windows 98 will install the appropriate driver.

Note, too, that if Windows 98 doesn't have a driver of its own, it may ask you to install a driver from the manufacturer's disk (or from a downloaded driver file).

The next couple of sections show you how to install a driver for legacy devices and for those few Plug and Play devices not immediately recognized by Windows 98.

Using Automatic Hardware Detection

Windows 98 has a Detection Manager component that checks ports, buses, SCSI controllers, and other hardware nooks for clues that a new device is present. The Detection Manager is usually pretty good at ferreting out new hardware. However, even if the Detection Manager fails to find a new device, you can always install the appropriate driver by hand. I'll discuss the latter in the next section. For now, here are the steps to follow to have Windows 98 check for new devices:

1. Open the Control Panel's Add New Hardware icon. This launches the Add New Hardware Wizard.

2. Click Next. The wizard lets you know that it will now look for Plug and Play devices.

3. Click Next. Windows 98 runs the Configuration Manager to check for Plug and Play devices. If it finds any, it will let you know and you may be asked to insert your Windows 98 CD to install a driver or two.

4. When the Plug and Play phase is complete, the wizard displays a dialog box with a list of the devices that were installed, if any. The wizard wonders whether your devices were installed:

Yes, I am finished installing devices: If Windows 98 found your new device, activate this option, click Next, and then click Finish to exit the Add New Hardware Wizard.

No, I want to install other devices: If Windows 98 didn't find your device, activate this option and click Next. The remaining steps assume you choose this option.

5. If you have any devices that have a problem, the wizard displays a list of those devices and offers two options:

   No, the device isn't in the list: If your device isn't in the list, activate this option and click Next.

   Yes, the device is in the list: If your device is listed, highlight it and click Next. In this case, the wizard will likely tell you that the device has a problem. Click Finish to display the device's property sheet, which will explain the problem and (probably) offer an Update Driver button.

6. The wizard now asks whether you want Windows 98 to search for new hardware:

   Yes (Recommended): Activate this option and click Next to have the Detection Manager scour your system for the new device. The remaining steps assume you choose this option.

   No, I want to select the hardware from a list: Activate this option and click Next to install a driver by hand (see the next section).

7. The wizard displays a dialog box that explains the detection process. Click Next. The wizard displays a Detection progress meter that shows you how much of the hardware detection is complete. Note that this process takes a few minutes.

8. When the detection phase is complete, the wizard lets you know whether it found any new devices. If it did, click the Details button to see a list of the installed devices. Click Finish.

Watch Out!
If the Detection progress meter doesn't change for several minutes, it's likely that the Detection Manager is stuck. Shut down your computer and leave it off for several seconds to give all your devices time to spin down and stop completely. Then turn your computer back on and try again. If the detection fails again, make sure you installed the hardware properly and that it's turned on (if applicable).

9. At this point, you may need to insert your Windows 98 CD or run through a configuration process for the new device.

10. If Windows 98 asks whether you want to restart your computer, click Yes.

Installing a Driver by Hand

As you saw in the preceding section, the Add New Hardware Wizard offers an option for installing a device driver by hand if Windows 98 couldn't find your device or doesn't have a driver for it. You can also opt to install the driver by hand if you have a manufacturer's disk or a downloaded file that includes the appropriate driver.

To get started, you usually have two choices:

- If the manufacturer's disk or downloaded file has a setup program, run that program to install the driver.

- Use the Add New Hardware Wizard, as described in the preceding section. When you get to step 6, activate the No, I want to select the hardware from a list option, and click Next.

If you choose the latter route, here are the steps to follow from here:

1. The Add New Hardware Wizard displays a list of various hardware classes. Use the Hardware Types list to highlight the appropriate class for your device, and then click Next.

2. Depending on the hardware class you selected, a new wizard may appear. (For example, if you chose the Modem class, the Install New Modem wizard appears.) In this case, follow the wizard's dialog boxes. Otherwise, the Select Device dialog box appears. Figure 22.1 shows the Select

Remember
Most large hardware manufacturers have an extensive collection of device drivers on their Web sites. In most cases, look for a link to the Technical Support area. You can also get drivers from the Windows Update Web site (click Product Updates and then click Device Drivers) and the Windows Hardware Compatibility List (http://www.microsoft.com/hwtest/hcl/). For the latter, search for your device and then look for a "Save" icon. Click that icon to see a list of downloadable drivers.

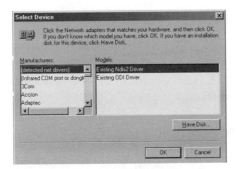

Figure 22.1
Use the Select
Device dialog box
to install a device
driver manually.

Device dialog box for network adapters.

3. If you have a manufacturer's disk or downloaded file, click Have Disk, enter the appropriate path and filename in the Install From Disk dialog box, and click OK.

4. Highlight your device. (In the default Select Device dialog box, first highlight the device's manufacturer in the Manufacturers list and then highlight the name of the device in the Models list.)

5. Click OK.

6. If prompted, insert your Windows 98 CD or run through a configuration process for the new device.

7. If Windows 98 asks whether you want to restart your computer, click Yes.

Working with the Signature Verification Tool

To ensure that device drivers work properly with Windows 98, Microsoft runs a Windows Hardware Quality Lab (WHQL), which has a Web site here:

```
http://www.microsoft.com/hwtest/
```

Vendors submit their devices to the WHQL for testing. If a device passes, the vendor gets the following benefits:

- A license to use the "Designed for Windows 98" logo on the device packaging

- A listing for the device in the Hardware Compatibility list

Watch Out!
Although Windows 98 was designed to work with a wide variety of hardware, you'll almost always have an easier installation if you purchase devices designed for Windows 98, or that meet the guidelines for the PC 98 or PC 99 standards (see `http://www.microsoft.com/hwdev/`). You should also check the Windows Hardware Compatibility List at `http://www.microsoft.com/hwtest/hcl/`.

- Distribution of the device's drivers via the Hardware Compatibility list

- A Microsoft digital signature certifying the driver meets the WHQL standards and has not been altered in any way since the testing

Most reputable manufacturers offer high-quality drivers. After all, if their drivers didn't work properly, people would simply stop buying their products. However, you can be sure you're getting a safe, high-quality, Windows 98-compatible driver if it has been digitally signed by Microsoft. How do you know? Well, if you download the driver from the Hardware Compatibility list or Windows Update, then you know automatically that you're installing a driver with a Microsoft digital signature. For all other drivers, you can set up Windows 98 to warn you of non-signed drivers, or to block their installation altogether, by following these steps:

1. In the System Policy Editor, select File, Open Registry.

2. Open the Local Computer icon.

3. Select Windows 98 System, Install Device Drivers, Digital Signature Check.

4. Select one of the following levels:

   Allow installation of all drivers: Select this level to disable the checking of digital signatures.

   Block installation of non-Microsoft signed drivers: Select this level to tell Windows 98 not to install any driver that doesn't come with a Microsoft digital signature.

   Warn installation of non-Microsoft signed drivers: Select this option to tell Windows 98 to warn you if you're about to install a driver that doesn't come with a Microsoft digital signature.

Undocumented
The level you choose is stored in the Registry in the HKEY_LOCAL_MACHINE\Software\Microsoft\Drive Signing key as the Policy DWORD value.

5. Click OK.

6. Select File, Save to put the option into effect.

What about drivers you've already installed? To see if they come with a Microsoft digital signature, you can use the new Signature Verification Tool to check your existing drivers. Here are the steps to run through:

1. To start the utility, use either of the following techniques:

    • Select Start, Run, type sigverif.exe, and click OK.

    • Select Start, Programs, Accessories, System Tools, System Information, and then select Tools, Signature Verification Tool.

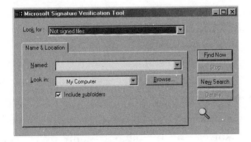

Figure 22.2
Use the Signature Verification Tool to check for installed drivers that don't have a Microsoft digital signature.

2. In the Microsoft Signature Verification Tool window that appears (see Figure 22.2), use the Look For list to select either Not Signed Files or Signed Files.

3. Use the Named text box to enter the filename of a specific driver or a filename specification. This is optional.

4. Use the Look In list to select the folder in which you want to check.

5. Click Find Now.

Using Automatic Skip Driver Agent to Bypass Troublesome Drivers

Windows 98 loads many virtual device drivers at startup. Many

Shortcut
If you don't restrict the name or location, the Signature Verification Tool will find many Windows 98 files that don't have a signature. For more useful results, use a specific filename or a folder that contains only a few files.

of these drivers, while still important for device functionality, are not considered critical to the operation of Windows 98. Critical drivers are those that, if they fail, will prevent Windows 98 from starting.

Windows 98 has a new feature called Automatic Skip Driver Agent that monitors the startup procedure and flags any device driver that causes Windows 98 to hang. Automatic Skip Driver Agent then disables that driver so that it gets bypassed at the next restart.

To see a list of the drivers that have been disabled (if any), run Automatic Skip Driver Agent by using either of the following methods:

- Select Start, Run, type `asd.exe`, and click OK.

- Select Start, Programs, Accessories, System Tools, System Information, and then select Tools, Automatic Skip Driver Agent.

If no critical failures have occurred on your machine, Automatic Skip Driver Agent displays a dialog box to let you know. Otherwise, the Automatic Skip Driver Agent window appears and displays a list of the drivers that failed to load. After you've solved the problem (usually by reinstalling the troublesome driver), use Automatic Skip Driver Agent to enable the disabled driver.

Getting Device Information

Undocumented
When Automatic Skip Driver Agent disables a driver, it records what it did in the text file Windows\Asd.log.

If you need data about the devices on your system—whether it's configuration information, device errors, or the drivers used by a device— Windows 98 offers a number of tools to get the job done. Here's a summary:

Device Manager: Organizes devices by hardware class. Displays device problems and driver information, and enables you to change drivers and resources (such as IRQ lines and I/O ports). Open the System icon in Control Panel (see the next section for a more detailed look at this tool).

System Information: Contains a Hardware Resources branch that details the resources used by devices, as well as a Components branch that lists the hardware installed in various categories. The items in the latter branch display driver details, associated Registry locations, and current driver problems. Also contains a History category that outlines the history of the system's device changes. See Chapter 15, "Crucial System Maintenance Skills."

See Also...
"The System Information Utility," p. 346

Hardware Diagnostic Tool: Displays data on each device's Registry key, allocated resources, and drivers using a color-coded system (see Figure 22.3). To start this utility, select Start, Run, type hwinfo.exe /ui, and click OK. The color codes used are as follows:

Green—Registry data

Pink—Driver file data

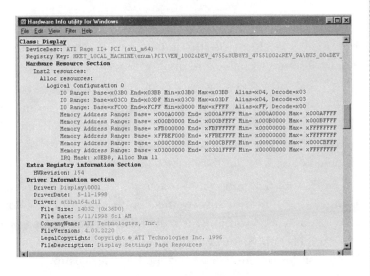

Figure 22.3
The Hardware Diagnostic Tool provides color-coded data about your installed devices.

Dark red—Configuration Manager (resource usage) data

Red—Device errors

Blue—Device warnings

Dealing with Device Manager

Of the three hardware information utilities listed in the preceding section, the most important is Device Manager because it not only provides comprehensive data about each device,

Figure 22.4
Device Manager
displays a list of
the hardware
classes installed
on your system.

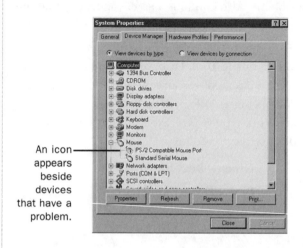

An icon
appears
beside
devices
that have a
problem.

Shortcut
You can also get
to Device
Manager by right-
clicking the desk-
top's My
Computer icon,
clicking
Properties, and
then displaying
the Device
Manager tab.

Undocumented
For a SCSI device
to be enumerated
properly at
startup, the
device must be
turned on. If you
forgot to turn on
a SCSI device,
you can let
Device Manager
know that it's
now available by
clicking Refresh.

but it also enables you to update device drivers, change resource settings, enable and disable devices, and more.

To view Device Manager, open the Control Panel's System icon and then display the Device Manager tab. As you can see in Figure 22.4, Device Manager displays a tree-like hierarchy of hardware classes. Opening a branch displays a list of the installed devices within that branch.

Note, too, that you can also activate the View Devices By Connection option to display the devices according to how they're connected within your system. If your computer has a Plug and Play BIOS, for example, you can use this option to see the list of devices enumerated by the BIOS at startup.

Below the list of devices, you see four command buttons:

Properties: Displays a property sheet for the highlighted device (see "Working with Device Properties," later in this chapter).

Refresh: Updates the Device Manager display.

Remove: Removes the highlighted device from the Device

Manager list. Use this button to tell Windows 98 when you're about to physically remove a legacy device from your system.

Print: Prints some or all of the Device Manager data. If you want to print only the data for a particular hardware class or device, select it before clicking this button. In the Print dialog box that appears, select System Summary (resource usage only), Selected Class Or Device (driver and resource usage for the highlighted hardware class or device), or All Devices And System Summary (driver and resource usage for all devices).

Device Manager is also useful as a troubleshooting tool. As you can see in Figure 22.4, Device Manager displays an icon beside the device name:

- A yellow icon with a black exclamation mark means the device has a problem.

- A white icon with a blue i means that a device's resources have been configured manually.

- A red X means the device is missing or disabled.

Highlight the device in question and then click Properties to see a description of the problem.

Viewing Devices by Resource

If your system isn't fully Plug and Play-compatible, you'll occasionally need to manipulate a device's IRQ lines, I/O ports, and other resources. To avoid conflicts with existing devices, it helps to get an overall view of the resources that are currently

Inside Scoop
The following Microsoft Knowledge Base article contains a description of the error codes used by Device Manager:
http://support.
microsoft.com/
support/kb/
articles/Q125/1/
74.asp.

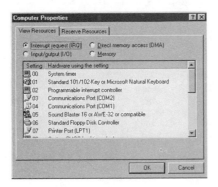

Figure 22.5
Use this dialog box to view devices by IRQ line, I/O port, DMA channel, and memory address.

See Also...
"Hot Docking and Hardware Profiles," p. 580

allocated on your machine. To do this in Device Manager, make sure My Computer is highlighted at the top of the Device Manager list, and then click Properties. Figure 22.5 shows the Computer Properties dialog box that appears. If a setting is missing in the list, it means that resource is available. The default view is Interrupt Request (IRQ). You can also view the devices by Input/Output (I/O), Direct Memory Access (DMA), and Memory.

Working with Device Properties

Each device on your system has a number of properties that you can view and, in some cases, manipulate. To view the property sheet for a device, highlight it and then click Properties. (You can also double-click the device.) The dialog box that appears will have two or more of the following tabs:

Watch Out!
Make sure you don't select a resource that conflicts with an existing device. Keep your eye on the Conflicting Device List area to watch for conflicts.

General: Gives you basic data about the device, such as the manufacturer's name and the hardware version. The Device Status group tells you whether the device is working properly or, if it's not, what the problem is. The check boxes in the Device Usage group are used for enabling and disabling devices in a hardware profile. (See Chapter 25, "The Ins and Outs of Windows 98's Notebook Features.")

Settings: Displays one or more controls for working with device settings.

Driver: Click Driver File Details to see a list of the driver files used by the device. To change the driver, click Update Driver.

Resources: Displays a list of the resources used by the

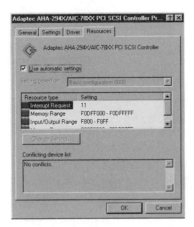

Figure 22.6
Use the
Resources tab to
view and change
a device's
resources.

device, as shown in Figure 22.6. To change a resource, deactivate the Use Automatic Settings check box and then use either of the following techniques:

- Select a different configuration from the Setting Based On list.

- Highlight the setting you want to change and then click Change Setting.

Essential Information

- To enable communication between a device and the processor or a device driver, four hardware features are used: interrupt request (IRQ) lines, input/output (I/O) ports, Direct Memory Access (DMA) channels, and memory addresses.

- A device driver is a small software program that implements the code necessary for Windows 98 to operate a device.

- For Plug and Play to work properly, your system must have a Plug and Play BIOS, Windows 98 (or some other Plug-and-Play-compatible operating system), and Plug-and-Play-compatible devices.

- Run the Control Panel's Add New Hardware icon to install

GET THE SCOOP ON...
Mouse customizations ▪ Working with Microsoft's
IntelliPoint software ▪ Setting keyboard options ▪
Working with keyboard layouts and languages ▪
Typing with extended characters ▪ Setting up joy-
sticks and other game controllers

Setting Up and Customizing Input Devices

Chapter 23

THE COMPUTER PRESS HAS BEEN abuzz of late with reviews of several new voice recognition packages. The promise of these packages is the ability to control Windows and software applications using only voice commands. This is something that computer folk have been anxiously awaiting since the days of the original *Star Trek* TV show. Unfortunately, the waiting continues because even though these newfangled voice recognition packages are the best yet produced, they're still too inaccurate and cumbersome for regular use.

Voice recognition will come (in fact, Microsoft has hinted that it will someday be built into Windows), but until then we're stuck with the same old, same old: the mouse, keyboard, and joystick. To help you get the most out of these devices, this chapter shows you how to configure them to your liking.

Working with Your Mouse

The mouse was invented at Xerox PARC in the seventies. However, like so many clever inventions from that bastion of the bright, no commercial applications of the then radical input device were ever created. It was left to Apple and its Macintosh computer and, later on, the Windows family, to bring the product into the mainstream and turn us all into mouse potatoes.

The mouse is now such an ubiquitous part of the computing landscape that most users take it for granted and barely notice that it's there. However, the mouse has a few properties you can manipulate, and a slight tweak here and there can do wonders for your productivity. This section examines those properties.

Customizing the Mouse

The standard Windows 98 mouse driver offers several customization options, including the ability to switch the mouse buttons, control both the double-click and pointer speeds, specify custom pointers, and much more. All of these options are available in the Mouse Properties dialog box, shown in Figure 23.1. You display this dialog box by opening the Control Panel's Mouse icon. (Note, however, that if you have Microsoft's IntelliPoint software installed, your Mouse Properties dialog box will have a layout different from the one shown in Figure 23.1. See "Working with the IntelliPoint Settings," later in this chapter.)

Exchanging the Left and Right Mouse Buttons

By default, Windows 98 sets up the mouse for right-handers:

- You left-click to select an object, left-double-click to launch an object (I'm assuming here that Web integration is off), and left-drag to move or copy an object.

Figure 23.1
Use the Mouse Properties dialog box to customize the operation of your mouse.

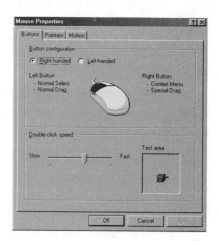

- You right-click to open an object's shortcut menu, and right-drag an object to open a special drag-and-drop shortcut menu when you drop the object.

These techniques are cumbersome for left-handers. For example, clicking and double-clicking must be done with the middle finger of the left hand instead of the more natural index finger. To correct this, switch the mouse buttons by activating the Left-handed option in the Buttons tab.

Adjusting the Double-Click Speed

The *double-click speed* is a time value that enables Windows 98 to differentiate between a double-click and two consecutive single-clicks. The default value is about half a second (452 milliseconds, to be precise):

- If two mouse clicks occur within that timeframe, Windows 98 interprets them as a double-click.

- If the second click comes after that much time has elapsed, Windows 98 interprets the two clicks as separate single-clicks.

You can adjust the double-click speed by dragging the slider in the Double-click speed group:

- If your reflexes aren't what they used to be, drag the slider toward the Slow end of the scale. This increases the time value so that Windows 98 will be more likely to catch your double-clicks.

- If you have quick reflexes, you may find that Windows 98 is often interpreting two quick single-clicks as a double-click (for example, when you try to single-click a filename twice in order to rename the file). In this case, drag the slider toward the Fast end of the scale to reduce the double-click threshold time.

Changing the Mouse Pointers

Windows 98 uses the mouse pointer to offer visual clues about potential mouse actions:

Undocumented
The slider value is stored in the Registry in the HKEY_CURENT_USER\ Control Panel\ Mouse key. The DoubleClickSpeed setting stores the current value, in milliseconds. The minimum value is 100 and the maximum value is 900.

- The standard arrow means you can click something to select it.

- A vertical bar appears when you're working with text and it means you can click to position the insertion point cursor, or drag to select text.

- A two-headed arrow appears on a window border or split bar and it means you can drag the border or bar to resize the window or pane.

- A hand with a pointing finger appears over a Web page link (or a filename or icon if Web integration is turned on) and it means you can launch the link by clicking it.

- When you drag an object, the universal "not" symbol (a circle with a diagonal line through it) appears over areas where you can't drop the object.

- An hourglass icon appears when Windows is busy.

You can change the look of the standard Windows 98 pointers by displaying the Pointers tab in the Mouse Properties dialog box and using any of the following techniques:

To change all the pointers: Select a pointer scheme from the Scheme drop-down list.

To change individual pointers: In the list of pointers, click the pointer you want to work with, click Browse, and then select a cursor file using the Browse dialog box. (Assuming they're installed, you'll find the Windows 98 cursor files in the Windows\Cursors folder.)

To create a custom pointer scheme: Select the individual pointers you want to use and then click Save As.

Adjusting the Mouse Pointer Speed

If you display the Motion tab of the Mouse Properties dialog box, you'll see a Pointer speed slider. This control doesn't so much set the speed of the pointer as the *acceleration rate* of the pointer. There are three general properties of this control to keep in mind:

- No matter what setting you choose, if you move the mouse slowly, the pointer moves slowly.

- If you move the slider all the way to the left (Slow) end, the pointer moves slowly no matter how fast you move the mouse.

- If you move the slider all the way to the right (Fast) end, the more quickly you move the mouse, the faster the pointer moves.

To understand how this works, you have to turn to the Registry's HKEY_CURRENT_USER\Control Panel\Mouse key. Here you'll find three settings:

MouseSpeed: This value determines the acceleration rate. The possible values are 0 (no acceleration), 1 (the acceleration is twice the normal speed), or 2 (the acceleration is four times the normal speed).

MouseThreshold1: This is a pixel value that determines when the double mouse speed kicks in. The default value is 4. This means that if you move the mouse more than 4 pixels between mouse interrupts, the mouse speed is doubled (assuming, of course, that MouseSpeed is 1 or 2).

MouseThreshold2: This is a pixel value that determines when the quadruple mouse speed kicks in. For example, if this value is set to 12, and then you move the mouse more than 12 pixels between mouse interrupts, the mouse speed is quadrupled (assuming that MouseSpeed is 2).

Table 23.1 shows the values of MouseSpeed, MouseThreshold1, and MouseThreshold2 that correspond to the seven possible slider positions.

Remember
You can also change the pointers using the Desktop Themes, if they're installed. Open the Control Panel's Desktop Themes icon and then choose an item from the Theme list. If you want to change only the pointers, deactivate every check box except Mouse pointers.

Inside Scoop
The *mouse interrupts* are regular IRQ messages sent from the mouse to the CPU. They tell the CPU where the pointer is as well as the current state of the mouse (such as having a button pressed).

TABLE 23.1: THE RELATIONSHIP BETWEEN THE POINTER SPEED SLIDER POSITIONS AND THE SPEED AND THRESHOLD REGISTRY VALUES

Slider Position	MouseSpeed	MouseThreshold1	MouseThreshold2
1 (Slow)	0	0	0
2	1	10	0
3	1	7	0
4	1	4	0
5	2	4	12
6	2	4	9
7 (Fast)	2	4	6

Activating Pointer Trails

The final options I'll examine in the standard Mouse Properties dialog box are in the Motion tab's Pointer trail group. If you activate the Show pointer trails check box, Windows 98 leaves behind a trail of pointers as you move the mouse. This is useful if your eyesight isn't what it used to be, if you're running Windows 98 on a small screen, or if you're using a screen that shows colors only as grayscale. Use the slider to adjust the length of the pointer trail.

Working with the IntelliPoint Settings

The Microsoft Mouse comes with IntelliPoint software that gives you a much wider range of customization options, including the ability to have the mouse pointer automatically point to the default dialog box button, wrap the pointer around the screen, and customize the wheel button found in the Microsoft IntelliMouse and compatibles.

The latest version of the IntelliPoint software is 2.2 and it's compatible with Windows 98. If you have IntelliPoint 1.1 or 2.0, you can get an upgrade from the following Microsoft Web site:

```
http://www.microsoft.com/products/hardware/mouse/driver/
```

After you install IntelliPoint 2.2, the Mouse Properties dialog box changes to the configuration shown in Figure 23.2.

Remember
If the Show pointer trails check box is grayed out, it means that your video card doesn't support the pointer trails feature.

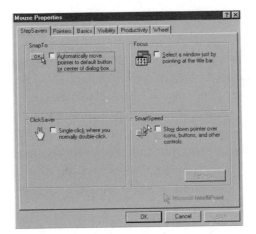

Figure 23.2
When you install
IntelliPoint 2.2,
the Mouse
Properties dialog
box changes to
the layout shown
here.

Shortcut
After you display
the new Mouse
Properties dialog
box, a new mouse
icon appears in the
system tray. You
can display the
Mouse Properties
dialog box again in
the future by
double-clicking this
icon. If you'd rather
not see the icon,
right-click it and
then click Remove
Icon.

Note that the settings from this dialog box are stored in a new Registry key:

```
HKEY_CURRENT_USER\Control Panel\Microsoft Input Devices\Mouse
```

The next few sections run through the new and changed controls in this dialog box.

StepSavers

The controls in the StepSavers tab are designed to reduce mouse clicks and mouse movements:

SnapTo: If you activate this check box, Windows 98 automatically moves the mouse pointer over the default command button when you open a dialog box.

Focus: Theoretically, if you activate this check box, Windows 98 will bring a window to the foreground if you hover the mouse pointer over that window's title bar. In practice, however, a bug in IntelliPoint 2.2 means this feature is effectively disabled in Windows 98. (The only thing it does is select a desktop icon if you hover the mouse pointer over it.)

ClickSaver: If you activate this check box, you can launch icons by single-clicking them (including the icons in the system tray). Note, however, that you don't get the same visual clues that Web integration uses to indicate that single-clicking is on: underlined icons and the hand-with-a-pointing-finger mouse pointer. Therefore, I suggest you

Watch Out!
SnapTo is a handy
feature, and I use it
all the time myself.
However, you need
to be a bit careful
with it. For one
thing, the default
command button
isn't always what
you expect, so
clicking too quickly
might mean you
select a button you
don't want. For
another, the mouse
pointer can sud-
denly disappear if a
temporary dialog
box appears briefly
on the screen.

leave this option deactivated and use Web integration to get single-click launching.

SmartSpeed: If you activate this check box, IntelliPoint slows down the mouse pointer when you move it over certain "clickable" objects, particularly icons and command buttons. (Click the Settings button to determine how much the pointer slows over these objects.) This is useful if you've set up a fast pointer speed because it prevents your overshooting common targets such as icons and buttons. (This option is unavailable if you have the Active Desktop turned on.)

Pointers

This tab is basically the same as the one in the standard Mouse Properties dialog box. The only difference is that you get quite a few more pointer schemes to choose from.

Basics

The controls in the Basics tab are variations on the controls in the standard Mouse Properties dialog box:

Pointer Speed: The new slider gives you finer gradations on the pointer speed. You can also click the Advanced button to set the acceleration rate (or turn off acceleration).

Double-Click Speed: You now set the double-click speed by double-clicking the Set picture. Use the Test picture to test the new speed.

Visibility

You can control the visibility of the mouse pointer by using the options in the Visibility tab:

Sonar: If you activate this check box, pressing the Ctrl key causes a series of concentric circles to appear around the mouse pointer. This is useful if you can't find the current pointer position.

Vanish: If you activate this check box, IntelliPoint hides the mouse pointer when you start typing. This is useful if you find the pointer getting in the way while you type. To make the pointer reappear, move the mouse.

Trails: As described earlier, activate the Display pointer trails check box to turn on mouse pointer trails. Click Settings to adjust the length of the trail.

PointerWrap: If you activate this check box, when you move the mouse pointer to the edge of the screen, IntelliPoint causes the pointer to wrap to the opposite edge of the screen.

Productivity

The Productivity tab is a bit of a misnomer because none of its options have all that much to do with productivity! There are three items to play with:

Odometer: If you activate this check box, IntelliPoint monitors all mouse movements and translates them into feet and miles. This strikes me as monumentally useless, and would be, in fact, a detriment to productivity (since, presumably, you'd want to check your "progress" from time to time).

Orientation: Click the Set Orientation button to launch the Orientation wizard. You use this wizard to specify a non-standard way that you move your mouse. (For example, the setup of your desk may mean that you prefer to move the mouse left and right to move the pointer up and down.)

ClickLock: If you activate this check box, you can drag an object without having to hold down the left mouse button. The idea is that you point at the object you want to move and then press and hold down the mouse button for a couple of seconds. You then release the mouse button and drag the object. To drop it, click the mouse button. To determine how long you must hold down the mouse button to "lock" the object, click the Settings button.

Wheel

The Wheel tab controls the new wheel "button" that comes with Microsoft's IntelliMouse (and compatible mouse devices). This button—for which Windows 98 has built-in support—enables you to scroll up and down in any object that

Remember
Some applications—such as Microsoft Word—automatically hide the mouse pointer when you type.

66

[Microsoft] first learned about the unfamiliar challenges that the home market posed in its Usability Lab.... Steve Ballmer was on hand when a user, who wanted to move the screen's cursor down, pulled the computer's mouse to the edge of the table—and then down the table leg.
—Randall E. Stross, The Microsoft Way

99

contains scrollbars. That is, instead of clicking the up and down scroll arrows or dragging the scroll box, you simply turn the wheel: Turn the wheel forward to scroll up; turn the wheel backward to scroll down. Note that this works only in the Windows 98 accessories and in applications that support the wheel (such as Microsoft Office 97 and later).

Here's a summary of the controls in the Wheel tab:

Inside Scoop
For faster scrolling, click the wheel. This locks the scroll feature so that you can scroll up and down by moving the mouse forward and back.

Turn on the wheel: This check box toggles the wheel functionality on and off. When it's on, click Settings to control the number of "lines" that scroll at a time when you rotate the wheel one notch. You can also reverse the scrolling direction.

Turn on the wheel button: This check box toggles the wheel button functionality on and off. Use the Button Assignment list to change what the wheel does when clicked. You can also click Settings to set how fast IntelliPoint scrolls when the button is clicked.

Turn on Universal Scrolling: This check box toggles IntelliPoint 2.2's Universal Scrolling feature on and off. When on, this feature enables you to use the wheel to scroll even in applications that don't natively support the wheel. (For my money, this feature alone is worth the download of version 2.2.) To specify an application that shouldn't use this feature, click the Exceptions button.

Setting the Tweak UI Mouse Properties

To complete our look at customizing the mouse, let's turn to Tweak UI. As you can see in Figure 23.3, the Mouse tab contains quite a few options for adjusting the mouse behavior:

Menu speed: This slider controls the speed at which a submenu appears when you hover the mouse pointer over the command that displays the submenu. Note that this applies only to submenus used in shortcut menus (those that appear when you right-click an object).

Double-click: Use this spinner to set the maximum number of pixels the mouse pointer can move during a double-click.

If the pointer moves farther than that, Windows 98 will assume you're using two single-clicks in two separate locations.

Drag: Use this spinner to set the maximum number of pixels an object is allowed to move before Windows 98 assumes you're dragging the object. This is useful if you find that you often move the mouse slightly when you click an object.

Use mouse wheel for scrolling: This check box toggles the IntelliMouse wheel on and off.

Scroll a page at a time: If you activate this option, each notch of the wheel becomes equivalent to pressing Page Up or Page Down.

Scroll by *x* lines at a time: If you activate this option, use the spinner to set the number of lines that are scrolled with each notch of the wheel.

Activation follows mouse (X-Mouse): If you activate this check box, Windows 98 activates whatever window the mouse pointer is currently over. Note, however, that the window is *not* brought to the foreground, so the usefulness of this feature is limited.

Undocumented
To get more control over the number of pixels the mouse is allowed to travel during a double-click, open the Registry Editor and find the following key: HKEY_CURRENT_USER\ Control Panel\ Desktop. Use the DoubleClickHeight and DoubleClick Width settings to specify the allowable number of vertical and horizontal pixels.

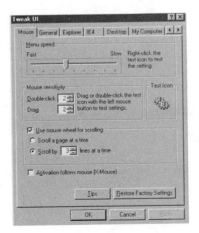

Figure 23.3
Use Tweak UI's Mouse tab offers a number of mouse-customization options.

Working with Your Keyboard

The mouse always seems to get most of the attention in Windows 98, but you probably spend much more time keyboarding than you do messing with your mouse. So, it makes sense to invest a little time in setting up the keyboard to your liking. The next few sections take you through a few useful keyboard customizations and features.

Customizing the Keyboard

Keyboards don't come with the bells and whistles that the mouse does, but there's still no shortage of customization options you can work with. This section looks at a few of those options, including the delay, repeat rate, and settings related to Num Lock, Caps Lock, and more.

Setting the Delay

As you know, an easy way to type multiple copies of the same character is to press and hold down the appropriate key. The amount of time that passes between the appearance of the first and second character is called the *delay*. This isn't usually an issue in regular typing, unless you want to enter multiple dashes or some other symbol. The delay is most important when using the arrow keys to navigate a document because you often press and hold down these keys.

There are two circumstances under which you might want to adjust the keyboard delay:

- If you find that you often get two or three copies of a character when typing regularly, you probably need to increase the delay.

- If you often hold down the arrow keys to navigate a document, you can speed up the navigation by using a shorter delay.

To change the current delay setting, follow these steps:

1. Open the Control Panel's Keyboard icon to display the Keyboard Properties dialog box shown in Figure 23.4.

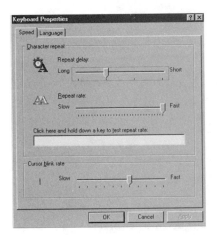

Figure 23.4
Use the Keyboard Properties dialog box to customize the delay and other keyboard settings.

2. Use the Repeat delay slider to set the new delay.

3. To test the new setting, use the Click here and hold down a key to test repeat rate text box.

4. Click OK when the delay is adjusted to the value you want.

Setting the Repeat Rate

The *repeat rate* is the rate at which characters repeat when you press and hold down a key. Again, you can increase the speed of your document navigating by increasing the value of the repeat rate. Here's how to do it:

1. Open the Control Panel's Keyboard icon.

2. Use the Repeat rate slider to set the new rate.

3. Use the Click here and hold down a key to test repeat rate text box to test the new rate.

4. Click OK when the repeat rate is set up the way you want.

Playing Tones When Toggling Caps Lock and Other Keys

One of the most frustrating keyboard conundrums is when you accidentally hit the Caps Lock key and end up typing a long string of all-uppercase characters. Equally annoying is accidentally turning Num Lock off and then trying to enter numbers using the numeric keypad. To help you avoid these

Shortcut
Windows 98 has dozens of useful keyboard short-cuts. I outline them all in Appendix C, "Windows 98 Keyboard Shortcuts."

scenarios, you can tell Windows 98 to play a sound whenever these keys (as well as Scroll Lock) are toggled on or off. Here's how:

1. Open the Control Panel's Accessibility Options icon to display the Accessibility Properties dialog box.

2. Display the Keyboard tab.

3. Activate the Use ToggleKeys check box.

4. Click OK.

Remember
The other options in the Keyboard tab are sometimes useful. The StickyKeys feature enables you to include Ctrl, Alt, and Shift in key combinations without having to hold those keys down. The FilterKeys feature enables you to tell Windows 98 to ignore repeated or very brief keystrokes.

Controlling Num Lock at Startup

Depending on your keyboard layout and the kind of typing you do, you may prefer to have the Num Lock key on or off all the time. Rather than trying to remember to set this key after Windows 98 starts, you can specify whether this key is on or off at startup. To do so, open Config.sys in a text editor and then add one of the following lines at the top of the file:

`NUMLOCK=ON`   Use this line to turn Num Lock on at startup.

`NUMLOCK=OFF`   Use this line to turn Num Lock off at startup.

Typing Extended Characters

The Windows ANSI character set defines 256 standard characters used by Windows 98. The first 32 characters (ANSI 0 to ANSI 31) are called *control characters*, and they have special uses within applications. (For example, the tab and the carriage return are represented within these control characters). The next 96 characters (ANSI 32 to ANSI 127) represent the letters, numbers, and symbols that you see on your keyboard. The 128 remaining characters (ANSI 128 to ANSI 255) are called the *extended characters* and they include accented letters (such as á and ö), foreign characters (such as æ and µ), punctuation marks (such as — and …), mathematical symbols (such as ÷ and ±), and other useful symbols (such as £ and ©). Table 23.2 lists all the extended ANSI characters.

TABLE 23.2: EXTENDED ANSI CHARACTERS

Code	Character	Code	Character	Code	Character	Code	Character
0128	□	0160	N/A	0192	À	0224	à
0129	N/A	0161	¡	0193	Á	0225	á
0130	,	0162	¢	0194	Â	0226	â
0131	ƒ	0163	£	0195	Ã	0227	ã
0132	„	0164	¤	0196	Ä	0228	ä
0133	…	0165	¥	0197	Å	0229	å
0134	†	0166	¦	0198	Æ	0230	æ
0135	‡	0167	§	0199	Ç	0231	ç
0136	ˆ	0168	¨	0200	È	0232	è
0137	‰	0169	©	0201	É	0233	é
0138	š	0170	ª	0202	Ê	0234	ê
0139	‹	0171	«	0203	Ë	0235	ë
0140	Œ	0172	¬	0204	Ì	0236	ì
0141	N/A	0173	_	0205	Í	0237	í
0142	Z	0174	®	0206	Î	0238	î
0143	N/A	0175	¯	0207	Ï	0239	ï
0144	N/A	0176	°	0208	Ð	0240	δ
0145	`	0177	±	0209	Ñ	0241	ñ
0146	'	0178	²	0210	Ò	0242	ò
0147	"	0179	³	0211	Ó	0243	ó
0148	"	0180	´	0212	Ô	0244	ô
0149	•	0181	µ	0213	Õ	0245	õ
0150	–	0182	¶	0214	Ö	0246	ö
0151	—	0183	·	0215	×	0247	÷
0152	š	0184	¸	0216	Ø	0248	ø
0153	™	0185	¹	0217	Ù	0249	ù
0154	→	0186	º	0218	Ú	0250	ú
0155	›	0187	»	0219	Û	0251	û
0156	œ	0188	¼	0220	Ü	0252	ü
0157	N/A	0189	½	0221	Ý	0253	ý
0158	z	0190	¾	0222	Þ	0254	þ
0159	Ÿ	0191	¿	0223	ß	0255	ÿ

To use any of these characters in an application, hold down Alt, type the four-digit ANSI code (including the leading 0), and release Alt.

Undocumented
Windows 98 has built-in support for the new Euro currency symbol. However, Character Map displays the wrong keyboard shortcut for this symbol (it says Ctrl+2). The actual keyboard shortcut is to press Alt+0128 on your numeric keypad (see Table 23.2). Note that this problem is fixed in Windows 98 Second Edition.

Another way to type some extended characters is to use a special keyboard layout called *United States-International.* This layout extends the regular United States 101 layout to include special key combinations that enter extended characters. Here's how to select this layout:

1. Open the Control Panel's Keyboard icon to display the Keyboard Properties dialog box.

2. Select the Language tab.

3. If you have multiple keyboard languages installed (as described in the next section), highlight the English (United States) language.

4. Click Properties to display the Language Properties dialog box.

5. Use the Keyboard layout drop-down list to select United States-International and then click OK.

6. Click OK and then follow the prompts to insert your Windows 98 CD.

Table 23.3 lists the key combinations that become available with the new layout. The two Ctrl+Alt columns mean that you hold down both Ctrl and Alt and then press the key. The two Ctrl+Alt+Shift columns mean that you hold down Ctrl, Alt, and Shift and then press the key.

TABLE 23.3: KEY COMBINATIONS AVAILABLE WITH THE UNITED STATES-INTERNATIONAL KEYBOARD LAYOUT

Key	Ctrl+Alt	Ctrl+Alt+Shift	Key	Ctrl+Alt	Ctrl+Alt+Shift
1	?	¡	I	í	Í
2	²	N/A	O	ó	Ó
3	³	N/A	P	ö	Ö
4	¤	£	[	«	N/A
6	¨	N/A	]	»	N/A
7	´	N/A	\	¬	⊥
8	p	N/A	A	á	Á
9	'	N/A	S	ß	§
0	˝	N/A	D	u	q

Key	Ctrl+Alt	Ctrl+Alt+Shift	Key	Ctrl+Alt	Ctrl+Alt+Shift
-	¥	N/A	L	ø	Ø
=	¥	÷	;	T	°
Q	ä	Ä	Z	æ	Æ
W	-	-	C	©	¢
E	é	É	N	ñ	Ñ
R	®	N/A	M	µ	N/A
T	w	t	<	ç	Ç
Y	ü	Ü	?	¿	N/A
U	ú	Ú			

Another feature of the United States-International layout is the ability to add accents to characters. This is accomplished by using several *dead keys*. These are outlined in Table 23.4. The idea is that you press and release a dead key and then press a letter. Windows 98 will then insert the accented letter. (If the letter and the accent don't go together, Windows 98 displays both the dead key and the unaccented letter.) To type a dead key, press the key and then the Spacebar.

Shortcut
Pressing the right Alt key is the same as pressing both Ctrl and Alt.

TABLE 23.4: CREATING ACCENTED LETTERS USING THE UNITED STATES-INTERNATIONAL LAYOUT

Dead Key	Accent	Example
~ (tilde)	Tilde	Press ~ and then n to get ñ.
` (back quote)	Grave accent	Press ` and then a to get à.
^ (caret)	Circumflex	Press ^ and then e to get ê.
" (quotation mark)	Dieresis	Press " and then i to get ï.
' (apostrophe)	Acute accent	Press ' and then e to get é.

Using Keyboard Languages

You saw in the previous section that the Keyboard Properties dialog box has a Language tab. Besides selecting a different keyboard layout, you can also use this tab to select different keyboard languages. This is useful if you ever have to write documents in a different language. Here are the steps to follow to install a keyboard language:

1. Open the Control Panel's Keyboard icon to display the Keyboard Properties dialog box.

2. Select the Language tab.

3. Click Add to display the Add Language dialog box.

4. Select the language you want to work with from the Language list, and then click OK.

5. If you want to set the language as the default for your applications, highlight it and click Set as Default.

6. In the Switch languages group, activate a keyboard shortcut for switching between languages. (Or, select None to do without a shortcut.)

7. To switch languages using an icon in the system tray, leave the Enable indicator on taskbar check box activated.

8. Click OK and then follow the prompts to insert your Windows 98 CD.

Figure 23.5 demonstrates this feature. As you can see, clicking the language indicator in the system tray displays a list of the installed languages. Click the one you want to use and your subsequent typing will use the language.

Figure 23.5
Click the language indicator in the system tray to select the installed language you want to type with.

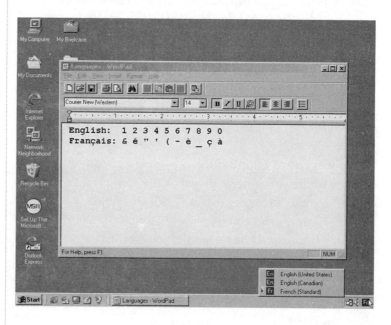

Calibrating a Game Controller

Joysticks and other game controllers need to be properly calibrated with Windows 98 to ensure accurate movement and responses. You tell Windows 98 about your game controller, as well as calibrate the controller, by using the Control Panel's Game Controllers icon.

Here are the steps to follow to tell Windows 98 what type of game controller you have:

1. Click Add. Windows 98 displays the Add Game Controller dialog box.

2. Use the Game Controller list to select your game controller or joystick:

   - If you're not sure what type of game controller you have, select a generic controller from those listed at the top of the list.

   - If you know what type of game controller you have, scroll down the list and select one of the specific models.

   - If your game controller isn't listed, click Add Other and use the dialog box that shows up to choose the manufacturer and model (or click Have Disk if you have a disk from the manufacturer).

3. Click OK. Windows 98 adds the controller to the Game Controllers dialog box.

With your game controller added, highlight it in the Game Controller list and then click Properties to bring up the controller's property sheet. Display the Test tab and check out the controller's axis movement, point of view hat, buttons, and so on to see if they function properly. If not, you need to calibrate the controller by following these steps:

1. In the game controller's property sheet, display the Settings tab.

2. Click Calibrate to display the game controller's Calibration dialog box.

3. The calibration process consists of a wizard-like series of dialog boxes that take you through setting the center position (see Figure 23.6), range of motion, point of view hat, and more.

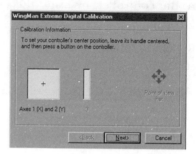

4. Click Finish when the calibration is done.

5. Display the Test tab once again and make sure your game controller works properly.

Essential Information

- Open the Control Panel's Mouse icon to exchange the left and right mouse buttons, adjust the double-click and pointer speeds, customize the mouse pointers, and activate pointer trails.

- If you have Microsoft IntelliPoint 2.2 installed, you can automatically move the mouse pointer to the default dialog box button, slow the pointer down over clickable objects, wrap the pointer around the screen edges, and set up the wheel button to work in all applications.

- Open the Control Panel's Keyboard icon to set the delay and repeat rate and to work with keyboard layouts and languages.

- To type foreign letters, symbols, and other extended ANSI characters, press Alt plus the four-digit ANSI code, use the Character Map accessory, or use the United States-International keyboard layout.

- Open the Control Panel's Game Controllers icon to add, test, and calibrate a game controller or joystick.

GET THE SCOOP ON...
Installing a driver for your graphics adapter ▪ Adjusting
the number of colors used and setting screen resolution ▪ Working with power management and other monitor features ▪ Expanding the Windows 98 desktop to
two or more monitors ▪ Using sound in Windows 98

Maximizing Multimedia Hardware

Chapter 24

THIS CHAPTER CONTINUES YOUR LOOK at specific hardware devices, this time in the multimedia category. I spend the bulk of the chapter discussing devices related to what you *see* on your computer. I begin with graphics adapters and show you how to install the appropriate driver. I also explain the important concepts of color depth and screen res-olution and show you how to configure these settings. From there, I move to monitors and show you how to configure a monitor and work with your monitor's power-management fea-tures, as well as show you the steps required to put together a multiple-monitor setup. The final stop on the tour of visual hardware shows you how to work with scanners and digital cameras.

The rest of the chapter focuses on what you can *hear* with your computer, including setting up a sound card, assigning sounds to system events, and recording and editing sound files.

Installing and Configuring a Graphics Adapter

The *graphics adapter* (sometimes called a *video adapter*) is a sys-tem component that usually comes in the form of a circuit board that plugs into a bus slot inside the computer.

(Therefore, the graphics adapter also is called a *graphics board*, a *graphics card*, and a *video card*. Note too that some graphics adapters are part of the computer's motherboard. Its job is to enable software to display text or an image on the monitor. The basic process works something like this:

1. The software alerts the CPU to let it know that the program has something to display on the monitor.

2. The CPU contacts the graphics adapter's device drive and passes along the instructions:

   - For older adapters, the CPU passes along specific instructions about not only *what* to display, but *how* to display it.

   - The vast majority of modern graphics adapters are *accelerated*, which means they have their own processor that can handle the specifics of displaying graphics primitives (lines, boxes, and so on) onscreen. In this case, the CPU has to send instructions only about what to display.

3. The driver uses an IRQ to contact the adapter and uses the system bus to pass along the instructions from the CPU.

4. The adapter builds the new screen image and stores it in a *frame buffer*: a piece of the adapter's onboard memory.

5. The adapter uses a *RAMDAC—random access memory digital-to-analog converter*—to convert the digital data in the frame buffer to analog data that the monitor can understand.

6. The monitor displays the screen image by converting the incoming signal into the colors that get displayed using individual screen pixels.

Based on these steps, you can see that there are three crucial components to consider if you want to optimize video performance:

- Make sure you get an accelerated graphics adapter. The graphics coprocessor on this type of board shoulders much of the graphics burden that would otherwise fall to the CPU, thus improving overall system performance.

- Get an adapter with as much video memory as you can afford. As you'll see a bit later when I discuss color depth and resolution, the higher these values are, the larger the frame buffer that's required. The more video memory you have, the larger the frame buffer can be and the more memory the adapter's processor has for performing calculations and other video procedures.

- Get an adapter that operates on a speedy bus. If your system has a PCI bus, then a PCI-based adapter is your best bet.

Changing the Adapter Driver

On the vast majority of systems I've worked with, Windows 98 has correctly determined the graphics adapter (even for non-Plug-and-Play cards) and installed the appropriate driver. So, chances are that your system will have the required driver installed and you won't have to worry about it. However, Windows 98 does occasionally miss an adapter and will, instead, install just a generic driver. Here's how to change the driver:

1. Open Control Panel and launch the Display icon. The Display Properties dialog box appears.

2. Display the Settings tab and click the Advanced button to get the adapter's property sheet onscreen.

3. Display the Adapter tab and click Change. Windows 98 launches the Update Device Driver Wizard.

4. Click Next.

5. Activate the Display a list of drivers... option and click Next.

Remember
Even faster than PCI cards are those based on the new *Accelerated Graphics Port* (AGP). The AGP enables the graphics adapter to come off the PCI bus, thus reducing bottlenecks that occur when several devices contend for the bus. AGP not only enables the CPU and the adapter to talk directly to each other, but it also gives the adapter access to system memory as a way of augmenting the existing memory on

Shortcut
Another way to get to the Display Properties dialog box is to right-click an empty section of the desktop and then click Properties.

6. Activate Show all hardware, and then use the Manufacturers and Models lists to highlight your adapter. (Alternatively, if you have a disk from the manufacturer, click Have Disk and follow the dialog boxes to display a list of the disk's drivers.)

7. Click Next and follow the wizard's remaining dialog boxes to install the driver files.

Configuring the Color Depth and Resolution

How images appear on your monitor is a function of two measurements: the color depth and the resolution. This section explains these concepts and shows you how to manipulate them in Windows 98.

The *color depth* is a measure of the number of colors available to display images on the screen. In general, the greater the number of colors, the sharper your screen image will appear (and the more processing power that will be required to display those colors). Color depth is usually expressed in either bits or total colors. For example, a 4-bit display can handle up to 16 colors (because 2 to the power of 4 equals 16). Table 24.1 lists the bit values for the most common color depths.

TABLE 24.1: BIT VALUES FOR SOME STANDARD COLOR DEPTHS

Bits	Colors
4	16
8	256
15	32,268
16	65,536
24	16,777,216
32	16,777,216

Inside Scoop
The 32-bit color depth yields the same number of colors as the 24-bit depth because the extra 8 bits are used for an alpha channel, which can hold transparency information.

The *resolution* is a measure of the density of the pixels used to display the screen image. The pixels are arranged in a row-and-column format, so the resolution is expressed as *rows by columns*, where *rows* is the number of pixel rows and *columns* is the number of pixel columns. For example, a 640 by 480 resolution means screen images are displayed using 640 rows of pixels and 480 columns of pixels. The higher the resolution, the sharper your images appear. Individual screen items—such as icons and dialog boxes—also get smaller at higher resolutions because these items tend to have a fixed height and width, expressed in pixels. For example, a dialog box that's 320 pixels wide will appear half as wide as the screen at 640 by 480. However, it will appear to be only one quarter of the screen width at 1,280 by 1,024 (a common resolution for larger monitors).

The key thing to bear in mind about all this is that there's usually a trade-off between color depth and resolution. That is, depending on how much video memory is installed on your graphics adapter, you might have to trade off higher color depth with lower resolution, or vice versa.

Why does the amount of video memory matter? Earlier I mentioned that each screen image is stored in a frame buffer. The size of that buffer is a function of the total number of pixels used in the resolution and the number of bits required to "light" each pixel. For example, a resolution of 640 by 480 means there are a total of 307,200 pixels. If each pixel uses a color depth of 16 bits, then a total of 4,915,200 bits are required to hold the entire screen image, or 614,400 bytes (600KB). If you bump up the resolution to 1,024 by 768, the total number of bits involved leaps to 12,582,912 or 1,572,864 bytes (1,536KB). If your graphics adapter contains only 1MB of video memory, you won't be able to select the 1,024 by 768 resolution unless you drop the color depth down to 8 bits (bringing the total number of bytes required to 786,432).

In general, you use the following formula to calculate the number of bytes required to display a screen:

*rows * columns * bits / 8*

rows	The number of rows in the resolution.
columns	The number of columns in the resolution.
bits	The number of bits in the color depth.

Remember
A *pixel* is a tiny element that displays the individual dots that make up the screen image ("pixel" is short for "picture element"). Each pixel consists of three components—red, green, and blue—and these are manipulated to produce a specific color.

Table 24.2 lists the most common resolutions and color depth values, and calculates the number of bytes required. When purchasing a graphics adapter, make sure you populate it with enough video memory to handle the resolution and color depth you want to work with.

TABLE 24.2: TRANSLATING RESOLUTION AND COLOR DEPTH INTO MEMORY REQUIRED

Resolution	Color Depth	Bytes
640 by 480	4 bits	153,600
640 by 480	8 bits	307,200
640 by 480	16 bits	614,400
640 by 480	24 bits	921,600
800 by 600	4 bits	240,000
800 by 600	8 bits	480,000
800 by 600	16 bits	960,000
800 by 600	24 bits	1,440,000
1024 by 768	4 bits	393,216
1024 by 768	8 bits	786,432
1024 by 768	16 bits	1,572,864
1024 by 768	24 bits	2,359,296
1280 by 1024	4 bits	655,360
1280 by 1024	8 bits	1,310,720
1280 by 1024	16 bits	2,621,440
1280 by 1024	24 bits	3,932,160
1600 by 1200	4 bits	960,000
1600 by 1200	8 bits	1,920,000
1600 by 1200	16 bits	3,840,000
1600 by 1200	24 bits	7,680,000

To change the color depth, follow these steps:

1. Open the Control Panel's Display icon to get the Display Properties dialog box onscreen.

2. Display the Settings tab, as shown in Figure 24.1.

Figure 24.1
Use the Settings
tab to set the reso-
lution and color
depth.

3. Select the color depth you want to use from the Colors drop-down list.

4. Click OK. The Compatibility Warning dialog box appears. Unlike previous versions of Windows, Windows 98 can perform color depth changes on-the-fly. However, some graphics applications might hang when you do this, so Windows 98 asks if you want to restart your computer before implementing the change.

5. Select the option you want (you probably don't have to restart), and click OK.

   To change the resolution, follow these steps:

1. Open the Display Properties dialog box and select the Settings tab again.

2. Drag the Screen area slider left or right.

3. Click OK. A dialog box tells you that Windows 98 will now resize the desktop.

4. Click OK. If you went ahead with the resolution change, Windows 98 performs the adjustment and then displays a dialog box asking if you want to keep the new setting.

5. Click Yes. (If your graphics adapter or monitor can't handle the new resolution, you'll end up with a garbled display. In this case, just wait for 15 seconds and Windows 98 will restore the resolution to its original setting.)

Inside Scoop
Rather than being prompted about restarting each time you change the color depth, you can define a default response. In the Settings tab, click Advanced to display the adapter's property sheet. In the General tab, select a default option from the Compatibility group.

Shortcut
If you plan on changing the color depth or resolution frequently, there's a way to do it without opening the Display Properties dialog box. In the Settings tab, click Advanced to display the adapter's property sheet, activate the Show settings on taskbar check box, and click OK twice. This adds a "monitor" icon to the system tray. Click this icon to display a list of all the possible resolution and color depth combinations, and then click the combo you want.

Remember
Rather than worrying about matching the monitor and adapter refresh rates, consider purchasing a *multisync* monitor, which adjusts automatically to the refresh rate generated by the graphics adapter.

Working with Windows 98's Monitor Features

As I explained earlier, your monitor shows the result of all the pixels pushed around by the graphics adapter. Having a high-end adapter with loads of video RAM won't do you a lick of good if your monitor can't handle what the adapter sends it. Not only that, but a cheap monitor is uncomfortable to look at and hard on the eyes in the long run. If you're in the market for a monitor, here are a few things to bear in mind:

- Get a monitor that's Plug-and-Play–compatible for easiest setup.

- To save energy, get a monitor that supports the Energy Star standard for power management. See "Using Your Monitor's Power Management Features," later in this chapter.

- Check that the monitor supports a *refresh rate* of at least 75Hz. The refresh rate measures the number of times per second that the screen is refreshed. If this rate is too low, the screen will flicker and the display will be hard on your eyes.

- Check that the monitor's refresh rate matches the refresh rate generated by the graphics adapter.

- Check that the monitor supports the same maximum display resolution as the graphics adapter. For example, if your graphics adapter supports 1,280 by 1,024 resolution, make sure your monitor supports that resolution as well.

- Look for a *noninterlaced* monitor. *Interlacing* means that the electron beam that generates the screen image uses two passes: first the odd lines and then the even lines. (The refresh rate determines the frequency of these passes.) Unfortunately, these separate passes can cause a slight flicker that makes the display hard on the eyes. To prevent this flicker, get a noninterlaced monitor that paints the entire screen during each pass.

- Look for a monitor with a *dot pitch* value of .28mm or less. The screen image is generated by the electron beam activating phosphors behind the monitor glass. The distance between each phosphor is the dot pitch. The smaller the dot pitch, the sharper the image.

Changing the Monitor Type

Windows 98 is pretty good at detecting Plug-and-Play–compatible monitors. In this case, all you need to do is plug in and connect the new monitor, turn it on, and then restart your computer. However, Windows 98 will occasionally fail to recognize such a monitor and will end up listing it as an Unknown Monitor. Here's how to fix this:

1. Open the Display Properties dialog box, select the Settings tab, and then click Advanced.

2. Display the Monitor tab.

3. Activate the Automatically detect Plug and Play monitors check box.

4. Click OK twice to return to the desktop.

5. Restart your computer to give Windows 98 a chance to redetect your monitor.

For non-Plug-and-Play monitors, you have to follow these steps to specify the monitor type:

1. Open the Display Properties dialog box, select the Settings tab, click Advanced, and then display the Monitor tab.

2. Click Change. Windows 98 launches the Update Device Driver Wizard.

3. Click Next.

4. Activate the Display a list of drivers… option and click Next.

5. Activate Show all hardware, and then use the Manufacturers and Models lists to highlight your monitor. (If you have a disk from the manufacturer, click Have Disk and follow the dialog boxes to display a list of the disk's drivers.)

6. Click Next and follow the wizard's remaining dialog boxes to install the driver files.

Using Your Monitor's Power Management Features

If your monitor supports the VESA Display Power Management Signaling (DPMS) specification (or if it's Energy Star-compliant), and if your graphics adapter driver supports the Advanced Power Management BIOS, then you can take advantage of certain monitor power management features. Specifically, you can make the graphics adapter driver turn off the monitor after a specified interval.

First off, you should make sure that your monitor's power management features are activated. To do this, open the Display Properties dialog box, select the Settings tab, click Advanced, and then display the Monitor tab. Activate the Monitor is Energy Star-compliant check box, if necessary, and then click OK twice to return to the desktop.

With that done, Windows 98 will manage the monitor's power and turn it off after a defined interval. Unfortunately, that defined interval is maddeningly short: only 15 minutes. To change this, follow these steps:

Shortcut
If you already have the Display Properties dialog box open, you can get to the Power Management Properties dialog box by displaying the Screen Saver tab and clicking the Settings button in the Energy saving features of monitor group.

1. Open the Control Panel's Power Management icon to display the Power Management Properties dialog box.

2. Use the Turn off monitor drop-down list to select the interval you want.

3. Click OK.

Setting Up Multiple Monitors

Windows' capability to multitask is indispensable, of course, but multitasking inevitably leads to a problem: screen overcrowding. For years I struggled with having word processor, email, Web browser, and dictionary/thesaurus programs vying for space on my monitor. Because I always run my word processor maximized, I had to constantly switch from one window to another, a process that grew tiresome even using the quick Alt+Tab switching method.

So when people ask me if Windows 98 has any truly compelling new features, I tell them that, for me, there's only one: multiple-monitor support. Running Windows 98 with a two-monitor setup for the past few months has made my life so much easier and has resulted in a significant productivity boost. Now I keep my word processor open on my main monitor, and I keep my email client open on the second monitor. If I'm doing research, I open the Web browser or CD program on the second monitor for easy referral.

So just what *is* multiple-monitor support? It means that you insert two or more graphics adapters into your computer and then attach a monitor to each card. The result? An expanded desktop that enables you to move windows from one monitor to the other, display the taskbar in either window, and much more. Windows 98 supports up to nine adapter/monitor combinations.

For a multiple-monitor setup to work, you have to use the appropriate graphics adapters:

- For the primary adapter, you can use just about any PCI adapter.

- For the secondary adapter(s), Microsoft maintains a list of PCI and AGP adapters that are compatible with this feature. These include many adapters from ATI, Number Nine, STB, and Diamond, as well as adapters that use the S3 ViRGE chipset. See the following Web page for the complete list:

  `http://support.microsoft.com/support/kb/articles/Q182/7/08.asp`

- You must use the graphics adapter device driver that comes with Windows 98.

After you've inserted the second adapter and connected the monitor, Windows 98 should recognize the new hardware and then display the following message on the second monitor at startup:

```
If you can read this message, Windows has successfully
initialized this display adapter.
```

```
To use this adapter as part of your Windows desktop, open
the Display option in the Control Panel and adjust the
settings on the Settings tab.
```

> 66
> With Windows 98, you can connect up to nine monitors to your computer. You can set up these monitors like one large desktop, or you can set them up to show a different program on each monitor. For example, you could have a financial report open in Word on one monitor, have a quarterly budget spreadsheet open in Microsoft Excel on another monitor, and refer to the budget while you write the report.
> —From the "Getting Started" booklet
> 99

Watch Out!
If you haven't
installed Windows
98 yet, you can still
insert the extra
graphics adapter
and Setup will find
it during installa-
tion. Note, however,
that you should *not*
install the extra
adapter if your sys-
tem uses an exist-
ing adapter that's
built into the moth-
erboard. If you do,
Setup might not
find the mother-
board adapter.

Figure 24.2
The Settings tab
takes on a new
look when you
have multiple
adapter/monitor
combinations.

You also might need to go through a driver setup procedure for the new monitor. After Windows 98 loads, follow
these steps to enable the new adapter/monitor combination:

1. Open the Control Panel's Display icon.

2. Select the Settings tab. As you can see in Figure 24.2, this
   tab now has a new look. Monitor 1 represents your primary adapter/monitor and monitor 2 is the secondary
   adapter/monitor.

3. Click monitor 2. Windows 98 asks if you want to enable this
   monitor.

4. Click Yes.

5. Click Apply. The second monitor activates and displays the
   extended desktop.

To work with an adapter/monitor combination, use either
of the following techniques:

- Click the monitor icon.

- Select the combination from the Display list.

After that's done, you can adjust the color depth, resolution, and advanced settings.

Multiple-monitor support does have a few quirks that you
need to be aware of:

- You can run only full-screen DOS programs on the primary monitor.

- When you run a DOS program full-screen, you can't use your mouse on the secondary monitor.

- Some programs display dialog boxes and shortcut menus only on the primary monitor. This can be a bit disconcerting if the programs are running on the secondary monitor.

- A few programs (graphics programs, mostly) just don't get along with multiple-monitors at all. If you try to drag the program's window into the second monitor, the program hangs, and can even take the system down with it. For example, I've experienced this problem with QuickTime for Windows.

- If you move a program window to the secondary monitor, that program will likely open in the secondary monitor the next time you launch it.

Working with Scanners and Digital Cameras

Windows 98 now comes with built-in support for still image devices, including scanners and digital cameras. This new still image architecture enables you to install a device and then have that device available to any TWAIN-compatible application, including the Imaging for Windows program that comes with Windows 98. (TWAIN is an industry standard protocol and applications programming interface for enabling graphics programs to interact with graphics hardware and acquire digital images. TWAIN stands for Technology Without Any Interesting Name.)

Installing a Scanner

To install a still image device, you have three choices:

- If the device is Plug-and-Play–compatible, just connect the device and turn it on. Windows 98 should recognize the device and install the appropriate drivers the next time you boot.

Inside Scoop
You also can change the relative positions of the two monitors by dragging the monitor icons.

Watch Out!
If you remove the secondary monitor, programs that are used to opening on the secondary monitor will still do so. In other words, those programs will no longer be visible. They still respond to keystrokes, however, so "activate" the window (using Alt+Tab) and then press Alt+Spacebar to open the program's control menu. Press m to select the Move command, and then use the arrow keys to move the window back to the primary monitor.

- If you already have a still image device installed, the Control Panel will have a Scanners and Cameras icon. Launch that icon and then click Add. This starts the Scanner and Camera Installation Wizard, which you can use to install either one of the supported Windows 98 models (there are only two: Kodak's DC-120 and DC-25 digital cameras) or a driver from the manufacturer's disk.

- If the device isn't Plug-and-Play–compatible and no other still image devices are installed, run the Add New Hardware Wizard.

After your still image device is installed, you can test it by using these steps:

1. Open the Control Panel's Scanners and Cameras icon.

2. Highlight the device and click Properties. The properties sheet for the device appears.

3. Click the Test Scanner or Camera button.

Undocumented

Depending on the device, the property sheet might contain one or more other tabs with options you can manipulate. For example, many scanners now support "push" scanning where you press a button on the scanner and the scanning software loads and scans the current image automatically. If your scanner supports this feature, you should be able to specify the scanning application within the property sheet.

Capturing Images

Windows 98 treats still image devices more or less the same. Therefore, the basic steps you take to initiate image capture are the same whether you're dealing with a scanner or a digital camera. Here are the steps to follow to initiate image capture using Windows 98's Imaging for Windows program:

1. Select Start, Programs, Accessories, Imaging. Windows 98 launches the Imaging for Windows application.

2. If you have multiple still image devices installed, choose the one you want to use by running File, Select Scanner, highlighting the device you'd like to use in the Select Scanner dialog box, and then clicking OK.

3. Select the File, Scan New command (or click the Scan New toolbar button).

Windows 98 now loads the image capture software that was installed with the device. From here, use the software to capture the image.

Wiring Windows for Sound

Windows 98 comes with drivers for hundreds of sound cards. If you install a Plug-and-Play–compatible sound card, Windows 98 should recognize it at startup and install the appropriate driver. For other cards, you'll need to run the Add New Hardware Wizard.

Once the driver is installed, use the following techniques to play and work with sounds:

- The default Windows 98 sound format is WAV (.wav files). When you double-click a WAV file, Windows 98 launches Sound Recorder and plays the file. You can run Sound Recorder by hand by selecting Start, Programs, Accessories, Entertainment, Sound Recorder.

- Windows 98 also supports MIDI files (.mid or .rmi files). Double-clicking a MIDI file launches Media Player to play the music. (Media Player also can play WAV files.) To run Media Player by hand, select Start, Programs, Accessories, Entertainment, Media Player.

- The ActiveMovie Control also supports .aif, .aiff, .aifc, and .au sound files. To open the ActiveMovie Control, select Start, Programs, Accessories, Entertainment, ActiveMovie Control.

- For any other sound files, you need a third-party application.

- To adjust the volume, click the Volume icon in the system tray and then use the Volume slider to set the volume level or mute the sound. For more control over the volume, select Start, Programs, Accessories, Entertainment, Volume Control. (You also can double-click the Volume icon.)

Assigning Sounds to Windows 98 Events

Windows 98 continuously monitors your system and then plays sounds when certain events occur. For example, one sound accompanies the appearance of a warning dialog box, another sound plays when a new email message arrives, and yet

Remember
After Windows 98 went to market, Microsoft released a program called Media Player 6, which is designed to replace not only the Windows 98 version of Media Player, but also the ActiveMovie Control and the NetShow player. It also supports several new sound and video formats, including streaming audio from RealAudio (only up to version 4.0). To download this new version of Media Player, go to the Windows Update Web site. Note, however, that Media Player is part of Windows 98 Second Edition (see Start, Programs, Accessories, Entertainment, Windows Media Player).

another sound is played when you exit Windows. All Windows 98's event-driven sounds are customizable, and there are even dozens of other events to which you can assign a sound. Windows 98 even defines a few different *sound schemes* for making wholesale changes to event-related sounds.

To work with these sounds, follow these steps:

1. Open the Control Panel's Sounds icon to get the Sounds Properties dialog box onscreen, as shown in Figure 24.3.

Figure 24.3
Use this dialog box to adjust Windows 98's event-related sounds.

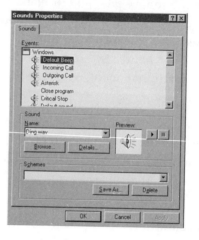

2. In the Events list, highlight the event you want to work with.

3. Use the Name list to select the sound file to play when the highlighted event occurs. Alternatively, click Browse to select the file from a dialog box. To hear the sound, click the Play button in the Preview area.

4. To save your changes as a sound scheme, click Save As, enter a name for the scheme, and click OK.

Rather than work with individual events and sounds, you can use the Schemes list to select one of Windows 98's predefined sound schemes. (If you see only No Sounds and Windows Default in this list, it means you didn't install the Multimedia Sound Schemes component when you installed Windows 98. Run the Control Panel's Add/Remove Programs icon to install the schemes, which are part of the Multimedia component.)

If you examine the Events list, you see that it includes application-related events for Windows Explorer, Sound Recorder, Media Player, and Microsoft NetMeeting. You can expand this list to include other applications by editing the Registry. Here's how it works:

1. Launch the Registry Editor and highlight the following key:

   `HKEY_CURRENT_USER\AppEvents\Schemes\Apps`

2. Select the Edit, New, Key command to create a new subkey.

3. Type the name of the application's executable file, without the extension, and press Enter.

4. Highlight the new subkey and then open its Default setting. Enter the name of the application (this text will appear as a heading in the Events list) and click OK.

5. Create new subkeys within this key for the events to which you want to define sounds. You have eight choices for the names of these subkeys:

   Close: Closing the application.

   Maximize: Maximizing the application.

   MenuCommand: Selecting a menu command in the application.

   MenuPopup: Pulling down a menu in the application.

   Minimize: Minimizing the application.

   Open: Opening the application.

   RestoreDown: Restoring the application after it has been maximized.

   RestoreUp: Restoring the application after it has been minimized.

6. Exit the Registry Editor.

Inside Scoop
Most of the events are straightforward. However, there are a few events that might seem strange at first blush, including Asterisk, Critical Stop, Exclamation, and Question. These are all dialog box-related events and the sounds are played when these types of dialog boxes are displayed by Windows 98 or an application.

To assign sounds to these events, open the Sounds Properties dialog box once again, find your new events, and then follow the procedure outlined previously.

Recording a WAV File

Most modern sound cards are capable of recording sounds, and most come with a microphone to enable you to record voice messages and other sounds. Here's how you do it:

1. Select Start, Programs, Accessories, Entertainment, Sound Recorder.

2. Sound Recorder starts with an empty sound file ready to record. If you'd prefer to add your recording to an existing file, open the file (using the File, Open command) and then use the slider to choose the position within the sound file where you want your recording to begin.

3. To set the quality level of the new sound file, select Edit, Audio Properties and then click Advanced Properties in the Recording group to display the Advanced Audio Properties dialog box. Use the Sample Rate Conversion Quality slider to set the quality level. Click OK until you're back in Sound Recorder.

4. Click the Record button and then use the sound card's microphone to make the recording.

5. When your recording is complete, click the Stop button.

6. Select File, Save. If you recorded a new sound file, the Save As dialog box appears.

7. To change the sound format, click Change and use the Sound Selection dialog box to set the format you want to use. (The easiest way to do this is to select a predefined format—CD Quality, Radio Quality, or Telephone Quality—from the Name list.)

8. Save the file.

Editing a WAV File

Sound Recorder doesn't hold a candle to professional sound editing software, but it does have a few bells and whistles for editing your bells and whistles.

For starters, the Edit menu offers the following commands:

Copy: Copies the current sound file to the Clipboard.

Paste Insert: Pastes a sound file from the Clipboard to the current position in the open sound file. (The existing file is expanded to include the pasted file.)

Paste Mix: Takes a sound file from the Clipboard and mixes it with the open sound file so that the two sounds play together.

Insert File: Inserts another sound file at the current position within the open sound file. (The existing file is expanded to include the inserted file.)

Mix with File: Combines another sound file with the open sound file so that the two sounds play at the same time.

Delete Before Current Position: Deletes everything from the current position to the beginning of the sound file.

Delete After Current Position: Deletes everything from the current position to the end of the sound file.

The Effects menu also offers a few interesting techniques:

Increase Volume (by 25%): Makes the sound's volume louder by 25%.

Decrease Volume: Makes the sound's volume quieter by 25%.

Increase Speed (by 100%): Doubles the speed of the sound.

Decrease Speed: Halves the speed of the sound.

Add Echo: Creates an echo effect.

Reverse: Plays the sound backward.

Inside Scoop
If you have trouble recording the file, the problem might lie in the sound card's hardware acceleration. Open the Advanced Audio Properties dialog box and use the Hardware Acceleration slider to reduce the acceleration.

Undocumented
Sound Recorder can record audio CDs. Just insert an audio CD in your CD-ROM drive and then start recording. (If the CD Player doesn't start automatically, select Start, Programs, Accessories, Entertainment, CD Player.)

Essential Information

- For maximum video performance, get an accelerated graphics adapter (that is, one with a built-in processor) that has as much video RAM as you can afford and that runs either on the PCI bus or the Accelerated Graphics Port (AGP).

- Color depth is a bit value that determines the maximum number of colors displayed, while resolution is a measure of the number of rows and columns of pixels used on the screen.

- When buying a monitor, look for one that supports the same resolution as your graphics adapter, has a refresh rate of at least 75Hz, is noninterlaced, has a dot pitch of .28mm or less, is Plug-and-Play–compatible, and supports the Energy Star standard.

- To use Windows 98's multiple-monitor support, you need two graphics adapters, once of which can be any PCI adapter, and the second of which must be on Microsoft's list of supported adapters.

- Use the Sounds Control Panel icon to assign sounds to system events.

- To set up application-specific events, add subkeys to the `HKEY_CURRENT_USER\AppEvents\Schemes\Apps` Registry key.

- Use the Sound Recorder program to play, record, and edit WAV files.

GET THE SCOOP ON...

Extending battery life by using Windows 98's notebook power management features ▪ Using hardware
profiles to manage a notebook docking station ▪
Inserting, removing, and configuring PC Card devices
▪ Sharing files between a notebook and a desktop
computer by synchronizing file transfers ▪ Configuring
an infrared port and using it for printing and file
transfers

The Ins and Outs of Windows 98's Notebook Features

Chapter 25

T HE PRICES OF NOTEBOOK COMPUTERS remain stubbornly
high compared to those of comparably equipped desktop machines. Yet notebooks are more popular than
ever. Why? The reason can be summed up in one word: mobility. For many of today's professional and managerial workers, it
isn't enough to have a desktop computer at work. These
employees also take work home, run presentations at client
sites, and travel to distant cities and countries. To do their jobs
properly, mobile workers also must make their work mobile,
which means packing a notebook case along with their briefcase or suitcase.

This trend was recognized long ago by Microsoft, so it
included many new notebook features in Windows 95. Those
features have been carried over into Windows 98 with few
changes. This chapter takes you through a half dozen of the
most important notebook niceties in Windows 98: power management, hardware profiles, PC Card devices, Direct Cable
Connection, Briefcase, and infrared ports.

Power Management for Notebook Users

Power management support in Windows 98 is a confusing mess of acronyms, standards, and tugs of war involving the operating system and the hardware. In an ideal world, notebook power management would be completely controlled by the operating system. In the so-called *OnNow Design Initiative* (see http://www.microsoft.com/hwdev/onnow.htm), every aspect of the machine—from the devices, to the buses, to the device drivers—is involved in the power management process. An OnNow-compliant machine would be immediately available for use when it was turned on, would turn itself off when not in use, would respond to "wakeup events" such as an incoming fax, and would offer precise control over the power state of every component. The latter feature is provided by the Advanced Configuration and Power Interface (ACPI) standard, which provides a hardware interface for power management (among other things).

Undocumented
Even if you upgrade your notebook's BIOS to make it compliant with ACPI, Windows 98 won't detect the change. To force it to detect ACPI, open the Registry Editor and head for HKEY_LOCAL_ MACHINE\Software\ Microsoft\Windows \CurrentVersion\ Detect. Add a new string value named ACPIOption and set its value to 1. After that's done, launch the Add New Hardware Wizard and have it detect the devices on your system.

Unfortunately, we live in the real world where support for OnNow is spotty, at best. The vast majority of notebook computers—including many new notebooks—don't support OnNow, or support only certain features. Vendors are coming out with BIOS upgrades, and 1999 is likely to see the full acceptance of OnNow in new machines.

In the meantime, most notebooks support an earlier and less-powerful standard called Advanced Power Management (APM). Windows 98 supports APM 1.2, which enables Windows to turn off some machine features (such as the display and hard disk), place the computer in *standby mode* (which shuts down the computer but preserves the operating system's current state), monitor battery life, and more. Muddying the APM waters is the fact that some notebooks support only APM 1.0 and APM 1.1.

To complicate matters even more, most notebooks support some kind of power management at the BIOS level. This often leads to conflicts because the operating system and the BIOS compete for power management supremacy.

The situation is, as I've said, a mess. Fortunately, power management is relatively straightforward for those systems that support either APM 1.2 or OnNow. For all other systems, Windows 98 offers a few workarounds to help prevent crashes and other undesirable behavior.

Putting the System into Standby Mode

If your notebook supports APM, you can put it into the low-power standby mode. Windows 98 offers three methods for putting the system into standby mode:

- Select Start, Shut Down, activate the Stand by option, and click OK.

- Set up a power scheme to place the system into standby mode after a preset interval of idle time. See the next section, "Setting Up a Power Scheme.

- Set up a battery alarm that places the system into standby mode when the battery level falls to a certain percentage. See "Monitoring the Battery," later in this chapter.

To resume operation from standby mode, press the notebook's power button or reset button. If you'd like Windows 98 to prompt you for your Windows password before resuming, follow these steps:

1. Open the Control Panel's Power Management icon.

2. Select the Advanced tab.

3. Activate the Prompt For Password When Computer Goes Off Standby check box.

4. Click OK.

Setting Up a Power Scheme

A *power scheme* is a collection of time intervals that control how Windows 98 works with the power state of several components:

> **Monitor:** Windows 98 can blank the notebook screen. (This also works for desktop systems using Energy Star-compliant monitors.)

Inside Scoop
One of the things you can do to make power management more manageable is to prevent Windows 98 and the notebook's BIOS from competing with each other. To do this, access the BIOS settings and turn off all the power management features. If there is no way to disable these features, set the time intervals higher than those you use in your Windows 98 power scheme (see "Setting Up a Power Scheme," later in this chapter).

Watch Out!
If your notebook hangs when entering or leaving standby mode, the likely culprit is the BIOS not implementing APM correctly. You can often resolve this problem by opening the Control Panel's System icon, displaying the Device Manager tab, opening the System devices branch, and then double-clicking Advanced Power Management support. In the Settings tab, activate the Force APM 1.0 mode check box.

Figure 25.1
Use the Power Schemes tab to set up a power scheme for your notebook.

Hard disk: Windows 98 can spin down the hard disk.

System standby: Windows 98 can put the system into standby mode.

To choose a predefined power scheme, follow these steps:

1. Open the Control Panel's Power Management icon.

2. Select the Power Schemes tab in the dialog box that appears. The tab you see depends on your system. Figure 25.1 shows the tab for a notebook computer that supports APM.

3. Select an item from the Power Schemes list.

4. Click OK.

To create your own power scheme, follow these steps:

1. Display the Power Schemes tab in the Power Management Properties dialog box.

2. Select System Standby intervals for when the notebook is Plugged In and Running on Batteries.

3. Select Turn Off Monitor intervals for when the notebook is Plugged In and Running on Batteries.

4. Select Turn Off Hard Disks intervals for when the notebook is Plugged In and Running on Batteries.

5. Click Save As, type a name for the new scheme.

6. Click OK.

Monitoring the Battery

If you're forced to run your notebook without AC (on an airplane, for example), maximizing battery life is crucial. That's why APM power schemes support different time intervals for when the notebook is plugged in and when it's on batteries. It's equally important to monitor the current state of the battery to avoid a shutdown while you're working.

To help you monitor battery life, Windows 98 displays a power meter in the system tray, as shown in Figure 25.2. When you're on batteries, the power meter is a yellow battery icon. As your notebook uses up battery power, the amount of yellow decreases accordingly. To see the exact level of battery power remaining, you have two choices:

- Double-click the power meter icon. Windows 98 displays the Power Meter dialog box, which shows the percentage of battery life still available.

- Hover the mouse pointer over the power meter icon. After a second or two, Windows 98 displays a banner that tells you the percentage of battery life available.

Besides monitoring the battery level manually, Windows 98 also enables you to set up alarms that are triggered when the battery level reaches specified percentages. Here's how to customize these alarms:

Inside Scoop
If your notebook has trouble entering or leaving standby mode, the Power Management Troubleshooter tool can help. This file is available on the Windows 98 CD in the tools\ mtsutil\pmtshoot folder. The latest version is available online at http://support. microsoft.com/ download/ support/mslfiles/ PMTSHOOT.EXE. After you install the tool, it runs automatically at startup. Suspend and resume your machine and, if you encounter a problem, examine the tool's readout (problems are shown in red text). Uninstall the tool when you're finished with it.

The power meter

Figure 25.2
Windows 98 displays the power meter as a battery icon when you run your notebook on batteries.

1. Open the Control Panel's Power Management icon.

2. Select the Alarms tab, shown in Figure 25.3.

3. In the Low battery alarm group, use the check box to toggle the alarm on and off.

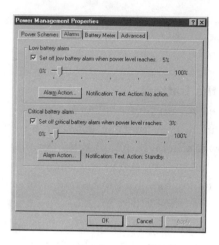

4. Use the slider to set the percentage at which the alarm is triggered.

5. To customize the alarm, click Alarm Action. The dialog box that appears contains the following options:

   Sound alarm: When activated, beeps the notebook's speaker when the alarm is triggered.

   Display message: When activated, displays a warning message when the alarm is triggered.

   When the alarm goes off, the computer will: When activated, performs the action selected in the accompanying list (Standby or Shutdown) when the alarm is triggered.

   Force standby or shutdown even if a program stops responding: When activated, initiates standby mode even if a running program stops responding to the system.

6. Repeat steps 3–5 for the Critical Battery Alarm group.

7. Click OK.

Hot Docking and Hardware Profiles

If you have a docking station to go with your notebook computer, then you have two distinctly different hardware configurations:

- When the notebook is docked, you might use an external monitor, keyboard, and mouse, the docking station might have extra ports and PC Card sockets, and it might contain boards such as a network card and sound card.

- When the notebook is undocked, you probably don't use the external devices; you probably use the built-in mouse, and you might use a different sound card and graphics adapter.

To handle these kinds of different hardware scenarios, Windows 98 enables you to set up separate *hardware profiles* that list the devices present in each configuration. This enables Windows 98 to configure the hardware resources accordingly and to install only the required drivers.

If you have a notebook with a Plug-and-Play BIOS, install Windows 98 while the notebook is docked. This ensures that Setup sees the docking station and all its attached devices. The notebook's Plug-and-Play BIOS also means that it probably supports *hot docking*, which enables you to dock and undock the computer while Windows 98 is running. The first time you undock the notebook, Windows 98 recognizes the change and runs the hardware detection module to see which devices are part of the undocked state. When that's done, Windows 98 creates separate profiles—named Dock 1 and Undocked—automatically.

If Windows 98 didn't set up these profiles automatically, here's how to do it manually:

1. If Windows 98 isn't yet installed, run Setup with the notebook docked. Otherwise, dock the notebook and run the Add New Hardware Wizard with full detection.

2. Open the Control Panel's System icon and select the Hardware Profiles tab.

3. Make sure Original Configuration is highlighted, and then click Rename, change the name to Docked, and click OK.

4. Click Copy, type Undocked, and click OK.

5. Shut down the notebook, undock it, and then restart.

Shortcut
Most notebooks that support hot docking also will add an Eject PC command to the Start menu. Selecting this command is the same as pressing the eject button on the docking station.

6. Because the current hardware configuration doesn't match either profile, Windows 98 won't know which profile to use. It will therefore display the following prompt:

```
Windows cannot determine what configuration your computer is
in.
Select one of the following:
1. Undocked
2. Docked
3. None of the above

Enter your choice:
```

7. Select the Undocked profile.

8. When Windows 98 loads, run the Add New Hardware Wizard to detect devices in the undocked state.

9. Open the Control Panel's System icon and select the Device Manager tab.

10. For each device not visible in the undocked state, double-click the device to display its property sheet, activate the Disable in this hardware profile check box, and click OK.

11. Restart your computer.

Windows 98 should now recognize the docked or undocked state and load the appropriate profile automatically.

Windows 98's PC Card Support

The small footprint of a notebook computer means it doesn't have the expandability of a desktop machine. To get around this, small credit card-sized modules called *PC Cards* (formerly PCMCIA cards) are used for a wide range of devices, including network interface cards, modems, hard disks, and SCSI controllers. These cards are inserted into special PC Card sockets, and most notebooks have one or two of these sockets.

If Windows 98 Setup recognizes a PC Card controller during installation, it will launch the PC Card (PCMCIA) Wizard to configure the controller. When you start Windows 98, you see a PC Card (PCMCIA) Status icon in the system tray, as shown in Figure 25.4.

The PC Card (PCM-CIA) Status icon

Figure 25.4
If Windows 98
Setup installed
support for a PC
Card controller, a
PC Card icon
appears in the
system tray.

PC Card devices are *hot swappable*, which means you can insert them while Windows 98 is running. The first time you do this, Windows 98 recognizes the new device and automatically installs the appropriate driver.

Note, however, that although PC Card devices are hot swappable, you should never just yank a card out of its socket. (If you do, Windows 98 displays a warning message.) To give Windows 98 a chance to reallocate the device's resources properly, stop the device before removing it. You have two choices:

- Click the PC Card (PCMCIA) Status icon, and then click the device you want to stop.

- Open the Control Panel's PC Card (PCMCIA) icon to display the PC Card (PCMCIA) Properties dialog box. In the Socket Status tab, highlight the device you want to remove and then click Stop.

Transferring Files Between Computers Using Direct Cable Connection

A common conundrum faced by notebook users involves transferring files between the notebook and another computer, usually a desktop system. For years, the only solution was to toss some files from one computer onto a floppy disk, insert the disk into the other computer, and then copy the files. The disadvantages of this method are obvious: It's slow, cumbersome, and limited by the relatively small capacity of the floppy. (Although the recent popularity of the 100MB Zip disk has solved the capacity problem to a certain extent.)

A more practical solution to this problem involved running a cable between the two machines and using that connection to transfer the files. A program called LapLink got this idea off the ground by providing a cable and a decent interface for the file transfer. Microsoft got on board by including the forget-

Shortcut
You also can get to the PC Card (PCMCIA) Properties dialog box by double-clicking the PC Card (PCMCIA) Status icon.

❝
sneakernet, noun:
The transfer of files from one computer to another using a floppy disk or other removable medium.
—The Word Spy
(http://www.
logophilia.com/
WordSpy/)
❞

table InterLink program in DOS. InterLink was jettisoned when Windows 95 debuted, and it was replaced by the Direct Cable Connection accessory. The idea behind Direct Cable Connection is relatively simple: Establish the connection between the two machines as a kind of one-way mini-network. This enables one machine—called the *guest*—to browse folders and other resources that have been shared by the other machine—called the *host*.

To use Direct Cable Connection, you must use a cable to connect the two computers using the same type of port on each machine. The port can be serial, parallel, or infrared. The type of cable you use depends on the type of port you use:

Serial port: In this case, you must use a *null-modem cable*. You cannot use a regular serial cable because the wires aren't set up properly for these kinds of direct data transfers. For example, on a regular serial cable, data enters the cable via the port's Transmit Data pin and stays on that wire for the entire journey through the cable. This means the receiving port gets the data on the Transmit Data pin, which won't work. (At this point, a modem would normally reroute the data to the Receive Data wire.) A null-modem cable accepts data from the Transmit Data pin, but then makes sure it arrives at the receiving end on the Receive Data pin. Serial port transfers have a theoretical bandwidth limit of 115,200bps, or about 14Kbps.

4-bit parallel port: This type of parallel port is found on older computers and is designed for one-way communications between the port and a printer. It requires a *parallel LapLink cable* or a *parallel InterLink cable* instead of the standard parallel printer cable. Output uses all 8 of the port's bits, resulting in a throughput of 80–120Kbps, but input is limited to 4 bits, for a throughput of 40–60Kbps.

8-bit parallel port: This has been the standard parallel port on computers for the past few years. It uses 8 bits for both input and output, for a throughput of 80–120Kbps. Again, you need a parallel LapLink cable.

Inside Scoop
To maximize serial port throughput, set up the port to transfer data at 115,200bps. To do this, open the Control Panel's System icon, display the Device Manager tab, open the Ports (COM & LPT) branch, and then double-click the serial port you'll be using—usually Communications Port (COM1). In the Port Settings tab, select 115200 in the Bits per second list.

Enhanced Parallel Port (EPP): This type of port was popular on notebook computers in the mid-1990s. It offers throughout of approximately 300Kbps using a parallel LapLink cable.

Extended Capabilities Port (ECP): This is similar to the EPP, but it uses a DMA channel for improved multitasking. It offers throughout of about 300Kbps with a parallel LapLink cable, and up to about 500Kbps with an ECP-compliant cable. This type of port is now standard on most new desktops and notebooks.

With your cable and port considerations resolved and the cable strung between the two machines, it's time to set up Direct Cable Connection. Your first consideration is to decide which machine is to be the host and which machine is to be the guest. Remember that the guest machine works with the shared resources on the host machine, but the host machine can't work with the guest computer's resources. (However, later on I'll show you an undocumented workaround that enables the host to peruse the guest under certain circumstances.) If one of the computers is already connected to a network, it would make sense to use it as the host because it presumably is already sharing resources.

Let's begin by configuring the host computer:

1. Select Start, Programs, Accessories, Communications, Direct Cable Connection. This launches a wizard that will take you through most of the configuration process.

2. Activate the Host option and click Next.

3. If you don't have Dial-Up Networking installed, you'll be prompted to install it here. In this case, run through the install, restart your computer, and then start the configuration again.

4. The wizard displays a list of ports. Highlight the port you want to use and click Next.

5. If your computer isn't already sharing resources, the wizard will let you know. In this case, click File and Print

Remember
To get the most out of your ECP, you should get an ECP-compliant cable. To ensure compatibility with your ECP, look for a *Universal Cable Module (UCM)* cable. For example, Parallel Technologies offers the Universal FAST Cable that boasts throughput up to 500Kbps. See `http://www.lpt.com/`.

See Also...
"Sharing Your Resources on the Network," p. 635

Sharing and then set up your shared resources, as explained in Chapter 28, "A Complete Tour of the Network Neighborhood." Restart your computer, share some resources, and then start the Direct Cable Connection configuration once again.

6. The wizard asks if you want the guest user to enter a password before accessing the host. If so, activate the Use password protection check box. To enter the password, click Set Password, type the password twice, and click OK.

7. Click Finish. Direct Cable Connection initializes and then waits for the guest. Click Close.

Next, you have to configure the guest computer:

1. Select Start, Programs, Accessories, Communications, Direct Cable Connection.

See Also...
"Step 3: Installing Network Protocols," p. 611

2. Activate the Guest option and click Next. (Again, you might be prompted here to install Dial-Up Networking.)

3. Highlight the port and click Next.

4. Click Finish. The guest attempts to connect to the host. Click Close.

To ensure that the two machines can communicate successfully with each other, you must set up at least one common networking protocol on both machines. NetBEUI and IPX/SPX are common choices. See Chapter 27, "Setting Up Your Own Local Area Network," to learn how to install networking protocols.

To connect the guest to the host, run Direct Cable Connection on both machines. On the host, click Listen, and then on the guest, click Connect. Depending on your setup, you might have to run through the following:

■ If the host is protected by a password, you have to enter a password.

■ The guest might need to log on to the network, if one exists.

- The guest might ask for the name of the host computer. This is the name specified in the Computer name text box in the Identification tab of the Network dialog box. (Open the Control Panel's Network icon.)

- The guest should automatically display a folder window showing the host's shared resources. You can display this window at any time by clicking the View Host button.

Using a Briefcase to Synchronize File Sharing

The need to share files between a notebook computer and a desktop computer also creates a problem: How do you ensure that both computers always have the most up-to-date copies of the transferred files? Windows 98's solution to this problem is a special folder called a *briefcase*. The files in a briefcase are always synchronized either with the original files (that is, the files copied to the briefcase from one computer) and with the working copies (that is, the files copied from the briefcase to the other computer). It takes only a simple command to update the briefcase files or the original files, so everything stays in sync.

Unfortunately, the briefcase feature has always suffered from an unnecessary complexity. What's the best way to send the original files to the briefcase? Do you move or copy the briefcase to the floppy disk (or whatever)? On the other computer, do you work with the files in the Briefcase or send them to the computer? Fortunately, I've developed a straightforward procedure that cuts through the usual complexity. It's still tedious, but that's due more to the design flaws inherent in the briefcase concept.

Let's begin with the case where you're transferring files using a floppy disk or some other removable medium. First, place a briefcase on the disk using either of the following methods:

- Move the desktop's My Briefcase icon to the disk.

- Open the disk in Windows Explorer and select File, New, Briefcase. Type a name for the new briefcase and press Enter.

Inside Scoop
Although there is no direct way for the host computer to work with the guest computer, it *is* possible to set this up. First, make sure that file and printer sharing is enabled on the guest and that some resources are shared. Also, provide a network name for the guest. (Open the Control Panel's Network icon, display the Identification tab, and enter the name in the Computer name text box.) When everything's ready, select Start, Run and enter *Name**share*, where *Name* is the guest computer's network name, and *Share* is the name of a shared resource.

With that done, follow these steps to use the removable disk to transfer and synchronize files:

1. On the source machine, send the files you want to work with to the briefcase on the removable disk. (If you right-drag and drop, make sure you click Make Sync Copy in the shortcut menu.)

2. Insert the removable disk in the target computer.

3. Send the files from the briefcase to a folder on the hard disk of the target computer.

4. Work on the files on the target computer.

5. Use Windows Explorer to open the briefcase in the removable disk.

6. Select Briefcase, Update All (or click the Update All toolbar button) and, when the list of the updates to be performed appears, click Update. This synchronizes the briefcase with the changed files on the target computer.

7. Insert the removable disk in the source computer.

8. Use Windows Explorer to open the briefcase in the removable disk.

9. Select Briefcase, Update All (or click the Update All toolbar button) and, when the list of the updates to be performed appears, click Update. This synchronizes the original files with the changed files in the briefcase.

If you're using Direct Cable Connection, follow these steps to transfer and synchronize files:

1. Connect the host and guest.

2. On the guest computer, copy the files you want to work with from the host computer to a briefcase on the guest.

3. Disconnect the host and guest (if necessary).

4. Work with the files from the guest computer's briefcase. (Don't move or copy the files to another folder on the guest.)

5. When you're ready to synchronize the files, connect the host and guest.

6. Open the guest computer's briefcase.

7. Select Briefcase , Update All (or click the Update All tool-bar button) and, when the list of the updates to be per-formed appears, click Update. This synchronizes the host computer's files with the changed files in the guest brief-case.

Notes About Infrared Ports

Many modern notebooks come with an infrared (IR) port that acts much like a serial port, only without requiring a cable. You can use IR ports to transfer files, send print jobs, connect to a network, and more.

Remember
To ensure proper communication between two IR devices, make sure the IR ports are directly facing each other and that they're no more than 3 to 9 feet apart.

Windows 98 comes with drivers for devices that support the Infrared Data Association (IrDA) standard, including Serial Infrared (SIR) and Fast Infrared (FIR) devices. If your note-book has a built-in IR port, Windows 98 Setup should recog-nize the port and install the appropriate drivers. In this case, you see an Infrared Monitor icon in the system tray, as shown in Figure 25.5. If Setup didn't recognize your device, run the Add New Hardware Wizard and set up the device by hand using the Add Infrared Device Wizard.

The Infrared Monitor icon

Figure 25.5
If Setup recog-nizes your note-book's IR port, the Infrared Monitor icon appears in the system tray.

To enable the IR port, follow these steps:

1. Open the Control Panel's Infrared icon, or double-click the Infrared icon in the system tray. The Infrared Monitor dialog box appears.

2. Display the Options tab.

3. Activate the Enable infrared communication check box.

4. Click OK.

The Infrared Monitor icon shown in Figure 25.5 is the one that appears when no other IR device is within range. When another device comes within range, the icon changes to the one shown in Figure 25.6.

Figure 25.6
The Infrared icon
changes when
another IR
devices comes
within range.

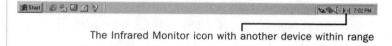

The Infrared Monitor icon with another device within range

For more information about the device (or devices) within range, open the Infrared Monitor dialog box and check out the Status tab. As you can see in Figure 25.7, this tab gives you some data on the device (or devices) within range.

Figure 25.7
The Status tab
gives you details
about any IR
device that's
within range.

The Infrared Monitor dialog box also boasts a few options for controlling IR communications. The Options tab has the following controls:

Enable infrared communication: Toggles the IrDA driver on and off.

Search for and provide status for devices within range: When activated, this check box tells the IrDA driver to watch out for other IR devices. Use the Search every *x* seconds spinner to set the frequency with which the driver searches for devices.

Limit connection speed to: If you activate this check box, you can use the accompanying list to select a maximum transmission speed for IR communications. This is useful if you find that IR communications are unreliable at the default speed.

Install software for plug-and-play devices within range: When activated, this option tells Windows 98 to install drivers automatically for any plug-and-play devices that appear within the IrDA driver's range.

The Preferences tab contains the following Infrared Monitor options:

Display the Infrared Monitor icon on the taskbar: Toggles the system tray's Infrared Monitor icon on and off.

Open Infrared Monitor when communication is interrupted: When activated, this check box tells Windows 98 to open the Infrared Monitor dialog box automatically whenever communication between the IR devices is interrupted. (The idea here is that you might want to use the dialog box settings to adjust the communication parameters and, hopefully, reestablish the connection.)

Play sounds when available devices come within range and when communication is interrupted: When activated, this check box tells Windows 98 to play a sound when communication between IR devices is established and broken.

The Identification tab contains just two controls:

Computer name: Identifies your computer to other IR devices (refer to Figure 25.7).

Computer description: Describes your computer to other IR devices (again, refer to Figure 25.7).

To transfer files using an IR port, you have two choices:

Direct Cable Connection: In this case, set up the host and guest to use the virtual IR port.

Infrared Transfer: This is a new Windows 98 utility that sends files over an IR connection.

To use the latter, highlight the file or files you want to send and then select File, Send To, Infrared Recipient. (You also can right-click the files and then click Send To, Infrared Recipient.) The target machine creates a new folder named My Received Files and uses it to store the incoming files.

Inside Scoop
If you installed an IR device after setting up Direct Cable Connection, click the Change button when you start Direct Cable Connection to run the Direct Cable Connection Wizard and update the connection. Note that when you get to the dialog box that asks which port you want to use, the IR ports won't appear. Click Install New Ports to add the new IR ports to the list.

Essential Information

- Windows 98 supports the OnNow initiative and ACPI for complete control over a system's power management, although most notebooks support only APM.

- Use the Control Panel's Power Management icon to select and create power schemes, monitor battery life, and set power management options.

- If you have a docking station, Windows 98 supports hot docking and it will set up separate hardware profiles for the docked and undocked states.

- Use the Control Panel's PC Card (PCMCIA) icon to set PC Card options and to stop PC Card devices before removing them.

- For fastest Direct Cable Connection throughput, use a parallel LapLink cable on an Enhanced Parallel Port, or a UCM cable on an Extended Capabilities Port.

- To use a briefcase efficiently, place it on a floppy disk and transfer files back and forth from the briefcase.

- After you have an infrared port set up and a connection established, you can transfer files by selecting the Send To menu's Infrared Recipient command.

Windows 98
Networking Skills

PART VII

Understanding Networking

Chapter 26

A FEW YEARS AGO, ANY DISCUSSION of networking required a preamble that justified why a network was necessary: You can share a printer or other peripheral with multiple machines; you can easily transfer files between machines; you can share disk drives and folders among machines; and you can easily back up files to another computer.

Nowadays, these and other networking benefits are well known, so the burning networking question is no longer "Why?," but "How?." The chapters here in Part VII are designed to answer that question. My focus will be on setting up a local area network (LAN) suitable for a small office or home. This chapter gets you started by running through some crucial networking concepts such as network types, network hardware and topology, and the various protocols that are available. Chapter 27, "Setting Up Your Own Local Area Network," gets practical by showing you how to set up workgroups and accounts, and gives you a step-by-step procedure for setting up each network client. Chapter 28, "A Complete Tour of the Network Neighborhood," takes you through some Windows 98 networking techniques, including logging on, accessing the Network Neighborhood, sharing resources, mapping resources, and network printing. Finally, Chapter 29, "Connecting Remotely with Dial-Up Networking," shows you how to connect to your network from remote locations.

Network Types: Client/Server Versus Peer-to-Peer

When designing your network, the first decision you have to make is what network type you want to use. You have two choices: client/server or peer-to-peer.

A *client/server* model is one that divides the network into two types of computers:

Clients: These are computers that require access to services such as printing, file storage, or security. To access those services, each computer must have *networking client* software installed.

Servers: These are computers that provide services such as a shared printer, shared disk drives or folders, and password authentication. Network servers typically run *network operating system* software such as Windows NT Server or Novell NetWare.

In a traditional client/server setup, a number of client machines connect to a single server. When deciding whether to implement this model, you have to ask yourself whether your network requires a dedicated server running a network operating system. The answer depends on whether your network has any server-specific needs. For example, although the Windows 98 networking model enables you to set up password protection for shared resources, it's a bit cumbersome to use. A much better system is called *user-level security*, but it requires a dedicated server. Similarly, if you want your network to implement an email server or Web server, most such software requires a true server.

Remember
Client computers also are known as *nodes* or *workstations*.

A *peer-to-peer* model is one in which no distinction is made between the computers attached to the network. In other words, every machine can act as both a client and a server. For example, computer A can act as a server by sharing a printer, and computer B can act as a client by using that shared printer. Conversely, computer B can act as a server by sharing a CD-ROM drive, and computer A can act as a client by accessing files on that drive.

This type of network doesn't implement a dedicated server running a network operating system. And because it's usually the server that adds the bulk of the complexity to any network setup, the peer-to-peer model is easier to set up and maintain than the client/server model. Note, too, that peer-to-peer is usually cheaper than client/server because network operating systems tend to be expensive, and they require a substantially greater hardware investment (lots of memory, for example).

Network Hardware: NICs, Cables, and More

A network is essentially a physical connection between two or more computers. That connection can be extremely simple. For example, if you read the previous chapter, you saw how running a humble null-modem cable between two machines was enough to establish a bare-bones network using Direct Cable Connection. To establish a *real* network—one that's substantially faster and more reliable than the Direct Cable Connection variety—you need to bump up the hardware. This section runs through the hardware you need to set up your small LAN.

The Connection Point: The Network Interface Card

Your network hardware considerations should always begin with what is almost certainly the most important component: the *network interface card* (NIC). The NIC is, for most machines, a circuit board that slips into a bus slot inside the computer. (For notebook computers, PC Card NICs are common.) The NIC's backplate contains one or more ports into which you plug the network cables, so the NIC acts as the network connection point for each node. Not only that, but the NIC brings some intelligence to that connection. Depending on the underlying network architecture, the NIC can detect whether data is being sent over the network. This helps to avoid data collisions and increase the overall reliability of the network.

When purchasing NICs, keep the following points in mind:

- For easiest installation, look for a NIC that's Plug-and-Play–compatible.

Remember
Windows 98 ships with a simple Web server called Personal Web Server. It's on the Windows 98 CD in the `\addons\pws` folder. See the following page on my Web site for a tutorial on setting up and using Personal Web : `http://www.mcfedries.com/books/cightml/pws4.html`.

- To avoid system bottlenecks, get 16-bit or even 32-bit NICs.

- For best performance, look for PCI-based NICs that support bus mastering.

The final consideration when planning NIC purchases is perhaps the most crucial one: the network architecture. Each NIC is designed to work with a specific architecture, and that in turn determines the throughput of the network and the specific methodology used to avoid data collisions. Although many such architectures exist, the most popular architecture by far (and the only one you should consider for your LAN) is called *Ethernet*. It actually comes in several flavors, but only two are relevant for small LANs:

Ethernet: The majority of the world's networks use standard Ethernet, which offers 10Mbps throughput. You have a choice of cables to use, as well as a choice of topologies (see "Network Topology: Star Versus Bus," later in this chapter).

Fast Ethernet: The majority of new and upgraded networks probably use Fast Ethernet, which offers 100Mbps throughput. This architecture requires Category 5 twisted-pair cable, a hub, and the star topology. (I discuss all these concepts later in this chapter.) Note that many NICs can support both Ethernet and Fast Ethernet, and can automatically switch between the two, depending on the network architecture.

> **"**
> Ethernet technology is ubiquitous. More than 83 percent of all installed network connections were Ethernet by the end of 1996 according to IDC.
> —Gigabit Ethernet Alliance (http://www.gigabit-ethernet.or**"**

The Connection: The Network Cable

After you've decided on the NICs you want to use for your LAN, your next consideration is what kind of network cable to use. The cable is what connects all the network nodes, so in one sense the cable *is* the network.

The two decisions actually go hand-in-hand because the type of cable you use will affect the specific NICs you must purchase. The cable attaches to a port on the NIC's backplate. However, as you see next, the two main types of cable require completely different ports. Therefore, you have to get NICs that have ports that match the cable. Note, too, that the cable decision also is affected by the type of network topology you want to use. (I discuss network topologies a bit later in this chapter.)

The two primary network cable types are *twisted-pair* and *coaxial*:

Twisted-pair: This type of cable consists of a pair of copper wires twisted together and surrounded by shielding. It uses RJ-45 jacks (similar to, but a bit larger than, the RJ-11 jacks used with telephone cables) that plug into complementary RJ-45 ports in a NIC's backplate (see Figure 26.1). Twisted-pair cable comes in various categories that determine the maximum bandwidth for data transmission along the cable. If you'll be setting up an Ethernet network, use Category 3 twisted-pair cable, which is rated at 10Mbps. For a Fast Ethernet network, use Category 5 cable, which is rated at 100Mbps. (Actually, to make a possible upgrade easier down the road, you should probably get Category 5 cable no matter what type of network you're setting up.) This cable is most often used with the star network topology. The maximum length for a twisted-pair cable is 100 meters.

Coaxial: This type of cable consists of multiple, stranded, copper wires at the core, surrounded by various insulating layers. There are two types available: *thinnet* and *thicknet*. Thinnet—also called *10Base-2*—is 0.2 inches in diameter and has a maximum length of 185 feet; thicknet—also called *10Base-5*—is 0.4 inches in diameter and has a maximum length of 500 feet. Both are rated for 10Mbps transmission. Figure 26.2 shows the connections used with coaxial cable. The NIC must have a BNC port on its backplate. To that you attach a T-connector that has a bayonet-style connector and two BNC ports. To those two ports you connect your coaxial cables. This type of cable is most often used with the bus network topology.

Shortcut
If you think you might change cables down the road (for example, it's common to start with coaxial cable and then switch to twisted-pair cable when your LAN gets a bit larger), purchase NICs that have multiple ports for the different cable types. For easiest configuration, get NICs that can automatically detect what kind of cable is attached.

Figure 26.1
The RJ-45 jack used by twisted-pair network cable attaches to the RJ-45 connector in the backplate of the NIC.

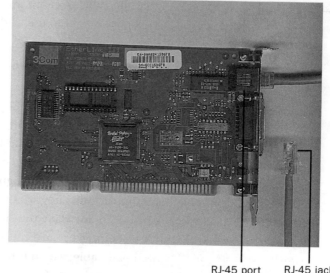

RJ-45 port   RJ-45 jack

Watch Out!
You can't use coaxial cable to connect computers in a "circle." Instead, the first and last computers in the network must use a special *terminator* (see Figure 26.2) to close the circuit created by the cables. See Figure 26.4 for a diagram of how this works.

Here are a few cabling tips to bear in mind when laying your cables:

- Don't run cables under carpet (they might get stepped on).

- To avoid disruption, don't run twisted-pair cable near phone lines, and avoid electromagnetic sources.

- If you're laying coaxial cable, make sure the connections are secure. The bayonet-style connectors are a bit tricky to use at first, and they can be easily installed incorrectly.

- Try not to leave excess cable lying in loops or coils that could generate an electrical field that disrupts transmissions.

- Don't pinch the cable. In particular, if the back of the computer is near a wall, make sure the machine isn't right against the wall or the cable could get pinched at the connection.

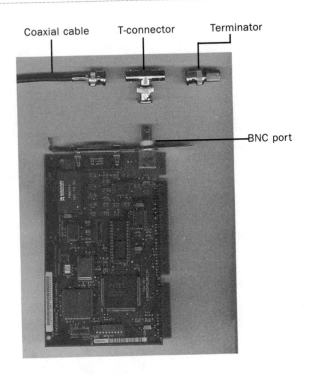

Coaxial cable   T-connector   Terminator

BNC port

Figure 26.2
To connect a
coaxial cable,
attach a
T-connector to the
NIC's BNC port,
and then attach
the cable to the
T-connector.

Other Network Hardware

A network can be as simple or as complex as you want to make
it. In the simplest case, you can use coaxial cable to connect
two computers. Here's what you need:

- Two NICs with BNC connectors

- A single coaxial cable long enough to reach both
  computers

- Two T-connectors

- Two terminators

From this humble beginning you can branch out to all
kinds of configurations and layouts. Depending on the number of clients in the LAN, the type of topology used, and the
extra features you require (such as a direct Internet connection), you might need some extra equipment. A complete list
of the extra networking goodies available would fill an entire
book. However, because we're just talking here about a small

LAN, there are only a few network knickknacks that you'll ever have to consider. Here's a summary:

Inside Scoop
Actually, there's a network setup that's even simpler: two computers connected by a single twisted-pair cable. Note, however, that the wiring of a standard twisted-pair cable prevents you from using it to connect computers directly. Instead, you must use a special *crossover cable*.

Hub: Also known as a *concentrator*, this device is a box that consists of 4 or more RJ-45 ports. When you're running twisted-pair cable, you use the hub as a central connection point for each client. That is, each twisted-pair cable is attached to the client's NIC at one end and to the hub at the other end. The hub serves only to pass along the network data, so each client can "see" the others that are attached to the hub. See Figure 26.3 for a diagram that shows how a hub is used in a star topology network. Here are two things to bear in mind when looking for a hub:

- If you think you might need to add a second hub down the road, make sure you purchase hubs that have an *uplink* port that can be used to attach the two hubs. Ideally, the uplink port should handle the crossover to the second hub automatically (that is, without requiring a crossover cable).

- Get a hub that supports the network type you'll be using. If you plan on using Fast Ethernet, for example, get a hub that supports 100Mbps transmissions. If you'll be using Ethernet, a hub that supports both 10Mbps and 100Mbps (and can automatically detect the transmission speed) gives you the most upgrade flexibility.

- Look for a hub that has LEDs that tell you when a workstation is on the network and that signal data collisions.

Repeater: Earlier I mentioned that each type of cable has a maximum length. Although you're unlikely to exceed those lengths in a small network, it might happen. In that case, you use a repeater to boost the signal. For example, if you're using twisted-pair cable, you need to add a repeater every 100 meters. Note, that many hubs (called *active hubs*) act as repeaters.

Bridge: This device connects two LANs. As your network grows, you'll likely find that the overall performance on the network drops. When that happens, split the network into two separate LANs and then use a bridge to enable the two networks to see each other. (If you have a server, you can create a de facto bridge by adding a second NIC to the server.)

Router: This is a box that routes network data by examining the address information contained in each network packet. If you'll be setting up a direct Internet connection (using, say, an ISDN line), you'll need a router so that incoming and outgoing data is sent to the correct IP address. Figure 26.3 shows a network setup that includes a router for a direct Internet connection.

Network Topology: Star Versus Bus

The final hardware aspect to consider is the layout of the network, or its *topology*. This describes how the network nodes are connected, and also affects the type of cabling you use and the other equipment you need. Although a number of topologies are available, only two are relevant to the small LAN:

> **Star topology:** In this topology, each workstation is connected to a hub. By far the most common setup is to run twisted-pair cables from each workstation to the hub. The main advantages of this kind of setup are that it's easy to add nodes (just run another cable to the hub) and the entire network stays up if one node goes down. The main disadvantages are the expense of the hub and the inability to add new nodes if you run out of hub ports. (Although, as I mentioned earlier, it's possible to expand by connecting a second hub to the first one.) The diagram in Figure 26.3 shows a typical star topology.

> **Bus topology:** In this topology, each workstation is usually connected to a main cable, which is known as a *bus* or a *backbone*. On a smaller LAN, that bus is usually formed by the various coaxial cables connecting each workstation. The main advantage of the bus topology is that it's inex-

Remember
There's a great deal of emphasis on small-office and home-networking these days, so many companies are coming out with affordable networking equipment that combines multiple devices into a single package. For example, as I was writing this book, ZyXEL (http://www.zyxel. com/) announced the Prestige 100MH, which combines a V.90 (56Kbps) modem with a four-port Ethernet hub and a router, all for about US $329.

pensive (no extra equipment is required). On the down side, if a single network node goes down, the entire network goes down. The diagram in Figure 26.4 shows a small-network bus topology using coaxial cables.

Figure 26.3
In a typical star topology, network workstations and other devices (such as a router) are connected to a central hub.

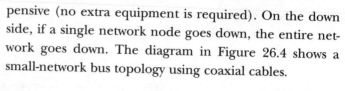
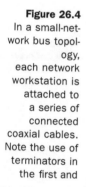
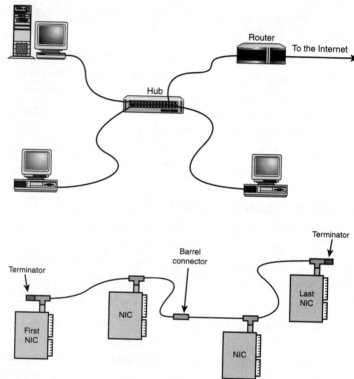

Figure 26.3
In a typical star topology, network workstations and other devices (such as a router) are connected to a central hub.

Figure 26.4
In a small-network bus topology, each network workstation is attached to a series of connected coaxial cables. Note the use of terminators in the first and

Network Protocols: NetBEUI, IPX/SPX, and TCP/IP

The final networking component to consider is software-based: the *network protocol*. The idea behind the protocol is to establish a common structure for the *packets* of data sent along the network. These packets contain information on the source (the computer from which the data was sent), the destination (the computer to which the data is being sent), as well as the actual data. The protocol also defines procedures to take if a packet doesn't arrive at the destination, if it arrives damaged, if a multi-packet transmission arrives out of order and needs to be reassembled, and much more.

The key thing about network protocols is that it really doesn't matter which one you use. However, all the clients must have *at least one* protocol in common. A number of protocols are available, but three are the most common:

NetBEUI: This is the NetBIOS Extended User Interface protocol, and it's supported by all Microsoft networks. It uses a simple and efficient structure that requires little or no configuration. Overall, it's ideally suited to small networks.

IPX/SPX: This is the Internet Packet eXchange/ Sequenced Packet eXchange protocol. It's most often used on Novell NetWare networks, but it's fully supported by Microsoft networks.

TCP/IP: T This is the Transmission Control Protocol/Internet Protocol. It's the protocol used on the Internet, but many companies also are implementing it on LANs because it's reliable, routable, and scalable. TCP/IP is a must if you plan on using your network as an intranet, or if you'll have a direct connection to the Internet and you want each workstation to be able to access the Internet via that connection. Note, however, that TCP/IP requires more effort to configure than either NetBEUI or IPX/SPX. See Chapter 18, "Getting on the Internet."

Inside Scoop
A *barrel connector* is a small component that consists of two BNC ports. (Think of a T-connector without the BNC connector.) As shown in Figure 26.4, you use a barrel connector to connect two coaxial cables.

Essential Information

- In a client/server network type, clients (also known as workstations or nodes) that require access to network services—such as file storage, printing, or security—interact with a server running a network operating system and providing access to network services.

- In a peer-to-peer network type, each computer can share resources with the network (that is, act as a server) and can access resources shared by other computers on the network (that is, act as a client).

- The network interface card (NIC) is an internal circuit board or PC Card that provides ports for connecting network cables.

- Two types of network architecture are commonly used with small LANs: Ethernet (10Mbps throughput) and Fast Ethernet (100Mbps throughput).

- For network cabling, use either twisted-pair (Category 5 is best) or coaxial (thinnet is the most common).

- The star topology normally uses twisted-pair cables attached to a central hub, while the bus topology uses a series of connected coaxial cables with terminators at both ends.

See Also...
"Installing and Configuring the TCP/IP Protocol," p. 430

- You can use any protocol on your network—NetBEUI, IPX/SPX, or TCP/IP—but just make sure that all the nodes have at least one protocol in common.

GET THE SCOOP ON...

Performing a few preliminary setup chores ▪ Installing various networking components ▪ Choosing between share-level and user-level access control ▪ Setting up a Microsoft Mail postoffice ▪ Sharing an Internet connection between clients

Chapter 27

Setting Up Your Own Local Area Network

IN THE PREVIOUS CHAPTER, YOU LEARNED THAT, at least at the small LAN level, networking is not all that complicated or expensive. (Networking doesn't become complex until you hit the enterprise level, and then the level of complexity rises exponentially.) Although I've been critical of many Windows 98 features in this book, small-LAN networking isn't one of them. Windows has been a decent small network client ever since Windows for Workgroups, and Windows 98 is the best client yet. This is particularly true if you have plug-and-play NICs combined with a plug-and-play BIOS. In this case, Windows 98 sets up everything for you automatically, although tweaks are still required because Windows 98's networking defaults include a few bad configuration decisions. Even if you don't have plug-and-play hardware, it's still not that difficult to get your small network up and running. This chapter tells you everything you need to know.

Some Preparatory Chores

Before getting to the heart of this chapter—setting up a computer as a network client—let's take a second and go through a few tasks that you might need to run to get your network ready:

- **Decide on the peer-to-peer servers:** If you'll be running a peer-to-peer setup, you need to decide which clients will share which resources. This applies not so much to folders and hard disks, but to devices such as printers, CD-ROM drives, and scanners. For example, it doesn't make sense to attach any of these devices to a notebook computer that might be disconnected from the network from time to time.

- **Establish workgroups:** A *workgroup* is a network subset that consists of a collection of related computers. On larger networks, workgroups usually comprise departments, floors, divisions, or some other logical or physical grouping. If your network consists of just a few computers, you don't need to create more than one workgroup. However, if you're administering a dozen or more machines, or if you know of a logical way that the clients should be grouped, workgroups may be the way to go. Fortunately, it's trivial to set up workgroups in Windows 98. You just provide the same workgroup name for the related computers when entering the network identification for each machine. See "Step 6: Identifying the Computer," later in this chapter.

- **Create server accounts:** If you decided on a client/server network setup, you'll need to install the network operating system (NOS) and perform other server setup chores. The details of this depend on the NOS and are beyond the scope of this book. However, one of the basic tasks you'll have to perform on any network server is to create accounts for each user. These accounts are used not only for logon purposes, but also for user-level security.

- **Create an Lmhosts file:** If you'll be running TCP/IP as a common protocol on a peer-to-peer network, you have to map each computer's network name (also known as its NetBIOS name) to its assigned IP address. To do this, create a text file named Lmhosts (no extension) and, for each machine, enter the IP address and the network name on a single line. This file must be copied to the Windows folder of each client. Here's an example:

```
127.0.0.1 localhost
123.45.67.89 nessman
123.45.67.90 tarlek
```

- **Enable WINS resolution:** WINS—the Windows Internet Name Service—maps each computer's network name to an IP address. If you plan on using TCP/IP as a common network protocol, and you're using Windows NT Server on a client/server network, you must enable WINS and use the WINS Manager to set up a mapping for each name/IP address combination.

An Eight-Step Guide to Setting Up a Network Client

With all the theory and decision-making out of the way, it's time to get to the meat of the matter by configuring the network clients. I'm assuming here that you've installed the network interface card (or PC Card, if you're working with a notebook). I've divided the client setup into a simple eight-step procedure. Remember, however, that plug-and-play NICs get configured automatically, so you may be able to skip some of these steps (or, at worst, tweak the default configuration).

All the configuring takes place inside the Network dialog box (see Figure 27.1), which you get onscreen by clicking the Control Panel's Network icon.

The list in the Configuration tab shows you which networking components are currently installed. Bear these points in mind when working with this list:

- As you'll see a bit later, many of the network components are bound to each other. For example, to use a particular protocol, you bind it to your NIC. If a particular item is bound to multiple components, the list of components signifies this by listing all components separated by an arrow (→).

Remember
Get all the NOS information you need from Que's *The Complete Idiot's Guide to Networking, Second Edition.*

Remember
Windows 98 ships with a file named Lmhosts.sam (it's in the Windows folder) that acts as a sample Lmhosts file. Note, too, that the 127.0.0.1 localhost entry in my sample file refers to the client on which the Lmhosts file resides. If you're running TCP/IP and you're having network problems, try pinging 127.0.0.1 to see if TCP/IP is configured properly on your machine.

Figure 27.1
All your network
client configura-
tion chores take
place in the
Network dialog
box.

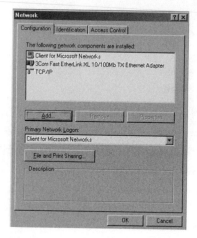

Shortcut
If you have a
Network
Neighborhood icon
on the desktop,
you can get to the
Network dialog
box by right-click-
ing Network
Neighborhood and
then clicking
Properties in the
shortcut menu.

- To add a new component to the list, click the Add button.

- To remove a component, highlight it and click Remove.

- To configure a component, highlight it and click Properties.

The next eight sections run through the steps required to use the Network dialog box to configure a network client.

Step 1: Installing a NIC Driver

Windows 98 should detect a plug-and-play NIC without any trouble. However, even non–Plug-and-Play NICs are usually found by the Add New Hardware Wizard's Detection Manager. In both cases, the required drivers are installed along with some bare-bones networking functionality.

On the odd chance that Windows 98 missed your NIC, follow these steps to install the driver by hand:

1. Click Add. The Select Network Component Type dialog box appears, as shown in Figure 27.2.

2. Select Adapter and click Add. Windows 98 displays the Select Network Adapters dialog box.

3. In the Manufacturers list, select the name of the company that made the NIC, and then select the name of the NIC in the Network Adapters list. (If you don't see your NIC

listed, click Have Disk and install the driver from the disk that came with your NIC.)

4. Click OK. The NIC is added to the list of installed components.

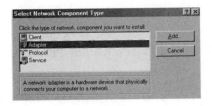

Figure 27.2
Use the Select
Network
Component Type
dialog box to
choose what type
of networking
component you
want to install.

Step 2: Installing a Network Client Driver

The network client driver handles the network logon, viewing computers in the Network Neighborhood, accessing shared resources, and more. Although Windows 98 comes with several clients, the best one to use with your small LAN is the Client for Microsoft Networks. This client should be installed automatically after your NIC is installed. If not, follow these steps:

1. In the Network dialog box, click Add to display the Select Network Component Type dialog box.

2. Select Client and click Add to display the Select Network Client dialog box.

3. In the Manufacturers list, select Microsoft.

4. In the Network Clients list, select Client for Microsoft Networks.

5. Click OK. The client is added to the list of installed components.

I'll discuss the properties associated with the Client for Microsoft Networks a bit later (see "Step 8: Specifying the Network Logon").

Step 3: Installing Network Protocols

I mentioned in the previous chapter that you must install at least one common protocol on all the network clients. TCP/IP should be installed by default. The following steps show you how to install other protocols:

Undocumented
Windows 98 can
handle up to four
NICs in a single
machine. This can
be handy if you
have to connect
your machine to
different networks.

1. In the Network dialog box, click Add to display the Select Network Component Type dialog box.

2. Select Protocol and click Add. Windows 98 displays the Select Network Protocol dialog box.

3. In the Manufacturers list, select Microsoft.

4. In the Network Protocols list, select the protocol you want to install (IPX/SPX-compatible Protocol, NetBEUI, or TCP/IP).

5. Click OK. The protocol is added to the list of installed components.

Although the NetBEUI and IPX/SPX protocols have a few configurable properties, you don't need to worry about them. For the TCP/IP protocol's properties, see Chapter 18, "Getting on the Internet."

Step 4: Installing Network Services

Most of the network services you'll need are provided by the Client for Microsoft Networks driver. However, another vital service—file and printer sharing—isn't installed by default. To install this or a different service, follow these steps:

1. In the Network dialog box, click Add to display the Select Network Component Type dialog box.

2. Select Service and click Add. Windows 98 displays the Select Network Service dialog box.

See Also...
"Installing and Configuring the TCP/IP Protocol," p. 430

3. In the Models list, select the service you want to install (such as File and Printer sharing for Microsoft Networks).

4. Click OK. The service is added to the list of installed components.

Step 5: Setting Up File and Print Sharing

The file and printer sharing service enables the workstation to share resources—such as a disk drive, folder, or printer—with the rest of the network. If you installed the service, you must now tell Windows 98 what in general you want to share:

1. In the Network dialog box, click File and Print Sharing. Windows 98 displays the File and Print Sharing dialog box, shown in Figure 27.3.

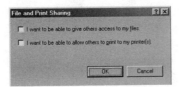

Figure 27.3
Use the File and Print Sharing dialog box to activate sharing for files and printers.

2. To share drives and folders, activate the I Want to Be Able to Give Others Access to My Files check box.

3. To share a printer, activate the I Want to Be Able to Allow Others to Print to My Printer(s) check box.

4. Click OK.

Step 6: Identifying the Computer

Each computer on the network must have a unique identity within a workgroup. Identifying the computer is handled by the Identification tab, shown in Figure 27.4. This tab offers three text boxes:

- **Computer name:** Use this text box to enter a unique name for the client. (This is the NetBIOS name that I mentioned earlier in the context of the Lmhosts file and WINS.) The name must be 15 characters or less, and you can use any alphanumeric character along with the following symbols (spaces aren't allowed):

    ˜ ! @ # $ % ^ & ( ) _ - { } ` .

- **Workgroup:** Use this text box to enter the name of the workgroup for this client. (Use the same naming rules that I mentioned for the computer name.) All clients that use the same workgroup name will appear together in the Network Neighborhood. If you're running a client/server setup with Windows NT Server, use this text box to enter the name of the client's domain.

- **Computer Description:** Use this text box to describe the client. This description will be visible to other network

Inside Scoop
Another service you might consider adding is the Remote Registry Service, which enables you to work with another computer's Registry over the network.
To add this service, click Have Disk in the Select Network Service dialog box, enter *drive*:\ tools\reskit\ netadmin\remotreg in the dialog box (where *drive* is the letter of a CD-ROM drive containing your Windows 98 CD), and click OK. Note that both your computer and the remote computer must have this service installed. See "Some Remote Administration Options," in the next chapter.

clients if they configure the Network Neighborhood to use the Details view. You can enter up to 48 characters.

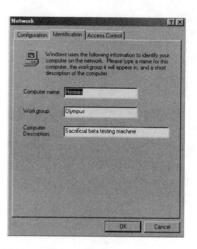

Step 7: Specifying Access Control

When you share resources with the network, you probably don't want the entire network to have complete access to those resources. Instead, you may want to allow full access to only a few users, allow read-only access to some other users, and deny access to the rest.

To enable this, Windows 98 offers two types of access control:

- **Share-Level Access Control:** This is a resource-by-resource method. For each shared resource on your system, you assign two passwords: one for full access and another for read-only access. (Windows 98 is flexible about this: You can assign the same password to both, assign only one of the passwords, or assign neither of them.)

- **User-level Access Control:** This is a user-by-user method. For each shared resource on your system, you specify one or more users in three access categories: full, read-only, and custom. For this to work, you must have a Windows NT server on your network and you must be running the Client for Microsoft Networks. When a user attempts to access a shared resource on the client, the person's username is sent to the server for validation. If they pass muster on the server, access is granted at the specified level.

To choose the access control method you want, display the Access Control tab, shown in Figure 27.5. Select either Share-Level Access Control or User-Level Access Control. For the latter, use the Obtain List of Users and Groups From list to enter your Windows NT domain or the name of the server.

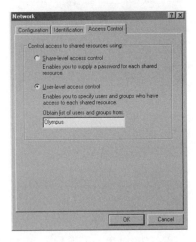

Figure 27.5
Use the Access Control tab to choose between share-level and user-level access control.

Step 8: Specifying the Network Logon

Your final task for setting up the network client is to specify the logon options. This involves just two steps:

1. In the Configuration tab, select Client for Microsoft Networks from the Primary Network Logon list. This logs you on to the network at startup.

2. In the list of installed components, select Client for Microsoft Networks and then click Properties. This displays the dialog box shown in Figure 27.6. There are two groups:

   • **Logon validation:** If you have a network server and you'll be logging on to a Windows NT domain, activate the Log On to Windows NT Domain check box, and then enter the name of the domain in the Windows NT Domain text box.

Watch Out!
Because you're probably not actually on the network just yet, Windows 98 may tell you that it can't find the "security provider" you entered after activating User-Level Access Control. If that happens, click Yes and then, in the Authenticator Type dialog box, select the type of object you specified: Windows NT domain or Windows NT server.

- **Network logon options:** These options determine how you're logged on to the network. Selecting Quick Logon doesn't reconnect network resources at startup, which makes Windows 98 load faster. Selecting Logon And Restore Network Connections takes a bit of extra time to reconnect all network resources, but that makes them available for use immediately.

Figure 27.6

Use this property sheet to specify some network logon options for the Microsoft Networks client.

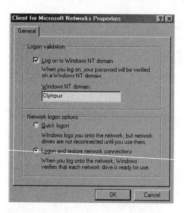

Finishing Up

With the client setup complete, click OK to close the Network dialog box, and then follow the prompts for inserting your Windows 98 CD. When you're asked whether you want to restart your computer, click Yes. I'll discuss logging on to the network, sharing resources, and other network techniques in Chapter 28, "A Complete Tour of the Network Neighborhood."

Creating a Microsoft Mail Postoffice for Network Email

A network isn't truly complete unless it has email capabilities. If you've put together a client/server network, you might consider a full-blown *email server*, such as Microsoft Exchange Server. If this route is too expensive or is overkill for your small network, or if you have a peer-to-peer setup, then you should consider a simple Microsoft Mail postoffice. This is a mini-server that runs on one network machine and is used to maintain a list of users and to store and forward email messages for those users. It's extremely simple to set up and maintain, and it works well on small networks. The only drawback is that you have to use Windows Messaging as the email client; you can't use Outlook Express for Microsoft Mail. This means that each workstation must run two email clients (assuming, of course, that the machines are already using Outlook Express for Internet email).

Installing the Postoffice

The Microsoft Mail postoffice isn't part of the regular Windows 98 package. Instead, it's available on the Windows 98 CD as part of the Windows Messaging component. To install both Windows Messaging and the Microsoft Mail postoffice, follow these steps:

1. Insert the Windows 98 CD.

2. In Windows Explorer, open the CD's `\tools\oldwin95\ message\us` folder.

3. Launch the `wms.exe` file. You are asked if you're sure you want to install Windows Messaging.

4. Click Yes. The license agreement appears.

5. Click Yes.

6. When the installation is complete, click OK.

Creating the Postoffice

With Windows Messaging installed, you'll find a new icon named Microsoft Mail Postoffice in the Control Panel. Follow these steps to create your postoffice:

1. Click the Control Panel's Microsoft Mail Postoffice icon. Windows 98 displays the Microsoft Workgroup Postoffice Admin dialog box.

2. Activate Create a New Workgroup Postoffice and click Next. The program asks you to enter a location for the postoffice.

Inside Scoop
One other client setup chore you may want to run through involves the various bindings set up by Windows 98. As I mentioned earlier, each protocol is bound to each NIC, as well as to the Dial-Up Adapter (used by Dial-Up Networking), if it's installed. Also, the client software and the network services are bound to each protocol. To turn these bindings on and off, open the component's property sheet and select the Bindings tab. You'll see a check box for each binding.

3. In the Postoffice Location text box, enter the drive and folder where you want the postoffice to be created. For example, if you enter `C:\`, the program creates a folder named `C:\wgpo0000` for the postoffice. Click Next.

4. When the program displays the location of the postoffice folder, click Next. The program prompts you to create your administrator mailbox, as shown in Figure 27.7.

Figure 27.7
Use this dialog box to provide the details for your administrator mailbox.

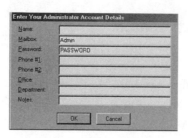

5. Fill in the fields (only Name, Mailbox, and Password are required) and click OK. The program creates the postoffice and displays a dialog box to remind you to share the folder.

6. Click OK.

7. Share the folder with full access, as described in Chapter 28.

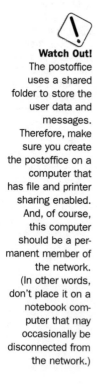

Watch Out!
The postoffice uses a shared folder to store the user data and messages. Therefore, make sure you create the postoffice on a computer that has file and printer sharing enabled. And, of course, this computer should be a permanent member of the network. (In other words, don't place it on a notebook computer that may occasionally be disconnected from the network.)

Creating User Mailboxes

The final step in setting up your postoffice is to add mailboxes for each user. The following steps show you how it's done:

1. In the Control Panel, click the Microsoft Mail Postoffice icon.

2. Leave the Administer an Existing Workgroup Postoffice option activated, and then click Next. The Admin program displays the location of the postoffice.

3. If, for some reason, the displayed location isn't correct, edit the information in the text box. Click Next. The program prompts you for your administrator mailbox name and password.

4. Enter the name and password for the administrator mailbox and click Next. The Postoffice Manager dialog box appears.

5. You have three choices:

   - To create a new user mailbox, click Add User, enter the Name, Mailbox, and Password (and any other data you want to include), and click OK.

   - To make changes to an existing user, highlight the name, click Details, use the dialog box to adjust the user's data, and then click OK.

   - To delete a user, highlight the name and click Delete. When you're asked to confirm, click Yes.

6. When you're finished working with the mailboxes, click Close.

Installing Microsoft Mail in Windows Messaging

To exchange email messages over the network, you have to install and configure the Microsoft Mail service in Windows Messaging. How you do this depends on how Windows Messaging was set up.

If you just installed Windows Messaging and haven't yet run the program for the first time, follow these steps:

1. Launch Windows Messaging by either selecting Start, Programs, Windows Messaging, or by clicking the Inbox icon on the desktop. The Inbox Setup Wizard appears.

2. Make sure the Microsoft Mail check box is activated, and then click Next. The wizard prompts you for the location of the postoffice.

3. To specify the location, you have two choices:

   - If you're setting up Microsoft Mail on the same computer that holds the postoffice, enter the drive and path of the postoffice folder.

See Also...
"Sharing Your Resources on the Network," p. 635

Watch Out!
Create only one postoffice for your network. Messages can be exchanged only between users in one postoffice, so if you create a second postoffice, the two groups of users won't be able to exchange messages.

Remember
The Name field is what the other users see when they view the postoffice address list.

• If you're setting up Microsoft Mail on another network workstation, enter the UNC path to the postoffice folder. I'll discuss UNC paths in more detail in
the next chapter. For now, enter the path as
server\wgpo0000, where *server* is the network name
of the machine hosting the postoffice.

4. The wizard displays a list of the user mailboxes on the
specified postoffice. Select the username for your mailbox
and click Next. The wizard prompts you for the mailbox
password.

5. Enter the password and click Next.

6. The next two wizard dialog boxes prompt you for the locations of your personal address book and personal message
store. Adjust the locations, if necessary, and click Next
each time.

7. In the final dialog box, click Finish. Windows Messaging
finishes loading.

If Windows Messaging is already installed and running on
your computer, follow these steps to add the Microsoft Mail
service:

See Also...
"Understanding
the Universal
Naming
Convention,"
p. 634

1. In Windows Messaging, select Tools, Services to display
the Services dialog box.

2. Click Add to display the Add Service to Profile dialog box.

3. Select Microsoft Mail and click OK. (If you don't see the
Microsoft Mail service listed, then you need to install
Windows Messaging from the Windows 98 CD, as
described earlier.)

4. In the Microsoft Mail dialog box, fill in the following tabs
(I discuss the other tabs in the next section):

• **Connection:** Use the Enter the Path to Your
Postoffice text box to specify the local or UNC path
to the postoffice folder.

- **Logon:** Enter your mailbox name and password. If you don't want to be prompted to enter your password each time you log on, activate the When Logging On, Automatically Enter Password check box.

5. Click OK. Windows Messaging tells you the service won't start until you log off and restart.

6. Click OK to return to the Services dialog box, and then click OK again to return to Windows Messaging.

7. Select File, Exit to quit Windows Messaging, and then restart the program.

Setting Microsoft Mail Options

The Microsoft Mail service has a large number of options you can work with to configure the service the way you like. To view the property sheet for the Microsoft Mail service, follow these steps:

1. Select Tools, Services to display the Services dialog box.

2. Select Microsoft Mail.

3. Click Properties.

Figure 27.8 shows the Microsoft Mail dialog box that appears. (If you have Dial-Up Networking installed, you'll see a few extra tabs.)

Inside Scoop
Messages sent to a user are first stored in the postoffice folder. When the user retrieves her messages, they're moved from the shared folder to the personal message store on her computer. The latter is a .pst file, which is usually C:\Exchange\ mailbox.pst. In Windows Messaging's list of services, the personal message store is listed as Personal Folders.

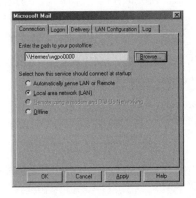

Figure 27.8
Use this dialog box to configure Microsoft Mail.

Remember
You can also add
and configure
services outside
Windows
Messaging. In the
Control Panel,
click the Mail icon
to display the
Windows
Messaging
Settings
Properties dialog
box. Use the
Services tab to
add new services
(click Add) or con-
figure an existing
service (select it
and click
Properties).

The Connection tab displays the path to the postoffice folder. Use the Enter the Path to Your Postoffice text box to adjust the path (or click Browse and use the Browse for Postoffice dialog box to pick out the postoffice folder). This tab also contains a few options that specify how the Microsoft Mail service connects to the postoffice during the Windows Messaging startup. Microsoft Mail can connect either via the network or via a remote Dial-Up Networking call, as determined by the following options:

- **Automatically Sense LAN or Remote:** Activate this option to have Microsoft Mail attempt to determine the type of connection automatically.

- **Local Area Network (LAN):** Activate this option to connect to the postoffice using only the network.

- **Remote Using a Modem and Dial-Up Networking:** Activate this option to connect to the postoffice using Dial-Up Networking only. (This option will be disabled if you don't have Dial-Up Networking installed.)

- **Offline:** Activate this option to tell Microsoft Mail not to connect to the postoffice.

Use the Logon tab to hold your mailbox name and password, and to specify whether you want Microsoft Mail to enter your password automatically. You can adjust your password by clicking the Change Mailbox Password button. In the Change Mailbox Password dialog box that appears, type in your old password and your new password (you enter the latter twice), and then click OK.

Use the Delivery tab to configure how Microsoft Mail works with incoming and outgoing messages:

- **Enable Incoming Mail Delivery:** Toggles the delivery of incoming messages on and off.

- **Enable Outgoing Mail Delivery:** Toggles the delivery of outgoing messages on and off. Note that you can still "send" messages. However, these messages are saved in Windows Messaging's Outbox folder until you enable outgoing messages again.

- **Enable Delivery To:** The idea here is to click the Address Types button to specify which types of email addresses can be sent to the postoffice. If you're running only Microsoft Mail, you don't have to worry about this.

- **Check for New Mail Every *x* Minute(s):** Sets the interval, in minutes, that Windows Messaging uses to check automatically for new messages.

- **Immediate Notification:** Activating this check box tells Windows Messaging to notify the recipients immediately when a message you send arrives in the postoffice. All the computers involved must support the NetBIOS protocol.

- **Display Global Address List Only:** Activating this option tells Windows Messaging to display only the postoffice addresses when you access the address book. When this option is deactivated, the contents of your personal address book are also displayed.

The LAN Configuration tab contains three check boxes:

- **Use Remote Mail:** Activating this check box enables Windows Messaging's Remote Mail feature, which tells Windows Messaging not to check for incoming mail automatically. This is useful if you're using a notebook computer that's no longer connected to the network. You can then use the Tools, Remote Mail command to connect to the network via Dial-Up Networking and download your messages.

- **Use Local Copy:** Activating this check box tells Windows Messaging to create a local copy of the postoffice address list. This is useful for composing messages offline.

- **Use External Delivery Agent:** Activating this check box tells Windows Messaging to deliver your messages using a program called EXTERNAL.EXE. Note, however, that this program is part of the Microsoft Mail Post Office Upgrade, available from Microsoft. This upgrades the Windows 98 postoffice to the full Microsoft Mail Server postoffice.

Shortcut
You can also open the Change Mailbox Password dialog box from within Windows Messaging. Select the Tools, Microsoft Mail Tools, Change Mailbox Password command.

Undocumented
To make the Immediate Notification feature work in Windows 98, all the computers must be running the IPX/SPX-compatible protocol. In addition, on all the computers you must click the Control Panel's Network icon, select the IPX/SPX-compatible protocol (the one that's bound to your NIC), and click Properties. In the NetBIOS tab, activate the I Want to Enable NetBIOS Over IPX/SPX check box.

Finally, the Log tab enables you to configure Windows Messaging to log your Microsoft Mail sessions so that you can check them for problems. You have two options:

- **Maintain a Log of Session Events:** This check box toggles the log on and off.

- **Specify the Location of the Session Log:** This text box specifies the name and location of the log file.

Sharing a Dial-Up Connection Between Network Clients

I look at networks as just big "sharing machines." The whole point of any network is to be able to share both information (for example, files and email) and devices (for example, printers and disk drives). This sharing machine gets extended even further when the Internet is involved. Two scenarios are common:

Remember
To refresh the postoffice address list, select the Tools, Microsoft Mail Tools, Download Address Lists command.

- You have a direct connection to the Internet using an ISDN line or some other technology. In this case, you need to include a router on your network and configure each machine's TCP/IP protocol for Internet access (see Chapter 18).

- You have a dial-up account and you want each machine to be able to access the Internet using that account. You *could* supply each machine with its own modem and split the phone line, but that is both costly and inconvenient. A better solution would be to share a single modem connection among all users. This can be done, although it's not supported directly by Windows 98.

The ability to have multiple network clients share a single dial-up connection is called *modem sharing*.

Using Internet Connection Sharing in Windows 98 Second Edition

If you have Windows 98 Second Edition, you can use the new Internet Connection Sharing feature to get modem sharing on your network. First, decide which computer will share the connection. This machine is called the *gateway*. Create an Internet connection on the gateway and make sure that you connect successfully. Now you must configure the gateway. Here's how you do it:

See Also...
"Installing and Configuring the TCP/IP Protocol," p. 430

1. Click the Control Panel's Internet Options icon. (Or, right-click the desktop's Internet Explorer icon and then click Properties.)

2. Display the Connection tab.

3. Click the Sharing button. The Internet Connection Sharing Wizard appears.

4. The first dialog box just gives you an overview of Internet Connection Sharing, so click Next.

5. In the next wizard dialog box, select the adapter you use for the Internet connection (for a dial-up connection, select the Dial-Up Adapter) and click Next.

6. Select the NIC you use for your network connection, and then click Next. The wizard tells you it's about to create a Client Configuration Disk, which you use to configure the other network clients.

7. Click Next.

8. Insert a floppy disk (the wizard suggests you label this disk "Internet Connection Sharing Client Disk") and then click OK.

9. When the disk is done, remove it and click OK.

10. In the final wizard dialog box, click Finish.

11. When prompted to restart your computer, click Yes.

When you're back in Windows 98, return to the Connection tab and click the Sharing button once again. This time, you see the Internet Connection Sharing dialog box shown in Figure 27.9. The following gives you a rundown of the settings:

- **Enable Internet Connection Sharing:** This check box toggles Internet Connection Sharing on and off.

- **Show Icon in Taskbar:** Activating this check box places an Internet Connection Sharing icon in the system tray. Double-click this icon to see how many clients are using the shared connection.

- **Connect to the Internet Using:** Use this list to select the networking component that you use to connect to the Internet.

- **Connect to My Home Network Using:** Use this list to select the NIC you use with your network.

You'll need the Internet connection established to configure the clients, so connect to the Internet now.

Figure 27.9
After Internet Connection Sharing is enabled, clicking the Sharing button displays this dialog box.

With all that out of the way, your next chore is to set up the client machines. Note, first, that each client must have the TCP/IP protocol installed, and that TCP/IP must be set up properly. For the latter, open the Network property sheet and then open the property sheet for TCP/IP bound to the NIC. You need the following to set up:

- In the IP Address tab, make sure that the Obtain an IP Address Automatically option is activated.

- In the WINS Configuration tab, makes sure that the Use DHCP for WINS Resolution option is activated.

- In the Gateway tab, make sure that no gateways are listed.

- In the DNS Configuration tab, make sure that the Disable DNS option is activated.

Click OK until you exit the dialog boxes, and then click Yes when asked to restart the client.

You're now ready to configure the client to use the gateway machine's Internet connection. Assuming the client can access the network successfully, follow these steps:

1. Insert the Internet Connection Sharing client disk.

2. Open Windows Explorer and display drive A:.

3. Double-click the file named `icsclset.exe`. This launches the Browser Connection Setup Wizard.

4. Click Next to get past the introductory dialog box. The wizard lets you know it will now change the client's browser settings.

5. Click Next. The wizard makes the changes and then displays its final dialog box.

6. If you want to connect to the Internet right away, activate the To Immediately Connect to the Internet Through Your Network... check box. To complete the wizard, click Finish.

Other Ways to Share an Internet Connection

Unfortunately, the original edition of Windows 98 offers no support for modem sharing right out of the box. However, there are several third-party applications available that can do this:

- **WinGate:** This application offers not only modem sharing, but also acts as a proxy server (which means each user doesn't require an IP address) and a firewall (to control the destinations of incoming and outgoing packets). WinGate is free for up to two users, and the price scales from there depending on the number of users.

  URL: `http://www.deerfield.com/wingate/`

Inside Scoop
Internet Connection Sharing uses Dynamic Host Configuration Protocol (DHCP) to assign IP addresses automatically to each client. However, when a client computer tries to access an Internet resource, Internet Connection Sharing uses the gateway's IP address so that DNS lookups are successful. When the data is returned, the gateway routes it to the correct client.

Watch Out!
If the client can't reach the Internet, make sure the gateway has a properly configured IP address. Open the Network property sheet and then open the property sheet for TCP/IP bound to the adapter that you're using to connect to the Internet. In the IP Address tab, make sure that Specify an IP address is activated. In the IP Address text box, enter `192.168.0.1`, and in the Subnet Mask text box, enter `255.255.255.0`.

■ **Trumpet FireSock:** This application offers both modem sharing and a firewall. Prices start at U.S. $35 for three users, and max out at U.S. $160 for 20 users.

URL: `http://www.trumpet.com/fsock.html`

■ **MidPoint Gateway:** This is the most full-featured of the applications because it supports modem sharing, can act as a proxy server and a firewall, and also has support for *modem teaming*. The latter enables you to increase your bandwidth by aggregating the throughput of multiple modems using multiple phone lines. Prices start at U.S. $299 for five users. (Note that there is also the MidPoint Companion, which offers modem sharing for only U.S. $199 for up to five users.)

URL: `http://www.midcore.com/`

Essential Information

■ Before configuring the network clients, decide which of the machines will be peer-to-peer servers, select your workgroups (if more than one is needed), and set up either an `Lmhosts` file or WINS resolution.

■ To configure a network client, click the Control Panel's Network icon (or right-click the Network Neighborhood icon and then click Properties).

■ To add a new NIC driver, client driver, protocol, or service, open the Network dialog box, click Add, select the component type you want to add, and then select the component from the dialog box that appears.

■ To establish a workgroup, supply each computer in the workgroup with the same workgroup name.

■ Share-level access control is a resource-by-resource method that assigns passwords to each shared resource, while user-level access control is a user-by-user method that gives individual users specific permissions for each resource.

■ To create and configure a Microsoft Mail postoffice, use the Control Panel's Microsoft Mail Postoffice icon.

GET THE SCOOP ON...
Logging on to the network with options ▪ Taking a
tour of the Network Neighborhood ▪ Sharing drives,
folders, and printers ▪ Mapping shared network drives
and folders ▪ Setting up a network printer ▪ Using
system policies ▪ Using remote administration

A Complete Tour of the Network Neighborhood

chapter 28

W ITH YOUR NETWORK planned, installed, and configured, you're ready to put it to good use. This chapter gets you started by showing you how to log on to
the network and access the Network Neighborhood. From
there, I'll show you how to share your resources with the network, work with resources shared by others on the network, set
up a network printer, customize the Network Neighborhood,
and monitor other computers remotely.

Accessing the Network

Let's begin with the basics of logging on to the network and
then take a look around the Network Neighborhood. Along
the way, I'll also show you how to set up automatic logons and
I'll explain the Universal Naming Convention and how to use
it to refer to network resources.

Logging On to the Network

After Windows 98 is set up for networking, you are prompted
to log on to the network each time you start or reboot your
computer. The logon dialog box you see depends on the type
of network you're using:

629

- **Peer-to-peer network logon:** In this case, you see the Enter Network Password dialog box shown in Figure 28.1. Your User Name should be filled in for you automatically, so enter your Password and click OK.

Figure 28.1
This logon dialog box appears if you're on a peer-to-peer network.

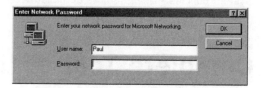

See Also...
"Step 8: Specifying the Network Logon," p. 615

- **Client/server network logon:** If, as described in the last chapter, you adjusted the properties of the Client for Microsoft Networks to log on to a Windows NT domain, you see the dialog box shown in Figure 28.2. Your User Name and Domain should be filled in for you automatically, so enter your Password and click OK.

Figure 28.2
This logon dialog box appears if you're on a client/server network.

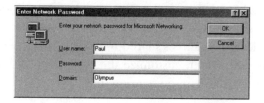

Logging On to Windows and the Network at the Same Time

If you have a Windows password set up, you may be forced to negotiate both the Enter Network Password dialog box and the Welcome to Windows dialog box at startup. It's possible to unify the logon so that a single dialog box logs you on to both the network and Windows 98. To do this, you need to set the same password for both logons by following these steps:

1. Click the Passwords icon on the Control Panel to display the Passwords Properties dialog box.

2. In the Change Passwords tab, click Change Windows Password.

3. If you log on to a Windows NT domain, a dialog box asks if you also want to change the password for Microsoft Networking. Leave the check box deactivated and click OK.

4. In the Change Windows Password dialog box, enter your existing password in the Old Password text box, and then enter your network password in both the New Password and Confirm New Password text boxes. Click OK.

5. When Windows 98 confirms that your password was changed, click OK to return to the Passwords Properties dialog box.

6. Click Close.

Setting Up an Automatic Logon

Because we're dealing with small networks here, there's a good chance that security isn't a huge issue for you. In that case, it's possible to set up Windows 98 to log you on to the network automatically. The following method applies to both peer-to-peer and client/server networks:

1. Click the Tweak UI icon on the Control Panel.

2. Display the Network tab, shown in Figure 28.3.

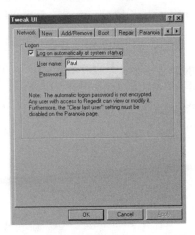

Figure 28.3
Use the Network tab to enable the automatic network logon.

3. Activate the Log On Automatically at System Startup check box.

4. Enter your User Name and Password.

5. Click OK.

Watch Out!
Before leaving Tweak UI, display the Paranoia tab and make sure the Clear Last User at Logon check box is deactivated. If it's not, the automatic logon feature won't work.

You may have noticed that Tweak UI's Network tab warns you that any user with access to Regedit can view or modify your password. What does this mean? To find out, open the Registry Editor and display the following key:

```
HKEY_LOCAL_MACHINE\Software\Microsoft\Windows\
CurrentVersion\Winlogon
```

Your username appears in the DefaultUserName setting, and your password appears in the DefaultPassword setting. The kicker is that the password appears as plain text, so anyone can read it or change it.

If you're on a client/server network where you log on to a Windows NT domain, and you're not comfortable having your network password in plain view, here's a workaround that stores your network password in the encrypted Windows 98 password list:

Inside Scoop
The Windows 98 password list is actually a .pwl file. The name of this file is user.pwl, where *user* is your user name. You'll find this file in the Windows folder.

1. Follow the steps outlined earlier to change your Windows password. (Again, don't change your Microsoft Networking password.) In this case, leave both the New Password and Confirm New Password text boxes blank. Click OK until you're back in the Control Panel.

2. Click the Network icon in the Control Panel.

3. In the Primary Network Logon list, select Windows Logon. (While you're in this dialog box, double-click Client for Microsoft Networks and make sure you're set up to log on to a Windows NT domain.)

4. Click OK.

5. When Windows 98 asks if you want to restart your computer, click Yes.

6. When the Enter Network Password dialog box appears, enter your Password, make sure that the Save This Password In Your Password List check box is activated, and then click OK.

How to Access the Network Neighborhood

Most of your network noodling occurs within the friendly confines of Windows 98's Network Neighborhood. This is a special folder that gives you access to the workgroups (or domains) and computers on your network. To get to the Network Neighborhood, Windows 98 offers two routes:

- **Windows Explorer**: Open Network Neighborhood in the All Folders list.

- **The desktop:** Click the Network Neighborhood icon.

Consider these notes about the Network Neighborhood's landmarks:

- The top-level folder displays Entire Network as well as a list of the computers in your workgroup or domain. As you can see in Figure 28.4, the Details view displays both the name of each computer and the description. (This is the data entered into the Identification tab of the Network dialog box.)

- If your network has multiple workgroups or domains, click the Entire Network item to see a list of those domains.

Shortcut
The Network Neighborhood is also available in the standard Windows 98 file dialog boxes. In the Open dialog box, select Network Neighborhood in the Look In list; in the Save As dialog box, use the Save In list. Note, too, that many 16-bit dialog boxes have a Network button that you can use to map a shared network drive.

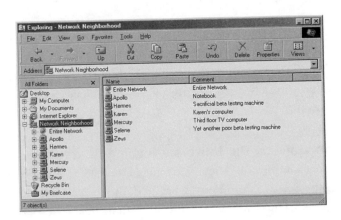

Figure 28.4
The top-level Network Neighborhood folder shows the machines in your workgroup.

- If you select a network computer, you see a list of the resources that it is sharing with the network. In Figure 28.5, for example, you can see that the computer named Selene is sharing a disk drive, a folder, a CD-ROM drive, a printer, and a Jaz drive.

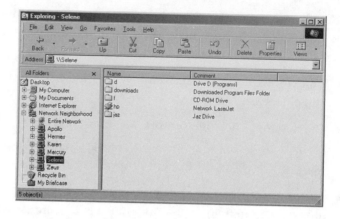

Remember

What you can do
with the remote
files depends on
the access rights
you have. For
example, if you
have just read-only
access, you won't
be able to delete
or add files.

- It's unlikely that you'll have trouble finding a computer on your small network. Just in case, however, Windows 98 offers a feature that can search the network for a particular machine. Select Start, Find, Computer to display the Find: Computer dialog box. Use the Named text box to enter all or part of the computer name you want to find, and then click Find Now.

- You use a remote shared drive or folder in much the same way that you use a local drive or folder. That is, you open the resource and then manipulate the files. Note, however, that you may need to enter a password to access a shared resource.

Understanding the Universal Naming Convention

If you examine the Address bar in Figure 28.5, you see that with the Selene computer highlighted, the displayed address is \\Selene. The leading \\ indicates that this is a network address. This notation is part of the Universal Naming Convention (UNC) for network addresses. UNC addresses use the following general format:

\\computername\sharename\path\file

computername	The name of the network computer.
sharename	The name of the shared resource.

path

A folder path within the shared resource.

file

A filename within the folder indicated by *path*.

For example, consider the following UNC address:

`\\Selene\jaz\memos\fiat19.doc`

This address points to the shared resource named Jaz on the Selene computer, and refers to the fiat19.doc file within the memos folder.

Consider these notes about working with UNC paths within Windows 98:

- If the shared resource is a folder or disk drive, you can open it in a folder window by selecting Start, Run, entering the UNC path, and clicking OK.

- You can use UNC addresses in DOS commands. For example, the following command copies the file fiat19.doc into the current directory:

  `copy \\Selene\jaz\memos\fiat19.doc`

- In Windows 98's standard Open and Save As dialog boxes, you can use UNC addresses in the File Name text box.

Sharing Your Resources on the Network

You've seen how the Network Neighborhood displays the resources shared by other computers. To be a good network citizen, you should share some resources of your own. The next couple of sections show you how to share drives, folders, and printers using both Share-Level Access and User-Level Access, as discussed in Chapter 27, "Setting Up Your Own Local Area Network."

Working with Share-Level Access

Peer-to-peer networks use Share-Level Access Control to share resources and set up individual passwords for each resource. (Nodes on a client/server network can also use Share-Level Access, but they're usually better off with User-Level Access Control, discussed in the next section.) To set up sharing, dis-

Inside Scoop
If you're working at the DOS prompt, you can open a shared folder or drive by typing start followed by the UNC address (for example, start \\selene\jaz).

See Also...
"Step 7: Specifying Access Control," p. 614

play the property sheet for the object you want to share and then display the Sharing tab.

Figure 28.6 shows a completed Sharing tab. Follow these steps to set up sharing for a disk drive or folder:

Figure 28.6
With Share-Level
Access Control,
the Sharing tab
appears as shown
here.

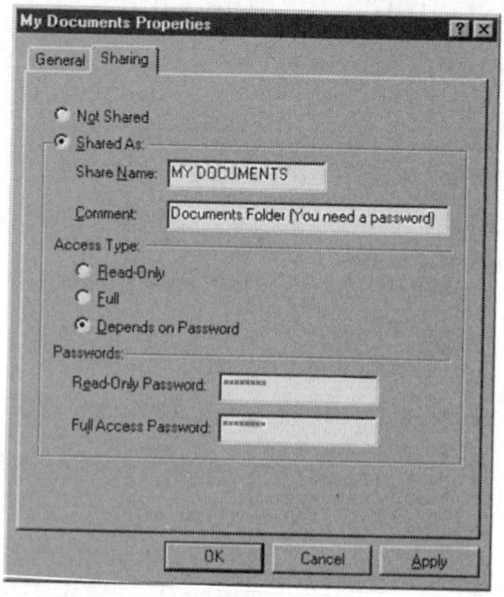

My Documents Properties	? X
General Sharing	

○ Not Shared
● Shared As:
Share Name: MY DOCUMENTS
Comment: Documents Folder (You need a password)

Access Type:
○ Read-Only
○ Full
● Depends on Password

Passwords:
Read-Only Password: ●●●●●●●
Full Access Password: ●●●●●●●

[OK]   [Cancel]   [Apply]

Shortcut
A quick way to the
Sharing tab is to
right-click the
object you want to
share, and then
click Sharing.

1. Activate the Shared As option.

2. Edit the Share Name, if necessary. This is the name that appears when other people open your computer in the Network Neighborhood. Names can be up to 12 characters long and can include spaces, all alphanumeric characters, and the following symbols:

   ~ ! @ # $ % ^ & ( ) _ - { } `

3. Enter a 48-characters-or-less description of the resource in the Comment text box. This description appears in the Network Neighborhood when remote users open your computer in Details view.

4. Use the Access Type options to select the access rights assigned to remote users:

   Read-Only: Allows users to view the resource contents, but does not let them modify those contents. In a folder or disk drive, for example, the user can open a file and save it locally. However, he can't delete or rename a file or folder, edit a file and then save it, or create a new file or folder.

Full: Gives users complete access to view and modify the resource contents.

Depends on Password: If you activate this option, the access rights assigned to the user depend on the password they enter when they attempt to work with the object.

5. If you activated either Read-Only or Depends on Password, enter the access password in the Read-Only Password text box.

6. If you activated either Full or Depends on Password, enter the access password in the Full-Access Password text box.

7. Click OK. If you entered a password, the Password Confirmation dialog box appears.

8. Reenter the password and click OK.

Note that, for every resource you share, Windows 98 adds a small hand icon underneath the object's regular icon.

To share a printer, you follow a similar set of steps:

1. Activate the Shared As option.

2. Edit the Share Name, if necessary.

3. Enter a description in the Comment text box.

4. Enter an optional password in the Password text box.

5. Click OK.

6. Confirm the password, if prompted, and then click OK.

Working with User-Level Access

Share-Level Access Control works well enough, but it's a bit cumbersome to use because you have to assign passwords to every shared resource and you have to distribute those passwords to the affected network users. This isn't a big deal if you have a small peer-to-peer network because your use of passwords will probably be limited. If you're on a client/server network, however, you have a more powerful alternative: User-Level Access Control. In this case, the server maintains a

Inside Scoop
For added security, you can hide a shared resource by adding a dollar sign ($) to the end of the share name. This tells Windows 98 not to display the share in the Network Neighborhood. I'll explain how authorized users can access the hidden share when I discuss mapping resources a bit later (see "Mapping a Shared Resource as a Local Disk Drive").

Remember
If you choose either Read-Only or Full, the password is optional. If you don't enter a password, the user automatically gains access to the resource using the specified rights. However, if you choose Depends on Password, then you must enter at least one of the passwords.

Watch Out!
If you've shared
your resources
using passwords,
don't forget to dis-
tribute those pass-
words to the
appropriate users.

list of the network users, and you use that list to select which users get access to each shared resource. After a user logs on to the network (a logon verified by the server), she can access any resource for which she is listed without having to worry about passwords. Note, too, that User-Level Access also gives you much finer control over the access rights granted to each user.

As before, you get started by opening the property sheet for the object you want to share, and then displaying the Sharing tab. As you can see in the completed tab shown in Figure 28.7, the layout is a bit different.

Figure 28.7
The layout of the
Sharing tab with
User-Level Access
Control.

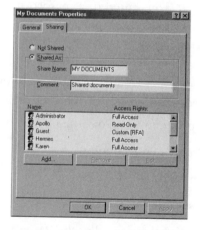

Watch Out!
The word "user"
means everyone
who has access to
the network, so
use this name with
caution.

Follow these steps to set up User-Level Sharing for a disk drive, folder, or printer:

1. Activate the Shared As option and edit the Share Name and Comment text boxes as required. (Use the same rules that I outlined earlier for Share-Level Access.)

2. Click Add to display the Add Users dialog box.

3. If your network has multiple domains, select the domain you want to use from the Obtain List From drop-down list.

4. In the Name list, select the user or users you want to add.

5. Click one of the following buttons:

Read Only: The selected users can view the resource contents, but they can't modify those contents.

Full Access: The selected users have complete access to view and modify the resource contents. Note that this is the only button available if you're sharing a printer.

Custom: The selected users have specific rights only within the resource. See step 8.

6. Repeat steps 4 and 5 until you've added all the users.

7. Click OK.

8. If you added a user with custom access rights, the Change Access Rights dialog box appears, as shown in Figure 28.8. Use the check boxes to spell out the specific rights this user has, and then click OK.

Figure 28.8
Use the Change Access Rights dialog box to set up custom access rights for a user.

9. To remove a user, select his name in the Sharing tab and then click Remove.

10. To change the access rights for a user, select his name and click Edit. Use the Change Access Rights dialog box to modify the user's access rights.

11. Click OK.

Mapping a Shared Resource As a Local Disk Drive

So far, you've seen two ways to access shared network resources: the Network Neighborhood and the UNC address.

These methods have some drawbacks, however:

- You often have to drill down a number of levels in the Network Neighborhood to find the resource you want.

- UNC addresses can get complex and unwieldy.

- Many older applications don't support either Network Neighborhood folders or UNC addresses.

You can solve all these problems by *mapping* a remote shared resource as a local disk drive. That is, you can take any shared disk drive or folder and have it show up on your system as a local disk drive. For example, if your system currently uses drives A through D, you can map a shared drive or folder so that it appears on your system as drive E. This gives you quick access to the resource, avoids UNC addresses, and appears as a local resource to older programs.

Mapping a Resource

Follow these steps to map a shared network resource to a local disk drive on your system:

1. Use the Network Neighborhood to highlight the shared resource you want to map.

2. Select File, Map Network Drive (or right-click the shared resource and click Map Network Drive in the shortcut menu). The Map Network Drive dialog box appears.

3. Use the Drive list to select the local drive letter to use for the selected resource.

4. To map the resource automatically each time you start Windows 98, activate the Reconnect at Logon check box.

5. Click OK.

6. If the resource is protected by a password, the Enter Network Password dialog box appears. Type the appropriate password and click OK.

Windows 98 offers an alternative mapping method that uses a UNC address instead of the Network Neighborhood.

Shortcut
Windows Explorer's toolbar can be customized to display two extra buttons: Map Drive and Disconnect. Choose View, Folder Options, display the View tab, activate the Show Map Network Drive Button in Toolbar check box, and click OK.

This is the method to use if you want to map a hidden shared resource. Follow these steps:

1. In Windows Explorer, choose Tools, Map Network Drive to display the Map Network Drive dialog box.

2. Use the Drive list to select the local drive letter.

3. Use the Path text box to enter the UNC address for the resource. For a hidden resource, don't forget to add the dollar sign ($) at the end.

4. Activate the Reconnect at Logon check box, if desired.

5. Click OK.

6. Enter a password, if prompted.

Disconnecting a Mapped Resource

When you no longer require a shared resource to be mapped to a local drive, use any of the following techniques to disconnect the share:

- Select the local drive that's mapped to the resource and then choose File, Disconnect. (You can also right-click the resource and click Disconnect.)

- In Windows Explorer, choose Tools, Disconnect Network Drive, select the drive in the dialog box that appears, and then click OK.

Printing Over the Network

If someone on your network has shared a printer, you can "install" that printer on your system and then print to it just as if it were a local printer attached directly to your computer. Windows 98 offers two methods for installing a network printer: the Add Printer Wizard and Point and Print.

To install a network printer using the Add Printer Wizard, follow these steps:

1. Select Start, Settings, Printers. Windows 98 opens the Printers folder.

Watch Out!
If you attempt to disconnect a mapped resource while you have open files from that resource, Windows 98 displays a warning. To avoid losing data, cancel the disconnect, close the files, and then attempt the disconnect again.

2. Click the Add Printer icon to load the Add Printer Wizard, and then click Next in the first dialog box.

3. Select the Network Printer option and click Next. The wizard prompts you for the location of the network printer.

4. In the Network Path or Queue Name text box, enter the UNC address of the printer, or click Browse and choose the printer from the Browse for Printer dialog box.

5. From here, you follow the same steps that you would for a local printer.

The Point and Print method enables you to install a network printer directly, which means you skip the first four steps of the Add Printer Wizard. If the network printer is attached to a Windows 95 or Windows 98 machine, Point and Print also installs the remote printer driver (so you won't have to insert your Windows 98 CD) and configures the printer using the remote computer's settings. Windows 98 offers a number of Point and Print methods:

Undocumented
If you have trouble printing to a network printer, try "capturing" the remote printer port so that it appears to be a physical port on your system. To do this, select the remote printer in the Network Neighborhood and then choose File, Capture Printer Port. In the dialog box that appears, select the port you want to use (such as LPT2) and click OK.

■ In the Network Neighborhood, select the remote printer and choose File, Install. (You can also right-click the printer and then click Install.)

■ In the Network Neighborhood, drag the remote printer and drop it inside your Printers folder.

■ Select Start, Run, enter the UNC address of the remote printer, and click OK.

■ Drag a document that you want to print and drop it on the remote printer.

In all cases, a shorter version of the Add Printer Wizard leads you through the driver installation.

Customizing the Network Neighborhood

The System Policy Editor offers a number of policies for customizing the Network Neighborhood. These policies control not only the look of the Network Neighborhood (for example, you can hide the Entire Network folder), but also how users work with the Network Neighborhood (for example, you can set a minimum length for passwords).

On the workstation you want to customize, run the System Policy Editor and open the local Registry. (See the next section to learn how to open a remote Registry from your own computer.) Click the Local User icon and then open the Windows 98 Network branch. The Sharing item has two check boxes:

Disable File Sharing Controls: When activated, prevents the user from using file sharing.

Disable Print Sharing Controls: When activated, prevents the user from using print sharing.

While still in the Local User Properties dialog box, open the Windows 98 System/Shell/Restrictions branch. You'll see three Network Neighborhood-related check boxes:

Hide Network Neighborhood: When activated, hides the Network Neighborhood both on the desktop and in Windows Explorer.

No 'Entire Network' in Network Neighborhood: When activated, hides the Entire Network folder in the Network Neighborhood. This is useful if you have a one-workgroup network that makes the Entire Network icon redundant (and possibly confusing for inexperienced users).

No Workgroup Contents in Network Neighborhood: When activated, hides the workgroup computers from the top-level Network Neighborhood folder. Users can still access the workgroup by opening the Entire Network folder.

The Local User Properties dialog box also enables you to customize the Network dialog box. Open the Windows 98 System/Control Panel/Network branch and activate the Restrict Network Control Panel check box. Three more check boxes become active in the Settings area:

Disable Network Control Panel: When activated, prevents the user from using the Network icon on the Control

Panel.

Hide Identification Page: When activated, hides the Identification tab in the Network dialog box.

Hide Access Control Page: When activated, hides the Access Control tab in the Network dialog box.

Click the Local Computer icon and then open the Windows 98 Network branch to see a long list of policy categories. Not all these categories apply to your small network, however. The rest of this section offers summaries of the ones that do.

The Access Control branch toggles User-Level Access Control on and off and, when it's on, enables you to specify the server name and authenticator type.

The Logon branch offers four check boxes:

Logon Banner: Activating this check box tells Windows 98 to display a dialog box before the Enter Network Password dialog box appears. You can specify both a Caption (the title bar text) and Text (the dialog box text). The default values warn the user not to log on unless he's an authorized user.

Require Validation from Network for Windows Access: When activated, this policy prevents the user from logging on to Windows 98 unless his network logon is validated by a server.

Don't Show Last User at Logon: When activated, this policy hides the name of the previous user who logged on. This is a security precaution that makes it a bit harder for unauthorized users to log on to the network because they must know both an authorized username and the corresponding password.

Don't Show Logon Progress: When activated, this policy prevents Windows 98 from showing things like mapped resource reconnects and system policy loading after the logon. This is a good idea if you think these items might confuse a new user, or if you don't want the user to cancel these tasks.

The `Password` branch has four policies related to user passwords:

Hide Share Passwords with Asterisk: When activated, this policy tells Windows 98 to display typed passwords as asterisks for security. If "shoulder surfing" isn't a concern, deactivate this check box to help inexperienced users enter passwords correctly.

Disable Password Caching: When activated, this policy prevents Windows 98 from saving passwords in the password cache.

Require Alphanumeric Windows Password: When activated, this policy forces the user to use both letters and numbers in her password. Passwords that mix both letters and numbers are much harder to crack than those that use letters only.

Minimum Windows Password Length: When activated, use the Length spinner to set the minimum number of characters that must appear in the password before it's accepted. The longer the password, the tougher it is to crack. (Most security experts advise using passwords that are eight characters long.)

The `Microsoft Client for Windows Networks` branch has policies for the logon and workgroup data:

Log on to Windows NT: When activated, this policy tells Windows 98 to log on to a Windows NT domain. Use the Domain Name text box to enter the domain. Activating Display Domain Logon Confirmation tells Windows 98 to display a dialog box letting users know they were logged on successfully. Activating the Disable Caching of Domain Password check box prevents Windows 98 from including the logon password in the cache. (This thwarts the second of the automatic logon methods I discussed earlier.)

Workgroup: Use this policy to specify the workgroup to which the user belongs. If you deactivate this check box,

❝

shoulder surfing
(present participle):
Stealing a computer password or access code by peeking over a person's shoulder while
they type in the characters.
—The Word Spy
(http://www.
logophilia.com/
WordSpy/)

❞

Inside Scoop
If password security is paramount, you can take other measures to prevent a password from being cracked. These include not using obvious words such as your name, using multiple words, and including some punctuation marks.

the user will not be able to participate in any workgroup.

Alternate Workgroup: If none of the users in the current workgroup are running file and printer sharing, activate this check box to specify a different workgroup that *does* have machines with file and printer sharing enabled.

The File and Printer sharing for Microsoft Networks branch has the same Disable File Sharing and Disable Print Sharing policies that I discussed earlier. Activating them here means that you're disabling sharing for *any* user on this computer.

Some Remote Administration Options

The method discussed in the preceding section for controlling policies on the other network workstations suffers from two serious drawbacks: You have to work directly with each computer and you have to install the System Policy Editor on each computer. You can overcome both problems by using Windows 98's *remote administration* features. These enable you to do a number of things:

- Open a remote machine's Registry using your local copy of System Policy Editor.

- Open a remote machine's Registry using your local copy of the Registry Editor.

- Track and work with connections on a remote machine.

- Monitor performance on a remote machine.

- Use the Network Neighborhood to add, modify, and remove shared resources on a remote machine.

Here are the steps to follow to enable remote administration:

1. Configure your machine and the remote machine for user-level security.

2. Install the Remote Registry service on your machine and the remote machine. In the Network dialog box, click Add, select Service, click Add, click Have Disk, enter *drive*:\tools\reskit\netadmin\remotreg (where *drive* is the letter of your CD-ROM drive, which should have your

Windows 98 CD inserted) and click OK.

3. On the remote machine, enable remote administration by opening the Passwords icon on the Control Panel, displaying the Remote Administration tab, and activating the Enable Remote Administration of This Server check box. Click Add to add the names of users or groups who are allowed to administer the machine.

4. Make sure you have at least one network protocol in common on both your machine and the remote machine.

Administering a Remote Registry

With remote administration enabled, use the following techniques to administer the remote machine's Registry:

Using the System Policy Editor: In your local copy of the System Policy Editor, choose File, Connect, enter the name of the computer you want to administer, and then click OK. If the System Policy Editor displays a list of users, highlight the user you want to work with and then click OK. The System Policy Editor opens the remote Registry. To disconnect, select File, Disconnect.

Using the Registry Editor: In your local copy of the Registry Editor, select Registry, Connect Network Registry, enter the name of the remote computer (or click Browse to select it from a dialog box), and click OK. The Registry adds a new branch with the top-level keys from the remote Registry. To disconnect, select Registry, Disconnect Network Registry, highlight the computer in the dialog box that appears, and then click OK.

Other Remote Administration Options

The following is a summary of the other remote administration techniques available with Windows 98:

Net Watcher: This program enables you to connect to a remote computer and then track the remote machine's shared folders, open files, and connected users. Select Start, Programs, Accessories, System Tools, Net Watcher. Select Administer, Select Server to connect to a remote

Undocumented
When you first connect to a remote machine using Net Watcher, the list of shared folders contains IPC$ and ADMIN$. These are hidden shared folders created when you enabled remote administration on the machine. Windows 98 uses them to communicate with the remote machine.

machine. Use the View menu to select the remote items you want to work with.

System Monitor: The System Monitor can monitor the same performance settings on a remote machine as it can a local machine. In System Monitor, choose File, Connect, enter the name of the remote computer, and then click OK.

Using the Network Neighborhood to work with remote shares: Remote administration enables you to use the Network Neighborhood to work with the shared resources on a remote machine. You can create new shared resources, make changes to existing shares, and stop sharing resources. To do this, open the Network Neighborhood, highlight the remote computer, and then choose File, Properties. Display the Tools tab and then click Administer. The folder window that appears contains the remote machine's existing shared folders, as well as its hard disks, which are displayed with a dollar sign, such as C$. Double-click this icon to see all the folders on that drive.

Essential Information

- To set up an encrypted automatic logon, change the default logon to Windows Logon, change your Windows password to blank, and then cache your domain password the next time you log on.

- You can access the Network Neighborhood via Windows Explorer, by opening the desktop's Network Neighborhood icon, or within the standard Windows 98 Open and Save As dialog boxes.

- The Universal Naming Convention (UNC) specifies remote addresses using the form \\computername\ sharename\path\file.

- To share a resource, open its property sheet, select the Sharing tab, activate the Shared As option, and then set up either a password or a list of users.

- To map a shared folder as a local disk drive, highlight the folder in the Network Neighborhood and then choose File, Map Network Drive.

- To use a network printer, either run the Add New Hardware Wizard and choose the Network Printer option, or use Point and Print to install the remote printer directly.

- To customize the Network Neighborhood, open the System Policy Editor either locally or on the remote machine and then adjust the various network-related properties.

GET THE SCOOP ON...

Setting properties for the Dial-Up Adapter ▪ Using Dial-Up Networking to create a connection for your network dial-up server ▪ Configuring Dial-Up Networking for easier connections ▪ Setting up a Windows 98 machine as a dial-up server ▪ Configuring and using Microsoft Mail over a dial-up connection

Connecting Remotely with Dial-Up Networking

BACK IN CHAPTER 18, "Getting on the Internet," I showed you how to create a Dial-Up Networking connection to the Internet. You can also use Dial-Up Networking to make a remote connection to your network, and I'll show you how it's done in this chapter. You'll see that the process is similar, but there are a few things you have to do differently when connecting to a LAN. If you're running a peer-to-peer network, this chapter also shows you how to configure a Windows 98 machine as a dial-up server. I finish by showing you how to use Microsoft Mail's remote features for sending and receiving messages on the road.

Configuring the Dial-Up Adapter

When you install Dial-Up Networking, Windows 98 installs a new network "adapter" called the Dial-Up Adapter, which appears in the list of networking components in the Network dialog box. The Dial-Up Adapter is really a network driver that acts as a kind of virtual network interface card. Before getting to the specifics of creating a Dial-Up Networking connection, let's quickly examine a few of the Dial-Up Adapter's properties.

651

Inside Scoop
Microsoft has released an updated version of Dial-Up Networking that includes enhanced security and password protection. Use the following address to download the update: http://support. microsoft.com/ download/ support/mslfiles/ Dun40.exe.

See Also...
"Using Dial-Up Networking,"
p. 417

Watch Out!
Make sure you have at least one protocol in common with the dial-up server. If not, you won't be able to negotiate a successful connection.

Open the Network dialog box (launch the Control Panel's Network icon), select Dial-Up Adapter in the list of networking components, and then click Properties. The property sheet that appears has three tabs:

- **Driver Type:** You can ignore this tab (Windows 98 doesn't use a 16-bit driver).

- **Bindings:** This tab lists the network protocols that are bound to the Dial-Up Adapter. Deactivate the check box beside any protocol that you don't need to connect to the dial-up server.

- **Advanced:** This tab contains a list of options for the Dial-Up Adapter. Select an item in the Property list and then select an item in the Value list. There are four properties:

Enable Point To Point IP: Toggles the Point-to-Point Tunneling Protocol (PPTP) on and off for the Dial-Up Adapter.

IP Packet Size: Sets the relative size of the Dial-Up Adapter's IP packets. Selecting the Automatic item is your best bet here.

Record a Log File: Toggles PPP logging on and off. If you change this to Yes, Dial-Up Networking uses a file named Ppplog.txt (it's in the Windows folder) to maintain a log of your dial-up sessions. This is useful for troubleshooting connections.

Use IPX Header Compression: Toggles IPX header compression on and off. IPX header compression is used only with CSLIP (Compressed Serial Line Interface Protocol) connections.

Creating and Configuring a Network Connection

As I mentioned before, creating a Dial-Up Networking connection for a remote network server isn't all that different from creating one for the Internet. Let's run through the basic steps:

1. Select Start, Programs, Accessories, Communications, Dial-Up Networking.

2. The next step depends on how Dial-Up Networking started:

   - If this is the first time you've launched Dial-Up Networking, the Welcome to Dial-Up Networking dialog box appears. In this case, click Next.

   - Each subsequent time you launch Dial-Up Networking, the Dial-Up Networking folder appears. In this case, click the Make New Connection icon.

3. Enter a name for your connection and, if you have multiple modems, choose the modem you want to use from the Select a Device list. Click Next.

4. Enter the dial-up server's Area code, Telephone Number, and Country Code, and then click Next.

5. Click Finish. An icon for your new connection appears in the Dial-Up Networking folder.

Now let's configure the new connection. Highlight the icon and then choose File, Properties to open the connection's property sheet. Display the Server Types tab and configure it as follows:

- I'm assuming here that you're dialing in to either a Windows NT Server machine, or to a Windows 98 machine configured as a dial-up server (as explained later; see "Setting Up Windows 98 as a Dial-Up Server"). Therefore, make sure the Type of Dial-Up Server list shows PPP: Internet, Windows NT Server, Windows 98.

- Make sure the Log On to Network check box is activated.

- Activate the other check boxes in the Advanced options group, depending on the configuration of the dial-up server.

- In the Allowed Network Protocols group, activate the check boxes for the networking protocols you need to

Inside Scoop
The IP Packet Size property is the value of the *Maximum Transmission Unit (MTU)*, which measures the size of the packets sent out by the Dial-Up Adapter. The Automatic setting means that Windows 98 uses 576-byte packets (the Internet default) for connection speeds below 128Kbps, and 1,500-byte packets for speeds greater than or equal to 128Kbps. The other available settings are Large (1,500 bytes), Medium (1,000 bytes), and Small (576 bytes).

Shortcut
Dial-Up Networking offers a couple of faster methods for opening a connection's property sheet. Either highlight the icon and click the toolbar's Properties button, or right-click the icon and then click Properties.

Shortcut
You can take some other routes to the Connect To dialog box. You can double-click the icon, highlight the icon, and then click the toolbar's Dial button, or you can right-click the icon and then click Connect.

See Also...
"Setting a Few More Connection Properties," p. 419

Undocumented
You can launch a Dial-Up Networking connection in the Run dialog box or a batch file by using the following syntax:

rundll
rnaui.dll,
RnaDial
connection

Replace *connection* with the name of the Dial-Up Networking icon you want to use. Note that this syntax is case sensitive.

communicate with the server. If you're using TCP/IP, click the TCP/IP Settings button and fill in your TCP/IP details (including your network's primary and secondary WINS servers, if any).

When you're done, click OK to return to the Dial-Up Networking folder.

Connecting to Your Network

After your Dial-Up Networking connection is configured, connecting to the network isn't much different from connecting to the Internet. Here are the steps to follow:

1. In the Dial-Up Networking folder, highlight the connection icon and then select Connections, Connect. The Connect To dialog box appears.

2. Make sure the User Name text box shows your network username.

3. Enter your network password in the Password text box. To cache the password, activate the Save Password check box. If necessary, use the Dialing From list or the Dial Properties button to adjust the dialing location. See Chapter 17, "Getting the Most Out of Your Modem."

4. Click Connect. Dial-Up Networking connects to the dial-up server and establishes a network connection.

5. Log on to the network in the usual manner. The Connection Established dialog box appears, and the system tray gets a new Dial-Up Networking icon.

6. Click Close.

To disconnect from the network, use any of the following procedures:

- Double-click the taskbar's Dial-Up Networking icon and then click Disconnect.

- Right-click the taskbar's Dial-Up Networking icon and then click Disconnect.

- In the Dial-Up Networking folder, right-click the icon and then click Disconnect.

Configuring Dial-Up Networking

To help ease your connection chores, Dial-Up Networking offers a few settings that can reduce the amount of effort you must expend to get connection. To view these settings, select Connections, Settings to display the Dial-Up Networking dialog box shown in Figure 29.1. You have the following options:

- **Show an Icon on Taskbar After Connected:** Toggles the taskbar's post-connection Dial-Up Networking icon on and off. Because you can use this icon to quickly disconnect from the network, it's probably a good idea to show it.

- **Prompt for Information Before Dialing:** If you deactivate this check box, Dial-Up Networking doesn't display the Connect To dialog box when you launch the icon. If you never change settings in this dialog box, deactivating this check box saves you an extra step when connecting.

- **Show a Confirmation Dialog Box After Connected:** If you deactivate this check box, Dial-Up Networking doesn't display the Connection Established dialog box after a successful connection. Because this dialog box serves no major purpose, deactivating it saves you an extra step.

Remember
For those times when your computer is off the network, create a second hardware profile that doesn't include your NIC. Otherwise, Windows 98 will always attempt to use the NIC to establish a connection to the network, and Dial-Up Networking will fail.

- **Redial:** Activate this check box if you want Dial-Up Networking to redial if the remote server is busy or if a connection can't be established. Use the Before Giving Up Retry spinner to set the maximum number of redials, and use the Between Tries Wait spinners to set the number of minutes and/or seconds between redials.

- **When Establishing a Network Connection:** These options determine what Windows 98 does when you attempt to access a network resource while not connected to the network. The default is Prompt to Use Dial-Up Networking, which displays a dialog box from which you can establish the Dial-Up Networking connection. To disable this prompt, activate the Don't Prompt to Use Dial-Up Networking option.

Figure 29.1
Use this dialog
box to configure
some Dial-Up
Networking set-
tings.

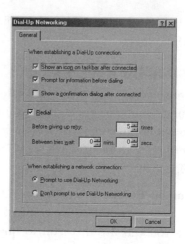

Setting Up Windows 98 As a Dial-Up Server

Dial-Up Networking assumes you have a dial-up server to connect to. On a client/server network, this usually means a
Windows NT Server machine running the Remote Access
Service (RAS). What do you do if you're just running a humble peer-to-peer network? In this case, you can configure one
of the Windows 98 machines as a dial-up server. You won't get
all the features of a RAS dial-up (for example, the Windows 98
dial-up server doesn't support the TCP/IP protocol), but it's
an easy (and inexpensive!) way to establish a remote connection.

Setting Up the Dial-Up Server

The Dial-Up Server is a kind of network resource, so you must
"share" it so that remote users can dial in. In this case, however,
"sharing" just means setting up the Dial-Up Server to allow
callers. As with the sharing of network resources, how you do
this depends on whether you're using Share-Level or User-
Level Access Control.

To get started, open the Dial-Up Networking folder and
then choose Connections, Dial-Up Server.

If you're using Share-Level Access Control, you'll see the
Dial-Up Server dialog box shown in Figure 29.2. Follow these
steps to configure the Dial-Up Server:

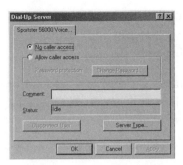

Figure 29.2
This version of the
Dial-Up Server dia-
log box appears if
you're using Share-
Level Access
Control.

1. If you have multiple modems installed, the Dial-Up Server dialog box shows a tab for each modem. Display the tab you want to use with Dial-Up Server.

2. Activate the Allow Caller Access option.

3. If you want to protect the dial-up with a password (a good idea), click the Change Password button and use the Dial-Up Networking Password dialog box to specify the password.

4. Use the Comment text box to add a description or other text related to the Dial-Up Server.

5. Click the Server Type button. Dial-Up Server displays the Server Types dialog box.

6. Make your choices from the following options and then click OK:

   Type of Dial-Up Server: If the incoming calls will be strictly from Windows 95 and Windows 98 machines, select the PPP: Internet, Windows NT Server, Windows 98 item. If there will also be Windows for Workgroups or Windows NT 3.51 dial-ups, select Default to let the Dial-Up Server figure out the correct type.

   Enable Software Compression: When this check box is activated, the server and the remote machine use software compression to exchange data.

   Require Encrypted Password: When this check box is activated, Dial-Up Server requires that the remote machine send its passwords in encrypted form (instead of plain text).

Remember
Dial-Up Server uses software compression and encrypted passwords only if both the server and the remote machine have these options enabled. For the remote computer, open the Dial-Up Networking connection icon, display the Server Types tab, and then activate the Enable Software Compression and Require Encrypted Password check boxes.

7. Click Apply. Dial-Up Networking adds the Dial-Up Server icon to the system tray and begins monitoring the modem for incoming calls.

If you're running User-Level Access Control, the Dial-Up Server dialog box appears as shown in Figure 29.3. Follow these steps:

1. If the dialog box displays multiple modem tabs, display the tab for the modem you want to use.

2. Select the Allow Caller Access option.

3. Click Add, and use the Add Users dialog box to select the users who are allowed to dial up the server. Click OK.

4. Use the Comment text box to add a description.

5. Click the Server Type button and fill out the Server Types dialog box as described previously.

6. Click Apply. Dial-Up Networking adds the Dial-Up Server icon to the system tray and begins monitoring the modem for incoming calls.

Monitoring the Connected User

With the Dial-Up Server configured, the Status box displays Monitoring to indicate that it's looking for incoming calls. When a call comes in, the Status line tells you who it is and when they connected, as shown in Figure 29.3. You can disconnect the user at any time by clicking the Disconnect User button.

Figure 29.3
This version of the Dial-Up Server dialog box appears if you're using User-Level Access Control.

Using Microsoft Mail Remotely

In Chapter 27, "Setting Up Your Own Local Area Network," I showed you how to set up a Microsoft Mail postoffice for network email, and I showed you how to configure Windows Messaging for the Microsoft Mail service. You can also access your mailbox on the road by dialing in to the server and then using Microsoft Mail's Remote Mail feature.

Creating a New Remote Mail Profile

As you'll see in the next section, the Microsoft Mail service has a number of remote options. Rather than configuring and reconfiguring these options depending on whether you're attached to the network or connecting remotely, you should create a separate profile to use with your remote sessions.

First, use these steps to create a new profile:

1. Click the Mail icon on the Control Panel. The Windows Messaging Settings Properties dialog box appears.

2. Click Show Profiles. The Mail dialog box appears.

3. Select your current Microsoft Mail profile and then click Copy. The Copy Profile dialog box appears.

4. Enter a name for the new profile and click OK.

You'll need the Mail dialog box in the next section, so leave it open for now.

Configuring Microsoft Mail for Remote Sessions

Now you need to modify the new profile's Microsoft Mail service to handle the rigors of remote sessions:

1. In the Mail dialog box, select the new profile and click Properties.

2. Select Microsoft Mail and click Properties. The Microsoft Mail dialog box appears.

3. In the Connection tab, activate Remote Using a Modem and Dial-Up Networking.

Watch Out!
The Dial-Up Server always answers incoming calls on the first ring, and there's no way to change that. Therefore, the Dial-Up Server may interfere with other communications software that answers incoming calls (such as Microsoft Fax).

❝
telework (noun): Computer work, particularly work that requires a dial-up connection to the Internet or a corporate network, performed from any remote location. 'Telecommuting' is telework performed at home.
—The Word Spy
(http://www. logophilia.com/ WordSpy/)
❞

4. Display the Dial-Up Networking tab (see Figure 29.4) and set the following options:

Figure 29.4
You can use the Dial-Up Networking tab to set a few options that determine how Microsoft Mail works with Dial-Up Networking.

- **Use the Following Dial-Up Networking Connection:** Select the Dial-Up Networking connection to use.

- **When Dial-Up Networking Fails to Connect:** Set the number of times to retry a failed connection, as well as the number of seconds to wait between each retry.

- **Confirm the Dial-Up Networking Connection Before Starting a Session:** Use these options to set when and if Windows Messaging prompts you for which Dial-Up Networking connection to use for your remote Microsoft Mail sessions. Note that if you select Confirm on First Session and After Errors, Windows Messaging displays the prompt only the first time you connect, or any time an error occurs.

5. Display the Remote Session tab (see Figure 29.5) and set the following options:

- **When This Service Is Started:** Activating this check box tells Windows Messaging to start the Dial-Up Networking connection as soon as you start Windows Messaging.

- **After Retrieving Mail Headers:** Activating this check box tells Windows Messaging to disconnect Dial-Up Networking after Remote Mail has downloaded the message headers.

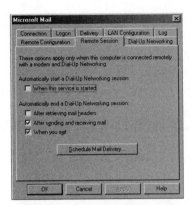

Figure 29.5
The options in the
Remote Session
tab control the
events that start
and stop the
remote Microsoft
Mail sessions.

■ **After Sending and Receiving Mail:** Activating this check box tells Windows Messaging to disconnect Dial-Up Networking after you've sent and received your Microsoft Mail messages.

See Also...
"Setting Microsoft
Mail Options,"
p. 621

■ **When You Exit:** Activating this check box tells Windows Messaging to disconnect Dial-Up Networking after you exit Windows Messaging.

■ **Schedule Mail Delivery:** Clicking this button displays the Scheduled Remote Delivery dialog box. Click Add to display the Add Scheduled Session dialog box, set up a mail delivery schedule, and then click OK.

6. Display the Remote Configuration tab. (Note that these are the same options covered back in Chapter 27.)

7. Click OK until you're back in the Mail dialog box.

8. Click Close.

Running a Remote Microsoft Mail Session

With Microsoft Mail now configured for remote sessions, you're ready to try it out. Follow these steps:

1. With Windows Messaging up and running, you have two ways to start:

   ■ To download received messages and upload sent messages, choose Tools, Deliver Now. (If you have multiple services installed, choose Tools, Deliver Now Using, Microsoft Mail.)

Remember
With your new profile configured, you should now tell Windows Messaging to prompt you for the profile to use. To do this, start Windows Messaging and then select Tools, Options. In the General tab, activate the Prompt for a Profile to Be Used option, and then click OK.

■ To download just the message headers, choose Tools, Remote Mail.

2. If Microsoft Mail is configured to prompt you for a Dial-Up Networking connection, you'll see a dialog box like the one shown in Figure 29.6. Use the drop-down list to select the connection you want to use.

Figure 29.6
This dialog box appears if you set up Microsoft Mail to prompt you for which Dial-Up Networking con-nection to use for the remote ses-sion.

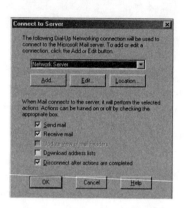

3. Use the following check boxes to specify the actions taken by Microsoft Mail after the connection is established:

■ **Send Mail:** When activated, sends any messages waiting in the Outbox folder.

■ **Receive Mail:** When activated, receives any messages wait-ing in your postoffice mailbox.

■ **Update View of Mail Headers:** When activated, displays only the headers of messages waiting in your postoffice mailbox. (This option is activated only if you selected the Remote Mail command.)

■ **Download Address Lists:** When activated, downloads the postoffice address list.

■ **Disconnect After Actions Are Completed:** When activated, tells Windows Messaging to disconnect the Dial-Up Networking session after the selected actions have been completed.

4. Click OK. Windows Messaging performs the selected actions.

5. Disconnect, if necessary.

Essential Information

- Dial-Up Networking uses the Dial-Up Adapter—a kind of virtual NIC—to connect to a remote dial-up server and log on to the network.

- To start your Dial-Up Networking connection, open the Dial-Up Networking folder and launch the Make New Connection icon.

- One of the key differences between an Internet connection and network connection is that the latter requires a network logon. In the property sheet for the Dial-Up Networking connection, display the Server Types tab and make sure the Log On to Network check box is activated.

- To connect to the dial-up server, highlight the connection icon in the Dial-Up Networking folder and choose Connections, Connect.

- To avoid the Connect To dialog box, choose Connections, Settings and deactivate the Prompt for Information Before Dialing check box.

- To configure the Dial-Up Server, run Dial-Up Networking and choose Connections, Dial-Up Server.

- To configure Windows Messaging for remote Microsoft Mail sessions, make a copy of your existing profile, open the copy, and then configure its Microsoft Mail service for remote connections.

Appendixes

PART VIII

A Glossary of Windows Terms

T<small>HIS</small> <small>GLOSSARY OF</small> W<small>INDOWS</small> terms is a subset from The Tech Word Spy Web site, a compendium of Windows- and Web-related words and phrases. The following address is part of my Web site:

`http://www.logophilia.com/TechWordSpy/`

accelerator key   The underlined letter in a menu name or menu command.

active partition   A disk drive's bootable partition. Its boot sector tells the ROM BIOS at startup that this partition contains the operating system's bootstrap code. The active partition is usually the same as the *primary partition.*

ADC   See *analog-to-digital converter.*

Advanced Power Management   A specification developed by Microsoft and Intel that enables the operating system, applications, BIOS, and system hardware to work cooperatively to manage power and extend battery life.

allocation unit   See *cluster.*

analog-to-digital converter   A chip in a sound card that converts analog sound waves to the digital audio format. See also *digital-to-analog converter.*

APM   See *Advanced Power Management.*

backup job   A Microsoft Backup file that includes a list of files to back up, the type of backup to use (*full, differential,* or *incremental*), and the backup destination.

baud rate   The number of signal changes (which might be variations in voltage or frequency, depending on the *modulation* standard being used) per second that can be exchanged between two *modems*. In most cases, this isn't the same as *bps*.

bi-directional printing   Printing in which not only can Windows 98 send data to the printer, but the printer can send data to Windows 98. For example, the printer could let Windows 98 know its configuration (say, how much memory it has installed), and the printer could keep the operating system informed of the current printer status (for example, out of paper). See also *Extended Capabilities Port.*

bitmap   An array of bits (pixels) containing data that describes the colors found in an image.

BootKeys   Shortcut keys or key combinations that either invoke the Windows 98 Startup menu or select a Windows 98 Startup option (such as *Safe mode*).

bps   Bits per second. The rate at which a *modem* or other communications device transmits data.

bridge   A *network* device that connects two *LANs,* provided that the two LANs are using the same *NOS.* The bridge can either be a standalone device or can be implemented in a server with the addition of a second network card.

CDFS   An *installable file system* for CD-ROM drives. CDFS uses a 32-bit *protected-mode VxD* (VCDFSD.VXD) that replaces MSCDEX.EXE, the 16-bit *real-mode* driver used in previous versions of Windows. See also *VFAT.*

CD-ROM File System   See *CDFS.*

client   In a *client/server network,* a computer that uses the services and resources provided to the network by a *server.*

client application   See *container application.*

client/server network   A *network* model that splits the computing workload into two separate but related areas. On the one hand, you have users working at intelligent "front-end" systems called *clients*. In turn, these client machines interact with powerful "back-end" systems called *servers*. The basic idea is that the clients have enough processing power to perform tasks on their own, but they rely on the servers to provide them with specialized resources or services, or access to information that would be impractical to implement on a client (such as a large database). See also *peer-to-peer network*.

Clipboard   A memory location used to store data that has been cut or copied from an application.

cluster   The basic unit of storage on a hard disk or floppy disk.

cluster chain   The sequence of *clusters* that defines an entire file.

cluster slack   The amount of unused *cluster* space taken up by a file. For example, if a system uses 4,096-byte clusters and a file is 3,000 bytes, its cluster slack is 1,096 bytes.

codec   A *co*mpressor/*dec*ompressor device driver. During playback of audio or video data, the codec decompresses the data before sending it to the appropriate multimedia device. During recording, the codec decompresses the raw data so that it takes up less disk space. Most codecs offer a variety of compression ratios.

color depth   Determines the number of colors (that is, the color palette) available to your applications and graphics. Color depth is expressed in either bits or total colors. See also *High Color* and *True Color*.

COM   See *Component Object Model*.

Component Object Model   The heart and soul of *OLE*. It defines not only the standards that server applications use to create objects, but also the mechanisms by which server and container applications interact when dealing with objects.

compound document   A *container* document that holds, along with its native data, one or more *objects* that were created using *server applications*.

compress   To reduce the size of a file by replacing redundant character strings with tokens. Windows 98 compresses data and manages the resulting *CVF* using the DriveSpace *device driver.*

compressed volume file   A hidden file on a *host drive* that contains the *compressed* files.

compression ratio   The ratio of the size of an uncompressed file to its compressed size. For example, a file that is 10,000 bytes uncompressed and 5,000 bytes compressed has a compression ratio of 2:1.

concentrator   See *hub.*

Configuration Manager   A Windows 98 component (Cnfgmgr.vxd) that enumerates the various *plug-and-play* devices on your system, identifies the *resources* used by each device, resolves resource conflicts, monitors the system for hardware changes, and ensures that the proper *device drivers* are loaded.

connection-oriented protocol   See *transport layer protocol.*

connectionless protocol   See *network layer protocol.*

container application   The application that you use to store a *linked* or *embedded OLE object* created with a *server application.* Also known as the *client application.*

context menu   A menu that appears when you right-click an object. The context menu gives you access to the properties and actions associated with that object.

cooperative multitasking   The *multitasking* mode used by Windows 3.*x* and 16-bit applications. It's up to the individual applications to decide when they will relinquish control of the system. See also *preemptive multitasking.*

cross-linked cluster   A *cluster* that has somehow been assigned to two different files, or that has two *FAT* entries that refer to the same cluster.

CVF   See *compressed volume file.*

DAC   See *digital-to-analog converter.*

data bits   In *modem* data transfer, the number of bits used to represent a character.

delay   When you press and hold down a key, the time interval between the appearance of the first character and the second character. See also *repeat rate.*

demodulation   The conversion into digital data of an analog wave (a series of tones) transmitted over a telephone line. This conversion is performed by a *modem.* See also *modulation.*

device driver   Small software programs that serve as intermediaries between hardware devices and the operating system. Device drivers encode software instructions into signals that the device understands, and, conversely, the drivers interpret device signals and report them to the operating system. See also *virtual device driver.*

Device Manager   A tab in the System property sheet that provides a graphical outline of all the devices on your system. It can show you the current configuration of each device (including the *IRQ, I/O ports,* and *DMA channel* used by each device). It even lets you adjust a device's configuration (assuming that the device doesn't require you to make physical adjustments to, for example, a DIP switch or jumper). The Device Manager actually gets its data from, and stores modified data in, the *Registry.*

DHCP   See *Dynamic Host Control Protocol.*

differential backup   Backs up only files in the current *backup job* that have changed since the last *full backup.* See also *incremental backup.*

digital-to-analog converter   A sound card chip that converts digitized audio back into an analog wave so that you can hear it. See also *analog-to-digital converter.*

directory entry   See *file directory.*

disk cache   A section of memory that stores recent or frequently used bits of program code and data. This improves performance by reducing the number of times the system has to retrieve data from the relatively slow hard disk.

Display Power Management Signaling   A specification that lets a *device driver* use the video adapter to send a signal to the monitor that can either blank the screen (standby mode) or turn off the monitor entirely.

DMA   Direct Memory Access. See also *DMA channel.*

DMA channel   A connection that lets a device transfer data to and from memory without going through the processor. The transfer is coordinated by a DMA controller chip.

DNS   See *Domain Name System.*

Domain Name System   On the Internet, a hierarchical distributed database system that converts *host names* into *IP addresses.*

dotted-decimal notation   A format used to represent *IP addresses.* The 32 bits of the address are divided into quads of 8 bits, which are then converted into their decimal equivalent and separated by dots (for example, 205.208.113.1).

dotted-quad notation   See *dotted-decimal notation.*

double-click speed   The time interval that Windows 98 uses to distinguish between two successive single clicks and a double-click. Anything faster is handled as a double-click; anything slower is handled as two single clicks.

DPMS   See *Display Power Management Signaling.*

dual-booting   Having the option, at startup, of running Windows 98 or some other operating system (such as Windows 3.*x*). See also *multi-booting.*

Dynamic Host Control Protocol   A system that manages the dynamic allocation of *IP addresses.*

ECP   See *Extended Capabilities Port.*

embedding   An *OLE* technique of inserting an *object* into a *container application's* document. An embedded object includes not only a pointer to the *server application,* but also the object's native data. See also *linking.*

environment   A small memory buffer that holds the DOS *environment variables.*

environment variables   Settings used to control certain aspects of DOS and DOS programs. For example, the PATH, the PROMPT, and the values of all SET statements are part of the environment.

Extended Capabilities Port A parallel port that provides support for high-speed printing; new devices that use parallel ports, such as CD-ROMs and modems; and *bi-directional printing*.

extended partition The hard disk space that isn't allocated to the *primary partition*. For example, if you have a 1.2GB disk and you allocate 300MB to the primary partition, the extended partition will be 900MB. You can then subdivide the extended partition into *logical DOS drives*.

extension In a filename, the part to the right of the period. Windows 98 uses extensions to determine the file type of a file.

FAT See *File Allocation Table*.

FIFO buffer A 16-byte memory buffer included with 16550 and later *UART* chips that lets a serial port handle high-speed data transfers while reducing retransmissions and dropped characters.

File Allocation Table A built-in filing system that is created on every formatted disk. The FAT contains a 16-bit entry for every disk *cluster* that specifies whether the cluster is empty or bad, or else points to the next cluster number in the current file.

file directory A table of contents for the files on a disk that is maintained by the *File Allocation Table*. The entries in the file directory specify each file's name, extension, size, attributes, and more.

File Transfer Protocol **(1)**In *modem* communications, this protocol governs various aspects of the file transfer ritual, including starting and stopping, the size of the data *packets* being sent, how errors are handled, and so on. Windows 98 supports seven protocols: Xmodem, 1K Xmodem, Ymodem, Ymodem-G, Zmodem, Zmodem with Crash Recovery, and Kermit. **(2)**An Internet protocol that defines file transfers between computers. Part of the *TCP/IP* suite of protocols.

font A unique set of design characteristics that is common to a group of letters, numbers, and symbols.

FTP See *File Transfer Protocol*.

full backup   Backs up all the files in the current *backup job*. See also *differential backup* and *incremental backup*.

gateway   A *network* computer or other device that acts as a middleman between two otherwise incompatible systems. The gateway translates the incoming and outgoing *packets* so that each system can work the data.

GDI   See *Graphical Device Interface*.

Graphical Device Interface   A core Windows 98 component that manages the operating system's graphical interface. It contains routines that draw graphics primitives (such as lines and circles), manage colors, display fonts, manipulate bitmap images, and interact with graphics drivers. See also *kernel* and *User*.

graphics adapter   The internal component in your system that generates the output you see on your monitor.

hardware flow control   A system whereby the computer and *modem* use individual wires to send signals to each other that indicate whether they're ready to receive data. To stop outgoing data, the modem turns off its CTS (Clear To Send) line. To stop incoming data, the processor turns off its RTS (Request To Send) line. See also *software flow control*.

hardware profile   Hardware configurations in which Windows 98 loads only specified *device drivers*.

High Color   A *color depth* of 16 bits, or 65,536 colors.

host   A computer on the Internet.

host drive   The hidden drive that contains the *compressed volume file* after a disk has been *compressed*.

host name   The unique name of an Internet *host* expressed as an English language equivalent of an *IP address*.

HTTP   See *Hypertext Transfer Protocol*.

hub   A central connection point for *network* cables. They range in size from small boxes with four, six, or eight RJ-45 connectors to large cabinets with dozens of ports for various cable types.

hyperlink   In the Windows 98 Help system, an underlined word or phrase that takes you to another topic or runs a program.

hypertext   In a World Wide Web page, an underlined word or phrase that takes you to a different Web site.

Hypertext Transfer Protocol   An Internet *protocol* that defines the format of *Uniform Resource Locator* addresses and how World Wide Web data is transmitted between a server and a browser. Part of the *TCP/IP* suite of protocols.

idle sensitivity   The amount of time that Windows 98 waits before declaring a DOS program idle. In the absence of keyboard input, Windows 98 just assumes that a DOS program is in an idle state after this predetermined amount of inactivity, and it then redirects the *time slices* to other running processes that it would otherwise devote to the DOS program.

in-place editing   See *visual editing*.

incremental backup   Backs up only files in the current *backup job* that have changed since the last *full backup* or the last *differential backup*.

installable file system   A file system that can be loaded into the operating system dynamically. Examples in Windows 98 are *VFAT* and *CDFS*.

Internet Protocol   A network layer protocol that defines the Internet's basic *packet* structure and its addressing scheme, and also handles routing of packets between *hosts*. See also *TCP/IP* and *Transmission Control Protocol*.

internetwork   A *network* that combines two or more *LANs* by means of a special device, such as a *bridge* or *router*. Internetworks are often called internets for short, but they shouldn't be confused with *the* Internet, the global collection of networks.

interrupt request   An instruction to the CPU that halts processing temporarily so that another operation (such as handling input or output) can take place. Interrupts can be generated by either hardware or software.

intranet   The implementation of Internet technologies such as *TCP/IP* and World Wide Web servers for use within a corporate organization rather than for connection to the Internet as a whole.

invalid cluster   A *cluster* that falls under one of the following three categories:

- A *FAT* entry that refers to cluster 1. This is illegal, because a disk's cluster numbers start at 2.

- A FAT entry that refers to a cluster number larger than the total number of clusters on the disk.

- A FAT entry of 0 (which normally denotes an unused cluster) that is part of a *cluster chain.*

I/O port   A memory address that the processor uses to communicate with a device directly. After a device has used its *IRQ line* to catch the processor's attention, the actual exchange of data or commands takes place through the device's I/O port address.

Io.sys   The *real-mode* portion of Windows 98. `Io.sys` processes `Msdos.sys`, `Config.sys`, and `Autoexec.bat`, reads the Registry, switches the processor into *protected mode,* and then calls on `Vmm32.vxd` to load the Windows 98 protected-mode drivers.

IP   See *Internet Protocol.*

IP address   The unique address assigned to every *host* and *router* on the Internet. IP addresses are 32-bit values that are usually expressed in *dotted-decimal notation.* See also *host name.*

IPX/SPX   Internet Packet eXchange/Sequenced Packet eXchange. IPX is a *network layer protocol* that addresses and routes *packets* from one *network* to another on an IPX *internetwork.* SPX, on the other hand, is a *transport layer protocol* that enhances the IPX protocol by providing reliable delivery. IPX/SPX is used by NetWare networks.

IRQ line   A hardware line over which peripherals and software can send *interrupt requests.*

Kbps   One thousand bits per second (*bps*).

kernel   A core Windows 98 component that loads applications (including any DLLs needed by the program), handles all aspects of file I/O, allocates *virtual memory* and works with the *Memory Pager,* and schedules and runs *threads* started by applications. See also *Graphical Device Interface* and *User.*

LAN   See *local area network.*

linking   An *OLE* technique of inserting an *object* into a *container application's* document. A linked object doesn't include the object's native data; instead, it includes only pointers to both the *server application* and the original data file. If the original data changes, the linked object gets updated automatically. See also *embedding.*

local area network   A *network* in which all the computers occupy a relatively small geographical area, such as a department, office, home, or building. All the connections between computers are made via network cables.

local resource   Any peripheral, file, folder, or application that is either attached directly to your computer or resides on your computer's hard disk. See also *remote resource.*

logical DOS drive—A subset of an *extended partition.* For example, if the extended partition is 900MB, you could create three logical DOS drives, each with 300MB, and they would use drive letters D, E, and F. You can assign up to 23 logical DOS drives to an extended partition (letters D through Z).

lost cluster   A *cluster* that, according to the *FAT,* is associated with a file but has no link to any entry in the *file directory.* Lost clusters are typically caused by program crashes, power surges, or power outages.

Map Cache   A Windows 98 feature that enables the system to execute program code directly from the *disk cache.* This saves memory and improves performance because the code doesn't have to be copied to memory.

master boot record   The first 512-byte sector on your system's *active partition* (the partition your system boots from). Most of the MBR consists of a small program that locates and runs the core operating system files (`Io.sys` and `Msdos.sys`).

Mbps   One million bits per second (*bps*).

MBR   See *master boot record.*

MDI   See *Multiple Document Interface.*

metafile   An image that consists of a collection of drawing commands from Windows 98's *GDI* component. These commands create the basic primitives (lines, circles, and so on) that make up the image.

MIDI   See *Musical Instrument Digital Interface.*

mini-driver   A small *device driver* that augments the functionality of a *universal driver* by providing the commands and routines necessary to operate a specific device.

miniport driver   A *device driver,* supplied by a SCSI controller manufacturer, that provides support for device-specific I/O requests. See also *mini-driver.*

modem   A device used to transmit data between computers via telephone lines. See also *modulation* and *demodulation.*

modulation   The conversion, performed by a *modem,* of digital data into an analog wave (a series of tones) that can be transmitted over a telephone line. See also *demodulation.*

Moore's Law   Processing power doubles every 18 months (from Gordon Moore, co-founder of Intel).

Msdos.sys   A text file that controls certain Windows 98 startup parameters.

multi-booting   Having the choice of three or more operating systems at startup. See also *dual-booting.*

multimedia   The computer-based presentation of data using multiple modes of communication, including text, graphics, sound, animation, and video.

Multiple Document Interface   A Windows 98 programming interface that lets applications display several documents at once, each in its own window.

multitasking   See *cooperative multitasking* and *preemptive multitasking.*

multithreading   A multitasking model in which multiple *threads* run simultaneously.

Musical Instrument Digital Interface A communications protocol that standardizes the exchange of data between a computer and a musical synthesizer.

name resolution A process that converts a *host name* into an *IP address*. See *Domain Name System* and *Windows Internet Name Service*.

NetBEUI The NetBIOS Extended User Interface *protocol*. (NetBIOS is an API that lets network applications—such as *redirectors*—communicate with *networking* protocols.) It's a combined *transport layer protocol* and *network layer protocol* developed by IBM and supported by all Microsoft networks. It's a simple, efficient protocol that works well in small *LANs*.

network A collection of computers connected via special cables or other network media (such as infrared) in order to share files, folders, disks, peripherals, and applications.

network adapter See *network interface card*.

network interface card An adapter that usually slips into an expansion bus slot inside a *client* or *server* computer. (There are also external *NICs* that plug into parallel ports or PC Card slots.) The NIC's main purpose is to serve as the connection point between the PC and the *network*. The NIC's backplate (the portion of the NIC that you can see after the card is installed) contains one or more ports into which you plug a network cable.

network layer protocol A *protocol* in which no communications channel is established between nodes. Instead, the protocol builds each *packet* with all the information required for the network to deliver each packet and for the destination *node* to assemble everything. See also *transport layer protocol*.

Network News Transport Protocol An Internet *protocol* that defines how Usenet newsgroups and postings are transmitted. Part of the *TCP/IP* suite of protocols.

network operating system Operating system software that runs on a *network server* and provides the various network services for the network *clients*.

network redirector   A *virtual device driver* that lets applications find, open, read, write, and delete files on a remote drive.

NIC   See *network interface card.*

NNTP   See *Network News Transport Protocol.*

node   A computer on a *network.*

NOS   See *network operating system.*

object   A separate entity or component that is distinguished by its properties and actions. In the *OLE* world, an object is not only data—a slice of text, a graphic, a sound, a chunk of a spreadsheet, or whatever—but also one or more functions for creating, accessing, and using that data.

object linking and embedding   A technology that lets you share data between applications. Data can be transferred from a *server application* to a *container application* via either *linking* or *embedding.*

OLE   See *object linking and embedding.*

open editing   In *OLE,* when you open an object for editing in a separate window. See also *visual editing.*

packet   The data transfer unit used in *network* and *modem* communications. Each packet contains not only data, but also a "header" that contains information about which machine sent the data, which machine is supposed to receive the data, and a few extra tidbits that let the receiving computer put all the original data together in the correct order and check for errors that might have cropped up during the transmission.

paging file   See *swap file.*

parity bit   In *modem* data transfers that use seven *data bits,* this is an extra bit that lets the receiving system check the integrity of each character.

Parkinson's Law of Data   Data expands to fill the space available for storage (from the original Parkinson's Law: Work expands to fill the time available).

peer-to-peer network   A *network* in which no one computer is singled out to provide special services. Instead, all the computers attached to the network have equal status (at least as far as the network is concerned), and all the computers can act as both *servers* and *clients*. See also *client/server network*.

point size See *type size*.

port driver A 32-bit *protected-mode device driver* that provides complete functionality for working with devices such as hard disk controllers and floppy disk controllers.

POST At system startup, the POST detects and tests memory, ports, and basic devices such as the video adapter, keyboard, and disk drives. If everything passes, your system emits a single beep.

Power-On Self Test See *POST*.

preemptive multitasking A multitasking model used by 32-bit applications in which Windows 98 uses a sophisticated algorithm to monitor all running processes, assign each one a priority level, and allocate CPU resources according to the relative priority of each process. See also *cooperative multitasking*.

primary name In a filename, the part to the left of the period.

primary partition The first partition (drive C) on a hard disk. See also *active partition* and *extended partition*.

property sheet A dialog box with controls that let you manipulate various properties of the underlying *object*.

protected mode An operating mode introduced with the 80286 microprocessor. Unlike *real mode,* which can address only up to 640KB of memory and gives a running program direct access to hardware, protected mode lets software use memory beyond 640KB. It also sets up a protection scheme so that multiple programs can share the same computer resources without stepping on each other's toes (and, usually, crashing the system).

protocol A set of standards that defines how information is exchanged between two systems across a *network* connection. See also *transport layer protocol* and *network layer protocol.*

real mode The operating mode of early Intel microprocessors (the 8088 and 8086). It's a single-tasking mode in which the running program has full access to the computer's memory and peripherals. Except for the Windows 98 Setup program (which uses real mode at first if you start it from the DOS prompt), Windows 98 doesn't use real mode. Real mode is also called *MS-DOS mode.* See also *protected mode.*

redirector   A networking driver that provides all the mechanisms needed for an application to communicate with a remote device, including file reads and writes, print job submissions, and resource sharing.

Registry   A central repository that Windows 98 uses to store anything and everything that applies to your system's configuration. This includes hardware settings, object properties, operating system settings, and application options.

remote resource   Any peripheral, file, folder, or application that exists somewhere on the *network.* See also *local resource.*

repeat rate   When you press and hold down a key, the speed at which the characters appear. See also *delay.*

repeater   A device that boosts a *network* cable's signal so that the length of the network can be extended. Repeaters are needed because copper-based cables suffer from attenuation—a phenomenon in which the degradation of the electrical signal carried over the cable is proportional to the distance the signal has to travel.

router   A device that makes decisions about where to send the *network packets* it receives. Unlike a *bridge,* which merely passes along any data that comes its way, a router examines the address information in each packet and then determines the most efficient route that the packet must take to reach its eventual destination.

routing   The process whereby *packets* travel from *host* to host until they eventually reach their destination.

RTS/CTS flow control   See *hardware flow control.*

Safe mode   A Windows 98 startup mode that loads a minimal system configuration. Safe mode is useful for troubleshooting problems caused by incorrect or corrupt device drivers.

sans serif   A *typeface* that doesn't contain the cross strokes found in a *serif* typeface.

serif   A *typeface* that contains fine cross strokes (called "feet") at the extremities of each character. See also *sans serif.*

server   In a *client/server network,* a computer that provides and manages services (such as file and print sharing and security) for the users on the network.

server application   The application that you use to create and edit an *OLE object.* Also known as the *source application.*

shortcut   A pointer to an executable file or a document. Double-clicking the shortcut starts the program or loads the document.

signature   A few lines of text at the end of an email message that identify the sender and include his contact information (such as his company name, email address, and fax number). Some people also include snappy quotations or other tidbits. Microsoft Exchange doesn't provide any method of adding a signature automatically. However, if you have WordMail, you can customize one of the included email templates with your signature.

Simple Mail Transport Protocol (SMTP)   An Internet protocol that describes the format of Internet email messages and how messages get delivered. Part of the *TCP/IP* suite of protocols.

software flow control   A system whereby the computer and *modem* send signals to each other that indicate whether they're ready to receive data. To stop the transfer, a device sends an XOFF signal (ASCII 19 or Ctrl-S). To restart the transfer, a device sends an XON signal (ASCII 17 or Ctrl-Q). See also *hardware flow control.*

source application   See *server application.*

special drag   Using the right mouse button to drag an object. When you drop the object, Explorer displays a *context menu* with various commands.

start bit   An extra bit added to the beginning of the *data bits* in a *modem* data transfer. This bit marks the beginning of each character. See also *stop bit.*

stop bit   An extra bit (or sometimes two) added to the end of the *data bits* in a *modem* data transfer. This bit marks the end of each character. See also *start bit.*

subnet mask   A 32-bit value, usually expressed in *dotted-decimal notation,* that lets *IP* separate a network ID from a full *IP address* and thus determine whether the source and destination hosts are on the same network.

swap file   A special file used by Windows 98 to emulate physical memory. If you open enough programs or data files that physical memory becomes exhausted, the paging file is brought into play to augment memory storage. Also called a *paging file.*

system tray   The box on the right side of the taskbar that Windows 98 uses to display icons that tell you the current state of the system.

TCP   See *Transmission Control Protocol.*

TCP/IP   Transmission Control Protocol/Internet Protocol. TCP/IP is the lingua franca of most UNIX systems and the Internet as a whole. However, TCP/IP is also an excellent choice for other types of *networks* because it's routable, robust, and reliable.

terminate-and-stay-resident   See *TSR.*

thread   A small chunk of executable code with a very narrow focus. In a spreadsheet, for example, you might have one thread for recalculating, another for printing, and a third for accepting keyboard input. See also *multithreading.*

topology   Describes how the various *nodes* that comprise a *network*—which include not only the computers, but also devices such as *hubs* and *bridges*—are connected.

Transmission Control Protocol   A *transport layer protocol* that sets up a connection between two *hosts* and ensures that data is passed between them reliably. If *packets* are lost or damaged during transmission, TCP takes care of retransmitting the packets. See also *Internet Protocol* and *TCP/IP*.

transport layer protocol   A *protocol* in which a virtual communications channel is established between two systems. The protocol uses this channel to send *packets* between *nodes*. See also *network layer protocol*.

True Color   A *color depth* of 24 bits, or 16,777,216 colors.

TSR   A terminate-and-stay-resident program. These programs load themselves into memory and remain there until a keystroke or some other prompt goads them into action. See also *device driver*.

type size   A measure of the height of a *font*. Type size is measured from the highest point (the "ascender") of a tall letter, such as "f," to the lowest point (the "descender") of an underhanging letter, such as "g." The standard unit of measurement is the point. There are 72 points in an inch. Also called *point size*.

type style   Extra attributes added to a font's *typeface*, such as **bold** and *italic*. Other type styles (often called type effects) include <u>underlining</u> and ~~strikeout~~ (sometimes called "strikethrough").

typeface   A distinctive design that is common to any related set of letters, numbers, and other symbols. This design gives each character a particular shape and thickness that is unique to the typeface and difficult to categorize.

UART   Universal Asynchronous Receiver/Transmitter. A special chip that resides inside every serial port (or sometimes on the computer's motherboard). (For an internal or PC Card modem, the UART chip sits on the card itself.) It's the UART's job (among other things) to take the computer's native parallel data and convert it into a series of bits that can be spit out of the serial port's Transmit Data line. On the other end, individual bits streaming into the destination serial port's Receive Data line are reassembled by the UART into the parallel format that the processor prefers.

Uniform Resource Locator An Internet addressing scheme that spells out the exact location of a Net resource. Most URLs take the following form:

`protocol://host.domain/directory/file.name`

`protocol`	The TCP/IP protocol to use for retrieving the resource (such as http or ftp).
`host.domain`	The domain name of the host computer where the resource resides.
`directory`	The host directory that contains the resource.
`file.name`	The filename of the resource.

universal driver A *device driver* that incorporates the code necessary for the devices in a particular hardware class to work with the appropriate Windows 98 operating system component (such as the printing subsystem). See also *mini-driver.*

URL See *Uniform Resource Locator.*

User A core Windows 98 component that handles all user-related I/O tasks. On the input side, User manages incoming data from the keyboard, mouse, joystick, and any other input devices that are attached to your computer. For "output," User sends data to Windows, icons, menus, and other components of the Windows 98 user interface. User also handles the sound driver, the system timer, and the communications ports. See also *Graphical Device Interface* and *kernel.*

user profiles Separate sets of customization options for each person who uses a computer. Each profile includes most of Windows 98's customization options, including the colors, patterns, wallpapers, *shortcut* icons, screen savers, and programs that appear on the Start menu.

VFAT An *installable file system* that works with the *block I/O subsystem* to access disk services. Because it's a 32-bit *protected-mode VxD* and is multithreaded, VFAT provides superior performance (especially compared to the 16-bit *real-mode* disk access found in Windows 3.1), enhanced reliability, and easier *multitasking.* In particular, VFAT avoids the slow processor mode switches between protected mode and real mode that plagued Windows 3.1. VFAT also supports many more drive and controller types than did Windows 3.*x*. However, it still uses the 16-bit *FAT* for physical storage of files and folders, so it inherits FAT's legendary fragility. See also *CDFS*.

virtual device driver   A 32-bit *protected-mode device driver.*

Virtual File Allocation Table   See *VFAT*.

virtual machine   A separate section of memory that simulates the operation of an entire computer. Virtual machines were born with the release of Intel's 80386 microprocessor. Thanks to *protected mode,* the 80386 circuitry could address up to 4GB of memory. Using this potentially huge address space, the 80386 allowed software to carve out separate chunks of memory and use these areas to emulate the full operation of a computer. This emulation is so complete and so effective that a program running in a virtual machine thinks it's dealing with a real computer. Combined with the resource sharing features of *protected mode,* virtual machines can run their programs simultaneously without bumping into each other.

Virtual Machine Manager   A Windows 98 driver (Vmm32.vxd) that allocates and manages the resources needed by your system's software—your applications and the various operating system processes. If a program or the operating system needs a resource—whether it's a chunk of memory or access to an I/O port—the Virtual Machine Manager handles the request and allocates the resource appropriately.

virtual memory   Memory created by allocating hard disk space and making it look to applications as though they are dealing with physical RAM.

visual editing   In *object linking and embedding,* when you double-click an embedded object, instead of the *server application's* being displayed in a separate window, certain features of the *container application's* window are temporarily hidden in favor of the server application's features. (Linked objects use *open editing.*) Here's a summary of the changes that occur in the container application:

- The document window's title bar changes to tell you what kind of object you're now working with. (Not all applications do this.)

- The menu bar (with the exception of the File and Window menus) is replaced by the server application's menu bar.

- The toolbars are replaced by the server application's toolbars.

VxD   See *virtual device driver.*

Windows Internet Name Service   A service that maps NetBIOS names (the names you assign to computers in the Identification tab of the Network property sheet) to the *IP addresses* assigned via *DHCP*.

WINS   See *Windows Internet Name Service.*

XON/XOFF flow control   See *software flow control.*

Online Resources for Windows 98

I F I'VE WHETTED YOUR APPETITE for even more Windows 98 know-how, the Internet is an excellent place to look. This appendix lists a few of my favorite official and unofficial Windows 98 World Wide Web sites and Usenet newsgroups.

The World Wide Web

The World Wide Web has tons of pages related to the various flavors of Windows. In this section, I give you addresses and descriptions of my favorite sites.

Microsoft Sites

Let's start with the "authorized" Microsoft sites:

Windows 98 Home Page

URL:	http://www.microsoft.com/windows98/
Content:	Files, how-to, news, shareware, troubleshooting
Comments:	This is the place to begin all your Windows 98 Web wandering. All the latest Windows 98 news from Microsoft, updates, new Windows 98 programs—it's all here.

Windows Update

URL:	http://windowsupdate.microsoft.com/
Content:	Files
Comments:	This site can check your system and let you know about new components, applications, and device drivers that are available. You should check this site regularly.

Microsoft Technical Support Search

URL:	http://support.microsoft.com/support/
Content:	How-to, troubleshooting
Comments:	If you're scratching your head over some weird Windows 98 behavior, chances are someone else has found the same thing and has asked Microsoft Tech Support about it, and the engineer has posted a solution in the Microsoft Knowledge Base. This Web site lets you search the Knowledge Base and other support content to track down a problem you might be having. Note that you have to register with Microsoft to use this site.

Windows 98 Software Library

URL:	`http://www.microsoft.com/` `windows98/downloads/default.asp`
Content:	Files
Comments:	This site contains miscellaneous Windows 98 files from Microsoft, including updated components, device drivers, and more.

Hardware Compatibility List

URL:	`http://www.microsoft.com/` `hwtest/hcl/`
Content:	Know-how
Comments:	This page presents the complete list of hardware that has passed muster with Microsoft and therefore has been deemed compatible with Windows 98.

Non-Microsoft Sites

Check out these links to "unauthorized" Windows 98 pages:

32BIT.com

URL:	`http://www.32bit.com/`
Content:	Files, how-to, news, shareware
Comments:	This site is dedicated to 32-bit operating systems, and has extensive Windows resources, particularly shareware.

Allen's WinApps List

URL:	`http://www.winappslist.com/`
Content:	Files, shareware
Comments:	An extensive collection of Windows software arranged in over 40 different categories.

AnchorDesk Windows Briefing Center

URL: http://www.zdnet.com/anchordesk/
                           bcenter/bcenter_303.html

Content: News, shareware

Comments: A collection of articles from Jesse
                           Berst's AnchorDesk newsletter.

Consummate Winsock Apps List

URL: http://cws.internet.com/

Content: Files, shareware

Comments: Not just your average list of Windows
                           98 shareware and files. This site
                           sticks out from the crowd thanks to
                           the in-depth reviews given to each
                           program by the site's proprietor:
                           Forrest Stroud.

DOWNLOAD.COM

URL: http://www.download.com /PC/Win95/

Content: Files, how-to, news, shareware, trou-
                           bleshooting

Comments: At the time of this writing, this site
                           was still geared toward Windows 95,
                           but I expect you'll find Windows 98
                           resources by the time you read this.

PC World Magazine's Windows 98 Page

URL: http://www.pcworld.com/workstyles/
                           win95/index.html

Content: How-to, news, troubleshooting

Comments: A huge list of Windows articles from
                           the pages of PC World magazine.
                           Includes a search engine.

PCWin Resource Center

URL: http://pcwin.com/

Content: Files, how-to, news, shareware, trou-
                           bleshooting

Comments: A nice collection of Windows 98
                           software.

Tech Support Guy

URL: http://www.cermak.com/techguy/

Content: How-to, troubleshooting

Comments: Thousands of troubleshooting arti-
                        cles, many of which are related to
                        Windows problems. Can't find your
                        answer? Ask the Tech Support Guy!

TUCOWS

URL: http://tucows.mcp.com/window95.html

Content: Files, shareware

Comments: One of the premier download sites
                        for Windows 95/98 shareware.
                        Approximately 70 separate software
                        categories.

Windowatch

URL: http://www.windowatch.com/

Content: News

Comments: Subtitled "Electronic Windows
                        Magazine of the Internet," this site
                        keeps you up-to-date on the latest
                        developments in the Windows
                        world.

Windows 98 Megasite

URL: http://www.winmag.com/win98/

Content: Files, how-to, shareware

Comments: This site is run by Windows maga-
                        zine and also includes discussion
                        groups, reviews, and access to the
                        rest of the Windows magazine Web
                        site.

Windows98.org

URL:	http://www.windows98.org/
Content:	How-to, news, shareware
Comments:	An excellent, well-organized site that also includes software reviews, discussion groups, a newsletter, and more.

WinFiles.com

URL:	http://www.winfiles.com/
Content:	Files, how-to, shareware
Comments:	This site has loads of useful links, and the shareware collection is second to none. The site's clever layout is designed to resemble the Windows 98 interface.

WinPlanet

URL:	http://www.winplanet.com/
Content:	How-to, news, troubleshooting
Comments:	This is one of the busiest Windows sites on the Net thanks to its large collection of tips and features related to the Windows world.

Usenet Newsgroups

Usenet newsgroups are usually populated with many enthusiastic users, so they're often a great source for getting answers to specific questions. The following Table B.1, is a list of the Windows 95/98 newsgroups that were available as this book went to press:

TABLE B.1: WINDOWS 95/98 NEWSGROUPS

Newsgroup	Description
alt.os.windows95.crash.crash.crash	The name sounds like a joke, but this group has plenty of serious posts related to troubleshooting issues.

Newsgroup	Description
alt.windows98	A catch-all group for Windows 98 questions and answers.
comp.os.ms-windows.apps.compatibility.win95	The place to look for help related to applications that won't run under Windows 98.
comp.os.ms-windows.apps.utilities.win95	Deals with issues related to the Windows 95 accessories.
comp.os.ms-windows.networking.win95	Check out this group if you need help with networking, Internet access, or other connectivity issues.
comp.os.ms-windows.setup.win95	Covers setup, configuration, and installation issues.
comp.os.ms-windows.win95.misc	Catchall group for other Windows 95 issues. A word of warning: This is a very busy group with hundreds of posts each day.
comp.os.ms-windows.win95.moderated	A high-signal, low-noise group that posts about one-tenth the number of messages that go through the misc group.
comp.os.ms-windows.awin95.setup	Another group related to installtion.

Microsoft also runs its own newsgroups. To view them, set up your newsreader to use the server msnews.microsoft.com. The following lists the newsgroups that deal with Windows 98 topics.

Newsgroup	Description
microsoft.public.win98.apps	Issues related to running applications in Windows 98.
microsoft.public.win98.comm.dun	Covers installation, configuration, and use of Dial-Up Networking.
microsoft.public.win98.comm.modem	Deals with issues related to modems, serial ports, HyperTerminal, Phone Dialer, and general telephony.

continues

TABLE B.1: CONTINUED

Newsgroup	Description
microsoft.public.win98. disks.general	Primarily a forum for disk drive issues, especially questions related to ScanDisk, DriveSpace, and DoubleSpace.
microsoft.public.win98. display.general	Discussions related to video cards and monitors.
microsoft.public.win98. display.multi_monitor	Covers Windows 98's support for multiple monitors.
microsoft.public.win98. fat32	Deals with the FAT32 file system.
microsoft.public.win98. gen_discussion	Miscellaneous Windows 98 topics.
microsoft.public.win98. internet	General Windows 98 Internet topics.
microsoft.public.win98. internet.active_desktop	Questions and answers related to the Active Desktop.
microsoft.public.win98. internet.browser	Discussions related to Internet Explorer and other browsers.
microsoft.public.win98. internet.netmeeting	Covers all aspects of NetMeeting conferencing.
microsoft.public.win98. internet.outlookexpress	Deals with email and newsgroup issues in Outlook Express.
microsoft.public.win98. internet.windows_update	Questions and answers related to the Windows Update Web site.
microsoft.public.win98. multimedia	Discussions on audio, video, and other multimedia.
microsoft.public.win98. multimedia.directx5	Covers multimedia topics related to DirectX version 5.
microsoft.public.win98. networking	Installation, configuration, and troubleshooting of Microsoft and NetWare networks.
microsoft.public.win98. performance	Deals with overcoming poor Windows 98 performance.
microsoft.public. win98.pnp	Windows 98's plug-and-play support.
microsoft.public.win98. power_mgmt	Questions and answers related to power management.
microsoft.public. win98.printing	Discussions about printing in Windows 98.
microsoft.public. win98.pws_4	Covers Personal Web Server.

Newsgroup	Description
microsoft.public.win98.scanreg	Deals with Windows 98's Registry Checker system tool.
microsoft.public.win98.setup	Covers issues related to Windows 98 installation.
microsoft.public.win98.setup.win31	Questions and answers related to upgrading to Windows 98 from Windows 3.1.
microsoft.public.win98.shell	Discussions on the Windows 98 shell and user interface.
microsoft.public.win98.sys_file_check	Covers the System File Checker utility.
microsoft.public.win98.taskscheduler	Deals with the Task Scheduler utility.
microsoft.public.win98.webtv	Questions and answers related to WebTV for Windows.

Windows 98 Keyboard Shortcuts

OFFICIALLY, WINDOWS 98 WAS made with the mouse in mind, so most day-to-day tasks are designed to be performed using standard mouse moves. Unofficially, however, this doesn't mean your keyboard should be ignored when you're not typing. Windows 98 is loaded with keyboard shortcuts and techniques that can often be used as replacements or enhancements for mouse clicks and drags. (These are also useful if your mouse goes south on you. I once saw an otherwise-competent manager panic badly when, just prior to an important presentation, his mouse died and he didn't know how to use Windows without it!) This appendix consolidates all of the Windows 98 shortcut keys and techniques in one place for handy reference.

Windows 98 Startup Keys

As described in Chapter 3, "Understanding and Controlling the Windows 98 Startup," the Windows 98 Startup menu offers several commands that control how Windows 98 starts. You can bypass the menu and run some commands directly by using the keys listed in Table C.1. In all cases, press the key or key combination immediately after you hear the beep that signals the end of the Power-On Self Test (POST).

699

See Also...
"Working with the
Windows 98
Startup Menu,"
p. 82

TABLE C.1: KEYBOARD TECHNIQUES FOR THE WINDOWS 98 STARTUP MENU

Press	To
F4	Boot to your previous operating system.
F5	Boot Windows 98 in safe mode.
Shift+F5	Boot to the DOS prompt in safe mode.
F8	Display the Startup menu. (You can also hold down Ctrl during the POST.)
Shift+F8	Boot Windows 98 using step-by-step confirmation.

Here are a few more startup keyboard techniques to bear in mind:

- Most computers enable you to press a key during the POST to invoke the machine's setup or CMOS settings. The key you press varies depending on the manufacturer, but Delete, Esc, and Ctrl+Esc are common. (You should see a message during the POST that tells you which key to press.)

- Hold down the Shift key during startup to bypass the items in your Startup folder.

- If you boot to the DOS prompt, press Ctrl+Alt+Delete to reboot your computer.

Interface Keys

Table C.2 presents a few keyboard shortcuts that you can use with the Windows 98 interface.

TABLE C.2: KEYBOARD TECHNIQUES FOR THE WINDOWS 98 INTERFACE

Press	To
Alt+Double-Click	Display the property sheet for the selected object.
Alt+Enter	Display the property sheet for the selected object.
Alt+Print Screen	Copy the active window's image to the Clipboard.
Ctrl+Alt+Delete	Display the Close Program dialog box.
Ctrl+Esc	Open the Start menu.
Print Screen	Copy the entire screen image to the Clipboard.

Press	To
Shift	Prevent an inserted CD from running its AutoPlay application. (Hold down Shift while inserting the CD.)
Shift+F10	Display the context menu for the selected object.
Shift+Right+Click	Display the context menu with alternative commands (such as Open With) for the selected object.

Application Keys

You'll spend most of your Windows life working within applications, so knowing a few keyboard shortcuts will save you all kinds of time in the long run. Table C.3 runs through the keys and key combinations available in most Windows applications.

TABLE C.3: KEYBOARD TECHNIQUES FOR APPLICATIONS

Press	To
	Working with Application Windows
Alt	Activate or deactivate the application's menu bar.
Alt+Esc	Cycle through the open application windows.
Alt+F4	Close the active application window.
Alt+Spacebar	Display the Control menu for the active application window.
Alt+Tab	Cycle through the active applications. Displays an icon for each application.
F1	Display context-sensitive Help.
F10	Activate the application's menu bar.
	Working with Documents
Alt+-(hyphen)	Display the Control menu for the active document window.
Alt+Print Screen	Copy the active window's image to the Clipboard.
Ctrl+F4	Close the active document window.
Ctrl+F6	Cycle through the open documents within an application.
Ctrl+N	Create a new document.
Ctrl+O	Display the Open dialog box.

continues

TABLE C.3: CONTINUED

Press	To
Ctrl+P	Display the Print dialog box.
Ctrl+S	Save the current file. If the file is new, display the Save As dialog box.
	Working with Data
Backspace	Delete the character to the left of the insertion point.
Ctrl+C	Copy the selected data to the Clipboard.
Ctrl+V	Paste the most recently cut or copied data from the Clipboard.
Ctrl+X	Cut the selected data to the Clipboard.
Ctrl+Z	Undo the most recent action.
Delete	Delete the selected data.

Dialog Box Keys

Table C.4 presents a few keyboard shortcuts that come in handy when working with Windows' dialog boxes.

TABLE C.4: KEYBOARD TECHNIQUES FOR DIALOG BOXES

Press	To
Alt+Down Arrow	Display the list in a drop-down list box.
Backspace	In the Open and Save As dialog boxes, move up to the parent folder when the folder list has the focus.
Ctrl+Shift+Tab	Move backward through the dialog box tabs.
Ctrl+Tab	Move forward through the dialog box tabs.
Enter	Select the default command button or the active command button.
Esc	Close the dialog box without making an changes.
F4	In the Open and Save As dialog boxes, open the Look In drop-down list.
F5	Refresh the current folder listing.
Shift+F1	Display "What's This?" help for the control that has the focus.
Shift+F10	In the Open and Save As dialog boxes, display the context menu for the selected object in the folder list.
Shift+Tab	Move backward through the dialog box controls.
Spacebar	Toggle a check box on and off; select the active option button or command button.

| Tab | Move forward through the dialog box controls. |

Drag-and-Drop Keys

You've seen in several places throughout this book that drag and drop is a useful and efficient method for performing many routine tasks within Windows 98. Unfortunately, its rules for copying, moving, and creating shortcuts are convoluted, to say the least. The keyboard techniques shown in Table C.5 can help you avoid drag-and-drop confusion.

TABLE C.5: KEYBOARD TECHNIQUES FOR DRAG AND DROP

Press	To
Ctrl	Copy the dragged object.
Ctrl+Shift	Display a context menu after dropping a left-dragged object.
Esc	Cancel the current drag.
Shift	Move the dragged object.

Windows Explorer Keys

Windows Explorer offers a large number of keyboard short-cuts, as shown in Table C.6.

TABLE C.6: KEYBOARD TECHNIQUES FOR WINDOWS EXPLORER

Press	To
+ (numeric keypad)	Display the next level of subfolders for the current folder.
- (numeric keypad)	Hide the current folder's subfolders.
* (numeric keypad)	Display all levels of subfolders for the current folder.
Alt+Left Arrow	Navigate backward to a previously displayed folder.
Alt+Right Arrow	Navigate forward to a previously displayed folder.
Backspace	Navigate to the parent folder of the current folder.

continues

TABLE C.6: CONTINUED

Press	To
Ctrl+Arrow Key	Scroll up, down, left, or right (depending on the arrow key used) while maintaining the highlight on the currently selected objects.
Ctrl+A	Select all the objects in the current folder.
Ctrl+C	Copy the selected objects to the Clipboard.
Ctrl+V	Paste the most recently cut or copied objects from the Clipboard.
Ctrl+X	Cut the selected objects to the Clipboard.
Ctrl+Z	Undo the most recent action.
Delete	Delete the selected objects.
F2	Rename the selected object.
F3	Display the Find dialog box with the current folder displayed in the Look In list.
F4	Open the Address toolbar's drop-down list.
F5	Refresh the contents of the Explorer window.
F6	Cycle the highlight among the All Folders list, the Contents list, and the Address toolbar.
Shift+Delete	Delete the currently selected objects without sending them to the Recycle Bin.
Tab	Cycle the highlight among the All Folders list, the Contents list, and the Address toolbar.

Internet Explorer Keys

Besides typing in the Address bar, most people only use their mouse within Internet Explorer. However, the program comes with quite a few keyboard shortcuts, as you can see from Table C.7.

TABLE C.7: KEYBOARD TECHNIQUES FOR INTERNET EXPLORER

Press	To
Alt+Left Arrow	Navigate backward to a previously displayed Web page.
Alt+Right Arrow	Navigate forward to a previously displayed Web page.
Ctrl+A	Select the entire Web page.
Ctrl+B	Display the Organize Favorites dialog box.
Ctrl+D	Add the current page to the Favorites list.

Press	To
Ctrl+F	Display the Find dialog box.
Ctrl+N	Open a new window.
Ctrl+O	Display the Open dialog box.
Ctrl+P	Display the Print dialog box.
Ctrl+Shift+Tab	Cycle backward through the Web page frames, the Address toolbar, and the Links toolbar.
Ctrl+Tab	Cycle forward through the Web page frames, the Address toolbar, and the Links toolbar.
Esc	Stop downloading the Web page.
F4	Open the Address toolbar's drop-down list.
F5	Refresh the Web page.
F11	Toggle between Full Screen mode and the regular window.
Shift+Tab	Cycle backward through the Links toolbar, the Address toolbar, and the Web page links.
Tab	Cycle forward through the Web page links, the Address toolbar, and the Links toolbar.

Doskey Keys

If you think you'll be spending much time at the DOS prompt, you'll definitely want to learn how to use the Doskey utility, which enables you to recall and edit DOS command lines. Table C.8 lists Doskey's command-recall keys.

TABLE C.8: KEYBOARD TECHNIQUES FOR COMMAND-RECALL IN DOSKEY

Press	To
Alt+F7	Delete all the commands from the recall list.
Arrow Keys	Cycle through the commands in the recall list.
F7	Display the entire recall list.
F8	Recall a command that begins with the letter or letters you've typed on the command line.
F9	Display the Line Number: prompt. You then enter the number of the command (as displayed by F7)

	that you want.
Page Down	Recall the newest command in the list.
Page Up	Recall the oldest command in the list.

Table C.9 runs through Doskey's command-line editing keys.

TABLE C.9: KEYBOARD TECHNIQUES FOR COMMAND-LINE EDITING IN DOSKEY

Press	To
Backspace	Delete the character to the left of the cursor.
Ctrl+End	Delete from the cursor to the end of the line.
Ctrl+Home line.	Delete from the cursor to the beginning of the
Ctrl+Left Arrow	Move the cursor one word to the left.
Ctrl+Right Arrow	Move the cursor one word to the right.
Delete	Delete the character over the cursor.
End	Move the cursor to the end of the line.
Home	Move the cursor to the beginning of the line.
Insert	Toggle DOSKEY between "insert" mode (your typing is inserted between existing letters on the command line) and "overstrike" mode (your typing replaces existing letters on the command line).
Left Arrow	Move the cursor one character to the left.
Right Arrow	Move the cursor one character to the right.

Windows Logo (▦) Keys

The Microsoft Natural Keyboard and most modern keyboards have a Windows logo key (▦). Table C.10 lists the keyboard shortcuts you can use with this key.

TABLE C.10: KEYBOARD TECHNIQUES FOR THE WINDOWS LOGO (▦) KEY

Press	To
▦	Open the Start menu.
▦+D	Minimize all open windows. Press ▦+D again to restore the windows.
▦+E	Open Windows Explorer.
▦+F	Find a file or folder.

Press	To
⊞+Ctrl+F	Find a computer.
⊞+M	Minimize all open windows, except those with open modal windows.
⊞+Shift+M	Undo minimize all.
⊞+R	Display the Run dialog box.
⊞+F1	Display Windows Help.
⊞+Break	Display the System Properties dialog box.
⊞+Spacebar	Scroll down one page (supported only in certain applications, such as Internet Explorer).
⊞+Tab	Cycle through the taskbar buttons.

Note, too, that the Microsoft Natural Keyboard and compatibles also have an Application key. It has a picture of a mouse pointer and a context menu. Pressing this key activates the context menu for the current object.

A

Accelerated Graphics Port (AGP), 22, 557
accelerator keys/rate, 243, 264, 539
accents, adding to characters, 551
access control
  custom, 639
  data devices, 528–529
  full, 637, 639
  handle, 332
  hard disks, 20
  Help feature, 37
  modems, 406
  passwords, 637
  read-only, 636, 639
  share-level, 614
  upper memory blocks (UMBs), 144
  user-level, 614, 644
Accessibility group (Internet Explorer)
  configuration, 456
  Options icon, 185–187, 189
  subkey, 194
  Wizard, 27
accessories, starting, 37
accounts
  Internet Connection Wizard, 13, 415–416
  ISPs, 412, 416–417
  servers, 608
ACPI (Advanced Configuration and Power Interface), 25
actions
  accelerator keys, 264
  file types, 262–265
  printing, 264
Active Channels page, 245, 501
Active Desktop, 230
  channels, 220
  converting to Web pages, 224
  creating, 224–225
  default settings, 223
  desktop items layer, 221–223
  enabling/disabling, 204–205, 222, 302
  HTML desktop background layer, 221
  icons, 221, 221
  installation, 500

Java applets, 223
memory, 12, 221
push media, 12
Registry, 105
active items
  hubs, 602
  scripting, 501
  windows, 700
ActiveMovie Control, 213, 569
ActiveX controls
  downloading, 315
  file types, 258
  signatures, 499
acute accent, 551
Adaptec SCSI adapter, 367
adding
  accents to characters, 551
  Address bar, domain suffixes, 443–444
  buttons, 442
  cabinet files, 109
  components, 66–67, 610
  Control Panel, 196–197
  Favorites folder sites, 445
  file types, 269
  folders, 242
  hardware, 523–524
  Java applets, 223
  keyboard languages, 551–552
  links to Web view templates, 217–218
  modems, 393–395
  Outlook Express 4, 484
  printers, 641
  programs, 130, 146–148, 186, 189
  remote administration, 646
  settings, 90
  shortcuts, 137, 238–239
  users to networks, 638
  WAV files, 573
  Web sites, 497
Address bar
  AutoComplete, 443
  domain suffixes, 443–444
  frames, 444
  Internet Explorer, 459, 462
  searches, 441, 444
  shortcuts, 443
  taskbar, 246
  updates, 442
  URLs, 437, 443

Index

Address Book
   backups, 55
   Internet Explorer, 27
   profiles, 502
   searches, 482
addresses
   memory, 290, 518
   Microsoft Mail Postoffice, 623
administration, remote
   enabling, 646–647
   hidden shared folders, 648
   monitoring, 646, 648
   Net Watcher, 647
   Registry, 646–647
   shared resources, 646, 648
   System Policy Editor, 647
Advanced Configuration and Power Interface (ACPI), 25
Advanced Connection Setting, 402–404
   cellular protocol, 403
   data compression, 403
   errors, 403
   flow control, 403
   log files, 404
   modulation type, 404
   S11 register, 404
advanced options, 61
Advanced Power Management (APM), 25
AGP (Accelerated Graphics Port), 22
alarms, batteries, 579–580
Allen's WinApps List Web site, 691
Allow F4 to boot previous OS (Tweak UI), 124
alphanumeric passwords (Network Neighborhood), 645
Always show boot menu (Tweak UI), 124
America Online, 412
analog lines, 388
AnchorDesk Windows Briefing Center Web site, 692
animations, 302, 461
anonymous logon, 502
ANSI character set, 548–551
antivirus software, 63, 359
   creating, 368
   updating, 362
APM (Advanced Power Management), 25

Appearance subkey (Registry), 194
applications
   16-bit, 149–151, 299
   32-bit, 299
   backups, 314
   closing, 571
   configuration files, 55, 128
   default settings, 136
   DLLs, 133–134, 148–149
   DOS, 302, 304–306
   exiting, 302
   extensions, 132, 267–268
   files, 15
   installation, 127–130
      Add/Remove Programs, 130
      AutoPlay, 130
      backups, 128
      bootable disks, 128
      custom, 129
      information files, 131
      MS-DOS mode, 131, 141
      paths, 132–133
      program settings, 132
      setup.exe file, 131
      user settings, 132
      viruses, 129
   keyboard shortcuts, 701–702
   launching, 20
   maximizing/minimizing, 136, 571
   memory, 294–296, 301
   menu commands, 571
   monitors, 566–567
   multitasking, 139
   opening, 134
      DOS prompt, 136
      double-clicking, 134–135
      in IFRAME, 501
      Quick Launch toolbar, 135
      Registry, 137–138
      Run dialog box, 135
      shortcuts, 135
      Start menu, 134
      Startup folder, 137
      Task Monitor, 322
      Task Scheduler, 135
      Win.ini file, 138–139
   Registry, 105
   restoring, 571
   unassociated, 260–261

uninstallation, 56, 134, 146–148, 313
unused, 301–302
archived files, 54, 314, 377
area codes, modem dialing locations, 406
arrows, shortcut icons, 282–283
assigning
    IP addresses, 413, 419, 429, 627
    logon scripts for Internet, 428
association file types, multiple extensions, 267–268
AT command modems, 396–398
attachments, 4, 472–475, 493
attributes, 178, 332, 372
audio CDs, recording, 573
authentication
    email, 504
    messages, 505, 508–509
    names, 644
    passwords, 502
AutoComplete, 443, 459
Autoexec.bat file, 367
    backups, 55, 371–372
    commenting out lines, 80
    configuration, 143–145
    copying, 54
    deleting, 80–81
    DOS, 140
    PATH statement, 81–82
    SET statement, 81
    startup, 78–79
    testing, 80
    see also Config.sys file
automating
    Infrared Monitor dialog box, 591
    installation, 61, 130
    logons, 502
    Msdos.sys file, 92
    Network Neighborhood, 631–632
    restarts, 86
    Skip Driver Agent, 527–528
    Startup menu, 94
AutoPlay install, 130, 701
Autorun ScanDisk (Tweak UI), 124
AutoScan (Msdos.sys file), 93, 462
AVI files, see video

B

Back button, 11, 202–203
background
    desktop, 230
    images, 200
    Outlook Express, 471
    printing, 462
    Web view, 207–209
backups
    8 millimeter tapes, 373
    address books, 55
    applications, 128, 314
    archived files, 54, 377
    Autoexec.bat file, 55, 371–372
    cabinet files, 110
    configuration files, 55, 87, 109, 129, 374
    creating, 374
    DAT tapes, 373
    data, 55, 377
    DC 6000 tapes, 373
    differential, 375–376
    digital line tapes (DLTs), 373
    DOS XCOPY command, 58
    EZFlyer, 377
    files, 37, 328, 372, 375
    floppy disks, 376
    full, 377
    hard disk, 58, 313
    HiFD, 377
    IDs, digital, 506
    incremental, 375–376
    installation, 54
    Jaz drives, 377
    online, 377
    opening, 374
    partitions, 341
    passwords, 375
    performance, 58
    personal folders, 55
    RAM, 371
    Registry, 106–107, 375
        availability, 108
        Checker utility, 17, 110
        daily, 107
    reports, 375
    restoring, 19, 108–109, 374, 377–379
    Setup, 57
    SparQ, 377
    SuperDisk, 376
    system files, 55, 109, 352

tape drives, 376
Travan tapes, 373
unattended, 376
utility, 18, 37, 373
verification, 375
Wide tapes, 373
Windows, 55, 58
Zip drives, 377
bad sectors, 317–318
bandwidth
NetMeeting, 16
serial ports, 584
banks, DIMMs/SIMMs, 291
basement area networks, 596
Basic group (Outlook Express 5),
485
Batch 98, 60–62
batch files
Dial-Up Networking, 654
shortcuts, 276
System Recovery utility, 380
batteries for notebooks, 579–580
baud rate, 389
billboards, 59
binary digits (bits), 388
binary files
editing, 372
file types, 269
Registry, 111, 114–115
testing, 372
values, 372
bindings, 431, 652
BIOS
code, 518
Plug-and-Play, 521
power management,
576–577
updating, 56
bitmapped images, 99–100
bits (binary digits), 388
blocking
device driver installation,
526
Outlook Express messages,
477
BNC connectors, 601
body of Web view templates,
211–214
bookmarks in Netscape, 446–447
boot disks
applications, 128
creating, 380
drive A, 76–77

floppies, 57
option (Tweak UI), 123
partitions, 46, 337–338
sector viruses, 358–359
write-protecting, 26, 362
booting
cold, 76
enabling, 95
files, 94–95
length, 124
operating systems, 124, 700
Startup menu, 124
see also dual-booting; triple-
booting
bottlenecks, 598
bps (bits per second), 388
breakpoints, 86, 88
bridges, 603
briefcases, 587–589
browsers
installation, 457
Internet Explorer, 13
windows, 458
browsing
configuration, 456–460
Favorites folder, 445–446
Internet Explorer, 30, 263
Links bar, 441
Outlook Express, 467
Web sites, 10, 437
buffers
controlling, 402
double-buffering, 89
files, 77
overriding, 78
startup, 77
bugs
Outlook Express 4, 475
security, 491
built-in items, Start menu,
241–242
buses
1394 (FireWire), 23–24
mastering, 518, 598
topology, 603
USB, 23
buttons on Links bar, 442
bypassing
logos, 97
proxy servers, 432, 497
Select Drive dialog box, 315
Startup folder, 700
bytes, screen display requirements, 559

C

C: drive, 54
cabinet files
    backups, 110
    extracting, 67–68
    Registry, 108
    strings, 109
cabling
    coaxial, 599, 601, 603
    connections, 600
    crossover, 602
    selecting, 598
    twisted-pair, 599, 602–603
cache
    memory limitations, 293
    Network Neighborhood
        passwords, 645
    passwords, 654
    Web sites, 454–455
    write-behind, 97
    see also RAM
calibration of game controllers,
    553–554
CALL command (DOS), 145
call waiting, modems, 406
calling cards, 407–408
canceling
    drag-and-drop, 160
    modem connections, 401
Caps Lock key, 547
capturing
    images, 568
    remote printer ports, 642
Carrier Detect (CD) serial ports,
    391
cascading windows, 244
[CD] section (Config.sys file),
    370
CD-ROM drives, 40
    initialization, 372
    letters, 371
cellular protocol, 403
certificates, 502–503
changing
    Favorites folders, 447
    files, 353
    graphics adapter drives,
        557–558
    monitor types, 563
    security zone levels, 498–502
    see also editing

channels
    Active Desktop, 220
    Definition Format (CDF),
        457
    DMS device drivers, 517–518
    full-screen mode, 459
    push technology, 220
    Web sites, 503
characters
    accents, 551
    filenames, 35
check boxes
    deactivating, 90
    ScanDisk, 319
checking security, 495
Chkdsk.exe file, 372
circuit boards, 291
circumflex, 551
class IDs, 195, 242
cleaning, 53–54, 56
Clear To Send (CTS) serial ports,
    391
ClickLock, 543
clients
    file sharing, 612–613
    Internet Connection
        Sharing, 626–628
    logons, 615, 617, 630
    networks, 596
        access control, 614
        NIC drives, 610–611
        services, 612–613
        workgroups, 613
    print sharing, 612–613
    protocols, 611–612
Clipboard
    active windows, 700
    memory, 302
    screen images, 700
clocks, 244
cloning hard disk, 58
closing
    applications, 571
    documents, 301
    folders, 457
    gates, 388
    programs, 57, 146, 700
    shortcuts, 279
    status bars/toolbars, 301
clusters
    chains, 320
    FAT, 333
    FAT32, 332, 338–339
    files, 321, 332

IALA, 322
    sectors, 333
    slack (overhang), 333–337
coaxial cables, 599, 601, 603
cold boot, 76
color
    desktop, 230–231
    folders, 208
    Hardware Diagnostic Tool,
        529
    menus, 369
    monitors, 558, 560, 567
    Registry, 105, 194
    system resources, 300–301
columns
    Registry Editor, 111
    Windows Explorer, 175
COM ports, 390
Command prompt only com-
    mand (Startup menu), 84
command-line editor
    DOS, 144
    startup, 78
    switches, 84
Command.com file, 96, 367
commands
    Briefcase, Update All, 588
    Connections, 641, 648, 654,
        656
    Dial-Up Networking,
        425–427
    DOS
        CALL, 145
        deleted, 43
        DEVICE, 308
        DEVICEHIGH, 308
        DIR, 129
        FC (File Compare),
            129–130
        FDISK, 46
        LOADHIGH, 308
        Lock, 144
        UNDELETE, 166–167
        XCOPY, 58
    Drive, Compress, 327
    Edit, 138, 157, 335
    File Manager, 57
    File menu
        Delete, 163
        Map Network Drive,
            640
        New, Folder, 162, 197
        New Shortcut, 276
        Open, 260

Open Registry, 120,
    192
Open With, 266
Properties, 276, 648
Quick View, 149
Rename, 162
Send To, 160–161
halt, 425
hiding, 241–242
New menu, 269
recall list, 705
restoring, 165, 378
settings, 59, 185, 259
shutdown, 98, 166, 577
Start menu, 98, 241–242
    Find, Files or Folders,
        168
    Run, 191
Startup menu, 83–84, 86
Toolbars, New Toolbar, 196
Tools, Remote Mail, 662
View menu
    Arrange Icons, 176
    Folder Options, 91,
        154, 177
    Status Bar, 154
    Thumbnails, 176
comment out, 191
commenting out, 80, 191
[COMMON] section (Config.sys
    file), 371
company names, 68
compatibility
    FAT32, 338
    mode, 88
    NICs, 597
    Plug-and-Play, 562
    System Recovery utility, 381
    Windows 98, 41
compatibility mode, 88
components
    adding, 66–67, 610
    deleting, 66–67, 314, 610
    options, 61
    System Information utility,
        347
compression
    data, 403
    Dial-Up Server, 657
    files/folders, 37, 325–328,
        361
    free space, 328–329
    headers, 652

partitions, 338
Serial Line Interface
    Protocol (CSLIP), 652
volume file (CVF), 326
CompuServe dial-ups, 429
computers
    clients, 613
    finding, 706
    infrared (IR) ports, 591
    Network Neighborhood, 634
    rebooting, 372, 700
    restarting, 523
concentrators, 602–603
Config.sys file, 367, 369
    backups, 55
    [CD] section, 370
    commenting out lines, 80
    [COMMON] section, 371
    configuration, 143–145
    copying, 54
    deleting, 80–81
    DOS, 140
    [HELP] section, 370
    menucolor section, 369–370
    menudefault section, 369
    [NOCD] section, 370
    testing, 80
    see also Autoexec.bat file;
        startup files
configuration
    Accessibility Wizard, 27
    adding, 90
    Autoexe.bcat file, 143–145
    backups, 87, 109, 129,
        374–375
    components, 610
    computers, 585–587
    Config.sys file, 143–145
    Control Panel, 190–191, 194
    Device Manager, 532
    Dial-Up Adapter, 651–652
    Dial-Up Server, 656–658
    digital IDs, 505–506
    editing, 90
    files, 128
        attributes, 372
        sharing, 612–613
        system, 352, 354
    hot docking, 581–582
    installation, 84
    IntelliPoint, 540–541
    Internet Connection
        Wizard, 13, 414, 625–628

Internet Explorer, 462
    Accessibility group, 456
    Browsing group,
        456–460
    HTTP 1.1 group, 460
    Java Virtual Machine,
        460–461
    Multimedia group, 461
ISPs, 417
keyboard rates, 546–547
logons, 631–632
modems, 187
    Advanced Connection
        Setting, 402–404
    dialing locations, 405
    port settings, 401–402
    Registry, 399
monitors, 567
    color depth, 558, 560
    multiple, 564–567
    resolution, 558–562
mouse, 535–536
New menu, 268
NICs, 599
Outlook Express, 468–469
Plug-and-Play devices,
    521–522
print sharing, 612–613
proxy servers, 430–431
Quick Launch toobar,
    245–246
Recycle Bin, 164–165
Registry, 68, 104–105,
    115–116
Remote Mail, 659–661
ScanDisk, 372
Share-Level Access Control,
    635
shell folders, 235
shortcuts, 33
sorting, 90
Start menu, 28, 34, 237
TCP/IP protocol, 432
time, 37
USB (Universal Serial
    Bus), 23
user profiles, 247
video cards, 232
VShield (McAfee), 360
Web settings, 205
Windows, 37, 175, 421–423
workgroups, 608–609
confirmation
    Dial-Up Networking, 655
    prompts, 84, 660

conflicting
    Device Manager devices, 531
    files, 355–357
connections
    attempts, 420
    cabling, 600
    computers, 37
    Dial-Up Networking
        establishing, 655–656
        sharing, 419
    disabling, 424, 427
    ISPs, 195, 424
        applications, 628
        direct, 624
        LANs, 429–430
        phone numbers, 412
        WinGate application,
          627
    Microsoft Mail Postoffice,
      622–623
    modems, 401, 403
    multiple, 420
    networks, 654
    Outlook Express, 468, 470
    passwords, 421
    Personal Web Server, 15
    remote administration, 646
    sharing, 30
    testing, 433
Consummate Winsock Apps List
  Web site, 692
Contacts list (Outlook Express 5),
  485
context menus, *see* shortcuts
Continue booting after *x* seconds
  (Tweak UI), 124
Control.ini file, 190–191
control ANSI characters, 548
Control menu, 223
Control Panel
    Accessibility Options icon,
      185
    adding, 196–197
    class ID, 242
    Control.ini file, 190–191
    cpl files, 190
    customizing, 192–193
    Date/Time, 186, 195
    Desktop Themes icon, 186
    dialog boxes, 189–190
    Display, 186, 195
    extension file, 188
    folders, 37, 184
    fonts, 186, 195
    Game Controllers icon, 186

    hardware, 184–185
    icons, 184–185, 192, 195,
      285
    Internet, 186, 195
    Keyboard icon, 186
    Mail icon, 186
    Microsoft Mail Postoffice
      icon, 187
    modems, 187, 195
    Mouse icon, 187
    Multimedia icon, 187
    Network icon, 187, 195, 643
    opening, 71
    Passwords icon, 187
    PC Card (PCMCIA), 187,
      195
    Power Management icon,
      187
    Power Meter icon, 195
    printers, 187, 196
    programs, 186
    Regional Settings icon, 188
    Registry, 193–194
    Scanners and Cameras icon,
      188
    settings, 194
    software, 184
    Sounds icon, 188
    system, 188, 196
    tabs, 193
    Telephony icon, 188
    Tweak UI, 188, 191
    Web view, 210
controlling
    buffers, 402
    Num Lock key, 548–549
    objects with property
      sheets, 36
    print jobs, 37
controls (Tweak UI), 123–124
conventional memory, 303,
  305–308
converting
    Active Desktop to Web
      pages, 224
    FAT16 to FAT32, 17
    FAT32 to FAT16, 339
    images, 100
    partitions, 340–342
cookies, 499–500
copying
    Autoexec.bat file, 54
    Config.sys file, 54
    EBD.CAB file to RAM drive,
      372

Outlook Express, 475
program code in memory, 324
RAM, 372
Registry, 105–106
Resource Kit Sampler, 348–349
screen images, 700
source files, 69
user profiles, 248
WAV files, 573
Web sites, 500
Windows Explorer, 157–158, 173–174
corrupted data/sectors, 107, 333, 337
cost
    MidPoint Gateway, 628
    modem connections, 401
    monitors, 22
    Trumpet FireSock, 628
    WinGate, 627
country codes for modem dialing locations, 406
cpl files, 189–190
crackers, 358
CRC (cyclical redundancy check), 352–353
creating
    Active Desktop wallpaper, 224–225
    Address bar, 443
    backups, 374–375
    bootable disk, 57, 380
    Dial-Up Networking, 652–654
    file types, 265–267
    images, 37
    Lmhosts file, 608
    logon scripts, 425–429
    Microsoft Mail Postoffice, 618–619
    modems, 406
    Optlog.txt file, 323
    Outlook Express, 480
    policies, 122
    power schemes, 578
    registration files, 118
    Registry, 116
    scripts, 29
    servers, 608
    Setup, 60–62
    shortcuts, 238, 275–276
    Start menu, 240
    startup disks, 65, 366–368

    user profiles, 249
    Web view, 207–210
    Windows Explorer, 161–162
cross-frame navigation, 492, 500
cross-linked files, 59, 317, 319
crossover cables, 602
CSLIP (Compressed Serial Line Interface Protocol), 652
Ctrl key, 82
cursors
    animated, 302
    moving, 706
    Registry, 194
customizing
    access, 639
    Control Panel, 191–193
    default settings, 183
    files, 143–145
    installation, 64, 129
    keyboard, 185
    Links bar, 441
    mouse, 185
    Network Neighborhood, 642
    shortcuts, 276–278
    system icons, 236–237
    Windows Explorer, 177
CVF (compressed file volume), 326
cyclical redundancy check (CRC), 352–353

D

DAT tapes, 373
data
    area, 318, 332
    backups, 55, 377
    bits, 389390, 401
    compression, 403
    devices, 528–529
    pasting, 501
    serial ports, 391
    terminal equipment (DTE), 400
    transferring, 517–518
date and time, 37, 65, 170, 186, 189, 195, 317, 332
DBLSPACE.BIN driver, 77, 96
DC 6000 tapes, 373
dead keys, 551
dead links, 280–281
debugging
    binary files, 372
    scripts, 457

default settings
    Active Desktop, 223
    applications, 136
    Autoexec.bat file, 143
    browsers, 270–271
    Config.sys file, 143
    customizing, 183
    databases, 356
    desktop, 232–233
    DOS, 140
    file types, 258
        actions, 263–265
        hiding, 256
        MIME content, 262
    Internet Explorer 5.0, 29–30
    logon banners, 644
    Outlook Express, 15, 30, 475
    passwords, 632
    PATH statement, 81
    Recycle Bin, 164
    shortcuts, 277
    start pages, 438
    user profiles, 247–248
    usernames, 632
    Web sites, 209, 439
    Windows Explorer, 178
defragmentation
    files, 37
    hard disk, 57, 296, 313,
      320–321
delay command, 425
delay rates for keyboard, 546–547
deleting
    application backups, 314
    Autoexec.bat file, 80–81
    boot sector viruses, 359
    characters, 706
    components, 66–67, 314,
      610
    Config.sys file, 80–81
    device drivers, 53, 530
    Favorites folder, 447
    files, 502
        empty, 314
        hard drive, 313–316
        system, 353
        temporary, 53
        types, 270
        zero-byte, 19
    folders, 19
    Links bar, 442
    Microsoft Mail Postoffice,
      619

    Outlook Express
        folders, 476
        mail rules, 480
        messages, 475, 477,
          484
    Registry, 116
    Start menu
        built-in items, 241–242
        shortcuts, 238, 240
    uninstallation files, 316
    users to networks, 639
    WAV files, 573
    Web sites, 454, 498
    Windows Explorer, 162–165
    Winundo.dat file, 314
Delivery tab (Microsoft Mail dialog box), 622
demodulation, *see* modems
deselecting Windows Explorer
  multiple objects, 157
desktop
    Active Desktop, 222–223
    background, 230
    color, 230–231
    default settings, 232–233
    files, 209
    fonts, 230–231
    icons
        editing, 227–229,
          232–233
        hiding, 231, 233
        InfoTip, 233
        lists, 231
        menus, 231
        selecting, 233
    Internet Explorer, 458
    layers, 221
    Network Neighborhood, 633
    Registry, 194
    screen savers, 230
    shell folders, 235–236
    shortcuts, 33
    startup, 33
    taskbar/toolbar, 244, 246
    themes, 186, 189, 302
    windows, 231
destination folders, 381
detection
    computers, 523
    corrupted data, 107
    hard disk errors, 63,
      316–319, 321, 372
    hardware, 26, 65, 347,
      522–524

terminate-and-stay-resident
  programs, 59
viruses, 53, 129
Device Bay support, 32
DEVICE command, 308
device drivers
  Automatic Skip Driver
    Agent, 527–528
  deleting, 53
  digital signatures, 526
  disabling, 528
  DMA channels, 517–518
  EMM386, 308
  HCL, 525
  I/O ports, 516–517
  installation, 521, 524–526
  IRQs, 514–516
  licenses, 525
  loading, 308–309, 519–520
  memory addresses, 518
  mini-, 520
  non-signed, 526
  Plug-and-Play, 520–521
  real mode, 519–520
  Registry, 105
  testing, 525
  types, 518
  universal, 520
  virtual (VxDs), 78, 519–520
  WHQL, 525–527
DEVICEHIGH command, 308
devices
  conflicting, 531
  data, 528–529
  deleting, 530
  drivers, 532
  hardware classes, 528
  printing data, 530
  property sheets, 530, 532
  refreshing, 530
  Registry keys, 529
  resources, 532
  SCSI devices, 530
  settings, 532
  System Information utility,
    347
  troubleshooting, 531
  viewing, 529–531
DHCP (Dynamic Host
  Configuration Protocol), 430
  enabling, 626
  IP addresses, 627
  Windows 98 Second Edition,
    422

Diagnostic startup option, 88
dial tone prompts on modems,
  401
Dial-Up Networking (DUN), 16
  accounts, 415
  address lists, 662
  bindings, 652
  commands, 425–427
  configuration, 651
  confirmation prompts, 655,
    660
  connections
    establishing, 655
    retry limit, 660
    sharing, 419
  creating, 652–654
  disconnecting, 660, 662
  DNS servers, 419
  driver types, 652
  Favorites, 451
  Internet Connection
    Wizard, 417–419
  IP addresses, 419
  IPX header compression,
    652
  log files, 652
  logon scripts
    assigning, 428
    creating, 425–429
    paths, 428
    prompts, 655
    testing, 428
  mail, 661–662
  modems, 418
  MTU, 653
  networks, 654
  opening, 195, 418, 423
  Outlook Express, 468
  packets, 652
  passwords, 423, 427
  phone numbers, 424
  PPP server, 419
  PPTP, 652
  property sheets, 652
  redialing, 655
  Remote Mail, 660
  security, 31, 421
  shortcuts, 284
  system variables, 427
  taskbar, 655
  TCP/IP protocol, 494
  updates, 652
  usernames, 423, 427
  variables, 427

VPNs, 31
Web view, 210
Windows 98 Second Edition,
    422
Dial-Up Server
    compression, 657–658
    configuration, 656–658
    encryption, 657
    passwords, 657–658
    type, 657
    users, 658
dialing locations, 405–408
dialog boxes
    Control Panel, 189–190
    keyboard shortcuts, 702
    tabbed, 37
    warnings, 495
dieresis, 551
differential backups, 375–376
digital cameras, 25, 188, 568
digital IDs, 503
    backups, 506
    configuration, 505–506
    messages, 507–509
    public key, 506–507
digital line tapes (DLTs), 373
digital signatures, 526
Digital Versatile Disc (DVD-
    ROM), 24
DIMMs (Dual In-Line Memory
    Modules), 291
DIR command (DOS), 129
Direct Cable Connection, 37, 584
    guest computers, 585–587
    host computers, 585–587
    infrared (IR) ports, 591
    protocols, 586
    serial ports, 584
direct connections, 624
Direct Disk Access, 144
Direct Memory Access channels
    (DMA), 517–518
directories, *see* folders
directory servers
    ISPs, 414
    passwords, 414
    Scanreg.ini file, 110
    searches, 482–483
disabling, *see* enabling/disabling
disconnecting
    Dial-Up Server users, 658
    idle time, 421
    ISPs, 429
    modems, 401

networks with Dial-Up
    Networking, 654
Remote Mail sessions, 660,
    662
shared resources as local
    disk drive, 641
DiskClone (Quarterdeck) Web
site, 58
disks
    bootable, 76–77
    cache, 144, 291
    cleaning, 19, 313–316
    defragmentation, 20, 37,
        320–323
    drives
        displaying, 326
        hiding, 326
        hosts, 327
        installation, 64
        local, 640–641
        protected mode, 85
        sharing, 636–637
        shortcuts, 284
        User-Level Sharing,
            638–639
    errors, 372
    formatting, 372
    repairing, 37, 372
    scanning, 372
    space, 44
    system, 57
displaying
    Address bar, 443
    alternate text, 456
    battery messages, 580
    Close Program dialog box,
        700
    context menus, 701
    disk drives, 326
    domains, 633
    file types, 263
    fonts, 463
    hard disk, 312
    Help, 706
    hidden files, 91
    HTTP error messages, 458
    icons, 186, 189, 195–196,
        463
    Internet Connection
        Sharing, 626
    Internet Explorer, 458
    Java console, 460
    License Agreement, 59
    logos, 97, 124

messages, 580
Microsoft Mail Postoffice, 623
object property sheets, 700
Outlook Express, 483
Power Management Signaling (DPMS), 564
Readme.txt file, 372
Run dialog box, 706
ScanDisk statistics, 318
screens, 124, 559
search engine results, 462
settings, 23
shortcuts, 229
Startup menu, 94, 124, 244, 700
System Properties dialog box, 707
URLs, 458
Web sites, 455
Windows Explorer, 154, 178
workgroups, 633
dithering images, 461
DLLs (dynamic link libraries)
applications, 149
functions, 52
GPFs, 53
installation, 52
shared, 133–134
storing, 52
subroutines, 52
uninstallation, 53
updating, 52
usage counters, 148
versions, 52
DMA channels, 517–518
DNS (Domain Name System) servers, 413, 419, 431
docking stations for notebooks, 580–582
documents, 241
centricity, 256
closing, 301
scraps (shortcuts), 284
dollar sign ($), 637
domains
Address bar, 443–444
displaying, 633
format, 201
names, 413, 431
DOS
applications, 151, 302
Autoexec.bat file, 140, 143–145

command-line editor, 144
commands
CALL, 145
deleted, 43
DIR, 129
FC (File Compare), 129–130
FDISK, 46, 340–341
LOADHIGH, 308
Lock, 144
UNDELETE, 166–167
XCOPY, 58
Config.sys file, 140, 143–145
default settings, 140
Direct Disk Access, 144
disabling, 145–146
disk cache, 144
Doskey, 279, 705–706
environment variable, 81
hidden files, 334
memory, 140
available space, 307
benchmarks, 306
conventional, 303, 307
environment variables, 305
expanded (EMS), 144, 304, 306–307
extended (XMS), 304, 306–308
high (HMA), 77, 304, 308
listing contents, 306–308
loading, 308
maximizing conventional, 306
MS-DOS protected-mode, 306
optimizing, 303, 308
pausing output, 306–308
PIF shortcut file, 304
property settings, 304, 306
reserved, 307
restricting conventional, 305
upper (UMA), 303, 307–308
write-protecting, 305
MS-DOS mode, 141–143
multitasking, 139
PIFs, 278–279
prompt, 136, 164, 700

restarting, 98
Setup, 62–63
shortcuts, 275–276, 283
system files, 334
UNC addresses, 635
upgrading from, 42–43
verbose mode, 334
Virtual Machine Manager
(VMM), 139
windows, 82
dot pitch, 563
dotless IP addresses, 492–493
double-buffering, 89, 96
double-clicking
applications, 134–135
mouse speed, 537
objects, 206
single-clicking, 10
Tweak UI, 544
DoubleBuffer (Msdos.sys file), 96
DOWNLOAD.COM, 692
downloading
ActiveX control signatures,
499
Dial-Up Networking, 652
Favorites subscriptions, 450
files
application, 315
hard drives, 491
security, 500
viruses, 358, 361
fonts, 500
images, 461
notifications, 458
Outlook Express, 470
Power Toys Set, 124
Remote Mail, 661–662
software, 501
DPMI (MS-DOS protected-
mode), 306
DPMS (Display Power
Management Signaling), 564
Dr. Watson utility, 383
drag-and-drop, 545
full-window, 232
keyboard shortcuts, 703
Start menu shortcuts, 240
Web site files, 500
Windows Explorer objects,
158, 160
Drive Image (PowerQuest) Web
site, 58
drivers
compression, 327
converting, 17, 341–342

DBLSPACE.BIN, 77
devices, 532
Automatic Skip Driver
Agent, 527–528
blocking installation,
526
deleting, 53
Detection Manager,
522–523
digital signatures, 526
disabling, 528
DMA channels,
517–518
EMM386, 308
HCL, 525
I/O ports, 516–517
installation, 521
IRQs, 514–516
licenses, 525
loading, 308–309,
519–520
manual installation,
524–525
memory addresses, 518
mini-, 520
non-signed, 526
Plug-and-Play,
520–521
real mode, 519–520
testing, 525
types, 518
universal, 520
virtual (VxDs), 78,
519–520
WHQL, 525–527
Dial-Up Adapter, 652
disabling, 528
DRVSPACE.BIN, 77
Fast Infrared (FIR), 589
LoadFailed lines, 83
Serial Infrared (SIR), 589
sound card, 569
drives
bootable disks, 76–77
drive C:, 54
free space, 327
graphics adapters, 557–558
hosts, 327
last drive letter, 78
network clients, 611
NIC, 610–611
Recycle Bin, 164
DriveSpace utility, 37, 77, 96,
325–329, 367
DSOUND driver, 83

Dual In-Line Memory Modules (DIMMs), 291
dual-booting
    enabling, 95
    FAT32, 338
    installation, 42
    Linux, 51
    OS/2Warp, 51
    Setup, 63
    Windows 3.1x, 44, 47–48
    Windows 95, 45
    Windows 98
        FAT32, 46–47
        other OSs, 45, 47–48, 51
        partitions, 46
        Windows NT, 49–51
    see also booting; triple-booting
DUN, see Dial-Up Networking
duplicate filenames, 317
DVD-ROM (Digital Versatile Disc), 24
DWORD, 111
Dynamic Host Configuration Protocol, see DHCP
dynamic link libraries, see DLLs
dynamic partitions, 337
dynamic virtual device drivers, 78

E

EBIOS driver, 83
echoing
    AT commands, 398
    PING utility, 432
    TRACERT utility, 432
    WAV files, 573
editing
    Batch 98, 62
    binary files, 372
    commands, 144
    desktop, 227–229, 232–233
    file types, 261–263
    FrontPage Express, 14–15
    History bar, 439
    images, 99–100
    Links bar, 442
    Microsoft Mail Postoffice, 619, 622
    monitors, 560–562
    mouse pointer, 538
    Msdos.sys file, 92
    Outlook Express 4/5, 480, 485–486

passwords, 187
profiles, 503
Registry
    binary values, 114–115
    company names, 68
    global, 117
    strings, 114
    usernames, 68
settings, 90
shortcuts, 278, 282–283
shutdown bitmap, 99
sound schemes, 569–570, 573
startup bitmap/options, 76, 99
strings, 138
text, 157, 335
turn off bitmap, 99
WAV files, 573
Windows Explorer, 155
Effects menu (Sound Recorder), 573
email
    authentication, 504
    encryption, 504
    IMAP account, 413
    Microsoft Mail Postoffice, 623
    new features, 15
    POP3 accounts, 413
    privacy, 504
    Remote Mail, 659
        address lists, 662
        configuration, 659–661
        confirmation prompts, 660
        Dial-Up Networking connections, 660
        digital IDs, 505–506
        disconnecting, 660, 662
        headers, 662
        mail delivery schedule, 661
        messages, 661
        profiles, 659
        receiving mail, 662
        retry limit, 660
        running, 661–663
        sending mail, 662
    S/MIME, 505
    servers, 616
    spoof, 504
    tampering, 504
    virus hoaxes, 490–491

emergency boot disk, 108, 365-366
EMM (expanded memory manager), 88, 304, 306–308
empty files/folders, 19, 314
EMS (expanded memory), 306
enabling/disabling
    Active Desktop, 204–205, 222, 302
    Address bar searches, 462
    animated cursors, 302
    antivirus software, 56
    automatic installation, 130
    AutoPlay, 701
    Autoscan, 462
    bad sector repair, 318
    booting, 95, 362
    check boxes, 90
    clock, 244
    Connect To dialog box, 424
    Connection Established dialog box, 424
    device drivers, 85, 528
    DHCP for WINS Resolution option, 626
    DOS, 145–146
    Doskey command-line editor, 279
    double-buffering, 96
    drivers, 302, 528
    dual-booting, 95
    fast shutdown, 89
    files, 258, 643
    HD IRQs, 88
    images, 461
    infrared (IR) ports, 589, 591
    installation on demand, 457
    Internet Connection Sharing, 626
    Internet Explorer, 270
    IPX/SPX, 419
    IrDA driver, 590
    ISPs, 413
    Java logging, 460
    Microsoft Mail Postoffice, 622
    modems, 406
    monitors, 564
    NetBEUI, 419
    Network Neighborhood, 643
    Num Lock key, 548
    Outlook Express, 480
    page hits/transitions, 457–458
    Pentium F0, 89
    policies, 121
    Post-Dial Terminal Screen, 429
    power management, 577
    print sharing, 643
    Profile Assistant, 502
    remote administration, 646–647
    ROM breakpoints, 88
    Safe mode, 95
    ScanDisk, 89
    script debuggers, 457
    security, 495, 499
    shared resources, 636–637
    shortcuts, 94, 282
    Show Files link, 219–220
    Startup menu, 89, 91
    swap files, 56
    synchronization, 457
    TCP/IP protocol, 431
    UDF, 89
    User-Level Access Control, 644
    wallpaper, 302
    Web integration, 57, 203–204
    Web view, 206–207
    Windows Explorer, 154
    WINS, 609
    write-testing, 318
encryption
    Dial-Up Server, 657
    email, 504
    Fortezza standards, 503
    keys, 504–505
    messages, 507–509
    security, 501
Energy Star standard, 562
Enhanced Parallel Port (EPP), 585
Entire Network folder, 643
enumeration, SCSI devices, 530
environment variables
    conventional memory, 305
    values, 81
errors
    corrections, 389
    detection, 316–319, 321
    hard disk, 63, 313, 347
    log files, 319
    messages, 458
    modems, 403
    MS-DOS mode name length, 319
    scripts, 457
Ethernet, 598

euro currency symbol, 31, 549
even parity, 389
events, sound schemes
    editing, 569–570
    Registry, 571–572
excluding file types from backups, 375
executing
    ActiveX control signatures, 499
    Add New Modem Wizard, 393–395
    antivirus software, 359–361
    Disk Defragmenter utility, 320–321
    DOS applications, 302
    full backups, 380
    Plug-and-Play, 520–521
    programs, 134, 137–138, 242, 654, 706
    Registry Checker utility, 109
    Remote Mail sessions, 661–663
    reports, 57
    ScanDisk, 59, 321
    System File Checker utility, 351
    uninstall feature, 71–72
exiting
    applications, 302
    MS-DOS mode, 86
    Windows, 37, 58, 97
Expanded Memory (EMS), 144
expanded memory manager (EMM), 88, 304, 306–308
Explorer.exe file (Windows Explorer), 179–180
exporting
    Favorites folders, 30, 446–447
    Netscape, 446–447
    registration files, 116–117
Ext.exe file, 372
extended ANSI characters, 548–551
Extended Capabilities Port (ECP), 585
extended memory, 64, 304, 306–308
extensions
    file types, 256–257
        displaying, 263
        enabling, 258
        hiding, 256, 263
        MIME content, 262
        multiple, 267–268
        registering, 265
        renaming, 256
        saving, 257
    files, 332
        links, 274
        shortcuts, 281–282
        registering, 265
        shortcuts, 275
External Jscript, 493
external modems, 391, 393, 400
extracting files, 18, 67–68, 354–355, 367, 372
EZFlyer backups, 377

F

Fast Ethernet, 598
Fast Infrared (FIR) drivers, 589
fast shutdown, 97, 89
FAT16, 17, 317, 339
FAT32, 17, 40, 46–47, 331–332, 337–342, 368
Favorites list
    browsing, 445–446
    exporting, 30, 446–447
    folders, 457
    frequently updated sites, 448
    importing, 446–447
    Internet Explorer 5.0, 13
    offline viewing, 452–454
    opening, 241
    research sites, 448
    sites, 445
    subscriptions, 448
        configuration, 453
        dial-up connections, 451
        downloading, 450
        logins, 451
        updated pages, 449, 452
    Web sites, 445, 447–448
FC (File Compare) command (DOS), 129–130
FCBS settings, 78
FDISK utility, 53, 340–341, 367
file allocation table, *see* FAT16; FAT32
File menu commands
    Connect, 648
    Delete, 163
    Disconnect, 641

Map Network Drive, 640
New, Folder, 162, 197
New, Shortcut, 276
Open, 260
Open Registry, 120, 192
Open With, 266
Properties, 276, 648
Quick View, 149
Rename, 162
Restore, 165
Send To, 160–161
FileList, 214
files
    access handle, 332
    actions, 258, 262–265
    ActiveX controls, 258
    adding, 269
    applications, 132, 315
    archived, 54, 314
    attachments, 493
    attributes, 332, 372
    Autoexec.bat, 54–55
    backups, 37, 55, 328, 352,
      372, 375
    binary values, 269
    blocks, 78
    buffers, 77
    cabinets, 110
    changed, 353
    clusters, 332–337
    commands, 269
    compression, 37, 325–328
    configuration, 54–55, 109,
      352, 354
    conflicting, 355–357
    Control Panel, 188
    creating, 265–267
    CRC values, 352–353
    cross-linked, 317, 319
    data, 55
    date and time, 332
    default settings, 258
    defragmenting, 37
    deleting, 53, 270, 313–316,
      353, 502
    describing, 262
    downloading, 491, 500
    editing, 261–263
    empty, 314
    extensions, 154–155,
      256–258, 267–268,
      281–282
    extracting, 372
    File Manager, 57
    finding, 37, 706

fragmentation, 316, 320
future use, 332
hidden, 91, 178
highlighting, 261
icons, 261
ignoring, 354
Information Utility, 348–349
initialization, 54
installation, 351
Internet Explorer, 263,
  270–271
last modified, 332
links, 274
Lmhosts, 608
location, 353–354
log files, 353
lost fragments , 319
maintenance, 167
Media Player, 31
MIME content, 262
naming, 35, 72, 155, 259,
  269, 317, 436
Netscape, 270–271
Network Neighborhood, 643
null, 269
opening, 10, 260–261
optimizing, 109
overwriting, 351
password list, 55
placeholders, 259
policies, 122
primary name, 332
printing, 264
programs, 20, 55
protecting, 350
Quick View, 262
Registry, 11, 105, 258–259
restoring, 351, 354, 356–357
scanning, 360
search criteria, 353
security, 494
selecting, 11, 349
Setup, 67–68, 354–355
sharing, 431, 587–589,
  612–613
shortcuts, 275
startup, 54, 367
storing, 59, 331
support versions, 350
temporary, 315
tracking, 333
transferring, 390, 459,
  584–585, 591
types, 275
undeleting, 37

uninstallation, 70–71, 316
updating, 354, 588–589
verification data file, 351, 354
versions, 350
viruses, 358, 361
Web sites, 201, 211, 436, 500
Win.ini, 55
Windows 3.1*x*, 47
Windows Explorer
   attributes, 178
   creating, 161–162
   date criteria, 170
   deleting, 162–165
   finding, 168–170
   hiding, 179
   pop-up descriptions, 178
   recovering, 165–167
   renaming, 162
   sorting, 176–177
   specifications, 169
   uppercase names, 179
Windows Messaging, 55
WordPad, 266
zero-byte, 19
filtering messages, 4, 30, 476–480
finding, 30, 241
   computers, 706
   files, 37, 367, 706
   folders, 706
   hardware, 523
   Network Neighborhood, 634
   Outlook Express messages, 475, 480–482
   shortcuts, 278–280
   Windows Explorer, 168–170
   see also searches
FireWire, *see* IEE 1394
FixSize() functions, 215
flagging Outlook Express messages, 474–475
Flashpt.sys file, 367
floppy disks
   backups, 376
   boot, 57, 128, 361–362
   formatting, 362
   objects, 164
   scanning, 360
   Windows Explorer, 171–174
flow control, 392, 403, 413
folders
   color, 208
   compressed, 361
   Control Panel, 184

editing, 485
empty, 19
finding, 706
formatting, 209
hiding, 485
host computers, 201
links, 12
listing, 129
Microsoft Mail Postoffice, 617
My Documents, 26
naming, 213
opening, 264
options, 204
Outlook Express, 467, 476
Scheduled Tasks, 363
shared, 636–637, 648
shell, 235–236
shortcuts, 33, 277, 284
Start menu, 79, 239, 242
user profiles, 250
User-Level Sharing, 638–639
viewing, 11, 213, 284
Web sites, 202, 205, 435–436
Windows Explorer
   creating, 161–162
   customizing, 177
   default settings, 178
   deleting, 162–165
   recovering, 165–167
   renaming, 162
   selecting, 155
   sorting, 176–177
   title bar, 178
   uppercase names, 179
fonts
   Control Panel, 186, 189, 195
   desktop, 230–231
   displaying, 463
   downloading, 500
   euro currency symbol, 31
   shortcuts, 279
Force Compatibility mode disk access, 88
foreground executing, 59
form submission
   security, 501
   Web sites, 503
formatting
   disks, 372
   drive C:, 54
   files, 372
   floppy disks, 362
   folders, 209
   numbers, 215

partitions, 54
URLs, 200
Windows Explorer, 171–173
Fortezza standards, 503
Forward button, 11, 202–203, 438
forwarding Outlook Express messages, 474
fragmentation, 316–317, 319–320
frames
    Address bar, 444
    buffers, 556
    Frame Spoof, 492, 501
    stack, 78
    Web sites, 444
free space, 308, 327–329
fritterware, 237
FrontPage Express, 14–15
FTP (file transfer protocol), 390, 459
full access, 637, 639
full backups, 377, 380
full-screen DOS applications
    channels, 459
    dragging, 232
    executing, 302
functions
    in DLLs, 52
    JavaScript, 215–216
    keys, 123, 700
future use of files, 332

G

game controllers, calibration, 186, 189, 553–554
gates, 388
gateways
    Internet Connection Sharing, 624–627
    IP addresses, 430
    TCP/IP protocol, 431
GDI (Graphical Device Interface), 79, 300
General Protection Faults (GPFs), 53
General tab (Folder Options dialog box), 204
global Registry editing, 117
Go button (Internet Explorer 5), 458
"Good Times" virus hoax, 490
GPFs (General Protection Faults), 53

Graphical Device Interface (GDI), 79, 300
graphics adapters
    Accelerated Graphics Port (AGP), 557
    BIOS code, 518
    drives, 557–558
    installation, 555–556, 566
    monitors, 565
    PCI bus, 557
    memory, 557
    RAM, 518
    Web TV, 556
    see also video
grave accent, 551
guest computers, 583, 585–587
GUI (graphic user interface), 94

H

hackers, 358
halt command, 425
hard disk
    accessing, 20
    backups, 313, 380
    cleaning, 19, 53–55
    cloning, 58
    clusters, 320, 333–337
    data area, 318
    defragmentation, 57, 313, 320–321
    errors
        checking, 313
        detection, 63, 316–319, 321
    FAT, 331–332
    files, 313–317, 332–333
    fragmentation, 320
    interrupt requests, 86
    memory, 56
    partitions, 40–41, 46, 53–54
    power schemes, 577
    properties, 312
    recovering, 379–380
    reliability, 311
    ScanDisk checks, 56
    sectors, 333
    Setup, 63
    source files, 69
    space, 339–340
    storage, 311
    swap files, 296–297
    system area, 318
    Web view, 312

hardware
    adding, 185
    Control Panel, 184
    detection, 26, 65, 522–524
    finding, 523
    flow control, 392
    Hardware Diagnostic Tool,
      529
    HCL, 525, 691notebooks,
      581
    Plug and Play, 65, 522
    processors, 40
    profiles, 77
    RAM, 40
    Registry, 105
    System Information utility,
      347
    VGA video card, 40
    WAV files, 573
    WebTV application, 41
    Windows 95/98
Have Disk dialog box, 120
headers, 211
    FixSize() functions, 215
    FormatNumber() functions,
      215
    Init() functions, 216
    Properties() functions, 215
    Remote Mail, 662
    style sheets, 214, 216–217
    variable declarations, 214
heaps, 298–299
height of images, 100
Help feature, 37, 242, 370, 372,
  706
hiding
    commands, 241–242
    compressed volume files
      (CVFs), 326
    Control Panel, 184, 192–193
    desktop icons, 231, 233
    disk drives, 326–327
    displaying, 91
    DOS, 334
    file types, 256, 263, 275
    folders, 648
    mapping, 641
    Network Neighborhood,
      643–645
    Outlook Express 5, 485
    passwords, 632
    Registry Editor, 111
    taskbar, 244
    Windows Explorer, 154,
      178–179

hierarchy, 111
HiFD backups, 377
high memory area (HMA), 77,
  304, 308–309
highlighting file types, 261
Himem.sys file, 367
history
    editing, 439
    folders, 457
    Internet Explorer, 438
    System Information utility,
      347
HKEY keys (Registry Editor)
    CLASSES ROOT, 112,
      258–259
    CURRENT CONFIG, 113
    CURRENT USER, 112
    DYN DATA, 113
    LOCAL MACHINE, 112
    USERS, 113
HMA (high memory area), 77,
  304, 308–309
hoaxes, virus email, 490–491
holders, 24
horizontal sizing
    taskbar, 245
    Web view templates, 213
hosts
    computers, 583, 585–587
    compressed data, 326
    domains, 436
    drives, 319, 327
    names, 431
hot docking, 580–582
hot swap, 23, 583
hovering, 11, 156, 202
HTML (HyperText Markup
  Language), 200
    desktop background layer,
      221
    editors, 14–15
HTTP (HyperText Transfer
  Protocol), 436, 458, 460
hubs, 602–603
HyperTerminal, 37, 195, 390
hypertext, *see* links
HyperText Markup Language,
  see HTML
HyperText Transfer Protocol
  (HTTP), 436, 458, 460

I

I/O ports, 516–517, 531
IALA (Intel Application Launch
  Accelerator), 322
icons
    Accessibility Options, 185
    Active Desktop, 186, 221
    adding to Start menu, 196
    color, 231
    Control Panel
    Date/Time, 186
    displaying, 186, 463
    editing, 227–229, 232–233
    file types, 261
    Fonts, 186, 231
    Game Controllers, 186
    hiding, 184, 192, 231, 233
    hovering, 11
    InfoTip, 233
    Infrared, 186
    IntelliPoint, 541
    Internet, 186
    Internet Connection
      Sharing, 626
    Internet Explorer, 232
    Keyboard, 186
    Mail, 186
    menus, 231
    Microsoft Mail Postoffice,
      187
    Modems, 187
    Mouse, 187
    Multimedia, 187
    My Briefcase, 232
    My Computer, 232
    My Documents, 232,
      234–235
    Network, 187
    Network Neighborhood, 232
    New Hardware, 185
    numbers, 229
    opening, 184
    Passwords, 187
    PC Card (PCMCIA), 187
    Power Management, 187
    Printers, 187
    Recycle Bin, 232, 235
    Regional Settings, 188
    selecting, 233
    Scanners and Cameras, 188

    shortcuts, 275, 278–279,
      282–283, 285
    Sounds, 188
    Start menu, 34, 244
    System, 188
    System Policy Editor,
      120–121
    Telephony, 188
    themes, 186
    titles, 196
    toolbars, 247
    Tweak UI, 188
    Windows Explorer, 175–176
IDE drives, 370
idle time
    ISPs, 421
    screen savers, 230
IDs, 613
IEEE 1394 (FireWire), 23–24, 521
IFRAME, 501
IFSHLP.SYS, 77
ignoring system files, 354
images
    background, 200
    capturing, 568
    converting, 100
    creating, 37
    dithering, 461
    downloading, 461
    editing, 99–100
    enabling, 461
    height, 100
    logo screens, 99
    scanners, 25
    thumbnails, 175
    Web sites, 438
    width, 100
IMAP email accounts, 413
importing
    Netscape bookmarks, 30,
      446–447
    Outlook Express mail
      accounts, 470
    registration files, 117–119
    Web sites, 446–447
improper shutdown, 124
Inbox Assistant (Outlook
  Express), 479
increasing memory, 302
incremental backups, 375–376
information files/panel, 131, 202,
  213
InfoTip, 233

infrared (IR) ports
  Control Panel icon, 186, 189, 195
  Direct Cable Connection Wizard, 591
  enabling, 589
  files, 591
  identification, 591
  IrDA standards, 589
  monitors, 590–591
  notebooks, 589
  plug-and-play devices, 591
  sound alerts, 591
  subkeys, 194
  transmission speed, 591
  see also serial ports
Init() functions, 216
initialization, 44, 54, 105, 372, 399, 404
Input/Output ports, 516–517
insert links, 213
inserting, *see* adding
Installable File System Helper, 77
installation
  Active Desktop items, 500
  antivirus software, 56
  applications, 127–130
    Add/Remove Programs, 130
    application-specific paths, 132–133
    AutoPlay, 130
    backups, 128
    bootable disks, 128
    custom, 129
    files, 128, 131–132
    MS-DOS mode, 131
    settings, 132–134
    viruses, 129
  automatic, 130
  backups, 54–55
  BIOS, 56
  configuration, 55, 84
  customizing, 64
  device drivers, 521
    Detection Manager, 522–523
    manual, 524–525
  disk drive cache, 64
  DLLs, 52
  dual-boot, 42
  extended memory manager, 64
  files, 57, 348–349, 351

floppy disks, 57
graphics adapters, 555–556, 566
hard disk
  cleaning, 53–56
  defragmentation, 57
  to FAT32 partition, 40
initialization files, 54
ISPs, 412
Microsoft Fax, 15
Microsoft Mail Postoffice, 617, 619–621
modems, 187, 392
  56Kbps transmission, 398
  Add New Modem Wizard, 393–395
  Registry settings, 395–399
network client drives, 611
NIC drives, 610–611
programs, 57
protocols, 611–612
ScanDisk, 56
scanners, 567–568
scripts, 61–62, 380–381
services, 612–613
Setup script, 60–62
shared printers, 641–642
software, 501
source folder, 381
startup files, 54, 56
swap files, 56
System Policy Editor, 120
TCP/IP protocol, 430
Temp directory, 56
Tweak UI, 122, 124
Web sites, 57, 457
Windows 98, 42–45
Windows Messaging, 15, 55
integrity check, 64
Intel, 293, 322
IntelliPoint
  ClickLock, 543
  configuration, 540–541
  feet/mile measurements, 543
  icons, 541
  orientation, 543
  pointers, 542–543
  SmartSpeed, 542
  SnapTo, 541
  Tweak UI, 545
  wheel, 543–544
  windows, 541

inter-window dragging, Windows
  Explorer objects, 160
interface, Windows 95, 204
interlacing monitors, 562
InterLink, 584
internal modems, 397, 400
internal Registry configuration,
  105
international calls, 408
International subkey (Registry),
  194
Internet
    connections, 195
        direct, 624
        MidPoint Gateway
            application, 628
        multiple, 420
        phone numbers, 412
        testing, 433
        Trumpet FireSock appli-
            cation, 628
        WinGate application,
            627
    Control Panel icon, 186, 189
    LANs, 429–430
    links, 217–218
    logon scripts, 425–429
    temporary files, 315
    zones, 497
    see also Dial-Up Networking;
        IPX/SPX network proto-
        col; ISPs
Internet Connection Sharing, 30
    clients, 626–628
    enabling/disabling, 626
    gateways, 624–627
    icons, 626
    IP addresses, 627
    NICs, 626
    Windows 98 Second Edition,
        624
Internet Connection Wizard
    accounts, 13, 415–416
    configuration, 414
    Dial-Up Networking,
        417–419
    opening, 414
    Windows 98 Second Edition,
        416–417
Internet Explorer 4.0/5.0
    Accessibility group, 456
    Address bar, 27, 441, 459,
        462
    alternate text, 456
    Back button, 438
    browsing, 13, 30, 456–460

cache, 454–455
certificates, 502
Channel bar, 459
cookies, 500
cross-frame navigation, 492
desktop, 232, 458
disabling, 270
dotless IP address, 492–493
downloading notifications,
  458
error messages, 458
Favorites list, 13, 30,
  445–448, 452–454
files, 457
    browsing, 263
    deleting, 502
    downloading, 491
    opening, 263
    storing, 502
    types, 270–271
FTP, 459
Go button, 458
History bar, 438
HTTP 1.1 group, 460
images, 461
Java Virtual Machine,
  460–461
keyboard shortcuts, 704–705
links, 438
Multimedia group, 461
Netscape bookmarks, 30
options, 61
Outlook Express, 466
printing, 462
Properties dialog box, 455
Quick Launch toolbar, 245
Radio Bar, 461
Registry, 105
Search feature, 29, 439–441,
  462
security, 462, 495, 497–499
shortcuts, 285
start pages, 438
subscriptions, 421
system caret, 456
Toolbar group, 462
updates, 13, 449, 452, 457
Web sites, 440–441, 401
Interrupt 13, 342
Interrupt Request lines, *see* IRQs
intranet addresses, 217–218, 432
invalid dates and times, 317
invalid site certificates, 503
Io.sys file, 78, 367–368
Iomega Jaz drives, 342

IP addresses
  assigning, 413, 419, 429
  current, 433
  DHCP, 627
  DNS servers, 419
  dotless, 492–493
  gateways, 430
  subnet masks, 413
  TCP/IP protocol, 430
IPX/SPX network protocol, 419,
  604–605, 652
IrDA (Infrared Data Association)
  standard, 589–590
IRQs (Interrupt request lines)
  conflicting, 531
  device drivers, 514–516
  hard disk controller, 86
  holders, 24
  interrupt vector tables, 515
  line assignments, 515
  programmable interrupt
    controller, 515
  steering, 24, 516
  virtual handlers, 88
ISDN lines, 624
ISPs (Internet service providers)
  accounts, 412, 416–417
  connections, 420, 424
  directory servers, 414
  disconnections, 429
  DNS servers, 413
  flow control, 413
  idle time, 421
  installation, 412
  Internet Connection
    Wizard, 415
  IP addresses, 413
  LDAP, 414
  modems, 413
  PPP connections, 413
items in Startup folder
  bypassing, 700
  disabling, 91
  selecting, 82

J

Java, 200
  adding to Active Desktop,
    223
  downloading, 315
  enabling, 460
  Java Virtual Machine,
    460–461

JIT Compiler, 460
  scripts, 501
  security, 500
  toggling, 460
JavaScript, 29, 200, 214–216
Jaz drive backups, 377
JIT Compiler, 460
joysticks, 553–554

K

kernel, 79
keyboard shortcuts, 277
  applications, 701–702
  dialog boxes, 702
  Doskey command-recall
    keys, 705–706
  drag-and-drop keys, 703
  function keys, 700
  Internet Explorer, 704–705
  logo key, 706–707
  Windows Explorer, 703–704
keyboards, 41
  ANSI characters, 548–551
  Caps Lock key, 547
  Control Panel icon, 186, 189
  customizing, 185
  dead keys, 551
  delay, 546–547
  languages, 551–552
  Num Lock key, 548
  objects, 156–157
  plaque, 546
  repeat rate, 547
  StickyKeys feature, 548
  United States-International
    layout, 550–551
keys, 112, 115–117, 504
Keys pane, 111

L

LabelCheck, 72
languages, 551–552
LANs (local area networks), 595,
  598
  configuration, 623
  Internet connections, 415,
    429–430
  Microsoft Mail Postoffice,
    622
  NetMeeting, 16
  Wake-On-LANs, 32
LapLink, 583, 584

large desktop icons, 231
lassoing Windows Explorer
  objects, 159
LASTDRIVE3DZ, 78
launching, *see* opening
LDAP (Lightweight Directory
  Access Protocol), 414, 482–483
LED indicators
    external modems, 391
left mouse button, 536
legacy devices
    Plug-and-Play, 520
length
    Network Neighborhood
      passwords, 645
Level 1 (L1) cache, 291
Level 2 (L2) cache, 292
    Intel's 430TX/430VX, 293
License Agreement
licenses
    device drivers, 525
    displaying, 59
Lightweight Directory Access
  Protocol (LDAP), 414, 482–483
LILO (Linux Loader), 51
Limit memory to *x* MB, 89
limitations
    FAT, 337
    Network Neighborhood, 639
links, 200
    dead, 280–281
    files, 274
    folders, 12
    hypertext, 437
    settings, 282
    Show Files, 219–220
    underlining, 206, 459
    Web sites, 201–202
    Web view templates, 217–218
Links bar, 246
    buttons, 437, 442
    customizing, 441
    shortcuts, 442
    subfolders, 442
Linux, 51
Linux Loader (LILO), 51
lists
    conventional memory con-
      tents, 306–308
    desktop icons, 231
    folders, 129
    search engines, 441
Lmhosts file, 608

loadings, 16
    Command.com, 96
    device drivers, 308–309,
      519–520
    DOS in HMA, 308
    Drvspace.bin, 96
    failures, 83
    GUI, 94
    mouse drivers, 59
    Registry, 105
    TSRs, 308–309
local items
    copy lists, 623
    disk drives, 640–641
    folders, 217–218
    icons, 120–121
    intranet zone, 497–498
    NetMeeting, 16
    pages, 10, 121, 437, 643
    TCP/IP protocol, 494
location
    shortcuts, 274
    system files, 353–354
Lock command, 144
lock icons, 495
lockups, 89
log files
    Dial-Up Adapter, 652
    Dr. Watson utility, 383
    Microsoft Mail Postoffice,
      624
    modems, 404
    ScanDisk, 319
    size, 323
Logged command (Startup
  menu), 83
Logitech mouse driver, 59
logons/logoff, 242, 622, 624
    anonymous, 502
    client/server network, 615,
      617, 630
    directory servers, 414
    Favorites subscriptions, 451
    Internet Connection
      Wizard, 416
    Java, 460
    Network Neighborhood,
      630–632, 644–645
    prompts, 65, 655
    scripts, 425–429
    user profiles, 249
    validation, 615
    welcome messages, 460
    Windows, 630–631

logos
    bypassing, 97
    displaying, 97, 124
    keys, 706–707
    screens, 99
long-distance calls, 408
lost file fragments, 316, 319
Low Resources dialog box
    (Resource Meter), 301

M

macros, 358
mail accounts (Outlook Express)
    configuration, 468–469
    connections, 468, 470
    deleting, 480
    Dial-Up connections, 468
    downloading, 470
    enabling/disabling, 480
    importing, 470
    messages, 476–477, 479–480
    order of, 480
    passwords, 468
    security, 470
    servers, 468–469
    usernames, 468
Mail dialog box, 659
mailboxes (Microsoft Mail
    Postoffice), 618–619
main memory, 291
Maintenance Wizard utility, 21,
    167
manual configuration
    device drivers, 524–525
    ISPs, 417
    uninstallation, 72–73, 98,
        149–151
MapCache, 325
mapping shared resources,
    640–641
MaxBackupCopies setting
    (Registry Checker utility), 109
maximizing
    applications, 136, 571
    display resolution, 562
    Windows Explorer icons,
        175
McAfee utilities
    VirusScan, 358–360, 368
    VShield, 360–361
Media Player, 31, 569

memory
    32-applications, 292
    Active Desktop, 12, 221
    addresses, 290, 518
    cache, 293
    Clipboard, 302
    conventional, 303
    DMA channels, 517–518
    DOS, 140, 303–308
    expanded (EPS), 144, 304,
        306–308
    extended (XMS), 304,
        306–308
    hard disk, 56
    high memory area (HMA),
        77, 304, 308
    I/O ports, 516–517
    increasing, 302
    modules, 291
    monitoring, 292
    networks, 303
    POST, 76
    program code, 324
    RAM, 289, 291–292
    Registry, 107, 109
    requirements, 294–296
    resolution, 559
    restricting, 89
    Run Registry key, 302
    speed, 290
    stacks, 515
    Startup folder, 302
    swap files, 296–298
    testing, 293
    upper memory area (UMA),
        86, 144, 303–304, 308, 310,
        518
    usage, 293–294
    virtual, 292
menus
    color, 369
    commands, 571
    default settings, 369–370
    desktop icons, 231
    shortcut, 35
    speed, 544
messages
    displaying, 483
        filtering, 476–480
        finding, 475, 480–482
        flagging, 474–475
        forwarding, 474
        Inbox Assistant,
            478–479
        mail rules, 476–480
        moving, 475, 484

printing, 475
priorities, 473
reading, 473–474
receiving, 473
redirecting, 477
replying to, 474
sending, 470–473
signature, 472
sizing, 484
sorting, 483
sorting, 484
storing, 467
width, 484
filtering, 30
Microsoft Mail Postoffice,
622–623
Outlook Express 4.0/5.0
attachments, 472–474
background, 471
blocking, 477
copying, 475
deleting, 475, 477
Microsoft
Diagnostics utility, 57
Fax, 15
newsgroups, 695–697
Mail Postoffice, 187, 466
addresses, 623
backups, 55
connections, 622
installation, 15, 617,
619–621
mailboxes, 618–619
messages, 622–623
passwords, 622
paths, 622
property sheet, 621
Remote Mail, 623
session events, 624
settings, 659
shared folders, 617
Plus! add-ons
VirusScan, 358–360
VShield, 360–361
Technical Support Search
Web site, 690
MIDI files, 569
MidPoint Gateway application,
628
MIME content, 262
mini-banner Web view, 207, 212
mini-drivers, 520

minimizing
applications, 136, 571
windows, 245, 706
Windows Explorer, 175
Missing Shortcut dialog box, 279
mixing WAV files, 573
MMX (Multimedia
Extensions), 23
modems, 189
Add New Modem Wizard,
393–395
baud rate, 389
bits, 388–390
call waiting, 406
calling cards, 407–408
cellular protocol, 403
COM ports, 390
compression, 403
configuration, 187
connections, 401, 403
Control Panel, 195
data terminal equipment
(DTE), 400
dial-tone prompts, 401
Dial-Up Networking, 418,
657
dialing locations, 405–408
errors, 389, 403
even parity, 389
external, 391
file transfer protocol, 390
flow control, 392, 403
gates, 388
HyperTerminal program,
390
initialization strings, 404
installation, 187, 392–393,
398
international calls, 408
Internet Connection
Wizard, 416
ISPs, 413
log files, 404
long-distance calls, 408
modulation standards, 389,
404
online sessions, 41
outside lines, 406
ports, 400–404
pulse dial, 407
Registry, 398–399
S11 register, 404
serial ports, 390–392
sharing, 624–627
speaker volume, 400

speed, 400, 404
starting, 37
teaming, 628
terminal emulation, 390
testing, 395–397
tone dial, 407
transmission, 388
XON/XOFF flow control,
  392
modes
  compatibility, 88
  MS-DOS, 86, 141–143
  protected, 76
    disabling, 85
    performance, 80
    Scanrequ.exe, 108
    startup, 78–79
  real, 76, 108
  standby, 576
  verbose, 334
modulation, see modems
monitoring
  application memory use, 301
  batteries, 579–580
  Dial-Up Server, 658
  log files, 322
  memory, 292
  remote administration, 646
  system resources, 299–301
monitors
  changing, 563
  color, 558, 560, 567
  configuration, 564–567
  costs, 22
  dot pitch, 563
  DPMS, 564
  Energy Star standard, 562
  graphics adapters, 565
  interlacing, 562
  maximum display resolution,
    562
  multiple, 22
  Plug-and-Play, 562–563
  power management, 564,
    577
  refresh rate, 562
  resolution, 558–562
motherboard
  banks, 291
  BIOS code, 518
  IRQs, 514–516
mouse, 187, 189
  acceleration rate, 539
  configuration, 535–536
  drivers, 59

IntelliMouse, 541–542
IntelliPoint
  ClickLock, 543
  configuration, 540–541
  orientation, 543
  pointer, 542
  speed, 542
  trails, 543
  Universal scrolling, 544
  wheel, 543–544
  left/right buttons, 536
  Microsoft, 41
  objects, 156
  pointer, 538–540
  speed, 537
  Tweak UI, 544–545
  Web sites, 201
  wheel mouse, 28
moving
  cpl files, 190
  cursor, 706
  desktop items layer, 223
  Favorites folder, 447
  Links bar, 442
  Outlook Express, 475–476,
    484
  system caret, 456
  taskbar, 245
  Web sites, 455
  Windows Explorer, 157–158
MS-DOS
  applications, 131, 141–143
  Autoexec.bat file, 143
  configuration, 142–143
  errors, 319
  exiting, 86
  high memory area, 308
  modes, 306
  SmartDrive disk cache, 303
  troubleshooting, 384
msbatch.inf file, 380, 382
Mscdex.exe file, 372
Msdos.sys file, 367
  editing, 92
  hidden files, 91
  options, 93–97
  paths, 93
  x lines, 93
MTU, Dial-Up Adapter, 653
multimedia, 187, 189
  configuration, 461
  extensions, 23
  NetShow, 29

multiple items
    files, 11, 267–268
    monitors, 22, 564–567
    user profiles, 249
multitasking, 139, 585
My Briefcase folder, 232, 587
My Computer folder, 210, 232, 284
My Document folder, 26, 232, 234–235

N

names
    files, 269
    Registry, 68
    shortcuts, 278
NDIS2SUP driver, 83
Net Watcher, 647–648
NetBEUI, 419, 604–605
NetMeeting, 15–16
Netscape, 30, 270–271, 446–447
NetShow, 28
Network dialog box, 430, 431, 609, 644
Network Neighborhood
    Access Control tab, 644
    computers, 634
    customizing, 642
    desktop, 232
    domains, 633
    Entire Network folder, 643
    file sharing, 643
    hiding, 643
    Identification tab, 644
    limitations, 639
    logons, 631–632, 644
    Network Control Panel, 643
    passwords, 645
    print sharing, 643
    remote administration, 648
    shortcuts, 633
    users, 644
    Wdesktop, 633
    Web view, 210
    Windows Explorer, 633
    Windows NT, 645
    workgroups, 633, 645, 646
networks
    adapters, 430
    architecture, 598
    basement area, 596
    BNC connectors, 601
    bridges, 603

cabling, 598–599, 601–603
client/server, 596, 630
    access control, 614
    drives, 611
    logon, 615, 617
    NIC drives, 610–611
components, 610
computers, 284, 613
connecting, 654
Control Panel icons, 187, 189
drives, 164, 178
Ethernet/Fast Ethernet, 598
file sharing, 612–613
hubs, 602
logons, 615-616, 630–631
Network Neighborhood, 195
NICs, 601
nodes, 32
operating system (NOS), 596, 608
options, 61
peer-to-peer, 596–597, 630
print sharing, 612–613
printers, 637, 641–642
protocols, 303, 604–605, 611–612
repeaters, 602
routers, 603
security, 596
services, 612–613
T-connectors, 601
terminators, 601
topology, 603
users, 97, 638–39
see also NICs
New Hardware icon (Control Panel), 185
New menu, 268–270
new messages (Microsoft Mail Postoffice), 623
New toolbar (taskbar), 246
newsgroups
    Microsoft, 695–697
    Usenet, 694–696
    Windows 98, 694–695
NICs (network interface cards), 597–598, 601
    architecture, 598
    bottlenecks, 598
    bus mastering, 598
    configuration, 599
    installation, 610–611

Internet Connection
  Sharing, 626
  Plug-and-Play compatibility,
    597
NNTP server, 414
Normal startup option, 88
Norton utilities, 58, 359
NOS (network operating system),
  596, 608
notebooks
  batteries, 579–580
  briefcases, 588–589
  Direct Cable Connection,
    585–587
  Fast Infrared (FIR) driver,
    589
  file sharing, 587–589
  hardware profiles, 581
  hot docking, 580–582
  infrared (IR) ports, 589–591
  parallel ports, 584–585
  PC Cards (PCMIA cards),
    582–583
  plug-and-play BIOS, 581
  power management, 576
  serial ports, 584
  standby mode, 576–577
  undocking, 581–582
Notepad, 210, 265
notifications, downloading, 458
null files, 269
null–modem cable, 584
Num Lock key, 548
numbers
  formatting, 215
  icons, 229

O

objects
  ADO, 663–664
  context menu, 701
  controlling, 36
  double-clicking, 206
  hovering, 156
  permissions, 265
  property sheets, 700
  selecting, 202, 204
  servers, 686
  shortcuts, 274–275
  single-clicking, 205
  tables, 876–888
  Web integration, 156

Windows Explorer
  deselecting multiple,
    157
  drag-and-drop, 158,
    160
  inter-window dragging,
    160
  lassoing, 159
  right-drag, 158–159
  selecting, 155–158
offline Microsoft Mail Postoffice
  connections, 622
OLE (Object Linking and
  Embedding), 105
online backups, 14, 377
OnNow Design Initiative, 576
opening
  ActiveMovie Control, 569
  applications, 134
  backups, 373–374
  browser windows, 458
  Control Panel, 71, 184,
    189–190
  default settings, 136
  Dial-Up Networking, 418,
    423, 653
  DOS prompt, 136
  double-clicking, 134–135
  files, 10, 167, 260–261,
    265–266
  folders, 264
  gates, 388
  IFRAME, 501
  Infrared Monitor dialog box,
    591
  Internet Connection
    Wizard, 414–415
  Internet Explorer, 263, 455
  ISPs, 416
  Media Player, 569
  MIDI files, 569
  Network Neighborhood, 633
  Outlook Express, 466–467
  programs, 20, 37, 324–325
  Quick Launch toolbar, 135
  Registry, 11, 110–111,
    137–138, 646
  Run dialog box, 135
  Setup, 62–66
  shortcuts, 33, 135, 278–279
  Sound Recorder, 569
  Start menu, 134, 700
  Startup menu, 82, 137
  system utilities, 87, 292

Task Monitor, 322
Task Scheduler, 135
Tweak UI, 122–123
WAV files, 569
Web sites, 202,205, 437, 458
Win.ini file, 138–139
Windows Explorer, 153, 706
WINIPCFG utility, 433
operating systems
    booting, 124, 700
    networks, 596
    previous, 85
    Windows 98, 45, 47–48, 51
optimizing
    conventional memory, 303
    programs, 323–324
    Registry, 109
options
    advanced, 61
    Disk Defragmenter utility,
        321
    Infrared Monitor dialog box,
        590
    Internet Explorer, 61
    Msdos.sys file, 93–97
    networks, 61
    Setup, 61
    shortcuts, 279
    System Configuration, 88–89
    Windows Explorer, 177–179
Optlog.txt file, 323–324
order of Outlook Express mail
    rules, 480
orientation, IntelliPoint, 543
OS/2 Warp, 51
outgoing messages (Microsoft
    Mail Postoffice), 622
outgoing security
    lock icons, 495
    warning dialog boxes, 495
Outlook Express 4.0/5.0
    Address Book, 27
    attachments, 472–475, 493
    authentication, 508–509
    background, 471
    Basic group, 477, 485
    connections, 468, 470
    Contacts list, 475, 485
    default settings, 15, 30, 475
    deleting, 475, 477
    Dial-Up connections, 468
    digital IDs, 505–506
    downloading, 470
    editing, 485

encryption, 507–509
filtering, 476–480
Find feature, 30, 475,
    480–482
flagging, 474–475
folders, 467, 476, 485
forwarding, 474
importing, 470
Inbox Assistant, 478–479
LDAP, 482–483
mail rules, 476, 480
messages, 30, 477, 483–484
moving, 475–476
opening, 466–467
Outlook bar, 485
passwords, 468
Preview Pane group, 486
printing, 475
priorities, 473
public key, 506–507
Quick Launch toolbar, 245
reading, 473–474
receiving, 473
redirecting, 477
reducing, 476
renaming, 476
replying to, 474
security, 470
sending, 470–473
servers, 468–469
signature, 472
Status bar, 485
storing, 467, 476
Tip of the Day, 486
toolbar, 485–486
updated features, 15
usernames, 468
Views bar, 485
window layout, 485
outside lines for modems, 406
overwriting
    DLLs, 52
    system files, 351

P

packets
    Dial-Up Adapter, 652
    protocols, 604
    sniffers, 490
    tracing, 432

pages
    frames, 304
    scrolling, 707
    transitions, 458
    Web site hits, 457
paging files, 56, 292, 296–298
Paint, 37
parallel cables/ports, 584–585
parity, 389, 401
Partition Magic (PowerQuest)
  Web site, 58
partitions
    clusters, 333
    converting, 341
    FAT32
        boot, 337
        compression, 338
        converting to, 340
        Drive Converter,
        341–342
        dynamic, 337
        FDISK, 340–341
    formatting, 54
    hard disk, 40–41, 53–54
    system files, 46
    Windows 98, 46
passwords
    access, 637
    alphanumeric, 645
    authentication, 502
    cache, 654
    caching, 645
    connections, 421
    Control Panel icon, 187, 189
    default settings, 632
    Dial-Up Networking, 427,
      657–658
    directory servers, 414
    editing, 187
    hiding, 632, 645–646
    host computers, 586
    ISPs, 412
    length, 645
    list, 55
    logons, 502
    Microsoft Mail Postoffice,
      622
    Outlook Express, 468
    prompts, 502
    screen savers, 230
    user profiles, 248
    variables, 427
pasting
    data, 501
    WAV files, 573

paths
    logon scripts, 428
    Microsoft Mail Postoffice,
      622
    sections, 93
    statements, 81–82
    variables, 50
    Web view templates, 211
pausing conventional memory
  output, 306–308
PBX systems, 406
PC 98/99 standards, 525
PC Cards (PCMIA cards), 187,
  195, 582–583
PC World Magazine, 692
PCI bus, 41
    graphics adapters, 557
    Plug-and-Play, 521
pcrestor.bat file, 382
PCT 1.0 (Private
  Communications Technology),
  503
PCWin Resource Center Web site,
  692
peer-to-peer networks, 596–597,
  608, 630
Pentium MMX (Multimedia
  Extensions), 23
Pentium processor, 290
performance
    improving, 58, 80–81
    protected mode, 80
    remote administration, 646
    swap files, 296–298
    User-Level Access Control,
      637
    video, 557
personal folders, 55
phone numbers
    Dial-Up Networking, 424
    Internet, 412
PIFs (program information files)
  shortcuts
    closing, 279
    creating, 276
    DOS, 275
    fonts, 279
    icons, 279
    naming, 278
    opening, 278–279
    options, 279
    property sheets, 279
    screens, 279
    settings, 304
    windows, 279

PIN number (Personal ID number), 408
PING utility, 432–433
pixels, 559
placeholders, 259
plaque, 546
Plug-and-Play
  BIOS, 521, 581
  configuration, 522
  executing, 520–521
  hardware, 65
  IEEE 1394 (FireWire)
    devices, 521
  infrared (IR) ports, 591
  legacy devices, 520
  monitors, 562–563
  NICs, 597
  PCI devices, 521
  storing, 521
  USB devices, 521
Point-to-Point Protocol (PPP), 413, 419
Point-to-Point Tunneling Protocol (PPTP), 652
pointer
  IntelliPoint, 541–543
  mouse, 538–540
policies, 121–122
polls, I/O ports, 516
pop-up descriptions, 178
POP3 email account, 413
ports
  I/O, 516–517
  modems, 400–404
POST (Power-On Self Test)
  Ctrl key, 82
  system memory, 76
Post-Dial Terminal Screen, 429
Postoffice, *see* Microsoft Mail Postoffice
power management
  Control Panel icon, 190
  disabling, 577
  monitors, 564
  notebooks, 576
  properties, 578
  troubleshooting, 579
power meter, 195, 579
power schemes, 577–578
Power Toys Set, 124
Power-On Self Test, *see* POST
PowerCfg subkey (Registry), 194
PowerQuest, 58

PPP (Point-to-Point Protocol) connections, 413, 419
PPTP (Point-to-Point Tunneling Protocol), 652
preferences
  infrared monitors, 591
  modem connections, 401
preserve state for cookies, 499
preventing lockups, 89
previewing
  panes, 486
  screen savers, 230
  Web views, 11
Previous version of MS-DOS command (Startup menu), 84
primary names for files, 259, 332
printers
  Control Panel, 196
  remote ports, 642
  shared, 637–639, 641–642
  shortcuts, 284
printing
  backgrounds, 462
  configuration, 462
  Control Panel icons, 187, 190
  controlling jobs, 37
  Device Manager, 530
  files, 264
  Outlook Express messages, 475
  .prn files, 383
  security, 494
  sharing, 612–613, 643
  System Information utility, 383
  Web view, 210
priorities, Outlook Express messages, 473
privacy, email, 504
Private Communications Technology (PCT 1.0), 503
private-key encryption, 504–505
.prn files, 383
processors, hardware requirements, 40
product IDs, 381
profiles
  editing, 503
  email, 659
  hardware, 77
  Profile Assistant, 502
programmable interrupt controller (IRQ2), 515

programs, 241
    closing, 57
    codes, 324
    group files, 55
    opening, 20, 37
    optimizing, 323–324
    settings, 132
    switching, 37
    Web view, 210
    see also applications; PIFs
progress meter, hardware detection, 65
prompts
    confirmation, 84
    modems, dial tone, 401
    passwords, 502
    security, 499
    Setup, 59
    usernames, 502
properties
    Device Manager, 530, 532
    Dial-Up Adapter, 652
    DOS settings, 304, 306
    hard disk, 312
    headers, 215
    Microsoft Mail Postoffice, 621
    objects, 36, 700
    opening, 455
    Recycle Bin, 164–165
    shortcuts, 274, 279, 419
    tabbed dialog boxes, 37
    taskbar, 244
    VShield (McAfee), 360
    Windows 98, 422
proprietary tags, 15
protected mode
    device drivers, 85
    performance, 80
    Scanreqw.exe, 108
    startup, 76, 78–79
protecting system files files, 350
protocols
    Direct Cable Connection, 586
    IPX/SPX, 604–605
    NetBEUI, 604–605
    network installation, 611–612
    proxy servers, 432
    selecting, 430
    TCP/IP, 604–605
    Web integration, 200

proxy servers
    bypassing, 432, 437, 497
    configuration, 431
    HTTP 1.1, 460
    protocols, 432
    Windows 98 Second Edition, 422
public-key encryption, 504–507
pulse dialing, 407
push media, 12
push technology, 220

Q–R

Quarterdeck, 58
Quick Launch toolbar
    Active Channel page, 245
    applications, 135
    Internet Explorer, 245
    Outlook Express, 245
    shortcuts, 246, 274
    WebTV, 245
Quick View utility, 149, 262

Radio Bar (Internet Explorer), 461
RAM (random access memory), 289
    backups, 371
    chips, 293
    EBD.CAB file, 372
    files, 367, 371
    hardware requirements, 40–41
    Level 1/Level 2 (L1/L2) cache, 291–293
    main memory, 291
    speed, 290
    Static RAM (SRAM), 291
    syntax, 372
    System Information utility, 347
    terminate-and-stay resident programs, 64
read-only access, 326, 636, 639
reading Outlook Express messages, 473–474
Readme.txt file, 128, 367, 372
real mode
    device drivers, 519–520
    Scanreq.exe, 108
    startup, 76
rebooting computers, 372, 700
recall list commands, 705

Receive Data (RD) serial ports, 391
receiving
buffers, 402
Microsoft Mail Postoffice messages, 623
Outlook Express messages, 473
Remote Mail, 662
recording WAV files, 572–573
recovering
hard disk, 379–380
System Recovery utility, 381–383
Windows Explorer files/folders, 165–167
Recycle Bin
configuration, 164–165
default settings, 164
desktop icons, 232
drives, 164
files/folders
deleting, 162–164
recovering, 165–167
undeleting, 37
properties, 164–165
renaming, 235
size, 165
Start menu, 242
Web view, 210
redialing Dial-Up Networking, 655
redirecting Outlook Express messages, 477
reducing Outlook Express folders, 476
refreshing
Device Manager, 530
Microsoft Mail Postoffice, 624
monitors, 562
toolbars, 247
Regional Settings icon (Control Panel), 188, 190
RegisteredOrganization setting, 69
RegisteredOwner setting, 68
registering extensions, 265
Registry, 11
applications, 137–138
backups, 106, 373, 375
daily, 107
full, 380

restoring, 108–110, 379
system files, 109
binary values, 114–115
cabinet files, 108–109
cleaning, 53
company names, 68
configuration, 68, 104–105
Control Panel, 193–194
device drivers, 105, 529
Editor, 110–111
file types, 105, 258–259, 262–265
global, 117
hardware, 105
HKEY_CLASSES_ROOT, 258–259
importance of, 104
integrity check, 64
keys, 111, 115–118, 138
memory, 109
modems, 398–399
OLE, 105
Registry Checker utility, 107–108
remote administration, 646–647
repairing, 109
Scanreg.ini file, 110
searches, 113–114
settings, 104, 109, 111, 115–116
shortcuts, 282–283
sound schemes, 571–572
source paths, 69
strings, 114
System Information utility, 347
users, 68, 105–106, 250–251
versions, 108–109
Windows, 44
Remote Mail, 659
address lists, 662
Dial-Up Networking, 660
headers, 662
mail, 662
messages, 661–662
Microsoft Mail Postoffice, 623
profiles, 659
sessions, 659–661
remote sessions
administration, 646–648
browsing, 10
email, 659–663

Microsoft Mail Postoffice, 622
pages, 437
printer ports, 642
removing
    desktop items layer, 223
    file attributes, 372
    folder formatting, 209
    Run Registry key items, 302
    Startup folder items, 302
    see also deleting
renaming
    file type extensions, 256
    Links bar buttons, 442
    operating system files, 85
    Outlook Express folders, 476
    Recycle Bin icon, 235
    Registry keys, 115
    Start menu, 31, 240
    Startup files, 85
    system files, 85
    Windows 3.1*x* files, 47
    Windows Explorer files/ folders, 155, 162
    see also names
repairing
    bad sectors, 318
    disks, 37, 372
    Registry, 109
repeat rates, keyboards, 547
repeaters, 602
repeating searches, 441
replacing logo screens, 99
replying to Outlook Express messages, 474
reports
    backups, 375, 378
    system, 57
Request To Send (RTS) serial ports, 391
reserved memory, 307
resizing taskbar, 246
resolution
    maximum display, 562
    monitors, 558–562, 567
    pixels, 559
    video memory, 559
    WINS, 609
Resource Meter
    Device Manager, 532
    GDI, 300
    Low Resources dialog box, 301
    Resource Kit Sampler, 348–349

system resources, 299–301
user values, 300
restarting
    automatically, 86
    computers, 523
    files, 372
    MS-DOS mode command (shutdown), 98
    system resources, 301
restoring
    applications after minimizing, 571
    backups, 109, 374, 377
        complete, 19
        Registry, 108, 379
        reports, 378
    Restore Wizard command, 378
    system files, 351, 354, 356–357
restrictions on memory
    conventional, 305
    usage, 89, 293–294
    site zones, 497–498
restructuring hard disk partitions, 53–54
retry limit (Remote Mail), 660
reversing WAV files, 573
revocation of certificates, 502
right mouse button, 536
right-drag Windows Explorer objects, 158–159
Ring Indicator, 391
RJ-45 ports, 602
ROM, 76, 86, 88
root directory, 337–338
root keys (Registry Editor), 112–113
routers, 603
rows in taskbar, 245
RS-232 ports, 390
RTS/CTS flow control, 392
running, *see* executing

S

S11 register, 404
safe mode, 700
Safe mode (Startup menu), 83–84, 86, 95, 700
Safe Recovery option, 64
saving
    Desktop setting, 235
    email attachments, 474

FAT32 disk space, 339–340
file type extensions, 257
Internet Explorer, 263
maintenance, 167
storing, 52
ScanDisk utility, 37
    bad sector repair, 318
    check boxes, 319
    configuration options, 372
    cross-linked files, 319
    disabling, 89
    error detection, 316–319
    executing, 59
    hard disk, 56, 63
    host drives, 319
    LabelCheck, 72
    log files, 319
    lost file fragments, 319
    running, 321
    shutdown, 93
    SpaceCheck, 72
    statistics, 318
    write-testing, 318
scanners, 25, 188, 190, 567–568
scanning
    directory codes, 110
    disks, 372
    downloaded files, 361
    emergency boot disk, 108
    upper memory blocks, 86
    VShield (McAfee), 360
Scheduled Tasks folder, 210, 242, 363
screens
    displaying, 559
    images, 556, 700
    logos, 99
    savers, 230
    shortcuts, 279
    system caret, 457
    Windows Explorer, 156
scripts
    active, 501
    ActiveX controls, 499
    Batch 98, 60
    creating, 29
    debugger, 457
    errors, 457
    installation, 61–62
    logon, 425–429
    Setup installation, 60–62
scrolling
    pages, 707
    smooth, 459
    Tweak UI, 545

    Universal, 544
    wheel, 28
    Windows Explorer, 175
SCSI, 89, 530
searches
    Address bar, 441, 444, 462, 482
    configuration, 462
    criteria, 353
    directory servers, 482–483
    engines, 441, 462
    Internet Explorer, 29, 439–441
    Registry, 113–114
    repeating, 441
    URL failures, 462
    Web sites, 438–439
sectors
    bad, 317, 318
    boot, 358, 362
    corrupted, 333
    floppy disks, 171
    root directory, 337
Secure Sockets Layer Level 2/Level 3 (SSL 2.0/SSL 3.0), 503
security
    Active Desktop items installation, 500
    ActiveX controls, 499
    anonymous, 502
    authentication, 502, 505
    bugs, 491
    certificates, 502–503
    channels, 503
    cookies, 500
    cross-frame navigation, 492, 500
    Dial-Up Networking (DUN) 1.3, 31
    digital IDs, 505–506
    disabling, 499
    dotless IP addresses, 492–493
    email, 490–491, 504
    enabling, 499
    encryption, 504–505
    file sharing, 494
    files, 500
    fonts, 500
    form submission, 501, 503
    Fortezza standards, 503
    frame spoof, 492, 501
    IFRAME, 501
    incoming, 495

Internet Explorer, 493
Java, 500
Local intranet zone,
   497–498
logons, 502
messages, 506–509
outgoing, 495
Outlook Express, 470, 493
packet sniffers, 490
PCT 1.0, 503
print sharing, 494
profiles, 502
prompts, 499, 502
Restricted sites, 497–498
screen savers, 230
Secure HTTP, 495
security checks, 421, 495
shared resources, 637
SSL 2.0/SSL 3.0, 503
TCP/IP protocol, 494
TLS 1.0, 503
Trusted sites, 497–498
Universal Naming
   Convention (UNC), 498
untrusted scripted paste, 491
updates, 491–494
users, 501, 596
viruses, 358
warning dialog boxes, 503
Web sites, 500–501
Windows Critical Update
   Notification, 494
zones, 495, 497–502
Security group (Internet
   Explorer), 462
selecting
   cabling, 598
   desktop icons, 233
   devices, 524
   drives, 315, 321
   files, 11, 349
   hovering, 11
   menu commands, 571
   objects
      banners, 213
      double-clicking, 206
      hovering, 202
      single-clicking,
         204–205
   power schemes, 578
   protocols, 430
   Startup menu items, 82
   Web integration, 156
   windows, 541
   Windows Explorer, 155–158

Selective startup option, 88
sending
   Microsoft Mail Postoffice
      messages, 623
   Outlook Express, 470–473
   Remote Mail, 662
Sequenced Packet eXchange, *see*
   IPX/SPX network protocol
serial ports
   bandwidth, 584
   Carrier Detect (CD), 391
   Clear To Send, 391
   Data Set Ready, 391
   Direct Cable Connection,
      584
   files, 584
   Infrared (SIR) drivers, 589
   Line Interface Protocol
      (SLIP), 413
   modems, 390
   null-modem cables, 584
   Receive Data (RD), 391
   Request To Send (RTS), 391
   Ring Indicator, 391
   signal Ground, 391
   throughput, 584
   Transmit Data (TD), 391
   UART, 392, 514
servers
   accounts, 608
   names, 644
   networks, 596
   Outlook Express, 468–469
   peer-to-peer, 608
   proxies, 497
services, network installation,
   612–613
sessions, 624, 659–663
SET statement, 81
Setramd.bat file, 367
settings, *see* configuration
Settings command (Start menu),
   241
Settings pane, 111
Setup
   application installation, 131
   backups, 57
   billboards, 59
   cabinets, 67–68
   commands, 59
   components, 61
   ease-of-use, 39
   error detection, 63

extracting files, 354–355
files, 67–68
hardware detection, 26, 65
installation, 60–62, 64
integrity check, 64
Internet Explorer options,
61
License Agreement, 59
log files, 70
logon prompts, 65
minimum disk space
requirement, 59
mouse drivers, 59
networks, 59, 61
opening, 63–66
options, 61
Safe Recovery option, 64
Setup, 63
source paths, 69
startup disks, 59
switches, 59
temporary files, 59
terminate-and-stay resident
programs, 64
time zones, 65
TSR programs, 59
versions, 77
WinAlign utility, 66
Windows 95/98, 45
share-level access control, 614,
635
shared resources
applications, 133–134
connections, 30
Dial-Up Networking, 419
disconnecting, 641
disk drives, 636–637
enabling, 636
files, 587–589, 612–613
folders, 636–637
full access, 637
hidden, 648
mapping, 640–641
Microsoft Mail Postoffice,
617
modems, 624–627
password access, 637
printing, 612–613, 637,
641–642
read-only access, 636
remote administration, 646,
648
security, 637
shell folders, 78, 234–236, 269

shortcuts
adding, 137
Address bar, 441, 443
All Files, 100
applications, 135
batch files, 276
Close Program dialog box,
146
CompuServe dial-ups, 429
configuration, 33, 129, 276
Connect To dialog box, 424
Control Panel, 285
copying, 158
creating, 275–276
cutting and pasting, 157
date and time, 195
desktop, 33
device drivers, 195, 520
Dial-Up Networking, 195,
284, 653
document scraps, 284
DOS, 275–276
enabling, 94
fast shutdown, 97
Favorites folder, 445
files, 168, 275, 281–282
folders, 154, 264, 277, 284
HyperTerminal, 195
icons, 195–196, 234, 278,
282–283
importing mail accounts,
470
Internet Explorer, 285
key combinations, 277
links, 280–281, 442
location, 274
logos, 97
menus, 35
minimizing windows, 245
network computers, 284
Network Neighborhood,
195, 633
Notepad, 265
opening, 33, 260
overlays, 283
PC Card (PCMCIA), 195
PIFs, 278–279
Plug-and-Play devices, 521
Previous version of MS-DOS
command, 85
printers, 196, 284
property sheets, 229, 274,
419
Quick Launch toolbar, 246,
274

registration files, 118
Registry, 114, 118
Safe mode command, 84
scanning for viruses, 360
Send To menu, 274
shell extension, 234
Shortcut to object, 282
signature verification, 527
Start menu, 273
    accelerator keys, 243
    adding, 238–239
    deleting, 238, 240
    folders, 239
    renaming, 31, 240
Startup folder, 79
Step-by-step confirmation
   command, 84
targets, 277–280
text wrap, 162
Web sites, 285
Windows, 154, 274–275
"shoulder surfing," 645
Show Desktop icon, 221
Show Files link, 219–220
Show Text/Title command
  (taskbar), 247
shutdown, 242
    alarms, 580
    applications, 301–302
    bitmaps, 99
    commands, 98
    fast shutdown, 89, 97
    improper, 93, 124
    proper procedures, 98
    ScanDisk, 124
    write-behind caching, 97
Signal Ground, 391
signatures
    ActiveX controls, 499
    Outlook Express, 525–527
    verification, 525–527
SIMMs (Single In-Line Memory
  Modules), 291
single-clicking, 10, 202, 204–205
single-key encryption, 504
sizing
    clusters, 333, 338–339
    desktop items layer, 223
    log files, 323
    Outlook Express, 484
    Recycle Bin, 165
    swap files, 296
    taskbar, 245
    toolbars, 247
    Web sites, 215, 455

SLIP (Serial Line Interface
  Protocol), 413
SmartDrive disk cache, 303
smooth scrolling, 459
sneakernet, 583
software
    antivirus, 56, 63
    compression, 657–658
    Control Panel, 184
    downloading, 501
    flow control, 392
    fritterware, 237
    installation, 501
    System Information utility,
      348
sorting
    Favorites folder, 447–448
    Outlook Express, 483–484
    search engines, 441
    settings, 90
    Windows Explorer, 176–177
sound
    ActiveMovie Control, 569
    card drivers, 569
    editing, 569–570
    icons, 188
    infrared (IR) ports, 591
    Media Player 6, 569
    MIDI files, 569
    opening, 569
    Registry, 571–572
    Sound Recorder, 569, 573
    volume, 569
    warning, 547
    WAV files, 569, 572–573
    Web sites, 461
source files/paths, 18, 69
spaces in filenames, 72
SparQ, 377
speakers, modems, 400
speed
    hard disk, 311
    memory, 290
    modems, 400, 404
    mouse
        double-clicking, 537
        pointer, 538–540, 542
    RAM, 290
    WAV files, 573
spinners, 298
spoof, 504
SRAM (Static RAM), 291
SSL 2.0/SSL 3.0 (Secure Sockets
  Layer Level 2/Level 3), 503
stack frames, 78, 515

Standard Buttons toolbar, 463
standards
    Infrared Data Association
        (IrDA), 589
    PC 98/99, 525
    VGA display driver, 89
standby
    alarm, 580
    mode, 576–577
    shutdown, 98
star network topology, 603
start bits, 389
Start GUI automatically (Tweak
    UI), 124
Start menu, 37
    accelerator keys, 243
    applications, 134
    built-in commands, 241–242
    commands, 98, 241–242
    configuration, 28, 34, 237
    Control Panel, 196–197
    folders, 242
    icons, 34, 244
    opening, 700
    Recycle Bin, 242
    Registry, 105
    Scheduled Tasks folder, 242
    shortcuts, 31, 238–240, 273
    Subscriptions folder, 242
    URL History folder, 242
start pages, 438
starting
    accessories, 37
    applications, 141
    Control Panel, 185
    file execution, 191
    folders, 259
    modems, 37
    searches, 168
    shut down, 166, 577
    System File Checker, 352,
        354
startup files/folders
    applications, 137
    bitmap, 99
    booting, 95
    buffers, 77–78
    cleaning, 56
    clusters, 322, 321
    cold boot, 76
    commands, 84
    configuration, 87
    creating, 65, 366–368
    DBLSPACE.BIN driver, 77
    diagnostic, 88

DOS3DHIGH statement, 77
double-buffering, 96
DRVSPACE.BIN driver, 77
dual-booting, 95
files, 78, 322
GDI, 79
GUI, 94
hardware, 77
HIMEM.SYS manager, 77
IDE drives, 370
IFSHLP.SYS, 77
installation, 54
items, 91, 302, 700
Kernel, 79
LASTDRIVE3DZ, 78
loading, 79
logos, 97
memory, 302
modes, 78–79
Msdos.sys file, 91–92
Normal, 88
Num Lock key, 548
options, 76
POST, 76
protected mode, 76
real mode, 76
Registry, 107–108
renaming, 79, 85
ROM BIOS, 76–77
Safe mode, 95
SCSI CD-ROM drives, 370
selective, 88
Setup, 59
SETVER.EXE program, 77
SHELL3DCommand.com/P,
    78
shortcuts, 94, 137
stack frames, 78
System Configuration utility,
    87
testing, 368
User component, 79
virtual device drivers
    (VxDs), 78
Win.com, 78
Win.ini file, 79
see also Autoexec.bat file;
    Config.sys file
Startup menu
    booting, 124
    breakpoints, 86
    commands, 83–84, 86
    displaying, 94, 124, 700
    enabling, 89
    items, 82

LoadFailed lines, 83
  opening, 82
  switches, 85–86
startup options, 19–20, 33
state, 499
Static RAM (SRAM), 291
static virtual device drivers
  (VxDs), 78
statistics, ScanDisk utility, 318
status bar
  closing, 301
  editing, 485
  infrared monitors, 590
  Outlook Express 5
  Web view templates, 213
  Windows Explorer, 154
steering IRQs, 516
Step-by-step command (Startup
  menu), 84
StickyKeys feature, 548
stop bits, 389–390, 401
storing
  archived files, 314
  backups, 110
  Control Panel, 194
  DLLs, 52
  Favorites folder, 445
  files, 331
  hard disk, 311
  Open dialog box, 52
  Outlook Express, 467, 476
  Plug-and-Play, 521
  Registry, 104–105
  Save As dialog box, 52
  screen images, 556
  Setup, 59
  swap files, 296–297
  system icons, 237
  Web sites, 454
strings, 109, 111, 114, 427
style sheets, 214, 216–217
subfolders, 442
subnet masks, 413
subroutines in DLLs, 52
subscriptions, 13, 242, 421, 452
$SUCCESS variable, 427
Suhdlog.dat file, 70
Super VGA video card, 41
SuperDisk backups, 376
support files/partitions, 337–338,
  350
suspend nodes, 32
swap files, 56, 292, 296–298
switches, 59, 84–86, 145
switching programs, 37

Symantec, 58
synchronization, 457
system files, 372
  Active Desktop, 302
  animated cursors, 302
  applications, 301–302
  area, 332
  backups, 55, 109, 352
  BIOS, 56
  boot partitions, 46
  caret, 456
  changed files, 353
  checking, 18, 351–354
  color codes, 300–301
  compressed volume files
    (CVFs), 326
  configuration, 19–20, 87–90,
    352, 354
  conflicting, 355–357
  Control Panel, 196
  crashes, 379–380
  CRC values, 352–353
  deleted files, 353
  desktop themes, 302
  documents, 301
  DOS, 334
  hard disk, 318
  heaps, 298
  icons, 188, 190, 236–237
  ignoring, 354
  installation, 351
  location, 353–354
  log files, 353
  Low Resources dialog box ,
    301
  monitoring, 299–301, 648
  overwriting, 351
  power schemes, 577
  properties, 707
  protecting, 350
  Registry, 106
  renaming, 85
  reports, 57
  restarting, 301
  restoring, 351, 354, 356–357
  search criteria, 353
  security, 494
  status bars, 301
  toolbars, 301
  transferring, 372
  uninstallation, 71
  updating, 354
  variables, 427
  verification data file, 351,
    354

versions, 350
wallpaper, 302
Windows 3.1*x*, 47, 298
Windows 98, 298
see also memory
System Information utility, 20–21,
528
    components, 347
    data, 383
    device information, 347
    hardware, 347
    history, 347
    opening, 292
    RAM, 347
    Registry key, 347
    software environment, 348
    troubleshooting, 346
    uptime, 347
    versions, 347
System Policy Editor, 119
    Control Panel, 192–193
    icons, 120–121
    installation, 120
    Local Computer/User, 121
    Network Neighborhood
        Access Control tab, 644
        Entire Network, 643
        Identification tab, 644
        logon banners, 644
        Network icon, 643
        customizing, 642
        file sharing, 643
        hiding, 643
        logon process, 644
        passwords, 645
        print sharing, 643
        user validation, 644
        usernames, 644
        Windows NT, 645
        workgroups, 643,
          645–646
    remote administration, 647
    settings, 235
System Recovery utility, 19, 379
    batch files, 380
    bootable disk, 380
    compatibility, 381
    destination folder, 381
    installation script, 380–381
    product ID, 381
    recovering, 381–383
System Settings group, 61

T

T-connectors, 601
tabbed dialog boxes, 37
tabs, hiding, 193
tags, *see* HTML
tampering with email, 504
tape drives, 376
targets, shortcuts, 277–280
Task Monitor (IALA), 322–323
Task Scheduler utility, 21, 135
task-switching, 35
taskbar, 37
    Address toolbar, 246
    buttons, 707
    Cascade Windows com-
      mand, 244
    clock, 37, 244
    Control Panel, 196
    desktop, 244, 246
    Dial-Up Networking icon,
      655
    hiding, 244
    Links toolbar, 246
    Minimize All Windows com-
      mand, 245
    moving, 245
    New toolbar, 246
    properties, 244
    Quick Launch toolbar, 245
    Refresh command, 247
    Registry, 105
    resizing, 246
    rows, 245
    Show Text/Title command,
      247
    sizing, 245
    Start menu, 244
    task-switching, 35
    Tile Windows
      Horizontally/Vertically
      command, 245
    toolbars, 34
    View command, 247
TCP/IP network protocol,
604–605
    configuration, 432
    dial-up connections, 494
    domain name, 431
    File and Print Sharing, 431
    gateways, 431
    host name, 431
    installation, 430
    IP addresses, 430
    LANs, 494

network adapters, 430
security, 494
WINS servers, 431
teaming modems, 628
Tech Support Guy Web site, 693
Technology W/O Any Interesting
Name (TWAIN), 567
Telephony icon (Control Panel),
188, 190
temporary files, 53, 59, 315
terminal emulation, 390
terminate-and-stay resident (TSR)
programs, 59, 64, 304, 308–309
terminators, 601
testing
Autoexec.bat file, 80
binary files, 372
Config.sys file, 80
connections, 433
device drivers, 525
logon scripts, 428
memory, 293
modem installation, 395–397
scanners, 568
startup disk, 368–371
text
alternate, 456
deleting, 706
Windows Explorer, 157–158
wrapping, 162
thicknet/thinnet cable
(10Base-5), 599
throughput, serial ports, 584
thumbnails, 175–176, 213
tilde, 551
tiling windows, 245
time, 37, 65, 170, 186, 189, 195,
317, 332
Tip of the Day (Outlook Express
4), 486
titles, 178, 196, 247
TLS 1.0 (Transport Layer
Security), 503
toggling, see enabling/disabling
tone dialing for modems, 407
toolbars
closing, 301
commands, 196, 641, 662
configuration, 462
editing, 485–486
icons, 247
refreshing, 247
taskbar, 34
titles, 247
topology of networks, 603

TRACERT utility, 432
tracks (floppy disks), 171
trails, mouse, 540, 543
transferring
data, 517–518
files, 584–585, 591
ISP accounts, 417
system files to disk, 372
transmission
buffers, 402
infrared (IR) ports, 591
modems, 388
serial ports, 391
string literals, 426–427
Transmission Control/Internet,
see TCP/IP
Transport Layer Security (TLS
1.0), 503
Travan tapes, 373
triple-booting, 51
Trojan horse viruses, 358
troubleshooting
archives, 377
batchfiles, 380
compatability, 381
data, 346, 377, 383
destination folder, 381
Device Manager, 531
Dr. Watson utility, 383
EZFlyer, 377
floppy disks, 376
full, 377
HiFD, 377
installation, 380–381
Jaz drives, 377
MS-DOS Report Tool, 384
online, 377
printing, 383
product ID, 381
recovery, 381–383
restoring, 377–379
source folders, 381
Startup menu, 20, 85–86
SuperDisk, 376
system crashes, 379
tape drives, 376
unattended, 376
virtual device drivers
(VxDs), 78
Windows Report Tool, 384
Zip drives, 377
Trumpet FireSock application,
628
Trusted sites, 497–498

TSRs (terminate-and-stay-resident) programs, 59, 64, 304, 308–309
TUCOWS Web site, 693
TWAIN (Technology W/O Any Interesting Name), 567
Tweak UI (Control Panel), 188, 190–191
    boot option, 123
    commands, 241
    controls, 123–124
    installation, 122, 124
    logons, 631
    mouse, 544–545
    opening, 122–123
    shortcuts, 282–283
twisted-pair cables, 599, 602–603

U

UART (Universal Asynchronous Receiver/Transmitter), 392, 402, 514
UCM (Universal Cable Module), 585
UDF (Universal Disk Format), 89
UMBs (upper memory blocks), 304
unassociated applications, 260–261
unattended backups, 376–377
UNC (Universal Naming Convention), 498, 634–635, 639
uncompressed hard disk, 296
undeleting files, 37, 166–167
underlining
    links, 206, 459
    Web integration, 201
undocking notebooks, 581–582
Uniform Resource Locals (URLs), *see* Web sites
uninstallation, 56, 313
    16-bit applications, 149–151
    32-bit applications, 146–148
    DLLs, 53
    DOS applications, 151
    executing, 70–72
    files, 71
    LabelCheck, 72
    manual, 72–73
    Setuplog.txt file, 70
    SpaceCheck, 72
    Suhdlog.dat file, 70
    system files, 71

Windows 98, 69–70, 316
Winundo.dat file, 71
United States-International keyboard layout, 550–551
universal drivers, 520
unread messages, 483
Untrusted Scripted Paste, 491
unused applications, 301–302
updates
    Address bar, 442
    antivirus software, 362
    BIOS, 56
    Dial-Up Networking, 652
    DLLs, 52
    Favorites, 452
    files, 354, 588–589
    Internet Explorer, 13
        cross-frame navigation, 492
        dotless IP address, 492–493
        downloading files, 491
        External Jscript, 493
        newer versions, 457
    Outlook Express, 15, 493
    security, 491–494
    subscriptions, 421
    synchronization, 457
    Web sites, 454, 492
    Windows Critical Update Notification, 494
upgrading, 40
    disk space, 44
    DOS, 42–43
    Windows 3.0, 42–43
    Windows 3.1*x*, 44–45
    Windows 95/98, 14, 45
uplink ports, 602
uploading Remote Mail messages, 661
upper memory area (UMA)
    accessing, 144, 304
    available space, 307, 310
    Command.com, 96
    Drvspace.bin, 96
    DOS, 303
    free, 308
    unused memory blocks, 86
uppercase names, 179
uptime for System Information utility, 347
URLs (Uniform Resource Locators), *see* Web sites
usage counters for DLLs, 148

USB (Universal Serial Bus), 23, 521
Use SCSI Double-buffering, 89
Usenet newsgroups, 694–696
User-Level Access Control, 637
    clients, 614
    Dial-Up Server dialog box, 658
    security, 596
users
    application installation, 132
    components, 79
    configuration, 247
    connections, 421
    custom access, 639
    data, 501
    default settings, 247–248, 632
    deleting from networks, 639
    Dial-Up Networking, 423, 427, 658
    files, 7, 105–106, 643
    folders, 250
    full access, 639
    ISPs, 412
    items, 248
    logons, 7, 249, 502
    multiple, 249
    names, 68, 644
    networks, 97
    Outlook Express, 468
    passwords, 248
    print sharing, 643
    prompts, 502
    Query Analyzer, 7
    read-only access, 639
    Registry, 68, 250–251
    Start menu, 240
    taskpads, 7
    Tools menu, 7
    values, 300
    variables, 427
UTF-8 standard, 457

V

validation
    logon, 615
    Network Neighborhood, 644
values
    binary, 111, 269
    Dial-Up Networking, 427
    environment variables, 81
    FAT, 332

GDI, 300
    string, 111
    user, 300
    Win.ini file, 79
variables
    declarations, 214
    Dial-Up Networking, 427
    environment, 305
    PATH, 50
VBScript, 29
verbose mode, 334
verification
    backup jobs, 375
    system files, 351, 354
VeriSign Web site, 507
versions
    Conflict Manager, 351, 355–357
    DLLs, 52
    files, 350
    Internet Explorer, 457
    Registry Checker utility, 108–109
    System Information utility, 347
vertical sizing of taskbar, 245
video
    cards, 232
    configuration, 232
    enhancements, 23
    memory, 518,557, 559
    performance, 557
    Super VGA, 41
    VGA monitor
        hardware requirements, 40
        System Configuration, 89
    Web sites, 461
    see also graphics adapters
viewing
    Device Manager, 529–531
    files, 247
    folders, 11, 91, 154, 177, 284
    icons, 176
    Microsoft Mail Postoffice property sheet, 621
    My Computer, 284
    Outlook Express, 485
    Registry Editor Keys pane, 111
    shortcut file extensions, 281–282
    Status Bar, 154
    thumbnails, 176

Web site folders, 205
Windows Explorer, 175,
177–179, 284
virtual device drivers (VxDs), 78,
519–520
virtual handlers, 88
Virtual Machine Manager
(VMM), 139–140
Virtual Memory Manager, 78–79,
292
virtual private networks
(VPNs), 31
viruses
antivirus software, 56, 63,
358–362
applications, 129
boot floppy disks, 361–362
compressed folders, 361
crackers, 358
detection, 53
email hoaxes, 490–491
files, 358, 361
floppy disks, 362
hackers, 358
macros, 358
Scheduled Tasks folder, 363
sectors, 358–359
security, 358
Trojan horse, 358
types, 357
Windows Update, 362
voice conversations, 15–16
volume
labels, 72
modems, 400
sound, 569
WAV files, 573
VPNs (virtual private networks),
31
VShield (McAfee VirusScan),
358–361
VxDs (virtual device drivers), 78

W

waitfor command, 425
Wake-On-LANs, 32
wallpaper, *see* Active Desktop
warning dialog boxes
Caps Lock key, 547
script errors, 457
security, 495, 503
WAV files, 569, 572–573

Web integration, 199
disabling, 57
domains, 201
enabling, 203–204
filenames, 201
Forward button, 203
HTML, 200
Java/JavaScript, 200
links, 200
mouse pointer, 201
new features, 10
objects, 156
tags, 200
underlining, 201
Web Publishing Wizard, 15
Web sites
32BIT.com, 691
Active Desktop, 224
adding to security zone
levels, 497
Address bar, 443
Allen's WinApps List, 691
AnchorDesk Windows
Briefing Center, 692
animations, 461
applications, 10
Back button, 203
background images, 200,
462
browsers/browsing, 10, 201,
437, 457
cache, 454–455
certificates, 502–503
channels, 459, 503
configuration, 205
Consummate Winsock Apps
List, 692
default settings, 439
deleting to security zone
levels, 498
Device Bay, 32
directories, 201, 436
DOWNLOAD.COM, 692
Favorites folder
browsing, 445–446
changing URLs, 447
deleting, 447
dial-up connections,
451
downloading, 450
exporting/importing,
446–447
logins, 451
moving, 447

offline viewing,
    452–454
research sites, 448
sorting, 447–448
storing, 445
updated, 448–449
files, 436, 500
folders, 202, 205, 208
form submission, 503
Frame spoof, 492
frames, 444
HCL, 691
host domains, 436
hypertext links, 437
images, 438, 461
Internet Explorer 5, 501
Java applets, 501
links, 201–202, 206, 459
local pages, 437
McAfee VirusScan, 359
Microsoft Technical Support
    Search, 690
mouse pointer, 201
Norton AntiVirus, 359
opening, 437
page hits/transitions,
    457–458
PC World Magazine, 692
PCWin Resource Center, 692
Personal Web Server, 597
PowerQuest, 58
Quarterdeck, 58
remote pages, 437
Search bar, 438–439, 462
security, 501
servers, 15
shortcuts, 285
sound, 461
Start menu, 242
start pages, 438
subscriptions, 13, 448-453
Symantec, 58
Tech Support Guy, 693
TUCOWS, 693
URLs, 200, 437, 457–458
userdata, 501
VeriSign, 507
video, 461
Windows 98, 362, 690–691,
    693–694
Windows Hardware Quality
    Lab (WHQL), 525
WinFiles/WinPlane, 694

Web view
    backgrounds, 207–209
    creating, 209–210
    Dial-Up Networking folder,
        210
    enabling, 206–207
    folders, 11, 205, 210
    hard disk, 312
    information panel, 202
    mini-banner, 207
    My Computer folder, 210
    Network Neighborhood, 210
    Notepad, 210
    previewing, 11
    templates, 209
        body, 211–214
        filenames, 211
        headers, 211, 214–217
        links, 217–218
        paths, 211
    windows, 215
WebTV, 28, 32
    graphics adapters, 556
    hardware requirements, 41
    Quick Launch toolbar, 245
welcome messages, 460
wheel mouse, 28, 543–544
WHQL (Windows Hardware
    Quality Lab), 525–527
width
    backup tapes, 373
    images, 100
    Outlook Express, 484
Win.com, 78, 85–86, 145
Win.ini file, 55, 79, 138–139
WinAlign utility, 20, 66, 324–325
Windowatch Web site, 693
windows
    browsers, 458
    cascading, 244
    configuration, 37
    desktop, 231
    DOS, 82
    full-window drag, 232
    layout, 485
    minimizing, 245, 706
    selecting, 541
    shortcuts, 278–279
    tiling, 245
    Tweak UI, 545
    Web view, 215
Windows
    Critical Update Notification,
        494
    dual-booting, 44, 47–48

exiting, 37, 58, 97
files/folders, 47, 210
initialization, 44
Internet Name Service
    (WINS), 430–431, 609
logo key, 706–707
logons, 630–631
popularity, 33
Registry, 44
Report Tool, 384
Setup, 63
shortcuts, 274–275, 283
swap files, 56
Start Menu folder, 197
system resources, 210, 298
triple-booting, 51
Update, 14, 362, 690
upgrading, 42–45
Windows 95/98
    compatibility, 41
    configuration, 421–423
    DHCP, 422
    Dial-Up Networking, 422
    dual-booting
        other OSs, 45, 47–48,
            51
        partitions, 46
        Windows NT, 49–51
    FAT32, 40, 46–47
    hardware requirements,
        40–41
    installation, 42–45
    Internet Connection
        Wizard, 416–417, 624
    interface, 204
    new features, 10
    newsgroups, 694–695
    property sheets, 422
    proxy servers, 422
    RAM, 40
    Registry, 44, 53
    Setup, 39, 45, 63
    Software Library, 691
    system resources, 298
    triple-booting, 51
    upgrading, 14
    VGA video card, 40
    Web sites, 690, 693–694
Windows Explorer, 37
    Address bar, 459
    commands, 91, 160–161
    files/folders
        attributes, 178
        creating, 161–162
        customizing, 177

date criteria, 170
default settings, 178
deleting, 162–165
display options, 178
Explorer.exe, 179–180
extensions, 154–155,
    178
finding, 168–170
hiding, 154, 179
opening, 264
pop-up descriptions,
    178
recovering, 165–167
renaming, 162
selecting, 155
sorting, 176–177
specification, 169
title bar, 178
uppercase names, 179
floppy disks, 171–174
icons, 175–176
keyboard shortcuts, 703–704
networks, 178, 633
objects
    drag-and-drop, 158,
        160
    lassoing, 159
    multiple, 156–158
    right-drag, 158–159
    single, 155–156
opening, 153, 706
Registry, 105, 111
screens, 156
status bar, 154
text, 157–158
views, 175, 177–179, 284
Windows Messaging, see Microsoft
Mail Postoffice
Windows NT
    dual-booting, 49–51
    logon, 645
    passwords, 632
    triple-booting, 51
WinFiles.com, 694
WinGate application, 627
WINIPCFG utility, 433
WinPlane Web site, 694
WINS (Windows Internet Name
    Service), 430–431, 609
Winset, 81–82
Winundo.dat/Winundo.ini files,
    71, 314
word processing, 37
WordPad, 37, 266
workgroups, 608, 633, 643, 645

workstations, 603
wrapping text, 162
write-behind caching, 97
write-protecting
      boot floppy disks, 361–362
      DOS settings, 305
write-testing, 318

X–Z

x lines, 93
XCOPY command, 58
XMS (extended) memory, 306
XON/XOFF flow control, 392

zero-byte files, 19
Zip drive backups, 377
zones, security levels, 495,
  497–502